SIXTH EDITION

Classroom Management Strategies

Gaining and Maintaining Students' Cooperation

BICENTENNIAL
1807
WILEY
2007
BICENTENNIAL

THE WILEY BICENTENNIAL—KNOWLEDGE FOR GENERATIONS

*E*ach generation has its unique needs and aspirations. When Charles Wiley first opened his small printing shop in lower Manhattan in 1807, it was a generation of boundless potential searching for an identity. And we were there, helping to define a new American literary tradition. Over half a century later, in the midst of the Second Industrial Revolution, it was a generation focused on building the future. Once again, we were there, supplying the critical scientific, technical, and engineering knowledge that helped frame the world. Throughout the 20th Century, and into the new millennium, nations began to reach out beyond their own borders and a new international community was born. Wiley was there, expanding its operations around the world to enable a global exchange of ideas, opinions, and know-how.

For 200 years, Wiley has been an integral part of each generation's journey, enabling the flow of information and understanding necessary to meet their needs and fulfill their aspirations. Today, bold new technologies are changing the way we live and learn. Wiley will be there, providing you the must-have knowledge you need to imagine new worlds, new possibilities, and new opportunities.

Generations come and go, but you can always count on Wiley to provide you the knowledge you need, when and where you need it!

WILLIAM J. PESCE
PRESIDENT AND CHIEF EXECUTIVE OFFICER

PETER BOOTH WILEY
CHAIRMAN OF THE BOARD

SIXTH EDITION

Classroom Management Strategies

Gaining and Maintaining Students' Cooperation

JAMES S. CANGELOSI

1807
WILEY
2007

BICENTENNIAL
BICENTENNIAL

John Wiley & Sons, Inc.

Vice President and Publisher: Jay O'Callaghan
Executive Editor: Chris Johnson
Acquisitions Editor: Robert Johnston
Production Manager: Dorothy Sinclair
Marketing Manager: Emily Streutker
Designer: Hope Miller
Media Editor: Sasha Giacoppo
Editorial Assistant: Eileen McKeever
Senior Editorial Assistant: Katie Melega
Production Management Services: Pine Tree Composition, Inc.

Typeset in 10/12 New Caledonia by Laserwords Private Limited, Chennai, India and printed and bound by Malloy Lithographers. The cover was printed by The Lehigh Press.

The paper in this book was manufactured by a mill whose forest management programs include sustained yield harvesting of its timberlands. Sustained yield harvesting principles ensure that the number of trees cut each year does not exceed the amount of new growth.

This book is printed on acid-free paper. ∞

Cangelosi, James S.
Classroom management strategies: gaining and maintaining students' cooperation, Sixth edition
ISBN 0-470-08452-9

Printed in the United States of America.

10 9 8 7 6 5 4 3 2 1

To
Jason, Ben, & Alli

Preface

The most commonly expressed school-related concern of students, teachers, parents, and school administrators involves a lack of pupil discipline, poor classroom management and control, and disruptive student behavior. A tenth grader remonstrates, "School is a joke! I don't learn anything because the teachers are so busy trying to keep order that they don't take time to teach." One seventh-grade teacher's comment is indicative of the feelings of thousands of her colleagues that teach at every level: "I became a teacher because I love knowledge and I wanted to help children. But these pupils don't want my help! They won't sit still long enough to learn anything—except how to drive me out of the profession!" "What am I supposed to do?" a social studies teacher asks. "Six of the 28 students in my fifth-hour class are classified as behavior disordered—and some of the others ought to be!" Another teacher's lamentations are all too common: "I used to look forward to each school day. Now, I start days hoping I can survive until school is out without being driven crazy, overly embarrassed, or physically harmed." A parent expresses his dilemma: "My taxes go to support public education, but I had to find a private school for my child where teachers controlled students with good old-fashioned discipline." A recent high school graduate suggests, "Teachers should exert more control. I just played around in school—rarely paid attention or did homework. Now I'm paying for my fooling around. I wish my teachers had made me work and learn." A school principal states emphatically, "The number one thing I look for when hiring a new teacher is the ability to maintain discipline and order. What good does it do teachers to know all the subject matter and pedagogy in the world if they can't control the kids?"

Not surprisingly, more than any other instructional variable, classroom observation instruments used in virtually every public school district for assessing teacher performance emphasize how teachers manage their students. Some teachers may blame student inattentiveness, lack of effort, disruptive behaviors, and general lack of cooperation on their students' own flaws or on the lack of support provided by society, families, and school administrators. Yet thousands of other teachers manage to overcome these seemingly impossible circumstances and elicit their students' cooperation in the face of unfavorable student attitudes and school conditions. These teachers orchestrate safe, productive classroom communities where students cooperate and enjoy learning.

How can you maintain your students' attention, effort, and cooperation? That is the question addressed by *Classroom Management Strategies: Gaining and Maintaining Students' Cooperation*. This text contains a wealth of information about classroom management strategies that successful teachers use to lead students to be on-task and engaged in lessons. The strategies are based on extensive school teaching experiences as well as on the findings of numerous studies in learning theory, social interaction, communication, developmental psychology, multicultural education, behavioristic psychology, motivation, student engagement, and violence prevention.

However, any strategy for maintaining students' cooperation can be understood and applied only by teachers who are exposed to examples demonstrating how the strategy is used in everyday, realistic classroom situations. Thus, this book not only explains such strategies but also brings them to life in 311 cases drawn from a wide range of actual elementary, middle, junior high, and senior high school teaching experiences. The cases demonstrate the principles of classroom management, as well as how teachers apply successful strategies and learn to modify strategies that are unsuccessful. Many cases "get inside" teachers' minds, following thought processes as solutions to discipline problems are formulated, revised, and fine-tuned to meet the needs of particular situations.

In this sixth edition of *Classroom Management Strategies: Gaining and Maintaining Students' Cooperation*, the practical orientation of prior editions has been retained with its pedagogy that leads you—the preservice or in-service teacher—to discover how to apply research-based strategies in your own classroom. You will be prompted to analyze, contrast, and compare the cases (311 of the 312 are actual—Case 7.1 is the only one that is not), leading you to develop strategies for (a) establishing safe, nurturing classroom communities, (b) efficiently managing classroom time, (c) fostering cooperative relationships and healthy productive interactions, (d) effectively communicating with students and their parents, (e) establishing and enforcing standards of conduct and procedures for classroom routines, (f) collaborating in the development and implementation of schoolwide safety and discipline policies, (g) working with individual differences among students, (h) accommodating students' exceptionalities, (i) utilizing the diversity among students to build strong, productive classroom communities, (j) teaching students to productively manage conflict, (k) motivating students to engage in learning activities, (l) conducting engaging learning activities, (m) effectively teaching students to supplant off-task behaviors with on-task behaviors, and (n) effectively dealing with misbehaviors—both nonviolent and violent.

However, the sixth edition is a major refinement of the fifth:

- Updated content is incorporated throughout that reflects recent advances in the research bases for classroom management strategies.
- Chapter 2, "Schools of Thought and the Research Bases for Classroom Management Strategies," is new to the sixth edition. It is designed to lead teachers to grasp some fundamental principles from the various academic areas of study that provide the research-based foundation for the classroom management strategies developed in subsequent chapters.
- Chapter 6's groundbreaking section, "Including Students with Characteristics Typically Disdained in So-Called 'Mainstream Society'," is new to the sixth edition.
- To accommodate the new content without appreciably increasing the book's length, Chapter 1 is considerably shorter in this edition than it was in the fifth, and the content from Chapters 6 and 7 of the fifth edition has been collapsed into a single chapter in this edition.

The book is presented in five parts with 12 chapters:

- Part I: The Research-Based Art of Leading Students to Cooperate
  - ► Chapter 1, "The Complex Art of Teaching," introduces you to an advanced organizer that will help you integrate techniques and suggestions presented in Chapters 2 to 12 into your work as a classroom teacher.
  - ► Chapter 2, "Schools of Thought and the Research Bases for Classroom Management Strategies," leads you to grasp some fundamental principles

from the various academic areas of study that provide the research-based foundation for the classroom management strategies you will be developing in your work with Chapters 3 to 12.

- Part II: Fostering Cooperation and Preventing Discipline Problems
  - ▶ Chapter 3, "Establishing a Favorable Climate for Cooperation," leads you to develop strategies for establishing a classroom climate that is conducive to students cooperatively engaging in the business of learning.
  - ▶ Chapter 4, "Establishing Cooperative Relationships," leads you to develop strategies for interacting and communicating with students and their parents in ways that foster productive, cooperative relationships.
  - ▶ Chapter 5, "Standards for Conduct, Routine Procedures, and Safe-School Policies," leads you to develop strategies for establishing standards for classroom conduct, procedures for classroom routines, and schoolwide discipline and safety policies.
  - ▶ Chapter 6, "Working with Individual Differences Among Students," leads you to develop strategies for working with the individual characteristics of your students in ways that foster cooperation and engagement in learning activities. Particular attention is paid to the inclusion and accommodation of students' exceptionalities, working with students for whom English is not a first language, working with and including students with characteristics typically disdained by so-called "mainstream" society, and using the cultural diversity of students to enhance classroom cooperation and student engagement.
- Part III: Motivating Students to Engage in Learning Activities
  - ▶ Chapter 7, "Conducting and Monitoring Engaging Learning Activities," leads you to develop strategies for conducting and monitoring learning activities so that students willingly and enthusiastically engage in them. Particular attention is paid to problem-based lessons as well as the following types of learning activities: lecture, cooperative learning, discussion, questioning, independent work, and homework.
- Part IV: Confronting and Solving Discipline Problems
  - ▶ Chapter 8, "Approaching Off-Task Behaviors Systematically," leads you to develop overall strategies for responding to students' off-task behaviors.
  - ▶ Chapter 9, "Modifying Off-Task Behavior Patterns," leads you to develop strategies for teaching students to supplant off-task behavior patterns with on-task behavior patterns.
  - ▶ Chapter 10, "Dealing with Nondisruptive Off-Task Behaviors," leads you to develop strategies for constructively dealing with the following types of students' off-task behaviors: mind wandering, daydreaming, refusing to participate in class activities, failing to complete homework assignments, failing to bring materials to class, being absent or tardy, and cheating on tests.
  - ▶ Chapter 11, "Dealing with Disruptive Behaviors," leads you to develop strategies for constructively dealing with the following types of students' off-task behaviors: interrupting, clowning, being discourteous, failing to

clean up, bullying, fighting, brandishing weapons, attacking teachers, and vandalizing.

- Part V: Making Classroom Management Strategies Work for You
  - ▶ Chapter 12, "Incorporating Classroom Management Strategies into Your Teaching Style," heightens your awareness of the complexities of teaching and the need to use classroom experiences to further cultivate what you've learned from your work with this textbook.

Chapters begin with a goal defined by a set of objectives. Embedded throughout chapters are prompts for you to engage in activities designed to enhance your talent for developing classroom management strategies. Included at the end of each of the first 11 chapters are synthesis activities and a transitional activity. The synthesis activities are designed to help you (a) bring together the various ideas to which you have been exposed throughout the chapter, (b) reinforce and extend what you have learned in the chapter, and (c) assess what you have gained from the chapter so that you can identify both your areas of proficiency and those areas you need to review. The transitional activity sets the stage for the chapter that follows.

This textbook is designed for college- and university-level courses aimed at helping preservice and in-service teachers lead their students to choose cooperative, on-task, and prosocial behaviors. For professors who incorporate this edition into their courses, an instructor's manual is available from John Wiley & Sons, Inc. The manual contains (a) suggestions for taking advantage of the book's features in a variety of course structures, (b) a detailed sample syllabus, (c) a sample sequence of class-meeting agendas and activities for a semester-long course, and (d) sample unit, midterm, and final tests with scoring rubrics for each.

Reviewers whose valuable suggestions and insights have contributed to the development of this book are acknowledged here with gratitude:

Byron Anderson—UW-Stout

Barbara A. Block—Florida Southern College

Mary Anne Christenberry—College of Charleston

Jurgen Combs—Shenandoah University

Carla Crippen—California State University, Stanislaus

Jane Diekman—California State University, Stanislaus

John Donaldson—Liberty University

Anne G. Dorsey—University of Cincinnati

Martha A. Drobnak—West Chester University

Kimberly Fields—Albany State University

S. Alfred Foy—William Carey College

Margaret Gray—Fontbonne University

Nomsa Gwalla-Ogisi—University of Wisconsin-Whitewater

Kathleen Holowach—San Diego State University

Sandra Jackson—DePaul University

Suzanne MacDonald—University of Akron

Kaye McCrory—West Virginia University

Susan Mintz—University of Virginia

John Moore—University of Western Kentucky

Juanita Moore—University of Portland

Dorothy Neathery—Sam Houston State University

Marilyn Nicholas—Towson University

Merrill M. Oaks—Washington State University

S. D. Parker—Academy of New Church College

Francine Peterman—Cleveland State University

Gerald Pratt—St. Mary's University

Elizabeth Raker—The University of Findlay

Robert Richmond—Florida Institute of Technology

Thomassine Sellers—San Francisco State University

Robert Shearer—Miami University of Ohio

John Shindler—California State University, Los Angeles

Toni Sills—Tulane University

Lois Silvernail—Spring Hill College

Marian Alice Simmons—University of Missouri, Kansas City

Bruce D. Smith—Henderson State University

Dorothy Stokes—Belhaven College

Will Weber—University of Houston

James C. Wenhart—Arizona State University

Karla B. Willis—Eastern Kentucky University

Table of Contents

Preface   vii

PART I

THE RESEARCH-BASED ART OF LEADING STUDENTS TO COOPERATE   1

CHAPTER 1
The Complex Art of Teaching   3

Chapter 1's Goal and Objectives   3
Teaching Experiences: Satisfying or Frustrating   3
Teaching Cycles   4
Allocated Time and Transition Time   9
Student Behaviors   9
   On-Task, Engaged, Off-Task, and Disruptive   9
   Prosocial and Antisocial   11
Taking Charge in Your Classroom   12
Synthesis Activities for Chapter 1   13
Transitional Activity from Chapter 1 to Chapter 2   16

CHAPTER 2
Schools of Thought and the Research Bases for Classroom Management Strategies   18

Chapter 2's Goal and Objectives   18
Students' Need to Be Taught to Cooperate   19
Implications from Learning Theory   20
Implications from Studies of Social Interaction
   and Communications   27
   Critical Communication Styles and Classroom
      Climates   27
   True Dialogues Instead of IRE Cycles   28
   Other Implications Regarding Communication
      Styles   34
Implications from Studies in Developmental Psychology
   and Multicultural Education   34
Implications from Behavioristic Psychology   37
   Learned Responses   37
   Behavior Modification   38
   Isolated Behaviors and Behavior Patterns   38
   Positive Reinforcers   39
   Destructive Positive Reinforcers   40
   Contrived versus Naturally Occurring
      Punishment   42

Differences Between the Effects of Naturally
      Occurring and Contrived Punishment   42
   Unwittingly Administered Punishment   44
   Destructive Punishment   44
   Negative Reinforcement   45
Implications from Studies Focusing on Motivation
   and Student Engagement   46
   Student Disinterest   46
   Intrinsic Motivation   46
   Extrinsic Motivation   46
   The Preferred Type of Motivation   48
Implications from Studies Focusing on Violence
   Prevention in Schools   48
Synthesis Activities for Chapter 2   49
Transitional Activity from Chapter 2 to Chapter 3   53

PART II

FOSTERING COOPERATION AND PREVENTING DISCIPLINE PROBLEMS   55

CHAPTER 3
Establishing a Favorable Climate for Cooperation   57

Chapter 3's Goal and Objectives   57
Creating a Businesslike Climate   57
   The Advantage of a Businesslike Atmosphere   57
   The Meaning of *Businesslike*   58
   Five Steps Toward a Businesslike
      Atmosphere   59
Beginning a New School Year   59
   Students' Perceived Notions   59
   Taking Advantage of Initial Uncertainty   59
   Planning for a Favorable Beginning   60
   Learning Activities Conducive to a Favorable
      Beginning   62
Displaying Withitness   71
Modeling Preparation and Organization   72
   The Importance of the Third and Fourth Stages
      of Teaching Cycles   72
   The Effects of Preparation on Classroom Climate
      and Efficiency   73
Orchestrating Smooth, Efficient Transitions   74
   Smoothness of Transitions and Momentum   74

Minimizing Transition Time   78
Dispensing with Administrative Duties   79
    Inefficient Use of Class Time   79
    Efficient Use of Class Time   80
Saving Time When Distributing Materials and Giving
        Directions   80
    Efficient Beginnings to Learning Activities   80
    Freedom from Having to Speak to the Whole
        Class   82
    Distributing Materials Ahead of Time   83
    Cues for Efficient Routines   83
Employing Technology to Enhance Classroom
        Efficiency   85
Saving Time With Intraclass Grouping   86
Accommodating Students' Completing Work
        at Different Times   86
Creating a Comfortable, Nonthreatening, and Safe
        Learning Community   87
    A Frightening Place   87
    Risking Self-Respect   88
    Disassociating Self-Respect from Achievement   90
Synthesis Activities for Chapter 3   90
Transitional Activity from Chapter 3 to Chapter 4   92

CHAPTER 4
Establishing Cooperative Relationships   93

Chapter 4's Goal and Objectives   93
Using Descriptive Instead of Judgmental Language   94
    Focused Descriptions, Not Characterizations
        or Labels   94
    Differences Between Descriptive and Judgmental
        Language   95
    The Consequences of Judgmental Language   96
        The Detrimental Effects of Characterizations   96
        The Fallacy of Labels   97
        Competition or Cooperation   98
Teaching Students to Listen to You   98
    The Richness of Descriptive Language   98
    The Judicious Use of Words   99
    Thinking Before Talking   100
    More and More Useless Words   101
    Speaking Only to Intended Listeners   102
    Body Language and Proximity   102
    Voice Tone   105
    Speaking Only to the Attentive   106
Listening to Students   107
Using Supportive Replies   108
    Accepting Feelings   108
    Relieving Frustration   108
    Defusing Conflict   109
Avoiding Unintended Messages   110

    The Risk of Misinterpretation   110
    Modeling a Businesslike Attitude   111
    Avoiding Disruptive Teacher Behavior   111
Being Responsible for One's Own Conduct   112
Communicating Assertively   115
    The Assertive Response Style   115
    Controlling Your Professional Life   117
    Teaching Students to Communicate Assertively   121
Communicating Evaluations   121
    Two Reasons for Communicating Evaluations   121
    Emphasizing Formative Evaluations   126
    Grades as a Form of Communication   130
Fostering Parents' Cooperation   130
    Focusing on Formative Evaluations   130
    Conferences   131
    Written Communications   132
Professional Confidence and Students' Rights   132
    Unprofessional Behavior   132
    Privileged Information   134
Synthesis Activities for Chapter 4   135
Transitional Activity from Chapter 4 to Chapter 5   139

CHAPTER 5
Standards for Conduct, Routine Procedures, and Safe-School Policies   140

Chapter 5's Goal and Objectives   140
Standards for Classroom Conduct   140
    Purposefully Stated Standards   140
    The Number of Standards for Classroom
        Conduct   142
Procedures for Smoothly Operating Classrooms   142
Necessary Standards for Conduct   144
    Four Purposes   144
    Justification of a Standard   144
    Politeness and Courtesy   145
    The Consequences of Unnecessary Standards   146
When to Determine Standards and Routine
        Procedures   147
Who Should Determine Standards?   147
Teaching Standards and Procedures to Students   148
Schoolwide Discipline Policies   151
Developing Safe-School Programs   153
    The Roots of School Violence   153
    Focus on Prevention Not Retribution   155
    Violence-Prevention Strategies   155
    Conflict Management and Resolution
        in Curricula   156
    Reducing Gang-Related Activities in School   163
    Gang Activities   163

Working with Gang-Affiliated Students and Eliminating Gang Activities in School   166
Gentle, Caring School Communities   168
Essentials of an Effective Safe-School System   172
   Eleven Elements   172
   Consensus within the Community   172
   Research and Periodic Safety Audits   173
   School-Safety Committee   173
   Team Approach   173
   Training for All School Personnel   174
   Coordination with Schoolwide Discipline Policies   174
   Provisions for Building Positive Relationships   175
   Provisions for Conflict Resolution   175
   Communication Systems   175
   Backup and Crisis-Support Resources and Procedures   176
   Traffic Control and Intruder Prevention   176
Synthesis Activities for Chapter 5   178
Transitional Activity from Chapter 5 to Chapter 6   179

CHAPTER 6
Working with Individual Differences among Students   180

Chapter 6's Goal and Objectives   180
The Key: Relating to Students as Individuals   181
Including Students with Characteristics Typically Disdained in So-Called Mainstream Society   185
   The Consequences of Students' Feeling Marginalized   185
   Strategies for Inclusion in Your Classroom   187
Special Populations   189
Legal Concerns Relative to Inclusion and Accommodation   191
   Classroom Management Implications of IDEA and Other Federal Statutes   191
   Zero-Reject and IEP Implications for Classroom Management   192
Accommodating and Including Students with Physical, Hearing, Visual, or Communication Impairments   193
Accommodating and Including Students with Learning Disabilities   206
Accommodating and Including Students with Emotional or Behavioral Disorders   212
Accommodating and Including Students for Whom English Is Not a First Language   215
Benefitting from Cultural Diversity   224

Synthesis Activities for Chapter 6   230
Transitional Activity from Chapter 6 to Chapter 7   231

PART III
MOTIVATING STUDENTS TO ENGAGE IN LEARNING ACTIVITIES   233

CHAPTER 7
Conducting and Monitoring Engaging Learning Activities   235

Chapter 7's Goal and Objectives   235
Problem-Based Learning   235
   Non-Problem-Based Approach   235
   Problem-Based Approach   236
   Intrinsic Motivation Via the Problem-Based Approach   238
Giving Directions   240
   Explicitness, Specificity, and Directness   240
   Nine Points about Directions   242
Monitoring Student Engagement   244
Variety of Learning Activities   252
Ideas for Lecture Sessions   252
   Student Engagement during Lectures   252
   Fourteen Points about Lectures   255
Ideas for Cooperative-Learning Sessions   258
   Students Learning from One Another   258
   Guidance and Structure for Maintaining Engagement   258
   Ten Points about Cooperative-Learning Sessions   260
Ideas for Discussion Sessions   262
   Student Engagement during Discussions   262
   Seven Points about Discussion Sessions   263
Ideas for Questioning Sessions   265
   Student Engagement during Questioning Sessions   265
   Six Points about Questioning Sessions   268
Ideas for Independent Work Sessions   270
   Student Engagement during Independent Work Sessions   270
   Four Points about Independent Work Sessions   272
Ideas for Homework Assignments   272
   Student Engagement in Homework Assignments   272
   Eight Points about Homework Assignments   275
Classroom Designs that Enhance Student Engagement   276
Synthesis Activities for Chapter 7   285
Transitional Activity from Chapter 7 to Chapter 8   287

PART IV

CONFRONTING AND SOLVING DISCIPLINE PROBLEMS 289

CHAPTER 8
Approaching Off-Task Behaviors Systematically 291

Chapter 8's Goal and Objectives 291
Deal with Off-Task Behaviors via the Teaching Cycles Model 291
   A Mechanism for Focusing 291
   More Elaborate Applications 293
   Staying Calm and Organizing Thoughts 296
Deal with Misbehaviors Before They "Get to You" 297
Either Respond Decisively to an Off-Task Behavior or Ignore It Altogether 297
Distinguish between Teaching Students to Be On-Task and Building Character 299
   A Teacher's Responsibilities and Capabilities 299
   Focusing on the Task 300
Distinguish between Isolated Off-Task Behaviors and Off-Task Behavior Patterns 300
Control the Time and Place for Dealing with Off-Task Behaviors 301
Provide Students with Dignified Options for Terminating Off-Task Behaviors 303
Avoid Playing Detective 304
Use Alternative Lesson Plans 305
Use the Help of Colleagues 305
Use the Help of Parents and Instructional Supervisors 306
   The Myth of the "Good Teacher" 306
   Assertiveness 307
Do Not Use Corporal Punishment 309
   Corporal Punishment 309
   Arguments for and against Corporal Punishment 311
   Corporal Punishment: A Poor Choice 313
Know Your Rights and Limitations 314
Maintain Your Options 314
Know Yourself and Your Students 314
Synthesis Activities for Chapter 8 315
Transitional Activity from Chapter 8 to Chapter 9 317

CHAPTER 9
Modifying Off-Task Behavior Patterns 318

Chapter 9's Goal and Objectives 318
Systematic Techniques for Changing Habits 318

The Formations and Elimination of Behavior Patterns 318
The Need for Systematic Observation 319
Applying the Principle of Extinction 320
   The Principle 320
   Unintentional Extinction 320
   Intentional Extinction 321
Alternative Behavior Patterns 322
Applying the Principle of Shaping 323
Maintaining Desirable Behavior Changes 324
   Reinforcement Schedules 324
   Fixed Schedules 324
   Intermittent Schedules 325
   Planned Schedules of Reinforcement 326
Cuing 327
Generalization and Discrimination 327
   The Idea 327
   The Principle of Generalization 328
   The Principle of Discrimination 328
   Distinguishing between Generalizing and Discriminating 328
Applying the Principle of Modeling 330
Applying the Principle of Satiation 331
Synthesis Activities for Chapter 9 332
Transitional Activity from Chapter 9 to Chapter 10 333

CHAPTER 10
Dealing with Nondisruptive Off-Task Behaviors 334

Chapter 10's Goal and Objectives 334
Nondisruptive Off-Task Behaviors 334
Mind Wandering and Daydreaming 335
   Detection and Response 335
   Strategies 336
Refusing to Participate in Class Activities 338
Failing to Complete Homework Assignments 342
   Meaningful Homework 342
   Strategies 343
Failing to Bring Needed Materials to Class 344
Being Under the Influence of Debilitating Drugs 345
   Teachers' Attitudes 345
   Strategies 346
Being Absent or Tardy 350
   Schoolwide Policies for Extrinsically Motivating Student Attendance 350
   Teachers' Policies for Extrinsically Motivating Student Attendance 351
   Irrationality of Some Popular Attendance Policies 351
   Strategies 352
Cheating on Tests 354
   Ten Incidents 354

Prevalence and Causes of Cheating   356
Strategies   357
Synthesis Activities for Chapter 10   359
Transitional Activity from Chapter 10
          to Chapter 11   360

CHAPTER 11
Dealing with Disruptive Behaviors   361

Chapter 11's Goal and Objectives   361
     Disruptive Behaviors   361
Dealing with Nonviolent Disruptions   361
     Disruptive Talking   361
     Interrupting   364
     Clowning   365
     Being Discourteous   367
     Failing to Clean Up   369
Dealing with Violent Disruptions   370
     Safe-School Programs in Place   370
     Bullying   370
     Fighting   372
     Attacks on Teachers   378
          Causes   378
          Strategies   380
     Vandalizing   381

Synthesis Activities for Chapter 11   382
Transitional Activity from Chapter 11
          to Chapter 12   382

PART V
MAKING CLASSROOM MANAGEMENT
STRATEGIES WORK FOR YOU   383

CHAPTER 12
Incorporating Classroom Management Strategies
into Your Teaching Style   385

Chapter 12's Goal   385
Building on Experiences   385
Instructional Supervision   386
Assessing Your Own Teaching   388
Action Research   389
Your Uniqueness   389

References   391

Index   399

PART I

THE RESEARCH-BASED ART OF LEADING STUDENTS TO COOPERATE

The Complex Art of Teaching

▶ CHAPTER 1'S GOAL AND OBJECTIVES

The goal of this chapter is to introduce an advanced organizer that will help you integrate techniques and suggestions presented in Chapters 2 through 12 into your work as a classroom teacher. Specifically, Chapter 1 is designed to lead you to achieve the following objectives:

1. Organize your teaching responsibilities within the teaching cycles model.
2. Examine your personal commitment to gaining and maintaining students' cooperation so that you enjoy satisfying teaching experiences and your students experience optimal learning opportunities.
3. Heighten your awareness of factors that need to be considered when developing classroom management strategies.
4. Distinguish between examples and nonexamples of each of the following: allocated time, transition time, student engagement, on-task behavior, off-task behavior, disruptive behavior, prosocial behavior, and antisocial behavior.

▶ TEACHING EXPERIENCES: SATISFYING OR FRUSTRATING

Some teachers orchestrate smoothly operating classrooms where students cooperatively and efficiently go about the business of learning with relatively few disruptions. Other teachers exhaust themselves struggling with student misbehaviors as they attempt to gain some semblance of classroom order. Those from the latter group who remain in the teaching profession eventually give up the struggle, deciding that today's students are so unmotivated and out of control that it is futile to attempt anything more than surviving the school day (Cangelosi, 2006; Clancy, 2005; Flannery, 2005). Whether your teaching experiences are satisfying or marked by frustrating struggles to get students to cooperate depends largely on your classroom management strategies and how you apply them. Through the application of such strategies, you are able to meet one of your primary instructional responsibilities: to provide students with a learning environment that is conducive to achievement and free from disruptions, distractions, and threats to their safety and well-being.

▶ TEACHING CYCLES

Before examining classroom management strategies for gaining and maintaining students' cooperation and effectively confronting discipline problems, briefly examine your role as a teacher. Classroom teaching is not brain surgery; teaching is far more complex. Brain surgery involves—with assistance—(a) studying a patient's symptoms and determining the need for surgery, (b) specifying what the surgery is to accomplish, (c) planning for the surgical procedure, (d) preparing for the surgery (e.g., sterilizing the tools and scheduling the operating facility), (e) conducting the surgery and monitoring the patient's progress, and (f) evaluating the outcome of the operation. Your work as a classroom teacher is conducted in cycles that parallel the stages of brain surgery. However, unlike the brain surgeon, you do not have the luxury of working with only one client (i.e., student or patient) at a time. Typically, a teacher deals with about 30 students at a time. Whereas the brain surgeon only engages in one surgery at a time, focusing on one aspect of the patient (e.g., removing an intraaxial neoplasmic tumor from the occipital lobe) while others (e.g., an anesthesiologist) monitor variables (e.g., the patient's respiratory rate), the teacher—usually with no assistance—is expected to concurrently engage in numerous teaching cycles with about 30 students while monitoring myriad variables (e.g., self-image, aptitude, motivation, achievement, attention level, interest in the lesson's content, progress toward long-range goals, success with moment-to-moment objectives, and on/off-task behavior).

Teaching is an extremely complex art; consider, for example, Case 1.1.

▶ CASE 1.1

Ms. Martinez, an English teacher at Carver High School, believes her students need to improve their abilities to communicate in writing. In her opinion, they should become aware of the different ways readers interpret what they write and be able to edit their own writing to convey their messages as unambiguously as possible. Thus, for one of her classes of 32 students, she designs a process writing unit with the following learning goal: "Students will be aware of the different ways their writing can be interpreted and will edit what they write in light of that awareness."

For the unit, she plans, prepares, and implements a number of learning activities over a 10-day period. For example, one day she divides the 32 students into five cooperative-learning groups of six or seven each. Within each group, one student reads a paragraph she or he wrote for homework. The other students then discuss the meaning of the paragraph as if the writer were not present. The writer, who is not allowed to enter into the discussion, listens and takes notes on how the classmates interpreted the paragraph. Later, the writer is to modify the paragraph in light of the discussion. This activity continues until all students have had a chance to read their paragraphs and hear them discussed.

Near the end of the 10-day unit, Ms. Martinez uses a posttest to help her evaluate students' awareness of readers' interpretations and how effectively students learned to edit what they wrote.

The idea for Ms. Martinez's unit grew from her belief that her students needed to improve their writing and editing abilities. Deciding to do something about that need, she determined a learning goal. To help her students achieve that goal, she designed learning activities and then prepared for them (e.g., rearranging her classroom to accommodate five groups working independently). The term *learning activity* refers to what a teacher plans for students to experience to help them achieve a learning goal. When Ms. Martinez's students were writing paragraphs, reading them in their groups, listening to others read, discussing what was read, taking notes, and rewriting paragraphs, those students were engaged in learning activities, and Ms. Martinez was conducting learning activities. Finally, Ms. Martinez evaluated how successfully her students achieved the unit's goal.

You, like Ms. Martinez, design and conduct teaching units by effecting the six stages of what is referred to throughout this textbook as *teaching cycles*:

1. Determine needs of students.
2. Determine learning goal.
3. Design learning activities.
4. Prepare for the learning activities.
5. Conduct the learning activities.
6. Determine how well students have achieved the learning goal.

Not only is each individual teaching cycle filled with complex decisions for you to make, you must also concurrently operate various stages of multiple teaching cycles as you teach. Two of the many concurrent teaching cycles Mr. Chacone operates are apparent in Case 1.2 (adapted from Cangelosi, 2000, pp. 2–4).

▶ **CASE 1.2**

While designing one of the mathematics units for his class of 26 second graders, Mr. Chacone thinks to himself, "For mathematics to be meaningful and useful to my students, they need to connect some key concepts to their own everyday lives. This unit involves some fundamental geometry. Circle is one of the key concepts with which this unit should deal. I don't want them just to remember that a circle is something that's round. They need to construct the concept of circle for themselves—internalizing the attributes of a circle and understanding how round is different from straight. Okay, if I think of some point as the center of my circle and some distance from that point as my radius, then my circle is made up of all the points in a plane that are that same distance from the center point. (See Figure 1.1) At this time in their school lives, they don't need a formal definition of circle with technical words like 'radius,' 'equidistant,' and 'plane' until they've conceptualized circles."

Mr. Chacone decides to include the following among the objectives for the unit he is planning: Students construct the concept of circle.

He then designs the lesson for the objective. Several days later, Mr. Chacone is with his students outside in the schoolyard engaging them in the lesson he designed. He places a soccer ball on the ground and marks a straight line about 15 meters from the ball. He directs the students to stand side-by-side on the line as shown in Figure 1.2 and explains the rules of a game they are about to play.

In the game, Mr. Chacone calls out two students' names in rapid succession. Upon hearing their names, those students race from their places on the line and, without contacting one another, try to kick the ball before the other. After each race, the ball is replaced and another pair of names is called. As Rosita waits for her name to be called following the second race, she shoves her way from an outside position on the line to one closer to the middle of the line. Mr. Chacone thinks, "It's good that Rosita has figured out that she gains an advantage by being nearer the middle of the line—that's going to help her discover the attributes of a circle. But she also needs to comply with my directions and behave politely or else someone could get hurt. To get her to learn to follow the rules and cooperate, I'll intervene by applying the principle of negative reinforcement." (Note that negative reinforcement is a principle that is explained in Chapter 2 of this text.) He calmly signals Rosita to come stand by him. After the third race, he tells her, "Rosita, you may rejoin the

Given a distance r, a circle with radius r is the set of all the points in a plane that are r from its center. Thus, the following figure is a circle with radius approximately equal to 2.1 inches. Its center, C, and the broken line segments indicating the length of the radius are not part of the circle.

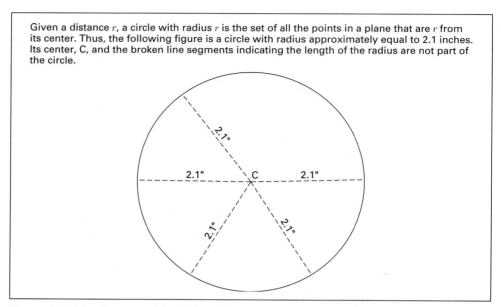

Figure 1.1. The Concept of Circle Mr. Chacone Wants His Second Graders to Construct for Themselves

Figure 1.2. Early in Mr. Chacone's Mathematics Lesson

Figure 1.3. Later in Mr. Chacone's Mathematics Lesson

game as soon as you make up your mind to keep your place in line and respect your classmates' rights." Rosita: "But it's not fair; Jamie is closer to the ball than me!" Mr. Chacone: "Yes, I know. You may rejoin the game as soon as you make up your mind to keep your place in line and respect your classmates' rights." After the fourth race, Rosita jogs over to her original place on the line. Through the next two races, Mr. Chacone observes her waiting to hear her name in compliance with the rules. To positively reinforce this on-task behavior, Mr. Chacone calls out her name along with a student's who is located even farther from the ball than Rosita.

Although students aren't shoving one another or getting out of line, they are squeezing closer to the middle of the line in anticipation of their names being called. As the races continue, they grumble about the game not being fair. Mr. Chacone calls a halt to the proceedings and engages them in a discussion to explain why they think the game isn't fair. They agree that everyone should be "just as close to the ball." Mr. Chacone directs them to change the rules so they are fair to everyone, but insists that they don't shorten the distance between the starting line and the ball because everyone needs the exercise. The students discuss the problem and decide that everyone would have the same distance to run if they lined up around the ball. They arrange themselves as shown in Figure 1.3 and continue the game under the revised rules.

The following day, Mr. Chacone continues the lesson in the classroom with the students describing and illustrating why and how they revised the game. Aware students knew the word "circle" prior to the lesson, he writes it on the board and has students list those things that make circles special. The list includes "circles are round and smooth," "circles are around something, always the same amount away," "circles are flat, unless you stand them up, which is when they're skinny," "circles have a huge hole in the middle," "a circle is like the outside of a hole which has been dug real even," and "circles don't have any wiggles in them." Such comments help Mr. Chacone to judge that most students are achieving the objective of the lesson.

As you work with students, you will orchestrate many interrelated teaching cycles. Engage in Activity 1.1.

▶ *ACTIVITY 1.1*

In Case 1.2, Mr. Chacone executed one teaching cycle by designing and conducting the lesson on circles. Using Figure 1.4 as a guideline, identify what he did for each of the six stages.

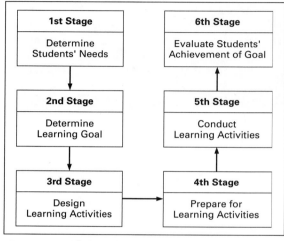

Figure 1.4. The Teaching Cycles Model

Compare what you identified to the following:

1. He recognized a student need when he decided, "For mathematics to be meaningful and useful to my students, they need to connect some key concepts to their own everyday lives. They need to construct the concept of circle for themselves—internalizing the attributes of a circle and understanding how round is different from straight."

2. He determined an objective that addressed the need by deciding to lead students to construct the concept of circle.

3. He decided how to lead students to achieve the objective by designing the lesson involving the racing game with the soccer ball.

4. Among other things, he obtained the soccer ball, reserved the playing field, and marked the field with the straight line.

5. He implemented the plan by engaging the students in the lesson that included the racing game with the soccer ball.

6. After observing students' activities and listening to their comments near the end of the lesson, he determined how well students achieved the objective by judging that most were in the process of learning.

Case 1.2 also relates another teaching cycle involving Mr. Chacone teaching Rosita to cooperate. Identify what he did for each of the six stages of that cycle.

Compare what you identified to the following:

1. He recognized a student need when he decided Rosita needed to comply with his directions and behave politely.

2. He determined an objective that addressed the need when he decided to lead Rosita to follow the rules and cooperate.

3. He decided how to lead a student to achieve the objective by planning to use the principle of negative reinforcement.

4. Case 1.2 doesn't indicate Mr. Chacone specifically doing anything in preparation for implementing his plan.

5. He implemented the plan by signaling Rosita to stand by him and interacting with her as described in Case 1.1.

6. He determined how well Rosita achieved the objective after observing her waiting at her place in compliance with the rules.

Note that Mr. Chacone's judgment that Rosita achieved the classroom management objective influenced him to initiate another teaching cycle—one with the objective of positively reinforcing Rosita's cooperation. Of course, Mr. Chacone was also in the process of orchestrating another teaching cycle by designing and implementing the teaching unit of which the lesson on circles was a part. The teaching cycles model will serve as an advanced organizer for systematically teaching students to supplant uncooperative behaviors with cooperative ones.

▶ ALLOCATED TIME AND TRANSITION TIME

The third stage of a teaching cycle requires you to design and plan your students' learning activities. Suppose that the learning activities you plan for one school period call for a group of students to (a) read a passage from a book, (b) discuss what they read, (c) listen to you give a brief lecture, (d) respond individually in writing to questions on a worksheet, and (e) read another passage and write a brief essay for homework. The intervals in that day when you *intend* to have your students engaged in these learning activities are referred to as *allocated times*. Obviously, allocated time cannot take up an entire school period. On the day you conduct the five learning activities, time must also be devoted to, among other things, (a) getting your students assembled and attentive, (b) assigning the reading and directing them to begin, (c) calling students' attention away from the reading and to the lecture, (d) after the lecture, getting the worksheets distributed and directing students to answer the questions, and (e) calling a halt to the worksheet activity and assigning the homework. The time intervals to take care of such tasks before and after scheduled learning activities (i.e., between allocated times) are referred to as *transition times*.

▶ STUDENT BEHAVIORS

On-Task, Engaged, Off-Task, and Disruptive

Consider the behaviors of the students in the following three cases:

▶ CASE 1.3

Mr. Isaac directs Buster and Elysia, two of his 28 first graders, to put on their aprons and remove their paints from their supply boxes in preparation for a learning activity. Buster puts on his apron, takes out his paints, and waits for directions. Elysia picks up a bottle of yellow paint and throws it across the room, splattering several students.

▶ CASE 1.4

Ms. Saunders, a high school history teacher, is in the midst of conducting a class discussion on why the U.S. Congress rescinded prohibition in 1933. Lia listens intently to the discussion, occasionally expressing her thoughts on the causes. Amy quietly sits at her desk daydreaming about riding horses.

▶ CASE 1.5

Coach Murphy directs 18 of his football players to take two laps around the field. Hewitt begins running while Ricky hides behind the blocking dummies until the others have completed the exercise.

Buster's, Lia's, and Hewitt's behaviors, as described in Cases 1.3 to 1.5, are cooperative. These three students were acting as their teachers had planned. Because they were attempting to follow their teachers' directions, their behaviors were *on-task*. Buster was on-task during transition time. Lia, during the time that Ms. Saunders had allocated for discussing why Congress had rescinded prohibition, seemed to be involved in the discussion. Hewitt, like Lia, became engaged in a learning activity by being on-task during allocated time. In general, students who are cooperating with a teacher and doing what the teacher planned for them to do are displaying on-task behavior. If on-task behavior occurs during a period of allocated time, the behavior is also referred to as *student engagement* in a learning activity. On-task behavior can occur during either allocated time or transition time. Engagement can occur only during allocated time. Elysia's, Amy's, and Ricky's behaviors in the cases were uncooperative. Elysia was *off-task* because she was not attempting to follow Mr. Isaac's directions. Amy's behavior was not disruptive like Elysia's, but Amy was still off-task because she was neither listening nor contributing to the discussion, as Ms. Saunders had directed. Unlike Elysia's, Amy's off-task behavior occurred during allocated time; thus, Amy was disengaged from a learning activity. Similarly, Ricky was off-task and not engaged in Coach Murphy's planned learning activity.

When Elysia flung her paint across Mr. Isaac's room, she was not only displaying off-task behavior, but her behavior also prevented or discouraged other students from being on-task. Amy's quiet daydreaming, however, probably did not disturb any of the other students or interfere with their chances of being on-task. The off-task behavior that Elysia exhibited is referred to as *disruptive*; Amy's off-task behavior was not disruptive. Off-task behaviors such as students talking to one another during times allocated for listening to a presentation, interrupting a speaker, being generally discourteous, clowning, and acting out violently are usually disruptive. Off-task behaviors such as students allowing their minds to wander from the topic at hand, daydreaming, being quietly inattentive because of the effects of drugs, failing to complete homework assignments, skipping class, and cheating on tests are usually nondisruptive. In general, a student's behavior is disruptive when it encourages or causes other students to be off-task.

Disruptive behaviors are the source of most teachers' greatest fears (Abernathy, Manera, & Wright, 1985; Obenchain & Taylor, 2005). Teachers who are considered by their supervisors and others to have poor classroom control and discipline problems are teachers whose students display high levels of disruptive behaviors. You have little choice but to deal one way or another with student disruptions. But unless you also deal effectively with nondisruptive off-task behaviors, (a) transition times will be inefficient, thus robbing you of allocated time, (b) disengaged students will fail to achieve your learning goals, and (c) nondisruptive off-task behaviors are likely to escalate into disruptions.

▶ *ACTIVITY 1.2*

With a colleague, reexamine Case 1.2 and respond to the following prompts about Rosita's behavior:

1. Identify one example in which Rosita's behavior was engaged.

2. Identify one example in which Rosita's behavior was on-task.

3. Although Case 1.2 does not specify an explicit example in which Rosita's behavior was on-task but not engaged, you can infer that at some point during the time in which Case 1.2 took place, Rosita did display such behavior. Describe an example that is consistent within the context of Case 1.2 in which Rosita is on-task but not engaged.

4. Identify an example in which Rosita's behavior is off-task.

5. Identify an example in which Rosita's behavior is disruptive.

Compare your responses to the following ones:

1. Among the possible examples in which Rosita displayed engaged behavior is the following: During the fifth and sixth races, she waits to hear her name; she races toward the ball in response to her name being called for the seventh race.

2. Engaged behavior is also on-task. Thus, Rosita was on-task in the example listed under "1" above.

3. Had Rosita cooperatively followed Mr. Chacone's procedure for moving with her classmates from the playing field back to the classroom, she would have been on-task during transition time. Thus, her behavior would be on-task but not engaged.

4. Rosita's behavior was off-task when she shoved her way toward the middle of the line following the second race.

5. Rosita's off-task behavior in the example listed under "4" above was also disruptive because it likely disturbed the on-task behaviors of other students.

Prosocial and Antisocial

Students' on-task, engaged, off-task, and disruptive behaviors directly affect the success of learning activities and, thus, lessons. However, because teaching is such of a complex art, you cannot only focus your attention on individual lessons. You are also in charge of establishing and orchestrating a learning community whose long-range success depends on its members routinely conducting themselves in a civil, safe, and cooperative manner. Social behaviors that are cooperative, peaceful, and mutually reciprocal among people are *prosocial*. Leading students to exhibit prosocial behaviors is, of course, a major reason for applying classroom management strategies. In Case 1.6 Ben demonstrates prosocial behavior:

▶ CASE 1.6

Ms. Greene has organized her class of 33 sixth graders into six collaborative teams; each examines a different aspect of the U.S. Patriot Act as renewed by Congress in 2006. Ben and Teshawn are assigned to the same team, but Teshawn is absent the day their team plans its report for the rest of the class. Without any prompting from Ms. Greene, Ben phones Teshawn that night to tell him about their team's discussion; Ben then e-mails Teshawn the plans for the report.

The next day, Tamra nervously prefaces her report to the class with, "This assignment just confused me. I wish Ms. Greene would just tell us if the Patriot Act is good or not. It's too hard for us to decide! Okay, what we—" Katrina, a member of Tamra's team, suddenly grabs the paper from Tamra's hand and yells, "You're such a wimp! Here I'll give the report." Ms. Greene intervenes, "Katrina, I need Tamra to present the report." Katrina throws the paper in Tamra's face, knocks over her team's display board, and yells, "Whatever, let the wimp do it!" Ben calmly rights the display board as Ms. Greene deals with Katrina's disruptive behavior.

The antithesis of prosocial behavior is *antisocial* behavior. Behavior is antisocial if it is hostile to the well-being of a community, aversive to others, and deviates from accepted standards of civility. Katrina's behavior in Case 1.6 is not only disruptive to Ms. Greene's learning activity, it is also antisocial. Tamra complained about Ms. Greene's collaborative group assignment, but she was only expressing her opinion, not threatening the well-being of the classroom community. Thus, Tamra's complaint shouldn't be considered antisocial.

Developing strategies for leading students toward prosocial, on-task, and engaged behaviors and away from antisocial, off-task, and disruptive behaviors is the major focus of the remainder of this text.

▶ TAKING CHARGE IN YOUR CLASSROOM

Considering the complexities of classroom and school communities, it's no surprise that behavior management and student discipline problems (e.g., lack of control and fighting) in schools continues to be, as it has been for at least the past 40 years, the number one concern of students, teachers, parents, and school administrators (Kumarakulasingam & Harrington, 2006). For typical classrooms, research studies suggest that the time allocated to learning activities averages about 60 percent of the time that students spend at school, and on the average, students are actually engaged in learning activities for about half that allocated time (Charles, 2005, p. 58; Weinstein & Mignano, 1993). Thus, the average amount of time in typical classroom situations that students spend actively engaged in learning activities is about 30 percent of the time they are at school. Why do students spend what appears to be an inordinate share of their time either off task or in transition between learning activities? Shouldn't they be engaged in learning activities for a larger portion of the school day?

When the proportion of allocated time that students spend engaged in learning activities is increased, students' achievement of learning goals increases (Fisher et al., 1980; Woolfolk, 1993, pp. 402–406). Some reports suggest that both the school year and the school day should be lengthened to accommodate more allocated time (Kapos, 1995, 1998; National Commission on Excellence in Education, 1983; Santini, 1998). Others, however, clearly show that through effective planning and organization teachers can increase allocated time, without lengthening either the school day or year, by minimizing transition time (Jones & Jones, 2004, pp. 282–298; Latham, 1984; Struyk, 1990). Furthermore, by applying fundamental classroom management and discipline techniques, teachers can lead students to be engaged in learning activities for more than 90 percent of allocated time (Cangelosi, 1990, pp. 13–20; Evertson, 1989; Fisher et al., 1980; Jones, 1979).

Major influences on how much of your students' time is spent cooperatively engaged in learning activities are (a) the goals you establish for your students to achieve; (b) the way you plan, prepare for, and conduct learning activities; (c) how you evaluate your students' achievements; (d) the way you organize and manage the classroom setting; and (e) the manner in which you communicate with students and their parents. Of course, other factors—many of which are out of your control—will also influence how well your students cooperate. Unsympathetic school administrators, uncaring parents, lack of needed supplies and facilities, too many students for one teacher, students with behavior disorders, the politics of high-stakes testing, and more work than is possible in 24-hour days are major culprits. But dwelling on causes outside your control will not be an efficient means for you to begin building productive learning communities in which students spend most of their time engaged in meaningful lessons. Instead, address this question: "What can I, the teacher in charge of students, do?" If you are willing to do what you can to gain and maintain your students' cooperation, then you are ready to work your way through the remainder of this text.

▶ SYNTHESIS ACTIVITIES FOR CHAPTER 1

The synthesis activities for each chapter are intended to (a) help you bring together the various ideas in the chapter, (b) reinforce and extend what you learned, and (c) assess what you gained from the chapter so that you can identify your areas of proficiency and the topics you need to review. Another purpose is to encourage you to articulate your thoughts about classroom management strategies in both writing and discussion. Understanding is enhanced through such activities (Knipper & Duggan, 2006; Paul & Elder, 2005; VanDeWeghe, 2005).

Here are the synthesis activities for Chapter 1:

I. Examine Case 1.7, and respond to the lettered prompts that follow in light of what you read.

▶ CASE 1.7

Because Ms. Kobayashi believes that most of her 33 home economics students do not adequately practice comparison shopping, she decides to conduct a learning unit designed to improve students' abilities to assess the cost-benefit value of products sold in stores. During one of the unit's learning activities, which involves students cutting ads out of newspapers, Corine and Gordon toss balled-up newspaper scraps at one another. Ms. Kobayashi decides to put a stop to their activity by speaking to them privately and directing them to clean up the area during the time when the rest of the class is taste-testing the fruit salad made during another learning activity. Both Corine and Gordon cooperatively clean up and do not disturb the class during subsequent lessons in the unit. Thus, Ms. Kobayashi concludes that they will be less likely to clown around in future class sessions. At the end of the unit, a test is given. Ms. Kobayashi decides that 11 of the 13 students who scored markedly higher than the test average are proficient at assessing the cost-benefit value of products.

A. In Case 1.7, Ms. Kobayashi completed two teaching cycles. One dealt with assessing cost-benefit values; the other dealt with a discipline problem. List what she did for each of the six stages of the cycle by answering the following questions:

1. *For the cost-benefit unit*: Ms. Kobayashi implemented the first stage of a cycle when she decided what? She implemented the second stage when she decided what? What did she decide when she implemented the third stage? What are some of the things she might have done while implementing the fourth stage? What are some of the things she probably did in carrying out the fifth stage? What did she decide when implementing the sixth stage?

2. *For dealing with the discipline problem*: Ms. Kobayashi implemented the first stage of a cycle when she decided what? She implemented the second stage when she decided what? What did she decide when she implemented the third stage? What are some of the things she might have done while implementing the fourth stage? What are some of the things she probably did in carrying out the fifth stage? What did she decide when implementing the sixth stage?

B. A number of instances of allocated time occurred in Case 1.7. What was one?

C. A number of instances of transition time were implied. What was one?

II. Compare your responses to Synthesis Activity I's prompts to those of a colleague; discuss similarities and differences. Because the questions posed by the prompts are open-ended, an exact answer key cannot be provided. Nevertheless, evaluate your responses in light of the following comments and sample responses.

In Case 1.7, Ms. Kobayashi followed the teaching cycle model in planning and conducting her unit on comparison shopping and also followed it to teach Corine and Gordon to be on-task. Applying the model to discipline goals in the same way that it is applied to academic learning goals may be a strange idea to many. But as Chapter 8 suggests, if you treat student displays of off-task behavior as indications that students need to learn something, you are more likely to deal effectively with discipline problems when they arise.

With respect to the cost-benefit unit, Ms. Kobayashi implemented the first stage when she decided that most of her students needed to be able to practice comparison shopping. The second was implemented when she set the goal for them to be able to assess cost-benefit values. The principal difference between the first and second stages is that a teacher who only determines that students have a particular need has not yet decided to do something about that need. As a teacher, you identify many needs that your students have that never lead to learning goals. You cannot, nor do you have the right or responsibility to, take care of all your students' needs. The student needs that fall within your responsibilities as a teacher and with which you are reasonably capable of dealing lead to learning goals. Ms. Kobayashi could have decided that other needs should take priority over learning to comparison shop, and she could have chosen not to move to the second stage. In this example, however, she decided to act on her recognition of that particular need. She implemented the third stage by planning to have students cut out newspaper ads and carry out other activities not given in the case. What she did to carry out the fourth stage (i.e., preparing for learning activities) is not described in Case 1.7. Try to imagine what she might have done. For example, she may have collected particular editions of newspapers with some especially helpful advertisements, distributed the papers and scissors, and grouped the students in a way that would benefit the smooth operation of the lesson. For the fifth stage, she explained what they were to do with the ads and supervised the cutting-out activities. In the sixth stage, she decided, probably among other things, that 11 of the 13 students who scored markedly higher than the test average were proficient at assessing the cost-benefit value of products.

With respect to the way she dealt with the discipline problem, it appears that Ms. Kobayashi decided, in the first stage of the second teaching cycle, that Corine's and Gordon's disruptive behavior should cease. There are times when a teacher may identify a need (e.g., that some off-task behavior should cease) and wisely choose not to deal with that need. Dealing with the unwanted behavior may itself create more disruption. But Ms. Kobayashi chose to deal with Corine's and Gordon's disruption and thus went on to the second stage of the model by deciding to get them to stop tossing paper balls. The third stage was implemented by deciding to speak to them privately and directing them to the clean-up task. You really have to use your imagination to fill in a fourth stage. Possibly, she saw to it that the rest of the class was able to remain busy while she directed Corine and Gordon to a private spot for the conversation. The fifth stage was, of course, speaking to them and directing them to clean up. Her evaluation that they had been adequately discouraged from repeating such behavior provided the sixth stage.

Regarding Prompts I-B and I-C, there are many examples you could have given. The time that Ms. Kobayashi planned to spend with students cutting out ads was an example of allocated time. Time spent directing the students from their newspaper-cutting activities to their salad-tasting activities was an example of transition time.

III. Following are some brief descriptions of student behaviors. Label each according to an appropriate combination of the following: (1) on-task, (2) off-task, (3) engaged, or (4) disruptive:

A. Ms. Romano directs her first graders to complete seven mathematics exercises on a task sheet. After working on only one or two of the exercises, several students begin doodling and drawing pictures.

B. Mr. Finegan tells his third graders that it is time for them to put away the materials with which they have been working at learning centers and get to their reading groups for the next lesson. Dale puts away the center materials and immediately goes to his reading group area and waits. Adonis places some of the colored rods from the learning center on Mary's head. Mary yells at Adonis, and the two begin arguing.

C. Charlene, Marion, and Rufus are eleventh graders engaging in a lively conversation as they wait for Mr. Bench to enter the classroom and begin chemistry class. Mr. Bench arrives, asks for silence, and asks Marion to demonstrate an experiment that had been tried for homework. Marion begins the demonstration. Except for Charlene and Rufus, who continue to socialize, class members watch and listen to the demonstration.

IV. Compare your responses to Synthesis Activity III's prompts to those of a colleague. Resolve differences. Evaluate your responses in light of the following comments:

Ms. Romano's students who doodled during time allocated for the mathematics exercises displayed off-task behavior. Doodling is usually not disruptive. The Mr. Finegan example involved transitional time rather than allocated time, so there was no opportunity for students to be engaged in learning activities as was the case in the Ms. Romano example. Dale's behavior appeared to be on-task, while Adonis's and Mary's seemed both off-task and disruptive. During the transitional time before Mr. Bench asked Marion to demonstrate the experiment, Charlene, Marion, and Rufus's talking did not seem inappropriate. When Marion began the demonstration, however, Charlene and Rufus's conversation became off-task and may have been disruptive, depending on whether or not others were distracted. Marion and those students who paid attention were displaying on-task, engaged behaviors during the demonstration.

V. Spend about an hour observing in an elementary, middle, or secondary school classroom. During that time, select a transitional time period and a period of allocated time to complete the following tasks:

A. Answer the following questions about the transition period:

a) For about how long did the transition period last?

b) What happened immediately before the transition period began?

c) What did the teacher do to get the students into the transition period?

d) What happened during the transition period?

e) What did the teacher do to get the students out of the transition period?

f) What happened immediately after the transition period?

B. Note one student, if there were any at all, who appeared to be on-task during the transition period and then complete the following task:

a) Describe those aspects of the student's behavior that led you to believe that she or he was on-task during the transition.

b) Describe the teacher's response to the student's apparent on-task behavior.

C. Note one student, if there were any at all, who appeared to be off-task during the transition period and then complete the following task:

      a)   Describe those aspects of the student's behavior that led you to believe that she or he was off-task during the transition.

      b)   Describe the teacher's response to the student's apparent off-task behavior.

D.   Answer the following questions about the allocated period:

      a)   For about how long did the allocated time period last?

      b)   What happened immediately before the allocated time period began?

      c)   What did the teacher do to get the students into the allocated time period?

      d)   What happened during the allocated time period?

      e)   What did the teacher do to get the students out of the allocated time period?

      f)   What happened immediately after the allocated time period?

E.   Note one student, if there were any at all, who appeared to be engaged in the learning activities of that allocated time period and then complete the following task:

      a)   Describe those aspects of the student's behavior that led you to believe that she or he was engaged in the learning activities.

      b)   Describe the teacher's response to the student's apparent engaged behavior.

F.   Note one student, if there were any at all, who appeared to be off-task during the allocated time period and then complete the following task:

      a)   Describe those aspects of the student's behavior that led you to believe that she or he was disengaged from the learning activities during the allocated time period.

      b)   Describe the teacher's response to the student's apparent off-task behavior.

G.   If you observed an example of prosocial behavior by a student, describe it and explain why you classified the behavior as *prosocial*.

H.   If you observed an example of antisocial behavior by a student, describe it and explain why you classified the behavior as *antisocial*.

VI.   Share, compare, and discuss your responses to Synthesis Activity V's prompts with those of colleagues. Make sure that as you discuss in-school observations that you do not violate professional confidences. Do not identify individual students by name; describe what you observed without making judgmental comments about the work of teachers.

▶ TRANSITIONAL ACTIVITY FROM CHAPTER 1 TO CHAPTER 2

The transitional activity from one chapter to the next is designed to set the stage for your work in the subsequent chapter. In preparation for your work in Chapter 2, collaboratively respond to the following prompts with two or more colleagues:

I.   Call to mind a child, preadolescent, or adolescent who is the age of a grade level you anticipate teaching and with whom you are familiar. Rank each of the following activities from first to 14th regarding your student's natural inclination to engage in that activity:

    A.   Play a computer game of her or his choice

    B.   Complete an arithmetic computation using a pencil and paper

C. Sit quietly in a desk and take notes as you present a lecture

D. Talk to one of her or his good friends

E. Read a textbook

F. Read a magazine about popular musicians

G. Play basketball

H. Daydream

I. Write responses to worksheet prompts about physical science

J. Write a note to a friend

K. Shop for clothes

L. Write a report on a short story assigned by a teacher

M. Sleep

N. Use a computer to respond to prompts from a computer-based language-arts learning program

With your colleagues discuss your respective rankings. Classify each activity according to whether or not it is typically associated with student engagement in classrooms.

II. Address the following question: What are some of the academic areas of study that provide the research findings that are the bases for sound classroom management strategies?

III. Compare and discuss two very different classroom management styles you experienced from teachers you've had during your years in elementary, middle, and secondary schools.

Schools of Thought and the Research Bases for Classroom Management Strategies

▶ **CHAPTER 2'S GOAL AND OBJECTIVES**

The goal of this chapter is to lead you to grasp some fundamental principles from the various academic areas of study that provide the research-based foundation for the classroom management strategies that you will be developing in your work with Chapters 3 through 12. Specifically, Chapter 2 is designed to lead you to achieve the following objectives:

1. Realize that on-task behaviors and engagement in learning activities are learned responses that you should plan to teach your students by employing researched-based strategies that you will learn as you work with Chapters 2 through 12.

2. Distinguish between the roles of inquiry and direct instruction in the development of classroom management strategies.

3. Distinguish between examples of true dialogues and teacher–student interactions dominated by IRE cycles and explain the advantages of teachers engaging students in true dialogues during inquiry-based learning activities.

4. Explain the following behavioristic principles: positive reinforcement, destructive positive reinforcement, punishment, contrived punishment, naturally occurring punishment, destructive punishment, negative reinforcement, isolated behavior, and behavior pattern.

5. Distinguish between examples of students being intrinsically and extrinsically motivated to engage in learning activities.

6. Heighten your awareness of the influence of studies from the following academic areas of study on the classroom management strategies that you will develop as a result of your work with this textbook: learning theory, social interaction and communication, developmental psychology, multicultural education, behavioristic psychology, motivation and student engagement, and violence prevention.

▶ STUDENTS' NEED TO BE TAUGHT TO COOPERATE

Contrast the engaged to the off-task behaviors in Cases 2.1 to 2.3.

▶ CASE 2.1

After being told by their second-grade teacher to work out the computations on a worksheet, Jaylene begins computing while Fred begins doodling and drawing pictures of robots on the task sheet.

▶ CASE 2.2

Instead of doing the push-ups his physical education teacher assigned for homework, Woodrow watches television and eats snacks.

▶ CASE 2.3

During history class, Janet listens to her teacher's lecture on the European Industrial Revolution while two of her classmates, Sophie and John, chat about their plans for going out that night.

Jaylene and Janet were on-task and engaged in learning activities; Fred, Woodrow, Sophie, and John were off-task. Which group, the on-task one or the off-task one, displayed behaviors that were more natural for people? Think about the contrasting behaviors of the two second graders, Jaylene and Fred. Would an eight-year-old, when handed a pencil and a sheet of paper containing numerals, be more inclined to begin manipulating the numerals or begin doodling and drawing? Is it surprising that Woodrow would prefer watching television and eating snacks to doing push-ups? Isn't it normal for two adolescents such as Sophie and John to be more interested in talking to each other than listening to a lecture on the European Industrial Revolution?

Sitting at a desk, thinking about academic topics, completing writing exercises, trying to memorize steps in a process, doing calisthenics, and discussing mitosis are simply not the kinds of things people are inclined to do in the absence of either the imposition of a special structure (e.g., a school) or extraordinary motivation. Keep in mind that students must *learn* to be on-task and engaged in the learning activities you plan for them. On-task behaviors are typically less natural than off-task behaviors. Consequently, you can expect your students to be on-task only if you have *taught* them to choose on-task behaviors over off-task behaviors.

How do you teach students to choose to be on-task? This question has been addressed by numerous reports, journal articles, books, and papers from which have emerged several schools of thought on the general topic of student discipline and classroom management. Sometimes mistakenly believed to contradict each other (e.g., the Ginott approach [Charles, 2005, pp. 27–30] versus the behaviorist approach [Ormrod, 2006, pp. 294–327]), these theories actually complement one another when the best ideas and insights from each are taken into consideration. This textbook's suggestions for developing classroom management strategies are synthesized from research-based principles from a wide range of areas of academic study, including learning theory, social interaction and communication, developmental psychology, multicultural education, motivation and student engagement, behavioristic psychology, group dynamics, violence prevention, and classroom organization.

▶ IMPLICATIONS FROM LEARNING THEORY

Because students need to learn cooperative conduct (i.e., on-task, engaged, and prosocial behaviors), you need to make use of teaching cycles to lead students to choose these behaviors just as you employ teaching cycles to lead them to achieve curriculum goals. Thus, an understanding of how people obtain knowledge, construct concepts, discover relationships, develop skills, acquire attitudes, formulate values, and make behavioral choices is foundational to the development of classroom management strategies. For example, the distinction between *inquiry* and *direct* instructional strategies and how they should be employed for different types of learning outcomes has critical implications in the classroom management world.

A teacher employs *inquiry instructional strategies* by engaging students in activities in which they interact with information, make observations, and formulate and articulate ideas that lead them toward discovery, concept construction, or invention. On the other hand, a teacher employs *direct instructional strategies* by exposing students to the information or process to be remembered and then engaging in repetitive activities to commit the information or process to memory (Cangelosi, 2003, pp. 172–227). Consider Case 2.4 (adapted from Cangelosi, 2000, pp. 10–30).

▶ CASE 2.4

Ms. Martin is planning the first class meeting for her third-period U.S. history class at Benjamin High School. The academic objective for her initial lesson is for students to discover that historians base their beliefs about the past on observations of today's phenomena and events, examinations of artifacts and documents, and interviews with people. She also has two classroom management objectives for the first two class meetings:

1. Students discover the importance of arriving to class on time and completing homework assignments by their due dates.

2. In order to begin building a productive learning community, students discover that in this course, each individual student's opinions, experiences, and responses to prompts presented by Ms. Martin are valued for their contributions to the class' understanding of U.S. history.

Because of her knowledge of learning theories, Ms. Martin understands that simply lecturing her students on the importance of being in class and completing homework assignments on time and telling students that she values their individual contributions to the class are not effective mechanisms for leading students to behave accordingly. Furthermore, she knows students have a history of teachers preaching to them about such matters, but they were still able to "get by" and that their individual opinions, personal experiences, and responses to prompts were hardly utilized in lessons. Ms. Martin will use direct instructional strategies to inform students of classroom procedures and standards of conducts as she will to inform them of names of historical characters. But for the two classroom management objectives and the academic objective she will target in the initial meeting, she employs inquiry instructional strategies.

She begins the first class meeting by directing students to complete the questionnaire displayed by Figure 2.1. Ms. Martin circulates about the room observing students as they respond to the questionnaire prompts. For example, she notes that instead of writing in #2's blanks, Tonja looks around the room, as shown in Figure 2.2, and asks students near her, "Why do we have to do this? I thought this was supposed to be history!" Ms. Martin walks to her and in a hushed, calm voice says, "Tonja, I need for you to fill in these blanks right away. I will use what you write to plan

Third-Period History 😊 Meeting #1

1. What is your name? _____

2. Think of something that happened before you were born that you think almost everyone in this room also knows about. In two sentences, tell what happened.

   _____
   _____
   _____
   _____

3. What makes you think what you just wrote actually happened?

   _____
   _____
   _____
   _____

4. Think of something that happened before you were born that you think no one else in this room (other than yourself) also knows about. In one or two sentences tell what happened.

   _____
   _____
   _____
   _____

5. What makes you think what you just wrote actually happened?

   _____
   _____
   _____
   _____

6. Explain one way in which you influenced history.

   _____
   _____
   _____
   _____

Figure 2.1. Questionnaire Ms. Martin's History Students Complete During the First Class Meeting

7. Suppose that you are walking down a path through a forest. Just around a curve, you look to your left and observe the scene pictured right:

Describe exactly what you see.

_____

_____

_____

_____

Now, explain what you would infer happened at this site at some time in the past before you arrived.

_____

_____

_____

_____

Figure 2.1. (*continued*)

Figure 2.2. Ms. Martin Observes Tonja's Reaction to the Questionnaire

tomorrow's class." Frowning, Tonja says before she begins to write, "Okay, but I don't see what this has to do with history!"

After collecting the questionnaires, Ms. Martin engages the class in a discussion about their responses, course expectations, and requirements for the course. She then distributes copies of a two-page essay by historian Mariya Jefferson and assigns the homework as follows:

> "Carefully read Mariya Jefferson's essay, 'Looking at the Past with Today's Eyes.' Note her descriptions of how she studies current events, artifacts, and documents, and how she talks to people in order to learn about the past. You will use your work from this assignment right after we begin tomorrow's class."

That evening in preparation for the second class meeting, Ms. Martin reads students' questionnaire responses, noting from each paper at least one comment that she would like to reference during upcoming learning activities. Figure 2.3 displays Reggie's responses.

Near the beginning of the second class meeting, Ms. Martin administers the test shown in Figure 2.4. Tonja spends most of the 15 minutes allotted for the test, as shown in Figure 2.5.

Reggie arrives to class 11 minutes late. As you hand him the test paper, he says, "I had to go to my locker to put away my orchestra stuff." He takes a seat and begins writing but time runs short. He complains, "I didn't have time to get started!" Acknowledging his complaint with a sincere, "Yes, I'm sorry; I wish we had more time for you to finish." She then begins playing off students' responses from the test prompts to engage the class in a discussion about how they use their own observations to make inferences about the past. During the spirited discussion, Reggie comments, "That Mariya woman said that she read old diaries and stuff to learn about things before she was born. That's kind of like when I look at old pictures of my great-grandma and stuff. That's how I know how they used to dress and look and stuff. I guess real historians like the one who wrote

Third-Period History ☺ Meeting #1

1. What is your name? *Reggie King*

2. Think of something that happened before you were born that you think almost everyone in this room also knows about. In two sentences, tell what happened.

   There was a huge musical festival called Woodstock that took place in the 1960's.

   Lots of popular bands played and people tore down the fences to get in.

3. What makes you think what you just wrote actually happened?

   I heard about it from others. There was a program on T.V. about it.

   Lately some big music producers tried t copy what Woodstock did.

4. Think of something that happened before you were born that you think no one else in this room (other than yourself) also knows about. In one or two sentences tell what happened.

   The boarded up building from across the street from where I live was built in 1912.

   It sued to be a fish market where people would buy fish to eat.

5. What makes you think what you just wrote actually happened?

   On top the building is carved "Erected in 1912" and below is "Seafood Emporium".

   I asked my mom what that meant and she said her dad said it was a fish market

   that closed a really long time ago.

6. Explain one way in which you influenced history.

   I taught my friend Drew to play the drum and now he wants to be a percussionist.

   Another was is because I was born, I change the data on the census and census

   will always be part of recorded history.

Figure 2.3. The Questionnaire with Reggie's Responses

7. Suppose that you are walking down a path through a forest. Just around a curve, you look to your left and observe the scene pictured right:

Describe exactly what you see.

I see a pile of ashes that looks like it's from an old campfire. I see rocks in a circle and an old log on the ground. There are trees going in the bakc.

Now, explain what you would infer happened at this site at some time in the past before you arrived.

Somebody lit a fire and probably sat by the fire and maybe cooked something or just sat around and stared at the fire. That's what I like to do.

Figure 2.3. *(continued)*

Opportunity to Demonstrate Your Understanding of
How We Discover History
☻
Meeting #2

1.   What is your name?

2.   Yesterday, when you answered the questionnaire at the beginning of class,
     you thought of two things that happened before you were born. For home-
     work, you read historian Mariya Jefferson's explanations of how she learns
     about the past.

     A.   What is one inference about the past that Jefferson related in her essay?

          _____

          _____

          _____

     B.   Describe a process she used to obtain information from which she
          made the inference you listed for "A" above.

          _____

          _____

          _____

     C.   What is one inference about the past that you have made? (It could be
          one of the ones you listed on the questionnaire yesterday, but it doesn't
          have to be).

          _____

          _____

          _____

     D.   Describe a process you used to obtain information from which you
          made the inference you listed for "C" above.

          _____

          _____

          _____

     E.   Explain how the process you described in "D" above was SIMILAR to
          the process you described in "B" above.

          _____

          _____

          _____

     F.   Explain how the process you described in "D" above was DIFFERENT
          from the process you described in "B" above.

          _____

          _____

          _____

Figure 2.4. Test Ms. Martin Administered on the Second Day

Figure 2.5. Ms. Martin Observes Tonja Taking the Test

that paper we read are more careful and scientific than we are when we just look at pictures or something." Ms. Martin asks Tonja, "Do you think Professor Jefferson is a bit more systematic when she formally studies history than when she's making everyday inferences about the past?" Tonja replies, "I didn't get to the homework; I didn't know we were going to be tested on it. Will we have a test tomorrow?" Ms. Martin says, "Yes we will. Now let's go back to Reggie's point paralleling the work of professional historians to what we do when we think about the past." The discussion continues.

Of course there are numerous other implications from learning-theoretic studies besides appropriately incorporating direct and inquiry instructional strategies to teach cooperative behaviors. Learning theory subsumes other areas of academic study that are alluded to in the remainder of this chapter and utilized throughout this book.

▶ IMPLICATIONS FROM STUDIES OF SOCIAL INTERACTION AND COMMUNICATIONS

Critical Communication Styles and Classroom Climates

The degree of success achieved by teachers as they attempt to engage students in learning activities—especially those utilizing inquiry instructional strategies—is highly dependent on two interdependent variables: (a) the types of communication styles teachers model as they interact with students and (b) the types of classroom climates teachers establish (e.g., the degree to which the classroom climate is such that students feel free to experiment with their ideas without fear that their personal worth will be judged according to the "correctness of answers to questions") (Cangelosi, 2003, pp. 62–63; Haefner et al., 2001).

The bases for strategies you will develop because of your work with Chapter 3, "Establishing a Favorable Climate for Cooperation," and Chapter 4, "Establishing Cooperative Relationships," are drawn primarily from studies that focus on the art of effective communication and social interaction. Bowers and Flinders (1990), for example, compared speech and thought patterns that typically occur in the classroom to those that are common in everyday problem-solving activities. Their findings suggest that you need to distinguish between *true dialogues* common in outside-of-classroom conversations and IRE-dominated exchanges typical in classroom discussions.

True Dialogues Instead of IRE Cycles

Discussion sessions are particularly valuable for inquiry lessons that target objectives requiring students to reason with subject content, not just remember it (Cangelosi, 2000, pp. 210–249). To stimulate students to reason rather than simply parroting what they think teachers will judge as "correct," teachers need to conduct discussion sessions so that students engage in *true dialogues*. Compare the dialogue in Case 2.5 to that in Case 2.6 (adapted from Cangelosi, 2003, pp. 64–65).

▶ **CASE 2.5**

Heidi and Shanna engage in the following conversation:

Shanna: Do you want to get something to eat before the movie?

Heidi: I'm not all that hungry, but we can go somewhere if you think we have time.

Shanna: The movie starts at 7:45, so we have over an hour to kill.

Heidi: But we still need to buy tickets. Darlene said they sold out last night before she got in.

Shanna: Oh! I didn't think of that. But maybe that was just because of opening night.

Heidi: Yeah, but I hate to take a chance—and besides I'd like to get there before the line gets too long.

Shanna: I wish I'd grabbed a bite before I left. But since you want to get there early, I'll just get something at the snack bar.

Heidi: The snack bar is just grease and sugar. Besides, they overcharge for everything. Maybe we should stop on the way—it'd be good for me to get a little something also so I won't get hungry in the theater and be tempted to overpay for that junk.

Shanna: Why don't we run by the theater to pick up the tickets and then go to that little deli on St. Charles Street? I'll get a salad and sandwich and you can grab something light to tide you over during the movie.

Heidi: That's a plan.

▶ **CASE 2.6**

As part of a unit on systems of linear functions, Ms. Cook had her algebra II students conduct experiments that produced data for comparing rates of change (e.g., Yasemin examined the speed at which two different quantities of water heated to 100°F on a burner). Ms. Cook plans to use their results to demonstrate how slopes of lines can be used to draw conclusions from data.

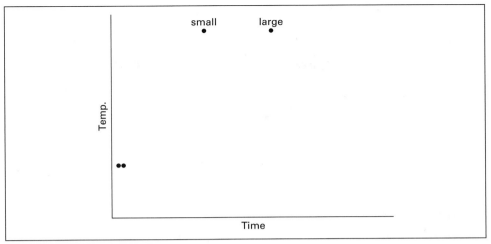

Figure 2.6. The Drawing Yasemin Brought to the Conversation with Ms. Cook

Yasemin's experiment resulted in the two pairs of plotted points shown by Figure 2.6 over which Yasemin and Ms. Cook have the following conversation.

Yasemin: Here's what I got.

Ms. Cook: Oh good! You graphed your results

Yasemin: Were we supposed to?

Ms. Cook: Yes, this really helps us compare the two differences. Draw the two lines determined by those two pairs of points.

        Yasemin produces Figure 2.7.

Ms. Cook: That's right; thank you. Now, how do the slopes of these two lines compare?

Yasemin: The one for the smaller pot is steeper.

Ms. Cook: Right. So, which line has a greater slope?

Yasemin: Uh, they'll both be positive, so—

Ms. Cook: That's right.

Yasemin: So the slope for the steeper line will be bigger.

Ms. Cook: Exactly. But why do you say "will be"? It *is* bigger, isn't it?

Yasemin: Well I haven't figured it out yet. Were we supposed to find the slopes?

Ms. Cook: No, that's fine. My point was that lines have slopes whether we compute them or not.

Yasemin: Oh, okay.

Ms. Cook: But to get back to how slopes can help us, the size of the slopes tells us which pot heated faster.

Yasemin: Okay, but could I ask something?

Ms. Cook: Of course.

Yasemin: I didn't know if we were supposed to do this, but I also took a few in-between measurements and I don't think the temperature went straight up.

Ms. Cook: Show me.

Yasemin: I didn't bring my graph because you didn't tell us to. But can I show you what I remember?

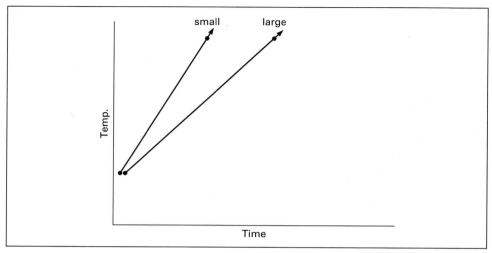

Figure 2.7. Yasemin Draws the Two Lines Determined by the Two Pairs of Points

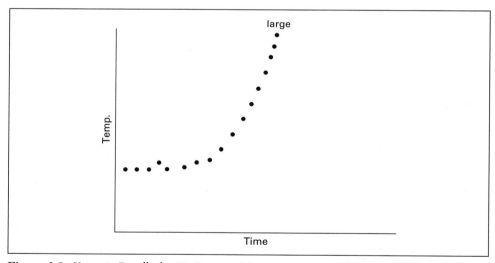

Figure 2.8. Yasemin Recalls the "In-Between" Points

Ms. Cook: Yes, please do.

Yasemin: The larger pot looked something like this.

Yasemin produces Figure 2.8 and then connects the points producing Figure 2.9.

Yasemin: So, what did I do wrong?

Ms. Cook: Oh, nothing. I'm glad you plotted these extra points. You see, water doesn't heat up the same number of degrees for every second. Your points not lining up in a straight line just shows that the water heated slower at first than it did later. The function isn't really linear.

Yasemin: So, how would I figure out exactly how fast it heated at the different times?

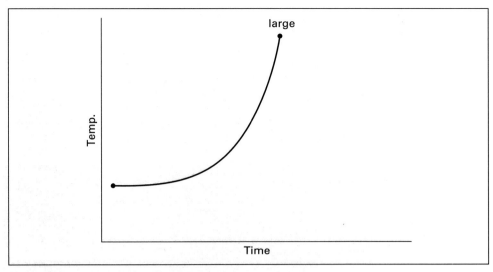

Figure 2.9. Yasemin Draws the Curve

Ms. Cook:	You could do that, but to get it down to the seconds, you need to use calculus.
Yasemin:	I don't plan to take calculus.
Ms. Cook:	You should think about taking it; it'll help you a lot.
Yasemin:	I hear it's too hard.
Ms. Cook:	You've done so well in algebra; calculus won't be too hard for you.

Case 2.5 is an example of the sort of natural conversation people ordinarily have in which they inform, clarify, persuade, identify problems, and address problems. Ideas evolve during these collegial interactions. As an aside, note how frequently Heidi and Shanna made quantitative or mathematical comparisons (e.g., amount of time it would take to eat with amount of time before the movie begins, waiting in a short line versus waiting in a long line, and combination of prices and nutritional value of snack bar food versus that for deli food).

Case 2.6 is an example of the kind of exchange that occurs between teacher and student in the classroom—one that doesn't have the same natural flow of typical outside-of-the-classroom conversations with people who are equally free to contribute ideas. Case 2.6 follows what McCormick and Pressley (1997, pp. 196–201) refer to as *"initiate-response-evaluation (IRE) cycles."* The teacher initiates by prompting students to respond (e.g., Ms. Cook directed students to collect data; Yasemin shows Ms. Cook her graph); the teacher evaluates the response (e.g., "Oh good!"). IRE cycles dominated the conversation. With IRE cycles, the students' role is to respond to the teacher's prompts in a way that merits a favorable evaluation. Although sometimes necessary, conversations dominated by IRE cycles discourage students from contributing their own thoughts for addressing problems; ideas don't evolve as when true dialogue is included (Bowers & Flinders, 1990; Cazden, 1988).

In Case 2.7 (adapted from Cangelosi, 2003, pp. 65–66), the teacher engages a student in a conversation that includes true dialogue that is not dominated by IRE cycles:

▶ **CASE 2.7**

As part of a unit on systems of linear functions, Ms. Galano had her algebra II students conduct experiments, as did Ms. Cook in Case 2.6. Joshua's experiment was the same as Yasemin's in Case 2.6. Looking at results similar to Figure 2.6, Joshua has the following conversation with Ms. Galiano:

Joshua: Here's what I got.

Ms. Galano: So the water in both pots began with the same temperature, but it looks like you took the smaller pot off the stove first.

Joshua: No, I kept it on the stove.

Ms. Galano: I thought you might have because the 100° bigger-pot-point is farther to the right than the 100° smaller-pot-point.

Joshua: Oh, I see why you thought that. But I just stopped testing the temperature of the big pot once the thermometer read 100°.

Ms. Galano: What if we drew the two lines determined by those points to picture how much farther the temperature in the bigger pot had to travel to get to 100°?

Joshua produces Figure 2.7.

Joshua: There, but the water didn't really travel anywhere.

Ms. Galano: Yeah, I see what you mean. Maybe, it's confusing to picture a speed like this as a distance. But you've still got me thinking. Does the differences in the slopes of the two lines picture the rate of increase in temperature?

Joshua: The faster one is steeper, but you know I found out that the water didn't heat straight up like that.

Ms. Galano: What do you mean?

Joshua: Well, look at this. I took some measurements in between the beginning and the end and the points lined up something like this.

Joshua produces Figure 2.8 and then Figure 2.9.

Ms. Galano: I see what you mean. I wanted for you to use these results to illustrate how the slopes of lines can be used to compare rates—like the rates the water in your two pots heated. But you've got to have a line—not a curve—to have a slope.

Joshua: Right.

Ms. Galano: That's too bad. Hmm, let's try something: Because two points determine a line and your curve is made up of points, pick out two points of the curve and name them something.

Joshua produces Figure 2.10.

Joshua: Here I called 'em *A* and *B*—Oh! I know what you're thinking; we can draw Line *AB* and it'll have a slope. So that sort of shows that the water was heating up slowly right in here because Line *AB* is flat.

Ms. Galano: Wow! I see what you mean. Where do you want to pick your next two points?

Joshua: Up here at the top where the lines are gonna have a bigger slope.

Ms. Galano: Should we do it for a pair of points in the middle?

Their drawings now look like Figure 2.11.

Ms. Galano: So are you suggesting that a curve has a lot of different slopes?

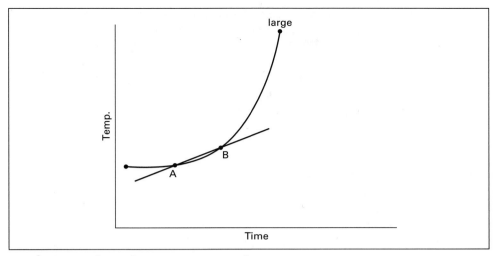

Figure 2.10. Joshua Picks Out Two Points on the Curve

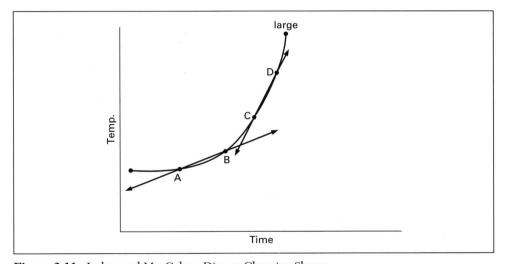

Figure 2.11. Joshua and Ms. Galano Discuss Changing Slopes

Joshua: I'm not sure. Is that possible?

Ms. Galano: Why don't you continue to mull this idea over and then let's share your thoughts with the class tomorrow and see if they're willing to think about expanding their idea of one slope per line to many slopes per curve.

Joshua: I don't know if I want to do that.

Ms. Galano: Think about it and let me know tomorrow.

Ms. Galano resisted the temptation to call Joshua an inventive mathematician in recognition of Joshua's beginning to develop a calculus technique; she was avoiding too many IRE cycles by not playing the role of evaluator. Ms. Galano wasn't ready to reveal that a technique had already been invented until Joshua and the class reaped the benefits of engaging in a true dialogue leading to discovery and invention. You help establish a favorable climate for meaningful inquiry instruction by engaging in real dialogues with students individually as well as in groups. Cooperative-learning activities are especially conducive to students engaging in true dialogues with one another. With true dialogues, students can share their own thoughts and try out ideas without the anxiety that each response will be met with an evaluation.

Other Implications Regarding Communication Styles

The treatise distinguishing true dialogues from discussions dominated by IRE cycles reflects only one example of studies in the field of social interaction and communication with implications for classroom management. Among others, the seminal works of the following are utilized throughout this text: Jacob Kounin (1977) on withitness, efficient transitions, multitasking; Thomas Gordon (1974, 1989) on active listening, I-messages, and conflict resolution; Haim Ginott (1965, 1972) on descriptive versus judgmental language and the detrimental effects of praising and labeling students; Lee and Marlene Canter (2002) on assertiveness and teachers' rights; William Glasser (1985, 2001) on individual responsibility and rational choices; Allen Mendler and Richard Curwin (2001) on addressing disruptive behaviors; Rudolf Dreikurs (1968) on mistaken beliefs about social acceptance; Fritz Redl and William Wattenberg (1959) on group dynamics; and Fred Jones (2001, 2002, 2003) on classroom organization.

► IMPLICATIONS FROM STUDIES IN DEVELOPMENTAL PSYCHOLOGY AND MULTICULTURAL EDUCATION

Your responsibility for keeping students on-task and engaged in learning activities is compounded by the fact that each student is unique. What motivates one student to be on-task does not necessarily motivate another. What discourages one from being off-task may encourage the off-task behavior of another. As a practitioner of the complex art of teaching, you are confronted with more variables to manipulate concurrently than is expected in any other profession (Cangelosi, 1992, pp. 2–35; Kobrin, 1992, pp. xii–xiv, 1–9).

The effectiveness of your strategies for leading students to be on-task and engaged in learning activities depends on how you interrelate with students as individuals and apply your understanding of their backgrounds. This is a major theme throughout this book and is the focus of Chapter 6. A wealth of studies from the fields of developmental psychology and multicultural education (see, for example, Heward [2006, pp. 136–585] and Ormrod [2006, pp. 18–180]) provide the foundation.

You should anticipate managing a classroom community of students with extreme differences with respect to the following variables—each of which has critical classroom-management implications.

- *Interest in learning*: You are interested in teaching your students, but you will be disappointed if you anticipate they will all be equally interested in learning. Children's and adolescents' interests in what schools offer range from obsessive avoidance to obsessive pursuit. Major challenges of teaching include

(a) motivating otherwise disinterested students to learn and (b) preserving and fostering the enthusiasm of those who are already motivated to learn.

- *Self-confidence*: Some students view learning tasks as opportunities to acquire new abilities and skills. Others approach learning tasks as competitive situations in which their existing abilities and skills are challenged. Unlike the latter group, the former group is not burdened with the fear that mistakes will bring ridicule, so these students are willing to pursue perplexing tasks and to learn from their mistakes. The amount of effort students are willing to invest in a learning task is not only dependent on the value they recognize in the task; it also depends on their perception of the likelihood that they will successfully complete the task (Parsons, Hinson, & Sardo-Brown, 2001, pp. 289–290). Problem solving, discovering relationships, analyzing academic content, and interpreting communications are cognitive tasks requiring students to work through perplexing moments. Those who are not confident in their own abilities tend to stop working on the task as soon as they become perplexed; more confident students tolerate perplexity longer and are more likely to continue with the task.

- *Perception of what is important*: Adults tend to value schools as vehicles for preparing their children for the future. "Study hard, and you'll be able to get a good job and make something of yourself when you're grown," a parent tells a child. However, most students are far more concerned with succeeding as children or adolescents than with succeeding as adults (Baenen, 2000; Ormrod, 2006, pp. 63–93). Today seems more important than tomorrow. Thus, many of your students will need to recognize immediate benefits in what you are trying to teach them before they will be motivated to engage in your learning activities. There is tremendous variation among what students consider immediately beneficial. For example, some students want to please their parents with their accomplishments; others find peer approval of their appearance far more important. Still others seek satisfaction within themselves and do not depend on outside approval or seek material rewards for their efforts. You may plan to use students' desires for success to motivate them to attempt a task, but some may be too fearful of failure to make the attempt. Their desire for success is overcome by their desire to avoid failure (Santrock, 2001, pp. 396–419). In any case, each student is driven by a unique combination of motives based on what she or he finds important.

- *Attitude toward school*: Some of your students will greet you as their friend, expecting to benefit from the experiences you provide. Others arrive with little regard for how you might help them and view you as an authority figure who interferes with what they would prefer to be doing.

- *Aptitude for reasoning*: Many of the learning activities you design for your students confront them with high-level cognitive tasks (e.g., inductive or deductive reasoning). Such requirements are quite arduous for some but present no difficulty for others. Whether you teach elementary, middle, or secondary school students, you will have to contend with a wide range of students' abilities to use various reasoning processes. Students who enjoy a history of successes with reasoning tasks are more likely to engage in high-level cognitive learning activities than those who come to you with a history of discouraging experiences.

- *Prior achievements*: Look at the initial chapters of a textbook designed for any grade level beyond the second. Note how the book begins with remedial material that overlaps the content of books for prior grades. Apparently, the author(s) recognized that having been exposed to content in prior courses does not guarantee that content was learned by all students. Most of your students will have failed to learn some content at a level you consider a prerequisite for what you want to teach them. Learning gaps vary from student to student. Furthermore, many students, although lacking some remedial skills and abilities, will have already acquired understanding of some advanced topics you are expecting to introduce to them. Your assessments of students' needs will detect differences among their motor skills as well as their cognitive abilities. Of particular concern to most teachers are differences in students' communication skills. Student engagement in most learning activities depends on students being able to both receive messages (e.g., by listening or reading) and send messages (e.g., by speaking or writing).

- *Experiences on which you can build*: Different students bring vastly different backgrounds to your classroom. Participating in sports, caring for younger children, repairing motors, tending gardens, working for money, traveling, experiencing major family upheavals, playing music, suffering from illnesses, and raising animals are only a few of the types of students' experiences to which you can relate the things you teach, thus motivating their engagement.

- *Home and social life*: Children and adolescents are under continual domestic and social pressures. The parenting of your students will range from supportive to neglectful, from healthy to abusive, and from constant to absent. For most students peer acceptance is of paramount concern (Ormrod, 2006, pp. 60–100; Tierno, 1994). Some have friends who encourage their pursuits of learning and cooperation with your efforts. Others may perceive that they risk acceptance of those whose friendship they value most by being studious and cooperative with you. Some may be involved in gang-related activities or in fear for their personal safety. Although it is important that you understand the pressures and influences with which your students live, keep in mind that because students live with disadvantages (e.g., abusive parents) does not mean that they cannot control their own behaviors, nor should it imply that you should expect less from them (Glasser, 2001; Pysch, 1991). However, variations in home and social life do create differences among students regarding such matters as how much time they have to devote to schoolwork, whether they have a place conducive to doing homework, and whether you can depend on their parents' cooperation and support.

- *Cultural background*: Schools in the United States serve a pluralistic society bestowed with multiethnic, multicultural communities. Your understanding of cultural diversity will serve you well as you develop strategies for motivating students to be on-task and engaged in learning activities. The application of classroom management strategies from a multicultural perspective is a major focus of this book—especially Chapter 6.

- *First language*: More than 13 percent of students in U.S. public schools speak a non-English language at home; the English proficiency of these students varies considerably from non-English proficient (NEP) to limited English proficient (LEP) to highly proficient in English. Differences in which language is native (e.g., Spanish or Vietnamese) also add to the diversity of your classroom. Chapter 3 illustrates ideas for building on that diversity to benefit the classroom climate as well as students' learning.

- *Exceptionalities*: Although you may not be a special education teacher, you can expect to have members of your classroom community whose special needs have been formally identified. Included among the special education classifications are specific learning disabilities, behavioral disorders, hearing impairments, speech or language impairments, visual impairments, emotional disturbances, orthopedic impairments, traumatic brain injury, and other health impairments. Besides accommodating the needs of students with special-education classifications, you can be assured that your "general education" students will also vary considerably in their abilities to hear, see, perform mental and physical tasks, control their emotions, and concentrate. A major focus of Chapter 6 is developing classroom management strategies that accommodate students' exceptionalities.

- *Substance abuse*: Inadequate study skills, boredom, lack of confidence, fatigue, hyperactivity, and nonacademic interests are just some of the many factors that can hinder students' willingness to engage in learning activities. Being either high or depressed from drugs at school or when trying to study is another hindrance to some students' academic work with which you must deal (Urdan, Ryan, Anderman, & Gheen, 2002). Strategies for mitigating such influences need to be incorporated into your classroom management plan. Chapter 10 addresses this issue.

- *Antisocial tendencies*: Students also vary considerably regarding their inclination to be hostile and violent or cooperative and prosocial. Antisocial behaviors are not only disruptive but also dangerous, posing a threat to the well-being of the school community. A focus of Chapter 11 is strategies for confronting antisocial behaviors in your classroom.

► IMPLICATIONS FROM BEHAVIORISTIC PSYCHOLOGY

Learned Responses

With initial impetus from the works of Watson (1914), Dunlap (1919), and others who focused attention on learned rather than instinctive human behavior, behavioristic psychology has flourished and provided a research-based foundation for today's theories and principles for teaching students to be on-task. Particularly notable are the investigations of B. F. Skinner (1953, 1954), who examined the effects of stimuli on learning when the stimuli occurred *after* a response or act. Such investigations led to the following general conclusion, which is fundamental to the behaviorist approach for managing behavior:

Behaviors (responses) that are followed by rewards—satisfying or pleasant stimuli—are more likely to be repeated than behaviors that are not. Aversive stimuli or punishment following a behavioral response tend to discourage that response from recurring.

Behavior Modification

Students' behaviors are complex sets of responses that have been conditioned by their environments. *Behavior modification* refers to the behaviorist approach by which students' environments are manipulated to increase the chances of desired behaviors' being rewarded while undesirable behaviors go unrewarded. Students are thus conditioned toward being on-task.

Detractors of behavior modification complain that the goal of behavior modification programs is to condition observable behaviors, thus neglecting character development while students learn to go through the motions of being well-behaved. Second, they are bothered that highly structured behavior modification programs often depend on extrinsic reward systems that have no natural association with the behaviors they are designed to encourage. Students, for example, may be given coupons for doing homework. Consequently, the students may learn to expect such prizes for simply meeting routine responsibilities. A third complaint proposes that conditioning students' behaviors treats human beings as if they are robots that lack free will.

Proponents of behavior modification answer the first of these three criticisms by noting that controlling students' behaviors cannot wait for character development. Moreover, by practicing desirable behaviors, one learns self-discipline. The second criticism is contested with the argument that students *initially* often need extrinsic rewards to choose to be on-task. After on-task behaviors become habitual, then the students begin to recognize the intrinsic values and no longer need to be "bribed." In the coupon example, the students eventually will find satisfaction from what they learn by doing homework—depending on the quality of the homework assignment. Thus, the intrinsic motivation (i.e., the satisfaction gained from learning) replaces the extrinsic motivation (i.e., the coupons). The third criticism, dealing with free will, involves questions that are more appropriately addressed in a treatise on philosophy.

The suggestions in this text are offered with confidence that they will work because of the wealth of research findings from behavioristic psychology (Ormrod, 2006, pp. 294–327) and other relevant schools of thought. Before you begin considering the specific methods for gaining students' cooperation, which are dealt with in subsequent chapters of this text, there are some concepts and principles with which you should be familiar. They include *isolated behaviors, behavior patterns, positive reinforcers, destructive positive reinforcers, punishment, contrived punishment, naturally occurring punishment, destructive punishment,* and *negative reinforcement.*

Isolated Behaviors and Behavior Patterns

Consider the four examples of student behavior in Case 2.8.

▶ CASE 2.8

While Ms. Bernstein is explaining to members of her sixth-grade class the upcoming homework assignment, Harry interrupts, "Oh no! That'll be boring!" This is one of the few instances in which Harry ever interrupts a speaker in class. It is atypical for Harry to interrupt.

Shortly after Ms. Bernstein continues her explanation, Valerie interrupts with a comment, as she has done on numerous other occasions over the past month.

After school, Dianne engages in the homework activity as she has for virtually every other one of Ms. Bernstein's homework assignments. Jessica also completes the homework, although she has only rarely bothered to do homework in the past.

By interrupting Ms. Bernstein, Harry displayed an off-task, disruptive behavior. Because such interruptions are not typical for Harry, that instance of being disruptive and off-task is said to be an *isolated behavior*. Valerie, on the other hand, habitually interrupts, so her off-task, disruptive behavior was just one display in a continuing *behavior pattern*. Similarly, Dianne was simply displaying what is a regular behavior pattern for her by choosing to be on-task and doing homework assignments. In the instance where Jessica did homework, she was deviating from her regular pattern and was thus displaying an isolated on-task behavior.

It is important for you to differentiate between behaviors that are part of a pattern students have incorporated into their general conduct and behaviors that are isolated displays and not habitual. Wouldn't you expect Ms. Bernstein to use one strategy for Harry's isolated instance of interruption and another to teach Valerie to break her habit of interrupting others?

Positive Reinforcers

Cases 2.9 to 2.13 are examples of behaviors, some of which are rewarded and some of which are not.

▶ CASE 2.9

Ever since Barry began regularly training with weights in physical education class, he enjoys the way he feels. He frequently receives comments from classmates about how good he looks and how strong he is.

▶ CASE 2.10

During class discussions, Sandra often interrupts speakers with wisecracks. Others in the class usually laugh at her remarks.

▶ CASE 2.11

Dale has a desire to lose weight. He attends a weight-reducing class several times with no resulting loss in weight. Dale ceases attending the class.

▶ CASE 2.12

A week ago, two-year-old Morris attempted to get his father, who was involved in a telephone conversation at the time, to pick him up. "Dad, Dad, hold me," Morris said in a calm voice. His father continued talking on the phone without paying attention to Morris. Morris persisted with his requests, becoming louder and sounding more and more distressed. Finally, Morris was lying on the floor screaming and kicking, so that his father could no longer hear the other party on the phone. At that point, Morris's father picked him up. Similar incidents have occurred since. Now when Morris wants to be picked up, he just throws himself on the floor and begins screaming and kicking.

▶ **CASE 2.13**

Nancy always does the written work assigned in Mr. Washington's class, where each paper is returned to her with comments and suggestions. Nancy hardly ever does the written work assigned in Ms. Taylor's class; Ms. Taylor never returns written work.

Barry, Sandra, Morris, and Nancy display voluntary behavior patterns. Barry continues to participate in weight lifting, Sandra frequently interrupts speakers, Morris routinely throws temper tantrums, and Nancy consistently completes Mr. Washington's written assignments. On the other hand, Dale no longer attends weight-reduction classes, and Nancy chooses not to do Ms. Taylor's written assignments. Why are some behavior patterns formed and continued, whereas others are discontinued or never established? Obviously, Barry perceives that his participation in weight-training classes is paying off. The way he feels and the compliments he hears *positively reinforce* his engagement in weight training. Similarly, Sandra's classmates' laughter serves as a positive reinforcer to her habit of interrupting speakers with wisecracks. Being picked up positively reinforces Morris's temper tantrums. Mr. Washington's helpful feedback on written assignments positively reinforces Nancy's behavior pattern of completing assignments.

People will not retain a behavior pattern or establish a new one in the absence of positive reinforcers. Dale no longer chooses to attend weight-reducing class when he perceives his attendance goes unrewarded. Nancy feels that doing Ms. Taylor's assignments is fruitless; thus, without positive reinforcement, she does not elect to do the work.

By definition, a *positive reinforcer* is a stimulus presented after a response that increases the probability of that response's being repeated in the future. In Case 2.9, the *response* is Barry's engagement in weight-training sessions; the *stimuli* are the way Barry feels and the compliments he receives from classmates. On-task as well as off-task voluntary behavior patterns are established because of the presence of positive reinforcers.

Destructive Positive Reinforcers

The positive reinforcers in Cases 2.14 to 2.16 may have undesirable side effects.

▶ **CASE 2.14**

Ms. Coco announces to her ninth-grade class, "Because you have been so cooperative with me today, I will not assign any homework for you to do tonight!"

▶ **CASE 2.15**

Students in Ms. Lambert's kindergarten class receive candy for completing assignments on time.

▶ **CASE 2.16**

Mr. Breaux asks his third graders, "Who can tell me why the man in the story did not want to leave his house in the morning?" A dozen of the students eagerly raise their hands. Mr. Breaux: "Jackie?" Jackie: "Because he didn't want to go to work." Some of the other students say, "No! Mr. Breaux, Mr. Breaux!" Mr. Breaux: "OK, Ory, can you help out Jackie?" Ory: "Because he thought his friend would come back to see him." Mr. Breaux: "Very good, Ory! That is correct! You are one of my very best readers!" Ory beams happily.

Teachers used positive reinforcement to encourage on-task behaviors in Cases 2.14 to 2.16. Ms. Coco's fifth graders were rewarded for their cooperation by being exempted from homework assignments. Ms. Coco's tactics probably served to encourage students' cooperation in the future. Unwittingly, however, she may also have taught her students that homework assignments are unimportant and not doing homework is better than doing homework.

In Case 2.15, the motivation of anticipating a piece of candy encourages Ms. Lambert's students to complete their assignments but may also teach them undesirable eating habits.

Mr. Breaux positively reinforced Ory's commendable answer with praise. But as will be explained in Chapter 4, Haim Ginott (1972) warned against getting students hooked on praise. In addition, Mr. Breaux may have unwittingly taught Ory to hope that others—such as Jackie—will be unsuccessful in order to enhance his own opportunity to be the star of the class.

In each of these three cases, the positive reinforcer for a targeted behavior (i.e., cooperation, finishing assignments, or comprehending a reading) had an undesirable side effect (i.e., teaching the unimportance of homework, unhealthy eating habits, or undue competitiveness among students). When a positive reinforcer for one behavior has undesirable side effects on other behaviors, it is referred to as a *destructive positive reinforcer*.

Engage in Activity 2.1.

► *ACTIVITY 2.1*

With a colleague, revisit Case 1.2 to respond to the following prompts.

1. After Rosita began to comply with the rules of the game, what did Mr. Chacone do in an attempt to positively reinforce that compliance?

2. What response did he want positively reinforced, and what was the reinforcing stimulus?

3. Speculate on one possible undesirable side effect that may have been a consequence of Mr. Chacone's strategy for positively reinforcing Rosita's on-task behavior—thus, causing the positive reinforcement to be destructive to some degree.

Compare your responses to the following ones:

1. He called out her name and that of another student who was farther from the ball than she was. She apparently wanted to be one of the students chosen for a race, and she wanted to win the race.

2. The response was her waiting at her place on the line; the stimulus was being called on to race with a high probability of winning.

3. One possibility is that Rosita is being encouraged to compete with classmates—a competitiveness that might interfere with subsequent cooperative learning activities. Such a side effect would make the positive reinforcement somewhat destructive, but that doesn't mean that Mr. Chacone's strategy was a mistake. Virtually all classroom management strategies have a downside. Teachers need to decide if the advantages outweigh the disadvantages. Rosita might also recognize that her disruptive behavior prompted special attention from Mr. Chacone that eventually increased her chances of winning a race. But if that occurred, it wouldn't be an example of a destructive positive reinforcer because in such a case, Mr. Chacone's action would be positively reinforcing to an off-task rather than an on-task behavior. Thus, Mr. Chacone's strategy would have backfired and would turn out to be a mistake. But the undesirable outcome would be a direct effect, not a side effect.

Selecting positive reinforcers for on-task behaviors that are not destructive is a main concern of Chapters 3, 4, 5, 7, 8, and 9.

Contrived versus Naturally Occurring Punishment

By definition, *punishment* is a stimulus presented after a response that decreases the probability of that response's being repeated in the future. Because they tend to affect students differently, you should distinguish between two types of punishment: (a) *contrived* and (b) *naturally occurring*. Here are two contrasting cases illustrating the difference:

▶ **CASE 2.17**

Leonard falls asleep while Mr. Tessier, his tenth-grade health teacher, lectures. After the lecture, Mr. Tessier directs Leonard to bring to class the following day a 1,000-word essay entitled "Why I Should Not Sleep in Class."'

▶ **CASE 2.18**

Bill falls asleep while Mr. Vasse, his tenth-grade health teacher, lectures. When Bill awakens, he realizes that he does not know what was explained during the lecture. The next day, Bill's fears are confirmed as he fails the test because he hasn't achieved the objectives covered by the lecture.

Oddly enough, if Leonard happened to find that writing the essay gave him an opportunity to be comical or vent some frustration, the assignment might positively reinforce the off-task behavior. Please assume, however, that this was not the case and writing the essay served as punishment for getting caught sleeping in class. Mr. Tessier designed the punishment specifically to get Leonard to regret having slept in class. But having to write an essay is not a natural consequence of sleeping when one should be paying attention in class. Thus, Mr. Tessier used *contrived punishment* in dealing with Leonard's disengagement from the learning activity.

In Case 2.18, Bill also received punishment, but his punishment was a natural consequence of sleeping when he should have been paying attention. Bill may make the connection: "If I miss out on Mr. Vasse's lecture, I won't learn what will be on the test." Thus, Bill suffered *naturally occurring punishment.*

Differences Between the Effects of Naturally Occurring and Contrived Punishment

In Case 2.19, a teacher uses naturally occurring rather than contrived punishment.

▶ **CASE 2.19**

Ms. Brock's kindergarten class is working in two groups: the Busy Bees and the Chipmunks. The Busy Bees have just finished working on a project in which they used scissors, paste, and cardboard. Ms. Brock tells them, "While I show a short filmstrip to the Chipmunks, I want each of you to put away your scissors and paste and then clean up these scraps from the floor and table. When I return, I will read this story to you." Ms. Brock displays a book. The Busy Bees eagerly anticipate hearing the story.

As Ms. Brock begins showing the filmstrip to the Chipmunks, the Busy Bees start giggling and playing instead of following her directive to clean up. Six minutes later, Ms. Brock returns to the Busy Bees with the storybook in hand. "Oh, my goodness! This floor is still a mess, and your scissors and paste are still out," she exclaims. "I am sorry, Busy Bees, but now I need to help you clean up this mess, and I won't have time to read the story to you." As she begins picking up along with the students, Ms. Brock continues, "I know you are disappointed. It is too bad that we still have to clean up and there won't be time left for the story."

If Ms. Brock consistently uses this strategy, her students will soon realize the automatic consequences of being off-task. Ms. Brock's words and manner communicated that she did not withhold the anticipated story because the students failed to pick up after themselves. She conveyed that the story was not read because the time set aside for the story would simply have to be used for cleaning.

The differences between contrived and naturally occurring punishment may seem so subtle as to be unimportant. But over time, the differences are monumental in terms of effects on students (Dreikurs, Grunwald, & Pepper, 1982, pp. 125–129; Weber, 1990, p. 271). In Case 2.20, Ms. Webb confronts a situation identical to that in Ms. Brock's example; however, Ms. Webb uses contrived punishment.

▶ **CASE 2.20**

As Ms. Webb begins showing the filmstrip to the Chipmunks, the Busy Bees start giggling and playing instead of cleaning up. Six minutes later, Ms. Webb returns to the Busy Bees with the storybook in hand. "Why is this mess still here?" she asks. "OK, because you didn't cooperate with me and pick up as I told you, I am not going to read this story. Maybe next time you'll know to listen!"

Do you see the subtle differences between Ms. Brock's and Ms. Webb's handling of the situation? Ms. Webb blamed her failure to read the story on the students' failure to follow directions. She turned the incident into something personal. Consistent handling of such situations will lead to an antagonistic rather than cooperative relationship between Ms. Webb and her students. In time, students will learn to avoid getting caught while still enjoying some of the benefits of being off-task. When Ms. Webb raises irrelevant questions such as, "Why is this mess still here?" they will have ready answers such as, "I was picking up, but Otis didn't!" and "I tried to pick up, but Nadine kept bothering me!"

In contrast, Ms. Brock blamed her failure to read the story on lack of time. Of course, the lack of time was a consequence of the area's not being clean. Ms. Brock focused on what must be done. The question of why the area had not been picked up was not raised. Rather than communicate an "I'll get you for this" tone, Ms. Brock shared the students' unhappiness at not having time to read the story.

Frankly, some teachers use contrived instead of naturally occurring punishment because some off-task behaviors do not have undesirable naturally occurring consequences. If, for example, a teacher assigns students to do work that has no meaningful benefit for them, then the students will not recognize any logical drawbacks for neglecting the work. Faced with such situations, teachers resort to the threat of contrived punishment to coerce students to cooperate.

Unwittingly Administered Punishment

You should keep in mind that on-task as well as off-task behaviors can be discouraged through punishment. Often, teachers are unmindful of such misfortunes when they do occur, as in Case 2.21.

▶ **CASE 2.21**

Barlow spends two hours figuring out and completing a computation exercise in which he is to find the products of 28 pairs of three-digit whole numbers. Barlow correctly executes almost all the steps in the process for the 28 items. But because he repeats a one-step error pattern in 19 of the items, only nine of his final answers are correct. Without explaining what he did wrong or indicating what he did right, Barlow's teacher returns his "corrected" work with 19 X-marks and "32% F" at the top of the paper.

Might the teacher's response have discouraged Barlow from making diligent efforts in the future? How could the teacher have avoided punishing his diligent efforts and still communicated to him that 19 of the answers were incorrect? Is there something that the teacher could have done to see that Barlow's efforts were positively reinforced although he had incorrect final answers? One solution is to score students' papers so that error patterns are identified but points are awarded (i.e., partial credit) for correct steps (e.g., see, Cangelosi, 2000, pp. 397–406).

Destructive Punishment

A positive reinforcer is destructive if it has undesirable side effects. Punishment can also be *destructive* if it produces undesirable side effects in addition to discouraging some targeted behavior. Cases 2.22 and 2.23 are examples. For each, identify the behavior that is being punished and a possible undesirable side effect.

▶ **CASE 2.22**

Mr. Norton is in the habit of assigning extra mathematics exercises to students who are disruptive in class.

▶ **CASE 2.23**

Ms. Chamberlain catches Quinn, one of her tenth graders, shooting paper clips across the classroom. She sends him to an assistant principal who administers three swats with a wooden paddle to Quinn's buttocks.

Mr. Norton's punishment—giving extra mathematics exercises for disruptive behavior—may effectively reduce incidences of disruptive behavior. But if it teaches students that mathematics is a form of punishment to be avoided, then the punishment is destructive. In addition to discouraging him from getting caught again shooting paper clips, Quinn's experience with the assistant principal may teach him that it is okay for one human being to strike another. The undesirable effects of corporal punishment are well documented (Andero & Stewart, 2002; Hyman & Wise, 1979) and are addressed in Chapter 8.

Negative Reinforcement

For many, but not nearly all, instances in which a student is off-task, negative reinforcement can be a powerful mechanism for getting that student to choose to be on-task. By definition, *negative reinforcement* is making the removal of punishment contingent on a specified change in the behavior of the individual who is being punished. Case 2.24 is an example.

▶ **CASE 2.24**

Ms. Dirks directs her preschool class to put away the musical instruments they've been playing and to wash up for their midmorning snack of bananas and carrots. Jay continues to blow his horn. Ms. Dirks goes over to Jay and says, "It's time to put your horn away and wash your hands." Jay slams the horn to the floor and screams, "No, no! I don't want to eat! I wanna play!" Ms. Dirks: "Jay, you don't want to eat. That's fine, but I want you to put away your horn, wash your hands, and sit with the rest of the children while they eat." Jay throws himself on the floor, kicks his feet, and yells incoherently. Ms. Dirks remains calm. With gentle firmness she gets Jay to his feet and walks him to the back of the room to a chair that faces away from the other students. Ms. Dirks: "Jay, you are to sit in this chair until you have decided to get control of yourself, put away your horn, wash your hands, and sit with the rest of us." She leaves him in the chair. It takes about four minutes for Jay to calm himself down. Then he hops off the chair, puts away his horn, washes his hands, and joins the group.

How does negative reinforcement relate to punishment and positive reinforcement? Like positive reinforcement and unlike punishment, negative reinforcement focuses on the behavior to be exhibited rather than the one to be inhibited. Ms. Dirks used punishment by having Jay sit in the chair, but she allowed Jay *to choose when* the punishment would be terminated. Ending the punishment served to positively reinforce the on-task behavior. Ms. Dirks would have used only punishment if she had told Jay to sit in the chair for five minutes or until she told him he could get up. Instead, she used negative reinforcement because the removal of the punishment was contingent on Jay's decision to cooperate.

Engage in Activity 2.2.

▶ *ACTIVITY 2.2*

With a colleague, revisit Case 1.2 to respond to the following prompts.

1. After Rosita shoved her way toward the center of the line, what did Mr. Chacone do in an attempt to apply the principle of negative reinforcement?

2. What was the aversive stimulus from which Rosita relieved herself by displaying the behavior targeted by Mr. Chacone's strategy?

3. What behavior did Mr. Chacone's application of negative reinforcement target?

Compare your responses to the following ones:

1. He prevented Rosita from participating in the game until she chose to comply with the rules.

2. She stood by Mr. Chacone instead of playing a game she wanted to play.

3. Cooperatively playing the game according to Mr. Chacone's directions.

Chapters 9, 10, and 11 will expose you to examples of teachers using negative reinforcement to teach students to supplant off-task with on-task behaviors.

▶ IMPLICATIONS FROM STUDIES FOCUSING ON MOTIVATION AND STUDENT ENGAGEMENT

Student Disinterest

"School is boring." "I hate history! Names, facts, dates—who cares?" "My teacher says geometry is supposed to teach us logical thinking, but all we do is memorize somebody else's proofs." "Why do we have to learn this? Nobody ever uses it!" "Why can't we study something we care about?" "The best thing happened today! There was a fire drill, so we didn't have to go to reading!" "Tomorrow, we don't have to study science because we're going on a field trip."

Do these student comments sound all too familiar? Often students do not cooperatively engage in learning activities because they find the activities uninteresting and not immediately valuable to them (Santrock, 2001, pp. 393–424). Teachers need not be entertainers, and learning activities should probably be more work than fun for students. Nevertheless, there are designs for learning activities that stimulate enthusiastic student engagement. The foundation for such designs are anchored in studies that address questions about human motivation (see, for example, Ormrod, 2006, pp. 364–430).

Intrinsic Motivation

Students are *intrinsically motivated* to engage in a learning activity if they recognize that by experiencing the activity they will satisfy a need. Intrinsically motivated students value engagement as *directly* beneficial. The learning activity itself is perceived to be valuable. The students are intrinsically motivated to engage in learning activities in Cases 2.25 and 2.26.

▶ CASE 2.25

Casey wants to stay healthy and avoid illness. He believes that a proper diet will contribute to his health. Thus, when his seventh-grade teacher directs his class to read a chapter on nutrition, Casey willingly completes the assignment.

▶ CASE 2.26

Samantha believes strongly that people should not hunt and kill wild animals. When her English teacher gives a lecture on how to write persuasively, Samantha listens intently because she wants to become an effective writer, able to use her writing to convince others not to hunt.

Students learn to recognize the value of learning activities from being positively reinforced as a direct result of being engaged.

Extrinsic Motivation

Students are *extrinsically motivated* to engage in learning activities not because they recognize value in experiencing the activity, but because they desire to receive rewards that have been artificially associated with engagement or want to avoid consequences artificially imposed on those who are off-task. Cases 2.27 and 2.28 are examples of students who are extrinsically motivated to engage in learning activities.

▶ **CASE 2.27**

James's seventh-grade teacher directs his class to read a chapter on nutrition. James completes the assignment because he wants to please his dad by making high grades in school. James believes that reading the chapter on nutrition will enhance his chances of raising his grades.

▶ **CASE 2.28**

Roy listens intently while his English teacher lectures on creative writing because he fears that if he doesn't listen, he will be embarrassed by not knowing answers when asked questions in class.

Students become extrinsically motivated to be engaged through experiences in which engaged behaviors are positively reinforced with rewards not directly related to the learning activity itself. Similarly, *contrived* punishments following off-task behaviors can teach a student to be extrinsically motivated to avoid being off-task.

Honor rolls, academic scholarships, academic competitions, letter jackets for students with high grade-point averages, and honor societies are just some of the ways that teachers and school administrators provide incentives for students to become engaged in learning activities. Typically, such attempts do not extrinsically motivate those students who are in greatest need of motivation because only students who have a history of academic success, and thus feel they have a reasonable chance of winning, vie for such awards. Teachers can, however, design learning activities with built-in extrinsic motivators for all students. Cases 2.29 and 2.30 are examples.

▶ **CASE 2.29**

To motivate her 28 second graders to study spelling words, Ms. Malaker holds team spelling tournaments. The class is divided into four teams—Protectors, Gobots, Starriors, and Bird People. On Monday, the Protectors stand in line at the front of the classroom. Ms. Malaker calls out the word "harp." The first Protector says, "H." The second says, "U." Ms. Malaker: "No, that's not it." The second Protector exclaims, "Oh, shoot!" and looks in anticipation at the third Protector who says, "A." The fourth one says, "R." The fifth says, "R." Ms. Malaker: "No." The sixth says, "P." Ms. Malaker: "Very well, the Protectors got four right and two wrong. Four minus two is two. So the Protectors have two points so far. The second word is 'tap.' " The seventh Protector says, "T." The first says, "A" and the second, "P." Ms. Malaker: "That's three right and zero wrong. So that's three more points, giving the Protectors a total of five points. The next word is 'biggest.' " The third Protector says, "B," and the tournament continues.

The Gobots have their turn on Tuesday, the Starriors on Wednesday, and the Bird People on Thursday. On Friday, all seven members of the highest-scoring team receive free passes to the zoo.

Ms. Malaker prefers this type of spelling contest to traditional spelling bees for three reasons: (a) Even the least-skilled spellers can contribute and be rewarded for a winning effort. (b) To compete, team members must listen to one another as letters are called out. (c) Students are not eliminated from the spelling drill for missing a letter as they are in traditional spelling bees.

▶ **CASE 2.30**

Mr. Landry meets individually with each of his 26 fifth graders once every two weeks. He spreads the conferences over a two-week period so he is not overloaded at any one time. During a conference, Mr. Landry and the student agree on a set of goals and rewards the student will receive if the goals are accomplished.

During one such conference, Mr. Landry and Mindy review how well previous goals were accomplished and begin establishing new goals. Mr. Landry shows Mindy a page from their science text and says, "I would like you to choose an experiment from this section. Figure out how to do it, set it up, and demonstrate it for the class on Wednesday. You'll get 20 science points for doing it at all and another 15 for following the steps exactly the way they appear in the book. Do you agree?" Mindy: "I don't know if I can have it done by Wednesday." Mr. Landry: "That's okay, but you won't get the points unless you do." Mindy: "Okay, I'll try." Mr. Landry hands Mindy a test paper and says, "You scored 14 on this pretest. Monday, we'll have the posttest. You bring that pretest score up at least 10 points to a 24 or better and you get a B. Bring it up more than 20 points and you get an A." Mindy takes notes on the goals and the rewards as the conversation moves to other subjects and goals.

The Preferred Type of Motivation

Ms. Malaker's and Mr. Landry's methods for extrinsically motivating student engagement were, of course, superior to not motivating students at all but inferior to having students intrinsically motivated (Cameron & Pierce, 1994; Gottfried, Fleming, & Gottfried, 2001). Students can be intrinsically motivated to engage in learning activities only when those activities are designed to help students achieve objectives that clearly meet their needs (i.e., when the teaching cycles model is followed). Nevertheless, just because the connection between your learning activities and your students' needs is obvious to you, you cannot assume that your students will be intrinsically motivated. To stimulate students' interest and intrinsically motivate engagement, you need to design problem-based lessons (Cangelosi, 2003, pp. 88–90). You will address the question of how to design problem-based lessons when you work with Chapter 7.

▶ IMPLICATIONS FROM STUDIES FOCUSING ON VIOLENCE PREVENTION IN SCHOOLS

Schools are the most common type of gathering place for young people. Consequently, antisocial conduct among children and adolescents occurs more frequently on school campuses than elsewhere (Ormrod, 2006, p. 504). Over the past 10 years, the popular media's attention to some horrific cases of shootings on school campuses (see, for example, Bradley, 2006) have lead many to believe that school violence is increasing. In fact, some studies suggest that the incidence of school violence (e.g., weapon possessions, assaults, and fights) has decreased over the past 10 years (DeVoe et al., 2003; Tonn, 2005). However, the validity of those findings has been questioned (Chandler, 2005; Roberts & Olinger, 2005). In any case, the more common forms of antisocial activity on campuses (i.e., bullying, destruction of property, and harassment directed at students because of their ethnicity, gender, sexual orientation, or appearance) present major challenges to teachers, instructional supervisors, and school administrators ("Boston High Schoolers," 2006; Dunne, Humphreys, & Leach, 2006; Kondrasuk, Greene, Waggoner, Edwards, & Nyak-Rhodes, 2005).

Over the course of your teaching career, you are likely to be responsible for teaching some students with antisocial tendencies and for managing classes of which such students are members. Maintaining a smoothly operating classroom in such cases will challenge your pedagogical and behavior management talents. However, as a teacher responsible for an entire class of students, you are in no position to treat conduct disorders or cure antisocial tendencies. The complex social setting of a classroom is not conducive to treating psychological disorders, nor are most classroom teachers trained to do so. Before the start of a school year, you should identify sources in your school district that can help you deal with students you suspect have antisocial tendencies. A school-administered mechanism for referring, diagnosing, and placing such students in a treatment program is a necessary condition for a safe school environment.

The manifestation of antisocial behaviors among students, criminal activities in school neighborhoods, intruders on school campuses, and gang warfare are unfortunate realities that have changed many schools from being peaceful sanctuaries to dangerous communities within our cities, suburbs, and rural areas.

As a teacher, you can apply strategies to reduce significantly the probability of violent activity occurring in your classroom and learn ways to intervene effectively when such frightening events occur. Such strategies, supported by a wealth of studies on violence prevention, are a major focus of this text. For your school to be a safe haven for learning, however, a schoolwide violence prevention program needs to be incorporated into a safe-school plan that is implemented and enforced by your entire school faculty, staff, and administration in cooperation with students, parents, community leaders, and law enforcement personnel. How to develop and implement a schoolwide safety plan is a question addressed in Chapter 5.

▶ SYNTHESIS ACTIVITIES FOR CHAPTER 2

I. Select the one best response for each of the following multiple-choice prompts that either answers the question or completes the statement:

A. For which one of the following objectives would it be appropriate for you to employ direct instructional strategies?

a) From their experiences observing or interacting with you following incidents in which their classmates violated a classroom standard of conduct, students discover that they can count on you enforcing those standards.

b) Students remember the six standards for classroom conduct.

B. For which one of the following objectives would it be appropriate for you to employ inquiry instructional strategies?

a) Students are able to predict the benefits of engaging in the learning activities you conduct for them.

b) Students know the procedure for learning content that they failed to learn due to an absence.

C. Behavior modification programs are based on the belief that _____.

a) human conduct is influenced by positive reinforcers that follow certain acts

b) extrinsic motivation is more important in shaping human behavior than is intrinsic motivation

c) human beings are like pigeons in that their conduct is primarily a function of instincts

d) environmental influences can explain all forms of human behavior

D. It is important for a teacher to identify whether a student's display of off-task behavior is isolated or part of a behavior pattern because _____.

a) behavior patterns are instinctive whereas isolated behaviors are learned

b) isolated off-task behaviors should be tolerated whereas habitual off-task behaviors should never be tolerated

c) students can control isolated behaviors, but others must control behavior patterns for them

d) a teacher should plan to confront an off-task behavior pattern differently from the way an isolated off-task behavior is confronted

E. If a student is rewarded for an off-task behavior, the reward is a _____.

a) positive reinforcer

b) negative reinforcer

c) contrived punishment

d) destructive positive reinforcer

F. Which one of the following is *not* an example of punishment?

a) After daydreaming during the time her teacher was giving directions, Jan feels lost because she doesn't know what to do.

b) Tony is unhappy that his teacher excluded him from a discussion because he repeatedly interrupted other students.

c) Charlie's teacher tells him he can rejoin the group whenever he decides to speak only when he has the floor.

d) Because she started a fight, Betty was required to meet with her teacher after school when she preferred to be socializing with her friends.

G. Which one of the following is *not* an example of positive reinforcement?

a) Lloyd talks to Carol in history class instead of being engaged in the learning activity. As a result of their conversation, Carol accepts an invitation to go out with Lloyd.

b) After studying diligently for an exam, Cynthia receives an *A*.

c) Tom enjoys the candy his teacher gave him for paying attention during class.

d) Isaac is relieved to find out that his teacher forgot to collect the homework that Isaac failed to complete.

H. Ted's teacher detects him talking and clowning during time allocated for quietly doing exercises in a workbook. The teacher tells Ted, "Go to the time-out area for 10 minutes. Maybe by then you will have decided to settle down and quietly do your work." Which one of the following ideas did Ted's teacher apply?

    a) Positive reinforcement

    b) Negative reinforcement

    c) Contrived punishment

    d) Naturally occurring punishment

I. A positive reinforcer is destructive when it _____.

    a) encourages an off-task behavior

    b) discourages an on-task behavior

    c) fails to increase the frequency of the target behavior

    d) has undesirable side effects

II. Compare your responses to Synthesis Activity I's multiple-choice prompts to the following key: A-b, B-a, C-a, E-d, E-a, F-c, G-d, H-c, I-d.

III. Reread Cases 2.6 and 2.7 in the section "True Dialogues Instead of IRE Cycles." In collaboration with a colleague, write scripts for two different dialogues in which you engage your students in a conversation about some subject content subsumed by one of your teaching specialties. Write them so that (a) IRE cycles dominate the first dialogue and (b) the second dialogue reflects a naturalistic conversation or true dialogue that is free of IRE cycles. Discuss the advantages of engaging students in the second rather than the first conversation.

IV. Describe an example of a teacher's dealing with a student's daydreaming in class using contrived punishment. Compare your example with those of colleagues. Here is a sample response:

> Discovering Amy daydreaming in class, Mr. Benson tells her, "Write a 500-word composition on what you were daydreaming about and turn it in to me tomorrow."

V. Describe an example of a teacher's dealing with a student's daydreaming in class using naturally occurring punishment. Compare your example with those of colleagues. Here is a sample response:

> Allison catches herself daydreaming and realizes that she's missed a critical portion of Ms. Thompson's lecture. Consequently, she does extra work to make up for what she missed.

VI. Describe an example of a teacher's dealing with a student's daydreaming in class using negative reinforcement. Compare your example with those of colleagues. Here is a sample response:

> Mr. Damato calls Amanda to his desk and begins describing what she did correctly and incorrectly on a paper she had turned in. As he explains, he notices that she is daydreaming instead of listening. He abruptly stops his explanation and says, "Here, Amanda! Take your paper to your desk and figure this out for yourself until you can

come back up here and attend to what I'm saying. I'll explain this only when you're ready to listen."

VII. Describe an example in which a student's on-task behavior is effectively encouraged by a destructive positive reinforcer. Explain why the positive reinforcer is destructive. Compare your example with those of colleagues. Here is a sample response:

> Ms. Byrnes holds a spelling contest between the boys and girls in her third-grade class. Keith's diligent studying pays off because he leads the boys to victory. The victory positively reinforces his diligent study habits but is also destructive because it plants the idea that boys are smarter than girls.

VIII. Chapter 1 contains the statement, "On-task behaviors are typically less natural than off-task behaviors." What does that statement mean? Do you agree with it? Explain why. If the statement is true, what are some of the major implications for how teachers plan their learning activities? Compare your response with those of colleagues. Discuss similarities and differences among your answers. Here is a sample response:

> The author referred to on-task behaviors as typically less natural than off-task behaviors because the activities students are directed to do in schools (e.g., quietly pay attention, solve computational exercises, do calisthenics, and discuss economics) are not what children and adolescents are usually inclined to do. Thus, teachers must devise plans to teach students to be on-task and engaged in learning activities.

IX. For each of the following examples, discuss with a colleague whether the student is intrinsically or extrinsically motivated.

A. Clyde carefully listens to the questions his teacher raises in class to avoid the embarrassment he feels when he's called on and doesn't provide an acceptable response.

B. Lynnae's mother tells her she can adopt a new kitten only if she does well on her next spelling test. Therefore, Lynnae diligently works on her spelling homework.

C. To impress her coach, Carmen spends extra time during basketball practice running up and down the bleachers.

D. To build up her endurance, Noel spends extra time during basketball practice running up and down the bleachers.

E. Because he wants to converse easily with his Spanish-speaking friends, Damien diligently works on assigned exercises in his Spanish class.

F. Madison carefully listens to and watches his teacher as she shows him how to write his name. He is anxious to write it himself on the Mother's Day card he's prepared.

G. To avoid being criticized by her teacher, Marnae carefully follows directions when completing a writing assignment.

H. To increase the chances that her teacher will display her essay on the bulletin board, Nadine carefully follows directions when completing a writing assignment.

I. Convinced that by learning arithmetic he can increase his chances of purchasing a better bicycle for less money, Anthony raises questions in class about how to complete a computation.

X.   In your responses to Transitional Activity IX's prompts, did you infer that the students in D, E, F, and I were intrinsically motivated and those in A, B, C, G, and H were extrinsically motivated?

XI.   In two paragraphs, describe the associations between (a) positive reinforcement and whether motivation is intrinsic or extrinsic and (b) whether punishment is contrived or naturally occurring and whether motivation is intrinsic or extrinsic.

XII.   Compare the paragraphs you wrote in response to Synthesis Activity XI's prompt with those of colleagues. They should include the following points. (a) When a behavior is positively reinforced by a naturally occurring reward, one tends to be intrinsically motivated to repeat that behavior. (b) When a behavior is positively reinforced by a contrived reward, one tends to be extrinsically motivated to repeat that behavior. (c) When a behavior is followed by naturally occurring punishment, one tends to be intrinsically motivated to avoid that behavior. (d) When a behavior is followed by contrived punishment, one tends to be extrinsically motivated to avoid that behavior.

▶ TRANSITIONAL ACTIVITY FROM CHAPTER 2 TO CHAPTER 3

In preparation for your work in Chapter 3, discuss with two or more colleagues the following questions.

I.   How does the climate of a classroom (that is, the prevalent attitudes of the students and the teacher about one another and the business of learning) influence students' inclinations to cooperate with one another and be on-task?

II.   What are some of the strategies employed by teachers to build and maintain a classroom climate that is conducive to cooperation and engagement in learning activities?

III.   What are some of the strategies employed by teachers to minimize transition time and maximize allocated time?

IV.   How is the classroom climate affected by students' embarrassment due to their failure to succeed with learning goals or being criticized in front of their peers?

PART II

FOSTERING COOPERATION AND PREVENTING DISCIPLINE PROBLEMS

Establishing a Favorable Climate for Cooperation

▶ CHAPTER 3'S GOAL AND OBJECTIVES

The goal of this chapter is for you to develop strategies for establishing a classroom climate that is conducive to students cooperatively engaging in the business of learning. Specifically, Chapter 3 is designed to lead you to achieve the following objectives:

1. Understand that students are more likely to be on-task and engage in learning activities in a classroom where (a) a businesslike climate exists so that the task of achieving learning goals is paramount, (b) the teacher demonstrates withitness, (c) transition times are efficient and students are busy, (d) students feel free to engage in the business of learning without fear of embarrassment, harassment, or violence, and (e) expectations for conduct are clearly established.

2. Develop organizational techniques and employ technologies for establishing a businesslike classroom climate, demonstrating withitness, and efficiently managing transition time.

3. Understand how to take advantage of a new school year or term to establish healthy and productive interrelationships and work habits.

▶ CREATING A BUSINESSLIKE CLIMATE

The Advantage of a Businesslike Atmosphere

Why would you want your classroom to have a businesslike atmosphere? I want a businesslike atmosphere in my classroom so I can do my job of leading student to achieve worthwhile, meaningful learning goals without spending inordinate amounts of energy and time dealing with matters that distract me from doing that job. Consider Cases 3.1, 3.2, 3.3, and 3.4. Which of the cases are conducive to teachers being able to efficiently do their jobs?

▶ CASE 3.1

Ms. Richard's 28 third graders are working in four reading groups when she calls a halt to the activity to begin a large-group Spanish lesson. Ms. Richard: "Okay, class! Class, listen up. Put your reading things away and get ready—Ilone, please listen to me! Margo, leave Frankie alone; he doesn't like that! OK, class, put your reading things away and set your desks up in one big group so we can start Spanish." Joey: "Ms. Richard, I didn't get a turn to read; you said we'd all have a turn!" Francine: "Get your desk outa my way! We're supposed to be startin' Spanish." Ms. Richard: "I'm waiting, class. Let's get these desks lined up. You're going to love what we're—Fred, put your reading things away and. . . ."

▶ **CASE 3.2**

Ms. Morrison's 28 third graders are working in four reading groups when she strikes a small gong situated on her desk. The students look up as she points to the word Spanish on a colorful poster displayed on a wall. Ms. Morrison then points to an icon on the poster that symbolizes a large-group arrangement for the students. The students put their reading materials away and rearrange their desks for a large-group session. They communicate with one another in whispers. Within four minutes Ms. Morrison is conducting the Spanish lesson.

▶ **CASE 3.3**

As the bell for third period rings at Fort George High, Mr. McMahon enters his room ready to teach Latin. "All right, enough already! Let's get in our seats; we've got a lot of work to do today," he shouts above the din. Some students begin to move to their places, but others continue to talk. "Shh, hush up!" is heard from some of the students. Mr. McMahon: "Hey, in here! Knock it off, ladies! Take your homework out and let's begin. . . . "

▶ **CASE 3.4**

As the bell for third period rings at Green Mountain High, Ms. Losavio enters her room ready to teach Latin. The students, who have been milling around and socializing, stop what they've been doing as soon as one student spots her and says, "She's here." Quietly they go to their places. Without a word from Ms. Losavio, they place their homework on their desks.

I assume that you like yourself well enough to prefer to teach in either Ms. Morrison's or Ms. Losavio's situations rather than in the other two. Neither Ms. Morrison nor Ms. Losavio had to struggle to get students to begin learning activities as Ms. Richard and Mr. McMahon did. Are some teachers simply fortunate enough to operate classrooms where students seem to go about the business of learning automatically, whereas other teachers fail to achieve even a semblance of order and efficiency? Good fortune, although it occasionally plays a role, is undependable. You, like Ms. Morrison and Ms. Losavio, must rely on your own initiatives to establish an efficiently operating, businesslike classroom.

The Meaning of *Businesslike*

To some people, the term *businesslike* connotes formality in manner and dress. Please do not make such an interpretation in this context. A businesslike classroom refers to a learning environment in which the students and the teacher conduct themselves in ways suggesting that achieving specified learning goals takes priority over other concerns. Surely, even with a businesslike atmosphere, activities other than learning activities take place. Lunch money may be collected, attendance may be taken, school announcements may be heard, visits may be made to the toilet, pleasant socializing may take place, a printer may be repaired, the room may be rearranged, and a joke may evoke laughter. In a businesslike classroom, however, such deviations from the business of learning are dispatched efficiently. Engagement in certain learning activities may be fun for some students but pure drudgery for others. But in either case, engagement is considered important, serious business. Purposefulness characterizes a businesslike atmosphere.

Five Steps Toward a Businesslike Atmosphere

How do you teach your students to consider their engagement in learning activities as serious, important business? How do you establish a smoothly operating classroom with a businesslike atmosphere? First, you must sincerely believe that the learning activities you plan for your students are vital to the achievement of worthwhile learning goals. Do not expect your students to place any more importance on learning activities than you do. But telling students that a learning activity is important is usually a waste of time. You communicate its importance by the behaviors you model and the attitudes you display. You establish a businesslike atmosphere in your classroom by (a) taking advantage of the beginning of a new school year or term to set the stage for cooperation; (b) being demonstratively prepared, organized, and with-it (Kounin, 1977); (c) minimizing transition time; (d) using a communication style that encourages a comfortable, nonthreatening environment where students are free to go about the business of learning without fear of embarrassment, harassment, or harm; and (e) clearly establishing expectations for conduct.

► BEGINNING A NEW SCHOOL YEAR

Students' Perceived Notions

Students arrive in your class on the first day of school with some preconceived notions about what to expect and what is expected of them. Even the vast majority of beginning kindergarten students know that they will be required to follow a teacher's directions and that antisocial behaviors (e.g., fighting) are unacceptable. Experience has taught older students that screaming, talking out of turn, leaving a classroom without permission, and blatant rudeness are among the things that teachers don't appreciate. Experience has also taught older students that teachers vary considerably regarding (a) how seriously they take their role of helping students to learn; (b) the specific student behaviors that are expected, demanded, tolerated, not tolerated, appreciated, unappreciated, recognized, punished, or rewarded; and (c) the consistency with which a teacher reacts to certain student behaviors (i.e., given a situation, can the teacher's behavior be predicted?).

Taking Advantage of Initial Uncertainty

No matter what age group you teach, your students come to you for the first time filled with uncertainties. Some will have developed a distaste for school and are hoping that somehow you might provide them with a different sort of experience. Others will expect a continuation of what they perceive to be meaningless, boring, and inane expectations thrust on them by previous teachers. Then there are those who appreciated previous contacts with schools and meet you with high expectations.

Because students are uncertain about you at the beginning of a new school session, they will be watching your reactions, evaluating your attitudes, predicting what the relationships among you and the students will be, assessing their individual places in the social order of the classroom community, and determining how they will conduct themselves. Take advantage of the attention that students afford you on the first days of a school session to begin establishing on-task and cooperative behavior patterns. During the beginning of a school year or term, you should strictly adhere to suggestions from this text and other sources that you choose to incorporate into your teaching. Later, after students better understand what to expect from you, allowing yourself an occasional transgression from the standards you've set for yourself may not harm the smooth operation of your classroom.

Planning for a Favorable Beginning

Do not simply hope for a favorable beginning; plan for it. At least two weeks before you prepare for the first class meeting, spend some time alone in your classroom. Visualize exactly what you want to be going on in that classroom during the middle of the upcoming school session. Picture yourself conducting different learning activities and managing transition times. What traffic patterns for student movement do you want followed? What sounds should be heard (e.g., one person talking at a time during large-group meetings and the soft tones of several students talking at once during small-group activities)? How should nonlearning activities be conducted (e.g., pencil sharpening, collecting money, and visits to the drinking fountain)? How should supplies get into and out of students' hands? How will you monitor students' learning? What modes of communication will be used? When do you want to spend time planning and completing aspects of your instructional work that do not involve interacting with students? Use the teaching cycle model—outlined in Figure 1.4—as a mechanism for organizing your thoughts about your responsibilities. You need to plan your operation so that you can efficiently meet those responsibilities. Anticipate problems that might arise (e.g., supplies that don't arrive and students' refusing to follow directions) and simulate alternative ways for you to respond to them. What backup does the schoolwide safety plan provide for crisis situations? Evaluate the different alternatives. Only after you've had a week or so to reflect on exactly how you want your class to operate are you ready to plan for the new school year or term. Case 3.5 is an example of a teacher who systematically plans for a favorable beginning.

▶ CASE 3.5

Mr. Zeltsman made a checklist that included the following questions for him to answer before planning to meet his middle school social studies class for the first time:

I.   *Classroom Organization and Ongoing Routines*

    A. What different types of learning activities (e.g., video presentations, large-group demonstrations, small-group cooperative-learning sessions, independent project work, and computer-based activities) do I expect to conduct this term?

B. What equipment (e.g., multimedia projector) and technologies (e.g., software) do I need?

C. How should the room be organized (e.g., placement of furniture, computers, resource materials, screens, and displays) to accommodate the different types of learning activities and the corresponding transition times?

D. What standards of conduct and routine procedures will be needed to maximize engagement during the different types of learning activities and on-task behaviors during transition times?

E. What standards of conduct and routine procedures will be needed to discourage disruptions to other classes or persons located in or near the school?

F. What standards of conduct and routine procedures are needed to provide a safe, secure environment in which students and other persons need not fear embarrassment, harassment, or harm?

G. How will standards and procedures be determined (e.g., strictly by me, by me with input from the students, democratically, or some combination)?

H. When will standards and procedures be determined (e.g., from the very beginning, as needs arise, or both)?

I. How will standards and procedures be taught to students?

J. How will standards of conduct be enforced?

K. What other parts of the building (e.g., the timeout room or other classrooms) can be used for separating students from the rest of the class?

L. Whom, among building personnel, can I depend on to help handle short-range discipline problems and long-range problems?

M. How do I want to use the help of parents?

N. What ongoing routine tasks (e.g., reporting daily attendance) will I be expected to carry out for the school administration?

O. What events on the school calendar will need to be considered as I schedule learning activities?

P. What possible emergencies (e.g., fire, student suffering physical trauma, or violent activity) might be anticipated? Considering school policies and the schoolwide safety plan, how should I handle them?

II. *One-Time-Only Tasks*

A. How should I communicate the schoolwide policies and safety plan to my students?

B. What special administrative tasks will I be required to complete (e.g., identifying the number of students on the reduced-payment lunch program and checking health records)?

C. What supplies (e.g., textbooks) will have to be distributed?

D. Are supplies available and ready for distribution in adequate quantities?

E. How will I distribute and account for supplies?

F. Are display cards with students' names ready?

G. How should I handle students who appear on the first day but are not on the class roster?

    H.   What procedures will be used initially to direct students into the classroom and to assigned places?

    I.   For whom on the student roster might special provisions or assistance be needed for certain types of activities (e.g., students with hearing loss and students confined to wheelchairs)?

    J.   For whom on the student roster will I need to schedule IEP conferences? For each, who is the relevant special education resource person?

III.   *Reminders for the First Week's Learning Activities*

    A.   Do lesson plans for the first week call primarily for learning activities that have (a) uncomplicated directions that are simple to follow, (b) challenge but allow all students to experience success, (c) built-in positive reinforcers for engagement, and (d) all students involved at the same time?

    B.   Do the first week's lesson plans allow me to spend adequate time observing students, getting to know them, identifying needs, and collecting information that will help me make curricula decisions and design future learning activities?

    C.   Do plans allow me to be free during the first week to monitor student activities closely, be in a particularly advantageous position to discourage off-task behaviors before off-task patterns emerge, and positively reinforce on-task behaviors so that on-task patterns emerge?

IV.   *Personal Reminders for Myself*

    A.   Am I prepared to pause and reflect for a moment on what I should say to students before I say it?

    B.   Am I prepared to observe exactly what students are doing and hear exactly what they are saying before making a hasty response?

    C.   Am I prepared to use descriptive rather than judgmental language as I interact with my students?

    D.   Am I prepared to act consistently and communicate assertively, being neither hostile nor passive?

    E.   Am I prepared to use a supportive response style?

    F.   Am I prepared to model a businesslike attitude?

Most of the questions in Mr. Zeltsman's list are dealt with in subsequent sections of this text (e.g., room arrangements in Chapter 7, standards for conduct in Chapter 5, and supportive response styles in Chapter 4). At this time, turn your attention to his three questions under heading III, "Reminders for the First Week's Learning Activities." Read them again.

Learning Activities Conducive to a Favorable Beginning

Engaging students in learning activities with easy-to-follow, uncomplicated directions during the early part of a new school session has two advantages: (a) Your students can immediately get to the business of learning without bewilderment about "What are we supposed to be doing?" (b) Students learn that your directions are understandable;

consequently, they will be willing to attend to them in the future. If students are confused by your initial directions, they are less likely to try to understand subsequent ones. Later, after students have developed a pattern of attending to the directions for learning activities, you can gradually introduce more complex procedures to be followed.

Students should find their first engagements with your learning activities satisfying. You want to leave them with the impression "I learned something; I can be successful!" The idea, of course, is to make sure engagement is positively reinforced so that patterns of engaged behaviors are formed. Later in a school session, it will be advantageous for you to have students working on individual levels, with some engaged in one learning activity while others are involved in a different learning activity. It is advisable, however, to involve all students in the same learning activity in the first stages of a school session. Having all students working on the same task allows you to keep directions simple, monitor the class as a whole, and compare how different individuals approach a common task. Moreover, until you get to know your students, you hardly have a basis for deciding how to individualize. In Case 3.6, a first-grade teacher begins setting a businesslike tone on orientation day and then plans opening-day activities that are ideal for students' initial experiences. Cases 3.7 and 3.8 provide additional examples.

▶ CASE 3.6

The faculty, administration, and staff of Eugene Street School conduct an orientation day for students and parents a few days before the beginning of the school year. The purpose is for students and their parents to meet the teachers, become acquainted with the campus, and learn schoolwide policies and procedures. Mr. Manda, a first-grade teacher, receives the preliminary roster for his class just in time for orientation day. He quickly examines the files of the students, noting if and where they attended kindergarten and if any had previously been retained in first grade. Although he does not have much confidence in the validity of standardized tests, he looks at the results of readiness and aptitude tests that are available. He also reviews any anecdotal records or notes in the files from parents, school administrators, or teachers. With the intent of communicating to his students "Welcome to your classroom! I am happy you are here and that we will be working together!" Mr. Manda displays a poster (see Figure 3.1) near the entrance to the classroom and, as shown in Figure 3.2, prepares a personalized storage station for each student.

Unfortunately, only 16 students visit the school on orientation day, and only 12 of those are accompanied by a parent. Mr. Manda engages in a warm, informative conversation with each student and gives them a letter for their parents. For example:

Mr. Manda: Hello, I'm Mr. Manda (shaking hands). What is your name?

Liu: I'm Liu.

Mr. Manda: I'm so happy to meet you. Please introduce me to this lady who is with you.

Liu: This is my momma.

Ms. Sun-Hu: Hello (shaking hands), I'm Fang Sun-Hu.

Mr. Manda: Thank you for coming. I'm Dustin Manda, Liu's first-grade teacher. Let's sit down over here by Liu's storage station. . . . Liu, you were in kindergarten at another school. Is that right?

Liu: Yes.

Ms. Sun-Hu: He was at Westview; we just moved into this district last month.

Mr. Manda: (turning to Liu) So these are exciting times for you—new neighborhood, a new place to live, and now a new school! Do you know your new school's name?

Liu: Eugene Street School.

Figure 3.1. Mr. Manda's Poster Welcoming 24 VIPs

Mr. Manda: Yes, it is. And here's a paper for you with the name of the school, my name—Mr. Manda—your room number—113—the names of the other students in your class, and some times and dates for you to go over with your momma later today. Bring this paper back here with you on Monday at 8:30 in the morning.

Ms. Sun-Hu: What do you say to your teacher?

Liu: Thank you.

Mr. Manda: You are welcome. Also, here is a letter for your momma; it explains some things about our class and Eugene Street School. Now, let's take a look around the classroom and then you and your mom can tour the building. What do you see against the wall there?

Liu: It's a picture of this room. Why . . .? (The conversation continues.)

The letter for Ms. Sun-Hu is shown in Figure 3.3. The form letters that parents receive appear personalized because of word-processing technology.

Mr. Manda maintains a high energy level throughout orientation day, but when the last student is gone and he is finished modifying his plans for opening day (based on ideas that came to him as he met with students and parents), fatigue takes over. He reflects on the day's activities and judges that the meetings were extremely useful for students, parents, and him. The rapport that was established with the students and the lines of communication opened with parents will pay dividends throughout the year. He's disappointed that some students and parents missed the experience. Out of concern for getting the first school day off to a smooth start and sending the message that learning is important business, he attempts to phone parents of the eight students who did not attend but manages to reach only five.

Figure 3.2. Personalized Storage Station in Room 113

On opening day he walks the students through Figure 3.4's tasksheet. Teacher directions for engaging the first graders in the tasksheet activities are included. Mr. Manda designed the opening-day activities and the tasksheet with the following purposes in mind:

- The students immediately get busy with school-like work that helps orient them to their new environment.

- The activity is relatively easy for Mr. Manda to monitor and cue individuals to be on-task.

- The students begin to develop the impression that schoolwork with Mr. Manda's guidance relates to their individual interests, they are expected to make judgments, and their judgments are valued.

- Mr. Manda can use students' responses from the tasksheets in subsequent lessons to help students understand academic content. For example, Mr. Manda intends to conduct a lesson on the concept of community during the second week. One of the activities he plans for that lesson is for students to compare their drawings from the tasksheet to demonstrate how different people in a community view things differently. From that idea, he will conduct a question–discussion session leading students to understand that communities need to accommodate differences among their members.

- He gains feedback about students' interests and skills that will be valuable for planning subsequent lessons. For example, as students respond to the tasksheet's prompts, he will

Eugene Street Elementary School
Southside School District

Dustin R. Manda

August 23, 2007

Ms. Fang Sun-Husan
Apartment #19
860 Shirley Avenue

Dear Ms. Sun-Husan:

The beginning of first grade marks a significant event in Liu's life. The year's experiences will influence his (a) attitudes about himself, (b) desire to learn, (c) work habits, (d) social attitudes and skills, (e) self-control, (f) academic abilities and skills, and (g) physical development. As his first-grade teacher, I will strive for Liu's school-related experiences to be as positive as possible. In carrying out this responsibility, my professional preparation should serve me well. But the success of the endeavor also depends on our working together cooperatively. To this end, we need to communicate routinely about how to work with Liu most effectively. I will use several means to keep you informed about my activities for the first-grade students of room 113:

1. Each month, I will send a newsletter to the parents. The letter will have four sections: (a) "Looking Back," summarizing class activities and achievements from the previous month; (b) "This Month," relating upcoming goals and activities; (c) "Looking Forward," previewing what's anticipated for upcoming months; and (d) "From the Students," presenting a sample of students' writings and artwork.
2. With approximately 25 students, I'm unable to contact individual parents as frequently as I would like. By phoning two or three parents each school-day evening, however, I can converse with a parent once every two weeks. Because of the constraints of work schedules, these periodic phone conferences must not exceed 10 minutes. Although brief, they allow me to apprise you of Liu's progress and enable us to exchange ideas on how we can effectively work with him.
3. The enclosed material includes an academic-year calendar for Eugene Street School. Note the four days set aside for parent-teacher conferences. Each time, you, Liu, and I will discuss his end-of-the-term progress report (the contemporary first-grade equivalent of a report card).
4. Several times a week, expect Liu to bring home samples of work he's completed in school. Liu needs to share his school accomplishments with you and hear your expressions of interest.
5. I'll assign homework three or four times a week. No more than 30 minutes in any one day should be spent on after-school homework. Typically, the assignment is for Liu to review a spelling-word list with you, collect materials or data to bring to school, or read a brief selection from a book.

Figure 3.3. Introductory Letter Mr. Manda Gives to Students' Parents

6. Occasionally we may need to schedule a conference to work out a solution to a problem cooperatively. The problem may involve helping Liu modify work habits or classroom behaviors. It could also be a pleasant problem such as how to help him nurture some of his special talents.

7. Anytime you feel the need to speak with me, please do not hesitate to set up an appointment by calling the school office (phone number 342-4065) between 7:45 A.M. and 4:45 P.M. on any school day. Ms. Sonya Hoyt, school office secretary, maintains a calendar for me and will be happy to take your calls and schedule appointments for us to meet in person or by phone.

8. You are welcome to visit our classroom and observe us in action anytime during the school day. Please familiarize yourself with the enclosed "Guidelines for Observers in Room 113" before your first visit. Note that school policy requires all visitors to stop by the school office and obtain a building pass before entering the classroom areas. This policy is designed to protect our children from intruders who might compromise the safety and security of the school environment.

Enclosed for your information are the following items:

1. Eugene Street School academic-year calendar.
2. Daily schedule of courses for the first-grade students of room 113.
3. Course descriptions for art and music, health and physical education, mathematics, reading, science, social studies, and writing and speaking.
4. A brief statement of my philosophy of teaching.

I am looking forward to working with Liu and you.

Sincerely,

Dustin Manda

Dustin R. Manda
First-Grade Teacher
Eugene Street School

enclosures

Figure 3.3. *(continued)*

note variations among students' performances in following directions, willingness to draw pictures, and what they enjoy doing.

► **CASE 3.7**

It is the opening day of a new term at Blackhawk Trail High School. The bell ending the second period rings, and the bell to indicate the beginning of third period will ring in five minutes. Mr. Stockton, in preparation for the arrival of his third-period earth science class, turns on a DVD player that shows a video on a prominently displayed monitor. The volume is turned up rather high. As required by school policy, Mr. Stockton stations himself just outside the classroom door between periods. As students enter the room, they hear his voice coming from the video monitor: "Please have a seat in the desk displaying a card with your name. If no desk has a card with your name, please sit in one of the desks with a blank card. There you will find a marking pen for you to

These 24 stickers are in an envelope attached to Olga's task sheet:

```
Olga Bailey
```

1.

2.

3.

Figure 3.4. Tasksheet with which Mr. Manda Engaged His Students on the First Day of School

Oral directions to be explained by the teacher to the students, one item at a time using an illustrative tasksheet:

1. Pinned to the sheet is an envelope with three kinds of stickers. Take out the stickers and find one with your name. Now put the others back in the envelope. Thank you. Now stick your name in this first box.

2. Now, draw a picture of your teacher—that's me, Mr. Manda—right here in this big box. Thank you. I like looking at these pictures of myself.

3. Now, picture in your head what the outside of our school building looks like. Now draw the outside of our school building in this big box. Thank you. I like looking at the different ways you pictured our school.

4. Now turn to the last page and look at all the pictures. Take the rest of the stickers out of your envelope. Put a smiley face sticker on each picture that shows something you don't like to do. When you're finished, put the leftover stickers back in the envelope and raise your hand so I can bring you something.

As each student finishes, Mr. Manda exchanges a picture to color for the completed tasksheet.

Figure 3.4. (*continued*)

print and display your first name. Once seated in your desk, please take out one sheet of paper and a pen or pencil. You will need them when the third period begins. I would appreciate you clearing your desktop of everything except your name card, pencil or pen, and paper. This message will be repeated until the beginning of third period. After the bell, the directions for today's first lesson will appear on the screen." The message, printed on the screen as Mr. Stockton's voice speaks it, is repeated until five seconds after the third-period bell. Mr. Stockton steps into the room. He moves among the students, gently tapping one inattentive student's desktop and pointing toward the monitor. Several times he gestures to the monitor in response to students who try to speak to him.

The message on the video changes. Mr. Stockton's image appears on the screen with this message: "I am about to perform an experiment. It will take six and a half minutes. During that time, carefully watch what happens. When the experiment is completed, you will be asked to describe in writing just what you observed. Remember these two words—*describe* and *observe*. They will be very important during this course in earth science. . . ."

As the experiment appears on the screen, Mr. Stockton watches the students. The video directs the students to spend seven minutes writing a paragraph describing what they saw. Then it ends. Mr. Stockton circulates around the room reading over students' shoulders as they write. At the end of the seven minutes, he calls on several students to read their paragraphs. Other students are then brought into a discussion session in which a distinction is made between describing observations and making judgments.

Mr. Stockton judges the activity a success because all students appear to realize that they had made and described observations. Mr. Stockton distributes copies of the course syllabus and goes over it item by item. As he discusses the goals of the earth science course, he makes frequent references to observing and recording results such as those they just shared.

Textbooks are distributed and some administrative chores taken care of before the period ends. Mr. Stockton indicates that standards for conduct and organizational procedures will be discussed at the next meeting.

By the way, while the students were viewing the video, Mr. Stockton checked the roll and posted the attendance report outside the classroom door for school office personnel to collect.

▶ CASE 3.8

Ms. Phegley spent most of the first two days of the school year helping her first graders get accustomed to their new surroundings. She spent the majority of the time getting to know these six-year-olds and teaching them how to adhere to standards for conduct and follow some basic routine procedures (e.g., for cleaning up after themselves and getting to and from the cafeteria).

On the third day, as the students are seated at their places, Ms. Phegley announces, "Everyone put your hands on your head like this." She puts both her hands on top of her head, and the students follow along. Ms. Phegley: "Now keep your hands up there until you see me take mine off my head." Smiling brightly, she surveys their faces with deliberation. Ms. Phegley: "Taped under your table is an envelope containing your very own word." Roger and Ethan begin to reach under their tables. Ms. Phegley: "My hands are still on top of my head. Thank you for waiting. Now look around the room. What do you see on the wall just above the boards?" "Posters!" "Cards!" "Words!" are some of the replies. Ms. Phegley: "Yes, I agree! There are posters and cards hanging all around the room with words on them. How many are there?" "Too many!" a student says. "One, two, three, four—ten; there are ten!" responds another. "No, more than ten!" says yet another student. Ms. Phegley interrupts, "There are as many words on the wall as there are of you. There's one for each of you. One of those words belongs to Louise, and one belongs to Granville, and one belongs to Marva—" "And one belongs to me!" shouts Mickey. "Which one is mine?" asks Gwynn. "Oh! I know," says Claudia. "The envelopes under our tables will tell us!" Ms. Phegley: "They sure will. When I take my hands off my head, that is the signal for you to take the envelope from under your desk and—Talya, look where my hands are—and find out which word on the wall it matches. Once you've found your word, you are to go and quietly stand under it. I'll tell you what we'll do next after everyone is quietly standing under her or his own word. Do you want to ask me anything before I take my hands off my head? . . ."

The learning activity continues, culminating with students' comparing similarities and differences in their words. Ms. Phegley chose this activity for the first week of school not only because it helps students develop some reading-readiness skills, but also because it gets them used to following her directions and lets them all achieve success. Some students are quicker than others to match the letters and locate where to stand. But this makes it easier for those who move slower because it reduces the number of places left to stand and thus the number of comparisons to be made.

Engage in Activity 3.1.

► *ACTIVITY 3.1*

Figure 3.4 displays a tasksheet Mr. Manda incorporated into the opening-day activities with his first graders. Reexamine Figure 2.1, which is the questionnaire Ms. Martin used with her high school history class in Case 2.4.

In both cases, the teachers used opening-day tasksheets designed to help establish the tone for the school year and provide insights about individual students' interests, attitudes, and skills.

Imagine a course or grade level that fits your educational specialty (e.g., fifth grade, middle school science,

or high school physical education) that you anticipate teaching in the near future. Design an opening-day tasksheet that you would consider incorporating in the first day's activities of that class. Keep in mind that the tasksheet should help you (a) communicate expectations and develop healthy attitudes and (b) get an early jump on knowing students as individuals.

Exchange your tasksheet with that of a colleague who is also engaging in Activity 3.1. Provide one another with feedback and suggestions on the tasksheets.

► DISPLAYING WITHITNESS

One of the purposes of using an opening-day tasksheet such as the one resulting from your engagement in Activity 3.1 is to get a jump on knowing your students. The better you know your students the better you're able to demonstrate what Jacob Kounin (1977) referred to as "withitness." Beginning in the 1950s and continuing into the 1970s, Kounin conducted studies examining the influence of certain teacher behaviors on the tendencies of students to be on-task (Kounin & Doyle, 1975; Kounin & Gump, 1974: Kounin & Sherman, 1979). These studies involved classrooms from kindergarten through college level.

One of the major implications of these studies involves the impact of teachers' withitness on students' behaviors. By definition, *withitness* is the degree to which a teacher is aware of what is going on in the classroom. Teachers whom students claim have "eyes in the back of their heads" display withitness. Kounin emphasized that teachers increase the likelihood of students' being on-task by demonstrating to students that they are with-it and can accurately detect classroom events. He found that the following conditions lead students to judge their teacher as having withitness:

- When discipline problems occur, the teacher consistently takes action to suppress misbehaviors of exactly those students who instigated the problems. (This response displays that the teacher knows what is happening. If, on the other hand, the students expect the teacher to blame the wrong person, they conclude that the teacher is not with-it.)
- When two discipline problems arise concurrently, the teacher typically deals with the more serious one first.
- The teacher decisively handles instances of off-task behaviors before the behaviors either get out of hand or are copied by others. (For example, if third-grader Bernie begins creating a tower out of the colored rods that he is supposed to be using to validate answers to multiplication exercises, a with-it teacher will likely take action to get Bernie back on-task before the tower tumbles over or other students begin building their own.)

To be with-it, it is important for you to manage a classroom so that you can deal with a number of events concurrently. Compare how the two teachers in Cases 3.9 and 3.10 handle instances of off-task behaviors.

▶ **CASE 3.9**

Ms. Farnsworth is explaining certain aspects of human digestive systems to her class of 31 tenth graders when she notices Ekpe and Ross whispering to one another. She stops her explanation and announces: "Please pay attention you two! It's very important for you to understand this. Now where were we? Oh, yes! As I was saying...."

▶ **CASE 3.10**

Ms. Gordin is explaining certain aspects of human digestive systems to her class of 31 tenth graders when she notices Rich and Jonathan whispering to one another. She continues with her explanations to the class as she moves nearer to Rich and Jonathan. They continue their whispering. Without the least interruption to her lecture, she moves between Rich and Jonathan and gently taps the top of Rich's desk. The two stop and appear to begin attending to the lesson. She continues to observe all the students, including Rich and Jonathan, as the explanation progresses.

How would you prefer to have handled the students' whispering—as Ms. Farnsworth did or as Ms. Gordin did? Ms. Gordin simultaneously handled two events: her explanation of digestive systems to the whole class and two students' off-task behaviors. Ms. Farnsworth, on the other hand, interrupted her lecture to take time to handle the whispering. Her failure to deal with both events at the same time caused other students to become disengaged from the learning activity.

▶ MODELING PREPARATION AND ORGANIZATION

The Importance of the Third and Fourth Stages of Teaching Cycles

Engage in Activity 3.2.

In Cases 3.7 and 3.8, Mr. Stockton and Ms. Phegley left their students with the impression that directions are to be strictly followed and learning activities are important business to be taken seriously. List some of the specific steps those teachers took that helped convey this impression to students. Now classify each step in your list according to its placement in the teaching cycles model. For example: (a) Mr. Stockton was operating within the third phase of a cycle when he decided to demonstrate an experiment at the very beginning of the class period. (b) Mr. Stockton was operating within the fourth phase of the cycle when he video recorded the experiment in preparation for the class meeting. (c) Ms. Phegley operated within the fourth phase of a cycle when she prepared the posters and hung them on the walls. (d) She was also within the fourth phase of the cycle when she taped the envelopes under students' tables before meeting her class.

I would guess that a large share of the steps in your list from Activity 3.2 fell within the purview of the third and fourth phases of the teaching cycle model (i.e., determining and preparing for learning activities). The way that Mr. Stockton and Ms. Phegley organized and prepared for their classes contributed to their smooth classroom operations and the desirable impressions left on students.

The Effects of Preparation on Classroom Climate and Efficiency

It took more preparation time for Mr. Stockton to demonstrate the science experiment on video than it would have to conduct the experiment live. But the extra effort in preparation made it much easier for him to start the first class session smoothly and have students engaged in a learning activity while he was free to manage the setting. The video presentation also added a professional touch that told students, "This is serious business. This teacher is serious enough to make the extra effort to organize and prepare thoroughly. The same is expected of students." Compare the message that such well-prepared sessions send to students with the message sent by sessions in which a teacher is prepared only with a whiteboard pen and a resolution that "students had better pay attention or else!" Or else what?

Preparing name cards for students was a simple matter for Mr. Stockton that made a major difference in how his initial meeting with students went. Name tags designating seating arrangements give students a hint of order in the classroom. Even though Mr. Stockton has approximately 160 students per term at Blackhawk Trail High, the name tags enabled him to call each student by name on the first day of school. Suppose, for example, that while he is going over the course syllabus, he notices that a student's attention is drifting; he is readily able to work that student's name into the explanations. Such a tactic can cue a student back on-task. "The guy in the green shirt" is not nearly as effective as "Ralph."

Secondary school teachers typically present information about course expectations at the beginning of a school term. Mr. Stockton prepared a course syllabus for distribution on the first day. Such documents, if professionally prepared, can provide at least four advantages in helping students to be on-task: (a) A course syllabus suggests to students that the course work is purposeful and gives them an idea of how it will benefit them. (b) A well-organized syllabus gives the impression that the course is well organized and will be conducted in a businesslike manner. (c) Throughout the term, the teacher can use the syllabus as a point of focus (e.g., Mr. Stockton can refer to it by saying, "Tonight's homework will move you to section 4 on page 5 of your syllabus."). (d) The syllabus provides an outline for the class meetings in which course expectations are discussed.

Figure 3.5 displays a syllabus developed by Ms. Fisher, a history teacher.

When Mr. Stockton was ready to discuss course expectations, he passed out copies of the course syllabus. Ms. Phegley's preparation for putting materials into her first graders' hands was a bit more elaborate. Instead of simply distributing word cards to her students in class, she placed them in envelopes and taped them under tabletops beforehand. What advantages did she gain by going to this extra trouble? (a) The first graders were able to discover "their very own" words at the same time without waiting for them to be handed out one at a time. (b) By being taped under the tabletops, the word cards were kept out of sight and thus did not become distracting toys before Ms. Phegley was ready for the students to work with them. (c) Having an unknown word located in an unusual place added an air of mystery that helped hold students' attention while Ms. Phegley relayed the directions for the learning activity. (d) Having the words already distributed before class gave Ms. Phegley more freedom during class to supervise and orchestrate the activities.

Generally speaking, the more work you put into your preparation before class, the less you will need to do to maintain a smooth operation during class. The benefits of exceptional preparation for highly organized learning activities increase over time for at least two reasons. (a) Materials prepared for one class (e.g., Mr. Stockton's videotape and Ms. Phegley's posters for displaying words) can be reused with or refined for subsequent classes. (b) The businesslike attitude that a well-prepared, highly organized teacher models for students has a lasting effect that will help establish on-task and engaged student behavior patterns.

▶ ORCHESTRATING SMOOTH, EFFICIENT TRANSITIONS

Smoothness of Transitions and Momentum

According to Kounin's studies, student engagement and on-task behaviors depend on how smoothly teachers move from one learning activity to another, how efficient transitions are, and how well momentum is maintained. Examine Cases 3.11 to 3.13.

▶ CASE 3.11

Mr. Condie is grading papers at a desk while his fifth-grade students individually work on a writing assignment at their places. Suddenly he announces: "Okay, class, you can finish that later; let's take out our history workbooks and start answering the questions beginning at the bottom of page 74. Jean, how would you answer number 1? ... " Some of the students who were involved with the writing assignment when Mr. Condie suddenly announced the new activity do not comprehend what was said. They continue to write, although history questions are being read. Others stop writing but inquire from classmates about the page number. There is a long delay before the majority of the class is engaged in the history lesson.

▶ CASE 3.12

Ms. Jesundas announces to her fourth-grade class: "I see that everyone is finished with the calculator drill. Please see that your calculator is off and put away in its box.—Thank you. Now we're going to begin working on something you'll really enjoy. I want everyone to get out one sheet

**Course Syllabus
for
U.S. History**

WHAT IS THIS COURSE ALL ABOUT?

The course is all about the history of the United States:
- Journeying through time taking us from the origins of our country to where we are today
- Discovering how to utilize the lessons of history to deal with today's issues and problems

WHAT IS HISTORY?

There are three aspects of history:
- All actual past events
- Methods used by historians to discover and describe past events and explain their causes and influences
- Documented references resulting from the work of historians

WHY SHOULD YOU LEARN U.S. HISTORY?

Every day of your life you make decisions about how to behave, what to do, where to go, who to see, what to eat, what to wear, and so on and so forth. Those decisions are influenced by your understanding of events in your past life (i.e., your own history). For example, you are more likely to choose to go places you found enjoyable in the past than to places where you were bored. Your understanding of past events helps you to control present and future events. As a world citizen, especially one living in the United States, you have an influence over present and future events in this country. Those events influence your everyday life. Understand events in this country's past and you'll be better able to influence its future.

There are also some more mundane reasons:
- Your success in other courses you take in high school as well as in any vocational school, technical school, or college you might attend depends on your understanding of history.
- A full year credit in U.S. history is required for a high school diploma in this state.
- An understanding of at least some U.S. history is expected of literate citizens in today's society and is needed in many occupations.

WITH WHOM WILL YOU BE WORKING IN THIS COURSE?

You will be working with Nancy Fisher, who is responsible for helping you and your classmates learn U.S. history. You will also be working with your classmates, each of whom will be making a unique contribution to what you get out of this course. In turn, you will contribute to what they learn by sharing your ideas, discoveries, insights, problems, and solutions.

WHERE WILL YOU BE LEARNING U.S. HISTORY?

You will draw your understanding of history from your entire environment whether at home, school, or anywhere else. Your classroom, room 203, at Rainbow High is the place where ideas about history are brought together and formalized. Room 203 is a place of business for learning history.

HOW WILL YOU BE EXPECTED TO BEHAVE IN THIS CLASS?

You and your classmates have the right to go about the business of learning history free from fear of being harmed, intimidated, or embarrassed. Ms. Fisher has the right to go about

Figure 3.5. Sample Course Syllabus Developed by Ms. Fisher

the business of helping you and your classmates learn history without disruption or interference. Thus, you are expected to follow five rules of conduct:

1. Give yourself a complete opportunity to learn history.
2. Do not interfere with the opportunities of your classmates to learn history.
3. Respect the rights of all members of this class (they include you, your classmates, and Ms. Fisher).
4. Follow Ms. Fisher's directions for lessons and classroom procedures.
5. Adhere to the rules and policies of Rainbow High as listed on pages 11–15 of the Student Handbook.

WHAT MATERIALS WILL YOU NEED FOR CLASS?

Bring the following with you to every class meeting:

- The course textbook:
  DiBacco, T. V., Mason, L. C., & Appy, C. G. (1991). History of the United States. Boston: Houghton Mifflin.
- A four-part notebook:
  1. Part 1 is for class notes.
  2. Part 2 is for homework and class assignments.
  3. Part 3 is for saving artifacts from independent and cooperative-group activities.
  4. Part 4 is for maintaining a reference for definitions and facts.
- A scratch pad
- Pencils, pens, and an eraser

You will also need five 5.25″ computer diskettes in a storage case. You will not have to bring these to class every day, but have them available at school (e.g., in your locker).

A textbook has been checked out to you for the school year. You are responsible for maintaining it in good condition and returning it to Ms. Fisher on the last day of class. The other materials can be purchased at the Rainbow High Bookstore or at other retail outlets.

WHAT WILL YOU BE DOING FOR THIS CLASS?

The course is organized into 22 units between one to three weeks each. During each unit you will be:

- Participating in class meetings
  Depending on the agenda for the meetings you will be:
  - Listening to Ms. Fisher speak and seeing her illustrations as you take notes on what is being explained
  - Listening to classmates speak and seeing their illustrations as you take notes on what is being explained
  - Explaining things to the class as your classmates take notes on what you say and show them
  - Asking questions, answering questions, and discussing issues with members of the class during questioning/discussion sessions
  - Working closely with your classmates as part of small task-groups
  - Working independently on assigned exercises
  - Taking brief tests
- Completing homework assignments
- Taking a unit test

WHAT WILL YOU LEARN FROM THIS CLASS?

Each unit will either introduce you to a new historical topic or extend your understanding of a previous topic. During the unit you will:

- Discover an idea or relationship
- Add to your ability to use historical methods

Figure 3.5. (*continued*)

- Acquire new information or add depth of understanding to previously acquired information
- Extend your ability to utilize the lessons in history to solve today's problems

Here are the titles of the 22 units:

1. Looking Ahead in Light of Past Lessons: Historical Methods
2. The First Americans, Exploration, and Colonization
3. A New Nation
4. The U.S. Constitution and the New Republic
5. Expansion
6. The Civil War and Reconstruction Eras
7. Emergence of Industrial America, New Frontiers
8. Urban Society and Gilded-Age Politics
9. Protests and the Progressive Movement
10. Expansionism
11. World War I
12. The Roaring Twenties
13. The Great Depression and the New Deal
14. A Search for Peace and World War II
15. A Cold Peace
16. The Politics of Conflict and Hope
17. The Civil Rights Movement
18. The Vietnam War
19. Dirty Politics
20. Toward a Global (and Cleaner) Society
21. The New Nationalism
22. Extending What You've Learned into a New Century

Units 1–12 are planned for the first semester, Units 13–22 for the second semester.

HOW WILL YOU KNOW WHEN YOU'VE LEARNED U.S. HISTORY?

Everyone knows at least some history, but no one ever learns it completely. History is being discovered. You will use what you learn in this course to further develop your ability to apply the lessons of history to everyday decision making.

The question is not whether or not you've learned history, but how well you are learning it. During this course, you will be given feedback on your progress through comments Ms. Fisher makes about work you complete, scores you achieve on brief tests, and the grades you achieve based on unit, midsemester, and semester tests.

HOW WILL YOUR GRADES FOR THE COURSE BE DETERMINED?

Your grade for the first semester will be based on 12 unit tests, a midsemester test scheduled between the sixth and seventh units, and a semester test. Your scores on these tests will influence your first semester grade according to the following scale:

- The 12 unit tests ....60% (5% each)
- The midsemester test 15%
- The semester test 25%

Your grade for the second semester will be based on 10 unit tests, a midsemester test scheduled between the 17th and 18th units, and a semester test. Your scores on these tests will influence your second semester grade according to the following scale:

- The 10 unit tests ....60% (6% each)
- The midsemester test 15%
- The semester test 25%

Figure 3.5. (*continued*)

of paper and a pencil.—Joseph, get those other things off your desk.—Thank you, Joseph. Okay, as I was saying, you should have just one sheet of paper—that's the way to do it, Mark!—You should have one sheet of paper and nothing else except for a pencil on your desk.—Oh! Rachel, your pencil needs sharpening. We'll take care of that in a moment. Now you're really going to like what we're going to do. Take your paper and. . . ."

▶ **CASE 3.13**

With the aid of an overhead projector, Mr. Saville is demonstrating to his accounting class one system for recording certain types of business transactions. While referring to an example involving consolidation of loans, Mr. Saville pauses and asks, "Have we ever explained what 'consolidation of loans' means?" Dorothy: "No, we never did get to that." David: "Yeah! What does that mean?" Mr. Saville: "I thought we had covered that, but I guess not.—Open your text to page.—Let's see—here it is! Page 139.—Everybody's got it?—Good! Now read the part under heading 6-4 on consolidating loans." Gwynn: "Mr. Saville, we already read this! This was a homework assignment." Other students express their agreement, while only a few suggest that they hadn't read the section. Mr. Saville: "In that case, put your books away and let's get back to our new recording system.—Now, as I was explaining before. . . ."

In Case 3.11 Mr. Condie failed to get all his students' attention before attempting to give them directions for an upcoming learning activity. The transition between the time allocated for the writing activity and the time allocated for answering history questions was not *smooth*. With some students continuing to work on the first activity, others changing activities, and still others beginning the new task, the transition time was marked by confusion. The teacher did not attend to details and attempted to make the transition between two learning activities too rapidly.

The problem with Mr. Condie's transition is in direct contrast to the one created by Ms. Jesundas in Case 3.12. She wasted so much of her students' time with minute details, taking care of isolated problems and trying to convince her students how enjoyable the activity would be, that her students got bored by what she had planned before they ever got to do it.

In Case 3.13 the transitions were inefficient; Mr. Saville failed to maintain *momentum* during learning activities. He interrupted one activity to begin another and then returned to the first while the second one was abandoned. Although such interruptions cannot always be avoided, they do make it difficult for students to remain engaged in learning activities. At least some of Mr. Saville's students were still thinking about who was right regarding the alleged homework assignment on consolidated loans when he was expecting their attention to be refocused on his demonstration.

Minimizing Transition Time

By minimizing transition time, you maximize allocated time. The more allocated time you have available, the more time students have for being engaged in learning activities. Of course, making more allocated time available does not necessarily result in greater achievement unless the learning activities are worthwhile and the additional allocated time actually results in additional engaged time.

Keeping transition time to a minimum has other benefits. Students' engagement levels are likely to be better when there is a smooth, rapid transition between learning activities than when transition time is extended or learning activities interrupted. By efficiently moving from one lesson to another and streamlining your procedures for dispensing with nonteaching, managerial, and administrative tasks, you can avoid having your students waste time waiting for the business of learning to start. Students waiting to get busy develop their own devices for relieving their boredom, such as attention-getting disruptions and daydreaming. Disruptive behaviors tend to extend the transition periods between learning activities and amplify the initial cause of the problem. Daydreaming, although not disruptive, makes it difficult for a student to become engaged in the learning activity when transition time stops and allocated time begins. Switching the focus of one's thoughts cannot always happen on cue.

The next five sections offer ideas on how to minimize transition time.

▶ DISPENSING WITH ADMINISTRATIVE DUTIES

Inefficient Use of Class Time

Case 3.14 would be incredible if it were not indicative of everyday occurrences in thousands of classrooms (Cangelosi, 2006).

▶ CASE 3.14

Ms. Rolando teaches fifth grade at a school where each day she is required to report to the main office the names of absentees and the number of students planning to eat lunch in the cafeteria that day—categorized by free lunch, reduced-payment lunch, and full-payment lunch. Students who were absent the previous day are required to display an admit slip signed by a school secretary before Ms. Rolando may permit their participation in class. Students not in the classroom by the second bell must show a signed late slip before being accepted into class.

It is now Monday morning, one that typifies most. Twenty-five of Ms. Rolando's 31 students are seated in their desks by the second bell. Four others come in during public-address announcements, which are followed by the *Pledge of Allegiance*. Ms. Rolando begins calling the roll: "Raymond?" "Here." "Melinda?" "Here." "Turner?—Turner!—Are you here, Turner?" "Oh! Yes, ma'am, I'm here." "Barbara?—I see Barbara's absent.—Frank?" "Yeah, I guess so!" "Frank, that's no way to answer the roll! OK, Melanie?—Where's . . . ?" It takes nine minutes to complete the roll call, during which time students sit idly or find ways to entertain themselves.

Ms. Rolando then asks, "Which of you on free lunch are eating in the cafeteria today? Okay, keep your hands high! One, two, three—Ralph, is your hand up?—six, seven. Okay, raise your hand if you're on reduced lunch." Turner: "I'm on reduced lunch, but I brought my lunch today. Should I raise my hand?" Ms. Rolando: "You know what I mean! No, Turner, keep your hand down unless you're eating in the cafeteria today." Turner: "What if I just want to get milk today?" Ms. Rolando: "Never mind, Turner. One, two—Willie, put your hand down; you're not on reduced lunch—three, four, six, eight. Now, the rest of you who are eating. . . ." Nine minutes later, Ms. Rolando has her lunch tallies.

"Those of you who came in late or were absent yesterday, bring your passes to me now," Ms. Rolando says as she dispenses with the admit and late slips in four minutes. All this time, her students are waiting for the business of the day to begin. As they wait, they become more and more restless and their moods change so that they are not as ready to be engaged in learning activities as they were before.

Finally, Ms. Rolando starts the transition into her mathematics activity with, "Take out your homework so I can come around and check on who did it and who did not."

Efficient Use of Class Time

Most public school teachers are burdened with administrative tasks that tend to extend transition time and detract from student engagement. But many teachers cope with this burden with only a minimal loss of allocated time. Case 3.15 is an example.

▶ CASE 3.15

Ms. Drexler teaches fifth grade at the same school as Ms. Rolando. She is also required to perform the same morning administrative duties. It's now Monday morning. Twenty-six of Ms. Drexler's 30 students are seated as the second bell rings and public-address announcements begin. As soon as the announcements and the *Pledge of Allegiance* are finished, Ms. Drexler directs her students to place their mathematics homework papers on top of their desks with "yes" written in the upper left-hand corner of the first page if they plan to eat in the cafeteria that day and "no" if they will not. She then distributes a written-response mathematics quiz that students begin immediately. As they respond to the quiz, Ms. Drexler circulates among the students, as she uses a hand-held electronic organizer to enter data regarding lunch count, attendance, and homework.

Because Ms. Drexler's electronic organizer is programed so that it indicates the lunch status of each student, the simple "yes" or "no" written on the homework paper is sufficient for her to provide the office with the categorized lunch tallies.

Ms. Drexler completes these tasks and transfers the data from her organizer to her computer, prints out the form that the main office expects, and takes care of other administrative duties before the students finish the mathematics quiz.

▶ SAVING TIME WHEN DISTRIBUTING MATERIALS AND GIVING DIRECTIONS

Efficient Beginnings to Learning Activities

Compare the efficiency of the transition in Case 3.16 to the transition in Case 3.17.

▶ CASE 3.16

Mr. Hansen's 38 fifth graders are filing into their classroom just after a recess break. He has planned a learning activity that involves pairs of students working with $350 in play money. Mr. Hansen believes that the students will enjoy and profit from what he has planned and eagerly waits for everyone to be seated so he can explain what to do. Speaking above the mild noise level created by the movement of bodies and a few conversations left over from recess, Mr. Hansen begins: "As soon as everyone's seated, I want your attention. Okay! Listen up. Hey, Bob, over here! Listen up—Okay, now. Find yourself a partner. Pull your desk next to his. The—" "What if it's not a 'him'?" asks Deborah. "That's right. Make that him or her," Mr. Hansen responds. He continues, "When everyone and his or her partner are seated together, I'll pass out some materials and tell you what we'll be doing."

Students move around identifying partners. Initially, some have no partners and others have two. Some friendly pushing occurs and comments such as, "I wanna be with Allison!" and "I always get stuck with Caesar!" are heard. Thirteen minutes after the start of the period, everyone seems to be with a partner, but the confusion concerns Mr. Hansen. Speaking louder than before, he says, "I have $350 of play money for you and your partner. You will need this for the problem you'll have to solve together." While he counts and distributes the money, students begin making remarks: "What are we going to do?" "Oh, shoot! This isn't real money!" "Yeah, Mr. Hansen, give us real money!" "Hey! Mr. Hansen, you only gave us $310!"

During the 14 minutes it takes for each pair to obtain the right amount, some students begin daydreaming, others doodle, and others pick up their conversations from recess. By the time Mr. Hansen is ready to explain the directions for the learning activity, enthusiasm for becoming engaged has waned.

▶ **CASE 3.17**

Mr. Jukola wants to conduct the same learning activity with his class of 30 fifth graders that Mr. Hansen was trying to begin in Case 3.16. But Mr. Jukola was more thoroughly prepared than Mr. Hansen. Before the students return from recess, Mr. Jukola places 15 different numerals (e.g., "63") at each of 15 workstations he has set up in the classroom. Thirty index cards (e.g., the one in Figure 3.6) are prepared so that each has a different numerical expression at the top but the same directions printed below. He selected the numerical expressions so that for each card there is only one other card in the deck that has an equivalent numerical expression. For example, a card with $(8 \times 8) - (3 \times 4)$ would match the card in Figure 3.6 because $(8 \times 8) - (3 \times 4) = 52$ as does 50% of $((303 + 9) \div 3)$.

As the students begin filing into the room, Mr. Jukola gives a card to each and softly announces to about five or six students at a time, "Please follow the directions on the card." Immediately on entering the room, the students are busy reading and computing. Because Mr. Jukola is not busy trying to give directions to the entire class, he is able to move among the students and respond to indications of off-task behavior.

Six minutes after the first student entered the room, all are busy working with their partners. Some started with the learning activity before others arrived because they did not have to wait for directions from Mr. Jukola. The very process for locating their materials and finding out the directions involved them in reading, computing, and acquiring a curiosity about the learning activity.

> ## 50% of ((303 + 9)/3)
>
> Go to the work station that is labeled with a number equal to the expression at the top of this card. There you will meet your partner. Next, find the envelope taped under the table top. Remove the envelope and open it. Inside you will find $250 in play money and instructions on what you and your partner should do with it. Good luck!

Figure 3.6. One of Mr. Jukola's 30 Index Cards

Freedom from Having to Speak to the Whole Class

In Case 3.16 Mr. Hansen tried to speak to his entire class at once to direct students into a planned learning activity. Students who were ready to listen for the directions right away had to wait for everyone else to be situated before finding out what to do. On the other hand, in Case 3.17, Mr. Jukola had the directions for students printed and duplicated on cards. By not having to tell everyone at once what to do, Mr. Jukola was free to move about the room to help, prod, and encourage individuals. Often you can achieve smoother, quicker transitions, free of hassles and off-task behaviors by using modes other than oral presentations to the whole group for communicating directions. Sometimes alternatives to talking about directions are not feasible. But when directions are complicated or individualized and students are able to read, approaches similar to Mr. Jukola's are usually more time efficient than Mr. Hansen's.

In any case, giving directions in a manner that doesn't depend on your having to speak to the class all at once has its advantages. (a) You are freer to supervise and manage the transition time before the learning activity begins. (b) Students do not have to wait for everyone else to be attentive before they begin following the directions. (c) You can save your voice and energy for times when it is more important to speak to the group as a whole. (d) The less you speak, the more attentive students will be when you do speak to them. (e) You can more efficiently clear up some students' misunderstanding of the directions.

The contrast between Cases 3.18 and 3.19 illustrates this fifth advantage.

▶ **CASE 3.18**

Ms. McDaniel announces to her 35 science students, "Each of you is to take your scale and individually weigh the five substances—beginning with the lightest-colored one, then the next lightest one, and so on until you've weighed the darkest one last. Any questions?" Xavier: "Then what do we do?" Ms. McDaniel: "I was coming to that." Carmen: "Why do we start with the lightest one?" Ms. McDaniel: "You'll see. Now, plot each weight on the sheet of graph paper. It is marked with the shades of colors on the vertical axis and the weights on the horizontal. Okay, get busy!"

Some students misunderstand the directions and begin weighing the substances according to which one feels lightest in weight, not by shade of color. April beckons Ms. McDaniel to help her: "I don't know what to do." Ms. McDaniel: "What don't you understand?" April: "What to do!" Ms. McDaniel: "I told you to weigh these substances, beginning with the one with the lightest color and. . . ."

Ms. McDaniel repeats the directions several more times before the end of the activity.

▶ **CASE 3.19**

Mr. Johnson wants his eighth-grade science class to carry out the same activity as Ms. McDaniel's class. But he has a copy of the directions printed on a slip of paper at each work station along with the substances and the graph paper. Students read the directions for themselves, and Mr. Johnson observes how well they are followed. When a student appears to misunderstand, Mr. Johnson simply points to the directive on the student's slip that is not being followed.

Mickey says to Mr. Johnson, "I don't understand what we're supposed to be doing." Mr. Johnson: "Read the second sentence just loud enough for me to hear." Mickey: "Line the substances up so that the darkest-colored one is fifth, the next darkest fourth, and so on until the lightest-colored one is first." Having already observed that Mickey had not followed that step, Mr. Johnson says, "Do what the second sentence says, and then do what the third sentence says."

Instead of repeating the directions over and over, as Ms. McDaniel did, Mr. Johnson refers unsure students back to the printed directions.

Distributing Materials Ahead of Time

Distributing materials (e.g., play money or documents) before they are needed for student use can reduce transition time. Mr. Jukola, in Case 3.17, took advantage of a recess break to distribute materials. In Case 3.20, Ms. Salley uses time near the end of one learning activity to distribute materials for the next:

▶ **CASE 3.20**

As Ms. Salley's health science students write their answers to questions during a reading activity on diseases of the ear, she circulates among them silently reading their answers and placing a closed box containing an otoscope under every other student's desk. She plans for partners to use the otoscope to examine each other's ears in the learning activity following this one. Because she has used this procedure for distributing materials before, the students know not to open the boxes without further directions and know not to ask, "What's this for?"

Cues for Efficient Routines

Once you have established a consistent, predictable routine for giving directions and distributing materials, student cooperation can be achieved with only a minimal effort on your part. Because certain directions occur over and over (e.g., "Look at the projector screen," "Form small groups of five or six," or "Take out your notebooks"), you may want to teach your students to respond to cues or signals for beginning certain routine procedures.

Cases 3.21 and 3.22 are examples.

▶ **CASE 3.21**

The variety of learning activities that Ms. Morrison uses in her work with 38 third graders frequently necessitates that students change from one type of grouping arrangement to another. To facilitate these transitions, Ms. Morrison has several posters clustered together on one wall of the classroom. When she is ready for her students to stop one activity and begin another, she strikes a small gong located near the cluster of posters. Her students have learned that this is the cue for them to stop what they are doing and silently pay attention to Ms. Morrison. Once Ms. Morrison has their attention, she uses the posters to give directions for the next learning activity.

For example, she will point to part of the poster pictured in Figure 3.7 to indicate whether or not talking is allowed. Pointing to one of the numerals in Figure 3.8 indicates the size of the group they are to form. If Ms. Morrison points to "1," the students know to work individually at their places. Pointing to "3" means they work in groups of three. "Whole class" means there will be a large-group session of the whole class.

Figure 3.7. Ms. Morrison's Poster for Signaling Whether or Not Talking Is Allowed

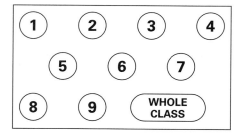

Figure 3.8. Ms. Morrison's Poster for Signaling How to Group for a Learning Activity

► **CASE 3.22**

Mr. Bowie reserves one section of the whiteboard for in-class assignments and another for homework assignments. His industrial arts students know where to find out the assignments without waiting to be told.

▶ EMPLOYING TECHNOLOGY TO ENHANCE CLASSROOM EFFICIENCY

Contrast Cases 3.23 and 3.24.

▶ CASE 3.23

Ms. Steele announces to her social studies class, "There are seven major features of the *Bill of Rights* with which we need to be familiar. Please jot each down in your notebooks as I put it on the whiteboard. Then we'll discuss the feature in some detail." With her back to the class, Ms. Steele lists the first feature on the board. The students try to copy from the board as she writes, but they must wait for her to finish writing and move out of their line of vision. Ms. Steele turns around ready to discuss the first feature, but the students are still copying. Some finish sooner than others. Ms. Steele begins her explanation of the feature after most look up from their notebooks, leaving only a few still writing.

With the discussion of the first feature completed, Ms. Steele again turns her back to the class and starts repeating the process for the second through seventh features. By the time she gets to the fourth feature, the whiteboard area that could be readily viewed by the students is exhausted, so she erases the first several features to make room. Erasing is time-consuming and prevents her from using the display of the descriptions of those earlier features later in the discussion. During the periods when Ms. Steele is writing on the board, some students amuse themselves by daydreaming or whispering. Some of those students have difficulty getting reengaged in the discussion each time Ms. Steele faces the class to explain and discuss another one of the seven features.

▶ CASE 3.24

Mr. Piowaty announces to his social studies class, "There are seven major features of the *Bill of Rights* with which we need to be familiar. Please jot each down in your notebooks as I display it on the wall. Then we'll discuss the feature in some detail." Mr. Piowaty watches the students ready their notebooks and then through the classroom's multimedia projector displays the first slide from his tablet laptop (i.e, a small portable computer that accepts input entered directly on its screen with an electronic pen). The first feature is displayed; he watches as the students make their copies. During the ensuing explanation and discussion of the feature, Mr. Piowaty writes notes and highlights phrases directly on the computer screen. He does this without ever turning his attention from the class.

The class is cued that it is time to attend to the second feature when Mr. Piowaty displays the next slide. The process is repeated for the remainder of the features without Mr. Piowaty's ever having to turn away from the class or the students having to wait for either the description of the feature to be written out or their line of sight to be cleared. Throughout the learning activity, Mr. Piowaty is able to control what the students can view on the wall. Descriptions of features not being discussed are not displayed. But Mr. Piowaty is able to bring back into view previously discussed features if he wants to draw comparisons or raise other points about them.

Because both the slides as well as what he wrote during the presentation are stored electronically, he can readily display them again, post them on the link for students on his Web page, or transmit them electronically to students (e.g., by e-mail).

Whenever feasible and practical, consider preparing visual displays, including ones with audio components (e.g., on a CD), before you are ready to use them in class. Because he did not have to take up students' time writing on the board with his back to the class, Mr. Piowaty minimized transition time and had a much easier time keeping students engaged than Ms. Steele did. Overhead projectors, interactive electronic whiteboards (Shorr, 2006), DVD players, visual presenters, and computer-based multimedia technologies (e.g., *Corel Presentation* or *Microsoft*

PowerPoint software, Web site downloads, and Web-based interactive learning tools [e.g., go to http://nlvm.usu.edu]) are some of the widely available and cost-effective devices that make it easier for you to conduct high-quality, professional demonstrations and presentations that (a) enhance the businesslike atmosphere of your classroom, (b) require little transition time, and (c) make it easier for you to supervise and attend to your students while they are engaged in learning activities. Some schools supply students and teachers with individual laptops that are networked with one another (Shaw, 2006). Such systems provide efficient mechanisms for interactive communications among teachers and students both inside and outside classrooms.

▶ SAVING TIME WITH INTRACLASS GROUPING

Intraclass grouping is the subdividing of the students within a class into individual task groups for a learning activity. In Case 3.25, students waste time waiting their turn to be engaged in a learning activity. In Case 3.26, the teacher uses intraclass grouping to keep students busily engaged.

▶ CASE 3.25

Coach McCreary is conducting drills on throwing two-hand chest passes for 13 junior high basketball players. The players are in a single line as the coach tosses the ball to Jan who is at the head of the line. Jan practices a two-hand chest pass as she throws the ball back to Coach McCreary who exclaims, "Nice job, Jan! Next!" Jan returns to the back of the line, and the next player has a try. As players take turns, the coach encourages them, acknowledges properly executed passes, and points out flaws in techniques.

▶ CASE 3.26

Coach Adomitis is conducting drills on throwing two-hand chest passes for 13 junior high basketball players. The players are divided into five groups of two and one group of three. Each of the six groups has a ball they use to throw two-hand chest passes back and forth between players in the group. Coach Adomitis encourages players, acknowledges properly executed passes, and points out flaws in techniques as she circulates among the groups.

While Coach McCreary's students spent more time waiting than practicing, Coach Adomitis kept her students busy due to the way she used intraclass grouping. Intraclass grouping is an especially effective means for accommodating individual differences among students within the same class (see, e.g., Cases 7.23 and 7.24).

▶ ACCOMMODATING STUDENTS' COMPLETING WORK AT DIFFERENT TIMES

Results of studies involving hundreds of elementary and secondary school classrooms in a wide variety of settings (e.g., inner city and suburban) indicate huge variations in the percentage of allocated time that is lost due to inefficient transitions and student off-task behaviors. The average appears to be about 50 percent (Cangelosi, 2006; Fisher et al., 1980; Jones, 1979; Struyk, 1990). Often time is wasted during independent-work sessions in which students individually work on a task as the teacher moves about the room providing individual help. Consider the dilemma Mr. Uter faces in Case 3.27.

▶ **CASE 3.27**

Mr. Uter distributes copies of a tasksheet containing 18 questions for his sixth graders to answer individually using their geography textbook as a reference. The students have 35 minutes to complete and turn in the assignment before discussing the questions in a large-group session.

After 15 minutes, several students have completed the work, but others are only through the first four questions. Those who finished sit idly waiting for the others. As more students complete the assignment, the noise level in the room increases and disturbs those still working. The noise bothers Mr. Uter, who finally puts an end to the exercise by saying, "Okay, it looks like most of you are finished. Everybody turn in your papers, and we'll discuss the answers."

How could Mr. Uter have planned the assignment so that his students' time would be more efficiently used? As one of many options, Mr. Uter might have made this a two-part assignment. The first part would consist of the 18 questions to be turned in at the end of the 35 minutes. Time permitting, the second part should be begun in class but would not be due until the next day (i.e., as homework). As a precaution against students' rushing through the first part to take advantage of the class time for homework, Mr. Uter could design the assignment so that successful completion of the second part would depend on the first part having been done well. At the end of the 35 minutes, work on either part of the assignment would cease, the first part would be turned in, students would put the second part away and out of sight, and then the first part questions would be discussed in a large-group session.

In general, your classroom will operate more efficiently if you sequence your learning activities so that independent tasks that need to be finished in class are followed by independent work that has flexible beginning and ending times. Mr. Uter made the mistake of scheduling the large-group discussion session immediately after the independent work session without accommodating for the fact that some students finish before others.

When you work with Chapter 7, you will develop specific strategies for keeping students engaged during independent-work sessions.

▶ CREATING A COMFORTABLE, NONTHREATENING, AND SAFE LEARNING COMMUNITY

A Frightening Place

You can cultivate a classroom climate that encourages on-task, engaged student behaviors by (a) creating a businesslike atmosphere; (b) being exceptionally prepared and organized, especially near the beginning of a new school term; and (c) minimizing transition time by efficiently dispensing with administrative tasks, efficiently distributing materials and giving directions, prudently utilizing technology, taking advantage of intraclass grouping, and sequencing learning activities to accommodate students who finish work at differing times. Nevertheless, unless students feel that it is safe for them to participate wholeheartedly in learning activities without being ridiculed, embarrassed, or harmed, the classroom climate will not be as conducive to on-task, engaged, and prosocial behaviors as you would like.

Why would a student ever be fearful of putting forth a concerted effort (i.e., becoming highly engaged) in a learning activity? The reasons are complex and varied.

Some preadolescent and adolescent students fear that their efforts to achieve learning goals will be ridiculed by peers who do not value academic achievement. Achieving the goal of acceptance by a peer group is typically more important in the minds of students in this age group than is achieving a learning goal determined by a teacher. Often academic learning goals appear long range, whereas a peer-acceptance goal seems immediate and urgent. Consequently, if students believe their peer group does not value school achievement, they may fear that engagement in learning activities will detach them from that group.

If students feel that a teacher has challenged or embarrassed them in front of their peers, they may consider engagement in learning activities to be tantamount to collaborating with a resented authority figure. Fears related to labeling compound the problems. Some students believe that if they put an effort into learning activities and still fail to achieve learning goals, they will either be labeled "stupid" or fail to live up to a previously acquired label of "smart." Consequently, they are afraid to risk failure, so often they do not try.

Due to threats from schoolyard bullies or outbursts of antisocial conduct (e.g., gang-related violence), school may be such a frightening place for some students that they worry more about protecting themselves than they do about learning. People can hardly be concerned with academics when they fear for their safety. Creating safe school campuses is a focus of Chapter 5. Your work with Chapter 11 will help you develop strategies for dealing with violent student behavior.

The lack of familiarity with a new school environment is a source of fear for many primary-grade children. For some, school is their first extended time away from the familiar surroundings of home and family.

The presence of these sources of fear does not excuse misbehavior or disengagement from learning activities. But being aware of them is the first step in developing and implementing strategies for mitigating their influences. Such strategies are suggested in subsequent chapters.

Risking Self-Respect

From their earliest moments, most children are inundated with storybook tales, television programs, poems, songs, adult talk, and other sources that leave them feeling that the degree to which a person is loved, appreciated, and respected by others and the worth of that person depend on how well she or he performs, accomplishes commendable deeds, and achieves desirable goals. *Rudolph, the Red-Nosed Reindeer*, for example, was an object of scorn among his peers until he achieved an act of heroism one Christmas Eve. Then he was "loved" and respected.

Many well-meaning but misguided parents attempt to motivate their children to achieve by displaying greater signs of love for their children after the children succeed in an endeavor than they display after the children fail. Consequently, the vast majority of students enter school believing that their personal worth and self-esteem depend on how well they perform in school. On the surface, such a phenomenon would seem to motivate students to be engaged in learning activities so that they will achieve. In reality, however, the phenomenon poses one of the greatest hindrances to students' willing engagement in learning activities. As a positive reinforcer for on-task behavior, the promise of love and self-respect can be effective in the short term but virtually always produces undesirable side effects over time (Ginott, 1972). Thus, rewards for achievement or on-task behaviors that communicate the message "You are a better, more loved person because you have succeeded or behaved as someone else wants you to behave" are destructive positive reinforcers. Similarly, withholding love and displaying disrespect after off-task behaviors are destructive punishments.

To understand why using love and respect as rewards is a destructive positive reinforcer that should be avoided, as should the destructive punishment of withdrawing love and respect, consider the following generalizations. (a) The acquisition and maintenance of love and esteem are two of a social person's more basic and compelling drives (Maslow, 1987; Ormrod, 2006, pp. 370–383; Parsons, Hinson, & Sardo-Brown, 2001, pp. 391–394). (b) Different students achieve learning goals at differing rates and degrees (Cohen & Lotan, 1995). When students are led to believe that the most successful among them will be loved and respected more than the least successful, their ego defense mechanisms discourage their participation in what seems to be a game with excessively high stakes and few winners. Why should anyone other than the more highly apt students be willing to jeopardize their self-esteem in a competition in which they cannot be best? Students who believe that they are worth less in the eyes of others when they are less than successful in school-related activities are defensive about engaging in those activities. Such defensiveness precludes the attitude of open cooperation that you would like to have prevail in your classroom. Cases 3.28 to 3.30 illustrate the problem.

▷ **CASE 3.28**

Ms. Davilio would like to find out just how well each of her Spanish-language students has achieved the learning objectives of an instructional unit. A knowledge of how well each has achieved will help her make wiser decisions regarding what should be retaught, what new objectives should be established, and who needs help with what. Like most teachers, Ms. Davilio uses tests to help her assess student achievement. But she has difficulty obtaining valid test results on her students' levels of achievement because many of them feel that their personal prestige and Ms. Davilio's fondness for them depend on their test scores. Consequently, some of these students display such anxiety when taking tests that their scores do not accurately indicate their achievement levels. Other students do not put forth the effort they should to prepare for tests because, consciously or unconsciously, they do not want to risk losing face by trying and failing. Other students even attempt to deceive Ms. Davilio into believing that they have achieved more than they actually have by either faking their way through test questions or directly cheating.

▷ **CASE 3.29**

Maunsell believes that his self-worth depends on his achievements. In time, he begins to resent Mr. Iverson and other teachers who seem to be continually judging him (whereas in reality some of those teachers are only judging Maunsell's achievement, not Maunsell himself). While using Socratic methods for one learning activity, Mr. Iverson asks Maunsell a question. Maunsell suddenly snaps, "Pick on somebody else; you're always trying to make me look bad!"

▷ **CASE 3.30**

Ms. Whalen assigns homework to her chemistry class, asking students to balance some equations. Theresa attempts the exercises at home and finds that she has difficulty completing them. Rather than return to school without the equations properly balanced, she feigns illness and does not attend school when the assignment is due. She prefers to miss class and not achieve the objective than face what she perceives to be a potentially embarrassing situation.

Disassociating Self-Respect from Achievement

Students would be much less defensive, and thus more likely to cooperate, if adults did not give them the idea that they risk their self-respect whenever they undertake tasks or are expected to behave in a prescribed manner. The destructive message from an authority figure that leads to student defensiveness is, "I love and respect you when you are successful (or behave properly)." In other words, "I do not love and respect you when you are unsuccessful (or misbehave)."

You can mollify a student's defensiveness by communicating that "I am happy when you are successful—or behave properly—because I love and respect you." In other words, "I am unhappy when you are unsuccessful—or misbehave—because I love and respect you."

It is not easy for you or any other teacher to communicate that a teacher's job involves judging behaviors and achievement exhibited by students rather than students themselves. Chapter 4 is designed to help you develop a particular style for communicating with students that, when consistently practiced, breaks through defensive student attitudes and leads to the type of classroom climate where students feel free to cooperate enthusiastically and engage in learning activities. Through appropriate communication techniques, you can (a) avoid the characterizations and labeling (such as "smart," "dumb," "bright," "slow," "good," "overachiever," and "underachiever") that lead students to be defensive about engaging in learning activities, (b) gain students' trust so that they understand that they are not gambling with their self-esteem by cooperating with you and engaging in the learning activities you plan, and (c) avoid the resentment and power struggles that occur as a consequence of students feeling embarrassed in the classroom.

▶ SYNTHESIS ACTIVITIES FOR CHAPTER 3

I.   Write one paragraph suggesting how the incident in Case 3.31 might influence, both positively and negatively, the businesslike atmosphere of Ms. Schott's class.

▶ CASE 3.31

While conducting a questioning strategy session with her class, Ms. Schott notices Ms. Byung-Lee, the school principal, beckoning her to the doorway of the classroom. Ms. Schott calls a halt to the learning activity, telling her class, "Excuse me, class, but I have some business with Ms. Byung-Lee. We'll finish up shortly. While I'm busy, please confine your talk to whispers." After six minutes in which Ms. Schott and Ms. Byung-Lee confer at the doorway, Ms. Schott directs the class, "Okay, now let's get back. . . ."

Exchange the paragraph you just wrote with that of a colleague. Discuss the implications, including the impressions students might infer regarding the priority that Ms. Schott affords the business of learning. Chapter 4's section "Avoiding Unintended Messages" elaborates further on these issues.

II.   Write two paragraphs explaining why the beginning of a new school year presents a teacher with an especially opportune time for establishing a classroom climate conducive to on-task behaviors. Compare your response with that of a colleague; discuss similarities and differences.

III.   Imagine yourself as a teacher about to begin a school year. Answer the first 14 questions from Mr. Zeltsman's list in Case 3.5. Exchange responses with those of a colleague; discuss similarities and differences.

IV.   Think of one of your teachers whom you consider to be with-it. Think of another whom you don't consider with-it. Write one or two paragraphs describing differences in their classroom behaviors that led you to think of one as demonstrating withitness and the other not. Exchange your description with that of a colleague who is also engaging in this activity. Discuss specific behaviors that cause teachers to demonstrate withitness.

V.   Develop a lesson plan for one day in the first week of a school year that fits Mr. Zeltsman's three "Reminders for the First Week's Learning Activities" in Case 3.5. Exchange your lesson plan with others who are engaging in this activity. In a discussion, share your thinking behind the specific plans you made so the lesson would fit Mr. Zeltsman's three reminders.

VI.   With one or two colleagues, discuss why you agree or disagree with the following statement: "The harder a teacher works within the fourth stage of the teaching cycles model, the less that teacher will have to work within the fifth stage to make learning activities effective."

VII.   Think of a teacher you once had who used an inefficient method of taking roll. Think of a second teacher you had who took roll more efficiently.

VIII.   List some of the advantages, relative to keeping students on-task, of directing students into learning activities using ways other than personally speaking to the entire class at once. Compare your list with that of a colleague.

IX.   Describe two examples in which a teacher uses a presentation technology (e.g., a computer in conjunction with a multimedia projector) to communicate information to students during a learning activity. Write a second example in which the teacher uses a different type of presentation technology to communicate that same information during the learning activity. Share your examples with a colleague. Compare the relative advantages and disadvantages of the choices for the particular learning activity.

X.   Plan a learning activity in which intraclass grouping is used to maximize allocated time and minimize transition time. Exchange your plan with a colleague; discuss your rationales for employing intraclass grouping.

XI.   Describe an example in which students in a classroom complete an assignment at differing times. Devise and describe a plan for that teacher to use so that students who finish the assignment early are kept busy with productive activities. Exchange and discuss examples with a colleague.

XII.   Carlotta is a student who feels more loved after scoring high on tests than she does after scoring low. Discuss with colleagues why such a feeling may eventually discourage her from enthusiastically engaging in learning activities.

▶ TRANSITIONAL ACTIVITY FROM CHAPTER 3 TO CHAPTER 4

In preparation for your work with Chapter 4, discuss with two or more colleagues the following questions.

I. How does a teacher's style of communication (e.g., whether the teacher tends to describe situations or judge people) affect the classroom climate?

II. What strategies can teachers employ to condition students to listen attentively to what is said?

III. When students express feelings of frustration, how can teachers help them deal with the frustrations and get on with the business of learning?

IV. How can teachers avoid being misinterpreted by students?

V. Are teachers' behaviors sometimes disruptive?

VI. How can teachers consistently send the message that each person is responsible for her or his own conduct?

VII. What are some of the strategies employed by teachers to elicit the cooperation of students' parents?

VIII. What role do grades play in motivating student engagement?

IX. What are teachers' professional responsibilities regarding privileged information about students?

Establishing Cooperative Relationships

▶ CHAPTER 4'S GOAL AND OBJECTIVES

The goal of this chapter is for you to develop strategies for interacting and communicating with students and their parents in ways that foster productive, cooperative relationships. Specifically, Chapter 3 is designed to lead you to achieve the following objectives:

1. Develop a descriptive rather than judgmental language style in communications with your students and their parents so that you (a) avoid the characterizations and labeling that lead students to be defensive about engaging in learning activities, (b) gain students' trust so that they understand they are not gambling with their self-esteem by cooperating with you and engaging in the learning activities you plan, and (c) avoid the resentment and power struggles that occur as a consequence of students feeling embarrassed in the classroom.

2. Incorporate techniques in your interactions with students that lead them to choose to attend to your messages for them—techniques that involve the judicious selection of words, body language, voice tone, active listening, and supportive replies.

3. Communicate that individuals are responsible for their own conduct and avoid communicating unintended messages that lead your students to misunderstand how you expect them to behave.

4. Develop an assertive communication style, avoiding both hostile and passive responses.

5. Develop strategies for leading students to use communication styles that foster cooperation in the classroom.

6. Emphasize formative rather than summative evaluations when communicating with students and parents about students' achievement of learning goals.

7. Recognize that the level of professionalism you display in your communications about students influences the trust and confidence students have in you.

▶ USING DESCRIPTIVE INSTEAD OF JUDGMENTAL LANGUAGE

Focused Descriptions, Not Characterizations or Labels

Haim Ginott (1965, 1972) offered solutions to common communication problems that parents experience with their children and teachers experience with their students. He emphasized that the messages adults send have a profound effect on children's and adolescents' self-concepts. What may seem to be only subtle differences in the ways teachers consistently use language can be a major determinant in how students view themselves and how willing they are to cooperate. Cases 4.1 and 4.2 provide contrasting examples to illustrate a major Ginott theme.

▶ CASE 4.1

Ms. Robinson is conducting a learning activity in which her sixth graders are discussing how reading a particular poem influenced them. "I began to remember back when I was only seven years old when—," Justin is saying, when he is interrupted by Theresa who blurts, "Yeah, because you still are seven! Who wants to hear what a baby like you thinks?" Ms. Robinson: "Theresa! What a rude little girl you are! Why can't you be more thoughtful? Continue, Justin. It is too bad that one discourteous person hurt your feelings! You are definitely not a baby. Please go on."

▶ CASE 4.2

Ms. Hebert is conducting a learning activity in which her sixth graders are discussing how reading a particular poem influenced them. "I began to remember back when I was only seven years old when—," George is saying, when he is interrupted by Lamona who blurts, "Yeah, because you still are seven! Who wants to hear what a baby like you thinks?" Ms. Hebert turns to Lamona and firmly but calmly says, "George has the floor right now. I am angry because your interruption stopped us from hearing what George was saying." Turning to George, Ms. Hebert says, "George, you were saying that the poem had you remembering when you were seven. I would like you to continue."

Ms. Robinson addressed Theresa's character; she labeled her as rude. Ms. Hebert, on the other hand, did not bring Lamona's personality into question, nor did she label Lamona. Instead, Ms. Hebert addressed the situation and targeted Lamona's rude behavior rather than Lamona herself. Lamona's rudeness needs to be eliminated rather than Lamona herself.

Paramount in Ginott's work is this principle: Teachers should verbalize to students descriptions of situations and behaviors but never value judgments about individuals themselves. Ms. Hebert described a situation when she said, "George has the floor right now." She also described her own feelings by saying, "I am angry because your interruption stopped us from hearing what George was saying." According to Ginott, teachers should recognize both their own feelings and those expressed by students. If, as a teacher, you are only rarely angry, you are more likely to prompt students' attention when you do get angry. Ginott suggests that you take advantage of such times to model just how you want your students to handle times when they are angry. Ms. Hebert acknowledged her anger but displayed complete control and never resorted to name-calling, insults, or sarcasm. She focused on getting back to the business at hand and getting students reengaged in the learning activity.

Teachers are often reminded (e.g., in psychology courses and professional journals) that they should avoid sarcasm and not associate students with undesirable labels (e.g., "dumb," "rotten," or "poor reader"). Ginott, of course, agreed that such a deplorable but common practice is detrimental to obtaining students' cooperation and maintaining on-task behaviors. But he also pointed out the dangers of characterizing or labeling students even with complimentary ones (e.g., "smart," "good," or "fast reader"). Consider Case 4.3.

▷ **CASE 4.3**

Upon returning one of her students' science test papers with a high score, Ms. Johnson remarks, "Whitney, you proved you are quite a scientist. Thank you for being such a good student!" Whitney feels proud about being praised in front of his peers. Jana, hearing Ms. Johnson's remark, thinks, "Because I had a low test score, I must be a bad student who can't do science."

Later Whitney gets nervous, fearing that he won't score high enough on subsequent science tests to live up to Ms. Johnson's label. When science gets difficult for him, he is tempted either not to try—lest he fail to live up to the label—or to cheat on tests to maintain his status in the class.

Instead of labeling Whitney as "quite a scientist" and a "good student," Ms. Johnson should focus on his work by *describing* his accomplishments. For example, she could say, "Whitney, your description for Item 3 clearly illustrates Newton's second law of motion."

You should acknowledge students' work and their desirable behaviors, not praise students themselves. Being praised motivates desirable student behavior only if students' self-esteem depends on the opinions of others. Ginott warned of the dangers of getting students hooked on praise. Their self-esteem should not depend on how they think others perceive them. In Case 4.1, Ms. Robinson suggested that Theresa had hurt Justin's feelings. She assured Justin that he was not a baby. In contrast, Ms. Hebert in Case 4.2 avoided suggesting for a moment that Lamona could influence how George felt about himself. She assumed that George was capable of determining for himself whether or not he was a baby.

Call to mind two other differences between Cases 4.2 and 4.1. Ms. Hebert responded to Lamona's disruptive behavior by describing the situation and then directing the students back on-task. Ms. Robinson, on the other hand, raised at least one irrelevant issue when she asked Theresa, "Why can't you be more thoughtful?" Unless Ms. Robinson wanted to waste class time listening to Theresa explain why she couldn't be more thoughtful, she should not ask that question. Why did she allow the exchange to get sidetracked, thus delaying the class's reengagement in the learning activity?

Differences Between Descriptive and Judgmental Language

Research studies indicate that students feel less threatened, less defensive, and more willing to engage in learning activities when working with teachers who consistently use descriptive language than they feel when working with teachers who use a judgmental language style (Van Horn, 1982). *Descriptive language* verbally portrays a situation, a behavior, an achievement, or a feeling. *Judgmental language* verbally summarizes an evaluation of a behavior, achievement, or person with a characterization or label. Judgmental language that focuses on personalities is particularly detrimental to a climate of cooperation (Ginott, 1972).

Teachers use descriptive language in Cases 4.4 and 4.5.

▶ **CASE 4.4**

Four-year-old Justin shows one of his paintings to Ms. Maeger, who exclaims, "The greens and browns in your painting make me think of being outside in a forest!"

▶ **CASE 4.5**

Mr. Zelezak turns to Joe, who has just interrupted Katrina while she was making a comment, and says, "It makes it difficult for me to concentrate on what Katrina is saying while you are talking."

Teachers use judgmental language in Cases 4.6 and 4.7

▶ **CASE 4.6**

Four-year-old Caroline shows one of her paintings to Ms. Murphy, who exclaims, "Why, Caroline, that's a beautiful picture! You are quite an artist!"

▶ **CASE 4.7**

Ms. Gordon turns to Mindy, who has just interrupted Greg while he was making a comment, and says, "You are very rude for interrupting Greg!"

The Consequences of Judgmental Language

The Detrimental Effects of Characterizations

To use a descriptive language style consistently, you must resist even silent thoughts that characterize students with labels such as "smart," "slow," "good reader," "well behaved," "problem child," "honest," "intelligent," "underachiever," and "overachiever." Instead of thinking of students according to labels, focus on learning tasks, circumstances, and situations.

Recall the failure of the teacher in Case 4.3 to separate judgments about what students do and accomplish from her judgments of students themselves. She again uses judgmental language in Case 4.8.

▶ **CASE 4.8**

Ms. Johnson tends to characterize her students and communicate her evaluations of them. For example, while orally giving directions to her class, Ms. Johnson notices Ursala talking to a neighbor instead of paying attention. Ms. Johnson tells her, "Ursala, you're always talking when you shouldn't! Why are you such a pain?" Ursala begins to feel uncomfortable in Ms. Johnson's presence as she now believes that Ms. Johnson has little respect for her. Ms. Johnson continues to respond to Ursala's displays of disruptive behaviors with judgmental language. In time, Ursala develops a disruptive behavior pattern as she lives up to what she perceives to be Ms. Johnson's expectations (Ormrod, 2006, pp. 66–67).

In a parent–teacher conference, Ms. Johnson tells Leo's father, "Leo is quite bright, but he tends to be lazy."

By consistently following their successes with ego builders and their failures with attacks on their personalities, Ms. Johnson confirms her students' belief that personal self-worth depends on success. Even those students who do not care about Ms. Johnson's opinions are influenced by the continual association between achievement levels and character judgments.

Compare Ms. Johnson's labeling of students in Cases 4.3 and 4.8 to Mr. Ramirez's use of descriptive language in Case 4.9.

▶ **CASE 4.9**

Mr. Ramirez distinguishes between a student's accomplishments and the value of that student. He does not view a student's display of off-task behavior as a reflection of character flaws. Mr. Ramirez believes that he is responsible for teaching each student to be on-task and achieve learning goals. He does not include judgment of students' characters among his responsibilities. His use of descriptive language helps students realize that he focuses on learning tasks, not on personalities.

Upon returning one of his student's science test papers with a high score, Mr. Ramirez remarks, "Mickey, this paper indicates that you understand the dependence of animal respiration on plant respiration."

While orally giving directions to his class, Mr. Ramirez notices Mary Frances talking to a neighbor instead of paying attention. Mr. Ramirez tells her, "Mary Frances, I would like you to stop talking and listen to these directions."

In a parent–teacher conference, Mr. Ramirez tells Nettie's father, "Nettie grasped the idea of multiplication right away. But she does not have all the multiplication facts memorized because she sometimes does not take the time to complete the drills that I assign in class."

Mr. Ramirez makes a concerted effort to use language that addresses specifically what has or has not been achieved, specific behaviors he expects students to exhibit, and specific behaviors that are unacceptable. He avoids implications that label or characterize personalities. Mr. Ramirez does not hesitate to communicate his feelings about specific behaviors or achievements of students; however, he never allows those feelings to influence the degree to which he respects, cares for, and values students.

The Fallacy of Labels

If a student does not comprehend the messages from several readings, that student is not necessarily a "slow learner" or "poor reader." The student simply does not comprehend the messages from those readings. The lack of comprehension might stem from a lack of interest in the content of the readings, thought patterns that tend to diverge from the authors', misconceptions regarding the contents, or myriad other reasons that do not fall under a general label such as "poor reader." If, however, students acquire the idea that they are poor readers, they are unlikely to read enthusiastically, even when they are interested in the content, do not think divergently from the author, have no misconceptions to overcome, and suffer no other interferences specific to that particular reading selection. Rather than blaming the lack of reading comprehension on the "poor reader" label, the teacher should focus on designing and helping students engage in learning activities that improve their reading skills.

If a student readily grasps what is generally a difficult-to-grasp scientific principle, the student is not necessarily "bright" or "scientifically minded." The student simply has a grasp of that particular scientific principle. To label such a student "scientifically minded" asks her or him to live up to someone else's image and encourages elitism. To label such a student "bright" is unwittingly to label those who do not grasp the principle "dull."

A student who is misbehaving is not a behavior problem; the misbehavior, not the student, is the problem. The distinction may seem trivial. Nevertheless, for you to be able to apply the suggestions for dealing with misbehaviors that are presented in Chapters 8 through 11, you need to perceive the behavior, not the student, as the problem to be eliminated. Students who perceive themselves as "behavior problems" cannot do away with the problems without doing away with themselves. Unless such students resort to suicide, they tend to protect themselves by wearing their "behavior problem" label with pride. On the other hand, students who learn that they are worthwhile people who choose behaviors that cause problems may be willing to alter those behaviors.

Competition or Cooperation

Classrooms where students feel that their abilities, skills, efforts, and activities are constantly being judged are classrooms that are not conducive to cooperative and discovery learning. By using judgmental instead of descriptive language, teachers are continually putting students on the spot—having to perform with answers or responses that will be judged as "good" or "wrong." This fosters an environment where students compete for favorable judgments rather than an environment in which students cooperatively construct concepts, discover relationships, solve problems, and pursue knowledge (Haefner et al., 2001). You were introduced to a powerful strategy for interacting with students in a way that fosters cooperative inquiry when you worked with Chapter 2's section "True Dialogues Instead of IRE Cycles."

▶ TEACHING STUDENTS TO LISTEN TO YOU

The Richness of Descriptive Language

Descriptive language is richer in information than judgmental language. In Case 4.10 Mr. Allred's comment is descriptive, whereas in Case 4.11 Ms. Mustaphos's comment is judgmental. Which is more informative to students?

▶ **CASE 4.10**

Mr. Allred and his second graders have just returned to their classroom from the school yard, where they conducted an experiment on erosion. He announces to the class, "After we finished the experiment, it took us only four minutes to collect our equipment and return to our places here in the room. We didn't disturb any other classes during that time. We will go outside again tomorrow and conduct an experiment with water."

▶ **CASE 4.11**

Ms. Mustaphos and her second graders have just returned to their classroom from the school yard, where they conducted an experiment on erosion. She announces to the class, "You are such good boys and girls! I'm so proud of you! Next time we do something like this, I know you'll be just as cooperative."

By listening to Mr. Allred, students gained specific knowledge about what they did and what they will be doing. They were able to associate how their specific behaviors (e.g., taking only four minutes to get situated) will influence future plans and opportunities (e.g., getting to perform another experiment outside the next day). By listening to Ms. Mustaphos, students found out only that their teacher was pleased with them. Although important, her message did not tell them anything they didn't already know. Hopefully, the students already know they are "good." Ms. Mustaphos can't really know that they will be just as cooperative next time, so why did she say that? Was she attempting to improve the chances that they would be cooperative next time? If so, there was a hint of dishonesty in her statement. Students don't care to listen to teachers who are not being forthright.

The Judicious Use of Words

In general, students are likely to pay attention to what you say if they have learned that, whenever you speak, you really have something to say. By judiciously using words that inform and avoiding inane talk, you leave your students with the idea that they miss something by not hearing you when you speak to them.

Unfortunately, students readily learn to tune out teachers because the majority of children are frequently exposed to meaningless talk from adults. Cases 4.12 and 4.13 are examples of inane adult talk.

▶ **CASE 4.12**

Five-year-old Holly is sitting down drinking a glass of milk. Her father sees her and says, "Don't spill your milk."

▶ **CASE 4.13**

Joshua is working on an individual assignment in Mr. Green's psychology class when he gets up and begins walking across the room. Mr. Green sees him and says, "Joshua, don't get up."

In Case 4.12, Holly's father's words neither taught nor reminded Holly that milk should not be spilled. She was drinking her milk with no intention of spilling it. She already knew that milk spilling is not allowed. Her father's words taught Holly that he sometimes says uninformative things; thus, she does not always need to pay attention to him. If, on the other hand, Holly's father notices her being careless with the milk by swinging the glass around with one hand, he might say, "Holly, it would be safer to hold that glass with two hands." Those words acknowledge that Holly already knows that milk should not be spilled and help her to think of ways to prevent spilling.

Engage in Activity 4.1.

▶ *ACTIVITY 4.1*

Discuss with a colleague why Mr. Green's comment to Joshua in Case 4.13 is inane and tends to condition students to not listen to him.

Compare ideas brought out in your discussion to the following: "Joshua was already up and walking when Mr. Green gave his directive. At that time, it was possible for Joshua to sit down but impossible for him to have never stood up. Mr. Green was unwittingly teaching Joshua not to pay attention to him by giving a command that he could not possibly obey. Mr. Green could have told Joshua to return to his place."

Rather than immediately reacting with the first words that come to mind, as Mr. Green did in Case 4.13, it is usually wise for teachers to pause and carefully frame words before speaking to students.

Thinking Before Talking

Often adults send inane messages to children because they react before becoming aware of some relevant circumstances. Case 4.14 is an example.

▶ **CASE 4.14**

As three-year-old Amanda goes to bed, her mother tells her, "Now, don't get up! You stay in bed." Several minutes later, Amanda's mother sees her out of bed and in the hall. She exclaims to Amanda, "I thought I told you to stay in bed! Get back to bed this instant!" Amanda: "But Momma, I have to make pee-pee!" Mother: "Okay, go to the bathroom and then get back to bed."

Had Amanda's mother first observed where Amanda was going before ordering her back to bed, she might have avoided that unnecessary exchange. Over time, Amanda may learn to attend to her mother's talk if the circumstances under which she is allowed to get out of bed (e.g., having to go to the bathroom) are initially clarified. The teacher in Case 4.15 could use the same advice as Amanda's mother.

▶ **CASE 4.15**

Mr. Prenn directs his fourth-grade class to read pages 17 through 21 silently. He notices Maureen talking to Walt and says, "Maureen, this is supposed to be silent reading. You know you're not to be talking." Maureen replies, "I'm sorry, but I was just telling Walt the page number." Mr. Prenn: "Then that's okay."

Exchanges such as the one between Maureen and Mr. Prenn cannot always be avoided. If they become common occurrences, however, they condition students to ignore listening to what a teacher is saying. If Maureen was only telling Walt the page numbers, the talking would have self-terminated without Mr. Prenn's intervention. Had he first waited to see if the talk would soon stop, he could have avoided the exchange of useless words.

Sometimes teachers and other adults teach students to tune them out by acting as if they are terminating self-terminating behaviors; Case 4.16 is an example.

▶ **CASE 4.16**

Peabody Junior High teachers are expected to stand in their doorways to enforce hall regulations, which include "no running." Mr. Adams notices Carol and Mark running toward the room across the hall from his door. Just as the two students get to their room, they hear Mr. Adams yell, "Stop that running!" They were about to stop running, not because of what Mr. Adams yelled but because they had reached their destination.

The incident in Case 4.16 was relatively harmless, but a more positive impact on how well students listen to Mr. Adams could have been realized had he either said nothing about the running or acted decisively to prevent it from recurring. Mr. Adams's words served only to remind the students that adults say a lot of meaningless things.

Why are adults sometimes so unthinking in their use of language? If they understood their reasons, they might be more careful with words. Here is one hypothesis about why Mr. Adams chose an ineffectual approach that may ultimately lead students to ignore his words:

From his location in the classroom doorway with a hall crowded with students, Mr. Adams is not in an advantageous position to enforce hall regulations. If he leaves his post to deal effectively with Carol's and Mark's running, he no longer will be serving as a reminder to the scores of other students in the hallway to follow regulations. He realizes that his mere presence is a cue to many students. Mr. Adams may not consider Carol's and Mark's running offensive enough to exert his time and energy to deal with it effectively. They were only running, not fighting. On the other hand, he doesn't simply ignore the self-terminating running because he feels obliged to announce to anyone in earshot that he is doing his duty. If Carol and Mark collide with something and injuries result, he can at least say, "I told them to stop running."

More and More Useless Words

Students also begin to learn to ignore teacher talk when teachers act as if they are initiating self-initiating behaviors, as in Case 4.17.

▶ **CASE 4.17**

Mr. Chapman's fourth graders eagerly begin working on a learning activity he has just explained to them. He then says, "Okay, get to work."

The unnecessary words that interrupted their engagement lead Mr. Chapman's students to place less importance on what he says. As a teacher, you should limit what you say to only what you intend to be heard.

Students may begin tuning out a teacher when that teacher makes judgments that only the students can make. Ms. White makes judgments for her students in Case 4.18.

▶ **CASE 4.18**

Ms. White is introducing a learning activity to her fifth graders. She says, "You're going to love this! This'll be more fun than what we've been doing! You won't want to stop after we begin to. . . ."

How long will Ms. White go on? Whether or not the students will enjoy the activity, find it fun, or want to stop is something for them to judge for themselves. Probably some will enjoy the activity, while others won't. Shouldn't Ms. White get on with the directions and quit trying to sell the activity? If the activity is truly enjoyable for the students, they will find this out for themselves when she stops talking and they become engaged. If Ms. White thinks she will enjoy the activity, she should quickly pass that information to the students by telling them, "I'm going to enjoy this; I hope you will also." The students would probably like to know how she feels. But she only wastes time and words by trying to inform them of their own feelings.

Speaking Only to Intended Listeners

The teacher in Case 4.19 is conditioning students to ignore him.

▶ **CASE 4.19**

Mr. Brunoski is sitting at his desk as his business law students silently read assigned passages from a textbook. Mr. Brunoski notices that Ali is doing chemistry homework instead. From his place at the front of the room, Mr. Brunoski says, "What do you think you're doing, Ali?" Ali: "I wasn't doing anything!" Mr. Brunoski: "Well, you sure weren't reading your business law! Put that stuff away before I confiscate it. Do the reading like everybody else." Ali: "Yes, sir."

Ali needed to be engaged in the reading; that was the message that he—not the others in the class—needed to hear. Shirley, for example, stopped reading when Mr. Brunoski spoke out. She then waited for the exchange between Mr. Brunoski and Ali to cease before becoming reengaged. The other students had to either ignore what Mr. Brunoski said or become disengaged in the learning activity. Had Mr. Brunoski dealt with the situation as Ms. Lowe does in Case 4.20, students would be more inclined to listen to him in the future.

▶ **CASE 4.20**

Ms. Lowe is sitting at her desk as her business law students silently read assigned passages from a textbook. Ms. Lowe notices that Woody is doing chemistry homework instead. Ms. Lowe walks over to Woody, squats down directly in front of him, and makes eye contact. She whispers, "Woody, it is time for you to be reading from your business law text." She stands, pivots, and returns to her desk as Woody puts away the chemistry homework and appears to read the business law text.

Ms. Lowe made it clear that what she had to say was meant only for Woody. Other students didn't need to stop their work to find out that Ms. Lowe's message didn't apply to them. Ms. Lowe doesn't speak to the entire class unless she expects all the students to listen. Her students are conditioned to stop and listen when she addresses them because they haven't had to block out her voice when her message was for someone else.

Body Language and Proximity

Through the use of eye contact, facial expressions, gestures, physical proximity to students, and the way you carry yourself, you can communicate that you are in calm control of the class and expect to be taken seriously. Direct eye contact between two people often makes those people uncomfortable. Consequently, teachers and students are inclined to look away when their eyes meet. Frederic Jones (1979), however, has found that control over a classroom situation is exerted when a teacher continually monitors the students, often pausing to look directly into the eyes of individual students. By focusing your eyes on individual students and managing to do this regularly for all students, you communicate that each student is an important part of what's going on in the classroom. Brief nonverbal acknowledgments (e.g., smile or thumbs-up gesture) when you have made eye contact helps communicate that you are aware, interested, and happy that the individual is there. By following Jones's suggestion about eye contact, you demonstrate Kounin's withitness.

As you might expect, students who see the teacher nearby are more likely to be on-task than students who are farther away. You should consider planning learning activities so that you are free to roam among your students rather than being stationary (e.g., as at a lecture stand or chalkboard or behind a lab table). Chapter 7 offers suggestions for conducting learning activities—even lectures and demonstrations—so that you are able to move among your students and encourage engagement.

Which teacher, the one in Case 4.21 or 4.22, displays more effective use of body language?

▷ **CASE 4.21**

Ms. Tramonte's students are working on individual assignments at their desks as she moves about the room answering questions and providing help. While explaining something to Charlie, Ms. Tramonte realizes that Bonnie and John, two students seated behind her, are off-task and becoming disruptive as they talk with one another. Without turning her body around, Ms. Tramonte looks over her shoulder and yells, "Knock it off! I don't want to hear any more yakking." (See Figure 4.1)

Figure 4.1. Ms. Tramonte's Body Language Fails to Communicate the Seriousness of Her Message

Figure 4.2. Mr. Brown's Body Language Leaves No Doubt that He Means What He Says

▶ **CASE 4.22**

Mr. Brown's students are working on individual assignments at their desks as he moves about the room answering questions and providing help. While explaining something to Iris, Mr. Brown realizes that Dustin and Annie, two students seated behind him, are off-task and becoming disruptive as they talk to one another. Mr. Brown softly tells Iris, "Excuse me, I'll be back within 40 seconds." Mr. Brown pivots and faces Dustin and Annie. He calmly walks toward them and squats down so his eye level meets theirs. With his shoulders parallel to Dustin's, he looks Dustin in the eyes and softly says, "I would like you to get to work without talking." (See Figure 4.2.) He immediately turns directly to Annie, achieves eye contact and repeats the message. Standing up, he pivots and returns to Iris.

Unlike Ms. Tramonte, Mr. Brown moved and positioned his body in a way that left no doubt as to whom his message was directed and no doubt that he was serious about having his directions followed.

Teachers sometimes make the mistake of saying one thing to students but communicating another through their body language. Case 4.23 is an example.

▶ **CASE 4.23**

At the whiteboard, Ms. Nagle is writing some sentences that she has directed her students to classify as either simple or compound. Writing with her back to the students, she is disturbed by loud talking from the class. "No more talking!" she says without pausing from her writing task. The students quit talking momentarily, but soon the noise level increases again. Continuing to write but now looking over her shoulder toward the class, she shouts, "I've had it with all this noise! I said, 'No more talking!'"

Ms. Nagle's students didn't take what she said very seriously. Her voice hinted at stress and indicated to them that she was not really in control. Her body language indicated that she was willing to continue with the learning activity although she hadn't obtained their cooperation. Because she didn't bother to face them and command their attention, they didn't attend to her demand for no more talking. Do you think Ms. Terrell in Case 4.24 will be more successful in getting her students to follow her directions?

▷ **CASE 4.24**

At the whiteboard, Ms. Terrell is writing some sentences that she has directed her students to classify as either simple or compound. Writing with her back to the students, she is disturbed by loud talking from the class. Ms. Terrell puts the marker down, pivots, and directly faces the class. She pans her eyes across the class, making eye contact with one student and then another. In a moment she feels they are ready to listen, and she says, "The talking is disturbing me and those of you who are trying to analyze these sentences." She pauses and observes them briefly before turning around to continue with her task.

Voice Tone

Like body language, the tone of voice you use influences how students receive your messages (Cangelosi, 2006). The voice tones of teachers in Cases 4.25 to 4.28 have undesirable consequences.

▷ **CASE 4.25**

In a high-pitched, patronizing, melodious voice, Ms. Moulding tells her fourth-grade students, "Okay, everyone take out your green folders so we can begin adding to our vocabulary list!" Just then, Mr. Evans, another teacher steps into the room and says to her, "Excuse me, Ms. Moulding, but here's that CD you wanted to use today." Speaking in a lower-pitched, adult-to-adult voice, she responds, "Thank you very much. You got this to me just in time." She then returns to her high-pitched, melodious, patronizing tone and tells the students, "Our first new vocabulary word for the day is . . ."

▷ **CASE 4.26**

Mr. Ferraro is explaining the directions for an upcoming library assignment. Julio raises his hand. Speaking with a disinterested, distant tone, Mr. Ferraro says, "Yes. You want to ask me something?" Julio: "How many references do we need?" Mr. Ferraro responds somewhat curtly, "At least 12." He then acknowledges Summer's raised hand with a warm, enthusiastic-sounding, "Yes, Summer!"

▷ **CASE 4.27**

Ms. Grandison is explaining the directions for an upcoming library assignment, when she notices Orlando take out his CD-player and slip on his earphones. While continuing her explanation she walks over to Orlando and changing to an irritated, challenging tone, she tells Orlando, "I need you to put that away!"

▶ **CASE 4.28**

Mr. Lopes is explaining the directions for an upcoming library assignment when he notices Charles take out his CD-player and slip on his earphones. While continuing his explanation he walks over to Charles and in a cracking, anxious-sounding, pleading tone, he tells Charles, "I need you to put that away!"

All the teachers in Cases 4.25 to 4.28 appeared to use words that were appropriate to the situation. However, their voice tones are likely to affect students more than what they said. In Case 4.25, Ms. Moulding's fourth graders discriminate between the businesslike, adult voice she used with Mr. Evans and the cutesy voice she uses with them. Children don't generally appreciate being treated like pets or subspecies that aren't taken as seriously as adults.

In Case 4.26, students will read the difference in Mr. Ferraro's tone as an indication that he favors Summer over Julio.

In Case 4.27, Orlando may feel challenged and insulted in front of his peers, not by what Ms. Grandison said but by the way she said it. He may feel obliged to take the perceived challenge to save face, thus, escalating an innocuous incident into a hostile confrontation.

In Case 4.28, the most likely lesson Charles learns from Mr. Lopes' communication is that Mr. Lopes is stressed and fears that Charles won't comply with this request. The experience of "getting to" Mr. Lopes and displaying power over Mr. Lopes' feelings may positively reinforce Charles' off-task behavior.

Engage in Activity 4.2.

▶ *ACTIVITY 4.2*

Think of two teachers you had whom you and other students tended to pay attention to and listen to what they said in class. Think of two teachers you had whom you and other students tended to ignore what they said in class. Now list behaviors of the two teachers to whom you paid attention that led you and your classmates to be attentive.

List behaviors of the other two teachers that led you and your classmates to be inattentive.

Share your lists with colleagues who are also engaging in this activity. Discuss teacher behaviors that encourage their students to listen to them.

Speaking Only to the Attentive

In Case 4.24, Ms. Terrell obtained her students' attention before trying to speak to them. Speak to people only when they are ready to listen. Sometimes, students may not be ready to listen to you because they do not think you understand them well enough to tell them anything that they would consider important. In other cases, they may be preoccupied by thoughts that they must dispense with before attending to your message. That is one reason why it is important for you to listen actively to students.

▶ **LISTENING TO STUDENTS**

Effective communication with students involves not only sending them messages but also receiving their messages. Students will become bored with your monologues sooner than with verbal interchanges with you. They are more likely to be attentive to what you are saying when you say it within a conversation rather than as part of a speech to which they are expected to listen passively.

Listening to students, observing their actions, and reading what they write are opportunities for you to learn what they think, believe, feel, know, understand, misunderstand, and value. You will also learn what they are willing and unwilling to try. A reasonably accurate understanding of your students' thoughts and attitudes is vital to your ability to identify students' needs, decide learning goals, design learning activities, evaluate how well learning goals are achieved and be with-it. You also need to understand students' thoughts and attitudes to decide what messages you should communicate and when and how each message should be communicated. By listening to students, you will discover how to get them to listen to you.

Contrast Case 4.29 to Case 4.30.

▶ **CASE 4.29**

Except for Billy, Ms. Lye's kindergarten students are following her directions by putting away the mathematics manipulatives with which they've been working and gathering around her in the reading corner to hear a story. Billy throws himself on the floor and screams, "I'm hungry! I wanna eat my candy!" Ms. Lye goes over to Billy, who is now yelling and crying incoherently. He flails his arms and legs and seems out of control. Ms. Lye grabs him and says, "Stop that, Billy! Pull yourself together. What's the matter with you anyway?" Billy continues crying, unintelligibly screaming something about candy. Ms. Lye is on her knees with Billy. Speaking loudly to be heard above the screams, she says, "That's enough! You know you can't have any candy right now. You haven't had lunch yet. Please calm down. I know you will like this story. You can sit on my lap while I read it." Billy doesn't even hear her as he continues the tantrum.

▶ **CASE 4.30**

Except for Lois, Ms. Medlyn's kindergarten students are following her directions by putting away the mathematics manipulatives with which they've been working and gathering around her in the reading corner to hear a story. Lois throws herself on the floor and screams, "I'm hungry! I wanna eat my candy!" Ms. Medlyn goes over to Lois, who is now yelling and crying incoherently. The child flails her arms and legs and seems out of control. Ms. Medlyn gets down on her knees and gently but firmly takes Lois by the shoulders and turns her so that the two are face to face. Without speaking, Ms. Medlyn observes and listens for some indications of what's on Lois's mind. Soon she catches the word *candy* amid all the child's noise. Speaking loudly, calmly, slowly, and distinctly and maintaining direct eye contact, Ms. Medlyn says, "You want some candy." Hearing the word *candy* seems to strike a chord with Lois, and she momentarily gains a semblance of composure. Ms. Medlyn seizes the opportunity to say, "As soon as you get control of yourself, we will talk about getting some candy." "But, I want my candy!" Lois says as she again starts to get upset. Ms. Medlyn: "Oh! You have some candy. Where is your candy?" Lois: "I left it." Ms. Medlyn: "You left it where?" Lois: "I don't know." Ms. Medlyn: "May I help you find it?" Lois is now relatively calm as she answers, "Yes." "Okay, I will. You put away your math things, and after I finish reading the story, we'll talk about finding your candy."

Lois was too upset to follow Ms. Medlyn's initial directions to the class. Nevertheless, because Ms. Medlyn actively listened to Lois's seemingly incoherent communications, the teacher was able to detect a key to obtaining Lois's attention. By saying something that Lois wanted to hear, Ms. Medlyn was able to help Lois be calm enough to hear what Ms. Medlyn had to say. The teacher did not try to get her own message across (i.e., put away the mathematics materials and prepare for the story) until Lois was able to receive that message. Note that Ms. Medlyn never promised Lois anything she was not prepared to deliver. When, to get Lois's attention, she said, "You want some candy," she was not telling Lois that she would give her candy or that Lois could eat candy before the mathematics materials were put away and the story was heard.

▶ USING SUPPORTIVE REPLIES

Accepting Feelings

Consider Case 4.31.

▶ CASE 4.31

Ms. Leonard is walking among her algebra students as they individually work on factoring polynomials. Paul tells her as she passes near his desk, "I can't figure these out! They're just too hard for me." Ms. Leonard replies, "Paul, these should be a piece of cake for a smart guy like you! Just do them like the example we did on the board. They're really simple. Let me show you. First, begin. . . ."

Ms. Leonard tried to encourage Paul and help him build his confidence. What impact do you think her response had on Paul's thinking? Her response denied Paul's feelings. He said the problems were hard; she said they were simple. She indicated that such problems were easy for smart people like him. Will he conclude that he is dumb? Will he conclude that when Ms. Leonard discovers that he can't do them, and is therefore not smart, she will no longer like and respect him? As Ms. Leonard tries to explain the algebraic process to Paul, he may not attentively listen because he feels she didn't hear him. In Paul's mind, Ms. Leonard doesn't understand the difficulty and frustration he is experiencing. Her response to his expression of frustration was an example of a *nonsupportive response* because it did not indicate that she understood and accepted his feelings. Expressions of feelings receive a *supportive response* when the listener indicates that the expression has been understood and accepted (Gordon, 1974, pp. 66–77).

Relieving Frustration

Ms. Palcic uses a supportive response in Case 4.32.

▶ CASE 4.32

Ms. Palcic is walking among her algebra students as they individually work on factoring polynomials. Bruce tells her as she passes near his desk, "I can't figure these out! They're just too hard for me." Ms. Palcic replies, "Factoring polynomials can really be difficult. I see that you're having trouble with these. Read number 5 to me. . . ."

Before trying to help Bruce with the factoring problems, Ms. Palcic let him know that she understood what he was going through and that he was perfectly fine, although he was experiencing difficulties with the problems. Frustration can be incapacitating, and sometimes a person must relieve the frustration before addressing its source. Having another person's empathy can relieve frustration. Contrast the nonempathetic, nonsupportive response style of the husband in Case 4.33 with the empathetic, supportive response style in Case 4.34.

▶ **CASE 4.33**

Theresa tells her husband, "I feel so tied down! The children have been off the wall all day long, and I'm just sick of being with them!" "Oh, come on! You know you love those kids," replies her husband. Theresa: "I never get a chance to get away from them and be with some adults." Her husband: "Now didn't I take you out to dinner Tuesday? Saturday, I'll stay home so you can go out and do whatever you like. You'll feel better."

▶ **CASE 4.34**

Eva tells her husband, "I feel so tied down! The children have been off the wall all day long, and I'm just sick of being with them. I never get a chance to get away from them and be with some adults." Her husband: "I don't know how you manage to do what you do all day. I got a taste of what you're talking about last Saturday, and you've been putting up with it practically every day!"

Eva's husband's reply was supportive. He let Eva know that he heard her and that it was okay to feel as she did. Theresa's husband, with his nonsupportive reply, found flaws in Theresa's statement and attempted to propose a solution to the problem before indicating that he understood the problem. Theresa, like Eva, needed understanding and the knowledge that her husband did not think less of her for feeling the way she did.

Defusing Conflict

In Case 4.35 the parent uses a nonsupportive response; the parent's response in Case 4.36 is supportive.

▶ **CASE 4.35**

Mr. Drake is driving his four-year-old daughter, Krisilen, home from preschool when they approach an ice-cream shop. Krisilen: "I want some ice cream! I want some ice cream!" Mr. Drake: "No, you don't! You haven't had your supper, and you never have sweets before supper." Krisilen: "Momma let me have some gum before supper one time!" Mr. Drake: "Don't argue with me; you're not getting any!" They drive past the ice-cream shop, but Krisilen continues to mutter, "I do want some."

▶ **CASE 4.36**

Mr. Fisher is driving his four-year-old daughter, Allison, home from preschool when they approach an ice-cream shop. Allison: "I want some ice cream! I want some ice cream!" Mr. Fisher: "Yes, I know you do. Ice cream would really taste good right now! It's too bad we haven't had supper yet." They drive past the ice-cream shop. Allison: "Can I watch *Sesame Street* when we get home?"

Both Krisilen and Allison simply expressed a desire for ice cream. In his supportive reply, Allison's father acknowledged that Allison wanted ice cream before he reminded her of the rule. Instead of acknowledging his daughter's desire for ice cream, Mr. Drake argued with Krisilen and perpetuated the conflict. By acknowledging students' feelings with supportive replies, you can often avoid arguments and dispense with excuses for not being on-task. In Case 4.37, Mr. Layton's nonsupportive reply leads to a useless argument. In Case 4.38, Ms. Malone's supportive reply avoids an argument while clearly communicating an expectation.

▶ **CASE 4.37**

Adrian to Mr. Layton, his physical education teacher: "Do I have to dress out today? I feel so stupid in these gym shorts. My legs are too skinny!" Mr. Layton: "Why, Adrian, you look just fine. Of course you want to dress out! Do you want to mess up your regular clothes?" Adrian: "I don't look just fine!" Mr. Layton: "Yes, you do." Adrian: "I don't mind messing up my clothes."

▶ **CASE 4.38**

Frank to Ms. Malone, his physical education teacher: "Do I have to dress out today? I feel so stupid in these gym shorts. My legs are too skinny!" Ms. Malone: "You don't like the way you look in those gym shorts. I wish I didn't have to wear these shorts either. Better hurry and get dressed; we're starting volleyball in six minutes."

▶ AVOIDING UNINTENDED MESSAGES

The Risk of Misinterpretation

As a teacher, you deal with many students at once. Some students' interpretations of what you say and do are likely to differ from those of other students. Obviously, you are continually risking misinterpretation. Unintended messages unwittingly communicated to students by teachers can cause many of the misunderstandings about expectations that lead students to be off-task. Miscommunicating with your students cannot be completely avoided. But you can reduce the frequency with which you send unintended messages to students by modeling a businesslike attitude and avoiding disrupting your own learning activities.

In Case 4.39, a teacher fails to display an adequate businesslike attitude with her students and consequently communicates that engagement in learning activities is not the highest priority.

▶ **CASE 4.39**

Ms. Coonley is conducting a lecture-discussion for her eleventh-grade health science class when her principal, Ms. Rodriguez, appears in the classroom doorway and beckons Ms. Coonley to her. Ms. Coonley tells her class, "Excuse me, I have some business with Ms. Rodriguez. Please be quiet until I'm through." Ms. Rodriguez then engages Ms. Coonley in a nine-minute conversation about a meeting to be held that night. In the meantime, the students' thoughts turn to things besides the contents of the health science lecture-discussion. When Ms. Rodriguez leaves, Ms. Coonley turns to her class and says, "Okay, let's get back to our discussion. Where were we?"

Modeling a Businesslike Attitude

In Case 4.40, Mr. Chenier's businesslike attitude tends to convince students that what goes on in class is of primary importance.

▶ **CASE 4.40**

Mr. Chenier is conducting a lecture-discussion for his eleventh-grade health science class when his principal, Ms. Meador, appears in the classroom doorway and beckons Mr. Chenier to her. Mr. Chenier turns to Ms. Meador and says, "Just a moment, Ms. Meador. Phil is responding to a comment about whether or not it is sensible to take decongestants." Phil takes 30 seconds for his response while Mr. Chenier listens intently. Mr. Chenier: "Class, keep Phil's thought in mind while I quickly check with Ms. Meador." Ms. Meador then tries to involve Mr. Chenier in a conversation about a meeting that night, but instead Mr. Chenier uses 40 seconds to arrange to speak with her at another time. He turns to the class: "Now that you've had a little time to think about Phil's concerns regarding the dangers of decongestants, do you think the warning label we looked at earlier is adequate? Okay, Audrey." Audrey: "Like Phil said. . . ."

Avoiding Disruptive Teacher Behavior

Teachers fail to model businesslike attitudes when they disrupt their own learning activities. Such disruptions carry the unintended message "disruptive behavior is acceptable." Contrast Case 4.41 with Case 4.42.

▶ **CASE 4.41**

Mr. Miller's sixth-grade students are busy with an interdisciplinary assignment in which each reads about a problem and writes out a proposal for a solution. The room is quiet when Robert and Chad begin talking to one another from their places in the back of the room. Mr. Miller, seated at his desk in front, notices them and in a loud voice announces, "This work is supposed to be done on your own. I don't want any talking until everyone is finished. Chad and Robert, cut out the talking right now." All Mr. Miller's students look up and listen during Mr. Miller's announcement. Some turn to see what Chad and Robert are doing when he mentions their names. Some continue to watch them for a while to see if they'll talk again.

▶ **CASE 4.42**

Ms. Toney's sixth-grade students are busy with an interdisciplinary assignment in which each reads about a problem and writes out a proposal for a solution. The room is quiet when Andrew and Julius begin talking to one another from their places in the back of the room. Ms. Toney quietly and discreetly walks over to them, catches their eyes, and whispers in a businesslike tone, "Get back to work." Only the students close to Andrew and Julius notice Ms. Toney's actions.

Mr. Miller disturbed his entire class, leading them to become disengaged, in order to get Robert and Chad back on-task. Ms. Toney, on the other hand, dealt with the disruptive talking without disturbing students who remained on-task.

▶ BEING RESPONSIBLE FOR ONE'S OWN CONDUCT

In the privacy of their school's conference room, two teachers have the conversation reported in Case 4.43.

▶ CASE 4.43

Mr. Green: Thanks for meeting with me. I want to talk to you about Bartell Hopkins. Wasn't he in your class last year?

Mr. Mena: Yes, and I'm glad you've got him this year instead of me! How's he getting along?

Mr. Green: Terrible! When I asked him for his homework today, he told me, it was—pardon me, I don't mean to be gross, but I'm just quoting—

Mr. Mena: Don't worry. I've heard everything after 14 years in the classroom, and most of it I heard from Bartell last year. What did he say?

Mr. Green: He told me it was up his ass, and I was welcome to come and get it.

Mr. Mena: Bartell is an abused child. Ever since he was a baby, he's had an uncle, his father—some father—and heaven knows who else take advantage of him in every grotesque way. It's a wonder the poor boy behaves as well as he does.

Mr. Green: I didn't know! No wonder he acts like that. I'm sorry I sent him out of the room today when he mouthed off at me. I'll begin to be more tolerant with him.

Mr. Green needs to be aware of some aspects of Bartell's background so he can better understand his behavior. According to William Glasser (1985, 2001), however, understanding why a student exhibits undesirable behaviors is no reason to tolerate them. Glasser emphasized that students are rational beings and quite capable of choosing to cooperate and be on-task. Mr. Green should never waver in his insistence on high standards of conduct from Bartell, despite Bartell's unfortunate background. He and other teachers may provide Bartell with his only opportunity to learn acceptable behaviors. The idea is for teachers to lead students to focus on their choices of behaviors while in school and never accept excuses for improper behaviors.

Canter and Canter (2002), Ginott (1972), and Gordon (1974), as well as Glasser and most other specialists in classroom discipline, emphasize that each individual is responsible and accountable for her or his own behaviors. Except for the relatively unusual cases where one person physically accosts another, one person cannot make another do something. Once students realize this, they are disarmed of virtually all their excuses for misconduct. To lead students to understand that only they are in control of their own conduct, you should consistently use language that is free of suggestions that one person can control another. Purge your language of statements such as these: "Be careful of what you say or you'll make Mia feel bad." "He made me lose control." "You made Allen cry." "Fred, don't get Tommy into trouble." "She got me so mad." "Vernon just can't get along without Martha." "She makes me happy."

Such language should be replaced with the following: "Be careful of what you say or Mia may think you don't enjoy her company." "I didn't maintain control when I saw what he did." "Allen was so unhappy about what you said that he cried." "Fred, don't encourage Tommy to do something he shouldn't." "I got so mad when I thought of what she did." "Vernon depends on Martha for help." "I'm happy to be with her."

When students say things such as, "I did it because they wanted me to," "She hurt my feelings," and "Make me happy," remind them that they control their own behaviors. Consider Case 4.44.

▶ **CASE 4.44**

During Ms. Martin's sports-literature class, the following exchange takes place:

Ms. Martin: Whom did you select for your sports personality, Luis?"
Luis: Carlos Arroyo.
Ms. Martin: Why did you decide on Arroyo for your report?
Luis: Because—
Jarvis: Because with a name like that, he must be a spic like fat-boy Luis here! Dumb spics stick together!

Engage in Activity 4.3.

▶ *ACTIVITY 4.3*

In a discussion with three or four colleagues, address the following questions:

1.   How should Ms. Martin respond to Jarvis' rude comment?
2.   How should Luis respond to Jarvis' rude comment?
3.   Did Jarvis insult Luis?
4.   Did Jarvis insult Latino people?
5.   Did Jarvis insult people who are fat?
6.   Was Luis harmed by this episode?
7.   Were Latino people harmed by this episode?
8.   How do you suppose Jarvis' remarks influenced other students' opinions about Luis?
9.   How do you suppose Jarvis' remarks influenced other students' opinions about Jarvis?
10.   How do you suppose Jarvis' remarks influenced other students' opinions about Latinos?
11.   How do you suppose Jarvis' remarks influenced other students' opinions about people who are fat?
12.   Who, if anyone, was harmed by this incident?
13.   Does Luis *need* an apology from Luis?
14.   Does Jarvis *need* to apologize to Luis?

In light of your discussions, readdress Questions #1 and #2.

In Case 4.45, three preservice teachers, Alandra, Jalini, and Nick engage in Activity 4.3.

▶ **CASE 4.45**

Jalini: Ms. Martin needs to respond decisively to Jarvis' rude comment. You can't expect to have a businesslike classroom conducive to cooperation if she allows students to insult one another.
Nick: At the least, she's got to get Jarvis to apologize to Luis.
Jalini: Yes, and follow it up with some intervention with Jarvis to teach him not to be rude again.
Alandra: I wonder if this is a disruptive behavior pattern or an isolated outburst. That would make a difference as to what Ms. Martin does to prevent the behavior from recurring.
Jalini: He probably does this to get attention and show off for his buddies. If they laughed at him, then the rudeness was positively reinforced.

Nick: You're all worried about helping Jarvis to improve his behavior—that's fine—but shouldn't we also do something for the victim? Luis was the target of Jarvis' rudeness.

Jalini: You said Ms. Martin should make him apologize. That's a start on soothing Luis' feelings.

Alandra: But if Jarvis is trying to show off, he might try to show off more by refusing to back down. Trying to get him to apologize may just escalate the confrontation. Why prolong the incident?

Jalini: Everyone will know the apology wouldn't be sincere anyway.

Nick: Well she's got to do something!

Alandra: Maybe it would be better to send Jarvis out of the room, get the class back on-task, and do something about Jarvis' behavior after school after she's had time to work out a plan—like with the teaching cycles model.

Nick: So how should Luis respond? That's the second question to discuss. He needs to defend himself or he'll lose face with the class.

Jalini: He could say, "At least I'm not a racist like you. And besides, I can always lose weight, but you'll always be ugly!"

Alandra: Then Luis would just be playing Jarvis' game. Why should he lower himself to Jarvis' level? Besides, Ms. Martin can't allow them to start going back and forth.

Nick: So, Luis should just keep quiet and beat the crap out of him after school.

Jalini: I hope you're kidding. Let's go to the next question.

Nick: The answers to Questions 3, 4, and 5 are "Yes," "yes," and "yes."

Alandra: After looking at Question 6, I'm not so sure I agree with you.

Nick: You don't think people can be harmed by insults?

Jalini: It depends on whether or not the person feels insulted. Some people will, others won't.

Alandra: I think Question 8 is key. How did Jarvis' rudeness influence other students' opinions about Luis?

Jalini: Jarvis was the one who displayed the bad behavior, not Luis. Jarvis' comments reflected on him, not on Luis. So, I think most students would lower their opinions about Jarvis rather than Luis.

Nick: But some might think of Luis as a wuss for not defending himself against insults.

Alandra: But he shows that he's not insulted because he's not ashamed of being Latino. What if he recognizes that Jarvis communicated tons about himself but nothing about Luis. Wouldn't that show strength?

Nick: But he called him fat and attacked Latinos! Doesn't he need to stand up to that?

Jalini: Maybe by letting it roll off of him and not lowering himself by playing Jarvis' game, he is standing up by demonstrating that Jarvis cannot control how he feels about himself.

Alandra: He is Latino and he might be fat. In any case, no words can make him ashamed of that. Were Latinos and people who are fat hurt by this episode? Absolutely not. Students in the class who were prejudiced won't be any more prejudiced because of Jarvis' remarks. Those who aren't prejudiced have actually benefitted because Jarvis has identified himself as someone who has racist attitudes and they'll know not to trust him. If Luis is comfortable with himself, the whole episode is win-win for the "good" guys.

Nick: Watch it! We're not supposed to label people.

Alandra: Okay, scratch my last remark and replace it with this one: Jarvis taught the class a lesson in how nasty some people can be. Depending on how Luis and Ms. Martin respond, it can also be a lesson that others don't have the power to insult us unless we give them that power.

Jalini: So should Jarvis apologize to Luis?

Alandra: Yes, not because Luis needs it but because Jarvis needs it.

Nick: What do you mean?

Alandra: I think we agreed that Jarvis victimized himself—not Luis. If he wants to repair relationships he harmed by his rude behavior, an apology might help others begin to reconnect with him. He helps himself by apologizing to Luis.

Jalini: If Luis requires Jarvis to apologize to feel better, then Luis is demonstrating that Jarvis really does have power over him.

Alandra: And that's why Ms. Martin shouldn't insist on an apology. Requiring an apology would communicate that Jarvis can control how Luis feels about himself.

Jalini: But part of her plan to teach Jarvis not to be rude in class might be to explain to Jarvis that he harmed his relationship with some of his classmates and by choosing to apologize to Luis he helps repair that relationship.

Nick: What you're saying makes sense as long as Luis' self-concept doesn't depend on what other say. But most kids haven't learned that lesson. So how does Ms. Martin help Luis if he is a typical kid who does feel insulted by others' rude remarks?

Alandra: I definitely agree that Ms. Martin needs to pull Luis aside and discuss some of the same points we've been discussing.

Jalini: Actually, more and more schools are integrating programs into curricula to teach students not to allow themselves to be victimized by the rudeness or comments of others. They focus on students using assertive communication styles just as teachers should.

The discussion continues.

▶ COMMUNICATING ASSERTIVELY

The Assertive Response Style

An *assertive* response style is characterized by openness, directness, spontaneity, and appropriateness. You are assertive by acting in your own best interests, standing up for your legitimate rights, and resisting coercion. Assertiveness builds healthy, constructive relationships (Alberti & Emmons, 1995).

Your communications are assertive when you send exactly the message that you want to send, being neither *passive* nor *hostile*. Your communication is passive rather than assertive if it fails to send the message you want to convey because you are intimidated or fearful of the recipient's reaction. Your communication is hostile rather than assertive if you intend it to be intimidating or insulting. To gain control over your professional life, you must be assertive with students, colleagues, administrators, and parents—neither passive nor hostile.

Ms. Wilford displays an assertive response style in Case 4.46.

▶ CASE 4.46

Russ, one of Ms. Wilford's students, initiates a discussion in history class:

Russ: Ms. Wilford, you know that report you wanted us to turn in Friday?

Ms. Wilford: Yes, Russ. What about it?

Russ: Couldn't we wait till Monday to give it to you? (Other students in the class chime in with comments such as, "Oh! Yes please, Ms. Wilford.")

Russ: (smiling) There's a game Thursday night, and I know you want us to support the team!

Marie: You wouldn't want us to miss the game?

Barkley: Be nice, just this once.

Ms. Wilford is tempted to "be nice" and enjoy the applause she knows she'll receive if she gives in. But she also realizes three things: (1) Delaying the assignment will cause the class to fall behind the planned lesson schedule. (2) If she doesn't get the reports until Monday, she won't be able to read and annotate them over the weekend; consequently, she would be inconvenienced. (3) If they will adjust their own schedules, the students are quite capable of completing the report on time without missing the game.

Ms. Wilford announces to the class, "I understand that you are worried about making it to this important game and still being able to finish the report on time. You have cause for concern. Because changing the due date will mess up our schedule and because I need the weekend to go over your papers, the reports are still due on Friday." That's not fair!" cries Dennis. Ms. Wilford: "Yes, it seems unfair to you. Now, let's turn our books to page 122. . . . "

Teachers who are less assertive than Ms. Wilford might have feared jeopardizing the relationship with the students by not complying with their request. In reality, Ms. Wilford's assertive reply is likely to enhance her relationship with the students for two reasons: (1) Students begin to realize that she takes their work seriously and that her plans for them are well thought out and not changed whimsically. (2) Had she changed her plans and not allowed herself the weekend to go over the reports, the personal inconvenience she suffered might have led to feelings of resentment directed at the students.

The recommended assertive response style is neither hostile nor passive. Ms. Wilford would have displayed hostile communications if she had responded to the students' request as follows: "You people are always trying to get out of work! Do you think your game is more important than schoolwork? Schoolwork will take you a lot farther in life than games. Besides, if you weren't so lazy, you'd have this paper finished in plenty of time for your game!"

Hostile communications encourage antagonistic feelings that detract from an atmosphere conducive to cooperation and learning. Passive communications erode the teacher's ability to control classroom activities. Ms. Wilford's communications would have been passive if she had responded to the students' request as follows: "Well, we really need to have these papers done by Friday. I really should be going over them this weekend. I wish you wouldn't ask me to do this because I—oh, okay, just this once—because this is an important game."

The teacher in Case 4.47 displays an assertive response. Hostile and passive responses are displayed in Cases 4.48 and 4.49, respectively.

▶ **CASE 4.47**

Lori yells during an independent work session, "Help! Mr. Clark, I can't do these!" Mr. Clark: "Instead of shouting, quietly raise your hand if you want me to help you."

▶ **CASE 4.48**

David yells during an independent work session, "Help! Miss Lancy, I can't do these!" Ms. Lancy: "You screech like a little girl! If you yell like that again, you're gone, Buster!"

▷ **CASE 4.49**

Tamara yells during an independent work session, "Help! Ms. Slovaki, I can't do these!" Ms. Slovaki: "Why must you yell at me? I hope you try to raise your hand next time."

Controlling Your Professional Life

To gain control over your professional life, you must be assertive with not only students but also colleagues, administrators, and parents. Case 4.50 is about a first-year mathematics teacher, Casey Rudd (adapted from Cangelosi (2003, pp. 43–45).

▷ **CASE 4.50**

Early in the school year, Mr. Rudd discovers the need to be assertive with his colleagues. For example, just before the second day's homeroom period, Mr. Rudd visits Ms. Barnes, who teaches the 4th-period health science class in Room 213, Casey's classroom in which he teaches the other five periods each school day. Mr. Rudd wants to discuss the problem her class created for him yesterday, but he would rather discuss it out of earshot of her homeroom students, some of whom are milling around the room. The conversation begins:

Mr. Rudd: Hello, Ms. Barnes, do you have a minute to talk?

Ms. Barnes: Of course, Mr. Rudd—always glad to meet with a colleague! What can I do for you?

Mr. Rudd: It's about your 4th-period class using Room 213. Could we step away from these students to discuss a problem I had yesterday with the room?

Ms. Barnes: Oh, don't worry about these kids; they're not interested in what we're saying. What's your problem?

Mr. Rudd: Well, it took me a long time to get the room ready yesterday for my 5th-period life-skills class.

Ms. Barnes: I thought all you math guys needed was a piece of chalk and you're ready!

Mr. Rudd: (laughing with Ms. Barnes) That's a common misconception, but really, I'd appreciate if you could—

A student comes up, interrupting Mr. Rudd by asking Ms. Barnes a question. She answers the student and they briefly converse as Mr. Rudd waits.

Ms. Barnes: Excuse me, Mr. Rudd—it's always something. You were saying?

Mr. Rudd: I'd really appreciate it if you could have your students put things back as they were when they came into the room.

Ms. Barnes: We took out all the extra chairs we brought in with us when we left. Were some left in?

Mr. Rudd: No, that was great. It's just that—

Another student interrupts; because the bell is about to ring, Mr. Rudd interrupts the student, to say, "Excuse me, Ms. Barnes, I've got to get to my homeroom."

Ms. Barnes: Thanks for coming by—I'm glad to help you out any way I can.

Mr. Rudd: Thank you, I appreciate it.

The room is in no better shape when Mr. Rudd arrives for 5th period than it was the first day; the problem persists for the remainder of the week. Realizing that he failed to tell Ms. Barnes what he wanted out of fear of creating ill feeling, Mr. Rudd is angry at himself for not communicating assertively. Over the weekend he phones Ms. Barnes:

Ms. Barnes: Hello.

Mr. Rudd: Hello, Marilyn, this is Casey Rudd. We spoke just before your homeroom Tuesday.

Ms. Barnes: Oh, hi, Casey. How are things going?

Mr. Rudd: Some things are going very well, others aren't. *We* still have a problem to solve regarding sharing *my* classroom. I'd really like to meet with you in *my* room so *we* can work out a solution.

Ms. Barnes: You want to meet on Monday?

Mr. Rudd: It has to be at a time when students won't be there to interrupt us. I can meet you any time today or tomorrow—or Monday at 7:15 in the morning would be okay too.

Ms. Barnes: You seem pretty serious; I'd better meet you today. Would an hour from now be okay?

Mr. Rudd: That would be great. See you in my room in an hour. Thank you very much.

Ms. Barnes: Good-bye, Casey.

Mr. Rudd: Good-bye, Marilyn.

Now that Ms. Barnes understands that Mr. Rudd is serious about the two of them solving what she now perceives as her problem as well as Mr. Rudd's, she is receptive to Mr. Rudd's explanations of just how the room should be left after 4th period. In the classroom, Mr. Rudd readily points out exactly what he expects. Mr. Rudd is pleased with the agreed-upon arrangement and the way Ms. Barnes leaves the room for the rest of the semester.

Mr. Rudd also learns to communicate assertively with parents. After school one day, Mr. Rudd passes one of his algebra students, Alphonse, walking with his father in the hallway:

Mr. Rudd: Hello, Alphonse.

Alphonse: Hi, Mr. Rudd. Mr. Rudd, this is my dad.

Mr. Rudd: Hello, Mr. Oldham, I'm Casey Rudd, very nice to meet you.

Mr. Oldham: So you're Alphonse's algebra teacher. You know, I tell my kids all the time, subjects like algebra and Latin—where you have to memorize—those are the subjects where you discipline the mind. Study algebra and you can make yourself do anything. Just because you don't use it much, today's kids don't want to learn it. They'd rather waste time with frilly subjects—but man needs to discipline his mind with stuff like algebra. It does for the mind what football does for the body! Isn't that right, Mr. Rudd; you tell him.

Smiling broadly at Mr. Oldham but quickly thinking to himself, "If only I had stayed in my room another 20 seconds, I would have avoided this dilemma. Mr. Oldham has the best of intentions and I'm happy he's trying to encourage Alphonse to study algebra. He wants to support my efforts and I really appreciate that. But he's sending all the wrong messages about the value of algebra. I don't want Alphonse to believe what he's saying, but then I hate to contradict what a father says in front of his child!" Not wanting to appear insulting, Mr. Rudd only continues to smile and says, "I agree that algebra is important for everyone to learn. It's a pleasure meeting you, Mr. Oldham. Thank you for introducing me to your father, Alphonse."

The next day in algebra class, during a discussion about using open sentences to solve real-life problems, Alphonse says, "Yeah, but the real purpose of algebra is to train your memory. That's what my dad says, and Mr. Rudd agreed with him yesterday."

After diplomatically attempting to correct the record about his beliefs relative to the purpose of algebra, Mr. Rudd resolves to be more assertive in communicating with parents and in responding to misconceived statements about mathematics.

Fortunately, Mr. Rudd's resolve is still fresh in his mind as he meets with Ms. Minoso about her daughter Melinda's work in geometry:

Ms. Minoso: You know, Melinda really has a lot of respect for you; she raves about your class. That's why I thought you should be the one to help me with this problem.

Mr. Rudd: What problem?

Ms. Minoso: Well, Melinda has got herself involved with this boy who is much too old for her. She keeps seeing him even though she knows I don't like it.

Mr. Rudd: I can see that you are concerned.

Ms. Minoso: I thought since she likes geometry so much, I could use that to get her to break it off.

Mr. Rudd: I'm not following you.

Ms. Minoso: Well, you know how math is harder for girls than boys. I told her if she keeps spending time with this boy, she was going to do bad in geometry. That's why girls don't do good in math because they get all wrapped up over boys. Do you see what I mean?

Mr. Rudd: Not really, ma'am, but please go on.

Ms. Minoso: Well, I thought you could back me on this. Tell her she's going to flunk if she doesn't spend more time studying geometry and less time fooling around with that boy.

Mr. Rudd: Ms. Minoso, I really appreciate you sharing your ideas with me, and I appreciate your concern for Melinda's welfare. You, being Melinda's parent, know far more about this situation than I. I'll confine my remarks to what I do know about. First of all, research studies clearly point out that girls do not have any more trouble learning mathematics than boys. It's a common misconception that they do, but they absolutely don't.

Ms. Minoso: But I had always heard that.

Mr. Rudd: If you're interested, I can give you some journal articles that explain the facts about girls and women in mathematics.

Ms. Minoso: Oh, that would be nice of you.

Mr. Rudd: Second, and more to the point here, my job is to teach Melinda and the other students mathematics as professionally and responsibly as possible. I cannot in good conscience base Melinda's grade on anything other than how well she achieves the goals of the geometry course.

Ms. Minoso: Well, I thought if you just told her, she'd listen.

Mr. Rudd: I'm flattered that Melinda would have that much confidence in what I say. But if I start lying to her, I'll lose her confidence.

Ms. Minoso: I don't mean for you to lie to her.

Mr. Rudd: I know, Ms. Minoso. You want what's best for your daughter.

In his classroom, Mr. Rudd encourages more interaction among students than they had been used to in mathematics courses with previous teachers. Early in the year, some students tended to take advantage of their freedom of expression by drifting off the current topic. Mr. Rudd, not wanting to alienate students or to discourage communications about mathematics, allowed some of the discussions to waste valuable class time. For instance, during a precalculus class, the difference between "negative x" and "x is negative" is being discussed:

Opal: If x is negative, then x has to be less than 0, so negative x could be a positive.

Bernie: That's too picky. It's like in Spanish class, what's the difference between "temar" and "temer"? Mr. Waiters makes such a big deal over whether you say "ar" or "er!" Who cares?

Rita: It's so he can have something to grade you on.

Bernie: He's not fair . . .

The discussion continues in this vein for several more minutes, with Mr. Rudd worrying about the appropriateness of Mr. Waiters being the topic of conversation and about time being spent on the topic at hand.

After a few similar experiences, Mr. Rudd resolves to be more assertive in such situations, and in subsequent weeks he is more likely to respond as he does in the following instance. During a geometry lesson about applying triangle congruence theorems to real-life situations, this conversation takes place:

Eric: In basketball there's a strategy you call the three-man game, in which you form a triangle. The triangle should be equilateral.

Vontego: Who cares about basketball? Eric's always got to talk about basketball. It's stupid!

Eric: You've got to be better to play basketball than to—

Mr. Rudd: Do not debate your opinions about basketball in here today. Even those that don't like basketball can learn something about equilateral triangles from Eric's example of the three-person strategy. Please repeat your example, Eric, without defending your opinion about basketball.

It is in meeting his most challenging responsibility of keeping students on task and responding to off-task behaviors that Mr. Rudd discovers the greatest need to be assertive. At times, he resents having to work continually to maintain students' interest and to teach students who tend to get off-task to be on-task. An expression of frustration prompts what turns out to be a productive private conversation with a faculty colleague Vanessa Castillo:

Mr. Rudd: Some days I'd just love to walk into class and discuss mathematics without having to worry about Frankie over in the corner who is going to fall asleep unless I'm either right near her or we're discussing a problem that strikes within the limited range of what she fancies! Or just once, getting through a session without having to deal with Brad's showing off or Christi's yakking with anyone who'll listen to her—wouldn't that be nice? But that's too much to ask for!

Ms. Castillo: Obviously, you're having one of those days!

Mr. Rudd: It's just that we were getting into our first formal proof in third period today, and they seemed so enthusiastic. But then they started to get a little noisy—some off-task talking. I let it go at first because I didn't want to put a damper on their enthusiasm. But then it became obvious that Christi and Livonia's conversation had nothing to do with geometry—right in the middle of my explanation!

Ms. Castillo: What did you do?

Mr. Rudd: I kept on explaining the theorem, and just moved near them and caught their eyes—that usually works for me.

Ms. Castillo: But it didn't this time.

Mr. Rudd: Oh, the two of them stopped as long as I stood there, but then other conversations broke out, and Christi and Livonia started up again as soon as I moved away. Five minutes later I'd had enough and made the mistake of threatening the class.

Ms. Castillo: What did you say?

Mr. Rudd: I told them if they didn't pipe down, they'd be sorry when the test came around. I knew that wasn't the right thing to say, but the noise just got to me and I reacted.

Ms. Castillo: Did they quiet down?

Mr. Rudd: Yes, but then Brad whispered something to Lin-Tau and she started giggling. That's when I jumped on them and called Brad a showoff. In other words, I handled it all wrong and made matters worse.

Ms. Castillo: So you weren't Mr. Perfect. You let things go too far and reacted with hostility instead of assertiveness—the way most of us react when we feel we've lost control.

Mr. Rudd: But I know better. I applied none of the stuff that's worked for me in the past—assertiveness, descriptive language, reinforcement principles—they all went out the window!

Ms. Castillo: I don't think you threw your principles out of the window; I think you waited too long to respond decisively. Most teachers wait until they are too near their threshold for tolerating noise or other annoyances before dealing with students' being off task.

Mr. Rudd: You're saying I should have stepped in and dealt with the early minor incidents before things escalated. I was passive in the beginning instead of being assertive. Then things got out of hand.

Ms. Castillo: And when things get out of hand, it's natural to be hostile.

Mr. Rudd: And that's why I'm really upset—at my own hostile behavior. I'm afraid I've lost some of the control and goodwill I've worked to build up to this point. I don't have much enthusiasm for tomorrow's class.

Ms. Castillo: What do you have planned?

Mr. Rudd: Before this, I was going to continue the session on proofs.

Ms. Castillo: I think you have two choices. You either go on with your original plan and conduct the class as if none of this happened—but have an alternative plan ready to go to as soon as they become uncooperative—you know, one where they have to work on their own while you monitor their every move. The second choice is to start the period off by expressing your feelings about what happened, even indicating that you're disappointed in your own behavior for letting things go too far and then acting with hostility as a result. But if you use this tactic, make sure to assertively demand their cooperation. If it turns out you don't get it even after clearing the air, then go immediately to the alternative learning-activity plan.

Throughout the year, Vanessa and Casey regularly share ideas on handling discipline problems, as well as other aspects of teaching. They even work out a plan by which Casey can send a student to Vanessa's classroom for custodial supervision when Casey needs to get that student out of his classroom until he has time to deal with the student's disruptive behavior. Casey reciprocates by providing the same service for Vanessa.

Teaching Students to Communicate Assertively

As Jalini alluded to in Case 4.45, classroom communities are more conducive to productive cooperation when students as well as teachers communicate assertively. In an attempt to create peaceful campus communities, some schools include programs for teaching students assertive communication and conflict resolution skills. Chapter 5 examines such schoolwide policies. Some individual teachers have successfully incorporated assertive communication units into their own subject content curricula. Figure 4.3 is an article that appeared in the *English Journal* in which Barbara Cangelosi (2000) relates a unit she incorporated into a high school English course.

▶ COMMUNICATING EVALUATIONS

Two Reasons for Communicating Evaluations

The sixth stage of the teaching cycles model involves evaluation of achievement. You evaluate students' achievement for two reasons: (a) You make *formative evaluations* during an instructional unit to gain feedback that will help you regulate how you

"Who You Dissin', Dude?"

At-Risk Students Learn Assertive Communication Skills

BARBARA R. CANGELOSI

It's 6:00pm on a May evening; I'm pumping gas at the self-service island while a man in his thirties fills his truck's tank. We make eye contact and smile innocuously. I finish, pay inside, and continue on my way four miles north to the mall. I get out of my car there and see this same man pull up alongside me, blocking my way to the mall entrance. Through his open truck window he says, "I just had to follow you to ask you your name," to which I respond, while briskly walking around him towards the relative safety of the crowded mall, "No, you don't," smiling stringently as I take in his face, truck type, and license and calculate the number of steps left to get inside—all along wondering whether or not his hidden hand is on a gun. I'm a forty-seven-year-old mother to three grown daughters. I think, "What would one of them have done had it happened to them?" Elise, thirty, would have torn him a new orifice (or two) while lambasting his gross impertinence and crudeness, unless he had looked like Brad Pitt, which terrifies me much more. Emmy, twenty, would have blanched and hyperventilated her way into the mall, seething at his rudeness and vulgarity—an old man like that behaving as if he were even in the running with a twenty year old! Jess, eighteen, would have turned beet red and stammered in the parking lot while she spelled her name for him, wanting desperately to get away but feeling trapped by her own awkwardness and discomfort.

I'm furious at the guy. Should I have lectured him at length about the inappropriateness of his acts and then called the police? Instead, I'd shined him on (as we used to say in the 70s). I effectively took the wind out of his sails, unruffledly shrugged off his advances, and left him, I believe, unoffended, unangered, but also unanswered. I took control of the situation without costing him a loss of respect, without venting a preachy put-down or further antagonizing a possibly dangerous situation.

On the campus of the alternative high school for at-risk students where I teach English, I've often observed students taunting one another—leaving some feeling victimized with threatened egos and diminished psyches. I've successfully (sometimes) hovered and smiled the group into an ending or remission of conflict. In my English classroom, students' safety from such unpleasant encounters is of paramount concern, and I demand strict adherence to appropriate verbal exchanges dealing with the business of the class curriculum at hand. I believe students welcome this strictness as a respite from personal hostilities. We focus on content rather than last weekend's drug bust or love fest. But am I helping these students prepare for the bumps and jostles of their real worlds—like the creepy, scary surprises encountered in mall parking lots? How quickly might my recent scenario have escalated had I not responded in a nonthreatening, face-saving way for him?

Since teens, especially at-risk students, often communicate inappropriately, assertive communication needs to supplant the typical passive-aggressive cycle. They want to be treated with respect but don't necessarily show respect to authority because they don't know how to do it without losing face. My years of experience teaching these students tells me that, to them, showing respect to authority is often confused with "kissing up," fawning favor. The fear of embarrassment and the loss of peer approval is immense. Consequently, the discomfort with their awkwardness and their desire to be one of the pack who is not to be singled out for any reason work against rational, calm interactions. That is not to say that most teens don't deal appropriately despite all these same factors, but my experience with at-risk students tells me they need instruction in assertive communication.

So I'm perceptive. I identify this need in the students. But there's a glitch: I also observe that

Figure 4.3. "Who You Dissn', Dude? At-Risk Students Learn Assertive Communication Skills"—An article from the May, 2000 issue of the *English Journal*, 89, 111–118 by Barbara R. Cangelosi (Copied with permission)

teach. (b) You make *summative evaluations* to provide periodic judgments on how well students have done as a result of instructional units that have been completed. Grades and reports of students' achievements (e.g., to their parents) result from teachers' summative evaluations.

In which Case, 4.51 or 4.52, is the teacher communicating a formative evaluation?

there's immediate and immense gratification in students' aggressive behavior—whether it's verbal or physical. It's very cathartic to deck that kid who's irritating, or shove her into the wall, or cuss him out if he's a problem; these kids are impulsive. It's the "act now, think later" syndrome. When they do think about it later, it's almost always as a victim: "I couldn't help it!" "She made me so mad!" "It's his fault!" Deflect responsibility; deny choice.

I begin to reflect on all these observations and this knowledge as I assess the students' needs and decide to use this power/control issue as it relates to respect as a guidelines for a unit of instruction. I decide to use the drawbacks or negative side-effects as the "hook" to engage the students and get them to buy into assertive communication. The drawbacks and negative side-effects include jail time, lawsuits, escalation of violence in retaliations, and increased likelihood of injury to themselves. I "sell" assertive communication to them as the mode of choice because it gives them power and control over a situation without the negative consequences. Punching somebody out is very satisfying at the moment, but the cost is too high—don't put yourself in a situation where it "costs" you. Assertive communication enables you to get what you need and take control without the problems of aggressive communication. Passive communication is ineffective also because the message does not get across due to fear and/or intimidation by others. It is characterized by whining, blaming, and labeling others. Assertive communication, on the other hand, is characterized by open, direct, honest communication without sounding intimidating or being intimidated by others. It empowers students appropriately to address issues of manipulation by others and stick to their opinions in the face of opposition. So, to teach my students assertive communication as a means of empowerment, a way of taking control and staying in charge of situations, I developed a four-week unit.

Organizing the Content and Implementing the Curriculum

I introduce the unit with a personal values inventory (see Figure 1) that I devised in anticipation of the unit's content: general communication information, the *Time* magazine article the students will be reading on emotional intelligence (EQ), the video they will watch about barriers and builders in communication, issues of personal responsibility, and issues of power and control. The inventory is a list of fifteen statements to which students respond by circling SA (strongly agree), AS (agree somewhat), DS (disagree somewhat), or SD (strongly disagree). After they silently respond individually, I call upon the class to walk with their inventories to the corner of the classroom that has the sign matching their answer for statement #1 (i.e., either "SA," "AS," "DS," or "SD"). I direct individuals to explain the reasoning behind their choices and, before continuing on to the next statement, ask individuals in an opposite corner to paraphrase the previous response and then give their points of view. The inventory now becomes a listening exercise, and listening is a key to respect in communication.

I introduce them to the concept of control theory through William Glasser's book, *The Quality School*, in which he states:

> ... control theory contends that all human beings are born with five basic needs built into their genetic structure: survival, love, power, fun and freedom. All of our lives we must attempt to live in a way that will best satisfy one or more of these needs. Control theory is a descriptive term because we try to control our own behavior so that we choose to do the most need-satisfying thing we can do at the time. (43-44)

Exposing the students to control as an issue in the outside world (e.g. in psychology) stresses its importance and relevance to them. Most of them work jobs, and many have been through counseling, therapy, and/or drug rehab. But they are not as adept as they should be at reading social situations. Since communication is overwhelmingly nonverbal (H. A. Smith 466) students need to get better at reading between the lines, inferring from words, tone, and body language what really is being communicated; thus, the students engage in a series of lessons and activities to build these skills.

Figure 4.3. (*continued*)

▶ **CASE 4.51**

Jay asks Ms. Motta, his basic chemistry teacher, "Do you think if I sign up for advanced placement chemistry, I'll do okay?" Ms. Motta: "I don't know. That's really up to you. But I am confident that you understand nearly everything we've covered in basic chemistry."

Figure 1. Five Items from Personal Values Inventory

1. I feel important in school.   SD   SA   DS   AS

2. My parents (siblings/girlfriend/boyfriend) can make me so mad that I hit them.   SD   SA   DS   AS

3. If I saw a homeless person on the street corner begging for food, I would ignore him.   SD   SA   DS   AS

4. If I'm at work and my boss screams at me for arriving late again, I would scream back at the boss in my own defense.   SD   SA   DS   AS

5. If an underage drunk driver kills a pedestrian, the driver's parents should be held legally responsible and should be successfully sued by the deceased's surviving family for a reasonable amount of money.   SD   SA   DS   AS

To illustrate the significance of nonverbal cuing in effecting communication, a series of activities demonstrate how difficult it is to be precise and accurate when certain aspects of communication are removed or thwarted. Examples include a peanut butter sandwich demonstration and an action-out-of-context transparency activity. In the former, one student goes to the front of the room, facing away from the class and blindfolded. Unbeknownst to this person, I place a loaf of bread, a jar of peanut butter, and a knife on a desktop in the rear of the room. I then direct the student to describe to me how to make a peanut butter sandwich, while signaling the rest of the class to silence. The student begins, "Well, I don't know—you get a piece of bread—" So I rip into the plastic bag of bread and tear off a two-inch piece "—and put some peanut butter on it." So I stab the knife through the plastic peanut butter jar and smear a gob on the two-inch piece of bread. "Then you get another piece of bread and put it on top of the other one, and you've got a sandwich." I tear off another two-inch piece of bread, stack it over the other one, and invite the student to remove the blindfold and eat the

delectable sandwich as I stand nearby sticky-fisted. Everybody hoots—mostly because I am such a mess! Then we discuss the lessons of this demonstration: Be careful with the assumptions you make in communication, be precise in your language use, and seek feedback to correct inaccurate information (e.g., if the student were able to see me tear off the two-inch piece of bread, the directions would be corrected by saying precisely, "one whole slice of bread").

The action-out-of-context series consists of ten to twelve overhead transparencies onto which have been traced individual photos, with only the body outlines of figures in the photograph and all background context removed (Figure 2).

The outlines are purposely kept gender-neutral, focusing on the body language. Students view each transparency and silently write down three logical guesses for each, reflecting what they think the person(s) could be doing given

Figure 2. Action-out-of-Context Outline

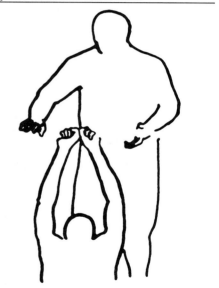

Figure 4.3. *(continued)*

▶ **CASE 4.52**

Larry asks Mr. Jones, his basic chemistry teacher, "Why did you give us so many problems to work for homework? You usually don't give half that many." Mr. Jones: "You seem to conceptualize the formulas very well, but you've been making a lot of computational errors. The best way I know for you to overcome that difficulty is to practice and practice."

that body language: positions of heads, arms, legs, and torsos. No facial expressions are shown and clothing is not detailed. I ask students to consider whether their answers would vary based on the gender of the person in the drawings. After they view all transparencies, students share their responses and the reasoning behind them. The class is treated to a wide variety of answers. Then I display the actual photos, emphasizing that there are no right or wrong answers. (Figure 3 is the photo corresponding to Figure 2.)

It is their use of logical application that is key. This activity reveals that meaning is shaped by our interpretation and past experiences. Assertive communication requires that students learn to be cautious in making assumptions about others, to seek feedback that they're getting the message across, to be precise in their language use, and to acknowledge that we are individuals with different experiences that shape our interpretation of the world around us.

Building on the success of the students' respectful interactions in the earlier activities, I ask them to read Gibbs's article "The EQ Factor" aloud together and complete a comprehensive study guide to help them organize its content. The phrase "emotional intelligence" was coined by psychologists Peter Salovey and John Mayer to describe qualities like understanding one's own feelings, empathy for the feelings of others, and "the regulation of emotion in a way that enhances living" (Gibbs 62). Gibbs quotes Daniel Goleman from his best-selling book, *Emotional Intelligence*. "When it comes to predicting people's success, brainpower as measured by IQ and standardized achievement tests may actually matter less than the qualities of mind once thought of as 'character'" (Gibbs 62). The article cautions:

> ...EQ is not the opposite of IQ...[but may be used to explain] how one's ability to handle stress, for instance, affects the ability to concentrate and put intelligence to use...Perhaps that most visible emotional skills, the ones we recognize most readily, are the "people skills" like empathy, graciousness, and the ability

Figure 3. Action-out-of-Context Photo

Seated: Casey Cangelosi; standing: Kasey Mitchell. Photo by Donna Karchner

to read a social situation. Researchers believe that about 90% of emotional communication is nonverbal. (63–65)

Randy, one of my students, wrote:

> The aspects of EQ [are something] I had thought about a lot this year. It was nice to know that someone wrote a book about it. I think that these aspects of life make life. It is when people become people and not just emotionally sensitive animals. It would be a nice society if everyone used the process of looking at their emotions and used them to better their own existence instead of letting their emotions control it. If you use assertiveness, it makes you have a better day.

Figure 4.3. (*continued*)

In Case 4.52, Mr. Jones indicated that he used his evaluations of what Larry did and didn't do well to influence the design of a learning activity. Thus, Mr. Jones's evaluation was formative. To be effective, teachers need to design learning activities in light of ongoing, frequent, formative evaluations that are regularly communicated to students (Cangelosi, 2000, pp. 42–118). Summative evaluations occur periodically (e.g., at the end of a learning unit), but they need not occur as frequently as formative evaluations. Nevertheless, when students and their parents think of teacher evaluations, they nearly always think of the summative variety because they think of grading.

To provide students with actual conversational tools for assertive communication, the class views H. Stephen Glenn's video "Empowering Others" in which communication barriers and builders are introduced and discussed. According to Glenn, people need to supplant the barriers they use in communications with the following builders instead:

1. assuming	→	1. checking it out
2. rescuing	→	2. exploring
3. directing	→	3. encouraging
4. expecting	→	4. celebrating
5. adultism	→	5. respecting

Students apply these techniques to original samples they write. (See Rinh's example in Figure 4).

Material from the book *Yes, I Can Say No* by Manuel J. Smith is presented as a model for assertiveness strategies to implement in the face of peer pressure and/or social criticism. Students learn techniques such as fogging, negative assertion, negative inquiry, workable compromise, positive assertion, broken record, and self-disclosure and apply them to sample dialogues between two fictional characters from *Ordinary People* and *I Know Why the Caged Bird Sings*, which the students rewrite in assertive style via Smith's strategies. The seven strategies are as follows:

1. Fogging: repeating and/or agreeing with a criticism (e.g., "You are stupid." "I sure could be smarter.")
2. Negative assertion: admitting a mistake (e.g., "Why are you so late?" "I know I'm late.")
3. Negative inquiry: questioning a criticism to exhaust the tormentor (e.g., "You are stupid." "What is it about me that is stupid?")
4. Self-disclosure: revealing your own personal feelings (e.g., "You're late again!" "I'm sorry; my car wouldn't start.")
5. Positive assertion: agreeing with a criticism using phrases like "Yes," "You're right," "You've got my number all right!" (e.g., "You are ugly." "You're right. I am ugly.")
6. Workable compromise: coming up with a middle ground proposal to resolve a problem or conflict (e.g., "You're late again! What's wrong with you? Can't you just get to work on time?" "What if I call you next time when I know I'm going to be late?")
7. Broken record: repeating your opinion in the face of opposition or manipulation (e.g., "I want to borrow your sweater. I have let you borrow my clothes before." "You have let me borrow your clothes before, but I'm not lending you my sweater.")

Following is a student sample of a revised excerpted conversation from *Ordinary People*:

Coach: Jarrett, you gotta be kidding me. I don't get it. I excuse you from practice twice a week so you can see some shrink. I work with you every damn night *at your convenience*; now what the hell more am I supposed to be doing for you?

Conrad: Nothing. I don't appreciate your derogatory use of the word shrink. I'm seeing a psychiatrist. (SELF-DISCLOSURE)

Coach: A bright kid like you with everything going for him. I don't get it. Why do you want to keep messing up your life?

Conrad: You're right. I have messed up before. What is it about my life you think I keep messing up now? (POSITIVE ASSERTION, NEGATIVE ASSERTION, NEGATIVE INQUIRY)

Coach: Well, you're quitting the team, you stupid jerk!

Conrad: I am a stupid jerk, but I don't think it'll mess up my life if I stop swimming. (FOGGING)

Coach: Okay, this is it. You are a big kid now and actions have consequences. You're messing up big time, but I'm not taking you back. You remember that.

Conrad: I'll remember, but I don't think it'll mess up my life if I stop swimming. (BROKEN RECORD)

Coach: You quit the swim team and you're seeing a shrink . . . I call that messing up your life.

Conrad: I'll tell you what'll straighten out this mess: I quit the swim team and *you* start seeing a psychiatrist for your complete lack of understanding and compassion! (WORKABLE COMPROMISE)

Figure 4.3. *(continued)*

Emphasizing Formative Evaluations

The grade consciousness that many students and their parents display can interfere with how well teachers are able to communicate formative evaluations to students. Consider Case 4.53.

The students' final writing assignment for this unit requires them to create at least thirty lines of original dialogue using assertive communication in the workplace scenario. Students can incorporate any of H. Stephen Glenn's barriers and builders techniques. Their original assertiveness in the workplace scenes are performed in front of the whole class. For example, one student, Trina, wrote "Employee Learns How to Deal with Angry Bosses." (The employer and manager are two different people here.):

Employer: Work faster, you good-for-nothing employee! You're working too slow.

Employee: Yes, I know I'm working a little slow today. (NEGATIVE ASSERTION)

Employer: Well, speed it up or you'll be finding yourself on the unemployment line!

Employee: I understand; I will snap out of my laziness. (SELF-DISCLOSURE)

Employer: Well, that makes me feel lots better, let me tell you.

Employee: I'm sure you have better things to do than to stand here and tell me to hurry up. I will speed up my pace. (NEGATIVE ASSERTION, FOGGING)

Employer: Stop feeding me B.S. You are the worst and slowest worker I've ever hired.

Employee: I'm sorry you feel that way, but what is it that makes you look at me so low? (SELF-DISCLOSURE, NEGATIVE INQUIRY)

Employer: Because you are a lazy employee.

Employee: I've changed; I just don't know why I'm being so slow today.

Employer: Just speed up your pace.

Employee: Yes, sir.

Manager: I told you to get to work.

Employee: You're right I should have listened to you. (FOGGING)

Manager: What can I do to make you work so I don't get in trouble?

Employee: You can try to get me a raise so I can work and it will be worth my while. (WORKABLE COMPROMISE)

Manager: No way! You don't deserve a raise!

Employee: If you get me a raise, I will work harder. (BROKEN RECORD, WORKABLE COMPROMISE)

Manager: I will do anything else, but you're not getting the raise.

Employee: I'm telling you, get me the raise and I will become a fast worker and you won't get in trouble. (BROKEN RECORD, WORKABLE COMPROMISE)

Manager: No way; now drop it.

Co-Worker: I heard that the manager came down hard on you.

Employee: Yes, I feel really miserable right now. (SELF-DISCLOSURE)

Co-Worker: I really need a favor from you, and that is I need someone to work for me on Saturday.

Employee: Don't look at me, I'm busy that night.

Co-Worker: Please . . . I will forever be in your debt.

Employee: No, I can't.

Co-Worker: Fine!

Employee: Why don't you try someone else, and I'll work for you some other time. (WORKABLE COMPROMISE)

Co-Worker: Well, OK, thanks for your help.

Employee: Anytime.

On the unit test students have access to all their notes and resources. Afterwards, they reflect on the unit in an evaluation questionnaire. Trina's written comment typifies the reflections of a significant segment of the class: "I feel that my attitude has changed. I feel that I don't lose my temper as fast and using these strategies keeps me calm. But it makes the other person upset because I'm not fighting back." Kevin stated, "I believe it has helped me out a little. Most of these things I already knew about except EQ. I am taking a lesson in anger management because I am aggressive most of the time or passive some of the time. I am not really assertive but have both of the others. I think if I were to become assertive it would help me out a lot." Jeff stated, "Now I often find myself using fogging, negative inquiry, and the others in conversations. I find myself talking to my mother in a more respecting way."

Figure 4.3. (*continued*)

▶ **CASE 4.53**

Mr. Wedington wants to find out exactly which steps in a long-division process his fifth graders can do and for which steps he needs to provide help. Thus, he meets with each student individually and has the student think aloud while working out a long-division computation. It is Stephanie's turn to demonstrate her skill with the process. Mr. Wedington: "Stephanie, I want to watch you

Figure 4. Barriers and Builders: Student Sample

Barriers	Builders
1. ASSUMING Mom: You broke the window; I can't believe you broke the window! Do you even have a brain in your head? How could you do that?	**1. CHECKING IT OUT** Mom: I noticed that the window is broken. Do you know what happened?
2. RESCUING Teacher: You idiot! I can't believe you dropped the books all over the floor! How could you have done that? Get out of here, so I can clean it up.	**2. EXPLORING** Teacher: I see the way you were carrying the books didn't work. Can you think of a better way to carry them?
3. DIRECTING Mom: Clean up your clothes, mop the floor, pick up the garbage, do the dishes . . .	**3. ENCOURAGING** Mom: I'm expecting company a little later on. Do you think you could help me with tidying up?
4. EXPECTING Mom: Why didn't you vacuum out the car and wash it like I told you to? You are so incompetent.	**4. CELEBRATING** Mom: Thank you very much for cleaning all of the garbage out of the car. That was very nice of you.
5. ADULTISM Boss: Why haven't you been producing as much as you're supposed to? Damn it! Why is that so hard for you?	**5. RESPECTING** Boss: I've noticed that your productivity has been slipping. Is there a reason for that?

Conclusions

Feedback from students throughout the unit, on the tests, and in their written evaluations of the unit was very positive and enthusiastic. Overall, they viewed the content as helpful and necessary; several students remarked how cool it was that we were learning about this sort of personally useful and practical communication that everyone needs daily to cope with others. Approaching the unit from the personal safety zone of the initial SA/AS/DS/SD inventory was productive because it opened the students to a tone of respect for their individual differences and presented a model for listening to those differences appropriately. Glasser's control theory provided an appropriate vehicle for the students' embracing assertiveness because of his basic needs component, which gave them a handle on the psychology behind the motivations for their choices and presented the notion that we are all responsible for our own decisions—nobody makes us do or say anything we haven't decided to do or say.

The idea of control as a means of gaining respect from others being the basis of assertiveness caused students to pause and think about how they themselves communicate and interact at home, at school, and in their social circles. Prior experiences in which they were manipulated by others' aggressive or passive communications hooked students into the unit. The EQ article enlightened students to the concept of emotional intelligence and addressed the very real need that exists in the work world for employees with people skills. Activities like the actions-out-of-context transparencies reinforced the need for assertive communication skills and precision in language. The barriers and builders presented by H. Stephen Glenn's video, *Empowering Others*, and the assertive response models from Manual J. Smith's book, *Yes, I Can Say No*, equipped the class with strategies for putting assertiveness into practice. Students worked assiduously on their writing assignments, shared examples and ideas with each other, and frequently checked with me for accuracy in their original scripts.

Figure 4.3. (*continued*)

divide 753 by 12. As you work it out here on your paper, tell me what you are thinking as you go through the steps." Stephanie writes down "$12\sqrt{753}$" but stops and says, "I don't know the answer." Mr. Wedington: "Neither do I. But I do know how to find the answer. I'd like you to begin to find the answer." Stephanie: "I can't while you're watching me!" Mr. Wedington: "Why not?" Stephanie: "Because I'll make a mistake and you'll lower my grade." Mr. Wedington: "This has nothing to do with your grade. I just want to see how you divide so that I can help you divide

I plan to incorporate support material such as CD-ROMs on this or related topics for use as enrichment and reinforcement of the unit objectives. The number of assertiveness strategy models would be expanded to include mirroring and other techniques Smith used in his book. In subsequent school terms, we will explore the theme of anger management in two young adult novels, *Iceman* by Chris Lynch and *Ironman* by Chris Crutcher, for which the previous implementation of assertive communication strategies lays a solid foundation. We will examine sample scenarios from the novels for communication styles and analyze them according to the assertiveness standards already studied.

Collaborating with a vocational teacher at the mainstream high shool, I'm investigating the idea of the at-risk students peer-teaching this same unit to a Teen Living and Life Skills class there. Both groups of students seem eager and enthusiastic about this cooperative project. You really know you've learned something if you can teach it to someone else.

Works Cited

Empowering Others. Videotape. Narr. H. Stephen Glenn. Sunrise Productions, 1990. 82 min.

Gibbs, Nancy. "The EQ Factor." *Time* 146 October 1995: 60-68.

Glasser, William. *The Quality School*. New York: Harper Perennial, 1992.

Simon, Sidney, Leland Howe, and Howard Kirschenbaum. *Values Clarification*. New York: Hart Publishing, 1978.

Smith, H.A. "Nonverbal Communication." *The International Encyclopedia of Teaching and Teacher Education*. Ed. Michael J. Dunkin. Oxford: Pergamon Press, 1987. 466-76.

Smith, Manuel J. *Yes, I Can Say No*. New York: Arbor House, 1986.

Barbara R. Cangelosi teaches at Logan South Campus School, Logan, Utah.

Figure 4.3. (*continued*)

better." Stephanie writes "6" as a partial quotient above the "5" in "753." Quickly, she puts down her pencil and asks, "Is that right?" Mr. Wedington: "Tell me why you decided to put '6' there." Stephanie begins to erase the "6," exclaiming, "Oh! It's not right!" Mr. Wedington gently touches the pencil, stopping her from erasing her correct response. Stephanie: "Oh! We're not allowed to erase...."

All Mr. Wedington wanted to do was to diagnose Stephanie's skill with long division so he would be in a better position to help. But Stephanie was so used to having teachers grade the outcomes of her efforts that she didn't understand that Mr. Wedington was trying to help her, not grade her.

How can you help students overcome their defensiveness about being evaluated and gain the cooperation you need to conduct ongoing formative evaluations? Here are three suggestions: (a) Use descriptive rather than judgmental language. (b) Clearly distinguish for your students those relatively infrequent tests that you use to make summative evaluations from the continual observations and tests used for formative evaluations. (c) Do not collect data for summative evaluations during learning activities.

Descriptive language helps convince students that you evaluate only their levels of achievement of specific learning goals, not the students themselves. Frequent assessments used to keep students apprised of their progress throughout learning units but that do not influence their grades help students to conceptualize, and thus cooperate in, formative evaluations. Those less-frequent assessments that do influence students' grades should be distinguished as extraordinary events for which their engagements in your learning activities and formative evaluations have prepared them.

You, like many teachers, may value student-centered learning activities in which students respond to your questions (e.g., with Socratic methods), solve problems, or take part in discussions. Sometimes students are reluctant to engage in such activities because they feel they're being graded. A comment from one seventh grader is typical: "Sure, Mr. Burke says, 'We learn by our mistakes.' But when we make mistakes, he's right there to take off points!" When performance during learning activities influences grades, students may not feel free to ask questions, try out answers, and risk making mistakes.

Grades as a Form of Communication

Although formative evaluations should be emphasized more than summative evaluations, summative evaluations must still be periodically communicated to students and their parents. Grades and report cards are common vehicles for such communications. Unfortunately, many teachers use grades for other purposes. Case 4.54 is an example.

▶ **CASE 4.54**

Ms. Carter bases 40 percent of her students' history grades on attendance. She believes this will motivate students to come to class. She also lowers a student's grade by one letter for every 10 demerits received during a term. A student receives demerits for getting caught exhibiting disruptive behaviors.

When teachers make grades directly contingent on attendance, effort, level of cooperation, or other factors different from student achievement of academic learning goals, the meaning of grades is lost. Is a *B* in history an indication of how well a student has achieved the goals specified by the history course syllabus? Or is the *B* a reflection of effort, willingness to cooperate with the teacher, and faithfulness to assignments? There are far more effective ways to motivate students to be on-task than artificially rewarding on-task behaviors with high grades and artificially punishing off-task behaviors with low grades. Specific suggestions for positively reinforcing on-task behaviors and punishing off-task behaviors without distorting the meaning of grades are included throughout the remainder of this text. In general, there is no need for you to manipulate grades artificially as long as you (a) make sure your learning activities provide students with effective means for achieving the stated learning goals and (b) the summative evaluations that you use to determine grades are based on assessments that are valid indicators of how well students achieved those same learning goals.

▶ FOSTERING PARENTS' COOPERATION

Focusing on Formative Evaluations

You should, but may not always be able to, depend on students' parents to help secure students' cooperation. Often you may want to discuss formative evaluations with parents to help them understand what you're trying to get their children to accomplish and how parents can contribute to that goal. Sometimes communications are thwarted by parents, who think all teacher evaluations are summative. In Case 4.55, Mr. Perkins attempts to gain Rolando's mother's cooperation. To do so, he must assertively steer the conversation away from summative and toward formative evaluations.

▶ **CASE 4.55**

Mr. Perkins does not have the time to confer with his fifth graders' parents as frequently as he would like. He does, however, maintain contact by routinely phoning one or two parents each school day. In this way, he is able to speak with a parent of each student at least once every three weeks. It normally takes two conversations before parents understand that Mr. Perkins's intentions are to inform them about what their children are doing, not to praise or criticize students. Here is an account of Mr. Perkins's first telephone conversation with Rolando Michot's mother:

Ms. Michot: Hello.

Mr. Perkins: Hello, Ms. Michot. This is Sal Perkins, Rolando's teacher. I hope you are doing well.

Ms. Michot: Oh, yes. And what about you?

Mr. Perkins: Just great! I'd like to take five to six minutes to let you know what Rolando's working on in fifth grade. Is this is a convenient time for us to talk?

Ms. Michot: I can talk now, but what kinda trouble is that boy giving you?

Mr. Perkins: Rolando is not giving me any trouble. I want to let you know about some things Rolando is working on in school.

Ms. Michot: I'm glad he's not troubling you. Is he going to pass? How are his grades?

Mr. Perkins: We're just beginning a lesson on how to use mathematics to find the best prices when shopping.

Ms. Michot: That's interesting. Do you think he'll learn it?

Mr. Perkins: Yes, and he should improve both his reading and mathematical skills as we start examining newspaper ads.

Ms. Michot: It'd be good for him to do more reading. He'd rather watch TV. I'm always telling him, "Turn off that boob tube, and go do some reading." But he just keeps watching.

Mr. Perkins: You've just given me an idea! Let's use his affinity for TV to build his interest in relating mathematics and reading to shopping. I'll assign Rolando to make a record of price-related information that is communicated in TV commercials. We'll use his notes during our mathematics lessons.

Ms. Michot: I'll make sure he has a pad and pencil with him when he's in front of the television.

Mr. Perkins: That'll be a help. Thank you.

Ms. Michot: Anything else?

Mr. Perkins: He'll be working on expanding his writing vocabulary and using dictionaries for another week.

Ms. Michot: How's his writing?

Mr. Perkins: Each day this week, I'll give him a list of between 5 and 10 new words and for homework ask him to write sentences using them. It should take him about 20 minutes each night to look up the words in his dictionary and write the sentences.

Ms. Michot: I'll see that he does it.

Mr. Perkins: Thank you. I'll call again in about three weeks, and we can further discuss what Rolando is doing in school.

Ms. Michot: That would be very nice. Thank you for calling.

Conferences

Conferences between parents and teachers are more common in elementary schools than in secondary schools. It is quite common for elementary schools periodically to devote entire school days to parent conferences. This practice is less common for secondary schools, but secondary teachers must also find time for conferences with parents. Consider the following suggestions whenever you plan a conference with one of your students' parents:

1. Prepare an agenda for the conference that specifies (a) the purpose of the meeting (e.g., to communicate summative evaluations relative to achievement of learning goals for the previous nine weeks or to develop a plan to increase the rate at which the student completes homework assignments), (b) a sequence of topics to be discussed, and (c) beginning and ending times for the conference.

2. Except for special situations, invite the student to attend and participate in the conference. (Healthier, more open attitudes are more likely to emerge when the student is included.)

3. Schedule the meeting in a small conference room or other setting where distractions (e.g,. a telephone) are minimal and there is little chance for outsiders to overhear the conversation.

4. Provide a copy of the agenda to each person in attendance. During the meeting, direct attention to the topic at hand by referring to the appropriate agenda item and using other visuals (e.g., material from the student's portfolio).

5. During the conference, concentrate remarks on descriptions of events, behaviors, and circumstances. Focus on needs, goals, and plans for accomplishing goals. Completely avoid characterizations and personality judgments.

6. During the conference be an active listener so that you facilitate communication and thus increase the likelihood that you (a) get your planned message across and (b) learn from the others at the meeting and pick up ideas for more effectively working with the student.

Written Communications

In addition to conferences with parents, which are necessarily infrequent, some teachers send home weekly or monthly newsletters designed to apprise parents of what their children's classes are doing. Figure 4.4 is an example.

By taking the time to write such form letters, you foster the goodwill and understanding of parents. Their understanding of what you, as a teacher, are trying to accomplish with their children will serve you well when you need to call on them to help you deal with behavior problems.

▶ PROFESSIONAL CONFIDENCE AND STUDENTS' RIGHTS

Unprofessional Behavior

What, if anything, bothers you about the behaviors of the teachers in Cases 4.56 to 4.58?

▶ CASE 4.56

Two teachers, Mr. Bates and Ms. Saddler, are talking in the 45th Street Sixth-Grade Center faculty room. Mr. Bates: "How's it going?" Ms. Saddler: "There must be a full moon! The kids are nuts

PARENTS' NEWSLETTER FOR AMERICAN HISTORY II

3RD PERIOD

From Jake Bertolli, Teacher

Vol. 1, No. 24, Week of March 16—20

Looking Back

Our last letter mentioned that we had begun a unit on late 19th century industrialism in the United States. I think a majority of the class were a bit bored with the material dealing with some of the major personalities (e.g., Carnegie and Rockefeller) that influenced industrialization in that era. However, I was quite pleased with the enthusiasm nearly everyone showed for the lessons on worker—management issues; especially when we studied the problems that led to the enactment of child labor laws. Based on my statistical analysis of the results, the test the class took last Friday seemed to provide a pretty accurate indicator of what most students achieved during the week. The class average on the test was 37.3, slightly higher than I had anticipated.

This Week

This week we will be discussing the rise of trusts in this country and move into the presidency of Woodrow Wilson. The relationship between the economic climate in the United States and the fighting of World War I will be a major focus of the class. One of the goals of the lesson is to help your daughter or son to understand how one event (e.g., a corporation in the U.S. decides to expand) influences another (e.g., strategic plans for a battle in Europe).

Homework assignments will include: (1) Read pp.588—661 from the textbook for Thursday's class; (2) Watch the show from 8:30 to 9:30 on Channel 7, Tues. night, and be prepared to discuss its content on Wednesday; (3) Complete a worksheet, to be distributed Thursday, and attach it to the test to be given on Friday; (4) Prepare for Friday's test.

Looking Forward

Next week, we will compare what we learned about the rise of industries and corporations near the turn of the century to today's world economic situation. In subsequent weeks, we'll return our attention to the 1920s and examine some causes of war and ways to achieve peace.

Figure 4.4. Sample Monthly Newsletter for Parents

today. Just hope you never have Arla Neville. She can't follow what's going on, so she entertains herself by bugging me. Why do I have to have all the retards?"

▶ **CASE 4.57**

Bill Kresie, a high school coach and social science teacher, meets one of his friends, Vickie Dobson, in the grocery store. Mr. Kresie: "Hi, Vickie." Ms. Dobson: "Well, hello, Bill. It's nice to see you. What have you been up to?" Mr. Kresie: "Same old stuff. How about you?" Ms. Dobson: "Well, you know my daughter, Christine—" Mr. Kresie: "Yes, lovely girl. How's she doing?" Ms. Dobson: "She just broke up with Ronald Boher and has taken up with Don Palmer." Mr. Kresie: "Really! Good move on her part. Ronald's a real loser. He went out for football, you know, and showed no guts at all. I had Don in American history. Bright, bright kid!"

▶ **CASE 4.58**

In a parent–teacher conference with Gary Mastoroni's father, Ms. Mauger tells him, "Gary is doing quite well. I wish all my students were like Gary. If I could get Elmo Thompson to cooperate like Gary, I'd jump for joy!"

Trust between a teacher and a student is an important ingredient in establishing a classroom climate that is conducive to cooperation, on-task behaviors, and engagement in learning activities. Teachers violate that trust when they gossip about students or share information obtained through their role as teachers with people who need not be privy to that information. Ms. Saddler in Case 4.56 was frustrated and obviously needed to talk about her difficult day. Her behavior was understandable, but was it professional? Was it excusable? Her use of the label "retards" displayed her disregard for at least some accepted professional standards. If all the teachers at her school understand that the faculty room is a place for teachers to vent some of their frustrations, and what is said does not leave the faculty room, then Ms. Saddler's comments may never get back to students. Once students acquire the idea that teachers gossip about them, they are unlikely to trust those teachers. In Cases 4.57 and 4.58, Mr. Kresie and Ms. Mauger can hardly hope that their comments about students will not be spread by the outsiders to whom they spoke.

Privileged Information

Of course, there are times when teachers should communicate information and express judgments about students' achievement levels and behaviors. Who should be aware of privileged communications? Typically, the following people are considered to have a right and a need to know:

1. In most cases, the student needs to be kept apprised of her or his own status regarding achievement of learning goals and evaluations of school conduct.

2. The student's parents need to be aware of their child's level of achievement and behaviors for two reasons: (a) Parents who are informed about exactly what their children are and are not accomplishing in school can better serve as partners with teachers to help their children cooperate and achieve. (b) Parents

are legally responsible for their children's welfare. They do, after all, delegate and entrust some of their responsibilities to teachers. They have a right to know how the school is influencing their children.

3. Professional personnel (e.g., a guidance counselor or another of the student's teachers) who have instructional responsibilities for that student sometimes need to know about the student's achievement and behaviors so that they are in a better position to help that student.

4. Professional personnel who supervise and evaluate the teacher's performance or provide the teacher with formative feedback on instruction sometimes need to understand specifics about individual students to meet their responsibilities to the teacher (see, e.g., Cangelosi, 1991, pp. 3–14).

5. Professional personnel whose judgments affect curricula and conduct of the school (e.g., the principal, subject-area supervisor, or curriculum director) sometimes need to be aware of an individual student's achievements or behaviors so that they will be in a better position to make school-level decisions.

6. Because a school often acts as an agency that qualifies students for occupations, other academic institutions, or other privileges (e.g., scholarships), it may sometimes be necessary for a representative of an institution to which a student has applied to have knowledge of evaluations of the student's achievements and behaviors. Nevertheless, school personnel should seriously consider following a policy stating that they will release information about an individual student's achievements or behaviors only with the student's and her or his parents' authorization.

▶ SYNTHESIS ACTIVITIES FOR CHAPTER 4

I. Select the one best response for each of the following multiple-choice prompts that either answers the question or completes the statement:

A. "Withitness" refers to how _____.

   a) well students respect the teacher

   b) enthusiastic a teacher is about the learning activities she or he conducts

   c) aware the teacher is of what is going on in the classroom

   d) well the teacher's students remain on-task and engaged in learning activities

B. Frederic Jones suggested that teachers should _____.

   a) avoid direct eye contact with one student at a time so as not to show favoritism

   b) not use hand gestures as a form of communication because they send ambiguous messages

   c) avoid stationing themselves at a distance from students during learning activities

   d) address all questions a student has when providing individual help

C. Ginott urged teachers to _____.

   a) avoid expressing personal feelings

   b) praise students for being on-task

       c)   describe situations for students

       d)   tolerate misbehaviors that are functions of students' family backgrounds

  D. Which one of the following remarks made by a teacher on a student's tests paper is most consistent with Ginott's suggestions?

       a)   "It appears that you should review the area-of-a-triangle formula."

       b)   "It appears that you are quite a mathematician."

       c)   "You didn't study hard enough."

       d)   "Apparently you are the kind of student who diligently prepares for tests."

  E. The assertive response style is characterized by ____.

       a)   concern for students' needs

       b)   honesty

       c)   hostility

       d)   passiveness

II.   Compare your responses to Synthesis Activity I's multiple-choice prompts to the following key: A-c, B-c, C-c, D-a, E-b.

III.   Reread Case 4.3. With a colleague, discuss how the effects of Ms. Johnson's praise of Whitney might differ if she had praised him privately rather than in front of the class. Following are some thoughts to consider:

> According to Ginott, praising students themselves rather than only their work is a mistake whether done publicly or privately. But group dynamics may compound the undesirable effects. Because the teacher called him a good student in front of peers, Whitney may feel compelled to maintain the label in not only Ms. Johnson's eyes but also those of his classmates. Another unfortunate possibility is for the group to begin resenting Whitney as a teacher's pet. Whitney may then respond to the group's resentment by demonstrating that he's really not a good student.

IV.   Following is a list of statements by teachers. Label each one as descriptive (D), judgmental of a person (JP), or judgmental of a behavior, achievement, or situation (J):

  A. "Xavier, you are very polite."

  B. "Xavier, that was a very polite thing for you to do for Richard."

  C. "Xavier, you allowed Richard to go first."

  D. "I am having trouble concentrating because of the noise in here."

  E. "All this noise shows that some people in here are inconsiderate."

  F. "Your score on this test makes you one of my best students."

  G. "Your score on this test was the highest in the class."

  H. "You did better on this test than anyone else in the class."

  I. "Pushing Ryan like that is not acceptable behavior."

  J. "Pushing Ryan like that is a violation of class rules."

K. "I am angry because you pushed Ryan like that."

L. "You're a bully for pushing Ryan!"

V. Compare your responses to Synthesis Activity IV's prompts with the following: A–JP, B–J, C–D, D–D, E–JP, F–JP, G–D, H–J, I–J, J–D, K–D, L–JP.

VI. Write a paragraph suggesting how the tactics that Ms. Price alludes to in Case 4.59 can backfire on her and eventually encourage students to be off-task in her class:

▶ CASE 4.59

Ms. Taylor asks Ms. Price in the faculty lounge, "How do you get your students to do their homework?" Ms. Price: "I embarrass them in front of their buddies if they come to class unprepared. I can make them feel like less than nothing for not doing what I assign."

Compare your paragraph with those of colleagues. Discuss similarities and differences.

VII. Students sometimes don't bother to listen to teachers because they've learned that adults often speak to them without really having anything of consequence to say. Categorize each of the following examples of teachers talking to students as *inane* or *informative*:

A. "Karl, your milk is dripping down the side of your glass."

B. "I am really enjoying myself!"

C. "You should behave while we're visiting the library."

D. "You really had a good time!"

E. Mr. Ballam notices one student in his class of 28 looking around during a written-response test. Mr. Ballam announces to the class, "Keep your eyes on your own paper."

F. "Until we get back to the room, stay within arm's length of your partner."

VIII. Compare your responses to Synthesis Activity VII's prompt with the following: A, B, and F are informative; C, D, and E are inane.

IX. Marcia, a sixth grader, comments to her teacher, "I don't want to take this test. I'll just flunk it." Provide a *supportive* response that Marcia's teacher could make and a *nonsupportive* response. In both responses, let Marcia know that she is expected to take the test as scheduled. Compare your responses with those of colleagues. Here is a possibility for a supportive response: "You seem nervous about taking the test, and it starts in only 40 seconds." Here's a possible nonsupportive response: "Oh, come on, Marcia! You'll do fine! Just relax; you'll see."

X. Write the letter of the comments that suggest that individuals are not completely responsible for their own conduct:

A. "Marla had trouble regaining her composure after Davalon spat on her."

B. "Evelyn's clowning in class is due to her lack of attention at home."

C. "He made me so ashamed!"

D. "Fred, your behavior will embarrass your mother!"

E. "I'm embarrassed!"

F. "Study hard and make me proud."

G. "I'll be very pleased to see you do well."

H. "He made me hit him."

I. "I was running so I wouldn't be late."

Did you list B, C, D, F, and H?

XI. Label each of the following teacher-made evaluations as *formative* or *summative:*

A. Mr. Jones decides to give Brenda a *C* in physical education.

B. Ms. Templeton judges that her learning unit on China went very well.

C. Ms. Blackstone decides that she should spend another day on an inductive activity for discovering a formula for the area of a triangle.

D. Ms. Collier decides not to allow Marcus to use paints for the rest of the week.

E. Mr. Larusso decides to reduce the planned homework assignment by one-third.

F. Ms. Banker decides that Juanita has made satisfactory progress.

XII. Compare your responses to Synthesis Activity XI's prompts to the following: A, B, and F are summative; C, D, and E are formative.

XIII. Write a one-page essay that presents positions both for and against the following policy:
The grade a student receives in a course should reflect *only* how well that student achieved the specified course goals.
Exchange your essay with that of a colleague and discuss similarities and differences in your responses.

XIV. Write a paragraph explaining the advantages that you, as a teacher, gain by maintaining a routine flow of information about your class to students' parents. Compare your paragraph with that of a colleague.

XV. Describe two examples in which teachers gossip about their students results in a loss of students' trust. Compare your examples with those of colleagues.

XVI. Ms. Jung's chemistry students are working in the laboratory when one student, Troy, turns up a Bunsen burner so that the flame is dangerously high. Troy laughs, saying, "Let's see how high this thing can go!"

A. Write an example of a *passive* verbal response that Ms. Jung might make.

B. Write an example of a *hostile* verbal response that Ms. Jung might make.

C. Write an example of an *assertive* verbal response that Ms. Jung might make.

Exchange your examples with those of colleagues. Here is a possible passive response:

"Troy, I really wish you wouldn't do that. That could be dangerous." A possible hostile response: "Troy, you're a menace to the safety of this class. What's the matter with you? Don't you have any sense at all?" A possible assertive response: "Troy, turn down that flame immediately. Thank you. Now shut off the Bunsen burner completely and come see me at my desk."

XVII. With three or four colleagues, describe how you might incorporate lessons that teach students assertive communication skills into your curricula.

► TRANSITIONAL ACTIVITY FROM CHAPTER 4 TO CHAPTER 5

In preparation for your work with Chapter 5, discuss with two or more colleagues the following questions:

I. Why is it important to distinguish between classroom standards of conduct and classroom procedures?

II. Why are classroom standards for conduct and procedures for classroom routines necessary?

III. Why should teachers avoid having unnecessary standards for conduct?

IV. Who should determine classroom standards for conduct?

V. What strategies do teachers employ to teach classroom standards of conduct and routine procedures to students?

VI. How should schoolwide discipline policies be formulated and enforced?

VII. What should be included in a safe-school program?

VIII. How should safe-school programs be developed and implemented?

IX. Access to what types of discipline-support, backup, crisis-support, and technology do teachers need in their classrooms so that they can conduct the business of teaching in a safe learning environment?

Standards for Conduct, Routine Procedures, and Safe-School Policies

▶ **CHAPTER 5'S GOAL AND OBJECTIVES**

The goal of this chapter is for you to develop strategies for establishing standards for classroom conduct, procedures for classroom routines, and schoolwide discipline and safety policies. Specifically, Chapter 5 is designed to lead you to achieve the following objectives:

1. Distinguish between necessary and unnecessary standards for classroom conduct and understand the consequences of having unnecessary standards.

2. Apply the teaching cycles model to help students comprehend standards of conduct, learn how to meet them, and predict the consequences of not meeting them.

3. Develop a plan for establishing and enforcing standards for classroom conduct as well as routine procedures for (a) maximizing on-task behaviors, (b) increasing safety and security, (c) preventing activities within your class from disturbing others outside your class, and (d) maintaining decorum among students, school personnel, and visitors to the school campus.

4. Collaborate with colleagues, parents, students, and community leaders to develop schoolwide discipline policies and a safe-school program.

▶ **STANDARDS FOR CLASSROOM CONDUCT**

Purposefully Stated Standards

Standards for classroom conduct are formalized statements that provide students with general guidelines for the types of behaviors that are required and those that are prohibited. Unlike a specific procedural rule that spells out a routine to be followed for a given situation, a standard is stated so that the focus is on its purpose. For example, a purposefully stated standard would serve the situation in Case 5.1 much more efficiently than the procedural rule the teacher uses.

Figure 5.1. Kay Manages to Stay in Her Seat But Still Disturbs Thau

▶ **CASE 5.1**

"All students are to remain seated during group-administered tests until the teacher has given the signal that all the papers have been collected" is included among the rules of conduct for Mr. Blanton's fifth-grade classroom. Thau is taking one such test sitting between Nikita and Kay, both of whom have finished the test and are waiting for the others. Kay rises and leans over Thau to hand Nikita a pencil, as shown by Figure 5.1. Mr. Blanton notices the disturbance and motions Kay to his desk where he asks, "Kay, what is the rule about getting out of your seat during a test?" Kay: "I was only returning the pencil I borrowed from Nikita. And besides, I never left my desk." Mr. Blanton: "How is it possible for you to give Nikita the pencil without leaving your seat?" Kay: "I leaned way over so my knee stayed on my seat." Mr. Blanton: "That's the same as leaving your desk." Kay: "Not if my knee was still touching. . . . "

The time that Mr. Blanton wasted in that inane conversation with Kay should have been more purposefully spent. It is ridiculous to argue about whether or not Kay left her seat. The concern should be with preventing disturbances to students such as Thau who are still taking the test. Mr. Blanton's rule to "stay in your seat" is too narrow to serve the purpose of "not disturbing others who are still taking the test." Kay focused on remaining in her seat when she should have been more thoughtful about not disturbing Thau. Instead of the specific procedural rule, Mr. Blanton should have had a purposefully stated standard such as, "Be careful not to disturb your classmates while they are taking a test." The focus of such a statement is on not disturbing classmates rather than being in or out of a seat.

The following are examples of purposefully stated standards for classroom conduct:

- Allow others opportunities to speak without being interrupted.
- Do nothing that risks injury, harm, or discomfort to you or another person.
- Respect the property of others.

The Number of Standards for Classroom Conduct

Four to 8 purposefully stated standards are preferable to a large number of narrow rules covering specific situations (e.g., "Do not sharpen your pencil during a class presentation.") because (a) a few standards are more likely to be remembered and understood than many rules, (b) each standard in a small set of standards is more likely to appear important than each standard in a large set, (c) purposefully stated standards appeal to the common sense of students and lead them to be thoughtful about their behaviors (e.g., "Would leaning over Thau disturb him during the test?"), and (d) purposefully stated standards focus attention on purposeful behaviors (e.g., how to be considerate) rather than on nonsensical technicalities (e.g., whether or not a student is seated). Teachers may sometimes fall into the trap of establishing too many narrowly focused rules instead of fewer standards because they confuse standards of conduct with routine procedures applicable to only specific situations (e.g., during group testing or class presentations).

▶ PROCEDURES FOR SMOOTHLY OPERATING CLASSROOMS

Routine procedures, like standards, should communicate expectations for behavior. Unlike a standard, however, a *routine procedure* applies only to a particular type of event and does not define a general principle for appropriate behavior. Standards for classroom conduct should be printed out and prominently displayed in the classroom (see, e.g., Figure 5.2), but routine procedures are usually learned through participation and need not be displayed in printed form. Routine procedures are the mechanisms by which students move through transition periods and learning activities.

Well-designed, efficient procedures are necessary for a smoothly operating classroom. The following is a small portion of the many types of routine classroom activities for which procedures need to be established.

- Students' arrival in the classroom at the beginning of a school day or class period
- Taking roll
- Completing administrative duties (e.g., accounting for materials distributed to students)
- Collecting assignments
- Students' speaking aloud in class
- Going to lunch
- Sharpening pencils
- Getting a drink

Standards for Conduct

1. Take advantage of learning opportunities.

2. Cooperate with your classmates and teacher in the business of creating learning opportunites.

3. Help create and maintain a comfortable, safe, and secure learning environment for all members of our classroom community.

4. Follow established classroom procedures as directed by your teacher.

5. Follow school policies.

Figure 5.2. Example of a Classroom Display of Standards for Conduct

- Going to the restroom
- Removing items from the storage area
- Making transitions from large-group to small-group sessions
- Cleaning up after oneself
- Leaving the room during class
- Returning to class after an absence
- Taking tests
- Retaking tests
- Borrowing materials
- Requesting individual help
- Scheduling conferences outside class hours
- Having guests in the classroom (e.g., a guest lecturer, visiting parent, supervisor, or observer from a college)
- Using computers
- Visiting the library and media center
- Turning in reports
- Fire and disaster drills
- Listening to announcements
- Responding to an outbreak of violence
- Leaving the room at the end of the school day

The list, of course, could be extended indefinitely. It may be helpful for you to begin with some general categories and list specific activities for which procedures are to be determined under each category. Categories might include (a) room use, (b) use of supplies, (c) large-group learning activities, (d) small-group learning activities, (e) independent learning activities, (f) transitions between learning activities, (g) crisis and emergency situations, and (h) administrative duties.

Engage in Activity 5.1.

▶ **ACTIVITY 5.1**

To help you think further about establishing routine procedures for your own classroom, classify each of the 27 types of activities from the previous sample according to the eight categories. Modify, delete, and add categories to fit your needs.

Share and discuss categories and lists with colleagues who are also engaging in this activity.

▶ NECESSARY STANDARDS FOR CONDUCT

Four Purposes

Does the situation in Case 5.2 seem familiar?

▶ **CASE 5.2**

As a youth, Mr. Tuft learned that hats should not be worn indoors. He remembers his father yelling at him, "Take that hat off your head! What kind of place do you think you're in? Ladies are present!" He remembers his parents laughing at old Mr. Busby for forgetting to take his hat off when he visited their home. When Mr. Tuft became a teacher, it seemed natural for him to establish a rule prohibiting the wearing of hats in the classroom. He didn't give it much thought.

Too often, Mr. Tuft interrupts his own learning activities to enforce his no-hat rule.

Teachers, as well as school administrators, sometimes establish unnecessary standards of conduct. A *necessary* standard for classroom conduct is one that serves at least one of the following purposes:

1. Maximizes on-task behaviors and minimizes off-task, especially disruptive, behaviors
2. Secures the safety and comfort of the learning environment
3. Prevents the activities of the class from disturbing other classes and persons outside the class
4. Maintains decorum among students, school personnel, and visitors to the school campus

Justification of a Standard

Which, if any, of the four purposes does Mr. Tuft's no-hat rule serve? Ordinarily, wearing hats does not interfere with students' being on-task. Of course, you can think of exceptions, such as a student who is wearing an outlandish hat that is excessively large or decorated with provocative pictures. But such exceptions can be covered under general standards such as "Dress for class so that your apparel does not distract others from their work."

Mr. Tuft's no-hat rule can hardly be justified as serving the second of the four purposes for standards of conduct. Hat wearing is unrelated to the safety and security of most classroom situations. Again, there are exceptions. For example, a hat dislodged from a student's head during a volleyball game could cause someone to slip. That situation, however, is better handled under procedures for specific learning activities. A hat that identifies its wearer's gang affiliation may also need to be prohibited, but a rule to keep gang-affiliation symbols off school property should be covered under schoolwide discipline and safety policies.

Classroom standards are established for the third of the four purposes out of consideration for persons who are not in the class but who are on or near the school campus. A lively discussion, even though on-task, can be disturbing to a neighboring class. Establish standards such as, "Be considerate of other classes; do not disturb them," as well as procedures for specific activities, such as, "While we are walking past those houses on the way to visit the science center, stay on the sidewalk and away from people's lawns." Prohibiting the wearing of hats does not seem to serve the third purpose for having standards for conduct.

If Mr. Tuft can justify his no-hat rule at all, he'll probably relate it to the fourth purpose. Maintaining decorum among students, school personnel, and visitors to the school campus is necessary to the development of a healthy, businesslike climate. Common courtesy is a critical ingredient for a smoothly operating classroom. But Mr. Tuft and other teachers should be careful that they do not use this fourth purpose as an excuse for imposing their personal biases and tastes on students.

Politeness and Courtesy

Decorum is necessary because polite interactions among students and teachers help maintain a classroom that is conducive to cooperation, whereas ill feelings are a consequence of impoliteness. But how do you decide which behaviors are polite and which are impolite? In all probability, your students come to you from a variety of backgrounds and subcultures. Although hat wearing in a building may be distasteful to one person, it may be in vogue to another and required by the religion of yet another. One approach is to define *politeness and courtesy* as behaviors that are exhibited as the result of thoughtful consideration for the rights and feelings of others. Such a liberal definition, as opposed to conventional dictionary definitions (e.g., "showing good manners; cultured; refined"), focuses on thoughtfulness toward others rather than on one group's opinion about what constitutes good taste. Even this advisable approach can lead to some difficulties in the complex classroom environment. Case 5.3 offers an example.

▶ **CASE 5.3**

During a discussion on nutrition in Ms. Oskoei's health class, Julie says, "There was something in the newspaper yesterday about some scientists saying we should be careful not to eat too much red meat." Dick: "I don't give a shit what any scientists say; I'm not gonna stop eating meat." Ms. Oskoei: "Dick, please don't use words like that while we're having class."

After class, Ms. Oskoei meets with Dick privately and says, "Which one of our standards for behavior did you violate today?" Dick: "I don't know." Ms. Oskoei: "I have one in mind that I think you did violate, and I want you to read through the list and guess which one I have in mind." Dick begins to read the list of standards displayed on the wall. Dick: "I don't know. Are you talking about the fourth one?" Ms. Oskoei: "Please read it aloud." Dick reads, "Before you act or speak, think of how your actions and words influence others. Act and talk in ways that others appreciate and not in ways they find offensive." Ms. Oskoei: "Yes, that is the one." Dick: "Because of what I said! Aw! Everybody says 'shit.' That doesn't hurt anybody." Ms. Oskoei: "I agree that it's no big deal. But there are people, including me, who just don't like to say or hear that word during class. Because you are quite capable of substituting words that others don't find offensive to express yourself, I do not expect you to violate Standard 4 again." Dick: "But Ms. Oskoei, we talk about bowel movements and urine in health class. Why is that okay?" Ms. Oskoei: "You've made an excellent point. I can't argue with your logic. But although our society considers it acceptable to refer to human waste material on television, as in laxative commercials, our society generally considers it unacceptable to say the word 'shit' on television. In fact, saying that word on television or in public places is a violation of obscenity laws in many locations. As long as our society frowns on public use of such words, people are going to feel uncomfortable hearing them spoken or written in formal, businesslike settings such as our classroom. I happen to be one of those people. Right or wrong, we violate Standard 4 by using words like 'shit' when other words that don't offend anyone can be used instead." Dick: "It doesn't seem right that something is okay one place but not in another." Ms. Oskoei: "It's like belching. Most everyone has a good healthy belch now and then. But most people in our society find other people's belching to be disgusting." Dick: "So belching is a violation of Standard 4 also." Ms. Oskoei: "A public display of belching, when it could be avoided, would indeed be a violation of Standard 4."

Did Dick violate Standard 4 in Case 5.3? Whether or not Dick's use of a word that is socially unacceptable to many people violated the standard depends on the degree to which others found his expression offensive. Ms. Oskoei did indicate to him that she, for one, found the term offensive. If you feel that Dick was within his rights in saying what he pleased as long as no one was really hurt or prevented from being on-task, then you may not want to include any standards for maintaining decorum. On the other hand, if you find it important to uphold community standards of courtesy in your classroom, then you should establish standards for all four purposes. In either case, please proceed with care. You want to make sure that you do not allow unnecessary standards to be established under the guise of maintaining decorum. The mistake of establishing unnecessary standards can cause you more problems than the mistake of failing to establish necessary rules.

The Consequences of Unnecessary Standards

When considering the inclusion of a particular standard of conduct for your classroom, ask yourself, "Which of the four purposes for having standards will it serve?" If the answer is "none," then that standard is *unnecessary* and should not be included. The inclusion of an unnecessary standard has three unpleasant consequences:

1. You will be responsible for enforcing a standard that does not have a defensible rationale. Thus, you put yourself in the position of teaching students to submit to unjustified regulations.

2. Once your students realize that one of the standards you enforce serves no important purpose, they will tend to generalize that other standards must be unimportant also.

3. Students who are penalized for resisting an unnecessary standard are likely to become disenchanted with school. Such students are often distracted from the business of learning because time that could be allocated for learning activities is used to deal with violations of standards.

Of course, you could choose to enforce only the necessary standards and ignore the unnecessary ones. This is inadvisable. Unenforced standards, even unnecessary ones, teach students that standards need not be taken seriously. It is more difficult to teach students to be on-task when they feel they can be selective about which standards to follow and which to ignore.

► WHEN TO DETERMINE STANDARDS AND ROUTINE PROCEDURES

Some teachers prefer to determine all standards for conduct and a large share of routine procedures at the very beginning of a school year or term. Others establish both standards for conduct and routine procedures as the need for them becomes apparent. The advantages of establishing standards and some of the routine procedures at the outset of a school term include the following: (a) Because expectations are formally communicated from the beginning, some off-task behavior patterns will not have time to emerge. (B) Students are more receptive to learning standards and procedures at the beginning of a school term than when they have become accustomed to a situation. (c) The sooner students know about standards and procedures, the more time they will have to practice following them.

On the other hand, there are advantages to establishing standards and routine procedures throughout the school term: (a) Waiting to establish some standards avoids prescribing standard-breaking behaviors for students who were positively reinforced for breaking regulations in previous classes. (b) Students are more likely to understand a standard or a procedure when it is established in response to a need that has just become apparent. (c) Students are more likely to appreciate the importance of individual standards and procedures that are established gradually rather than thrust on them all at once.

You will probably want to use some combination of the two approaches by establishing several purposefully stated standards of conduct and some basic routine procedures at the outset and then developing a more comprehensive list over time. The younger your students are, the more time you will need to establish and teach standards and procedures at the very beginning of a school year.

► WHO SHOULD DETERMINE STANDARDS?

Do standards more effectively serve their four purposes when teachers determine them or when students agree on them? Should you use an authoritarian process, a democratic process, or some combination of the two to establish rules? You have four options for who establishes standards. How well each option works depends more on how you go about implementing it than on which one you choose (Cangelosi, 2006). They are as follows:

1. You decide all standards, making sure that each is purposefully stated and necessary and not confused with a routine procedure.

2. You determine all standards yourself, but your determinations are influenced by the recommendations of students.

3. Standards are proposed and voted on by students. You are responsible for establishing the structure for democratic decision making; providing leadership to encourage the establishment of necessary, purposefully stated standards; and ensuring that every student has the opportunity to participate in decisions.

4. Some combination of the other three methods is used. Typically, you impose a few fundamental guidelines for behavior; students participate in decisions about more specific standards that fall within the purview of those guidelines.

Engage in Activity 5.2.

▶ **ACTIVITY 5.2**

With two or three colleagues, discuss the relative advantages and disadvantages of each of the aforementioned four options for who determines classroom standards of conduct. Discuss experiences you've had with various options employed by teachers. Compare differences in classrooms where methods for establishing standards of conduct were clearly understood and classrooms where standards were either established haphazardly or not at all.

▶ TEACHING STANDARDS AND PROCEDURES TO STUDENTS

Establishing standards for conduct and routine procedures for activities is one thing; teaching them to students is quite another. Students must first learn what the standards and procedures are and how to follow them; then they must be willing to follow them. The teaching cycles model applies to teaching standards and procedures just as it does to teaching academic subjects.

Case 5.4 is an example of a teacher who successfully establishes, teaches, and uses standards and procedures.

▶ CASE 5.4

Ms. Williams autocratically establishes some basic routine procedures and standards of conduct for her third-grade class at the very beginning of the school year. She plans to spend a major share of the first two weeks teaching these guidelines. She uses the word "rules" instead of "standards" with her students because she thinks "rules" is more familiar to them.

On the second day of the new school year, Ms. Williams announces to her 27 students, "There are four rules that you are required to follow anytime you are at school. Here is the first one." Ms. Williams displays a bright orange poster with "RESPECT THE RIGHTS OF OTHERS" boldly printed and a drawing of a cluster of happy faces. Touching each word on the poster as she says it, Ms. Williams continues, "'Respect the rights of others!' That is our first rule. I will hang this reminder for you right here on the wall. Connie, please help me." The bright orange poster is permanently displayed. "Now read this with me as I point to each word," Ms. Williams directs the class. Together the class recites with her, "Respect the rights of others." Ms. Williams. "What does it say, Allen?" Several students, including Allen, shout out, "Respect the rights of others!" Ms. Williams. "I'm sorry; there were too many people talking for me to understand Allen. Allen?" Allen: "Respect the rights of others." Ms. Williams. "Thank you. Now, I want everyone to quietly think to herself or himself what the rule means before we discuss it." Ms. Williams waits

30 seconds and says, "OK, let's share our ideas about what it means to respect the rights of others. We'll begin with Reginald." Reginald: "Being nice to them." Ms. Williams. "And what are some of the ways that we can be nice to others? What do you say, Jaylene?" Jaylene: "You don't pick on 'em." Ms. Williams. "Tell us what you think Jaylene means, Antonio?"

The discussion about the first standard continues until Ms. Williams is satisfied that her students have a reasonable understanding of the types of behaviors this standard requires and the types it forbids. Ms. Williams then teaches her students the procedures she will use for dealing with violations of Rule 1.

To deal with violations of standards, Ms. Williams has made arrangements with Mr. Demery, who teaches another third-grade class at her school, to combine their two classes for 40 minutes every afternoon just before dismissal. During that 40-minute period, some type of activity that the students find especially enjoyable is conducted. One day there may be supervised recreation in the gym, playground, or auditorium. Another day, the children may view a video or play computer games. Mr. Demery supervises the combined classes for the first 20 minutes of these sessions. Ms. Williams reserves that first 20 minutes to meet individually with any of her students who have violated standards or failed to follow procedures. At these conferences, Ms. Williams and the students work out a plan for preventing such violations or failures in the future. Ms. Williams supervises the second half of these 40-minute periods to allow Mr. Demery to work out plans with any of his students who violated standards or failed to follow procedures.

In teaching her students the procedures for dealing with violations of the first standard, she does not, of course, attempt to relate all the details of the arrangement with Mr. Demery. In time, the students will learn this for themselves. She does tell them, "Anytime I recognize that someone has not respected the rights of another, I will tell that person, 'Meet with me to discuss the first rule when it's time to join Mr. Demery's class.' "

On the third day of the new school year, Ms. Williams introduces the second standard with a bright green poster with one happy face and the message "RESPECT YOUR OWN RIGHTS." Ms. Williams's experiences have taught her that she should include this second standard to urge students to be more assertive in protecting their own rights and not allowing themselves to be abused. Students engage in role-playing to begin learning Standard 2.

One such lesson begins when Ms. Williams announces to her class, "Ron and Frankie will perform our next skit to help us better understand the second rule. Imagine that they're out in the schoolyard waiting for the first bell to ring. Ron will be playing the part of Joe, who is a fifth grader. Frankie will be Bob, a second grader. OK, fellows, you're on!" Holding his lunch box, Bob walks near Joe. Joe grabs Bob by the shoulder and says, "Hey! Where you going, Buddy?" Bob: "To my room." Joe lets go of Bob and asks, "You wanna be my friend?" Bob: "I guess so." Joe: "Good! I'd like to be your friend too. Whatcha got in the box?" Bob: "My lunch." Joe: "Let me look at it. You might have something for me." Bob: "No! I gotta get to my room." Joe (holding up his fist to Bob): "Look! You'd better let me check out your lunch, or you'll be sorry." Ms. Williams interrupts the skit at that point saying, "Thank you. Let's stop the drama for a few minutes to discuss what we've seen. I want each of you to think of what Bob can do so that he won't break the second rule." A discussion ensues in which suggestions are made about how Bob can protect his rights from Joe's bullying behavior. Later, Ms. Williams has Ron and Frankie act out two different endings to the skit. In one, Bob violates the second standard by allowing Joe to take his lunch. In the second, Bob protects his rights.

On subsequent days, Ms. Williams introduces and teaches Standard 3, "GIVE EVERYONE A CHANCE TO LEARN," and Standard 4, "FOLLOW PROCEDURES." Standard 3 is primarily concerned with preventing disruptive behaviors during learning activities. Standard 4 serves as a general guideline that leads to many of the procedures governing both transitional and allocated time. The following episode illustrates this relationship.

In the second week of the school year, Ms. Williams directs her students to complete individually a journal-writing activity at their places. As they work, students begin to yell out for

Ms. Williams to help them or interrupt her while she is helping another. Other students grow impatient waiting for Ms. Williams to get to them and begin talking among themselves. The noise disturbs those trying to complete the tasks.

Concerned, Ms. Williams develops a procedure for independent work sessions and decides to teach it to her students the next time such a session is scheduled. After some preparation, it is time for the independent work session. Ms. Williams. "Class, may I have your attention please?" She looks directly into students' eyes until everyone appears to be ready to listen. Ms. Williams. "Thank you. Do you remember what happened the last time we wrote in our journals in class?" Because Ms. Williams had previously established a procedure for speaking in a large-group arrangement, students raise their hands to signal that they would like to answer her questions. No one yells out. Ms. Williams. "Sadi, what do you remember?" Sadi: "It got very noisy, and you couldn't get around to help all of us." Other students provide more detail as Ms. Williams conducts a discussion in which the problems with which she wants to deal are articulated by the students. Finally, Ms. Williams says, "It seems to me that we didn't give everyone a chance to learn last time. We need a procedure so we won't break the third rule when we are working individually at our places. I'll explain the procedure now." She takes a bag from the storage closet and holds it up for the class to see. Ms. Williams. "In here is something to help us give everyone a chance to learn when we are working at our places." Barbara: "Is it candy? Are you going to give us candy for cooperating?" Ms. Williams looks directly at Barbara sternly and raises her finger to her lips. Barbara receives the message and does not pursue her question. Ms. Williams pulls a device from the bag that the students have never seen before. The device consists of a holder with a clip that can be attached to a student's desk. The holder contains three flags—red, blue, and yellow. Each flag can be rotated up or down. Ms. Williams gives each student one device for his or her desk and teaches them the following procedure for class assignments in which they are to work quietly at their places:

As long as a student is progressing through the assignment and does not want to be disturbed, that student is to display the yellow flag. When a student wants to be helped, a red flag should be displayed. When a student has completed the work and is also willing to provide help to others, she or he should display a blue flag. Ms. Williams is to move quietly from one student displaying a red flag to another. She also directs students displaying blue flags to provide help.

Ms. Williams chooses this seemingly elaborate flag-raising procedure over a more conventional "raise your hand" procedure because she believes the following: (a) The formality of the flags will help teach students just how seriously she expects them to follow the procedure. (b) Students who want help can simply display their red flags and continue to work without having to hold up their hands. (c) It provides a quiet, efficient method for using cooperative learning strategies with students who finish the assignment before others.

Because of her arrangement with Mr. Demery, Ms. Williams has a useful structure for dealing with violations of standards and failure to follow procedures. Standards and procedures that are not enforced are counterproductive. How Ms. Williams conducts the conferences to work out plans to prevent repeat offenses is, of course, a critical factor influencing the effectiveness of her standards and procedures. The question of how to deal with students after they have violated standards or failed to follow procedures is addressed in Chapters 8 to 11.

Case 5.5 is an example of a teacher whose decisions about procedures are influenced by students' suggestions.

▶ **CASE 5.5**

Ms. Tseu tells her seventh-grade class, "I have received three separate complaints from other teachers that their lessons were disturbed by some of us who were making trips to the library. If those reports are accurate, we were in violation of our standard of not bothering people outside our group. We still need to make trips to the library. Do I need to develop a procedure that guards against our bothering other classes?" Some students raise their hands.

Ms. Tseu: Dale?

Dale: The trouble is three or four of us go at once. Maybe you should allow only one to go at a time.

Ms. Tseu: I will seriously consider that suggestion. Jim?

Jim: Find who's causing the trouble and don't let them ever go to the library again.

Yolanda: But we really weren't doing anything wrong! Mrs. Crooks, she's always trying to get us in trouble.

Ms. Tseu: I'm more concerned with what we're going to do than what has already happened. Let's make sure we don't disturb others in the future.

Jean: Do we really need a special procedure if we just promise to keep quiet from now on?

Ms. Tseu: That's what I'd like to decide. How many of you think we need a special procedure for going to the library? Raise your hands. One, two, three—most of you believe we need one. Okay, I would like each of you to take out a sheet of paper and suggest what I should do in one to three sentences. Please do not put your name on the paper. I'll take your papers home tonight and consider your suggestions. I'll have a decision for you tomorrow.

In Case 5.6 the teacher uses a democratic process for determining procedures.

▶ **CASE 5.6**

Mr. Brown has organized his fourth-period health-science class so that large-group sessions and collaborative learning activities are confined to Mondays, Tuesdays, Thursdays, and Fridays. Wednesdays are saved for individual, catch-up, and enrichment work. Every Wednesday, students are free to determine how they spend their time as long as they are in the classroom doing independent work that involves health-science. The classroom has 12 computers to accommodate the 29 fourth-period students.

A month into the course, Mr. Brown discovers that on Wednesdays the student demand for use of the computers exceeds the availability. Students complain that some classmates are monopolizing the machines and cluttering up the desktops and hard drives with personal files and programs. To address the complaints, Mr. Brown calls a "class community meeting." Whenever such meetings are held, the students know that they operate under *Robert's Rules of Order* (Robert, Evans, Honemann, & Balch, 2004) and can raise issues of common concern. At this meeting, Mr. Brown describes the recurring difficulty with computer use; he entertains motions to resolve the problem. Several students' proposals are discussed. After some debate, a motion spelling out a procedure for computer use is moved, seconded, and passed.

▶ **SCHOOLWIDE DISCIPLINE POLICIES**

Your classroom standards of conduct and routine procedures should not conflict with schoolwide policies. Unfortunately, students in some departmentalized schools have to deal with standards for one teacher that are inconsistent with those for another (Cangelosi, 1980, 2006). Many schools have rules that are unnecessary according to the definition presented herein. Banning hats, prohibiting boys from wearing earrings, and regulating boys' facial hair are typical examples of schoolwide regulations that are difficult to justify under the four reasons for standards of conduct. Your responsibilities as a teacher are further complicated by being required to enforce unnecessary policies.

Many schools have uniform discipline policies that allow teachers to establish their own classroom standards of conduct but still have two major advantages over no schoolwide policy at all. First, the schoolwide discipline policy can establish general guidelines for individual teachers' classroom standards for conduct. Ideally, these guidelines are flexible enough to allow teachers autonomy while providing enough direction to prevent one teacher's standards from conflicting with another's. Second, the schoolwide discipline policy can establish a support service for enforcing individual teachers' classroom standards. Case 5.7 is an example.

▶ CASE 5.7

A month before the opening of a new school year, the faculty of Unity High School meets for five days to develop policies and plans for the year. One agenda item is to agree on (a) guidelines for teachers to follow in establishing classroom standards of conduct and (b) how the school administration can support teachers' enforcement of their standards of conduct.

After sharing ideas and working with a consultant on student discipline, Unity High's teachers and administrators agree to the following policies:

1. Each teacher is responsible for establishing standards of conduct for his or her own classes. Those standards should focus on (a) maximizing on-task behaviors, (b) increasing safety and security, (c) preventing class activities from disturbing others outside that class, and (d) maintaining acceptable standards of decorum.

2. Assistant Principal Coombs will serve as the chief administrator of the schoolwide discipline program.

3. Teachers should post standards (e.g., on their Web pages) as they are established and share them with Ms. Coombs so that she is in a better position to provide support services for teachers.

4. The school will maintain a time-out room to which teachers may send students to wait until the beginning of the next period of the day. No one teacher may send more than two students to the time-out room during a single period. A paraprofessional will supervise the time-out room.

5. There will be an in-school suspension program in which students who have been officially suspended from a class spend that class time in a special supervised classroom. There they work on independent-work assignments for the class they are missing. The following steps lead to an in-school suspension:

    A. Because of an alleged rule violation, a teacher chooses to write up the violation on a form supplied by Ms. Coombs's office.

    B. The student takes a copy of the form to Ms. Coombs's office where an appointment is set up with the student and Ms. Coombs.

    C. If the appointment cannot be arranged before the student is scheduled to return to the class for which she or he was written up, then the student spends the period when the class next meets in the in-school suspension classroom until the conference can be held.

    D.   At the conference, the student and Ms. Coombs attempt to work out a plan for returning to class.

    E.   The plan, which is designed to prevent a recurrence of the incident leading to the write-up, is forwarded by Ms. Coombs's office to the teacher. If the teacher agrees to the plan, the student is readmitted and is no longer on in-school suspension.

    F.   If the teacher does not agree to the plan, then a meeting of the three parties (i.e., the student, the teacher, and Ms. Coombs) is held to work one out.

    G.   If a plan is still not agreed on, the student's parents are brought into another session to arrange a plan. In the meantime, the student remains on in-school suspension.

Note that the plan may involve both students and teachers altering behaviors. If it appears that no reasonable plan will be worked out in the near future, arrangements are made for the student to be transferred out of that class.

The policies and a disclosure statement for due process are published in the *Unity High School Student, Parent, and Faculty Guidebook*.

► DEVELOPING SAFE-SCHOOL PROGRAMS

The Roots of School Violence

Robert Watson (1995, p. 57) asked a high school teacher who three months earlier had witnessed an intruder shoot one of her students outside her classroom door if she felt prepared to deal with such acts of violence. He reports that she replied, with tears in her eyes, "I resent the question. I did not come into this profession to be prepared to deal with violence. I am here because I love children and I love my subject, choral music." Motivated by a desire to serve children and share your knowledge, you might also question why you should have to worry about protecting yourself and your students from hostile, dangerous, and criminal activities. After all, you are a teacher, not a law-enforcement officer. I agree that you *should* not have to worry about preventing violence or dealing with violent activities at your school. Today's realities, however, dictate that being prepared to do so is necessary to succeeding as a teacher. Fortunately, there is an emerging body of research-based literature that provides guidance to school personnel for developing strategies to reduce the incidence of violence on campuses and effectively respond to violent activity when it does occur (Brown & Brown, 2006; Salmivalli, Kaukiainen, & Voeten, 2005; Steffenhagen, 2005; Stevahn, Munger, & Kealey, 2005; Whitted & Dupper, 2005). To be in a position to develop such strategies, you need to examine the roots of school violence.

Brendtro and Long (1995) identified four factors that lead to chronically violent behaviors: broken social bonds, stress and conflict, a culture of violence, and unhealthy brains. By *broken social bonds*, the authors refer to the lack of healthy human attachments in the lives of many children. Through secure social bonds children learn trust, self-management, and prosocial behaviors. Brendtro and Long (1995, p. 53) stated (Reprinted by permission):

Early in this century, psychiatrists, including David Levy and Lauretta Bender, found that children reared in depersonalized orphanages developed "affect hunger" or "affectionless personality" (Karen, 1994). When the social bond between child and adult was not nurtured, conscience was impaired and children did not internalize values. These unbonded children were labeled antisocial, primitive-unsocialized, or sociopathic.

Today, the orphanages are gone, but we are mass-producing hordes of adult-detached children. More families are disrupted by divorce, abuse, poverty, drugs, and other forces that interfere with normal parenting. Adults whose own lives are chaotic cannot effectively monitor and manage children's activities or affiliations. Nor can they spend time with children, teach conflict-resolution skills, or communicate consistent behavioral expectations (Walker, 1993).

Historically, extended families or tribes provide social bonds. Theologian Martin Marty observes that even though parents often were too young and immature, or may have died early, the tribe carried on cultural values. Today, having lost our tribes, we rely on a tiny nuclear family of one or two overstressed parents. Schools are now being asked to become new tribes, but seldom are prepared to play this role. When families fail, however, the only alternative institution for re-education is prison.

Angry adult-wary youths do not fare well in factory schools. They gravitate to other alienated people—gangs and other negative peer subcultures, or predatory adults like pimps, pedophiles, or criminal mentors. In these "artificial belongings," they acquire training and support for antisocial lifestyles. Relishing freedom from adult authority, they never gain true independence because they have not known secure dependence. "Nobody tells me what to do!" they shout, masking the reality that nobody really cares. Since they do not care either, their violence can be calculated and cold-blooded, motivated by money, power, status, revenge, racism, and hedonistic pleasure and aggression.

Although understanding teachers could offer surrogate bonds, these children's behavior drives most adults away. Moreover, school discipline rooted in punishment or exclusion only further estranges these students.

Stress and conflict, in manageable doses, are normal products of living that most children deal with reasonably well. The benefits of students' managing to cope with stress and constructively resolve conflicts through systematic cooperative learning activities are well documented (Guerrero, 2005; Johnson & Johnson, 1994). But when stress is severe and prolonged, some youths are overwhelmed, responding in self-destructive and antisocial ways. They develop defensive behavior patterns, display hostile biases toward adults, and bring a menacing interpersonal demeanor to school. For many, the school environment stimulates stress; students may fear peer rejection, bullies, and classroom failures. Not knowing how to secure self-esteem in positive ways, some seek status by acting out with hostility (Brock, Sandoval, Lewis, 2001, pp. 253–270). For students with stress accumulated from their homes and neighborhoods, schools need to be a refuge where they can find a semblance of balance in their lives (Garbarino, 1992).

Long (1990) developed a conflict cycle model to teach students, parents, and educators how to prevent stressful situations from escalating. Untrained students and adults who fail to recognize that an aggressive person is under stress tend to respond to aggressiveness with aggressiveness. For example, a typical response to "Go to hell!" is *"You* go to hell!" Analyses of crisis incidents suggest that the roots of most stressors originate outside school but escalate to violence because participants fail to disengage from confrontations (Brendtro & Long, 1995).

Anticrime laws cannot counter the pervasive proviolent messages of a *culture of violence*. The proliferation of weapons, daily news telecasts, television dramas, motion pictures, video games, sports, and music lyrics are only some of the reflections of society's infatuation with violence. A television set affords you the opportunity to witness a dramatized murder, fight, assault, or rape virtually any time of the day.

Unhealthy brains can lead to neurologically triggered aggression. Control of angry impulses, rational thought, and perception are impaired by intoxication, neurological trauma, disease, or chemical imbalances. The complex social setting of a classroom is not conducive to treating psychological disorders; however, strategies for preventing substance abuse problems from interfering with the school and classroom learning environment need to be incorporated into schoolwide safety programs as well as classroom management plans.

Focus on Prevention Not Retribution

When students' out-of-turn talking disrupts a learning activity, their teacher should apply strategies for terminating their disruptive behaviors, reengage the class in the learning activity, and teach the students to choose more appropriate times to talk. Chapters 8 through 11 explain and illustrate strategies for confronting and preventing off-task behaviors in the classroom. Most forms of off-task behaviors (e.g., out-of-turn talking) are generally considered to be conduct that students need to supplant with on-task behaviors (e.g., attending to an in-class presentation). After all, talking per se is not generally considered a criminal or immoral act. But some off-task behaviors (e.g., cheating on tests, stealing, and assaulting others) carry the additional complication of being considered immoral or criminal by most people. Violence is one of those moralistic concepts that people tend to react to with anger, outrage, indignation, and condemnation. Such an emotional response to activities that endanger us, violate our rights, and dilute our freedoms is understandable and, in my opinion, appropriate. Nevertheless, such a natural response also may interfere with our collective abilities to develop sound strategies for preventing violence. The National Council on Crime and Delinquency proposes replacing the rhetoric of moral condemnation with a preventive public health approach (Krisberg & Austin, 1993). Doing nothing more than attempting to catch violent offenders so that they can be punished or removed from the school environment has not worked (Lindquist & Molnar, 1995; Skiba & Peterson, 1999).

Violence-Prevention Strategies

Although effecting major social reforms leading to a gentler, less-violent society is beyond the purview of schools, each school's faculty is positioned to achieve major victories in the war against violence by concentrating on its own group of students. Troubled behaviors are self-perpetuating. Students who act as bullies by harassing peers should be targeted for early intervention. Bullying is an early predictor of lifelong antisocial tendencies, often leading to adult criminal activities (Ballard, Argus, & Remley, 1999; Dunn, 2001). Increasingly, bully-proofing strategies are incorporated into schoolwide violence-prevention programs (Hoover & Juul, 1993; Opotow, 2000; Salmivalli, 2001; Willert, 2002).

Traditional rehabilitation programs for violent offenders have proven inadequate. But the trend away from such programs in favor of removing troubled and violent students from schools only transfers problems from our education systems to penal systems. Traditional rehabilitation approaches focus on controlling deficiencies and deviance, whereas newer reclaiming strategies focus on developing strength and resilience. Schools, however, are not equipped to apply these strategies without significant outside resources. Success depends on collaborative efforts involving professional mental health workers, drug-abuse counselors, law enforcement and justice personnel, and educators. The collaborative role of students themselves must be emphasized. Adult-dominated solutions won't work with adult-wary students. Students rebel against adult coercion and form antisocial subcultures. By enlisting students as partners in their war on violence, schools create prosocial youth–adult bonds (Shaprio, Burgoon, & Welker, 2002).

By meeting children's needs for consistent, loving, safe environments, we begin to repair broken social bonds. Communities must develop comprehensive family support centers and redesign schools to restore the sense of tribe. Programs where all children learn self-discipline should begin in the primary grades and continue through secondary schools. Charney (1993) proposes a curriculum for ethical literacy in which teachers create cultures of nonviolence and teach self-discipline by playing off naturally occurring conflicts and problems. Schoolwide conflict resolution programs teach children to manage conflicts and address problems through negotiations and peer mediation. Hostile school climates have been transformed into gentler, safer communities via programs for developing conflict resolution skills (Sandy & Cochran, 2000; Stevahn, Munger, & Kealey, 2005).

Conflict Management and Resolution in Curricula

Keys for successful programs can be culled from the literature. One key is to incorporate *conflict management and resolution* techniques throughout the school curriculum. Rather than denying or backing off from conflicts, Johnson and Johnson (1995, pp. 64–65) suggested using naturally occurring conflicts as instructional tools (reprinted by permission):

> The elimination of violence does not mean the elimination of conflict. Some conflicts can have positive outcomes (Johnson & Johnson, 1991, 1992). They can increase achievement, motivation to learn, higher-level reasoning, long-term retention, healthy social and cognitive development, and the fun students have in school. Conflicts can also enrich relationships, clarify personal identity, increase ego strength, promote resilience in the face of adversity, and clarify how one needs to change.
>
> It is not the presence of conflict that is to be feared but, rather, its destructive management. Attempts to deny, suppress, repress, and ignore conflicts may, in fact, be a major contributor to the occurrence of violence in schools. Given the many positive outcomes of conflict, schools need to teach students how to manage conflicts constructively.
>
> The best conflict resolution programs seek to do more than change individual students. Instead they try to transform the total school environment into a learning community in which students live by a credo of nonviolence.
>
> Two contexts for conflict are possible: cooperative and competitive (Deutsch, 1973; Johnson & Johnson, 1989). In a competitive context, individuals strive to win while ensuring their opponents lose. Those few who perform the best receive the rewards. In this context, competitors often misperceive one another's positions and motivations, avoid communicating

Figure 5.3. Two Peer Mediators Help Two Other Students Resolve Their Conflict

with one another, are suspicious of one another, and see the situation from only their own perspective.

In a cooperative context, conflicts tend to be resolved constructively. Students have clear perceptions of one another's positions and motivation, communicate accurately and completely, trust one another, and define conflicts as mutual problems to be solved. Cooperators typically have a long-term time orientation and focus their energies both on achieving mutual goals and on maintaining good working relationships with others.

In addition to incorporating conflict management and resolution techniques in school curricula, schools need to implement a formal, schoolwide conflict-resolution system. One system involves use of students as trained peer mediators. *Peer mediation* is a method for peacefully resolving conflicts without coercion among students. In this approach, students voluntarily bring their disputes to panels of peers who facilitate agreements among the disputing parties (see Figure 5.3). Schrumpf, Crawford, and Usadel (1991) developed a program in which students are trained to serve as panel members (i.e., mediators) so that they learn to be unbiased, respectful, and empathetic listeners who lead the disputants through the following stages of mediation sessions: (a) set the tone for the session and agree on protocols (e.g., no interrupting or name-calling), (b) gather information, (c) focus on common interests, (d) create options, (e) evaluate options and choose a solution, and (f) write the agreement and close. Typically, participants agree to keep sessions confidential.

Examine Case 5.8.

▶ **CASE 5.8**

Besides its schoolwide discipline policies alluded to in Case 5.7, Unity High School also has a safe-school system in conjunction with those policies. Incorporated in that system is a peer-mediation program. Five years ago, several teachers proposed the program to the faculty and school administrators. After an in-service workshop and a year of planning, a diverse group of students were recruited to be trained as mediators. The training focused on (a) understanding the causes and effects of conflicts; (b) developing descriptive, assertive, and supportive communication styles; (c) understanding the role of the mediator (i.e., to facilitate civil, productive communications between disputants in a neutral, nonjudgmental manner); and (d) practicing the role of mediator in the peer mediation process.

With the leadership of Ms. Rubin, a faculty member who is given a reduced teaching load to serve as peer-mediation director, the program has expanded each year since its inception with experienced mediators helping train new ones. About four cases a week are now being submitted to peer mediation. The one involving Garth and Theo is an example.

For about a week, Garth and Theo have exchanged threatening remarks—clearly directing anger toward one another. Just before the first bell one morning, they are posturing as if they are about to fight when a mutual friend, Corina, steps up and engages them in the following conversation:

Corina: As soon as one of you throws a punch, you're both going to end up suspended.

Garth: Not before I take his ass apart!

Theo: Yeah! You'd like to git'n my ass; you must be a faggot!

Garth: That's it! You–

Corina: Stop it now! Don't get yourselves into trouble.

Garth: You heard what he called me!

Corina: Okay, so you're both angry and behaving stupidly. Try one thing before you decide to fight.

Theo: Looks like Corina don't want to see your blood all over this sidewalk.

Corina: You guys sound like you're reading from a bad movie script. Let's go over to Ms. Rubin's office and fill out a peer-mediation request like we should've done a week ago.

Because of seminars, presentations at school body meetings, and word-of-mouth from participating students, Theo and Garth understand what Corina is suggesting. Soon they are in Ms. Rubin's office completing Figure 5.4's form.

The following morning during second period, the confidential peer-mediation session is conducted by the pair of mediators, Eturo and Marie, with Ms. Rubin as faculty observer. Eturo initiates the first phase to set the tone of the meeting and agree on protocols:

Eturo: Marie and I have read the peer-mediation request forms you both completed and understand that you have a legitimate conflict to be resolved. Our job is to provide a forum for you to discuss the issues so that you resolve the conflict in a way that works for you both. Marie will go over what we'll be doing as well as the rules under which we'll operate this session. Marie.

Marie: Thanks, Eturo. This 50-minute session will have four phases. After this introduction, each of you will take turns explaining to us what the conflict is all about and just how you are feeling about it. During that second phase, Eturo and I will be trying to understand the conflict without making any judgments about who is right or wrong. That's not our job. We don't even care who is right or wrong; we care about helping you move forward in a positive direction. We'll be taking notes as you talk to try to capture the main issues that need to be addressed.

Garth: Who gets to speak first?

Eturo: You'll both have more than one turn to speak, but we'll just flip a coin to see who starts—right after Marie goes over the rules.

Confidential Request for Peer Mediation Session

Unity High School

Date: _____ Your name: _____ Homeroom # _____

Name of the person with whom you have a conflict to be mediated:

_____

From your point of view, please describe the conflict to be mediated:

_____

_____

_____

_____

Please indicate special circumstances, If any, you would like Ms. Rubin to be aware of when she selects two mediators for your session and schedules the time for the session:

_____

_____

_____

_____

_____

Thank you very much.   Office use only
                              Day & Time: _____
                              Mediators:
                              _____ & _____
                              Other: _____

Figure 5.4. Unity High's Peer-Mediation Request Form

Marie: Keep in mind that Eturo, Ms. Rubin, and I will not share anything that goes on during this with anyone else with the exception of any information that involves drugs or weapons on the school campus. By law, Ms. Rubin is obligated to report any such criminal activity to Principal Washington but not anything else. You also should agree to maintaining the confidentiality of this session. We have six rules: First, you will try to find a way to peacefully manage the conflict. Do both of you agree to abide by that rule?

Garth: Yes.

Theo: Yes.

Marie: Thank you. Rule 2 is no-name-calling during the session. Do you agree?

Garth: Yes.

Theo: Yes.

Marie: Thanks. Rule 3 is to allow the other to speak uninterrupted when it's his turn to talk.

Theo: Yes.

Garth: Yes.

Marie: Rule 4 is to be honest—only say what you believe is true.

Theo: You got it.

Garth: Yeah.

Marie: Thank you. And Rule 5 is no physical fighting or threatening one another.

Garth: Sure; that's why I'm here.

Theo: Okay.

Marie: And do you agree to keep what is said in here only among us?

Garth: Yeah; you already said that.

Theo: I'll keep my mouth shut.

Eturo: Now that we all agree to abide by the rules we can get started.

Ms. Rubin: Excuse me, Eturo and Marie. We didn't finish outlining the agenda for Theo and Garth.

Marie: Oh, yes; I got sidetracked. After you've explained the conflict to Eturo and me, we go to the third phase. That's when we make a list to identify issues causing the conflict. During this phase you talk directly to each other—not just to Eturo and me. And then finally, there's the fourth phase in which you come to an agreement, which we all sign.

Eturo: Thank you. Do you have any questions before we begin? Okay, flip the coin, Marie.

Garth: He can go first.

Eturo: Do you want to go first, Theo?

Theo: Yeah, sure.

Marie: Okay, Theo explain to us the conflict from your point of view.

Theo: It started when he started showing off for these asses he's trying to get tight with—

Garth: That's a bunch a—

Marie: Stop. You agreed not to interrupt and not to name-call.

Theo: I didn't call him a name.

Eturo: You didn't, but please don't call anyone else names either.

Theo: Okay, I won't. Like I was saying, me and him was buds—hanging out and stuff, havin' a good time until these dudes come around—he thinks they're this one dude's posse or something—that's supposed to make them cool or something. Anyway, they come around and all of a sudden he's disrespecting me—like he don't even hang with me. You know what I'm sayin'?

Eturo: Okay, thank you. Garth, you take a turn and Theo can continue after you talk about the conflict.

Garth: It wasn't me who was makin' fun and shit. He's the one that came at me and made me look bad in front of those dudes.

Theo: Not until you—

Marie: Theo, we agreed not to interrupt.

Theo: Okay, I'm sorry.

Garth: See he gets all hot and mad at me for nothing. I really don't know why he started hating me. We were fine before he got jealous of those dudes liking me better than him. I don't know; I'd like for us to be buds again, but he can't be jumping on me in front of my friends.

Eturo: Theo, go ahead and tell us more about how you see the situation.

Theo: What he didn't say is that before I came at him, he was disrespecting me.

Marie: Excuse me, but what did he do that you found to be disrespectful toward you?

Theo: As soon as the guys come around, he like changes from being my bud to—like my enemy who—I don't know—just acting like I'm not there and then putting me down.

Marie: Okay, let's take a break for a few minutes while Eturo and I discuss this with one another. Please just listen to us talk to one another and then we'll ask you some questions. Is that okay with you?

Theo: Yeah.

Garth: Okay.

Marie: I'm getting the impression that Theo feels that Garth acts one way when it's just the two of them, but another less-respectful way when those other guys are around.

Eturo: And I think Garth is more focused on Theo's angry response than on his own change in behavior. (turning to Garth) Garth, you heard what Marie and I were discussing and you heard what Theo said. Do you think you treat Theo differently when those guys are around than when it's just the two of you?

Theo: That's because he treats me differently—getting all mad and everything.

Eturo: Theo, do you act different with Garth when he's around those guys?

Theo: Well, yeah, but you would too if he was making fun of you.

Marie: I think it's time for us to move to the third phase and have you two speak politely with each other. We'll take notes and remind you to stick to the rules. I'd like for us to begin with Theo asking Garth a question.

Theo: What question?

Marie: Do you want to know if Garth thinks he acts differently toward you around those guys and, if so, why he chooses to act differently?

Theo: Okay, what she said.

Garth: Yeah, I guess I do. And then you get mad and that just makes me embarrassed.

Theo: So, I wouldn't get mad if you didn't act like that.

Garth: Yeah. I guess I get embarrassed and try not to show it.

Theo: So if I stopped getting mad, you wouldn't get embarrassed?

Garth: I guess that's not all of it. You're okay when you're not mad, but you just don't fit in with those guys. They're in a different direction.

Theo: So what do they say about me?

Garth: Nothin' really. Just—oh, nothing.

Theo: What un—really do they say about me?

Garth: It's stupid.—You're just not their type. And I guess I have to show them that I am—so I guess—I don't know.

Theo: So, what do I do to be their type?

Garth: Nothin' because you don't like what they like or dress like them. But that's fine for you and me too, but not them.

Eturo: Excuse me, Marie and I have been taking notes. Here's what we hear you guys saying: First, both of you really want to hang together. Second, Garth also wants to hang with these other guys, but doesn't feel they'd hang with him unless he shows he's different from Theo. Third, Theo recognizes this and shows it by getting angry. Are we missing anything?

Garth: No.

Marie: Okay, so what do you need from each other to resolve this conflict?

Theo: I want Garth to respect me when those guys are around just like he does when they're not.

Garth: But I can't 'cause they won't want to hang with me.

Theo: So, what if I changed and started dressing and acting like them? Then we could all hang together.

Garth: Yeah, I guess so, but I'm not asking you to change.

Theo: Good, because I'm not going to.

Garth: I want us to still be buds, but just not hang out when I'm with them. Then there would be no conflict.

Theo: Right, but I need you to stand up for me and not disrespect me to them even when I'm not there.

Garth: That's what I should do—but I don't think I can—not until I get in with them.

Theo: I'm not angry at you anymore, but I also don't want to hang with you at all—not until you can stand up for me.

Garth: I wish I could, but not until those guys know me.

Marie: It's time to come to agreement. I think we all understand the cause of the conflict. What should we put in the agreement, Garth?

Garth: Like I said, I want us to still hang out, but for him to give me space when I'm with those guys.

Theo: And like I said, I'm not ready to hang out until he's ready to be a real friend.

Eturo: And I heard you say you might be ready to be a real friend to Theo later on but not right now. Is that right, Garth?

Garth: I'm sorry!

Eturo: But there's no reason to fight. You can still be civil to one another—just not hang out for awhile.

Theo: That's right.

Marie: I suggest we make a month-long agreement in which you guys don't hang out and just be civil schoolmates who aren't like "best friends" and then we meet again in a month to see if you want to modify the agreement.

Eturo: I like that idea. We wouldn't have to have big-deal formal peer-mediation session like this one, just an informal meeting to review the agreement and see if there is a reason to change it. What do you think?

Theo: I like that.

Garth: Me too.

Eturo: Marie and I will write up the agreement. Let's meet here at 7:55 tomorrow morning to sign it.

Marie: Congratulations to both of you. You really did a fantastic job of identifying the real problems and coming to a practical solution. Good luck.

All parties shake hands and head for the third-period classes.

The success rates of peer-mediation programs that are implemented in the spirit of Case 5.8 are extremely encouraging with reports of about 92% of the cases resulting in a positive resolution and students exhibiting long-range conflict management skills (Bodine & Crawford, 1998; Guanci, 2002; Johnson & Johnson, 1995; Lee Canter & Associates, 1994f). One of the confounding factors in estimating the effectiveness of programs is that sometimes people confuse peer-mediation programs with schoolwide programs for dealing with misbehaviors and violations of schoolwide policies and standards of conduct (e.g., involving fighting). Sometimes, school personnel make the mistake of referring students to "peer mediation" as an alternative to punishment for fighting (Cangelosi, 2006). Student-court programs whereby students serve as jurists to deal with other students' violations of conduct codes are sometimes confused with peer-mediation programs. Keep in mind that peer mediation is a mechanism to teach students how to manage conflicts *before* they escalate into violations of violence or conduct standards. In-school suspension and student court are mechanisms for responding to violations after they have occurred.

Reducing Gang-Related Activities in School

Gang Activities

A critical function of a safe-school system is to identify and eliminate *gang activities* from the school campus. A gang is a group of allied persons who engage in criminal behavior such as assault, vandalism, theft, drug trafficking, and extortion. Typically, a gang claims a territory (i.e., an area of the community) and defends it against intrusion from other gangs. The gang has a name, and its members distinguish themselves from other gangs and nongang members with a combination of signs usually revealed in their clothing, gestures, haircuts, tattoos, and graffiti. The knowledge base regarding gangs includes the following (Dishion, Nelson, & Yasui, 2005; Walker, Colvin, & Ramsey, 1995, pp. 376–377).

- Gangs date back to the beginning of organized society. (Descriptions of elders being victimized by youth groups are included in the *Book of Proverbs*.)
- The proliferation of gangs is associated with a disintegration of family units, an increase in urbanization, drug abuse, the reduction of meaningful jobs for youth and young adults, racial discrimination, alienation, and conflict.
- Gang members are three times more likely to engage in violence than youth who are not in gangs.
- Gang violence is a community problem requiring comprehensive, community-based solutions.
- Incarceration and suppression strategies alone are inadequate responses to gang problems; community organization, outreach programs, and vocational training programs are also needed.
- A large share of gang activity is driven by a motivation to control members, neighborhoods, and turf and capitalizes on fears about gangs.
- Gangs are highly cohesive and communicate through markings, graffiti, dress, language (verbal and nonverbal), tattoos, hand signs, and behavioral codes or rules.
- Males outnumber female gang members by nearly 20 to 1; however, the number of female gang members is increasing dramatically.
- There are two major types of gangs: traditional (neighborhood-based) and non-traditional (profit-oriented; often organized around drug dealing, car theft, and burglary).
- Ethnic orientation is one factor around which many gangs organize and often leads to gang-related racial violence.
- Schools are important recruiting sites for new gang members. Gangs compete with communities for the lives of youth. Peer pressure to join gangs can be extremely powerful and difficult to resist.
- Gang membership is reinforced by recognition, peer status, social support, shared values, family tradition or history, protection, and perceived opportunity.
- Gang members generally range in age from 12 to 40.
- Hate crimes committed by loosely affiliated youth groups and gangs are increasing.

- Gang members who are students tend a have a low rate of participation in cocurricular activities. It is relatively rare for gang members to bond or identify with a significant adult at school.

- Individual members are unlikely to leave their gangs. Youths need alternatives to gang membership that are attractive and accessible.

- Currently, Latino gangs are the largest in the United States.

Indicators of a gang's emergence at a school include the following (Lee Canter & Associates, 1994e).

- *A tradition of gangs in the community.* Communities that have experienced gang activities are likely to continue to confront gang problems. The tradition of gang membership often runs in families, passed on from parents and older siblings.

- *Increase in ethnic conflicts.* Gangs often form among individuals with similar ethnic backgrounds, possibly because they are isolated from and afraid of other ethnic groups. An escalation of ethnic conflict at a school could be symptomatic of increased gang activities.

- *Displays of graffiti on and near the school campus.* Graffiti is a principal language of gangs. You increase your awareness of gang-related activities by reading graffiti. Educators need to comprehend the language through which gangs communicate to anticipate problems and plan effective measures. Graffiti written by gangs tends to (a) be angular in style, (b) follow a predictable pattern, (c) introduce a gang's presence in a neighborhood, and (d) identify the gang names of the graffiti writers. Crossed-out graffiti (see Figure 5.5) is a signal to

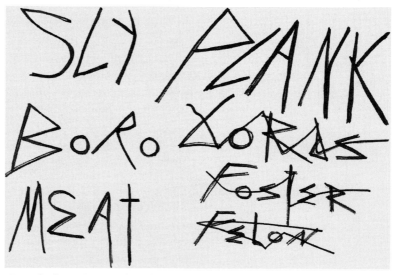

Figure 5.5. Plank Gang Members Sly, Boro, and Meat Have Crossed Out the Names of Foster and Felon of the Lords

an opposing gang that a rival gang has been in its territory. School personnel should be alerted that this action signals a confrontation is about to occur unless steps are taken to stop it. Note that the writing of taggers tends to be more circular than gang graffiti is. Tagging is done strictly for recognition and is typically unrelated to gang activities. It includes code names identifying the taggers. Nevertheless, it is a form of vandalism and should not be tolerated at school.

- *Extensive drug use.* Drug use at or near schools leads to deviant behaviors and the presence of individuals who have no legitimate business on campus. Furthermore, because gangs are often involved in drug trafficking, they may engage in turf wars over the drug business at schools where school personnel fail to stop drug use and drug-related activities.

- *Hostile confrontations.* Previolence confrontational behaviors common among members of opposing gangs include *hard looks* and *sweating*. Hard looks often begin with one individual staring down another. A hard look (see Figure 5.6) is perceived as a challenge to which the victim feels compelled to respond. Individuals delivering hard looks say nothing. They may walk away and round up fellow gang members to surround the victim. At that point a physical confrontation is likely. "Sweating" is the name for an act of intimidation in which a gang member stands with his or her face up against an opposing gang member's face and provokes a confrontation with insults and accusations. Gang codes dictate that the victim is compelled to respond violently. Backing down is unacceptable.

Figure 5.6. Hard Looks Are a Sign of Impending Violence

- *Increasing truancy rates.* High levels of gang activity off campus (such as crack parties or gang meetings) increase the chances that students will be absent or late for school.

- *Availability of weapons.* Weapons are a principal tool used in gang activities. They may be stored in backpacks or hidden in bushes or cars on campus.

- *Show-bys.* A show-by occurs when gang members from outside a neighborhood approach an area (e.g., your school campus) and reveal weapons to announce their presence. Show-bys are a sign that gang conflict is accelerating in the area.

Whenever there is evidence of gang activity at a school, the faculty and administration must either act decisively to eradicate it or expect school activities to be controlled by the gangs. Vigilance is necessary even when there is no evidence of gang activity.

Working with Gang-Affiliated Students and Eliminating Gang Activities in School

To combat gang activities in schools, teachers must apply strategies for obtaining compliance from gang-affiliated students. Attempts to convince gang members to disassociate themselves from their gangs are generally futile (Dishion, Nelson, & Yasui, 2005; Torok & Trump, 1994). Your responsibility as a teacher is to lead students—whether gang members or not—to conduct themselves appropriately at school, be on-task in your classroom, and engage in the learning activities you plan for them. The strategies explained throughout this book for obtaining such cooperation apply to students who are gang members as well as to your other students. Gang-affiliated students, however, may have a more difficult time complying with your requests to cooperate. A key to obtaining their compliance is to focus on three gang values that are congruent with your own values: fairness, respect, and loyalty (Lee Canter & Associates, 1994e). Because gang members understand and live by those values, they will be more likely to cooperate with your requests if you treat members with fairness, respect, and loyalty.

Too often, gang members perceive that they have not been given a fair chance to succeed and will look for opportunities to validate this perception. Thus, you can hardly overemphasize the importance of fostering a climate of *fairness* in your classroom and being fair when dealing with students. Use language that clearly expresses your intent to be fair, especially in cross ethnic situations. A teacher might say, for example, "I work the same way with the Latino students as I work with the Anglo students. Every time. Ask Jorge or Martin. Ask your friends." Your students will recognize whether or not you harbor prejudices. You make it easier to be fair by setting clear limits on behavior and posting standards for conduct. Appropriate behaviors and standards for conduct are the same for everyone no matter what their race, religion, gang affiliation, cultural background, gender, or status. Of course, wherever there are standards to which we hold individuals, there must be due process. Students need mechanisms through which they can tell their side of the story when conflicts arise. Providing ongoing opportunities for problem solving gives students alternatives to confrontation and violence.

As important as fairness is mutual *respect* in relationships among students and teachers. You can't expect gang-affiliated students to show respect for you if you do not show respect for them. You model respect for students by consistently being assertive (neither hostile nor passive), using descriptive instead of judgmental language, speaking directly to your intended listeners, protecting professional confidences, using supportive replies and active listening techniques, and avoiding actions that lead students to feel embarrassed in the company of their peers.

Loyalty may be the most powerful value in the gang code. Many gang members will do whatever they feel is necessary to protect or defend what they perceive to be the honor of fellow gang members. Developing trusting and respectful relationships is the key to cultivating loyalty. You begin by listening to students' concerns, treating them with fairness and respect, showing that you are sensitive to the issues that are important to them, and validating their thoughts and feelings. Students who are loyal to you are unlikely to victimize you or allow you to be victimized when they can control the situation. Students whose loyalty you have cultivated may also share critical information about serious, impending gang activities.

McCray (Lee Canter & Associates, 1994e) suggested that teachers be proactive when working with gang members and potential gang members. They should

- Know students' names. Some students go through the entire day without ever hearing their name. Addressing students by name helps to give them a sense of connectivity in the school setting.

- Use cooperative learning strategies to create opportunities for students to work with others they wouldn't have otherwise. This provides an opportunity for them to interact with individuals or small groups of students in a positive, supportive way and helps them build positive peer relationships.

- Institute clubs. Clubs offer an opportunity for students to interact with teachers in an unconventional and nonthreatening capacity. This creates an opportunity for you to get to know each other as human beings, not simply teacher and student.

- Speak informally outside class. Take time during lunch or before class to build a rapport with students and foster positive relationships with them. This interaction allows you to acknowledge other students without expecting anything in return.

- Let students know you are available to help them solve problems. They turn to peers when adults are not accessible. When students know you will be there for them, they will begin to confide in you and may offer information regarding gang-related activity.

Of course, individual efforts by teachers need to be consistent with and supported by a schoolwide safety program that incorporates gang-activity prevention measures. For example, a no-graffiti policy should be enforced with provisions for removing graffiti from the campus as soon as it is detected. The dress code should prevent students from declaring their gang affiliation on campus. The campus is the turf of the entire school community, an escape from gang activities.

As educators, we may only be able to manage the behavior of gang-affiliated students while they are at school under our supervision. But for nongang members, especially the young ones, we can reduce the chances that they will turn to gangs for their needs (e.g., security, connection, identity, empowerment, role models, status, material gain, and tradition). With redesigned schools we may be able to attend to some of the basic needs of children, providing a consistent, safe, loving environment with the sense of tribe suggested by Brendtro and Long (1995).

Gentle, Caring School Communities

Possibly the most critical key to a successful violence-prevention program is for the school to be a model community filled with caring, gentle relationships (see Figure 5.7). Dill and Haberman (1995, pp. 69–70) explain (Reprinted by permission):

How can schools help violent students envision a gentler way to live? How can we provide them with a better way to see and experience life? Our school must take the lead in introducing these students to an alternative culture of nonviolent options through gentle teaching and moral vision. We must help them discover new ways to solve social problems and to make empathetic decisions.

Students grasp the vision of a new way of behaving by (a) experiencing teacher patterns of communication that are gentle; (b) observing how "gentle" teachers respond to threats, verbal abuse, given stimuli, or typical environmental violence; and (c) seeing what teachers value.

To counter the culture of violence in school, we must model gentle responses to aggression—it may be the only glimpse of another way of doing business that aggressive students will ever witness. It will take a lot of work, considerable vision, and extreme perseverance.

It is imperative that principals and teachers learn how to scrutinize their interpersonal relationships and how these relationships either demonstrate new opportunities for kids or reaffirm a bleak suspicion.

Teachers must avoid patterns that are characteristic of violent environments: an authoritarian and directive approach in which the teacher overpowers the student.

Typically, the teacher and student rap out a well-rehearsed exchange. Teachers ask or tell; students respond and comply. No one needs to think. When students become unbearably

Figure 5.7. Schools Can Be a Model Community of Gentle, Caring Relationships

bored or the rewards of escaping become irresistible, noncompliance and elimination from the class ensues. Students reward teachers for not making them think by not getting in trouble; students punish teachers for making them think by disrupting the class.

Overly directive teaching limits time for interaction and reduces opportunities for modeling prosocial behaviors. Lecturing, giving directions, assigning and checking homework, taking roll, punishing noncompliance, marking papers, and similar activities permit little time for conversation, reasoning, or discussion of consequences. Further, responding dictatorially will only increase antisocial behavior....

Thoughtless authoritarian responses do not relieve the fear, distrust, verbal threats, and physical pain many children bring to school—conditions that interfere with learning. Ejecting students from the class may increase alienation and, in an atmosphere already concentrated on outcomes, inadvertently and ironically increase students' likelihood of academic failure, their need for hyper-alertness, the likelihood of violence in school, and the loss of hope.

Case 5.9 is adapted from an example reported by Dill and Haberman (1995, p. 70). In it, a teacher models an assertive, respectful, and reasoned response to a hostile student comment. The teacher manages her anger, defusing aggression and not affording the student and his peers the satisfaction of an exchange of insults.

▶ **CASE 5.9**

Ms. Dole shared with her class the fact that her child is Korean. A few days later, a 16-year-old asked her, "Heh, Miss, how's that little egg roll?" Caught off guard and simmering with anger, Ms. Dole considered a repertoire of possible responses. She was tempted to deliver a curt comeback she knew the student would find embarrassing. But instead of being baited into the student's power game, Ms. Dole decided to generate some options.

A response that expressed her feelings and those of other students would be appropriate, for example, "I became upset when you made that remark. Have you ever experienced racial prejudice? Was it your intent to have me feel sad?" If the student replied affirmatively, she could calmly say, "Well, it's not appreciated," and continue with the learning activity. She also thought about quietly and respectfully setting up a meeting with the student and her child, which would provide an opportunity for the student to see her child as an individual without the influence of his peers.

Having quickly considered these options, she calmly asked the student to meet her briefly after class. At the meeting she asked him, "Have you ever felt hurt?" "Yes," he responded. "Did you like feeling hurt?" she asked. "No," he said. "That's how I felt too. Why did you say that?" she asked gently. "I wanted to show the other guys," he answered. She realized he was just posturing for peers.

Ms. Dole modeled respect for the student while critically examining his behavior. She demonstrated that she values feelings and differentiates between emotional reactions and reasoned responses. The rude remark was not positively reinforced, and hostilities were derailed instead of escalated.

To provide a gentle, prosocial classroom community for your students, you need to project a confident, caring, and assertive communication style. Nevertheless, it is hardly possible for you to develop such a classroom confidently and assertively unless the school itself is reasonably secure and safe. The school also needs to provide you with a backup and support system that you can depend on for crisis situations. In contrast with Case 5.10, Case 5.11 has such a system in place.

► **CASE 5.10**

Mr. Kennedy directs his prealgebra class to begin working on a test he's just distributed. Instead of quietly beginning the test like most students, Polly takes out her portable CD player, turns to Daryl seated behind her, and says, "Listen to this," handing him the earphones. Still seated and facing Daryl, she begins moving to the music, snapping her fingers. Mr. Kennedy walks over to the two students and tells Polly, "Please put that away. You need to begin your test quietly and allow Daryl to begin his." Ignoring Mr. Kennedy, Polly continues moving to the music, face-to-face with Daryl. Positioning himself between them, Mr. Kennedy repeats, "Polly, please put that away. You need to begin your test quietly and allow Daryl to begin his." Polly to Mr. Kennedy: "Don't get in my face! We're listening to this!" Mr. Kennedy steps back and addresses Polly again: "It's not time to listen to your music right now; it's time to take this test." "I heard you the first time, dude!" Polly says in an agitated voice. Mr. Kennedy: "Let me hold your player for you until we've finished the test." Standing up and squaring off to Mr. Kennedy, Polly yells, "You're not stealing my CD!" Mr. Kennedy: "Let's step outside and discuss this calmly while the rest of the class takes the test." Polly: "Fuck off, dude! I ain't going anywhere with you, and you can't make me!" Mr. Kennedy gently reaches for Polly's arm as if to usher her toward the door. Polly jerks away and yells, "Don't touch me!" Mr. Kennedy: "Polly, you're out of control. You don't have to step outside with me, but you do have to go to the office and wait there until you calm down. Here, I'll give you a note for Ms. Tarmoni." Polly: "I don't have to do anything except listen to this with Daryl." All the other students are watching this drama unfold rather than taking the test. Assessing the situation, Mr. Kennedy quickly goes to his desk and writes a note to Ms. Tarmoni requesting that she immediately send someone to his room to escort Polly to the office, where she is to wait for him until after the current class period. He takes the note to one of the students seated in the rear of the classroom and says, "Here, Akeem, please take this note to Ms. Tarmoni right away. Don't delay."

Mr. Kennedy then directs Daryl to move to another area of the room and begin his test; he leaves Polly who now has on the earphones and is standing up dancing to the music. The teacher announces to the class, "The rest of you, please go to work on the test; we only have 25 minutes left." In a few minutes, Akeem returns and tells Mr. Kennedy, "Ms. Tarmoni was busy, but Ms. Beemon told me to ask you what the problem was." "I don't have time to explain the problem to Ms. Beemon," Mr. Kennedy says in frustration. "I just want Polly escorted out of the room so the rest of us can take our test!" Frustrated, Mr. Kennedy goes over to Polly and says, "Let's go. You're not going to continue to disrupt my class!" Polly: "Fuck off, you can't make me!" Mr. Kennedy: "I don't appreciate your using that kind of language in here." Polly: "So don't appreciate it; then go fuck off!" Some students laugh aloud; Polly grins and makes eye contact with a few of the students enjoying the show. Most of the students, however, find the lack of control more frightening than funny. With no help forthcoming from the office, Mr. Kennedy feels like he's run out of options. He knows better than to try physically to force Polly or any other students into complying with his directions.

► **CASE 5.11**

Mr. Huff directs his prealgebra class to begin working on a test he's just distributed. Instead of quietly beginning the test like most students, Dawnette takes out her portable CD player, turns to Emile seated behind her, and says, "Listen to this," handing him the earphones. Still seated and facing Emile, she begins moving to the music, snapping her fingers. Mr. Huff walks over to the two students and tells Dawnette, "Please put that away. You need to begin your test quietly and allow Emile to begin his." Ignoring Mr. Huff, Dawnette continues moving to the music, face-to-face with Emile. Positioning himself between them, Mr. Huff repeats, "Dawnette, please put that away. You need to begin your test quietly and allow Emile to begin his." Dawnette to Mr. Huff: "Don't

Figure 5.8. Mr. Huff Depends on Backup Help from Security

get in my face! We're listening to this!" Mr. Huff steps back and addresses Dawnette again: "It's not time to listen to your music right now; it's time to take this test." "I heard you the first time, dude!" Dawnette says in an agitated voice. Mr. Huff: "Let me hold your player for you until we've finished the test." Standing up and squaring off to Mr. Huff, Dawnette yells, "You're not stealing my CD!" Mr. Huff: "Let's step outside and discuss this calmly while the rest of the class takes the test." Dawnette: "Fuck off, dude! I ain't going anywhere with you, and you can't make me!" Mr. Huff: "Please step outside to talk this over, or else I will need to call security to have you removed from the room. Which option do you choose?" Dawnette: "I'm not going anywhere with you!" Mr. Huff walks directly to the security phone located near his desk (see Figure 5.8). With one push of the button, the security officer on duty is alerted that there is a crisis situation in the room. Over the phone, Mr. Huff says, "I need a security escort for Dawnette Martineau. She needs a supervised place to wait until I have time to sit down with her and one of the counselors."

In less than a minute, two security officers are in the classroom to usher Dawnette from the room.

In addition to the obvious advantages of being able to terminate an intolerable situation without teachers' having to confront students physically, the school-level backup and support system affords teachers a sense of confidence that makes it possible for them to deal assertively and gently with students. How to deal effectively with disruptive behaviors, including violent ones, in the classroom is a major focus of Chapters 8, 9, and 11. Included in those chapters are suggestions for keeping yourself from becoming a victim of violence. You are hardly in a position to provide a safe haven from violence for your students if you are in fear for your own safety or absent from your classroom because you have been hurt in a violent confrontation.

Essentials of an Effective Safe-School System

Eleven Elements

To be effective, a safe-school system must include the following.

1. The program is developed with the support of a consensus of school personnel, students, parents, community leaders, and community agencies—including law-enforcement agencies.

2. The initial design of the program is based on the results of research studies on school safety and school-safety audits.

3. A school-safety committee is organized and activated to plan, monitor, and redesign the program.

4. The program uses a team approach, with all school personnel working collaboratively with students, parents, community leaders, and community agencies.

5. All school personnel receive ongoing training in the art of making the program successful.

6. The program is coordinated with schoolwide discipline policies.

7. Provisions for building positive relationships among students, teachers, and other school personnel are included.

8. A schoolwide system for resolving conflicts is implemented.

9. Communications networks are installed using modern technology so that school personnel can rapidly communicate with one another.

10. Backup and crisis-support resources and procedures are in place.

11. Procedures are in place for controlling traffic on campus and preventing intruders from disrupting school business.

Consensus within the Community

Watson (1995, p. 58) stated,

> The first step in improving school safety is open discussion about the need for it. A school or school district should arrange a forum that includes all interested members of the school community—parents, businesspeople and chamber of commerce, and school improvement groups.
>
> Participants should know that school violence has many faces: it may occur in a series of small, observable incidents, or suddenly and brutally; it may arise from student conflict, community conflict, or simple criminal behavior. Whatever the nature of the problem, the discussion should focus on the fact that this is *our* problem and that we must do something about it. Schools themselves, not legislators, must identify the problems and the solutions.

A base of community support needs to be built from the onset of the development of the safe-school program. Parents, community leaders, and agencies, especially law enforcement, are needed for their ideas, political backing (e.g., initiating activities and using resources that have not been traditional for the school), funds (e.g., for communication technologies, teacher training, and security personnel), support and backup services (e.g., police response to suspicious activities on campus), and understanding (e.g., parents' cooperation in enforcing no-gang-apparel policies). Cooperation is more likely from persons who have been involved in the program's development from the beginning. Community participants need to understand that besides the highly publicized violent student outbreaks (Bucher & Manning, 2005), school violence occurs in many forms. Some faces of bullying are invisible to the casual observer. A culture of cyberbullying is now entrenched. Web sites are used to target specific groups, promote hate crimes, defame individuals, and identify targets for violence (Keith & Martin, 2005).

Research and Periodic Safety Audits

A research-based literature on how to develop safe schools has emerged (Brock, Sandavol, & Lewis, 2001). The initial design of the program should be based on an understanding of tenable theory and knowledge of what has succeeded and failed at other schools. Thus, a review of literature as well as observations and interviews at sites with existing programs should be conducted. Furthermore, a safety audit of the school campus should be undertaken.

Watson (1995) recommended that safety audits be conducted by school-safety consultants who are not themselves members of the school's community. The auditors inspect the campus and the neighboring areas, identifying potential danger points (e.g., areas of the building where criminal activity would be difficult to detect or campus areas easily accessed by outsiders), strategic points that can be used in crisis situations (e.g., a location that can be readily isolated from the rest of the campus), and indications of a potential for violence (e.g., evidence of gang activity). They survey and interview students, parents, teachers, school administrators, staff members, and neighbors for information and opinions that will influence the design of the program. A needs assessment is included for communications and monitoring technology, personnel resources, modification of the physical plant, and training of personnel.

Once the program is implemented, periodic safety audits continue to be conducted to provide feedback for regularly modifying the program to improve it and adjust it to changing needs.

School-Safety Committee

The design, development, implementation, management, evaluation, and ongoing modification of a school-safety program will not happen without specified people in charge. Although school safety is a community responsibility requiring a commitment from every faculty and staff member, a person or group of persons must officially oversee the program. For a large school with complex safety problems, a full-time school-safety director may be necessary to conduct day-to-day operations. In other situations, the directorship might be only one of many responsibilities assigned to a school administrator. In any case, a committee comprised of representatives of the faculty, students, parents, administrators, and the community served by the school needs to work with the director and be ultimately responsible for planning, evaluation, and modification (Watson, 1995).

Team Approach

A crucial but difficult-to-obtain attribute of a successful program is having every member of the school faculty, staff, and administration cooperate as a team to make the program work. If one teacher fails to follow through on a school-safety policy (e.g., allowing a student to have a pager in a classroom in violation of a no-pagers-on-campus rule), then it is difficult for other teachers to enforce policies (e.g., "Ms. Dodson lets me have my pager, so why won't you?"). If one teacher fails to be respectful and assertive with students, then students are more likely to feel hostile toward teachers in general. The effectiveness of school-safety programs depends on the vigilance of school personnel and their willingness to back up and aid one another in stressful situations and emergencies.

Training for All School Personnel

All school personnel should receive intensive training in how to fulfill their roles in the safe-school program. Faculty and staff must be able to (a) take advantage of the specific features of the program (e.g., know how to call for backup in a crisis situation), (b) build positive relationships with students, (c) teach and apply conflict-resolution strategies, (d) detect criminal activity, (e) lead students to manage anger and de-escalate hostility, (f) respond effectively to violent situations (e.g., by applying suggestions from Chapter 11 on how to intervene safely in fights), (g) protect themselves from becoming victims of violence, (h) contribute to the development of a gentle school community, and (i) enforce schoolwide discipline policies.

To be successful, inservice training must go far beyond a few weeks of lecture and demonstration sessions before the start of the school year. Workshop activities should include analysis of actual cases, role playing, and interaction with students and parents. Comprehensive simulations of crisis situations involving law enforcement and emergency-response teams have proven successful (Brock et al. 2001). The initial sessions should provide a foundation for in-service work that continues throughout the school year. During the year, teachers and other school personnel meet to analyze and learn from actual events and discuss strategies for dealing with problem situations.

Coordination with Schoolwide Discipline Policies

Obviously, the effectiveness of schoolwide discipline policies and the success of the safe-school program are interdependent. Garrison (Lee Canter & Associates, 1994b) stated,

> Research indicates a direct correlation between the lack of order in an environment and the potential for violence. The more orderly the school environment, the better behaved students are, and the safer everyone in the school community is. Allowing students to engage in disruptive, noncompliant behavior, regardless how minor, teaches students that they are not expected to follow the rules. When students break the rules and don't receive any consequences, they learn that they can get away with anything at school. Students who are potentially more aggressive and prone to violent behavior will take advantage of such an environment and escalate their behaviors to more serious levels.
>
> It is critical to develop a schoolwide discipline plan to establish a safe, orderly violence-free environment at school. A schoolwide discipline plan spells out rules students are expected to follow in the common areas of the school—the halls, the cafeteria, the yard and rest rooms—and consequences they will receive for not following the rules.

Safety audits conducted as part of the safe-school program have the potential of providing feedback that has implications for schoolwide discipline policies. For example, after a safety audit, the Unity High School faculty decided to modify its policies (see Case 5.7) by adding a section regulating certain student behaviors. Among those regulations is one requiring students to store their backpacks and other bags in their lockers during the school day (i.e., they may not carry the packs with them during the school day).

Lockers may also be searched by administrators at any time. The audit revealed that some students were concealing things such as illegal drugs, weapons, and spray paint in their bags. Specific consequences were spelled out for noncompliance with these regulations.

Provisions for Building Positive Relationships

By establishing a businesslike classroom environment, applying communications strategies suggested in Chapter 3, and establishing and enforcing necessary standards of conduct, you build positive relationships with your students and create a gentle community in your classroom. For a gentle, safe school, however, those approaches need to be applied by faculty and staff throughout the campus. Students tend to behave respectfully, cooperate, and comply with requests of teachers with whom they've established trusting, businesslike relationships. Teachers who have not fostered such relationships are more likely to be victimized by students (Dill & Haberman, 1995; Lee Canter & Associates, 1994b, 1994d). In addition to providing school personnel with in-service training in establishing positive relationships, the safe-school program should include activities in which students, parents, faculty, and staff have opportunities to interact socially (e.g., working together on community-service projects).

Provisions for Conflict Resolution

Conflicts among students that are not constructively resolved or managed are one of the major causes of violence. Thus, an effective school-safety program includes mechanisms for students to get help dealing with serious conflicts before they breed violence. As previously suggested, inclusion of conflict resolution in curricula and peer-mediation programs is critical.

Communication Systems

Recall Case 5.11 in which Mr. Huff used the crisis line on the telephone in his classroom to call for backup to help him deal with a student who refused to leave his classroom. Unfortunately, the classrooms in many schools not only lack telephones but also have no workable two-way intercom systems for such situations (Cangelosi, 2006). Traditionally equipped classrooms tend to isolate teachers from other adults.

One purpose for building consensus for a school-safety program is to develop the politically powerful support base needed to pay for program necessities such as communication and monitoring devices (e.g., telephones in classrooms, video monitors in hallways, and walkie-talkies for security personnel). To be able to enforce standards of conduct assertively and peacefully in your classroom, you need to know that you can readily call for backup support.

As explained in Chapter 8, some teachers are burdened by what Canter and Canter (1976) refer to as the "myth of the good teacher," which is the belief that good teachers should be able to manage any problems with students on their own within the confines of their classrooms. Case 5.11 illustrates that the belief is a myth. Mr. Huff was not foolish enough to try to bully Dawnette into complying with his request. Dawnette knew that Mr. Huff would be in more trouble than she if he tried to use physical force to remove her from the room. Mr. Huff understood the limits of his authority and knew when to call for support. Even if you never need to use your classroom telephone, just having it available will help build the confidence you need to confront unpleasant challenges to your authority without engaging in power struggles.

Backup and Crisis-Support Resources and Procedures

Of course, Mr. Huff's telephone would hardly be valuable in Case 5.11 if no one was available to receive his call and respond efficiently to his request. Had he gotten the same sort of counterproductive response that Mr. Kennedy received to his request for assistance in Case 5.10 ("Ms. Tarmoni was busy, but Ms. Beemon told me to ask you what the problem was"), then Mr. Huff would have wasted valuable time on the phone. Because of schoolwide planning, security personnel were available in Case 5.11, and a procedure had been worked out and practiced so that assistance was dispatched to Mr. Huff's classroom without the need for time-consuming explanations. Because of prior training, Mr. Huff and the support staff understand that calls for backup are not made capriciously. Unwarranted requests for crisis support will need to be explained by the teacher but not until after the response and the threat of any crisis has been averted or resolved.

In Case 11.21, a teacher intervenes in a fight in a common area of a school. As you will note when you read it, that school has a procedure in place in which students are used to locate nearby teachers to assist a teacher who is dealing with a violent activity.

Traffic Control and Intruder Prevention

Visitors to the campus pose a special problem to the school community. On one hand, visitors should be treated as welcome guests when they are at school to conduct legitimate business (e.g., parents who have scheduled conferences or classroom observations with teachers, guest speakers, classroom observers from teacher-preparation programs, delivery personnel, and school-supply sales representatives). On the other hand, intruders who do not have legitimate business at the school are a major threat to the tranquility of the campus community. Unwanted intruders include (a) outsiders with criminal intent (e.g., dealing drugs and weapons or sexually exploiting children), (b) outsiders intending to conduct gang-related business involving students in their own gangs or students in rival gangs, and (c) former students or students from other schools who are on campus to show off, socialize, flirt, or harass.

To distinguish between welcome guests and unwanted intruders, most schools require visitors to report to the main administrative office to identify themselves and their business before they are allowed access to other parts of the campus. At many schools, however, especially those in suburban and rural locations, the visitor policies are not consistently enforced (Cangelosi, 2006). Enforcement is self-imposed; visitors are expected to read the posted request to report to the office and voluntarily comply. Obviously, people without legitimate business are not likely to comply.

An effective safe-school program includes mechanisms for controlling traffic onto and off the campus. Case 5.12 is an example.

▶ CASE 5.12

A security fence is installed around the campus of Willburg Middle School so that there is only one entrance–exit point to the school grounds. Several security officers are stationed at the point to monitor movement onto and off the campus during the hour before the first period of the day when a mass of students is entering the campus. After the school day starts and traffic onto and off the campus slows, only one security officer is stationed at the entry–exit; additional officers are used again in the hour after the last period of the day. Regarding visitors to campus, the following procedures and regulations are included in Willburg Middle School's safe-school program:

1. All members of the school community who have regularly scheduled business on campus are issued and wear picture-identification badges. These are persons who are normally on campus at least once a week (e.g., students, faculty, custodians, cafeteria workers, receptionists, administrative assistants, secretaries, teacher assistants, maintenance workers, security officers, resource personnel, school-district specialists, regular parent volunteers, and student teachers).

2. The school administration publicizes its safe-school program, explaining—among other things—that visitors with business at Willburg Middle School should telephone the school office ahead of time so that temporary badges can be ready for them to pick up from the security officer at the entrance to the campus. These temporary badges—without photos but with the visitor's name and times for which the visit is authorized—are to be worn during the visits and returned to the security officer upon leaving campus. Provisions are made for visitors with legitimate business on campus who find it impractical to call ahead.

3. All members of the school community remain vigilant for persons on campus who are not wearing authorized badges. The presence of such a person on campus is immediately reported to a school security officer, teacher, administrator, receptionist, or administrative assistant, who then directs the unauthorized person to the school security office, where the person will either receive clearance and be issued a badge or escorted off campus. If the person refuses to comply, the security office is immediately called to provide assistance.

It's 10 A.M. on a Tuesday. Ms. Burch is the security officer stationed at the entrance gate when Lamont Dunn, a preservice teacher from the local college, arrives. Ms. Burch: "May I help you, sir?" Mr. Dunn: "I'm Lamont Dunn; I arranged last week to observe Ms. Long's third-period language arts class today." Ms. Burch: "Yes, Mr. Dunn. We've been expecting you. Here is your authorization badge. Please display it right here on your shirt during your stay with us. Return it to me or the officer on duty right here when you leave campus—let's see—that'll be about 12:30. Will that be enough time for you?" Mr. Dunn: "Yes, thank you very much." Ms. Burch: "To get to Ms. Long's room, enter the building through the northwest corner door, and you'll see a sign directing you toward rooms 130 to 144. Ms. Long's room is 138."

In a few minutes, a woman without a badge walks to the gate. Ms. Burch says, "Excuse me, ma'am; you need an authorization badge to enter the campus." The woman pauses and in a pleasant tone displays a business card and replies, "It's okay. I'm a financial consultant. I just want to speak with some of the teachers about a new tax-saving program." As the woman continues moving toward the school, Ms. Burch says, "Stop." The woman complies and hears Ms. Burch say, "I can give you an authorization badge to visit the main administrative office and speak with the receptionist to inquire about making appointments with teachers." The woman: "I'll just go to the faculty lounge and speak with teachers on their breaks." Ms. Burch: "No, ma'am, you need to make appointments either by calling or visiting the main office." The woman says as she leaves, "Thank you. I'll try another school."

A young man whom Ms. Burch estimates to be about 16 years old arrives. She says, "Yes, sir, may I help you?" He replies, "No, I'm just here to see my brother." He walks briskly toward the school building. Ms. Burch: "Please stop. I need to speak with you first." Continuing to walk he mumbles, "Don't worry about it; it's okay." Once more, Ms. Burch demands, "Stop," removing the walkie-talkie from her belt. Staying at her post while watching the intruder, she radios the security office and tells the officer responding to her call, "I have a code 4. A white male about 16 years old is entering the northeast door. He's wearing a navy blue baseball hat, white collarless shirt, and baggy navy-blue shorts. He's doesn't appear to be carrying anything. He's about six feet tall and thin. He just entered via the northeast door. Repeat—it's a code 4." Two security officers meet the young man just inside the school building and escort him back out. He leaves the premises after being told that he has the option of leaving immediately or waiting for the police patrol car to arrive. When Ms. Burch gave the code-4 signal, the school security office alerted the local police that assistance could be needed if the situation wasn't resolved in the next few minutes.

Ms. Burch is then met at the entrance by another teenage boy who says he's bringing his younger sister the homework she forgot to bring with her to school. After quickly viewing the homework documents, she gives him a badge authorizing him to go to the main office for 10 minutes. She radios the main office, telling the receptionist to greet the young man, receive the homework papers, and see that they are passed on to his sister.

▶ SYNTHESIS ACTIVITIES FOR CHAPTER 5

I. In a paragraph, explain the differences between a standard for classroom conduct and a routine procedure. Exchange your paragraph with one written by a colleague. Compare them in a discussion.

II. In a paragraph, explain why the literal meaning of the following statement fails to communicate anything about expected conduct: "You are allowed to come into the room after the first bell." Exchange your paragraph with one written by a colleague. Compare them in a discussion.

III. Which of the following standards for conduct are stated in purposeful terms?

  A. When you have been recognized to speak (e.g., to answer or ask a question) during a large-group meeting, speak so that everyone in the room can hear you.

  B. Do not chew gum in the classroom.

  C. Avoid doing anything that dirties, mars, or damages the classroom, its furniture, and its equipment.

  D. Sit straight with both feet on the floor.

  E. Use expressions such as "thank you," "pardon me," and "please"; refer to adults as "sir" and "ma'am."

  F. Do not bring toys to school.

  G. Respect everyone's right to learn.

  H. Be considerate of others' feelings

IV. Compare your response to Activity III's prompt to the following: Statements A, C, G, and H are stated in purposeful terms.

V. To a colleague, describe two alternative procedures you would consider for routinely checking your students' homework. Discuss the relative advantages and disadvantages of each.

VI. To a colleague, explain the answer to the following question: According to this text, what is the difference between a necessary and an unnecessary standard of conduct?

VII. Obtain a list of the standards of conduct established by another classroom teacher. In your opinion, which ones are necessary? Discuss your response with a colleague.

VIII. Decide whether you agree or disagree with the following statement: "The mistake of establishing unnecessary standards can cause a teacher more problems than the mistake of failing to establish necessary standards." Provide a rationale for your decision in a paragraph. Exchange your response to this item with that of a colleague; discuss similarities and differences.

IX.   With a colleague, discuss the advantages and disadvantages of establishing all standards and procedures at the very beginning of a school term.

X.   With a colleague, discuss the advantages and disadvantages of having students democratically determine standards of conduct.

XI.   With four or five colleagues, collaboratively design a schoolwide discipline policy for the type of school in which you are or will be teaching. Have another group of colleagues critique the plan.

XII. With a colleague, visit a school site. Interview a teacher and a school administrator to find out what steps have been taken to secure the safety and tranquility of the school community.

XIII. With four colleagues, role-play a peer-mediation session. Two of you take the part of two disputants, deciding first on what conflict you'll be discussing. Two others play the role of the peer mediators, and one should act as the teacher/observer who gives the peer mediators feedback on the session. Afterward, discuss with one another what you learned from placing yourselves in the roles of students in such a situation. Compare your session with those of other groups of colleagues who are engaging in this activity.

XIV. Visit an elementary school, a middle or junior high school, and a high school. At each, make note of the security procedures relative to visitors to the campus (e.g., clearance steps you had to complete to gain access to the building) and other security-related practices or technology (e.g., emergency telephones and security cameras) in the building. Interview both students and teachers regarding school-safety policies and about how safe and secure they feel on campus. Share and discuss your findings and compare them with those of your colleagues who are also engaging in this activity.

► TRANSITIONAL ACTIVITY FROM CHAPTER 5 TO CHAPTER 6

In preparation for your work with Chapter 5, discuss with two or more colleagues the following questions.

I.   How do some teachers manage to accommodate individual differences in a classroom of diverse students?

II.   What legal considerations relative to including and accommodating students with special needs must teachers take into account when applying classroom management strategies?

III. What are some effective classroom management strategies for including and accommodating students with physical, hearing, visual, or communications impairments?

IV.   What are some effective classroom management strategies for including and accommodating students with learning disabilities?

V.   What are some effective classroom management strategies for including and accommodating students with behavioral disorders?

VI.   What are some effective classroom management strategies for including and accommodating students for whom English is not their first language?

VII. What are some effective classroom management strategies for reaping the benefits of cultural diversity in a classroom?

Working with Individual Differences among Students

▶ CHAPTER 6'S GOAL AND OBJECTIVES

The goal of this chapter is for you to develop strategies for working with the individual characteristics of your students in ways that foster cooperation and engagement in learning activities. Specifically, Chapter 6 is designed to lead you to achieve the following objectives.

1. Explain why the effectiveness of strategies for leading students to be on-task and engaged in learning activities depends on how you interrelate with students as individuals.

2. Develop strategies for interrelating with students so that the individual differences among them enhance classroom cooperation and learning opportunities.

3. Explain the consequences of students feeling marginalized within your classroom community and develop strategies for including students with characteristics that are disdained by the majority of so-called mainstream society.

4. Explain the legal implications of your classroom management strategies relative to the inclusion and accommodation of special needs students, especially in light of the Individuals with Disabilities Education Act (IDEA).

5. Develop strategies for the inclusion and accommodation of students with physical, hearing, visual, or communication impairments that enhance classroom cooperation and student engagement.

6. Develop strategies for the inclusion and accommodation of students with learning disabilities that enhance classroom cooperation and student engagement.

7. Develop strategies for the inclusion and accommodation of students with emotional or behavioral disorders that enhance classroom cooperation and student engagement.

8. Develop strategies for the inclusion and accommodation of students for whom English is not a first language that enhance classroom cooperation and student engagement.

9. Develop strategies for using the cultural diversity of your students to enhance classroom cooperation and student engagement.

▶ THE KEY: RELATING TO STUDENTS AS INDIVIDUALS

In Case 6.1, a preservice teacher conducts a microteaching session for a group of students whom he does not know as individuals.

▶ CASE 6.1

For an assignment in the special teaching methods course he is taking at a university, Shandon Russell develops a lesson plan with the objective of leading middle school students to discover certain attributes of magnets (e.g., that magnets attract material made of iron but not of copper). The methods course professor, Joyce Chementier, discusses the plan with Shandon:

Prof. C.:   You've built in the necessary elements for a sound lesson plan. What part of the lesson would you like to present for your microteaching session for your field experience out in the schools?

Shandon: I thought I'd do the cooperative group activity in which they play the game where they use magnets to help them decide what different objects are made of.

Prof. C.:   Excellent choice! Students in the middle grades love to play games. And the key to them being engaged is having hands-on activities that keep them busy.

Through the university's field experience office, Shandon schedules his microteaching session for 30 minutes in Ms. Palmer's seventh-grade science class at Sunrise Middle School. On the eventful day, Shandon nervously delivers the directions and distributes the materials for the cooperative group work as Ms. Palmer observes. The students begin playing the game as Shandon supervises, moving among the groups. Nine minutes into the activity, Ms. Palmer is unexpectedly called out of the room by an administrator. Just as Shandon is moving from the group in which Atwan is supposed to be working and toward another group, Shandon hears Atwan say, "This is stupid; I ain't doing this no more!" Shandon turns to see Atwan slide his desk away from the group and put his head down on his desk. Shandon goes over to Atwan and in a low but firm voice says, "Young man, I need you to return to your group and continue playing the game." Burying his head even further into his arms on the desk top, Atwan mutters something that Shandon doesn't hear well enough to understand. Shandon: "I'm sorry, I couldn't understand what you said." Atwan picks up his head and exclaims, "You are a sorry bastard! I don't have to listen to what your white ass tells me!" Embarrassed in front of the other students, Shandon is stricken with panic; he says, "You can't talk to me that way!" Atwan: "I just did!" Shandon: "Maybe so, but you'll be sorry you did!" Shandon turns to the rest of the class and says aloud, "All right, let's get back to work playing the game in your groups. Ms. Palmer may be testing you on what you're supposed to be learning." Most students comply; Atwan puts his head back on his desk appearing to sleep. Ms. Palmer returns and Shandon relates the incident to her. Ms. Palmer apologizes for leaving and tells Shandon to finish the lesson while she deals with Atwan's disruption.

The following day, Shandon discusses the incident with Professor Chementier and the other preservice teachers in the teaching methods class.

Shandon: Even before I said "You can't talk to me like that," I knew that was the wrong way to respond. But not knowing what to do, I just fell into the trap of mimicking what I remember some of my teachers saying. First I was passive, then hostile. I should have been assertive, but I didn't know how. What should I have done? How should I have handled the situation?

Prof. C.:   Of course, I wasn't there, but we might have a case of a student from a subculture in which rebelling against an authority figure representing the dominant social structure is reinforced. I don't think we should be surprised to have such a student challenge us, especially in the context of a competitive game such as the one you were having them play.

Shandon: So what should I have done? That kind of disrespect shouldn't be tolerated, and there's no place for that kind of language in the classroom!

Mariane: Of course, we know students will respect us only if we respect them.

Shandon: But I was never disrespectful to this or any other student!

Prof. C.: I know you well enough that you would never intentionally be disrespectful to anyone.

Shandon: What do you mean "intentionally"?

Prof. C.: Well, what is a sign of respect in one culture—like looking at someone when you speak to her or him—may be interpreted as disrespect in another culture. You know, like in some Native American cultures it is disrespectful to make eye contact. And I agree that the kind of language the student used with you is inappropriate for a classroom. However, in some cultures, language that is unacceptable to some of us is not only tolerated, but reinforced as part of posturing during competitions.

Shandon: So what was I supposed to do? Oh, never mind! Let's talk about somebody else's microteach.

Considering Shandon's question about how to handle the off-task behavior, what principal factors are missing from the preceding discussion? Professor Chementier talked about a "dominant social structure" and cultural differences. Mariane reminded everyone that she is aware of the truism, "Respect breeds respect." But no one in the methods class discussed the two things that most needed to be addressed because they lacked firsthand knowledge of them: (a) the student, Atwan, and (b) the unique social environment and group dynamics of Ms. Palmer's classroom. Even without information about Atwan's ethnicity and cultural background, we know that Shandon's choice of strategies should have been based on his understanding of the unique characteristics of Atwan and the classroom situation—not on some sociological principles applicable to a culture as a whole rather than to individual members of that culture. Of course, knowledge of cultural similarities and differences is critically important to helping us explain the characteristics of individuals. However, the key to gaining and maintaining students' cooperation is recognizing and relating to them as individuals.

Compare Case 6.2 to Case 6.1.

▶ CASE 6.2

Rita Simon is a professor at a university where she conducts a special teaching methods course for preservice teachers. The course is designed to be field-based so that Professor Simon holds regular class meetings with the group of preservice teachers from 7:30 to 8:20 A.M. at Eastside Middle School. During the middle school's first period, which begins at 8:30 A.M., the preservice teachers work in various classrooms as follows: The 16 preservice teachers enrolled in the course are organized into eight pairs with each pair assigned to a first-period class run by one of the middle school teachers. At the very beginning of the school year, each pair spends most of its time in the classroom observing, tutoring, and performing other types of activities that help them gain insight into the students, the social dynamics of the classroom, and the manner in which the inservice teacher conducts the class. Their interactions with students also provide opportunities for the students to get to know the preservice teachers and establish expectations, roles, and trusting relationships. As the preservice teachers learn more about teaching from the combination of work with Professor Simon and experiences in the classrooms, they begin designing and conducting lessons—first with small groups of students, and then with larger groups. As one member of a pair conducts a learning activity, the other monitors students' engagement, responses, and interactions.

During the first period, Professor Simon moves among the eight classrooms, depending on what the various preservice teachers are doing on that day.

Amos Eisley and Maggie Goldstein are the preservice teachers assigned to work in Ms. Rose's first-period science class. During the first week of the school year, Amos and Maggie observe as Ms. Rose applies suggestions from this book's Chapter 2, "Creating a Favorable Climate for Cooperation." For example, on the first day, Ms. Rose gets a jump start on getting to know her students individually by engaging them in activities similar to those used by Mr. Stockton in Case 2.7. In the ensuing weeks, Amos and Maggie learn how Ms. Rose accommodates students with special needs, works with students with limited English proficiency, and takes advantage of the cultural diversity in her classroom. They become familiar with Ms. Rose's classroom management program, participating in the establishment and enforcement of standards for classroom conduct. A framed poster listing the five standards for conduct (similar to the sample display shown in Figure 5.2) hangs on the wall near the entrance to the classroom. Everyone in the class has learned that when Ms. Rose recognizes a student in violation of one of the five standards, that student is required to meet with her after school to work out a plan for preventing future violations.

It is now the fourth week of school, and Amos is directing the students into a cooperative group activity. Ms. Rose has just stepped out of the classroom, so Amos and Maggie are supervising the students. In the transition period, students are arranging their desks into several small circles. Margo is following Carter as they both carry their desks, then Margo trips and crashes into the back of Carter, causing him to fall over his desk and bang his shin against one of the metal desk legs. Sprawled on the floor and in pain, Carter screams, "Ow! What are you doin'?" Margo says, "I'm sorry," as she reaches down to help Carter. "Don't touch me, you dumb ho!" Carter screams. In the moment it takes Amos to move to the point of the incident, he thinks to himself, "Carter likes to play the role of the cool, in-control character in the class. He must be terribly embarrassed falling over and hurting himself like that. It's natural for him to transfer his embarrassment to anger toward Margo. He and I have worked together before; I think he'll calm down if I calmly and firmly step in and get between the two of them. I don't think he likes to be touched, so I'll just help him turn the desk upright and move it into the circle. Once he's calm and I get the class back on-task, I can deal with the disrespectful way he spoke to Margo." "Here, I'll help you with the desk," Amos tells Carter. Carter suddenly leaps to his feet and gets face-to-face with Amos and shouts, "Help me! You're just protecting that ho! You her pimp or somethin'?" Amos hears some of Carter's buddies laughing. Because Amos feels the class has learned to trust him, he's not embarrassed by Carter's attack; the laughter causes him to think, "Carter is dealing with his embarrassment by trying to impress his buddies with what he thinks are clever comebacks." Amos calmly turns toward the class and says, "Everyone, continue to arrange your desks and begin your group work as it's spelled out on the tasksheets I gave you." Quickly, he thinks to himself, "I see that 'help you' was the wrong phrase for me to have used with Carter. I'll put that bit of knowledge to productive use in the future. But I have to deal with the situation right now. Carter still hasn't backed off, although I've turned away from him. He looks unwilling to make the transition into the group activity. Maggie can supervise the activity while I deal with Carter. I can handle this myself, but it would be better if Ms. Rose were here in case the situation escalates." Amos then beckons Jason, a student on whom he's learned to depend, and says, "Please go down to the faculty workroom and ask one of the teachers to locate Ms. Rose and ask her to come in here as soon as possible." Turning to Maggie he says, "Ms. Goldstein, would you take over for me please?" Maggie: "I'll be happy to, Mr. Eisley."

Amos wants to speak with Carter privately away from his "audience." However, he thinks Carter is not yet ready to comply with a request to "step outside the door for a discussion." Amos believes that after Carter has had a few minutes to calm down he will be more likely to comply—especially if Ms. Rose is present. Carter is standing by himself in the middle of the room. Amos grabs a notepad and writes, "Carter, I need to speak with you just outside the door. Meet me there." Just as he's about to hand the note to Carter, Ms. Rose comes into the room and asks,

"Is there a problem, Mr. Eisley?" "Yes, but I believe Carter and I can work it out. Would it be all right if Carter and I step out in the hall for about five minutes?" Amos asks. Ms. Rose, knowing Amos well enough to trust what he'll do, says, "Yes, I'll help Ms. Goldstein work with the groups while you and Carter address the problem." Confident that Carter will follow him, Amos walks directly to the poster with the five standards for conduct hanging by the door, removes it from the wall, and takes it with him as he and Carter leave the classroom. In the hallway, Amos leans the poster against the wall and the two engage in the following conversation:

Carter: (in a harsh tone) What?

Mr. Eisley: (calmly) Are you angry with me?

Carter: No!

Mr. Eisley: The tone of your voice right now makes me think you're angry.

Carter: It's that dumb ho, she—

Mr. Eisley: I think you should stop before you violate our third standard for conduct again. I'd like for you to read our third standard right now.

Carter silently frowns and looks down at his feet.

Mr. Eisley: Do you choose to read it to me or should I read it to you?

Carter: You told me to stop, so I did.

Mr. Eisley: I don't want you to stop talking, I just want you to stop using rude names in our classroom because calling Margo a "dumb ho" and getting in my face and asking me if I'm a "pimp" are violations of Standard 3. You've already violated it today and I don't want you to do it again. I'll read it to you. Standard 3: Help—

Carter: I don't need you to read it.

Mr. Eisley: Very well, please read it to me.

Carter: "Help create and maintain a comfortable, safe, and secure learning environment for all members of our classroom community." So what?

Mr. Eisley: What happens when we violate one of our standards of conduct?

Carter: But she dissed me.

Mr. Eisley: Margo tripped and fell into you. It hurt you.

Carter: So then she's the one that violated Standard 3. It's not safe around her.

Mr. Eisley: I can understand why you got upset. When Ms. Rose, you, and I meet after school today, we should think of ways of remaining respectful to one another even when we're upset. Meet Ms. Rose and me at 2:55 right here.

Carter: Okay. Can I go back in now?

Mr. Eisley: Yes. Do you want to join one of the groups or would you rather work on your own until the rest of the class finishes the group work?

Carter: I'll just go sit at my desk.

Mr. Eisley: Okay, thanks for working with me.

The following morning, Amos and Maggie share the experience with Professor Simon and the other preservice teachers at the teaching methods course meeting. Advantages and disadvantages of various strategies for responding to such situations are discussed.

Unlike the discussion that took place in Professor Chementier's class following the incident with Atwan in Case 6.1, Professor Simon's class was able to engage in a more productive discussion of the events in Case 6.2 because some class members had firsthand knowledge of Carter, of Margo, of Ms. Rose's strategies, and of the social structure and dynamics of her classroom. For example, the discussion took into account the roles played by three critical elements that were in place prior to the incident: (a) the relationship Amos had established with Carter, (b) the students' comprehension of the third standard for conduct, and (c) Ms. Rose's system for following up on violations of the standards.

Your knowledge of general principles regarding how people respond to situations as a function of their age, cultural backgrounds, special needs, gender, and other circumstances is critical to your ability to develop a classroom management program that leads students to cooperate. However, the effective application of that knowledge to any unique classroom situation depends on the insights you gain and the relations you establish from your interactions with students as individuals. You must see students for *who* they are individually, not simply as a sample of some combination of abstract sociological categories. No two students will bring to your classroom the exact same combination of needs, abilities, attitudes, experiences, background, interests, motivations, energy, genetics, chemistry, aptitudes, resources, perceptions, beliefs, and so on. Furthermore, for any one student, that combination of attributes is in a constant state of flux. Consequently, not only do you need to take into account individual differences among students as you apply classroom management strategies, but you also need to be aware of how students change over time. As Kounin (1977) pointed out, withitness is essential for successful classroom management.

▶ INCLUDING STUDENTS WITH CHARACTERISTICS TYPICALLY DISDAINED IN SO-CALLED MAINSTREAM SOCIETY

The Consequences of Students' Feeling Marginalized

Consider Case 6.3.

▶ CASE 6.3

As part of their efforts to discourage students from using illicit drugs, administrators at Bear Creek Middle School kick off their annual antidrug campaign by having students view a slickly produced video program in which teenage and young adult celebrities repeatedly urge viewers to stay off of drugs. Each celebrity is thin, has unblemished skin, is dressed and groomed stylishly, smiles incessantly, flashes sparkling white and perfectly formed teeth, is—by Hollywood standards—gorgeous looking, and generally urges middle school students that they can be the same way if they'll only avoid drugs. A darkly tanned male Euro-American snowboarder urges, "It's not cool to do drugs. So just don't do them!" An African-American rapper with light-tan skin exclaims, "I don't hang with fools that do drugs!" A female and a male model who appear to have some romantic interest in one another credit their success to "staying clean." Similar testimonies are delivered by a basketball star, surfing champion, actress, academic scholarship winner, junior-Olympic medalist in gymnastics, and drummer for an up-and-coming band.

Jennifer, one of the students watching the video, is—like the vast majority of her middle-school classmates—very self-conscious of and unhappy about her appearance. She is displeased with pimples that spread across her face, the 120 pounds she carries on her 64-inch frame, uncooperative hair, clothes that "just won't hang right," and shyness about ever being seen or heard. In her mind, she is nothing like the smooth-talking "cool role models" paraded in front of her. Jennifer would like to feel as happy as the personalities on the video act, but thinks to herself, "No wonder they're smiling. They're cool and successful so people love them. I've never done drugs but I'm nothing like them." Jennifer associates her own appearance and personality more with the pock-marked face, sad-looking, unstylish, and—by Hollywood standards—ugly looking people pictured on posters plastered on Bear Creek Middle School walls with captions reading, "Drugs ruined my life!" than with those "cool people" on posters with the caption, "It's uncool to do drugs!" In her mind, Jennifer's life is already ruined, and she doesn't even have the luxury of blaming drugs.

Neither does Andrew feel that he can ever live up to the standards set by the "role models" his school is pushing on him. Like the model couple in the video, he knows that he is "supposed" to be attracted romantically to the opposite sex. But for reasons he doesn't understand, he finds males more sexually appealing.

The widely accepted precept that young people tend to imitate the behavior of individuals whom they admire is readily observed and supported by research (Ormrod, 2006, pp. 337–338). Thus, it is understandable that well-intentioned adults try to use individuals who are considered popular to convey important messages and exhibit behavior they want students to imitate. However, teaching is an extremely complex art, and teachers need to be aware of combinations of side effects that cause simplistic strategies to backfire (e.g., recall your study of destructive positive reinforcers and destructive punishment when you worked with Chapter 2). Typical, simplistic efforts to display "ideal role models" in an attempt to motivate students to achieve learning goals and exhibit desirable behaviors may have the side effect of perpetuating some unhealthy myths developed through continual contact with commercial media: (a) "Success determines self-worth." (b) "Being fat is uncool. All popular girls are thin." (c) "People are judged by their clothes." (d) "Cool people are desired by the opposite sex." (e) "Although politically correct speech displaying acceptance of diversity is cool, the physical appearances of really cool people is limited to those displayed by professional models (e.g., in television and magazine ads)." (f) "Being popular is the ultimate goal; it is why we want to achieve and display acceptable behavior."

But Jennifer and Andrew from Case 6.3 are keenly aware that studying harder or behaving appropriately (e.g., avoiding drugs) will not cause them to morph into one of the "role models" their teachers parade in front of them. Maybe one day, Jennifer will invest in a cosmetic makeover and Andrew will continue to suppress his sexual preferences. But for now (which is the point in time that is most important to them) being popular is not an attainable target. A classroom where such commercially promoted myths are perpetuated is not conducive to building a cooperative, safe, productive community of learners where students are comfortable being themselves. Resentment builds inside students who feel marginalized; resentment may erupt in antisocial conduct that catches teachers, parents, and peers by surprise. Recall an incident in which a student acted with hostility and you heard someone make a comment similar to the following: "I never imagined she[he] would ever do something like that. She[he] was so easygoing." More common than resentment erupting into overt hostility is for students to turn off teachers whom they view as trying to turn them into people they can never be.

Strategies for Inclusion in Your Classroom

Although you cannot change students' feeling marginalized by mainstream society, you can develop strategies to increase the chances that students with characteristics disdained outside your classroom will not feel marginalized inside your classroom. The strategies will not be simplistic. You are unlikely to develop successful strategies if you harbor personal prejudices about people who are fat, gay, unattractive looking, belong to certain religions, or any one of other common targets of mainstream biases. Here are some thoughts to keep in mind as you develop your strategies.

1. As emphasized in the previous section of this chapter, it is of paramount importance to think of each student as the unique individual she or he is. This principle reminds us of the well-worn saying, "Look for the good in everyone," but without the aspect of judging a person's traits as "good" or "bad."

2. As emphasized in Chapter 4, consistent use of descriptive, nonjudgmental language helps communicate acceptance of individuals for who they are without associating achievement with self-worth. Supportive replies convey acceptance of individual feelings while maintaining a focus on the business of learning. Assertive communications promote openness without hostility.

3. Nonjudgmental communications include being nonjudgmental about students' appearances. Counter the continual barrage of judgments about people's looks by avoiding discriminations related to appearance. It won't be easy to break the habit of complimenting people on their looks, because dispensing such complements is a habit most have developed to gain the favor of others. You will need to supplant comments such as, "Jodie, you look really nice today," with ones that emphasize behavior rather than appearance (e.g., "Jodie, you're showing a lot of energy today."). In Case 6.4, Ms. Arnell refuses to discriminate on looks.

▶ **CASE 6.4**

Emina enters Ms. Arnell's classroom with a new outfit. Brynja exclaims, "Hey Amina, you really look hot today. Don't you think Amina looks hot today, Ms. Arnell?" With a warm smile, Ms. Arnell replies, "All my students look equally beautiful."

4. The link between the "ideal look" and the alarming prevalence of eating disorders among young people is solidly established (Jansen, Smeets, Martijn, & Nederkoorn, 2006; Skemp-Arit, 2006). It is particularly critical to steer away from judgments associating beauty and weight. Avoid, for example, complimenting students for looking thin.

5. Recall your work with Chapter 2's section, "Destructive Positive Reinforcers." It is still common practice for teachers, especially in elementary schools, to "reward" students' achievements and on-task behaviors with food snacks (Cangelosi, 2006). Commonly adopted school mathematics textbooks are filled with colorful images of food. Pizzas, for example, provide appealing examples of circular regions for sectioning and measuring. I am not suggesting that you avoid references to food altogether, but as you develop curricula and design

lessons, keep in mind that weight-conscious students need attention to food balanced with a wide variety of other types of reinforcers and examples.

6. Read Case 6.5. What, if anything, concerns you about Mr. Moody's example? His activity follows sound principles of learning theory (e.g., he leads students to discover a critical relationship using inquiry strategies before employing direct instruction to help them remember it), and true to suggestions herein, he avoids IRE cycles as he interacts with students. But teaching is an extremely complex art in which undesirable side effects are always a concern. Mr. Moody's choice of example—a mathematically sound one—may send the unintentional message that the only acceptable type of dance couple is one that matches a female with a male. Gay students may feel marginalized, and all students are encouraged to perpetuate a myth. Another concern is that using the personal example of dance couples within the class may prompt undesirable quips (e.g., "Barry is too short to dance with Grace."). Dancing may be frowned on within the religion of some students, consequently, they feel excluded. Of course, there is no engaging, interesting example that's free from undesirable side effects. You don't need to limit yourself to sterile uninteresting examples, but be vigilant for potential side effects and vary your examples so that there is a balance of potential negative side effects. Over time, your students will recognize that you don't harbor divisive biases.

▶ **CASE 6.5**

As part of a unit on probability, Mr. Moody is attempting to lead prealgebra students to discover that multiplication can be used to count the number of ordered pairs extracted from two sets. He begins a discussion:

Mr. Moody: Count the number of young women we have with us today, Angela.

Angela: Okay, let me see. Uhh, one, six, and then—okay, we have 14.

Mr. Moody: Thank you. And how many young men, Mehmet?

Mehmet: Let's see—12, unless we count Mr. Moody, then it's 13.

Mr. Moody: Because I'm not so young, let's make it 12. Now, suppose we were going to have a dance. Given the 26 students among us, how many different possible dance partners could there be? Without counting or thinking about this very much, do you think it would be a number close to 26 or would it be less or would it be a lot more than 26? What is your guess, Vincent?

Vincent: At first I was thinking it would be small because we're cutting the class in half, but then—I don't know.

Tawni: I think it'd be a big number because there are a lot of different matches.

Mr. Moody: Let's run with Tawni's thought for a moment. So, let's look at the number of men that are potential dance partners for Dawnette. How many, Alasandra?

Alasandara: There are 12 guys; so, 12. Oh! I see where we're going with this. There are 14 different girls and 12 different guys so it's 12 times 14 possible couples.

The discussion continues.

7. As suggested by your work with Chapter 5's section, "Necessary Standards for Conduct," antiharassment standards need to be enforced in your classroom.

Of course, such reprehensible behavior that occurs outside your classroom affects the health of your learning community. Students who are gay are far more likely to be bullied and harassed in schools than their straight peers ("School Bullying," 2005; Stainburn, 2005). What can you do to combat such a campuswide problem? Teachers tread on tenuous legal ground by engaging in classroom discussions that deal with what might be perceived as sexuality. On the other hand, school administrators have a legal obligation to protect the safety of all students, even if it requires "antibias training" for school personnel and students (Marco, 2006; Norris, 2005; Reid, 2005; Underwood, 2004; Velez, 2006). Thus, consider using your influence as a faculty member to initiate or strengthen schoolwide programs that promote understanding and inclusion of all students (Caldwell, 2005; Henneman, 2005; "Teaching Tolerance," 2005).

8. When you worked with two of Chapter 4's sections, "Being Responsible for One's Own Conduct" and "Teaching Students to Communicate Assertively," you were exposed to strategies for teaching students to protect themselves from verbal harassment. Besides implementing those strategies in your own classroom, consider initiating or strengthening schoolwide programs that lead students to develop personal strategies for not allowing themselves to be victimized. A research-based literature is emerging that examines strategies for combating prejudice and including students with characteristics disdained by so-called mainstream society (see, e.g., Singer, 2005).

▶ SPECIAL POPULATIONS

It is essential for you to see and interact with each of your students as a unique individual, regardless of whether the student is classified "regular education" or "special education." However, when students' exceptionalities interfere with their abilities to remain on-task and engaged in learning activities, you will need to adjust how you apply classroom management strategies to accommodate these students. If you don't, you will be faced with discipline problems. Case 6.6 is an example.

▶ CASE 6.6

Heather, a seventh grader, has a hearing impairment for which her hearing aids only partially compensate. When Mr. Paisley, her social studies teacher, orally delivers directions or explanations to the class, Heather can hear only part of what he says, and much of what she does hear is distorted. For example, when he directs students to turn to page 143 in their textbooks and to write answers to questions 3, 4, 9, and 11 in their notebooks, Heather figures out what to do by watching what her classmates do. She looks to see what page they have open. Finding out what to do with page 143 requires more ingenuity on her part. Heather gets tired of always being several steps behind and taking more time to get through transitions than most of her classmates. Mr. Paisley's oral explanations to the class are even more difficult for her to follow than his directions. Unable to comply with directions that she doesn't understand and missing critical explanations, Heather is often disengaged from learning activities. More and more, she deals with her frustration, as well as with the boredom of sitting through lessons she is not following, with disruptive behaviors. The increase in disruptive behaviors prompts Mr. Paisley to recognize that Heather has a need that must be addressed; otherwise, his classroom management problems will continue to escalate.

Mr. Paisley confers with several of Heather's other teachers. Both her science and English teachers indicate that "she's slow to grasp some things," but presents them with "no discipline problems." The conversation with her art teacher, Mr. Howard, includes the following:

Mr. Howard: After seeing her struggle a few times with directions I presented to the whole class, I began deliberately standing in front of her and enunciating words more carefully. This has helped immensely.

Mr. Paisley: So you think the problem has to do with hearing. But don't her hearing aids work?

Mr. Howard: Apparently not well enough for us to teach as if she can hear as well as anybody else.

Mr. Paisley: But John [the school principal] said that kids who are mainstreamed should be taught just like everybody else.

Mr. Howard: As with most things, John seems to have this one backwards. By law, students with disabilities are supposed to be provided with learning opportunities just like everybody else. If we don't do something different to accommodate their exceptionalities, we're not providing them with the same opportunities to learn as everybody else. If we don't consider each student's individual differences as we plan instruction—whether the student is regular ed or special ed—we're not teaching to everyone. Why don't you check with Grace—Heather's homeroom teacher—who probably has a copy of the IEP [individualized education program]. Every student with a special education classification is supposed to have an IEP worked out collaboratively with the student, a parent, special education teacher, and regular education teacher. In Heather's case, it should include procedures for accommodating Heather's hearing impairment.

Mr. Paisley: Have you ever seen it?

Mr. Howard: No, John erroneously thinks that the IEP should be kept confidential. So rather than fight him on such things, I work out my own ways of accommodating students' special needs.

Mr. Paisley: I can't allow that child to keep falling further and further behind. Besides, my classroom management problems are escalating. Thanks. I'll see what Grace has to say.

Mr. Howard: Good luck!

Grace informs Mr. Paisley that she signed Heather's IEP at the beginning of the school year, but she's unable to locate her copy. She also mentions that John insists IEPs should remain confidential. Mr. Paisley plans to confer with the special education teacher as well as with the school district's educational audiologist. Once he gets their advice, he plans to work out a plan with Heather and her parents. However, because of schedule conflicts, his extremely busy schedule, and some broken appointments, the meetings are postponed. Realizing the importance of addressing the problem immediately, Mr. Paisley begins trying out a few strategies on his own. He tries putting more of his directions for activities in writing on tasksheets for students to read and depending less on giving directions orally. When speaking to the class, he makes a concerted effort to enunciate words clearly and to stand directly in front of Heather. As he employs more visual media to communicate and uses speech more carefully than before, he's amazed not only at the improvement in Heather's level of engagement, but also at improvements in how the whole class follows his directions and explanations.

Mr. Paisley shares his success story with the two specialists and with Heather's mother when he finally meets with them. He finds out that, under the state-administered program for adhering to special education–related federal statutes, he should not only have access to the IEP but also be one of the collaborators in the development of the IEP. Encouraged by the success of his initial efforts, Mr. Paisley tries out additional strategies with Heather as well as with his other students with special needs. He now thinks more about how he directs students into learning activities.

Each week he assigns a partner to Heather who is responsible for clarifying directions during transition periods. Most of the students tend to be extra attentive to directions themselves when they serve as Heather's partner.

In Case 6.6, Mr. Paisley not only addressed classroom management problems and led students to cooperate by making accommodations for students with special needs, but he also obeyed the law under the Individuals with Disabilities Education Act (IDEA) (Heward, 2006, pp. 19–31; Silver & Hagin, 2002, pp. 4–10; Turnbull & Turnbull, 1998, pp. 13–102). IDEA requires schools to accommodate students' special needs so that their educational opportunities are maximized in the least-restrictive learning environment. Under this series of federal statutes (i.e., enactments beginning in 1974), the 10 special-needs categories for students aged 6 through 21 are as follows: mental retardation, hearing impairments, speech or language impairments, visual impairments, emotional disturbances, orthopedic impairments, autism, traumatic brain injury, other health impairments, and specific learning disabilities.

► LEGAL CONCERNS RELATIVE TO INCLUSION AND ACCOMMODATION

Classroom Management Implications of IDEA and Other Federal Statutes

IDEA requires each state to have a plan by which public education agencies can provide the following services.

- *Identification and evaluation*: Extensive efforts are made to screen and identify all children and youth with disabilities. Nondiscriminatory evaluations of students suspected of having a disability are conducted fairly so that socioeconomic, language, or other such factors do not bias the results.

- *Service at public expense*: Every student with a disability is provided with an appropriate education at no extra cost to his or her parents.

- *Due process*: An evaluation conducted for the purpose of determining the special education classification of a student requires parental consent. If the student's parents contest the results of the evaluation, the special education placement, or the school's methods of complying with the provisions of the IDEA program, the parents are entitled to an impartial due-process hearing at which an arbitrator attempts to resolve the disagreements.

- *Parent and student participation*: The student and his or her parents are consulted about the special education placement and plan.

- *Confidentiality*: Access to records pertaining to a student's special education evaluation, placement, and program is available only to the student, her or his parents, and the professional educators who are responsible for delivering the services.

- *Individualized education program (IEP)*: An IEP is developed for each special education student by that student's IEP team. Members of the IEP team include the student's parents, at least one regular education teacher, at least one special education teacher, a representative of the school who is qualified to supervise specially designed instruction to meet the unique needs of the student, and other individuals deemed appropriate by the parents or school administrator. An IEP is a written agreement between the parents and the school that specifies an assessment of the student's present level of functioning, the long- and short-term goals, the services to be provided, and the plans for delivering and evaluating those services.

- *Appropriate education in the least-restrictive environment*: The student's educational needs are met, so far as reasonably possible, in the same environment as that of students in the general education population.

- *Zero reject*: A system of free, appropriate public education is available to every student with a disability. The education is provided so that exceptionalities are accommodated.

- *Personnel development and in-service*: Training and in-service education are provided for teachers and other professional personnel relative to meeting the needs of students with disabilities.

The combination of federal statutes known as "IDEA" (e.g., 20 U.S.C., Ch. 33, §§ 1400–1497 [1997]), other civil rights legislation (e.g., Section 504 of the Rehabilitation Act of 1973 and the Americans with Disabilities Act of 1990), local and state regulations, and the rulings from hundreds of litigations relative to adherence to IDEA (notably, *Honig v. Doe*, 484, U.S. 305 [1988]) provide a complex maze of implications for how you should employ classroom management strategies. Questions about your legal responsibilities—what you are required to do and what you may not do—should be directed to the professional responsible for administering your school district's special education program. Regarding classroom management practices, two aspects of IDEA play a particularly significant role: (a) *zero reject* and (b) the *IEP*.

Zero-Reject and IEP Implications for Classroom Management

Traditionally, the ultimate sanction that school administrators can impose on a student for serious misbehaviors is expulsion. When a student is expelled from a school, the school ceases to provide that student with educational services. The extent of a school's power to "play that last card" is curtailed by the zero-reject provision of IDEA. To understand the specifics of the zero-reject provision, consult with special education supervisors at your school or see references such as Heward (2006, pp. 19, 30, 436) and Turnbull and Turnbull (1998, pp. 60–64).

IDEA may seem to pose challenges to standard classroom management practices. At least it should cause you to pause and consider alternatives before responding to the misbehavior of a student with a special education classification by excluding her or him from a learning activity. By exerting your right to assert yourself as an active member of your students' IEP teams, you can use IDEA to help you manage your classroom. As a written contract, an IEP should not only specify the instructional services you are required to provide, but it should also specify the resources, services, support, and authority you require to enable you to deliver those instructional services. Your efforts seeking resources, services, and support from administrators, supervisors, parents, and specialists are more likely to be successful when those responsible for delivering such services are spelled out in IEPs.

Examples of teachers assertively influencing and making productive use of IEPs are explained in subsequent sections of this chapter.

▶ ACCOMMODATING AND INCLUDING STUDENTS WITH PHYSICAL, HEARING, VISUAL, OR COMMUNICATION IMPAIRMENTS

The huge, complex special education category of *physical impairments* includes some *neurological disorders* (e.g., cerebral palsy, seizure disorder, spina bifida, traumatic brain injury, and Tourette's syndrome), *musculoskeletal diseases* (e.g., muscular dystrophy and juvenile rheumatoid arthritis), and *other conditions affecting health and physical ability* (e.g., AIDS, asthma, cancer, cystic fibrosis, and fetal alcohol syndrome).

A student with a *hearing impairment* is either deaf or hard of hearing. Students who are *deaf* cannot successfully process linguistic information through audition even with a hearing aid. Students who are *hard of hearing* (e.g., Heather, in Case 6.6) are unable to detect a normal range of sounds, but their residual hearing is sufficient to enable them to process linguistic information through audition. Of course, there is extreme variation in the severity and effects of hearing impairments. Furthermore, the means by which students learn to manage their hearing impairments vary considerably. Only a relatively few are proficient with speech reading. Some deaf students depend on one form or another of manual communications (e.g., American Sign Language); others have been in programs that emphasize oral communications. Some hard-of-hearing students have well-maintained hearing aids that significantly enhance what they hear; the hearing aids of others are hardly useful, either because of the nature of the hearing loss or because the device itself is improperly maintained.

A student is considered *legally blind* when both eyes have visual acuity of 20/200 or less, even with corrective lenses, or when field of vision is so narrow that its widest diameter subtends an angular distance no greater than 20 degrees. The vision of most legally blind students is adequate for them to read print with some type of assistance (e.g., magnifying glasses or large-print books). The vision of some students is so severely impaired that they can read only using Braille or aural methods (Hallahan & Kauffman, 1997, pp. 354–356).

According to the American Speech-Language-Hearing Association (1993, pp. 40–41), a communication disorder is a disorder of speech, language, or a combination of both:

> A *communication disorder* is an impairment in the ability to receive, send, process, and comprehend concepts or verbal, nonverbal and graphic symbol systems. A communication disorder may be evident in the processes of hearing, language, and/or speech. A communication disorder may range in severity from mild to profound. It may be developmental or acquired. Individuals may demonstrate one or any combination of communication disorders. A communication disorder may result in a primary disability or it may be secondary to other disabilities.
>
> A. A *speech disorder* is an impairment of the articulation of speech sounds, fluency, and/or voice.

1. An *articulation disorder* is the atypical production of speech sounds characterized by substitutions, omissions, additions, or distortions that interfere with intelligibility.

2. A *fluency disorder* is an interruption in the flow of speaking characterized by atypical rate, rhythm, and repetitions in sounds, syllables, words, and phrases. This may be accompanied by excessive tension, struggle behavior, and secondary mannerism.

3. A *voice disorder* is characterized by the abnormal production and/or absences of vocal quality, pitch, loudness, resonance, and/or duration, which is inappropriate for an individual's age and/or sex.

B. A *language disorder* is impaired comprehension and/or use of spoken, written, and/or other symbol system. The disorder may involve (1) the form of language (phonology, morphology, syntax), (2) the content of language (semantics), and/or (3) the function of language in communication (pragmatics) in any combination.

How can you accommodate students with physical, hearing, visual, or communication impairments? The array of impairments, with each type ranging from mild to severe, is far too complex an issue to address in any other way than as follows: Each case is unique, and thus, classroom management strategies need to be individually tailored. Your involvement as the regular education teacher on IEP teams is absolutely critical. Your first task as a member of an IEP team is to find out what you can about the student and her or his condition from the specialists, the parents, and the student. Your second task is to determine what needs to be done to accommodate each student's disability in a way that contributes to the smooth and successful operation of your classroom. Of course, you make this determination in consultation with other team members and trusted professionals as well as relevant sources of ideas (e.g., professional journals and Web sites). Your third task is to influence the design of the IEP so that what you require for the planned accommodation to be successful is spelled out in the contract. Your fourth task is to fulfill your part of the agreement and to make formative evaluations relative to how, if at all, the program should be modified. Over the course of the school year, the team should routinely meet to assess progress and consider modifications in the IEP. Case 6.7 is an example.

▶ **CASE 6.7**

Just before the opening of the school year, Ms. Corona meets with the IEP teams for several of her fourth-grade students. Figure 6.1 displays the IEP that Jasmine's team developed with assertive leadership from Ms. Corona.

The first few weeks working with Jasmine and the other fourth graders provide Ms. Corona with profound learning experiences. She identifies additional resource and equipment needs that were not anticipated when Jasmine's initial fourth-grade IEP was developed. Here are three examples:

- Many of Ms. Corona's classroom activities involve students standing and moving about the room to do such things as making presentations, writing on the whiteboard, posting displays on the wall, and using computers. To facilitate Jasmine's engagement in such activities, Ms. Corona requests that handrails similar to ballet bars be installed along parts of the walls. This, she reasons, would provide more opportunities for Jasmine to stand and move about the room even when the arthritis in her lower extremities is flaring up.

Edgewater School District

Individualized Education Program (IEP)

Student: Jasmine L. Dornier   **School:** San Juan Elementary   **IEP#:** 7   **Date:** 8/17/06
Birthday: 12/8/97   **Grade:** 4th   **Reg. Ed. Teacher:** Sonia Corona   **Sp. Ed. Teacher:** David Hatch
IEP Team: Jasmine L. Dornier (student), Tabrina Dornier-Grey (mother), Sonia W. Corona (reg. ed. teacher), David Hatch (sp. ed. teacher), Elwood L. Shinkle (Assistant Principal), Narvonia G. Clay (orthopedic therapist).

I. Description of the Exceptionality

When she was 5, Jasmine was diagnosed with juvenile rheumatoid arthritis. Most of the time, there is inflammation in most of her joints (especially in the joints of the lower extremities). The severity of the condition fluctuates throughout most days. The stiffness in her joints makes movement uncomfortable and restricted. At times, it is so uncomfortable for her to move some parts of her body (most often her hips, knees, and ankles) that she uses unconventional methods of loco-motion (e.g., using her hands to slide herself from one point to another) or needs to use a wheelchair (with which she is very proficient).

Unpredictably, the severity of the inflammation varies. This is especially true for joints above the hips which can be functioning with no apparent stiffness or dis-comfort for hours at a time followed by a sudden attack (usually lasting from 5 to 20 minutes) in which only slight movements and external contacts (e.g., bumping into another person) result in extreme discomfort. On the other hand, the severity of the condition in her hips and the joints of her lower extremities varies within a smaller range—never disappearing, but hardly ever reaching the extreme levels she occasionally experiences in her upper-body joints.

The causes of juvenile rheumatoid arthritis are unknown and, as of this date, no cure has been invented. However, Jasmine engages in a daily program of physi-cal therapy, medication, and pain-management therapy that, at this time, appears to help her reduce the debilitating effects of the condition.

Although the condition restricts Jasmine's psychomotor activities and the therapy requires about 3 hours a day, she's able to engage in cognitive activities to the same degree as anyone else. In fact, she can read, view videotapes, operate a computer, and be involved in other learning activities while concurrently involved with at least some of her physical therapy.

See Attachment 1 to this document for a more detailed description of Jasmine's condition and treatment program.

Figure 6.1. IEP for Jasmine

II. Present Functioning Level

A. Psychomotor Achievement:

Over the past two years, Jasmine has consistently obtained scores on standard-ized physical fitness tests that are about average or slightly above average (5th or 6th stanines) with respect to the national norm for her age and gender in the fol-lowing areas: cardiovascular endurance, body composition, muscular strength and endurance, static balance, power, and reaction time. In the following areas (all of which are directly affected by her exceptionality) her scores are consistently markedly below the national norm for her age and gender (1st or 2nd stanines): flexibility, dynamic balance, coordination, and speed. These scores are consistent with the observations of Patricia Howell (her third-grade teacher) and of Ms. Clay.

Jasmine's ability to engage in everyday psychomotor activities varies depending on the severity and location of arthritic flare-ups. Generally speaking, she can nearly always perform many complex psychomotor tasks that do not require sud-den or prolonged joint extensions. She should not participate in contact sports.

In the past 4 months, Jasmine has improved her physical fitness and psychomo-tor skills to a remarkable degree. Her faithful attention to her therapy program has been a major factor in this progress.

B. Affective Achievement (including motivation, effort, conduct, and cooperation):

Jasmine has made remarkable progress managing her continuing disappointment with being excluded from some of the activities in which her peers engage (e.g., playing basketball and roughhousing with friends). She is extremely assertive in communicating her needs relative to her exceptionality. She willingly responds to inquiries about how rheumatoid arthritis affects her. She loves challenges, viewing them as opportunities to grow, learn, and extend her capabilities even when her performance falls short of the high expectations she sets for herself. Often, she gets tired of the discomfort caused by her condition and tends to withdraw from in-teractions with others—seeming to be gathering herself for the next herculean ef-fort. Bouncing back from disappointment is a Jasmine trademark.

She cooperates extremely well in the classroom, but there are times when she does not want to be pushed. She knows when she needs time to "catch her breath" and is assertive enough to stop others (including teachers) from pushing her to attempt a task before she's ready. Four years of therapy has taught her self-discipline and about how far she should push herself. She possesses an ideal combination of the motivation to excel and the understanding of her moment-to-moment limitations. Using a sports metaphor, she plays within herself.

Jasmine's third-grade portfolio (which she is happy to share with anyone inter-ested in it) includes reflection papers and artwork that provide insights into her attitude about family, school, and community and her outlook on life, likes, and dislikes. A copy of the portfolio's table of contents is Attachment 2 to this docu-ment. Items 4c and 17b are particularly indicative of her affective achievement.

Figure 6.1. (*continued*)

C. Cognitive Achievement:

Jasmine's performance in all academic areas exceeds the average of that for beginning fourth-grade students. Summative evaluation reports and work samples indicative of her academic achievements are included in her third-grade portfolio. Items 5, 6e, and 17a are an excellent reflection of how she constructs concepts, discovers relationships, and demonstrates process skills. Note how she integrates what she learns from different subject areas into a cohesive whole and applies it to address meaningful problems.

III. Goals for the School Year

A. Psychomotor Achievement:

Jasmine will continue with her current rate of progress with respect to the goals of increasing flexibility and improving the fluidness of her movements. More specific goals are listed in Attachment 1. School-based goals emphasize fine motor skill development that facilitate engagement in classroom activities. Psychomotor goals for the 4th-grade class are listed in Attachment 3; only the ones marked with a star are for Jasmine. They are the class goals that can be achieved without risking physical contact and without movements that are often uncomfortable for Jasmine.

B. Affective Achievement (including motivation, effort, conduct, and cooperation):

The affective goals for Jasmine to achieve during the 2006–2007 school year are the same as those for the rest of Ms. Corona's 4th-grade class. See Attachment 3 for a list of goals categorized by subject-content areas.

C. Cognitive Achievement:

The cognitive goals for Jasmine to achieve during the 2006–2007 school year are the same as those for the rest of Ms. Corona's 4th-grade class. See Attachment 3 for a list of goals categorized by subject-content areas.

IV. Plan for Accomplishing the Goals from III while Accommodating the Exceptionality

Jasmine will engage in learning activities as directed by Ms. Corona as is expected of other students in the class but with the following provisions:

1. Whenever a class activity is likely to cause physical discomfort related to her exceptionality or pose an undue risk of unpleasant physical contact either because of the nature of the activity itself or because of momentary flare-ups in Jasmine's condition, Ms. Corona will provide an alternative learning activity that is related to the lesson's objective, but without the aforementioned consequences.

Figure 6.1. (*continued*)

2. Ms. Corona and Jasmine will collaborate on teaching other students in the class how to behave so that Jasmine's comfort related to her exceptionality is not compromised.

3. Ms. Corona will orchestrate transitions between learning activities in a way that Jasmine is able to avoid discomfort related to her exceptionality.

4. Each week, Ms. Corona, in consultation with Ms. Clay and Mr. Hatch, will work out a schedule for Jasmine to engage in 30 minutes of physical therapy a day that minimizes interruptions to Jasmine's inclusion in regular class activities.

5. Each week, Ms. Corona, in consultation with Ms. Clay and Mr. Hatch, will integrate regular classroom activities designed to develop Jasmine's psychomotor skills.

V. Special Resources and Support Required to Implement the Plan from IV

Architectural Accommodations: Alterations to Ms. Corona's classroom are required to facilitate Jasmine's movements especially during transition periods. The entrance is to be widened to provide more clearance for Jasmine's wheelchair (on days that she uses it) and also to reduce the risk of Jasmine striking the door frame or being jostled by other students. Furthermore, a door is to be installed in the exterior wall of the classroom so that Jasmine can enter and exit the classroom without the threat of being bumped and jostled when negotiating a crowded hallway. Other alterations may be required that cannot be anticipated prior to opening of the school year. Mr. Shinkle will be responsible for acquiring funds for architectural accommodations through grants available for removal of architectural barriers. (These grants are administered through the State Office of Education and funded by Congress [20 U.S.C § 1405].)

Consultation and Support Personnel: Jasmine, Ms. Dornier-Grey, Mr. Hatch, and Ms. Clay will keep Ms. Corona apprised of Jasmine's changing needs and conditions. They will also be readily available for consultation with Ms. Corona as she plans units and class activities. Mr. Shinkle will see that a paraprofessional is available to help Ms. Corona supervise transition periods at least in the beginning of the year until other students have developed accommodating behavior patterns and also for particularly risky situations. Mr. Shinkle will also be responsible for providing administrative backing for the added classroom management burden of teaching students behavior patterns that accommodate Jasmine's exceptionality.

VI. Goals for weeks ___1 – 4___ of the School Year

A. Psychomotor Achievement:

Refer to the objectives that are marked "J-P" (for "Jasmine-psychomotor") in the unit plans of Attachment 4 to this document.

Figure 6.1. *(continued)*

B. Affective Achievement (including motivation, effort, conduct, and cooperation):

Refer to the objectives that are marked "J-A" (for "Jasmine-affective") in the unit plans of Attachment 4 to this document.

C. Cognitive Achievement:

Refer to the objectives that are marked "J-C" (for "Jasmine-cognitive") in the unit plans of Attachment 4 to this document.

VII. Plan for Accomplishing the Goals from VI while Accommodating the Exceptionality

Refer to the learning activities and descriptions that are marked "J" (for "Jasmine") in the unit plans of Attachment 4 to this document.

VIII. Special Resources and Support Required to Implement the Plan from VII

Refer to the items on the list of resource and support items marked "J" (for "Jasmine") in the unit plans of Attachment 4 to this document.

Provisions of this IEP agreed to by the IEP Team as indicated by the following signatures:

_____ / _____   _____ / _____
Jasmine L. Dornier   date   Tabrina Dornier-Grey   date

_____ / _____   _____ / _____
Sonia W. Corona   date   David Hatch   date

_____ / _____   _____ / _____
Elwood L. Shinkle   date   Narvonia G. Clay   date

Attachments:

1. Selected excerpts from Jasmine's medical and therapy records.
2. Table of contents for Jasmine's 3rd-grade portfolio.
3. Ms. Corona's goals for her 2006–2007 4th-grade students.
4. Ms. Corona's unit plans for Weeks 1–4 for her 4th-grade class.

Figure 6.1. (*continued*)

- Ms. Corona notices that the small tables in the room where students often sit for small-group activities are not of a shape and height that allow Jasmine to sit close to the table facing her fellow workers from her wheelchair. Thus, she wants to replace two of the tables with ones that better accommodate students in wheelchairs.

- Ms. Corona struggles with strategies for teaching students to interact with Jasmine and include her in their activities without risking her comfort. This problem is compounded by the fact that Jasmine's condition fluctuates unpredictably. The success of classroom management strategies depends on consistency and predictability; however, it might be comfortable for Jasmine to be touched one minute, but not the next. Jasmine accepts the responsibility for letting others know when it is okay to touch her and when it is not. But this is quite burdensome and nearly impossible in a classroom filled with fourth graders. Ms. Corona tries to think of an efficient nonverbal cue that Jasmine could use to let everyone know the status of her condition. She recalls seeing an excerpt from a videotape on a televised sports program showing a professional football team practicing. She noted that a few of the players practiced with jerseys with a large red-cross emblem. The emblem signaled to the coaches and other players on the field that those players were in the process of recovering from injuries and should not be hit, blocked, or tackled as would players who are not wearing the special jerseys. Ms. Corona considers playing off that idea and having a brightly-colored easy-to-slip-on-and-off vest that Jasmine would have available to put on as a signal that her condition is such that others should avoid making physical contact with her. Ms. Corona would like to introduce the idea to the class by showing a video clip of a professional football team practicing. If Jasmine and the rest of the IEP team agree, she'll need to obtain two vests for Jasmine—one for backup. The video clip is easily acquired without expense to the school.

Ms. Corona submits the requests for the handrails and the replacement tables to Mr. Shinkle and discusses her idea about using the vests. Mr. Shinkle suggests that she charge the vests to a school account, but that there are no funds for the furniture and installation of rails. However, they agree that by routing the requests through the IEP team, special education grant money can be used for funding. At the next IEP team meeting, the proposals are discussed, approved, and reflected by additions to the IEP.

In the ensuing weeks, Ms. Corona is pleased to discover how the procedures for accommodating Jasmine's exceptionality are affecting other students' behaviors. Apparently, by learning to be more aware of Jasmine's needs, they are becoming more aware and considerate of the needs of everyone in the classroom. Ms. Corona notices that some students are being more thoughtful about how they touch one another.

Figure 6.2 is an IEP for another student in Ms. Corona's class, Uschi, who has a hearing impairment. As with Jasmine, Ms. Corona discovers that accommodations for Uschi's exceptionality lead to benefits for the entire class. For example, because of Uschi's IEP, Ms. Corona obtained sound-field FM devices and had sound-enhancement material installed on the ceiling and walls. This has improved Uschi's, as well as everyone else's, ability to follow oral instructions, presentations, and discussions. The sound-field FM devices make class discussions easier for Ms. Corona to control. Four small microphones are located in the room. Ms. Corona has a fifth mike as well as a device located on her belt with which she controls which one of the five mikes is live. During class discussions, when a student is recognized by the discussion leader, the student moves to the nearest mike, Ms. Corona activates that mike, and the student speaks. The procedure is designed to accommodate Uschi's exceptionality by amplifying the speech of the speaker who has the floor and by making it easier for Uschi to identify who is speaking—she can see who is at the microphone and is cued to look at the speaker. Initially, Ms. Corona feared that the procedure would be clumsy and slow down the discussion. Instead, she discovered that the procedure added an air of order to discussions. Students were inclined to follow the process of being recognized so they could use

Edgewater School District

Individualized Education Program (IEP)

Student: Uschi Sample   **School:** San Juan Elementary   **IEP#:** 3   **Date:** 8/23/06
Birthday: 8/13/97   **Grade:** 4th   **Reg. Ed. Teacher:** Sonia Corona   **Sp. Ed. Teacher:** Candace Diggart
IEP Team: Uschi Sample (student), Amy Sample (mother), Derek Sample (father), Sonia W. Corona (reg. ed. teacher), Candace Diggart (sp. ed. teacher), Elwood L. Shinkle (Assistant Principal), Jim Messina (educational audiologist).

I. Description of the Exceptionality

A series of hearing tests conducted at State University in the spring of 2004 and followed up at Lakeside Audiology revealed that Uschi has a hearing impairment in the mild to marked range. Generally her better functioning ear does not detect speech frequencies below about 55 dB. Diagnostic findings suggest a conductive hearing impairment caused by nonsupperative otitis media.

Uschi is hardly able to hear and decipher conversational speech unless the speaker is face to face with her at a distance less than 6 feet. Speech must be louder than normal and clearly articulated to be processed by audition. Her hearing aids significantly improve her ability to process linguistic information. However, the effectiveness of the devices varies considerably depending on the sources and complexity of sounds and on other factors not yet understood.

Remarkably, Uschi's speech seems to be unaffected by her hearing impairment.

See Attachment 1 to this document for excerpts from Uschi's audiology assessment report.

II. Present Functioning Level

A. Psychomotor Achievement:

Uschi's physical fitness and psychomotor skills generally appear to be superior to what is considered average for her gender and age. She consistently scores markedly above average for her age and gender on fitness tests (usually about the 7th stanine) with respect to cardiovascular endurance, body composition, muscular strength and endurance, flexibility, coordination, speed, static and dynamic balance, power, and reaction time. Her exceptionality does not appear to affect her psychomotor achievement.

Figure 6.2. IEP for Uschi

B. Affective Achievement (including motivation, effort, conduct, and cooperation):

Apparently, Uschi's experiences of not hearing oral instructions have tended to reinforce a shutting-out type of response in the classroom. Rather than assertively communicating her need for speakers to speak clearly, loudly, and directly to her, she tends to ignore oral speech. Consequently, she is frequently off-task in the classroom and disengaged from learning activities. She doesn't seem to want to bother others (including her teachers) with her needs, nor does she seem to enjoy calling attention to herself. Consequently, her off-task behaviors are nearly always non-disruptive.

At times, she becomes frustrated with others' lack of consideration for or sensitivity to her being hard of hearing. When her passiveness turns aggressive, she responds with hostility—sometimes with verbal attacks, but more often by turning away with disgusted gestures and looks. She is much more likely to respond this way toward peers than with adults. She needs to learn to assertively communicate her needs (e.g., ask speakers to face her); once she develops a pattern of assertive behavior the passive-hostile cycle she falls into now should be less of a problem.

She neither flaunts nor tries to hide her exceptionality. She also appears very appreciative of others' efforts to make themselves understood.

C. Cognitive Achievement:

Uschi possesses an exceptional aptitude for learning. She reads at a level that is markedly better than what is considered average for beginning fourth graders. She excels more in subject areas with which she can depend on independent reading than in areas requiring algorithmic skills. Her scores and grades in mathematics are lower than in language arts and social studies. Traditional tests do not seem to reflect her cognitive achievement levels as well as performance or alternative assessments.

III. Goals for the School Year

A. Psychomotor Achievement:

The psychomotor goals for Uschi to achieve during the 2006–2007 school year are the same as those for the rest of Ms. Corona's 4th-grade class. See Attachment 2 for a list of goals categorized by subject-content areas.

B. Affective Achievement (including motivation, effort, conduct, and cooperation):

Besides the affective goals listed in Attachment 2, Uschi is to work toward the following goals during the 2006–2007 school year:

1. In situations in which she needs to understand speakers, she will assertively communicate to the speakers what they need to do in order for her to comprehend what they are saying.

Figure 6.2. (*continued*)

2. She will be more tolerant of others' lack of consideration for and sensitivity to her hard-of-hearing exceptionality.

3. She will significantly reduce the frequency with which she "shuts out" what is going on in the classroom.

C. Cognitive Achievement:

The cognitive goals for Uschi to achieve during the 2006–2007 school year are the same as those for the rest of Ms. Corona's 4th-grade class. See Attachment 2 for a list of goals categorized by subject-content areas. Note that among the cognitive goals listed in Attachment 2 are two that relate to developing assertive communications skills. These should complement the three affective goals enumerated above.

IV. Plan for Accomplishing the Goals from III while Accommodating the Exceptionality

Uschi will engage in learning activities as directed by Ms. Corona as is expected for other students in the class but with the following provisions:

1. Whenever addressing the class as a whole, so far as reasonably possible, Ms. Corona will locate herself within 6 feet of Uschi, positioned so that Uschi can see Ms. Corona's face, and articulate her words distinctly and loudly.

2. Ms. Corona will use more visual media than she has typically used in the past to communicate directions and explanations.

3. Ms. Corona will incorporate strategies into learning activities that will lead other students to speak in a way that facilitates Uschi processing and understanding what they are saying.

4. The acoustical characteristics of the classroom will be architecturally enhanced.

5. During large group classroom discussions, FM sound-field devices will be employed.

6. Working in collaboration with Ms. Corona, Uschi will complete the *Assertive Communications Strategies* module (Cangelosi & Petersen, 1998) over the course of the year.

V. Special Resources and Support Required to Implement the Plan from IV

Architectural Accommodations: Acoustical materials to reduce room reverberations are to be installed in appropriate locations of the room as directed by Mr. Messina (in consultation with an acoustical engineer.)

Figure 6.2. (*continued*)

Equipment: An adequate sound-field FM amplification system with 5 portable mini-microphones, a clip-on control device, and appropriate accessories.

Consultation and Support Personnel: Uschi will keep Ms. Corona apprised as to what needs to be done to help her listen in the classroom. This involves both immediate and overall needs. Mr. Messina will check Uschi's hearing aids and prescribe adjustments as needed at least twice a month. Uschi and her parents will be responsible for keeping her hearing aids in effective working order. Mr. Shinkle will facilitate the installation of equipment and acquisition of resources required by this plan. Uschi, Ms. Sample, Mr. Sample, Ms. Diggart, and Mr. Messina will be readily available to consult with Ms. Corona.

VI. Goals for weeks __1 – 4__ of the School Year

A. Psychomotor Achievement:

Refer to the objectives with psychomotor designations in the unit plans of Attachment 3 to this document.

B. Affective Achievement (including motivation, effort, conduct, and cooperation):

Refer to the objectives with affective designations in the unit plans of Attachment 3 to this document. Also refer to A-3, A-4, and B-2 of Attachment 4.

C. Cognitive Achievement:

Refer to the objectives with cognitive designations in the unit plans of Attachment 3 to this document.

VII. Plan for Accomplishing the Goals from VI while Accommodating the Exceptionality

Refer to the lesson descriptions from Attachment 3 and note the special provisions relating to Uschi.

VIII. Special Resources and Support Required to Implement the Plan from VII

Refer to the items on the list of resource and support items marked "U" (for "Uschi") in the unit plans of Attachment 3 to this document.

Figure 6.2. (*continued*)

Provisions of this IEP agreed to by the IEP Team as indicated by the following signatures:

_____ / _____		_____ / _____
Uschi Sample date		Amy Sample & Derek Sample date
_____ / _____		_____ / _____
Sonia W. Corona date		Candace Diggart date
_____ / _____		_____ / _____
Elwood L. Shinkle date		Jim Messina date

Attachments:

1. Selected excerpts from Uschi's audiology assessment records.
2. Ms. Corona's goals for her 2006–2007 4th-grade students.
3. Ms. Corona's unit plans for Weeks 1–4 for her 4th-grade class.
4. List of objectives for the *Assertive Communications Strategies* module.

Figure 6.2. (*continued*)

the microphone rather than blurting out comments and interrupting others. The process did slow down the pace of discussions, but because they were more orderly, the discussions tended to be more efficient and productive.

Engage in Activity 6.1.

▶ *ACTIVITY 6.1*

With two or three colleagues, discuss the following questions in light of Case 6.7.

1. In what ways did Ms. Corona's assertiveness serve her classroom management needs, Jasmine's needs, Uschi's needs, and the needs of other students in her class?

2. What does Jasmine's IEP require Ms. Corona to do that she would not do if Jasmine were not in her class?

3. What does Jasmine's IEP require the school administration to do for Ms. Corona that would not be required if Jasmine were not in Ms. Corona's class?

4. What does Uschi's IEP require Ms. Corona to do that she would not do if Uschi were not in her class?

5. What does Uschi's IEP require the school administration to do for Ms. Corona that would not be required if Uschi were not in Ms. Corona's class?

6. How does the need to accommodate Jasmine's exceptionality complicate Ms. Corona's classroom management strategies?

7. How does Ms. Corona's accommodation of Jasmine's exceptionality help her keep other students on-task and engaged in learning activities?

8. How does the need to accommodate Uschi's exceptionality complicate Ms. Corona's classroom management strategies?

9. How does Ms. Corona's accommodation of Uschi's exceptionality help her keep other students on-task and engaged in learning activities?

▶ ACCOMMODATING AND INCLUDING STUDENTS WITH LEARNING DISABILITIES

Generally speaking, the academic achievements of students with *learning disabilities* fall far short of the levels of achievement that are normally expected of students with their academic aptitudes. Psychological processing problems (e.g., perceptual disturbances causing deficits in the ability to perceive and interpret visual or auditory stimuli, distractibility, and hyperactivity) are major culprits leading to discrepancies between intellectual abilities and academic performance. This extremely difficult-to-pinpoint, often-misunderstood category of disorders is associated with frustrated students and frustrated teachers. Consider Case 6.8.

▶ CASE 6.8

"What was the story about that we just read?" Ms. Hinkley asks her fourth-grade students. Roy thinks to himself, "Ms. Hinkley wants us to—she's wearing earrings today; she didn't yesterday—wants us to tell her 'what was'—that means it happened already—'the story'—that must be from a reading—Why is Lisa turning around right now?—'we'—that's all of us in here—'just read'—that means the one we read last . . . so, the answer must be about when the day is about to be dark—that's called—Ms. Hinkley's writing something on the board—that's called 'dusk.'. . ." During the time Roy is processing Ms. Hinkley's question, she calls on Ismail who answers "dusk." Ms. Hinkley then writes the first sentence from the story on the board: "I saw a bat on top of a pole." She then turns to the class as Roy finishes processing her initial question. "Why do you suppose the author begins with this sentence, Roy?" Roy answers, "Dusk." A few of the students giggle. Roy thinks, "Why are they laughing? The story is about dusk." Ms. Hinkley: "Don't just repeat what Ismail said. Listen to my question. Why do you suppose the author begins with the sentence on the board?" Roy thinks to himself, "But I listened to her question and I answered it." Roy repeats, "Dusk." More students laugh this time, and Roy is embarrassed, but he's not sure why. He blurts out, "Dusk is between light and dark." "Very good!" Ms. Hinkley replies, "But the question is about the sentence on the board." A few other students begin to answer aloud, but Ms. Hinkley stops them with, "No, don't answer out of turn. Roy needs to figure this out for himself. Roy, read the sentence on the board." "I was a tab no pot—" Hearing laughter, he abruptly stops. Ms. Hinkley scolds the students for laughing, "Don't encourage his clowning.—Roy, this time read it right." Roy: "I'm sorry, I'm trying to read it right." Ms. Hinkley: "Then you're just not concentrating. Look at the words carefully; they make sense. 'I was a tab' makes no sense." Roy tries again, "I was—" Ms. Hinkley: "The word is 'saw.'" Roy: "I saw a tab—" More laughter erupts. Roy is concentrating so hard trying to read the sentence that his head is beginning to hurt. The restless movements of the students around him are making it harder for him to figure out the right words to say that will satisfy Ms. Hinkley. He wants to cooperate with her efforts to help him, but he can't figure out what she wants. In his mind, she said "saw," but she wrote "was." "And besides," he thinks, "the first sentence was something to do with a bat—why did she write 'tab'?" Frustrated with Roy's inexplicable responses, Ms. Hinkley calls on another student and Roy is left in a state of confusion.

Whereas Roy's learning disability had not yet been diagnosed in Case 6.8, a little more than 5% of the students in U.S. public schools, ages 6 to 17, are classified as having learning disabilities (Hallahan & Kauffman, 1997, p. 168; Heward, 2006, p. 191). About half of all students identified for special education fall into this category. Silver and Hagin (2002, pp. 110–113) suggested that about 15% of first graders have learning disabilities—most of which have not been diagnosed. *Learning disability* is defined in the Federal Register (1977, p. 65083) as follows:

> "Specific learning disability" means a disorder in one or more of the basic psychological processes involved in understanding or using language, spoken or written, which may manifest itself in an imperfect ability to speak, read, write, spell, or to do mathematical calculations. The term includes such conditions as perceptual handicaps, brain injury, minimal brain dysfunction, dyslexia, and developmental aphasia. The term does not include children who have learning problems which are primarily the result of visual, hearing, or motor handicaps, of mental retardation, of emotional disturbance, or of environmental, cultural, or economic disadvantage.

The National Joint Committee on Learning Disabilities (1989, p. 1) offers the following definition:

> Learning disabilities is a general term that refers to a heterogeneous group of disorders manifested by significant difficulties in the acquisition and use of listening, speaking, reading, writing, reasoning, or mathematical abilities. These disorders are intrinsic to the individual, presumed to be due to central nervous system dysfunction, and may occur across the life span.
>
> Problems in self-regulatory behaviors, social perception, and social interaction may exist with learning disabilities but do not by themselves constitute a learning disability.
>
> Although learning disabilities may occur concomitantly with other handicapping conditions (for example, sensory impairment, mental retardation, serious emotional disturbance) or with extrinsic influences (such as cultural differences, insufficient or inappropriate instruction), they are not the results of those conditions or influences.

Students with learning disabilities experience academic achievement problems in ways that are dissimilar to those of other students. Particularly prevalent are reading difficulties stemming from an inability to detect associations among certain letters, sounds, and letter sequences or from difficulty processing visual symbols. Learning disabilities often interfere with students' achievements in writing, speaking, and doing mathematics.

The academic problems of students with learning disabilities are often compounded by social difficulties stemming from an ineptness with conversation. Awkwardness with social interactions, an inability to maintain a flow of communications, and a tendency to misperceive what others say are characteristics of most students with learning disabilities—not characteristics that engender social acceptance.

Disorders of attention and hyperactivity are classified as learning disabilities. Hallahan and Kauffman (1997, p. 179) pointed out, "Students with attention problems display such characteristics as distractibility, impulsivity, and hyperactivity. Teachers and parents of these children often characterize them as being unable to stick with one task for very long, failing to listen to others, talking nonstop, blurting out the first things on their minds, and being generally disorganized in planning their activities in and out of school."

Another common learning disability is the inability to simultaneously engage in two cognitive tasks, such as listening and writing. Yet another is the inability to select efficient strategies for undertaking a learning task and self-monitor progress toward task completion. Hallahan and Kauffman (1997, p. 182) explained how these and other learning disabilities lead to motivational problems:

> Another source of problems for many persons with learning disabilities is their *motivation*, or feelings about their abilities to deal with life's many challenges and problems. People with learning disabilities may appear content to let events happen without attempting to control or influence them. These individuals have what is referred to as an *external*, rather than an *internal, locus of control*. In other words, they believe their lives are controlled by external factors, such as luck or fate, rather than internal factors, such as determination or ability (Hallahan, Gajar, Cohen, & Tarver, 1978; Short & Weissberg-Benchell, 1989). People with this outlook sometimes display *learned helplessness*: a tendency to give up and expect the worst because they think that no matter how hard they try, they will fail (Schunk, 1989; Seligman, 1992).
>
> What makes these motivational problems so difficult for teachers, parents, and individuals with learning disabilities to deal with is the interrelationship between cognitive and motivational problems (Borkowski, 1992). A vicious cycle develops: To begin, the student learns to expect failure in any new situation, based on past experience. This expectancy of failure, or learned helplessness, may then cause him or her to give up too easily when faced with a difficult or complicated task. As a result, not only does the student fail to learn new skills, he or she also has another bad experience, reinforcing feelings of helplessness and even worthlessness—and so the cycle goes.

Obviously, including and accommodating students with learning disabilities in your classroom poses a major challenge. Although the causes and mechanisms of learning disabilities are not well understood, important knowledge about learning disabilities and how to mitigate and circumvent—but not overcome—their effects has been gained over the last 35 years. Some of the adaptive teaching strategies with names such as "cognitive training," "scaffolded instruction," and "structure and stimulus reduction" are familiar to special education teachers—one of the reasons it is critical for special education teachers to be protagonists on IEP teams. Some of the simpler strategies they can suggest for accommodating students' learning disabilities can provide amazing results. Case 6.9 is an example.

▶ CASE 6.9

Chad is a high school student who has been diagnosed as having a condition that impairs his abilities to process information presented verbally and to focus concurrently on multiple tasks. Often word sequences become distorted by his reception mechanisms, but once he manages to decipher the symbols, Chad comprehends messages as well as most students. Prior to the opening of the school year, Ms. Fisher, who is Chad's U.S. history teacher, and Ms. Eng, his special education teacher, engage in the following conversation:

Ms. Fisher: I read your analysis of Chad's exceptionality. Tell me what adjustments I need to make in my teaching and in how I manage my classroom.

Ms. Eng: Of course, you decide just how to work out the exact accommodations that fit not only Chad's needs, but also what works for you and the other students in your unique classroom situation. I'd like to suggest a few basic ideas now, and then give you some time to mull them over and work up some details. Then let's go over your plan.

Ms. Fisher: That'll work for me. What are the basic ideas?

Ms. Eng: In Chad's case, we should focus on strategies for accomplishing four things: First, provide extra time for him to process verbal information—especially directions for learning activities. Second, avoid surprising him in class. Use techniques that allow him to prepare for what you expect him to do. He's easily caught off guard because he struggles with transitions from one event to the next. Third,—

Ms. Fisher: Slow down, I'm trying to take notes.

Ms. Eng: Oh! I'm sorry.—Okay, third, don't expect him to do two things at once—like you're doing right now—listening and taking notes.

Ms. Fisher: Maybe I'm learning disabled.

Ms. Eng: You may well be, but even if you aren't, you can see that having people with disabilities in our classes tends to heighten our awareness of some of the complexities of tasks we expect of all our students—like the need to slow down a lecture to facilitate note-taking. Students without disabilities also benefit from such tactics.

Ms. Fisher: But from my understanding of Chad's disability, I shouldn't expect him to take notes while listening to me no matter how slowly I speak.

Ms. Eng: Right. And besides, if you accommodate Chad's needs by pausing between every sentence, then rewording it to facilitate his processing and then directing him what to write down, that would help him quite a bit, but you'd probably lose the rest of the class. You aren't expected to do anything that harms other students' opportunities to learn.

Ms. Fisher: What were you saying about rewording sentences?

Ms. Eng: I'm sorry, I'm getting ahead of myself. This is something we all do in our verbal communications. We mention something—like I just did—before it's been properly introduced. Then we go back and try to recover missing pieces—and even worse—we do what I'm doing right now—which is to bring up another topic altogether before we address the question at hand.

Ms. Fisher: In other words, normal verbal communications aren't very linear.

Ms. Eng: Exactly! And normal nonlinear verbiage is impossible to follow for people with disabilities like Chad's.

Ms. Fisher: So, one accommodation I need to make is to use very direct communications with him and to use a much more linear flow of ideas with him than I typically use with other students.

Ms. Eng: Yes. That was going to be my fifth point.

Ms. Fisher: This conversation is rather nonlinear. Go ahead and list your first three points again and then give me the rest in order.

Ms. Eng: The first is to provide time for him to process verbal communication; the second is to avoid surprises. The third is to avoid expecting him to do two cognitive tasks at once. The fourth is to avoid pressure situations—especially in front of his peers. Chad gets quite flustered when he feels he's being judged by how quickly and smoothly he responds to prompts. Pressure aggravates the effects of his disability.—Fifth, as far as reasonably possible, use simple linear, short, and direct communications as we just discussed.—The sixth one is the one you asked me about before but we got sidetracked. Sometimes all Chad needs to understand what seems to us a simple verbal direction is to have the directions reworded and possibly demonstrated. Let me think of an example.—Okay, suppose you say to Chad, "Run the program on the Constitution from this CD-ROM disk," as you hand him the disk, and he just looks confused for a minute. After you think he's finished thinking about your first directive, you might follow up with, "Put this in your CD-ROM drive." Sometimes that's all it takes to get directions across—not most of the time, but often enough to try it. That brings us to number seven: Provide opportunities for Chad to experience success in processing verbal information and directing his own learning. This is one that's especially difficult to finesse—finding surefire simple things that lead him to gradually build his confidence to try more complex tasks.—Eighth, work out a system of cues between you and Chad that will facilitate the first six points. For example, you always stand directly in front of him for several minutes before you ever call on him in class. This signals him to prepare himself for a response. When he wants you to call on him, he might use a sign he can send you without anyone else even being aware of what's going on. Maybe you could teach him the hand sign for "now" in American Sign Language.

Ms. Fisher: And ninth?

Ms. Eng: The ninth idea involves accommodations you need to make for administering tests to Chad. That's it.

Ms. Fisher: Give me an example of how I might adjust my testing procedures.

Ms. Eng: Chad really labors trying to comprehend directions for test prompts. Often the problem can be addressed simply by having the directions rephrased and presented in a second format—such as having written directions rephrased orally—and allowing Chad more time to interpret and respond to prompts than most students need. He absolutely needs more time to take tests than other students. Also, it is nearly impossible for him to concentrate on test prompts in a classroom surrounded by other students. He's too easily distracted.

Ms. Fisher: So this means we have to make provisions for giving him extra time in a location away from the rest of the class. But is this fair to the other students? They'll also want extra time.

Ms. Eng: What isn't fair, or even legal for that matter, is for Chad's achievement to be tested under conditions that do not accommodate his exceptionality, which is something the other students don't have to cope with. Besides, unless we make these accommodations, the results of the tests are not valid—that is, they won't accurately reflect what Chad has learned.

Ms. Fisher: Of course, you're absolutely right. But I'm going to insist that we spell out the resources and support I need to make these accommodations right in Chad's IEP. The IEP should specify that the school will provide an area outside my classroom for Chad to take tests over an extended time period with a supervisor—other than me—who would be available to clarify directions for prompts without influencing Chad's responses to those prompts once the directions were understood.

Ms. Eng: I'll support your position when you make that argument next week at the IEP team meeting.

Ms. Fisher: I'll get to work on the details of my plans. When can you meet with me to go over them?

Ms. Eng: How about Thursday afternoon? Do you have an opening on your schedule?

Ms. Fisher: Four o'clock works for me. That will give us time to work up the needed provisions we're going to propose at the IEP meeting.

Ms. Eng: One other thing. I'd like to invite you to look at this videotape program.

Ms. Fisher views the videotape program *Understanding Learning Disabilities: How Difficult Can This Be? The F.A.T. City Workshop* (Lavoie, 1989). The program simulates some of the experiences students with perceptual disabilities suffer in classrooms in which their exceptionalities are not accommodated. She replays the 70-minute tape, selecting certain segments to study repeatedly. Now stimulated with ideas, she works out plans to discuss with Ms. Eng.

At the IEP team meeting, only one IEP is developed that is generic to all five classes Chad will be taking during the first term of the school year as well as to other special education commitments. Ms. Fisher insists on an attachment that specifically refers to her history class. Figure 6.3 displays that attachment; the course syllabus referred to in the attachment is displayed in Figure 6.2.

Attachment 3

Goals Relative to U.S. History
Class Conducted by Ms. Fisher

As indicated in the course syllabus, the U.S. History course is organized into 22 units. Each unit has a goal. The primary goals for Chad to achieve as a result of his participation in U.S. History are those 22 unit goals. Besides those primary goals, Chad will progress toward the following auxiliary goals related to managing his exceptionality:

A. Gain proficiency with respect to communicating about history.

B. Develop and apply strategies for learning history.

C. Develop and apply strategies for helping Ms. Fisher teach U.S. History while effectively accommodating his exceptionality.

D. Develop historical-research skills upon which he may be able to form a basis for building an area of scholarly expertise.

Plans for Accomplishing
the 26 Aforementioned Goals

Chad will engage in learning activities as directed by Ms. Fisher as is expected of other students taking the course but with the following provisions:

1. During the first week of the school year, Chad and Ms. Fisher will work out a procedure for using signals during class meetings by which (a) Chad indicates to Ms. Fisher how well he is understanding what he is supposed to be doing at the moment, (b) Ms. Fisher indicates to Chad that he should prepare to respond to a forthcoming prompt (e.g., call on him), (c) Chad indicates to Ms. Fisher whether or not he is prepared to respond to one of her prompts, (d) Chad acknowledges the reception of a signal from Ms. Fisher, and (e) Ms. Fisher acknowledges the reception of a signal from Chad.

2. Once a week, Chad, Ms. Fisher, and Ms. Eng will meet for approximately 45 minutes to (a) assess the previous week's accomplishments regarding the 4 auxiliary goals and (b) plan what they will do to make further progress with those goals during the upcoming week. At least one of Chad's parents will participate in every other one of these meetings.

3. Chad, Ms. Fisher, Ms. Eng, and Chad's parents will abide by agreements that are worked out during these weekly meetings. (An example of an agreement might be that Ms. Fisher will modify Chad's homework assignments to allow for the extra processing time he needs and one of Chad's parents will work with Chad as he completes the assignment to clarify directions and supervise his work.)

Figure 6.3. Attachment to Chad's IEP Specifically Relating to Ms. Fisher's U.S. History Class

4. Whenever Ms. Fisher administers tests to the class that have a bearing on course grades, Chad will take his test for an extended period of time (mutually agreed to by Chad and Ms. Fisher) under the supervision of a paraprofessional (who has been trained by Ms. Fisher in administering her tests and clarifying her directions for Chad) in an appropriate testing location provided by the school administration.

5. Chad engages in the special-education resource activities prescribed by Ms. Eng specifically designed to help him manage his exceptionality and facilitate Ms. Fisher's accommodation of his exceptionality for the U.S. History course.

Special Resources and Support to Implement the Plan

Assistant Principal Crane will make the paraprofessional and testing facility available to Ms. Fisher so that Provision 4 is possible. Ms. Fisher will be provided release from one non-instructional faculty responsibility (e.g., cafeteria supervision) to provide additional time for the conferences and planning alluded to in the provisions. Chad, Chad's parents, and Ms. Eng will be available at reasonable times to consult with Ms. Fisher. Ms. Eng will serve as a resource for ideas and materials.

Figure 6.3. (*continued*)

Engage in Activity 6.2.

▶ *ACTIVITY 6.2*

With two or three colleagues, discuss the following questions in light of Case 6.9.

1. In what ways did Ms. Fisher's assertiveness serve her classroom management needs, Chad's needs, and the needs of other students in her class?

2. What does Attachment 3 to Chad's IEP require Ms. Fisher to do that she would not do if Chad were not in her class?

3. What does Attachment 3 to Chad's IEP require the school administration to do for Ms. Fisher that would not be required if Chad were not in Ms. Fisher's class?

4. How will Ms. Fisher's accommodation of Chad's exceptionality help her keep other students on-task and engaged in learning activities?

▶ ACCOMMODATING AND INCLUDING STUDENTS WITH EMOTIONAL OR BEHAVIORAL DISORDERS

Emotional or behavioral disorder (EBD) refers to a disability that is characterized by affective responses and conduct in school that are so deviant from acceptable age-appropriate norms that educational performance in one or more of the following areas is adversely affected: academics, classroom behavior, personal and work adjustment, self-care, and socialization. To be classified EBD the condition usually is (a) persistent, not only a temporary response to stress; (b) consistently exhibited in at least two settings, one of which is school-related; and (c) unresponsive to the types of interventions typically available in the general education setting (Hallahan & Kauffman, 1997, pp. 214–215; Kerr & Nelson, 1998, pp. 7–10).

For some students, EBD is manifested by *internalizing,* in which they withdraw out of fearfulness and anxiety. Students that internalize tend to be easily embarrassed and hypersensitive. Students who are more readily identified with EBD are those who *externalize*. With externalizing, students act out aggressively with antisocial tendencies. In the classroom, internalizing generally prevents students from engaging in learning activities but without being disruptive. Of course, externalizing generally leads to classroom conduct that is extremely disruptive.

Estimates suggest that between 6% and 10% of the U.S. school-age population suffers from serious emotional or behavioral disorders (American Psychiatric Association, 2000; Brandenburg, Friedman, & Silver, 1990; Kauffman, 1997), with the prevalence of EBD between three and 10 times greater for boys than girls (Heward, 2006, p. 439). The percentage of students who are diagnosed with EBD and provided special education services is somewhat lower (U.S. Department of Education, 2003).

Your classroom management strategies are designed, of course, to encourage students to cooperate with on-task behaviors and discourage them from being off-task. Having students in your classroom with special education classifications other than EBD (e.g., a hearing impairment or learning disability) presents you with classroom management challenges that are indirectly related to the disabilities. For example, Ms. Fisher in Case 6.9 plans strategies (e.g., signaling Chad ahead of time when she wants to call on him) that make it possible for Chad to focus on being on-task. In contrast, when students with EBD are off-task, the behavior is a direct manifestation of their exceptionalities. The classroom management problems you face with the student classified EBD are practically indistinguishable from the disability itself. On one hand, it may be more difficult for you to empathize with the misbehaviors of a student with EBD than with the misbehaviors of students with other types of disabilities. On the other hand, the misbehaviors of a student with EBD are the focus of the special education services as spelled out in the IEP. Thus, support and resources directly related to addressing classroom management problems may be easier for you to obtain for your work with students with EBD than for your work with other students.

A variety of approaches for managing the behaviors of students with EBD are used (see, e.g., Hallahan & Kauffman, 1997, pp. 233–253; Kerr & Nelson, 1998; Levin & Shanken-Kaye, 1996; Lewis & Doorlag, 1991, pp. 206–308). The special education teachers with whom you work on your students' IEP teams should be in a position to suggest prescriptions for the unique needs of each of your students with EBD. Of course, these prescriptions must not only legally accommodate the students' exceptionalities (Turnbull & Turnbull, 1998, pp. 60–64), but they also should contribute to—not distract from—the smooth operation of your unique classroom. The suggestions for dealing with off-task behaviors explained in Chapters 8 through 11 of this textbook should prove helpful in formulating specific prescriptions in IEPs as well as for everyday classroom applications.

Consider Case 6.10.

▶ **CASE 6.10**

Victor Laberta is an eighth-grade student at Sweetbriar Junior High School; he is classified EBD. His IEP team consists of him, Mr. Pitts (his science teacher), Ms. Cedeno (his English teacher),

Ms. Richen (his special education teacher), Ms. Laberta (his mother), and Ms. Krapol (the assistant principal). The initial team meeting to develop the IEP near the opening of the school year is underway. Following is a small part of the conversation:

Ms. Richen: As you can see from copies of the report, Victor has a history of truancies, disruptive classroom behaviors—marked by aggressiveness and hostility toward classmates and teachers—and involvement in fights. There is documented evidence that on three occasions he deliberately damaged school property—

Victor: Don't pretend I was the only—

Ms. Richen: Excuse me, I need to finish speaking without being interrupted. There is documented evidence that on three occasions he deliberately damaged school property and one incident in which he was detained by city police officers for being in possession of stolen school property. There are also accounts of alleged criminal offenses not directly related to school activities. However, I suggest we limit our discussion here to Victor's school-related behaviors—that is, how he will conduct himself so that he affords himself opportunities to succeed here in school and respects the rights of his classmates to learn and of teachers to teach. Of course, we want to build in safeguards to protect his safety as well as the safety of everyone else who is a member of this school community.—Thank you for waiting for me to finish. Victor, is there something you would like to say right now?

Victor: No.

Ms. Krapol: How much of the detail in this report do we need to include in the IEP?

Ms. Richen: The report provides background information to help us describe Victor's exceptionality in section I of the Edgewater School District IEP form. I don't think we should even attach it to the IEP. Let's concentrate on how we will all work together to make progress with Victor managing his behavior in very positive ways. Victor, I would like for you to learn from your history—not be weighed down by it.

The meeting continues as team members discuss what should be included in each section of the IEP. At one point, the following exchange takes place:

Mr. Pitts: I'm happy to have an opportunity to work with Victor in science class. I am concerned about how to accommodate Victor's exceptionality while consistently enforcing classroom standards of conduct equitably for all students. It makes it difficult for my classroom management strategies to work if I have to have one set of behavior expectations for Victor and another set for everybody else.

Victor: Yeah, you do that—you know what I'm sayin'—everyone is gonna think I'm goofy.

Ms. Krapol: And there's the issue of maintaining confidentiality. Victor's exceptionality is no one else's business other than those of us who are directly involved in helping him manage it.

Mr. Pitts: The first priority has to be securing the safety of the classroom environment. The success of our efforts in the classroom depends on establishing a classroom community in which all can be comfortable—without fear of being disrespected or harmed in any way.

Victor: You don't have to be afraid of me. As long as nobody messes with me—you know what I'm saying—I don't bother nobody.

Ms. Laberta: Mr. Pitts isn't afraid of you. He could handle you. Right, Mr. Pitts?

Mr. Pitts: It doesn't matter whether I can or not. I don't tolerate any use of physical force in my classroom—either by me or anyone else. What we need are assurances that physical force will never be needed for us to conduct the business of teaching and learning in a safe and secure classroom.

Victor: I guess it'd be trouble for you—you know what I'm sayin'—if you ever laid a hand on me.

Mr. Pitts: Understand this: No one has the right to hurt another person. I don't have the right to try to hurt you. However, I am responsible for protecting my own safety and the safety of my students—including you—and I'll do what it takes to protect our safety. To do that, I need to make sure that backup is readily available to me so that I can protect our safety without having to use physical force. I will respect you and I expect you to respect me. Just in case someone forgets how to be respectful, I'm insisting that the school provide our classroom with reliable security support and backup for emergency situations.

Ms. Krapol: You have your classroom telephone to call for backup from the office.

Mr. Pitts: Last year, teachers couldn't depend on the phone for emergencies because the system can only handle two calls at a time. Furthermore, the office staff is not always able to respond immediately. If I'm going to conduct a businesslike classroom, I need assurances that I can get competent security help at a moment's notice.

Ms. Cedeno: I feel the same way about my classroom.

Ms. Richen: I've worked with Victor enough to know that he believes a dependable security system would work to his benefit. Victor, I would like for you to share with the group what you told me about how you need help to stay in control.

Victor: Well, you know—sometimes I just hate it when I get mad and—you know what I'm sayin'—I just wish somebody would be there to get me to—like—you know what I'm sayin'—like another planet or something—just make me get away for a while.

Ms. Richen: If we work out a sound procedure, properly trained security personnel could help Victor get away from situations before he acts out in ways he'll regret.

Ms. Krapol: Okay, I'm convinced we need to shore up our phone and security system. Let's make it a provision in as many IEPs as we can. For now we'll dip into the emergency fund and then hopefully we can reimburse ourselves from special ed grants.

Additional provisions are discussed. Finally, everyone has an opportunity to make suggestions about what should be included in each section of the IEP form.

Ms. Richen agrees to develop a first draft for the team to review. In light of the team's feedback, Ms. Richen develops the IEP shown in Figure 6.4, and the team approves it during its next meeting.

Engage in Activity 6.3.

▶ ACTIVITY 6.3

In a discussion with two or three colleagues, respond to the following prompts in light of Case 6.10.

1.   In what ways did Mr. Pitt's assertiveness serve his classroom management needs, Victor's needs, and the needs of other students in his class?

2.   Explain how, if at all, Mr. Pitts adhered to Chapter 4's suggestions (e.g., regarding descriptive, assertive, and supportive communications) in his interactions with Victor during the initial meeting of the IEP team.

3.   What does Victor's IEP require Mr. Pitt to do that he would not do if Victor were not in his class?

4.   What does Victor's IEP require the school administration to do for Mr. Pitt that would not be required if Victor were not in Mr. Pitt's class?

5.   How will Mr. Pitt's accommodation of Victor's exceptionality as specified by Victor's IEP help him keep other students on-task and engaged in learning activities?

▶ ACCOMMODATING AND INCLUDING STUDENTS FOR WHOM ENGLISH IS NOT A FIRST LANGUAGE

More than 15% of students in U.S. public schools speak a non-English language in their homes; the English proficiency of over half of these students is too limited for them to

Edgewater School District

Individualized Education Program (IEP)

Student: Victor J. Laberta   **School:** Sweetbrier Jr. High School   **IEP#:** 1   **Date:** 8/23/06
Birthday: 10/10/93 **Grade:** 8th **Reg. Ed. Teacher:** (6 different teachers) **Sp. Ed. Teacher:** Kathleen Richens

IEP Team: Victor J. Laberta (student), Mildred Laberta (mother), Kathleen Richens (sp. ed. teacher), Natrone Pitts (science teacher), Arlene Cedeno (English teacher), Aretha Kranpool (assistant principal).

I. Description of the Exceptionality

In March 1999, Victor was diagnosed as having a behavioral disability characterized by antisocial conduct directed at classmates and to a lesser degree at teachers and other school personnel. Victor has a habit of "reading into" comments and actions of others as "disrespecting" him. He tends to respond to what he perceives as being "disrespected" with anger that is difficult for him to responsibly manage. He frequently acts out his anger by directing abusive language and threats at others that too often lead to dangerous physical confrontations.

Besides the threat of violent behavior that Victor poses in the classroom, Victor struggles with complying with common standards of classroom conduct. It is extremely difficult for him to follow routine classroom procedures, especially when they require him to patiently wait his turn or allow others to be the focal point. He has a much easier time complying with directions when they require no more than very few, brief steps rather than complex procedures that tax his patience.

Victor appears to respond very defensively when teachers prompt him to engage in any type of task with which he has not previously been successful. He resists attempting tasks which he has never before attempted or which he perceives he has failed with in the past. He is likely to respond to a teacher's directions to attempt such tasks with a verbal attack toward the teacher for presenting the task and toward other students for complying with the teacher's directions.

His unwillingness to attempt new or difficult tasks is linked to poor rate of engagement in classroom activities, low rate of doing homework assignments, and high absentee rate.

Victor applies a destructive strategy to protect himself from what he perceives as "disrespect" by lashing out at others who put him in a position where he must either risk failure with a task or fail to take the risk.

Figure 6.4. IEP for Victor

II. Present Functioning Level

A. Psychomotor Achievement:

Victor's psychomotor functioning level is excellent. It is not affected by his exceptionality.

B. Affective Achievement (including motivation, effort, conduct, and cooperation):

Victor's exceptionality interferes with his progress with affective achievement. Consequently, this is the area in which he has major needs for remediation. His level of functioning regarding the following is inadequate for him to successfully work in school:

- socialization with others—especially peers—and especially how he responds to fear of being "disrespected"
- willingness to attempt school-related tasks
- anger management
- anti-social responses
- willingness to stay with tasks
- assertiveness

Victor functions in the following affective areas extremely well:

- aesthetic appreciation—especially with respect to music and visual arts
- willingness to help others—especially at times when he's not angry or responding to a perception of being "disrespected"

C. Cognitive Achievement:

As suggested by his school academic records (e.g., summative evaluation reports), Victor's academic performance has been unsatisfactory. His achievements in the language arts and social studies appear to be superior to those in mathematics, science, and technical education. It is difficult to assess the cause-and-effect relationship between his exceptionality and cognitive achievement.

III. Goals for the School Year

A. Psychomotor Achievement:

The psychomotor goals for the school year for Victor are the same as those for the general 8th-grade population at Sweetbrier Junior High School. See appropriate curriculum guides for details.

Figure 6.4. (*continued*)

B. Affective Achievement (including motivation, effort, conduct, and cooperation):

Besides subject-specific affective goals stated in curriculum guides for the courses Victor is taking, Victor is to work toward the following goals during the 2006–2007 school year:

1. Victor will be willing to consider alternative interpretations of others' behaviors and communications—alternatives to interpretations suggesting that he is being "dis-respected."
2. Victor will be willing to manage anger in a pro-social manner.
3. Victor will progressively increase the rate at which he is on-task in the classroom (i.e., complying with teachers' directions and engaged in learning activities) and reduce the rate at which he is off-task.
4. Victor will progressively increase the rate at which he complies with classroom standards of conduct for which teachers are responsible for enforcing.
5. Victor will progressively increase the rate at which he interacts with students, teachers, and other school personnel in an assertive (as opposed to a hostile or passive) manner.
6. Victor will avoid physical confrontations (e.g., fights), choosing instead to resolve conflicts in a prosocial manner (e.g., by utilizing the Sweetbrier Junior High Peer Mediation program).
7. Victor will collaborate with his mother, Ms. Richens, and other teachers to develop and apply strategies for accomplishing these six affective goals.

C. Cognitive Achievement:

Besides subject-specific cognitive goals stated in curriculum guides for the courses Victor is taking, Victor is to work toward the following goals during the 2006–2007 school year that involve the development of the skills necessary to put the 7 aforementioned affective goals into practice:

1. Victor will increase his understanding of why people choose to behave and interact as they do and his knowledge of fundamental principles of interpersonal communications.
2. Victor will develop anger-management skills.
3. Victor will develop specific study skills.
4. Victor will develop specific techniques for communicating assertively and avoiding the passive-aggressive cycle.
5. Victor will develop conflict-resolution and peer-mediation skills.

**IV. Plan for Accomplishing the Goals from III
while Accommodating the Exceptionality**

Victor will engage in learning activities as directed by his teachers as is expected for other students in his classes but with the following provisions:

Figure 6.4. (*continued*)

1. Whenever Victor believes that in one of his classes he is on the verge of "losing it" (i.e., is in serious danger of mismanaging his emotions [e.g., anger]), he will politely, discreetly, and assertively signal to the teacher that he needs to go directly to the school's "time-out" room where he can remain quietly with the "time-out" counselor until he feels well enough in control to engage in classroom activities. As long as Victor follows the required procedures, the teacher will allow Victor to go to the "time-out" room. Similarly, whenever a teacher believes Victor may be on the verge of mismanaging his emotions, the teacher will politely, discreetly, and assertively signal Victor to go directly to the school's "time-out" room until the teacher sends word to the "time-out" counselor that Victor should return to class. As long as the teacher follows the required procedures, Victor will comply with the directive.

2. Victor will enroll in the training program for peer mediators and serve as a peer mediator when called upon to do so.

3. For any serious conflicts he experiences with other students, Victor will submit requests for mediating the conflict with the school's peer mediation program.

4. Working in collaboration with Ms. Richens, Victor will complete the *Assertive Communications Strategies* module (Cangelosi & Petersen, 1998) over the course of the year.

5. Teachers will provide Ms. Richens with weekly progress reports regarding Victor's classroom conduct and level of cooperation. Ms. Richens will consult with teachers as well as work with Victor in light of these reports.

6. At least twice a month, Victor's IEP team will meet to assess progress, consider changes in the IEP plan, and to devise short-term goals and plans for reaching those goals.

Any violations of schoolwide discipline and safety codes or violations of teachers' standards for classroom conduct will be handled as they would be for other general education students. However, any disciplinary action involving exclusion from regular classroom activities for more than part of a single class period will be immediately called to Ms. Richens's attention by the parties involved in the decision. As needed, Ms. Richens will consult with teachers and school administrators regarding adherence to IDEA policies.

V. Special Resources and Support Required to Implement the Plan from IV

- School-provided supervised "time-out" room for designated students to get away from their classrooms to "cool off" or to wait until the teacher in charge has time to work individually with the student.
- School-provided dependable, efficient security and intra-school communication system by which teachers can immediately obtain backup support for crisis classroom situations.

Figure 6.4. (*continued*)

- Cooperation and support of the school administration and Victor's IEP team for implementing this IEP plan.
- Inservice training and consulting services for teachers who work with students with EBD.

Provisions of this IEP agreed to by the IEP Team as indicated by the following signatures:

Uschi Sample	date	Amy Sample & Derek Sample	date
Sonia W. Corona	date	Candace Diggart	date
Elwood L. Shinkle	date	Jim Messina	date

Figure 6.4. (*continued*)

participate fully in learning activities in which the English language is the primary means for communicating (Reeves, 2006). Spanish is the first language of approximately 75% of students classified as limited English proficient (LEP). Vietnamese, Hmong, Cantonese, Cambodian, or Korean is the first language of 10% of LEP students. Native American languages are spoken by about 2.5 percent of LEP students (Fleischman & Hopstock, 1993).

Grossman (1995, p. 50) stated,

> In many schools, students with limited English proficiency are placed in the regular education program, where they are taught in English without regard to their linguistic needs instead of being placed in an English as a second language (ESL) program or a sheltered English program. Submerged in English without the skills necessary to profit from instruction they receive, these students are at risk for joining the ranks of students who tune out their teachers, misbehave, cut classes, and drop out of education before graduating from high school.

Grossman (1995, pp. 116–117) further stated,

> Research indicates that instructing students for part of the day in their native language while they are learning English as a second language helps them adjust better than if they attend school where almost every transaction is in English (Silva, 1985). The Bilingual Education Act of 1988 provides that limited-English-proficient students may be instructed bilingually for 3 years and up to 5 years, if needed, to bridge the transition from their native language to English. When bilingual education is not a viable option, students can be placed in programs that combine sheltered English instruction, in which basic English is used to teach students their academic subjects, with English as a second language instruction to improve their advanced English skills. While not as desirable as bilingual education, these programs are

preferable to merely submerging non-English-proficient students in regular classes taught in English, where they either sink or swim.

Adapting your instructional and classroom management techniques to the learning styles of these students while they acquire the skills necessary to learn in American classrooms can enhance their learning. It may also reduce the likelihood that students will be frustrated, angry, anxious, or resentful in class.

Typically, students who are in the process of learning English as a second language develop their conversational skills with English much faster than they develop their proficiency for profiting from academic lessons taught in English (Khisty, 1997). Thus, don't assume that because a student is able to converse with you one-to-one in English that the student can follow complex, multifaceted instruction in English requiring her or him to listen, read, write, speak, and employ other communication structures (e.g., interpret body language and illustrations).

Of course, the success of your strategies for accommodating and including students for whom English is not a first language depends on your understanding of each student as an individual. Case 6.11 is a continuation of Case 6.2, in which Professor Rita Simon conducts a teaching methods course that is field-based at Eastside Middle School.

▶ **CASE 6.11**

For Ms. Rose's science class, Amos Eisely demonstrates an experiment designed to lead the students to discover Newton's Third Law of Motion. He then directs the students to work in groups of three to formulate hypotheses based on the results of the experiment. Throughout the time Amos conducts the lesson, his teaching partner, Maggie Goldstein, carefully monitors students' engagement.

The following morning in the teaching methods class meeting, Amos and Maggie are in the midst of discussion with the other preservice teachers and Professor Simon about the lesson Amos conducted:

Maggie: Nearly all the students really seemed to get into the lesson. I'd say 90% of the time in which Amos was explaining and demonstrating the experiment, 25 of the 29 students were highly engaged. The engagement rates fluctuated more, but stayed very high, during the group work. And at no time did I detect any disruptive off-task behaviors—unless you consider Cindy's, Lorita's, and Lena's constant, but low, talking disruptive.

Amos: It disrupted their own engagement, but not that of the other students because they kept to themselves and their voices down.

Maggie: They talked among themselves incessantly—during Amos's explanations as well as during the group activity—but I don't think the conversations had much to do with Newton's Third Law of Motion.

Henry: What were they talking about?

Maggie: I can't be sure because I don't understand Spanish.

Prof. S.: This would be a good time for Maggie and Amos to tell us about Cindy's, Lorita's, and Lena's special circumstances in Ms. Rose's class.

Maggie: Cindy speaks Spanish only—no English at all. Lorita is bilingual with Spanish as her first language, but she's fluent with English. Lena is also bilingual with Spanish as a first language. Lena's conversational English is functional, but she has limited English proficiency. Her functioning level as far as reading and writing in English and comprehending presentations in English like the one Amos gave yesterday is pretty low.

Amos: Ms. Rose, their regular teacher, nearly always has the three of them working together so that Lorita can help the other two—especially Cindy—know what's going on.

Henry: Shouldn't they learn English before we're expected to teach them?

Amos: Lorita functions just fine with English or Spanish, but Cindy for sure needs to be in an intensive English program.

Malinda: Is Cindy in Eastside's bilingual education program?

Maggie: All three are so that they can experience some instruction in their native language. But this particular program doesn't include much in the way of intensive English instruction.

Henry: Unless we speak Spanish ourselves we can't teach students like Cindy. And even if we could, what about all the other LEP students whose first languages are Tongan, Vietnamese, Chinese, and so on. No one can expect us to teach in all those languages.

Jana: The solution is to pull Cindy out of her classes and have her concentrate on a good intensive English course. Then, after a while, she'll be ready to return to regular classes.

Maggie: So, Jana, you think we should recommend that Cindy, and possibly Lena, be referred to an intensive English course?

Jana: Right, until their English is up to speed.

Prof. S.:   If Cindy were removed from the class to take intensive English, Amos and Maggie would no longer be faced with the classroom management dilemma of keeping her engaged in learning activities. That would solve the problem. Hmm, that makes me think about something.—You know, I've seen Cindy walking to school in the morning. There's always the possibility that she could be hit by a car or something crossing the street, and then she wouldn't be in class tomorrow when Amos is scheduled to teach another lesson. That would keep us from having to face the—

Amos: That's a horrible thing for you to say Dr. Simon! I'm shocked that you would even imagine such a terrible event! Cindy is a sweetheart that we've grown to care for over the past weeks! That's an awful thing for you to say!

Prof. S.:   It was a terrible thing for me to say. But the direction this conversation was going got me to thinking that the probability of having Cindy transferred out of Ms. Rose's class and into an intensive English class before your next lesson is a whole lot lower than the probability that a catastrophic event will keep Cindy from being in class and, thus, keep us from having to address the problem.

Amos: The problem being how to plan the lesson so that Cindy is included despite her being unable to function in English. I see your point. I apologize for attacking you; I was just so shocked at the thought of something so awful happening to that darling Cindy.

Prof. S.:   No apology needed. I would have been disappointed if you had reacted any other way. The fact of the matter is that you know Cindy as a unique individual—not simply some data point labeled "NEP" or "non-English proficient"—that can be dealt with via some administrative referral process.

Henry: So you think it's a bad idea to have her referred to an intensive English program?

Prof. S.:   To the contrary, not only do I think it's a good idea to refer Cindy to an intensive English program, I think it's imperative that we speak with Ms. Rose about doing so. But that doesn't mean she has to be excluded from her regular classes. And even if it did, I guarantee you it won't happen before tomorrow when Amos is scheduled to teach the class. Cindy is a living and breathing person who, if we're fortunate, is going to show up in class today and tomorrow, and Amos will be faced with the problem of teaching her in a way that accommodates her exceptionality. Amos, you've got a pedagogical and classroom management problem. How are you going to get it solved by tomorrow when you have a lesson to teach?

Maggie: On one hand, I think it would be a good idea to break up the trio of Cindy, Lena, and Lorita to increase their involvement with the rest of the class. At least Lorita could be engaged without having to worry about explaining things to Cindy and Lena.

Amos: If only that's what she really did. But more and more they just gab away in Spanish, hardly ever talking about anything to do with the lesson.

Maggie: That's why I think the trio should be split up for activities. But on the other hand, Ms. Rose indicated that they are more comfortable in class in one another's company. Cindy, in particular, is completely left out of things without Lorita or Lena there to give her some ideas of what's going on. No one else in the class knows enough Spanish to work with her.

Carrie: All of us agree that Cindy should learn to function with English. So why don't you and Amos come up with a plan in which you model learning in a second language yourself—namely Spanish. What if you got Cindy—with Lorita's or Lena's help—to teach some Spanish to the rest of the class?

Amos: That's cool! Or what if I got Cindy with both Lorita's and Lena's help—I'm not yet ready to break up the trio—to demonstrate and explain a science experiment to the class in Spanish? Remember this a science class—we need to keep the focus on science as we begin to pull Cindy into the class with an activity that uses the communication medium with which she is most comfortable. Great idea, Carrie! Thank you.

Jana: But how will the other students be able to engage in an activity conducted in Spanish?

Carrie: For one thing, they'll learn an appreciation for what Cindy goes through every day and maybe they'll learn something that'll lead them to work better with Cindy and Lena.

Amos: But even from a learning-science perspective, I think the idea has merit. One of the major pushes in the national curriculum standards for teaching science is to have students communicate about science. Having a scientific demonstration accompanied by explanations in a strange tongue could prompt students to raise a lot of questions leading to back-and-forth translations among Cindy, Lena, or Lorita, and the rest of the class. This could have some real advantages relative to precision of communication with science—something very important to scientific thinking.

Anastasia: Won't Cindy feel strange trying this? Does she know enough science to pull it off?

Maggie: She would, of course, have to be willing to give it a try. Knowing her, I think with some assertive prodding from us she'll be okay with it.

Amos: The demonstration and explanation would have to be very brief—not more than 10 minutes. We'd have to pick a science topic that would be new to the class, but something we could teach Cindy to do with Lena's and Lorita's help ahead of time.

Maggie: Let's figure out a straightforward experiment, then work it out with the three of them so that they all know exactly what to do. Cindy will conduct the demonstration and the explanations while Lena and Lorita are nearby to clarify and fill in the holes. It would turn into a mixture of Spanish and English. I love it.

Amos: But we've got a lot of planning to do even before we run the idea by Ms. Rose for her approval.

Prof. S.: One question before you ask me to be excused to start planning for this event: Is this going to be a one-time-only event or will you continue to put Cindy on stage for subsequent lessons?

Maggie: I think we ought to try this out with the one brief demonstration and then decide how to proceed later in light of what we learn. The whole thing could backfire.

Amos: I agree. What I hope will happen is that we decide to rotate the presentations among all the students, with even the English-speaking students mixing in some Spanish into their explanations.

Henry: How would that be possible?

Amos: Lorita and Lena could serve the same role they serve for Cindy's demonstration for other students as well—only in reverse—you know, filling in with some Spanish when the demonstration is in English just as they fill in with some English when the demonstration is presented in Spanish.

Maggie: Understand that they wouldn't be doing full translations—just plugging in a clarification here and there so that all students would be picking up both English and Spanish explanations that go along with the demonstrations. Everybody can see what's going on with the demonstration and hear which Spanish or English words go along with what they see.

Henry: I'm starting to see how this might have a slight chance of working with two languages. But what if you've got a bunch of other kids in class whose first language varies from Korean to Russian to Italian?

Amos: I wouldn't know what to do. Fortunately, we don't have that problem in Ms. Rose's class. I guess you have to tackle each unique classroom situation head-on to come up with a unique solution to each unique problem. I don't think there are any generic solutions.

Maggie: Dr. Simon, may we—

Prof. S.: Maggie and Amos, I think you should excuse yourselves and get to work on your plan for tomorrow's activities.

Engage in Activity 6.4.

► *ACTIVITY 6.4*

In a discussion with two or three colleagues, respond to the following prompts in light of Case 6.11.

1. Explain why the productive learning experience Professor Simon's preservice teachers had was possible because her methods course was organized so that they worked with students for an extended period of time rather than only for a one-time microteach as in Professor Chementier's methods course in Case 6.1.

2. What do you think Professor Simon was trying to accomplish with her provocative comment about the possibility of Cindy being hit by a car? What are the advantages and disadvantages of using such a tactic?

3. Critique the strategy Maggie and Amos planned to use to accommodate Cindy's exceptionality.

► BENEFITTING FROM CULTURAL DIVERSITY

In Case 6.11, Amos and Maggie addressed a classroom management problem emanating from a difference in the language experiences of students. They realized that to gain and maintain all students' engagement they had to rethink their instructional practices. Their plan for building on Cindy's Spanish skills and Lorita's and Lena's bilingual skills turned a classroom management dilemma into a pedagogical advantage. As Amos envisioned the lesson stemming from Carrie's idea, the science learning of all students in the class will benefit because of the difference in languages.

Besides the science-education benefits of the plan, there is, of course, the advantage of the classroom community valuing Spanish—a deeply rooted part of Cindy's, Lena's, and Lorita's culture. By conducting learning activities in ways that take advantage of language differences as well as other multicultural traits, you encourage cooperation and on-task behaviors. Students are more likely to be cooperative participants in a classroom community that is in harmony with their origins and families. Students with different cultural experiences are more likely to cooperate with one another if they understand, value, and learn from one another's differences. If they don't, misunderstanding of differences leads to fear, mistrust, divisiveness, and even hostility.

Your own understanding and appreciation of cultural diversity will serve you well as you develop strategies for motivating students to be on-task and engaged.

Furthermore, you are hardly in a position to elicit students' cooperation unless you are aware of differences that cause an action or communication to be perceived as a compliment within one subculture and an insult within another. The success of your teaching depends on staying abreast of multicultural issues and instructional strategies. Fortunately, a massive reservoir of instructional materials and ideas on how to implement multicultural instructional strategies exists in professional literature and media sources (e.g., see Avery [2005], Banks & Banks [2001], Black [2006], Carnes [1999], Franklin [2001], Peebles-Wilkins [2006], and Setati [2005] as well as the Web site www.teachingtolerance.org).

In Case 6.12, a teacher takes advantage of the cultural diversity in her geometry class.

▶ CASE 6.12

Building on ideas generated from working with this book's Chapter 3, "Establishing a Favorable Climate for Cooperation," Ms. Willis creates the tasksheet shown in Figure 6.5 and administers it to her high-school geometry students on the first day of class.

Ms. Willis designed the tasksheet with several goals in mind:

- The students will begin to get the following impressions about the course:
    - The geometry they will be learning is related to their own individual interests, backgrounds, and experiences.
    - The are expected to make judgments, and their judgments are valued.
    - They are expected to write about geometry.
    - Their experiences in this course will be different from those they've had in previous mathematics courses.
- Students will begin doing geometry by having to describe what they see in terms of relationships among figures imbedded in real-world images.
- Ms. Willis will begin to gain some insights about their individual personalities, tastes, interests, families, neighborhoods, and backgrounds.
- Ms. Willis will elicit some information that will help her begin to identify aspects of their individual cultural experiences on which she can build and incorporate into lessons she plans to teach throughout the course.
- Students' initial experience in the course will expose them to multicultural aspects of the world they'll be examining from a geometer's perspective.

Throughout the course, Ms. Willis draws on her knowledge of her students' cultural experiences to design her lessons. For example, as part of a unit on geometric constructions, she asks each student to apply congruence theorems by creating an image using only a compass and a straightedge. The image is to reflect a significant aspect of the student's family, neighborhood, or home. One student's work, reproduced in Figure 6.6, reflects the fact that his father works in a plant that manufactures rocket boosters.

As part of a unit on slope, Ms. Willis has students examine the pitch on various structures in their neighborhood. One student lives with her uncle who moves about in a wheelchair. She reports on the angle of inclination of the ramp that her uncle uses to enter and exit their apartment. This and other such units help students connect schoolwork to their family backgrounds and neighborhoods. The strategy also helps foster an understanding and appreciation for the diversity in the classroom. The benefit to Ms. Willis is a smoother-operating classroom where students are inclined to cooperate with one another.

1. What is your name? _____

2. Carefully look at the following two pictures of artwork:

Write a description of how one of the pieces of artwork looks different from the other.

_____

_____

_____

_____

_____

Write a description of how one of the pieces of artwork looks the same as the other.

_____

_____

_____

_____

_____

Figure 6.5. Tasksheet Ms. Willis Administered to Her Geometry Students the First Day of Class

3. Carefully look at the clothing worn by the people in the following two pictures:

Write a description of how the clothing in one of the pictures looks different from the clothing in the other picture.

_____

_____

_____

_____

_____

Write a description of how one of the pieces of clothing looks the same as the other.

_____

_____

_____

_____

_____

4. Carefully look at the following two types of writing characters:

שמזוהדגבא פמלנמשעת	AaBZwqLT utjpCdeRfm

Figure 6.5. (*continued*)

Write a description of how one of the types of characters looks different from the other.

_____

_____

_____

_____

_____

Write a description of how one of the types of characters looks the same as the other.

_____

_____

_____

_____

_____

5. Carefully look at the following two types of buildings:

Write a description of how one of the buildings looks different from the other.

_____

_____

_____

_____

_____

Figure 6.5. (*continued*)

Write a description of how one of the buildings looks the same as the other.

_____

_____

_____

_____

_____

6. List three things about your family, your neighborhood, or your home that you think are different from most of the other students' families, neighborhoods, or homes.

1) _____

_____

2) _____

_____

3) _____

7. List three things about your family, your neighborhood, or your home that you think are the same as most of the other students' families, neighborhoods, or homes.

1) _____

_____

2) _____

_____

3) _____

8. List three important questions about which you're going to have to make a decision during the next nine months.

1) _____

_____

2) _____

_____

3) _____

Figure 6.5. (_continued_)

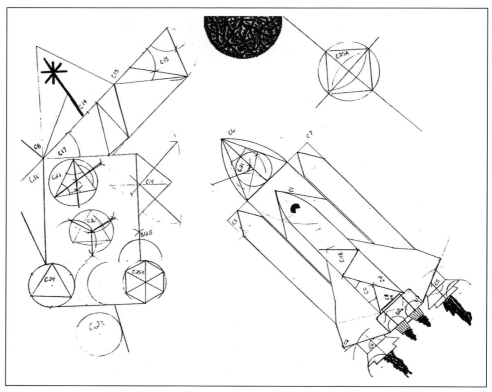

Figure 6.6. The Compass-and-Straightedge Image Produced by a Student Whose Father Works at a Rocket-Booster Production Plant (Reprinted with permission from Johnson [1997].)

▶ SYNTHESIS ACTIVITIES FOR CHAPTER 6

I. Reflect back on an academically and pedagogically sound lesson plan that you once designed. Address the following questions about the lesson plan:

    A. When you designed the lesson, did you do so for a specific group of students with whom you had previously worked and observed, and, thus, whom you had gotten to know individually?

    B. How does the design of the lesson incorporate strategies for encouraging student engagement?

    C. If your answer to Question A was "yes," how did your knowledge of the individual students in the class influence both your design of the lesson and your plan for incorporating classroom management strategies? If your answer to Question A was "no," think of a unique group of students with whom you have worked in the past—that is, students whom you know individually. Then redesign your lesson plan specifically for that group of students.

II. Share and discuss your responses to Synthesis Activity I with several colleagues who also engaged in that activity.

III.   In collaboration with a colleague, critique the way Mr. Eisley deals with Carter's disruptive behavior in Case 6.2.

IV.   With several colleagues, discuss the advantages and disadvantages of the IEP provision of IDEA.

V.   Interview two in-service teachers. Ask them how having students with special education classifications in their classrooms affects their classroom management strategies. Also ask about the extent of their participation on students' IEP teams.

VI.   While being careful not to violate the confidentiality of individual classroom situations, discuss the outcomes of the interviews you and your colleagues conducted when responding to Synthesis Activity V.

VII.   Obtain and view a copy of the videotape, *Understanding Learning Disabilities: How Difficult Can This Be? The F.A.T. City Workshop* (Lavoie, 1989).

VIII.   Reexamine Ms. Willis's tasksheet in Figure 6.5. Resurrect the opening-day tasksheet resulting from your engagement in Activity 3.1. Consider modifying the tasksheet so that it better takes advantage of the cultural diversity in your classroom.

IX.   Visit the Web site http://www.teachingtolerance.org. Familiarize yourself with the wealth of resources available to you at no cost.

▶ TRANSITIONAL ACTIVITY FROM CHAPTER 6 TO CHAPTER 7

In preparation for your work with Chapter 7, discuss with two or more colleagues the following questions.

I.   What strategies do teachers employ to motivate students to be on-task and engaged in learning activities?

II.   Why is it that a subject (e.g., history, mathematics, or science) that seems so boring in the hands of one teacher can be so exciting and interesting in the hands of another teacher?

III.   What strategies do teachers employ to help students understand and follow directions?

IV.   What strategies do teachers employ to keep students engaged in each of the following types of learning-activity sessions?

- Lecture
- Cooperative learning
- Discussion
- Questioning
- Independent work

V.   What are the preferable methods of motivating students to do homework assignments?

VI.   How should classrooms be arranged for smooth, efficient operation of the business of learning?

PART III

MOTIVATING STUDENTS TO ENGAGE IN LEARNING ACTIVITIES

7

Conducting and Monitoring Engaging Learning Activities

▶ CHAPTER 7'S GOAL AND OBJECTIVES

The goal of this chapter is for you to develop strategies for conducting and monitoring learning activities so that students willingly and enthusiastically engage in them. Specifically, Chapter 7 is designed to lead you to achieve the following objectives.

1. Develop ideas for designing problem-based lessons so that students are intrinsically motivated to engage in learning activities.

2. Develop techniques that encourage students to be on-task when you are directing them into learning activities.

3. Develop ideas for conducting learning activities so that you are able to monitor student engagement and demonstrate withitness.

4. Develop techniques that encourage students to be engaged during the following types of learning activity sessions: (a) lecture, (b) cooperative learning, (c) discussion, (d) questioning, (e) independent work, and (f) homework.

5. Develop ideas for creating classroom arrangements that facilitate students' on-task behavior and engagement in learning activities.

▶ PROBLEM-BASED LEARNING

Non-Problem-Based Approach

Unlike the other cases in this book, Case 7.1 is purely fictitious; it never happened, and let's hope it never will.

▶ CASE 7.1

Mr. Doe teaches a high school carpentry course by first conducting a unit on inserting nails into wood with a hammer. The second unit is on sawing lumber. Subsequent lessons include measuring planks, squaring corners, joining ends, selecting materials, sanding, inserting screws, the care of a drill, workshop safety, and using a drill press. Mr. Doe's students study and practice each skill in isolation from the other skills.

What do you think of Mr. Doe's fictitious course? It is organized ridiculously. Industrial arts teachers don't teach skills in isolation. Typically, carpentry teachers have students undertake a project through which they learn necessary skills by applying them to some task. Projects may be individualized; perhaps one student builds a bookcase, another a doghouse. In some cases, the entire class may focus on one large project, such as the construction of a portable classroom building. Unlike Mr. Doe, most all industrial arts teachers provide students with learning activities that teach students special skills and the integrated applications of those skills to solve real-life problems (e.g., how to build something people need).

Like all other cases in this book—except for Case 7.1—Case 7.2 reflects an actual event.

▶ **CASE 7.2**

Mr. Ullrich conducts a mathematics unit on equivalent fractions for his sixth graders by (a) lecturing on the importance of understanding fractions, (b) explaining the rules for expressing fractional equivalents, (c) demonstrating several examples on the overhead projector, (d) assigning practice exercises, (e) providing individual help with exercises, (f) assigning textbook exercises, and (g) reviewing the homework in class.

Mr. Ullrich's learning activities are fairly standard for academic subjects (Cangelosi, 2003, pp. 130–138; Jesunathadas, 1990). As in Mr. Doe's fictional lesson, techniques and ideas are often taught in isolation from their real-world applications. Mr. Ullrich lectures students on the importance of what they are to learn, but do you really think his students will be intrinsically motivated to be engaged in the learning activities on fractions because of what he says? If Mr. Ullrich follows the example of most industrial arts teachers and designs his unit so that it focuses on problems that students are concerned with, then students would discover the value of learning about fractions for themselves.

Problem-Based Approach

In Case 7.3, the problem-based approach is used to teach sixth graders about equivalent fractions.

▶ **CASE 7.3**

Ms. Olson has observed her 24 sixth graders at Westdale School long enough to understand what interests them. In planning a mathematics unit on equivalent fractions, she decides to take advantage of (a) the interest some have in the basketball season, (b) a class social for which they are planning to bake three cakes, and (c) physical education activities in which students are running various distances for time.

She begins by assigning six students to the basketball group, nine to the cake group, and nine to the running group. While the other 18 are working on assignments, she engages the basketball group in a conversation:

Ms. Olson: How do you think our Westdale boys' basketball team is doing this year?
Antoine: Oh! We're doing okay. We're gonna beat Sixth Avenue today. You watch!

Ms. Olson: I will. What's our record?

Mary: We've won three.

Gene: Yeah, and lost two.

Antoine: Yeah, but we would've won those if it wasn't for the refs.

Ms. Olson: What's your favorite NBA team, Alphonse?

Alphonse: The Utah Jazz! I like the Utah Jazz!

Antoine: Aw, I like the Lakers.

Ms. Olson: Who's doing better this year—the Jazz or Westdale?

Antoine: The Jazz may be better, but we win more.

Mary: You're crazy! The Jazz have won a lot more games.

Antoine: Well, sure! They play more.

Marcia: Yeah, they also lose more.

Ms. Olson: Okay, wait a minute. We have a game today. Antoine, your mathematics assignment is to report Westdale's win-loss record to the class tomorrow.

Antoine: I can tell you that now. It'll be four and two; you watch.

Ms. Olson: Alphonse, your job is to look up the Jazz's record in the morning paper and report it to the class.

Mary: What for?

Ms. Olson: We're going to figure out who is having a better year, Westdale or the Jazz.

In a similar fashion, Ms. Olson meets with the cake group. She directs some of those students to report figures from recipes that are designed to serve seven. The recipes will be used to bake cakes for Ms. Olson and the class of 24.

Her meeting with the running group leads them to report times for different distances they are to run during physical education that afternoon.

The following day, Ms. Olson uses the groups' data to confront the class with a number of problems. Including the following ones. (a) Which team is doing better—Westdale in their 6 games or the Jazz in their 44 games? (b) According to the recipe for seven, how much flour should the class buy to have enough cake to serve 25? (c) Do we run faster in a 30-meter race or a 60-meter race? Ms. Olson uses inductive questioning techniques to help her students discover that such problems can be efficiently solved by using equivalent fractions.

Later in the unit, Ms. Olson explains the rules for expressing fractional equivalents, demonstrates examples, and assigns and reviews exercises. At no point does she bother to tell students how important it is for them to be able to use equivalent fractions skillfully. They have already discovered that for themselves.

According to *Webster's Third New International Dictionary* (1986, p. 1807), a *problem* is a perplexing or difficult question that needs to be answered or something difficult that must be worked out. Because problems suggest difficulties, people are often inclined to think of problems as undesirable. But the existence of problems serves as a strong motivator for human endeavor. A perfectly satisfied person, one who recognizes no problems. Lacks motivation to change and thus to learn. Why would anyone want to learn to read unless that person felt a need to receive a written communication? Why would someone want to learn how to drive nails unless there is a need to build or repair something? Do people ever write unless they have something to communicate? Outside a mathematics course, do people ever work with equivalent fractions without first being confronted with problems they are motivated to solve?

Intrinsic Motivation Via the Problem-Based Approach

Students can be intrinsically motivated to engage cooperatively in learning activities when those activities focus on problems the students feel a need to solve. Learning activities, such as those typically conducted by industrial arts teachers and by Ms. Olson in Case 7.3 that confront students with real-world problems are *problem-based learning activities.* The goals of some teaching units may not lend themselves to problem-based learning activities. For such situations, you need to use extrinsic motivators to ensure student engagement. When well-organized problem-based activities are used, however, obtaining students' cooperation and engagement is usually a much easier task for a teacher. Cases 7.4 and 7.5 are examples of teachers using problem-based learning activities.

► **CASE 7.4**

Ms. Piscatelli designs a two-week unit to help her high school history students better understand the activities of the U.S. Congress in the first third of the twentieth century. Ms. Piscatelli observes her students to identify current issues that concern them. She decides to focus on the following problems: (a) Should marijuana be legalized? (b) What should the federal government do about unemployment? (c) What should Congress do to ensure the rights of ethnic minorities? (d) Does the United States need an equal rights amendment? (e) What should the federal government do about abortions? (f) What stand should the federal government take on combating pollution?

The learning activities include the following:

1. Ms. Piscatelli assigns each class member to one of six cooperative task groups. One group, consisting of five students, is directed to examine how Congress handled the prohibition of alcohol in the first third of the twentieth century and then relate those lessons of history to the current question about marijuana. The group is to report on Congress's rationale for repealing prohibition and identify similarities and differences between the question of alcohol prohibition then and marijuana prohibition now. Each of the other five task groups examines one of the other problems in a similar manner.

2. Each cooperative task group is provided with an organizational structure within which to operate, a list of resources from which to acquire information, a list of deadlines for specific subtasks, and directions on how findings are to be reported to the rest of the class and Ms. Piscatelli.

3. To obtain an overall picture of the climate within which the Congress operated in the first third of the twentieth century and thus be better able to compare problems of that era to current problems. All students are assigned to read the text chapter dealing with the period from 1901 to 1935.

4. Each group reports to the class according to the schedule.

5. After each group reports, other class members discuss the report and propose a solution for solving the current problem.

► **CASE 7.5**

Mr. Cefalo often combines intraclass grouping techniques with problem-based learning activities to accommodate the variety of achievement levels and interests displayed by the 34 tenth graders in his English class. As part of a unit designed to improve students' creative writing abilities, he groups students into pairs and assigns each pair a topic on which information is to be gathered and reported on in writing. Mr. Cefalo uses what he has learned about the students to design the assignment. Herb, for example, is an avid motorcycle racing fan who has not displayed much desire or ability to write. Ron, on the other hand, displays both a knack for and interest in writing but knows hardly anything about motorcycle racing. Thus, Mr. Cefalo pairs Herb with Ron and directs them to write a report on motorcycle racing as it exists in the local community.

Mr. Cefalo figures that Herb will become engaged in the activity because Ron needs his knowledge of motorcycle racing. Ron, who already possesses quality writing skills, should be challenged by the problem of having to write about an unfamiliar topic. Because of their diversity of interests and achievement levels, Herb and Ron both contribute to the completion of the task.

The strategy of confronting students with real-life problems to motivate engagement intrinsically has proven successful at virtually every grade level and school subject. Cases 7.6 to 7.12 are some brief examples.

▶ CASE 7.6

Mr. Byers involves his fourth-grade students in a project to build a scale model of the schoolyard to teach them about ratios and proportions.

▶ CASE 7.7

Ms. Groves discovers that 12 of the juniors in her literature class read below the third-grade level. Realizing that nine of them want to pursue a driver's license, she provides them with the state driver's manual and uses it as a textbook for improving their reading skills. While they focus on learning how to pass the test for a driver's license, they steadily improve their reading levels.

▶ CASE 7.8

Mr. Gervin takes advantage of his fifth graders' desire to decide their own rules for classroom conduct to teach them principles of democratic government.

▶ CASE 7.9

Ms. Robique's suggestion to her kindergarten students that they make greeting cards for their parents is met with considerable enthusiasm. That enthusiasm helps keep them engaged in a learning activity designed to teach them to form manuscript letters while working on greeting cards.

▶ CASE 7.10

While some second-grade students manage a classroom store and others make purchases from it, they acquire some needed computation and reading skills.

▶ CASE 7.11

Mr. Orborson realizes that his seventh graders have an avid interest in television but virtually no interest in history. To stimulate their interest in history, he designs a learning activity in which they are assigned to analyze certain TV shows for historical accuracy. For example, one student is to compare the dress of the actors on two "old West" shows to the dress of persons from that era who appear in history-book photographs.

▷ **CASE 7.12**

While caring for and feeding the inhabitants of the classroom aquarium, preschoolers polish their counting and grouping skills.

Engage in Activity 7.1.

▶ *ACTIVITY 7.1*

Recall two examples of problem based lessons you experienced as a student. What motivated you to engage in those lessons' learning activities? Contrast those lessons to some of the many lessons you experienced that were not problem based. What motivated you to engage in the learning activities of some of those non-problem-based lessons?

Share your examples with a colleague. Discuss how lessons designed from a problem-based approach differ from other lessons.

▶ GIVING DIRECTIONS

Explicitness, Specificity, and Directness

Indirect, nonlinear communications are appropriate for teachers to use as they conduct inquiry-based learning activities designed to stimulate students to reason, appreciate, discover, or create. Case 7.13 is an example.

▷ **CASE 7.13**

During a problem-based learning activity, Ms. Southworth is trying to help her junior high students discover principles of physics that make it possible for airplanes to fly. At one point in the lesson, Judy asks, "What would happen if the wings of the plane were curved on the bottom like they are on top?" Ms. Southworth: "Hmm, I wonder. Let's think about it. In that case, would the air pass over the top surface faster or slower than it would over the bottom surface?" Judy: "I guess that. . . ."

Ms. Southworth knew the answer to Judy's question, but instead of answering it directly, she probed with another question. Nonlinear, evasive communication was appropriate in this situation because Ms. Southworth's objective was to lead Judy to reason, not simply to know the answer. But when instead of stimulating thinking, you are providing students with directions for an upcoming learning activity, your communications should be linear, explicit, specific, and direct.

Ordinarily, you give directions during transition periods just before the start of a learning activity. Directions must be explicit, precise, and concise so that transition time is minimized and allocated time is not wasted because students failed to follow the directions for the learning activity. Consider Cases 7.14, 7.15, 7.16, and 7.17. In which two cases are the teachers' directions clear and to the point? In which two will student engagement in the upcoming learning activity be impaired because the directions don't fully communicate exactly what is to be done?

▷ **CASE 7.14**

Ms. Aldomat is holding a gymnastics class on the basketball court of the Saddle Hill School gym. Just as her 18 third graders complete their routine warm-up and stretching exercises, Ms. Aldomat briskly walks directly to a point in the middle of a foul-shot line on the basketball court. She pivots, faces her students, and blows her whistle for an instant. She holds her hand high above her head with the palm facing the students. The students have learned from previous class periods that the whistle signals an end to one activity and Ms. Aldomat's hand signal means to line up in front of her to wait for directions. As the students quickly move toward her, she says, "Line up on the half-court line, one arm's length apart, facing me." She watches them intently as they line up facing her. As soon as everyone is in position, she drops her hand and points to Jenny who is standing first on the left-hand side of the line. Ms. Aldomat: "Jenny, please do four cartwheels directly forward and then wait on the baseline behind me, facing us." Jenny obliges. Ms. Aldomat: "Thank you. Stay there, Jenny." She continues speaking to the group: "When I say 'start,' I want the rest of you to begin taking turns doing four cartwheels and waiting on the line as Jenny did. We'll begin on this end with Frank. As soon as Frank starts his third cartwheel, Freda goes, then Tamara, and so on down the line. Remember to watch the person to your left. You go as soon as he or she begins the third cartwheel. Ready—start!"

As the students take their turns, Ms. Aldomat positions herself so that she is just out of the way of the student who is about to begin. That helps signal the students to wait for their turns. If a student is late starting, she says nothing but simply gestures with her hand.

▶ **CASE 7.15**

Ms. Duncan is holding a gymnastics class on the basketball court of the Cedar School gym. Just as her 18 third graders complete their routine warm-up and stretching exercises, Ms. Duncan announces, "Okay, okay, that's enough. All right, listen up now. Let's do something else." The last student stops stretching, and the students gather around Ms. Duncan as she says, "We're going to practice our cartwheels now." "Good! Good!" Rhonda yells, jumping up and down. Tommy: "I hate cartwheels! Can't we jump on the trampoline?" "Yeah! Yeah! Let's jump on the trampoline, Ms. Duncan," exclaims Dustin. Ms. Duncan: "We'll do the trampoline another time; it's time to work on cartwheels. Here's what we'll do. Go over to the middle of the court and—" Several students run over to the center circle of the basketball court. The others, not knowing what to do, hesitate before rushing over themselves. Ms. Duncan reluctantly follows and says, "I didn't say to go yet. Now listen. I'm only going to say this once. Form a line." The students form something of a semicircle as they bunch themselves around the center-court circle. Ms. Duncan: "Spread out. Come on! You know what I mean." Finally, the students are positioned and ready to hear Ms. Duncan, who says, "Now one at a time, I want you to do several cartwheels. We'll start on one end and go one at a time. It's your turn when the one ahead of you is halfway through. Okay, let's go."

▶ **CASE 7.16**

Mr. Boudreaux wants to lead his third-period English students through the literal, interpretative, and analytical stages of reading poems. After completing a brief lecture on reading poetry, he directs the students into the next learning activity by distributing copies of Edwin A. Robinson's poem, "Richard Cory," and saying, "I want you to read this wonderful poem carefully and be prepared to discuss it when everyone is finished." Some of the students are beginning to read the poem as Mr. Boudreaux continues to provide direction. Mr. Boudreaux: "Now wait, don't start yet—Anthony, pay attention! Thank you. Okay, now, as I was about to tell you, when you come across a word in the poem that you don't know, look it up in the dictionary and write down the definition." Denise: "Where should we write them?" Mr. Boudreaux: "Just on a sheet of paper—no! I've got a better idea. Write them on the back of your copy of the poem. Then you'll have them together for our discussion. Any other questions? Good! Let's get started."

▶ **CASE 7.17**

Mr. Rice wants to lead his third-period English students through the literal, interpretative, and analytical stages of reading poems. After completing a brief lecture on reading poetry, he distributes a three-page document to each student containing (a) directions on the first page, (b) the poem "Richard Cory" on the second page, and (c) a list of questions for discussion on the third page. Watching their faces closely and seeing that everyone has the document, Mr. Rice raises his hand signaling the students that he expects their attention. Mr. Rice: "Thank you. Let's go through the directions on the first page." Seeing that Blanche is thumbing through the pages, he gently taps her desk top and whispers, "First page." When everyone appears attentive, he reads the following directions aloud, occasionally pausing to clarify or emphasize points:

"After receiving the signal to start, you have 14 minutes to:

1. Take out your pocket dictionary.
2. Read the poem 'Richard Cory' on the next page. As you read it, circle with your pen each unfamiliar vocabulary word. Look it up in your dictionary. Decide for yourself which of the meanings given in the dictionary Robinson meant for that word. Get the number of the page from your dictionary where that word appears. Jot the page number just over the word on your copy of the poem. Be ready to explain your choice of definitions to the class.
3. Read through the questions on the third page of this document.
4. Reread the poem. But this time read it so that you are prepared to discuss the answers to the questions with the class.
5. After the 14 minutes are up, we will have a two-part class discussion. The first part will focus on the vocabulary words. The second part will focus on the questions.

'Richard Cory' is rather brief; the third page consists of the following questions:

1. What is meant in the poem by the following?
    - 'he was always human when he talked' (line 6)
    - 'he glittered when he walked' (line 8)
    - 'And went without meat and cursed the bread' (line 14)
2. Was Richard Cory happy? Why or why not?
3. How did others think of him? Did they think he was happy? What lines from the poem support your answer?"

Nine Points about Directions

Ms. Aldomat's and Mr. Rice's explicit directions communicated what students were to do during learning activities more exactly and efficiently than either Ms. Duncan's or Mr. Boudreaux's. Ms. Aldomat and Mr. Rice took advantage of the following:

1. The students of teachers who display businesslike attitudes are more likely to follow directions efficiently than students of teachers who seem lackadaisical and less organized. Both Ms. Aldomat and Mr. Rice appeared to know exactly what tasks students were expected to complete and had well-organized plans for accomplishing those tasks.

2. As Jones (1979) has pointed out, teachers' body language is a powerful medium for communicating expectations to students. By briskly walking to the point where she wanted to give directions, deliberately positioning herself, directly facing students, and establishing eye contact with her shoulders parallel to the students', Ms. Aldomat communicated that her directions were to be heard and strictly followed.

3. Because giving directions is a frequent, routine occurrence in a classroom, teachers can minimize transition time, streamline communication procedures, display a more businesslike attitude, and reduce the amount of teacher talk in classrooms by establishing signals or cues that instantaneously communicate certain recurring expectations to students. Nonverbal signals are particularly effective. From their prior experiences in her class, Ms. Aldomat's students knew exactly how to respond to her whistle, her hand over her head, and even her body language. Similarly, Mr. Rice had conditioned his students to react appropriately to certain signals.

4. Speaking to students who are not attentively listening is not only a waste of time and energy but also encourages inattentive behavior patterns. By deliberately gaining at least the appearance of everyone's attention before providing directions, teachers communicate the seriousness of the directions and increase the chances that the directions will be followed. Both Ms. Aldomat and Mr. Rice achieved eye contact with students to ascertain that students were ready to listen and to signal that they expected to be heard before beginning to speak. Had students' attention not been obtained quickly, then they would have resorted to more decisive methods for dealing with student inattentiveness—a topic of Chapters 8 to 11.

5. Students who have learned that their teacher usually says things only once tend to listen the first time the teacher speaks. Ms. Duncan said, "I'm only going to say this once," but she probably repeated herself anyway because her initial directions were so vague.

6. Students are more likely to listen carefully to the directions of teachers who restrict their remarks to exactly what students need to know to engage successfully in the upcoming learning activity. Neither Ms. Aldomat nor Mr. Rice mixed uninformative, inane words with directions, unlike Mr. Boudreaux who included, "Okay, now, as I was about to tell you. . . ."

7. When teachers are providing directions, they are not conducting a discovery lesson or any other sort of higher-cognitive-level learning activity. Efficiently communicated directions in which transition time is minimized do not normally allow time for students to debate the pros and cons of what is to be done. Unlike Ms. Duncan, Ms. Aldomat never gave students an opening for arguing about the upcoming learning activity. She had Jenny demonstrate the cartwheels before the class even knew they would be doing cartwheels instead of jumping on the trampoline.

8. Students are far more likely to follow directions that provide specific guidelines for exactly what is to be done than to follow ambiguously worded general directions. Ms. Aldomat told her students, "Line up on the half-court line, one arm's length apart, facing me," rather than "Form a line." She directed students to

do "four" cartwheels instead of "several." Mr. Rice's time limit of "14 minutes" communicates something more specific to students than "in a while," "several minutes," "when everyone is finished," "10 minutes," or "15 minutes." Numbers such as 10 and 15 appear less specific. Unlike Mr. Boudreaux, who only told his students to be prepared to discuss the poem, Mr. Rice provided specific guidelines for how to prepare for the discussion.

9. The more senses (e.g., seeing and hearing) that a teacher uses to communicate directions, the more likely students are to understand them. In addition to telling her students what to do, Ms. Aldomat had Jenny demonstrate what was to be done. Mr. Rice's students heard and read his directions. If students had questions about the directions or appeared to misunderstand them, Mr. Rice could simply point to the relevant statements on the first page of the document he distributed.

Engage in Activity 7.2.

▶ **ACTIVITY 7.2**

Recall your experiences with a teacher whose directions for complex learning activities were almost always clear to you and most of your classmates. Now recall a teacher whose directions were often unclear to you and your classmates. In a discussion with a colleague, contrast the two teachers' methods for delivering directions in the transition time before a complex learning activity. Compare the differences to the aforementioned nine points about directions.

▶ MONITORING STUDENT ENGAGEMENT

You are in a far better position to monitor what students are doing and thinking when you are circulating among them than when you are confined to a single area of the classroom (e.g., at the board or behind an overhead projector). Thus, consider organizing learning activities—even large-group presentations—so that you are free to move about the classroom. During Ms. Snyder's learning activity in Case 7.18, she is hardly in a position to monitor her students' engagement and demonstrate withitness. By contrast, Mr. Heaps conducts an activity in Case 7.19 so that he can monitor engagement and be with-it (adapted from Cangelosi, 2003, pp. 104–108).

▶ CASE 7.18

Ms. Snyder has designed an integrated mathematics and science lesson for the purpose of leading her sixth-grade students to achieve the following objective:

Students discover that the speed of a moving object can be measured by dividing the distance the object traveled by the time it took the object to travel the distance.

The lesson plan calls for Ms. Snyder to use an overhead transparency to display a path with equally spaced grid lines and to move a tiny image of a car at a slow steady speed along the path as depicted by Figure 7.1. She will have a student use a stopwatch to time how long it takes the image to cross a number of grid lines. Then she'll repeat the demonstration several times, but with each trial she either moves the image at a different steady speed or varies the number of grid lines the image crosses. All along, she plans to raise questions and provide explanations that will lead students to discover the relationship specified by the objective. By recording the number of

Figure 7.1. Ms. Snyder Uses an Overhead Transparency to Demonstrate the Speed of a Moving Object

lines crossed (i.e., the distance) and the time it took for each trial on the board, she hopes to get students to make comparisons demonstrating that the faster the image moves, the greater the ratio of distance to time.

Ms. Snyder is now standing in front of the class conducting the planned demonstration on the overhead projector. See Figure 7.2. "Now count how many lines the car crosses this time," she directs the class as Yoshi operates the stopwatch.—"There, 8 lines that time. What was the time, Yoshi?" she asks. Yoshi: "A little over 12 seconds." Ms. Snyder: "So that time the car took about 12 seconds to cross 8 lines. How does that compare to the last trip when it took about 17 seconds to cross 8 lines?" Manny quickly answers loudly, "This time the car went faster." "I agree with Manny. The car went faster this time because it took less time to cross the same number of lines," Ms. Snyder says as she turns to add the results of this latest trial to the data already on the whiteboard. Based on Manny's response, she thinks that he answered "faster" because he recognized that the car crossed just as many lines in less time. However, while she is writing on the board and starting the next trial, she doesn't hear the following exchange between Manny and Frank who is sitting next to him off to one side of the room:

Frank: How did you know the answer?

Manny: Couldn't you see her move her hand faster that time? I didn't count no lines. I don't know what she's talking about.

Figure 7.2. Ms. Snyder Misses Some Important Opportunities to Monitor Student Engagement

Occupied at her place in the front of the room, Ms. Snyder also didn't notice Rosalina in the back of the room starting to raise her hand when Manny blurted out his answer. If Rosalina had the opportunity to respond she would have said, "The time before, the car took 17 seconds to go 8 lines. That's about 2 seconds for one line. But this time, the car took only 12 seconds to go 8 lines; that's like $1\frac{1}{2}$ seconds for one line."

Consequently, Ms. Snyder makes an erroneous formative evaluation about Manny's progress and misses an opportunity for feedback relevant to Rosalina's understanding. More importantly, the whole class would have profited from a discussion stimulated by Rosalina's thoughts had she shared them.

After completing all the trials using the overhead, she summarizes:

Ms. Snyder: So you see we find out the distance by counting the number of lines crossed and the time with our watch. Then the rate of speed is the distance, or number of lines crossed, divided by the time. When the car crossed 15 lines in 5 seconds, its speed was 3 lines per second. What would its speed be if it took 10 seconds to go 15 lines?

Mindy: 1.5 lines per second.

Ms. Snyder: Does everyone understand how Mindy found the speed?

Some students nod positively; others stare straight ahead or look down.

Ms. Snyder: Any questions? Yes, Parker.

Parker: I see how Mindy got 1.5, but I don't know why.

Ms. Snyder: Because the rate of speed is the distance, or number of lines crossed, divided by the time. Do you understand, now?

Parker: Uhh,—okay, yeah.

Throughout the activity, Ms. Snyder was so busy from her place by the overhead projector and the whiteboard that she missed myriad indicators of who was on-task, who was off-task, who had insightful comments to make, who was following the discussion, and who got lost in the process.

▶ **CASE 7.19**

Mr. Heaps devises a lesson plan for his sixth-grade students that targets the same objective as Ms. Snyder's in Case 7.18. His approach is similar to hers. But instead of standing in the front of the classroom by the overhead projector and whiteboard, he has a student, Nakisha, operate the overhead projector with the gridded pathway and image of a car. Another student, Jorge, records data from the trials on the whiteboard while Jason operates the stopwatch as Yoshi did in Case 7.18.

Because he is not busy at the overhead in front of the room, Mr. Heaps is free to move among the students as shown by Figure 7.3. He gives step-by-step directions to Nakisha on how to perform each trial. Everyone in the classroom also hears the directions, thus, making it easier for them to understand the procedure. Furthermore, he has the students at their places respond to the prompts on the tasksheet shown by Figure 7.4.

At one point in the activity, Mr. Heaps directs Nakisha: "For this third trial, start the car at the Second line on the path and move it at steady pace for 10 seconds. Wait until Jason gives you the signal to start. The rest of us will count how many lines the car crosses." As the trial is performed,

Figure 7.3. Mr. Heaps Conducts the Activity So He Is Free to Monitor Engagement

Trial #1:

    Number of lines crossed _____

    Time in motion _____

Trial #2:

    Number of lines crossed _____

    Time in motion _____

Trial #3:

    Number of lines crossed _____

    Time in motion _____

Trial #4:

    Number of lines crossed _____

    Time in motion _____

During which of the four trials did the car travel fastest? _____

    Why do you think your answer is correct? _____

    _____

    _____

    _____

During which of the four trials did the car travel slowest? _____

    Why do you think your answer is correct? _____

    _____

    _____

    _____

    Write a number that indicates the speed of the car during:

    Trial #1 _____   Trial #2 _____

    Trial #3 _____   Trial #4 _____

Figure 7.4. Tasksheet Mr. Heaps' Students Use During the Activity

Mr. Heaps observes who is following the procedure; then he directs the class to fill in the data for the third trial on the tasksheets. He quickly surveys a sample of the students' responses, noting that most wrote down "18"and "10 seconds," as did Jorge on the whiteboard, but that Brett wrote nothing for Trial 3 and Mitsuko wrote "10" for the number of lines crossed and "18" for the time. Quickly and discreetly, he puts his finger on the blanks on Brett's tasksheet and then points to the data on the whiteboard. Quietly, he sends Mitsuko a hand signal indicating that she should transpose the two numbers. He notes that they both comply with his directions—directions that hardly anyone else in the class noticed.

As students work on the tasksheet after the fourth trial, Mr. Heaps walks around the room sampling their responses and watching them use their calculators in response to the last four-part prompt of the tasksheet. Figure 7.5 contains three of the completed tasksheets he read.

<u>Woofa's</u>

Trial #1:

      Number of lines crossed _____8_____

      Time in motion _____15.4 sec._____

Trial #2:

      Number of lines crossed _____8_____

      Time in motion _____7 1/2 sec._____

Trial #3:

      Number of lines crossed _____18_____

      Time in motion _____10.0 sec._____

Trial #4:

      Number of lines crossed _____8_____

      Time in motion _____9.0 sec._____

During which of the four trials did the car travel fastest? _____#3_____

      Why do you think your answer is correct? _____because it crossed the most_____

      lines _____

      _____

      _____

During which of the four trials did the car travel slowest? _____#1 and 2_____

      Why do you think your answer is correct? _____#1 and 2 because_____

      _____

      _____

      _____

      Write a number that indicates the speed of the car during:

      Trial #1 _____52_____   Trial #2 _____11_____

      Trial #3 _____18_____   Trial #4 _____17_____

Figure 7.5. Woofa's, Julie's, and Saul's Tasksheets

<u>Julie's</u>

Trial #1:

      Number of lines crossed _____8_____

      Time in motion ___15.4 seconds___

Trial #2:

      Number of lines crossed _____8_____

      Time in motion ___7.5 seconds___

Trial #3:

      Number of lines crossed _____18_____

      Time in motion ___10 seconds___

Trial #4:

      Number of lines crossed _____15_____

      Time in motion ___9 seconds___

During which of the four trials did the car travel fastest? _3_____

      Why do you think your answer is correct? ___*Because it took only about half*___

___*a second to cross a line. The others took longer for a line. #4 took*___

___*just a little longer #2 took about 1 second and #1 took about 2*___

___*seconds*___

During which of the four trials did the car travel slowest? _#1_____

      Why do you think your answer is correct? ___*Because of what I said above*___

_____

_____

_____

Write a number that indicates the speed of the car during:

Trial #1 ___1.92___   Trial #2 ___.93___

Trial #3 ___.55___   Trial #4 ___.6___

Figure 7.5. (*continued*)

At this stage of the lesson, he only expects a few students to have discovered that speed can be measured by dividing the number of lines crossed by the number of seconds. He sees that Woofa has used her calculator to compute the actual number of lines per second as indicated by the numbers at the bottom of her tasksheet. But he also interprets her explanations of why the speed was fastest in the third trial and her choice of Trials 1 or 2 for the slowest as indicative of a

Saul's

Trial #1:

     Number of lines crossed _____8_____

     Time in motion ___*15.4 seconds*___

Trial #2:

     Number of lines crossed _____8_____

     Time in motion ___*7.5 seconds*___

Trial #3:

     Number of lines crossed _____18_____

     Time in motion ___*10 seconds*___

Trial #4:

     Number of lines crossed _____15_____

     Time in motion ___*9 seconds*___

During which of the four trials did the car travel fastest? *1*_____

     Why do you think your answer is correct? ___*15.4 is the most times*___

_____

_____

_____

During which of the four trials did the car travel slowest? *9*_____

     Why do you think your answer is correct? ___*9 seconds is the shortest*___

_____

_____

_____

Write a number that indicates the speed of the car during:

Trial #1 ___*?*___   Trial #2 ___*?*___

Trial #3 ___*?*___   Trial #4 ___*?*___

Figure 7.5. (*continued*)

misconception. Apparently, she only considered number of lines crossed without considering how much time it took to cross those lines. But yet, she computed the correct rates.

    From Julie's explanations of her choices for fastest and slowest trials, Mr. Heaps judges that she's developed very sophisticated insights about the targeted relationship. However, he's confused by the numbers written at the bottom of her sheet. Instead of the expected higher numbers for higher speeds, she has lower numbers for higher speeds.

Saul's responses suggest to Mr. Heaps that Saul reasoned that the greater the number of seconds, the faster the speed. Because he judges Saul's progress with the lesson's objective to be behind the progress of the vast majority of the class, he decides to not discuss Saul's responses at the moment, but rather to work with Saul individually at a more convenient time.

He begins a class discussion by having Julie read her explanations for her choices of Trial 3 as the fastest and Trial 1 as the slowest. A comparison of Julie's responses to those of some other students leads the class to agree that speed is a function of distance and time. Then Mr. Heaps asks Julie to explain what he considers mysterious numbers at the bottom of her sheet. She says, "My numbers tell us the average number of seconds the car took to cross one line." Now Mr. Heaps realizes that her computations are perfectly consistent with her explanations. Each of the numbers is a ratio of time to distance rather than the ratio of distance to time as he had anticipated.

A very productive discussion ensues, with most students recognizing that either Julie's method or the more conventional method provide equally accurate measures of speed. Rather than raise general vague questions, such as, "Does everybody understand?" Mr. Heaps directs focused queries at specific students to gauge their progress. For example, he asks, "Since Woofa's numbers are different from Julie's, how could they both be equally good indicators of how fast the cars were going?"

▶ VARIETY OF LEARNING ACTIVITIES

In Case 7.17, Mr. Rice conducted a lesson consisting of a variety of learning activities. He began with a brief lecture followed by a 14-minute independent work session and a two-part discussion session. If you incorporate too many types of learning activities into a single lesson, you'll find yourself spending an inordinate amount of time in transitional periods giving directions. But an optimum mix of different types of sessions—as in Case 7.17—guards against the monotony that leads to student boredom. Subsequent sections of this chapter focus on ideas for keeping students engaged during various types of learning activity sessions.

▶ IDEAS FOR LECTURE SESSIONS

Student Engagement during Lectures

For students to be engaged in a lecture, they must attentively listen to what a teacher is saying. Taking notes and attempting to follow teacher-prescribed thought patterns may also be components of student engagement for many lecture sessions. Such engagement requires students to be cognitively active while physically inactive. Sustaining this type of attention is difficult for older students and virtually impossible for younger students. Lectures that continue uninterrupted for more than five minutes are not advisable for elementary school students. Older students' attention can be maintained somewhat longer, but not easily.

In Case 7.20, the teacher is not likely to maintain even older students' attention during her lectures. In contrast, the teacher in Case 7.21 uses lecture techniques designed to obtain and maintain student engagement.

▶ CASE 7.20

Ms. Haenszel has prepared a lecture designed to help her junior high mathematics class understand, know, and apply the arithmetic mean statistic. The 28 students quietly sit at their desks, 12 of them poised with paper and pencil for note taking, as Ms. Haenszel begins from her station near the whiteboard at the front of the room. Ms. Haenszel: "Today, class, we are going to learn about a statistic for averaging data. It is called the arithmetic mean; many of you are probably already familiar with it. Here's the definition." She turns to the whiteboard and writes as she says, "The arithmetic mean of N scores equals the sum of the scores divided by N." She keeps the side of her body to the class so that she can easily look over her shoulder and still see what she writes on the board. Continuing, she says, "For example, to compute the mean of 30, 25, 20, 30, 40, 30, 60, 10, 0, and 15, we would first add all the numbers to find the sum. Let's see, adding those 10 numbers on my calculator I get—260. Because there are 10 scores, we divide 260 by 10 and get 26.0. The mean in this case is 26. The arithmetic mean is a very important statistic. For example, if we had a second string of data, say 25, 18, 15, 20, 70, 10, 10, 8, 30, and 15, and we wanted to know which of the two strings is greater, then we could compare their means to find out. In the second case, the sum is—221. And 221 divided by the number of scores, which like before is 10, is 221 divided by 10, which is 22.1. So the arithmetic mean of the first string of scores, although containing a zero and no number as large as 70, is on the average bigger. This is because 26.0 is greater than 22.1."

▶ **CASE 7.21**

Mr. Dwyer has prepared a lecture designed to help his junior high mathematics class understand, know, and apply the arithmetic mean statistic. After directing students to have their calculators available and distributing the form appearing in Figure 7.6, he faces the class from a position near the overhead projector and says, "I'm looking at you people, and I just can't get one question out of my mind." Very deliberately he walks in front of the fourth row of students and quickly but obviously looks at their feet. Then he moves in front of the first row and repeats his odd behavior with those students. "I just don't know!" he says, shaking his head as he returns to his position by the overhead.

He switches on the overhead, displaying the first line of Figure 7.6, and says, "In the first blank on your form, please write, 'Do the people sitting in the fourth row have bigger feet than those in the first row?'" He moves closer to the students, obviously monitoring how well his directions are followed. Returning to the overhead as they complete the chore, he says, "Now I've got to figure a way to gather data that will help me answer that question." Grabbing his head with a hand and closing his eyes, he appears to be in deep thought for a few seconds and then suddenly exclaims. "I've got it! We'll use shoe sizes as a measure. That'll be a lot easier than using a ruler on smelly feet!" Some students laugh, and one begins to speak while two others raise their hands. But Mr. Dwyer quickly says, "Not now, please, we need to collect some data." He flips an overlay off the second line of the transparency, exposing "data for row 4."

Mr. Dwyer: "Each of you in the fourth and first rows, quickly jot down your shoe size on your paper. If you don't know it, either guess or read it off your shoe if you can do it quickly. Starting with Jason in the back and moving up to Becky in the front, those of you in the fourth row call out your shoe sizes one at a time so we can write them down in this blank at our places." As the students volunteer the sizes, he fills in the blank on the transparency as follows: 6, 10.5, 8, 5.5, 6, 9. Exposing the next line, "data for row 1," on the transparency, he asks, "What do you suppose we're going to do now, Melanie?" Melanie: "Do the same for row 1." Mr. Dwyer: "Okay, you heard her; row 1, begin with David and move up the row one at a time so we can fill in this blank." The numbers 8.5, 8, 7, 5.5, 6.5, 6.5, 9, and 8 are recorded and displayed on the overhead.

Mr. Dwyer: "Now I've got to figure out what to do with these numbers to help me answer the question." Several students raise their hands, but he responds, "Thank you for offering to help, but I want to figure this out for myself." Pointing to the appropriate numbers on the transparency, he seems to think aloud, saying, "It's easy enough to compare one number to another. David's 8.5 from row 1 is greater than Jason's 6 from row 4. But I don't want to just compare one individual's number to another. I want to compare this whole bunch of numbers [circling row 4's set of

Question to be answered: _____

_____

Data for Row 4: _____

Data for Row 1: _____

Treatment for Row 4's data:

Treatment for Row 1's data:

Treatment to compare the two sets of data:

Results: _____

_____

Conclusions: _____

_____

Figure 7.6. Form Mr. Dwyer Uses During an Interactive Lecture Session

numbers with an overhead pen] to this bunch [circling row 1's]. I guess we could add all of row 4's numbers together and all of row 1's together and compare the two sums—the one with the greater sum would have the larger group of feet."

A couple of students try to interrupt with "But that won't wor—" but Mr. Dwyer motions them to stop speaking and asks, "What's the sum from row 4, Terri?" Terri: "—45." Mr. Dwyer: "Thank you. And what's the sum for row 1, Haeja?" Haeja: "59." "Thank you. So row 1 has the bigger feet because 59 is greater than 45," Mr. Dwyer says as he writes, "59 > 45." Mr. Dwyer: "I'll pause to hear what those of you with your hands up have to say. Vanessa?"

Vanessa: That's not right; it doesn't work.

Mr. Dwyer: You mean 59 isn't greater than 45, Vanessa?

Vanessa: 59 is greater than 45, but there's more feet in row 1.

Mr. Dwyer: All the people on row 1 have only two feet just like the ones on row 4. I carefully counted [students laugh]. Now that we've taken care of that concern, how about other comments or questions—Jeremy?

Jeremy: You know what Vanessa meant! There's more people on row 1. So what you did isn't right.

Mr. Dwyer: Let me see if I now understand Vanessa's point. She said we don't want our indicator of how big the feet are to be affected by how many feet, just the size of the feet.—So I've got to figure out a way to compare the sizes of these two groups of numbers when one has more numbers. I'm open for suggestions. Jung?

Jung: You could drop the two extra numbers from row 1; then they'd both have 6.

Mr. Dwyer: That seems like a reasonable approach. I like that, but first let's hear another idea—maybe one where we can use all the data. Alice?

Alice: Why not do an average?

Mr. Dwyer: What do you mean?

Alice: You know, divide row 4's total by 6 and row 1's by 8.

Mr. Dwyer: How will dividing help, Cito?

Cito: It evens up the two groups.

Mr. Dwyer: Oh, I see what you people have been trying to tell me! Dividing row 4's sum of 45 by 6 counts each number 1/6. And dividing row 4's sum of 59 by 8 counts each number 1/8. And that's fair because 6 one-sixths is a whole, just like 8 one-eighths is a whole. How am I doing, Jason?

Jason: A lot better than you were.

Flipping over another overlay, Mr. Dwyer displays the next two lines of Figure 7.6 and says, "Let's write, 'The sum of row 4's numbers is 45.' 45 divided by 6 is what, Becky?" Becky: "7.5." Mr. Dwyer: "Thanks. And on the next line we write, '59 divided by 8' is what, Henry?" Henry: "7.375." Mr. Dwyer: "Because 7.5 is greater than 7.375, I guess we should say that row 4's feet are larger than row 1's feet. That is, of course, if you're willing to trust this particular statistic—which is known as the VAJJ. Any questions?—Yes, Haeja." Haeja: "Why the VAJJ?" Mr. Dwyer: "Because I just named it that after its four inventors—Vanessa, Alice, Jung, and Jeremy. They're the ones who came up with the idea of dividing the sum."

Mr. Dwyer shifts to direct instruction to help students remember the formula, practice using it, and remember its more conventional name, arithmetic mean, during the remainder of the session.

Fourteen Points about Lectures

Please consider the following thoughts when designing lectures:

1.   Students are more likely to be engaged during a lecture session if the teacher has provided clear directions for behavior. Students need to have learned how to attend to a lecture. Questions about how to take notes, if they will be taken at all, should be answered before the lecture begins.

2.   Some sort of advanced organizer to direct students' thinking helps students actively listen during a lecture. A written outline of topics to be covered or problems to be addressed, such as the form that Mr. Dwyer distributed in Case 7.21, can be useful in focusing students' thoughts.

3.   Signals, especially nonverbal ones, can efficiently focus students' attention during a lecture. Mr. Dwyer used at least two such signals. He directed students to a particular item on the form and had them write specific things down from time to time during the lecture. This helped students stay on track, preventing some mind wandering. His use of the overhead projector also helped maintain students' focus. Turning the projector on signals students to look. Turning it off signals students to focus their eyes elsewhere. The use of transparency overlays controls what students see.

4. Lectures are useful learning activities for teachers who want to have a group of students concurrently follow a common thought pattern. Lectures, such as Mr. Dwyer's, that are designed to do more than just feed information to students, run the risk of becoming discussion or questioning sessions. Thus, some means for staying on track should be considered when planning a lecture. One method is to have signals worked out with students so that they clearly discriminate between times when the teacher is strictly lecturing and times when discussion or questions are welcome. Mr. Dwyer divided his lecture into two parts. In the first part, he presented the problem to be addressed, collected data, and focused thoughts on how to manipulate the data. During this first part, he had students speak, but they did not enter into a discussion session or raise questions. They simply provided him with data that he used in the lecture. Between the first and second parts of the lecture, Mr. Dwyer conducted a brief discussion session in which the students discovered the formula for the arithmetic mean. After the discussion, when he was again lecturing, he did entertain Haeja's question, but he had set up the students to ask such a question to achieve a smooth transition into the formal statement of the formula. Mr. Dwyer let his students know when their comments and questions were welcome by saying things such as, "But let me try and figure this one out myself" and "I'll pause to hear what those of you with your hands up have to say."

5. Voice volume, inflection, pitch, rhythm, and pace should be strategically modulated according to the message you want to send and the level of students. Even when the message itself is important and exciting, a monotone speech is a recipe for boredom. Punctuate key sentences with voice variations. Follow key statements and questions with strategic pauses. Pauses indicate points to ponder. Pace your speech so that sessions move briskly but students still have time to absorb your messages and take notes. Quina (1989, p. 143) suggested that between 110 and 130 words per minute is optimal. The type of lesson you're teaching, of course, should influence pace. A lecture for an inquiry learning activity would ordinarily proceed at a slower pace than one using direct instruction.

6. Students are more likely to follow lectures that use professional-quality communications technology. Students can hardly be engaged when the learning activity requires them to read, see, or hear something unintelligible. Technological advances make computerized, multimedia, and sound-enhanced presentations cost-effective for everyday classroom use.

7. At least three advantages can be gained from videorecording lectures ahead of time and playing them for students in class. (a) Video-recorded lectures avoid some of the interruptions in thought that occur when students make comments or ask questions. (b) The teacher can more attentively monitor students' behavior and effectively respond to indications of disengagement. (c) Kinks and mistakes in the presentation can be corrected and improvements made before the lecture is played for the class. With record-and-play devices, teachers can easily start, interrupt, replay, terminate, modify, and repeat presentations.

8. Entertaining is not teaching. But lectures that interject a bit of humor or contain other attention-getting devices do keep students more alert than a straight monologue. Be careful, however, that the attention-getting devices don't distract attention from the goal of the lesson.

9. Students are more likely to follow a lecture alertly when the lecturer maintains eye contact with them. This, of course, was one advantage that Mr. Dwyer's use of the overhead in Case 7.21 had over Ms. Haenszel's use of the whiteboard in Case 7.20.

10. Mind wandering and daydreaming are major causes of student disengagement during lectures. Teachers can deal more effectively with mind wandering and daydreaming during a lecture when they move about the room as they lecture. Rather than encouraging teachers to stand behind a lectern, Quina (1989, pp. 141–142) suggests purposeful movements, with the room divided into quadrants:

> Beginning teachers sometimes unconsciously pace the floor, moving from one side of the room to another. The observing students' heads move as though they are watching a tennis match. To avoid this, think where you want to be standing as you develop parts of your lecture. You can divide the room into quadrants and intentionally move into each quadrant at different stages of your lecture. For example, after introducing the question "Why do we need to communicate?" the teacher may move to the left side of the room, give some information on communicating in pantomime, provide a quick pantomime, then move to the right side of the room to discuss ways we designate things, illustrate by pointing to objects, and then ask a related question, "How is pointing and acting things out like using words?" The teacher may then walk to the back of the room and ask even more pointed questions: "What would happen if we did not have words? What would it be like if words were not available right now?"
>
> The shift in position in the room corresponds to the development of the lecture, providing a spatial metaphor for organization. As the teacher walks back to the front of the room to sum up, the very return to the front of the room, to the beginning point, suggests a completion, a completed square, circle, or other shape. These movements are intentional. They can be planned in advance or they can be used spontaneously. Either way, they are intentional—not random pacing.

11. Students who hear their names are usually alerted to listen to what is being said. Thus, many teachers purposefully interject the names of individual students into their lectures. For example, during a lecture in a Spanish class, a teacher might say, "Suppose George wanted to tell Louise that her hair had just caught on fire. He could begin by . . ."

12. To be engaged in lectures, students need to do more than just passively sit and listen. They need to be actively listening, trying to follow the teacher's thought patterns. Mr. Dwyer realized this, so he appeared to be thinking and reasoning aloud. Teachers can facilitate engagement by verbally walking students through cognitive processes that lead to information and answers. Such an approach is akin to the spirit of problem-based learning activities.

13. As teachers lecture, they should frequently monitor their students' comprehension of what is being said. Planned breaks in a lecture, in which students are asked questions, can provide the teacher with formative evaluation information that should guide subsequent stages of the lecture.

14. Sometimes students become disengaged during a lecture because the teacher used an unfamiliar word, expression, formula, or symbol. The teacher continues, assuming that students understand; the students are no longer listening to what the teacher is saying because they are busy trying to figure out the unfamiliar expression. Teachers should make themselves aware of knowledge and skills that are prerequisite to following a planned lecture and teach for those prerequisites before giving the lecture.

Engage in Activity 7.3.

▶ **ACTIVITY 7.3**

Recall your experiences with teachers delivering lectures. Think of one whose lectures were particularly engaging for you and your classmates. Think of one whose lectures were such that students tended to be disengaged. In a discussion with a colleague, contrast the two teachers' methods for conducting lecture sessions; point out what they did differently. Compare the differences to the aforementioned 14 points about lectures.

▶ IDEAS FOR COOPERATIVE-LEARNING SESSIONS

Students Learning from One Another

For some learning activities, it may be more efficient for you to organize your class into several subgroups rather than a single large group. Intraclass grouping arrangements in which students in each group work on a common task give students greater opportunities than whole class activities to interact with one another, allowing tasks to be tailored to special interests or needs and a wide variety of tasks to be addressed during class.

Cooperative-learning activities in which students learn from one another have proven to be quite successful (Ormrod, 2006, pp. 467–468). Students can engage in cooperative-learning activities in large-group settings, but small task-group sessions are particularly well suited for students who are teaching one another. A variety of task-group patterns are commonly used to facilitate cooperative learning, including (a) *peer instruction groups* in which one student teaches others by presenting a brief lesson, tutoring, or providing help with a particular exercise; (b) *practice groups* in which students review, drill, and provide one another with feedback as part of a knowledge-level or skill-level lesson; (c) *interest or achievement-level groups,* which are organized around interests (as in Case 7.3), achievement levels, or combinations of interest and achievement (as in Case 7.5); and (d) *problem-solving groups* in which students use a team approach to undertake projects or formulate solutions (as in Case 7.4).

Guidance and Structure for Maintaining Engagement

Research studies examining how students spend their time in classrooms indicate that students tend to have poor engagement levels in small-group learning activities unless the teacher is actively involved in the session (Fisher et al., 1980). But a teacher cannot be in the middle of several groups at once, and often subgroups fail to address their tasks due to a lack of guidance. Consider Case 7.22.

▷ **CASE 7.22**

As part of a science lesson for her fourth graders, Ms. Keene demonstrates the property of density by adding oil and then maple syrup to a container of water. She directs the students to form four groups of six to discuss why the syrup settled below the water while the oil floated on the water's surface. After six minutes spent in on-task discussion, the students in one group no longer bother with questions related to their observations of Ms. Keene's demonstration and instead socialize with one another. Ms. Keene, who is explaining the questions to another group, hardly notices that the first group is off-task. A third group becomes quite noisy, and Ms. Keene raises her voice from her position with the second group and announces, "Better keep it down in here. You won't discover a very important property of matter unless you keep your discussion on-task." In the fourth group, Terri dominates the first five minutes explaining to the others why heavier substances sink. She stimulates Shirley's interest, and the two of them engage in a conversation about the demonstration. The other four members of the group are doing things unrelated to the lesson's topic.

After managing to get the second group on track, Ms. Keene moves to the noisy third group, saying, "You people aren't following directions; you're supposed to be discussing your observations of the experiment." She then tells the group about the property of density she intended them to discover for themselves.

After spending four minutes with the second group, Ms. Keene calls a halt to the activity and announces, "Okay, class, let's rearrange our desks back to where they were. Now that you understand the idea of density, I want to show you how to. . . ."

Ms. Keene failed to initiate student engagement because her directions did not spell out the tasks and exactly how to go about completing each one. Contrast her strategies with those of Ms. Turkolu in Case 7.23.

▷ **CASE 7.23**

Ms. Turkolu is in the midst of a science unit for her fourth graders. Convinced that students have adequately achieved objectives involving weight, mass, and volume, she introduces the concept of density—without using the word "density"—by displaying two identical sealed cardboard boxes, each with the dimensions 60 cm × 37 cm × 30 cm. Unknown to the students, Ms. Turkolu has tightly packed one box with a neat stack of newspapers. The other box is filled with loosely crumpled balls of newspaper.

Students examine the two boxes without touching them, agreeing that the boxes appear to have the same capacity. Ms. Turkolu announces that both boxes are filled from top to bottom and side to side with newspapers. After instructing them about how to lift heavy objects carefully with back straight and knees bent, she directs students to lift one box and then the other. They agree that one is much heavier than the other but don't understand why, given what Ms. Turkolu told them about the boxes' contents.

The following day, as students enter the room, Ms. Turkolu hands each a blue, green, orange, or pink card with directions to go directly to the work station matching the color on the card. Her strategy for getting students organized into small task groups is similar to Mr. Jukola's in Case 3.17. Each card also spells out the role that the student will play in the group. The roles are (a) *chairperson,* who is responsible for conducting the group's activities and reminding group members to stay on-task; (b) *communicator of directions,* who reads the directions for completing the task to the group and answers questions regarding what to do; (c) *custodian of materials,* who cares for, distributes, and collects materials Ms. Turkolu has made available at the work station; (d) *reporter,* who writes up the group's activities and finalizes the report to the rest of the class; (e and f) *two workers,* who actually carry out the physical aspects of the assigned task.

Ms. Turkolu has arranged the four color-coded work stations so that, as the students find their places and begin reading their directions, the class is partitioned into four cooperative groups. Each group of six is able to perform its individual task out of sight of the other three. The tasks are as follows.

- The Blue Group is provided with two identical boxes, 100 soft rubber balls, a roll of packing tape, and a scale for weighing the boxes. Each member of the group is assigned a specific role. As directed, they fill one box completely with 25 balls and cram the remaining 75 balls into the second box, which means that the balls must be squeezed nearly flat to fit into the box. The students are motivated to keep their voices low as they work with one another because Ms. Turkolu's directions indicate that they are to keep their activities secret from the other three groups in the room. They seal both boxes and weigh each. The cooperative group member in charge of recording the procedures and results of the experiment completes the group's written report.

- The Green Group operates similarly, except that one of its boxes is one-third the size of the other. In this case, students are directed to fill both boxes completely with the same number of balls, which means they have to cram them into the smaller box. Both boxes are sealed and weighed and a brief report written.

- The Orange Group operates much like the Blue Group, but instead of filling boxes with balls, they fill two garbage bags of equal capacity—one with empty round aluminum cans, the other with flattened aluminum cans. The bags are sealed.

- The Pink Group operates much like the Green Group but fills one large garbage bag with unaltered aluminum cans and one small garbage bag with the same number of flattened aluminum cans. The bags are sealed.

As the groups work, Ms. Turkolu moves about the room, occasionally reminding chairpersons that someone needs a reminder to stick to her or his role but never allowing herself to become part of the group. For example, as she passes by the Orange Group, Zach asks, "Ms. Turkolu, how many of the cans are we supposed to stuff in here?" Ms. Turkolu turns to Sara, who's chairing the group, and says, "You'd better have your communicator of directions make a decision on Zach's question."

Later, in a large-group arrangement, the products of each group's experiment are examined—without unsealing the containers—by the other three groups. Ms. Turkolu then conducts a large-group inductive questioning session in which students make conjectures about what groups did to create the observed phenomena (e.g., two objects with equal volume but different mass). Using probing questions, Ms. Turkolu leads students to discover the concept of density. No one uses the word "density," but the students agree to name the idea "squishiness." The students formulate a definition of *squishiness* in terms of volume and mass. They apply their newly formulated concept to explain the mystery of the two boxes with which they worked the previous day.

Ten Points about Cooperative-Learning Sessions

Consider the following when designing cooperative-learning sessions.

1. Expect the sort of off-task behaviors that Ms. Keene's students exhibited in Case 7.22 unless you clearly define not only tasks for each cooperative group, but also the individual responsibilities of each group member.

2. As in Case 7.23, all group members should be jointly accountable for completing the shared task, with each member responsible for fulfilling an individual role.

3. Efficient routine procedures for making transitions into and out of small-group activities (e.g., Mr. Jukola's in Case 3.17, Ms. Morrison's in Case 3.21, and Ms. Williams's flag-raising routine in Case 5.4) avoid the time-wasting chaos that follows a direction such as "Let's move our desks so that we have four groups of five or six each."

4. Tasksheets and advanced organizers direct students' focus and provide them with an overall picture of what they are expected to accomplish in their groups.

5. To avoid interrupting cooperative group work to clarify directions the whole class should hear, specify the task and directions for everyone before attentions are turned to individual group activities.

6. Monitor groups' activities, providing guidance as needed without usurping individual students' responsibilities for designated tasks. In Case 7.23, Ms. Turkolu moved from one group to another, cuing students on task without actually becoming a member of any one group.

7. Model active listening techniques. Students do not automatically know how to listen to one another without your showing them. From classes they have taken with other teachers, they may have acquired the misperception that anything of academic importance (i.e., anything that will be on the test) is said by teachers, not peers. Thus, you should demonstrate that you intently listen to them and make use of what they say. Case 7.24 is an example.

▶ **CASE 7.24**

As he monitors a cooperative-learning activity in which his marketing education class is organized into five task groups, Mr. Lau-Chou stops to sit in with one group as they struggle with one of the questions from a tasksheet. As Malinda is commenting, Horace attempts to engage Mr. Lau-Chou with his own private question: "Mr. Lau-Chou, this doesn't make—" But Mr. Lau-Chou uses a frown and hand motion to cue Horace to be quiet. Then he says to the group, "Excuse me, Malinda, would you repeat that last part about adding the two prices? I missed what you said about that." Malinda repeats and finishes her comment. Mr. Lau-Chou says, "Thank you. That should shed some light on Horace's concern. Horace, raise your concern with the group." Horace: "To me, the question ought to be. . . ." Later, in the large-group session, Mr. Lau-Chou plays off different comments that students made in their groups.

8. Use formative feedback to regulate activities. Engaged behaviors during cooperative task-group sessions are observable because students should be involved in discussions and working on a specified task. Thus, formative feedback for regulating the activities is relatively easy to obtain.

9. Closure points are needed for lengthy sessions. As with other types of sessions, students need to experience climactic moments to positively reinforce engagement. Having a sequence of subtasks rather than one overall task facilitates this need if you provide students with feedback as they complete the subtasks.

10. Individual group work should be followed up and used during subsequent learning activities. In Case 7.23, Ms. Turkolu brought together the products of the four groups so that students could induct a concept in the follow-up activity with the whole class.

Engage in Activity 7.4.

▶ **ACTIVITY 7.4**

Recall your experiences as a student participating in cooperative-learning activities. Think of one cooperative-learning session in which you and your classmates were highly engaged. Think of another in which students were not highly engaged. In a discussion with a colleague, contrast how the two cooperative-learning sessions were organized and conducted. Compare the differences to the aforementioned 10 points about cooperative learning sessions.

▶ IDEAS FOR DISCUSSION SESSIONS

Student Engagement during Discussions

The success of cooperative-learning strategies typically depends on students focusing on a particular topic during discussion sessions. For students to be engaged in a discussion activity, they must attentively listen to what classmates say and be willing to make comments and raise questions pertinent to the topic. Discussions can be conducted in small intraclass groups or in large-group meetings of a whole class; Case 7.25 provides examples of both.

▶ CASE 7.25

To help her 26 third graders develop both their skills and interest in reading, Ms. Torres directs the class to read silently a three-line story entitled "Making Things" from page 97 of one of their readers. In 35 seconds everyone is finished, and Ms. Torres begins a brief questioning session that leads into a large-group discussion.

Ms. Torres stands in front of the class holding her copy of the reader open to page 97 in one hand and her bookmark held high over her head with her other hand. Ms. Torres: "Please put your bookmark on page 97, close your book, and keep it on your desk." She follows her own directions with her copy of the reader as she watches the class do the same. Ms. Torres: "I would like everyone to think about the answer to the question I'm about to ask. What was the reading about?" Most of the students raise their hands. Ms. Torres recognizes Gail, who says, "Making things." Ms. Torres moves about the room as she asks, "What did Gail say? Doris." Doris: "She said, 'making things.'" Ms. Torres: "Why would anyone want to make things? Jamal." Jamal: "It's fun." Ms. Torres: "Todd?" Todd: "You don't have to pay for them." Ms. Torres: "Put your hand up if you never, ever, like to make anything." No hands are raised. Ms. Torres: "It looks like we agree that we sometimes like to make things. We are about to have a *discussion* on making surprises for other people. Who remembers what we do when we have a class discussion?" About half the class raises hands. Ms. Torres says, "First we'll hear from Veda, then Morris, then Simon." Veda: "Only one talks at a time." Morris: "You hafta raise your hand to talk." There's a pause, so Ms. Torres motions to Simon, who says, "That's what I was going to say." Ms. Torres: "Tell me, who calls on people who raise their hands to talk? Jessie." Jessie: "The last one that talked." Ms. Torres: "Thank you. Remember in a discussion, I don't call on you. Whoever has the floor calls on the next person to speak."

Ms. Torres: "Let's talk about making things, but not just anything. Let's talk about making things to surprise someone with something he or she likes. We'll begin the discussion with Marvell. Marvell, you have the floor to start the discussion on making surprises for others to enjoy." Fourteen students eagerly raise their hands beckoning Marvell to call on them. Marvell: "I like to make drawings and surprise my Momma. She hangs them up on the wall. Okay, Lydia." Lydia, who is seated near where Ms. Torres is standing, begins speaking directly to Ms. Torres: "My brother lost the pick for his guitar, so I cut out a piece of this stuff and wrapped it up in a box for him." As Lydia speaks, Ms. Torres moves to a point across the room from her so that most of the other students are positioned between Ms. Torres and Lydia. This encourages Lydia to project her voice and speak to the class rather than Ms. Torres only. The discussion continues for 12 minutes with Ms. Torres continually moving about the classroom, occasionally motioning students to speak up and politely reminding them of the topic.

After the discussion, Ms. Torres conducts an activity in which students take turns reading aloud from a three-page story titled "Surprise Pancakes." Ms. Torres then divides the class into four groups. Each group is assigned a section of the room where they meet sitting on the floor in a circle. After all four groups are in place, Ms. Torres says to all the groups at once, using body language and gestures to help students understand her directions, "Austin, you are the discussion leader for this group. Veda, you're the leader there. Marvell, here. Zeke, there. Your group is to think of five things we could make to bring home as a surprise for our parents. The surprises have to be something that we could all make here at school. You have nine minutes to decide, and we've already used four seconds."

Ms. Torres moves from one group to another. When she stops to listen to the discussion in Veda's group, Jo asks her, "Is it okay if we cook something, like the kids did in the story?" Ms. Torres: "What do the rest of you think about cooking something?" Veda: "I didn't think we could, but. . . ." Seeing that Veda's group is again talking to one another, Ms. Torres quickly moves to Austin's group where Mary Jo and Freda are involved in a private conversation about cats. The other five appear to be on-task. Ms. Torres: "What are you thinking about making?" Austin answers as Mary Jo and Freda continue their conversation: "Greg thinks we should make up a song." Zane: "That's stupid!" Ms. Torres: "Freda, what do you think about our making up a song?" Freda: "What?" Ms. Torres: "Explain your idea to Freda one more time, Greg." Ms. Torres sees that everyone in the group is now listening to Greg, so she moves to another group.

After nine minutes, the alarm of the chronograph on Ms. Torres's wrist rings and she says, "Time's up. Just stay where you are, and we'll have each group give us its list." She positions herself by a whiteboard and makes a list of the 16 "things to make" as they are told to her. Only one group has exactly five suggestions; the others have one, three, and seven, respectively. Several suggestions appear in the list more than once. Ms. Torres: "We will leave this list on the board until tomorrow when we decide which ones we will actually make as surprises for our parents. Right now, I would like you to return to your places and open your readers to page 101." Once the students are in their places with their books open and ready to listen, Ms. Torres says, "What is the name of the story beginning on page 101? Barton." Barton reads, "Things to Make at School." Ms. Torres: "Thank you. Class, I want you to take this reader home tonight and read 'Things to Make at School.' We will discuss it tomorrow before we decide which things from our list we will make."

Seven Points about Discussion Sessions

Keep these thoughts in mind when planning discussion sessions:

1. Efficient use of time allocated for a discussion session partly depends on how clearly the directions communicate the exact procedures to be followed. If a teacher consistently follows the same procedures for all discussions, students

learn from repeated experiences to follow those procedures automatically without elaborate directions. For the first few discussion sessions with her class, Ms. Torres needed to spend time directly teaching her procedure for speaking to the group; now, only occasional reminders are necessary.

2. Student talk is likely to stray from the topic of a discussion unless that topic is specified and the purpose of the discussion is understood. Ms. Torres led into the large-group discussion with a questioning session in which she controlled the subject. She had her students thinking about making things before she began the discussion intended to deal specifically with "making things to surprise someone." The small discussion groups were directed to complete a specific task.

3. The focus of a discussion is more likely to be maintained when students perceive that the discussion is purposeful. The purposefulness of discussions can be appreciated by students when the teacher uses lead-in activities to set the stage for the discussion and when outcomes of the discussion are used in activities subsequent to the discussion. The readings and the questioning session had Ms. Torres's students focusing on the topic before the discussion. She used the list produced during discussions on the following day.

4. Students have a tendency to direct their comments to the teacher. Seating arrangements in which students face one another and the teacher is not a focal point encourage students to speak and listen to one another. During the large-group discussion, Ms. Torres moved about so that most of the class was between her and whoever had the floor at the time.

5. With only a minimal disruption to discussions, teachers can silently use hand signals to remind individuals to attend to a speaker or motion a speaker to direct comments to the group, speak up, or slow down.

6. By using the comment of one student to involve another, teachers model active listening behavior while encouraging participation. Ms. Torres, for example, asked Freda about Greg's idea.

7. Especially during discussion sessions that are part of lessons in which you are employing inquiry instructional strategies, engage students in true dialogues that are void of IRE cycles (refer to Chapter 2's section, "True Dialogues Instead of IRE Cycles.").

Engage in Activity 7.5.

▶ *ACTIVITY 7.5*

Recall your experiences with teachers conducting discussion sessions. Think of one whose discussions were particularly engaging for you and your classmates. Think of one whose discussions were such that students tended to be disengaged with only little quality participation. In a discussion with a colleague, contrast the two teachers' methods for conducting discussion sessions; point out what they did differently. Compare the differences to the aforementioned seven points about discussion sessions.

▶ IDEAS FOR QUESTIONING SESSIONS

Student Engagement during Questioning Sessions

For students to be engaged in a questioning activity, they must attentively listen to each question asked by their teacher, attempt to formulate answers to that question, and either express their answers in a manner prescribed by the teacher or listen to others express their answers. *Recitation* is one type of questioning session that teachers use to help students memorize. Case 7.26 is an example.

▶ **CASE 7.26**

Ms. Caldaron asks her fourth graders, "What is the capital of Mississippi? Eva." Eva: "Jackson." Ms. Caldaron: "What is the capital of Louisiana? Vincent." Vincent: "New Orleans." A number of students raise their hands, and Ms. Caldaron calls on Rosalie, who says, "Baton Rouge." Ms. Caldaron: "That is correct; Baton Rouge is the capital of Louisiana. Now, what about the capital of . . ."

In general, *reasoning-level questioning sessions* are more interesting and helpful to students than recitations because they are designed to stimulate students to think, discover, and reason. Case 7.27 is an example.

▶ **CASE 7.27**

Mr. Becnel is conducting a reasoning-level questioning session to help his 28 eighth graders understand how writers use facts to support their opinions. He displays an overhead transparency listing eight statements taken from a magazine article the class recently read (see Figure 7.7).

X	"There are about 20 varieties of barracuda."
O	"Barracuda are fearless."
X	"Some of the barracuda of the Southern Atlantic weigh over 60 pounds."
X	"Some people eat sun-cured barracuda meat."
O	"Barracuda meat is not as tasty as more commonly eaten fish."
O	"Fishing for barracuda is an exciting sport."
X	"Barracuda have numerous sharp teeth."
O	"Barracuda are ferocious."

Figure 7.7. List of Statements Used in Questioning Sessions Conducted by Mr. Becnel, Mr. Mongar, Ms. Kranz, and Ms. Dzildahl

Mr. Becnel initiates the questioning session: "The eight statements on the screen are from the reading. Notice that some of the statements are marked with Os, others with Xs. Can anyone tell me why the X statements belong together and why the O statements belong together? How are the X statements like each other but different from the O statements?" Jamal, Traci, and Sidney eagerly have their hands up, even before Mr. Becnel completes his questions. Without pausing after his questions, Mr. Becnel calls on Sidney. Sidney: "The ones with the Xs have numbers in them." "No, no!" cries Jamal. Traci is waving her hand to get Mr. Becnel's attention as three other students raise their hands.

Mr. Becnel: Easy, Jamal. Let's give Sidney a chance. Does the fourth one have a number in it?

Sidney: No.

Mr. Becnel: But is it an X statement?

Sidney: Yes.

Mr. Becnel: Then what can you conclude?

Sidney: My idea's not right.

Mr. Becnel: I agree that you've managed to disprove your hypothesis.

Jamal: The ones with the Os are things that everyone doesn't agree on.

Mr. Becnel: What do you mean? Give us an example.

Jamal: My aunt doesn't think fishing is exciting. She hates fishing. And who knows if barracuda are fearless? Did anyone ever ask a barracuda?

Mr. Becnel: Can't the same thing be said for the X statements?

Sidney: No, because each of the X ones we can know for sure.

Mr. Becnel: For example?

Sidney: You can weigh a barracuda and count his teeth.

Murray: Not me! I ain't gonna count no monster's teeth! [Laughter erupts in the class.]

Mr. Becnel: Barracuda are monsters. Is that an X statement or an O statement? Okay, Jamal.

Jamal: That's an O statement because that's just what Murray thinks. Some people may think they're pretty.

Mr. Becnel: Statements of what some people think, but that can't be determined as true or false, are statements of what? What is the word for ideas we don't all agree to—for all the O statements?

Traci: Opinions! O for opinions.

Mr. Becnel: Are all the Os statements of opinions?

Jamal: Yes.

Sidney: What do the Xs stand for?

Mr. Becnel: [to Sidney] Think of a word for something we can absolutely know to be true. It doesn't begin with X, but it fits all our Xed statements.

Sidney: Theories?

Traci and Jamal raise their hands.

Mr. Becnel: But do we know all theories to be true?

Traci: Facts.

Mr. Becnel: Who agrees with Traci?

Sidney, Jamal, and two others raise their hands.

Mr. Becnel: I agree also. All of the X statements are called what?

Jamal: Facts.

As the questioning session continues, a number of Mr. Becnel's 28 students discover the relation between the author's use of facts and opinions.

What did you think of Mr. Becnel's use of questioning, or Socratic methods, for stimulating students to reason? The session was probably very valuable to Jamal, Sidney, and Traci. But what about the other 25 students; what did they learn? Mr. Becnel seemed to know how to use questioning strategies effectively, but only a relatively small portion of his class became involved. For reasoning-level questioning sessions to be effective for all students, each student must attempt to answer the questions posed by the teacher (Tobin, Tippins, & Gallard, 1994). It is unnecessary for all students to express their attempted answers to the teachers, but they should at least attempt to formulate answers in their minds. Because Mr. Becnel called on Sidney immediately after asking his first set of questions, most students did not have enough time even to try to answer the questions. They quit thinking of their own answers to hear Sidney's answer and the ensuing discussion.

In Case 7.27, Mr. Becnel, like most teachers, did not allow enough time to elapse between the end of his question and his acceptance of a student's answer to the question. The average time that teachers wait for students to respond to their in-class questions is less than 2 seconds (Cangelosi, 2006; Tobin et al., 1994). After experiencing a few sessions like Mr. Becnel's, in which they are asked questions that they don't have the opportunity to answer, most students learn not to attempt to formulate their own responses. Some politely listen to the responses of the few; others entertain themselves with off-task thoughts; and others, if allowed, entertain themselves with disruptive behaviors.

Mr. Becnel should not discard Socratic methods. Reasoning-level questioning sessions are the primary mechanism to lead students to achieve higher-cognitive learning objectives (Cangelosi, 1992, pp. 68–115; 2003, pp. 172–266). What Mr. Becnel should do is reorganize his questioning sessions and apply techniques that lead all students to address all questions raised. Such techniques are demonstrated in Cases 7.28, 7.29, and 7.30.

▷ **CASE 7.28**

Mr. Mongar is conducting a reasoning-level questioning session to help his 28 eighth graders understand how writers use facts to support their opinions. He displays an overhead transparency listing eight statements taken from a magazine article the class recently read (see Figure 7.7).

Mr. Mongar says to the class, "I am going to ask you some questions, but I don't want anyone to answer aloud until I call on someone. Answer each question in your mind. Here are the first two questions. How do you think the X statements are alike but different from the O statements? How are the Os alike but different from the Xs?"

Two students eagerly raise their hands and say, "Oh, Mr. Mongar!" Mr. Mongar is tempted to call on them and positively reinforce their enthusiasm, but he resists and they sit quietly after seeing his stern look and gesture. He waits, watching the students' faces. Finally he says, "Tom, do you have an answer?" Tom nods. Mr. Mongar: "Good! How about you, Linda?" Linda: "Yes." Mr. Mongar: "Fine. Are you ready, Thelma?" Thelma: "No, I don't know." Mr. Mongar: "I'd like you to think aloud. What are your thoughts about how the X statements and O statements are different?" Thelma: "I don't see any difference; they're all about barracuda." Mr. Mongar: "That's an important similarity among all the statements. Now I'd like some volunteers to share their answers with us. Okay, Rita." Rita: "Well, it seems to me that. . . ."

▶ **CASE 7.29**

Ms. Kranz is helping her 28 eighth graders understand how writers use facts to support their opinions. She distributes to each student a list of eight statements taken from a magazine article the class recently read (see Figure 7.7).

Ms. Kranz: "At the bottom of the handout you just received, each of you is to write one paragraph describing why you think the X statements go together and why the O statements go together. How are the Xs alike but different from the Os? How are the Os alike but different from the Xs?" As the students think and write out answers, Ms. Kranz moves about the room, reading what students write from over their shoulders. Some students write nothing until Ms. Kranz comes by their desk and silently motions for them to write. After noticing that everyone has written something, she asks, "Would you please read to us what you wrote, Pete?" Pete reads, "The ones with the Xs are more specific. The other ones, with the Os, are general." Ms. Kranz: "Judy, please read yours." Judy: "I don't think this is right; I wasn't—" Ms. Kranz interrupts and says, "I would appreciate your just reading exactly what you wrote." Judy: "The O statements are more critical of barracuda than the other ones are. The X statements are more straightforward." Ms. Kranz: "Crystal, I'd like you to compare what Pete read to what Judy read. Is there anything about Judy's answer that is similar to Pete's?" Crystal: "It seems that. . . ."

After the discussion on her first set of questions, Ms. Kranz raises follow-up questions and again has the students silently write out answers. Because she reads some responses as she circulates around the room, she can select the responses to be read that will better stimulate discussion and help make points she wants made.

▶ **CASE 7.30**

After subdividing her class of eighth graders into five cooperative groups of five or six each, Ms. Dzildahl distributes to each group a list of eight statements (see Figure 7.7) taken from a magazine article the class recently read. She directs each group to decide on the differences and similarities between the X and O statements and gives them 11 minutes to prepare and present their decisions to the rest of the class. Ms. Dzildahl moves from one group to the other and monitors them as they work.

Six Points about Questioning Sessions

Here are some thoughts for you to keep in mind when designing questioning sessions.

1. Provide for periods of silent thinking during reasoning-level questioning sessions. Unlike recitation sessions, student engagement during reasoning-level questioning sessions requires students to take time to think about questions posed by teachers before expressing responses.

2. Having all students write out their responses to questions you pose has at least four advantages over having only students who are called on express answers: (a) Students have to organize their thoughts to write out answers, thus providing an additional learning experience. (b) Allowing time for students to write serves as a silent period for all students to be thinking about how to respond to questions. (c) Written responses make it possible for teachers to preview students' answers and decide which ones should be read to the class. (d) Having written responses available to read to the class avoids some of the stammering

and grasping for words that are typical of students who are answering aloud in front of their peers.

3. By directing a question at a particular student before articulating the question, you may discourage other students from carefully listening to that question. The teachers in Cases 7.27 to 7.30 posed most of their questions before designating someone to answer aloud. None of these teachers, for example, phrased questions such as "Johnny, is this an *X* or an *O* statement?" If they had, students other than Johnny might not have bothered to listen to the question.

4. Teachers need to move quickly from one student to another so that as many students as possible express answers aloud. With reasoning-level questions, however, some students' answers are complex and need to be discussed in some detail; answers are not simply right or wrong. To involve more students, maintain a single focus, yet have some particular answers fully discussed, teachers should use the responses of some students to formulate subsequent questions for other students. Mr. Becnel applied this technique by using Murray's characterization of barracuda as "monsters" in his next question for the class. Ms. Kranz asked Crystal to compare Pete's response to Judy's.

5. Students are more likely to engage in questioning sessions in which (a) questions relate to one another and focus on a central theme or problem rather than appear isolated and unrelated and (b) questions are specific rather than vague. The teacher-raised questions in Cases 7.27 to 7.30 focused on the relation between facts and opinions as used in a particular selection that all students had read. Vague questions such as, "Do you understand?" and "Is the statement 'Barracuda are monsters' an *X* or an *O* statement?" do not focus thought.

6. Learning activities conducted before questioning sessions can maintain the focus of the questioning session. In addition, students learn the importance of engaging in questioning sessions when the sessions culminate in problem resolutions that are applied in subsequent learning activities. In Cases 7.27 to 7.30, the reading of the passage on barracuda set the stage for the questions. What students discover about how the author supported opinions with facts should be used in follow-up assignments. Subsequent activities might include assignments in which students (a) read a new passage and analyze it—pointing out where the author supported opinions with facts—and (b) write an opinion piece in which they use facts to support their positions.

Engage in Activity 7.6.

▶ *ACTIVITY 7.6*

Recall your experiences with teachers conducting questioning sessions. Think of one whose sessions were particularly engaging for you and your classmates. Think of one whose questioning sessions were such that students tended to be disengaged with only little quality participation. In a discussion with a colleague, contrast the two teachers' methods for conducting questioning sessions; point out what they did differently. Compare the differences to the aforementioned six points about questioning sessions.

▶ IDEAS FOR INDEPENDENT WORK SESSIONS

Student Engagement during Independent Work Sessions

Engagement in an independent work session requires a student to complete some assigned task without disturbing others also working on the task. Typically, students work individually with the teacher available for help. When you plan for such sessions, two potential problems should be taken into account: (a) How do you accommodate students completing the task at differing times? (B) How can you efficiently provide the individual help that students may need to remain engaged with the task?

Failure to solve the first problem led to the disruption of Mr. Uter's learning activity in Case 3.27. In Case 7.31, Ms. Soulier fails to solve the second.

▶ CASE 7.31

Ms. Soulier's eleventh graders are individually working at their places on an exercise factoring algebraic polynomials. About 12 of the 27 students have their hands raised beckoning Ms. Soulier's help as she moves among them tutoring one and then another. She gets around to Brenda:

Brenda: I don't know how to do these.
Ms. Soulier: What is it you don't know how to do?
Brenda: I don't understand enough to know what I don't know!
Ms. Soulier: Let's look at number 3 here. Did you look for a factor common to all the terms?
Brenda: Well, all the terms have 3 as a factor.
Ms. Soulier: Then what can you. . . .

In the meantime, other students are waiting and feel they cannot continue with the exercise until Ms. Soulier helps them. But she doesn't get around to all those requesting help, and more and more students, bored waiting for help, become disengaged from the learning activity (see Figure 7.8).

Teachers were observed providing individual help, as did Ms. Soulier, and then they were asked how much time they thought they averaged with each student they helped. The vast majority thought they spent between one and two minutes; actually they averaged about four minutes with each student (Jones, 1979). Four uninterrupted minutes is too long to spend with one individual student while others are waiting for help.

In Case 5.4, Ms. Williams. Flag-raising procedure helped solve the problems experienced by Ms. Soulier as well as Mr. Uter. Case 7.32 also illustrates how independent-work sessions can be efficiently conducted.

▶ CASE 7.32

Ms. Evans distributes a tasksheet with the following directions to each of the 34 students in her Spanish class:

1. Please take out your translation notebook, pencil, textbook, and Spanish–English dictionary.

2. Translate into English each of the six sentences under the heading "A orillas del lago" on page 63 of your text, using the following procedure:

Figure 7.8. Students Become Disengaged Waiting for Ms. Soulier to Get to Them

A.   Look at the entire sentence. Lightly circle with your pencil each word whose English meaning you don't remember.

B.   Look up the meaning of each word you circled in your dictionary and write down the short meaning in your notebook.

C.   Locate the verb in the sentence.

D.   Determine the tense of the verb. If you need help in determining the tense, turn your text to page 39 and follow the directions for "Verb Tenses."

E.   Write a *literal*, word-by-word translation of the sentence in your notebook.

F.   Write an *interpretative* translation of the sentence right under the literal one in your notebook.

3.   In 17 minutes we will go over the translations of the six sentences.

4.   If you finish the six sentences before 17 minutes are up, please begin your homework assignment, which appears in the usual place on the whiteboard.

Ms. Evans reads through the directions with the students, and the students begin the task at their desks. Soon several students raise their hands. Ms. Evans walks over to Brad, who tells her, "I can't do these." Ms. Evans notices that Brad has all his materials out with the text and notebook open to the appropriate pages but that he has neither circled any words nor written anything down. She says, "I'll be back to see what you've done in 70 seconds. In the meantime, do this." She points to line 2-A on his copy of the directions. Ms. Evans goes over to Anna Mae, who says, "What's *lugar* mean?" Ms. Evans says nothing but points to the words "Lightly circle with your pencil each word that you don't remember in English" in line 2-A of the directions. As Anna Mae circles *lugar,* Ms. Evans picks up Anna Mae's dictionary, hands it to her, and moves to another student.

Four Points about Independent Work Sessions

By keeping the following thoughts in mind, you may improve the chances that your students enjoy high levels of engagement during the independent work sessions that you plan and conduct.

1. Clearly define the task in the first place. In this way you will avoid many of the nagging questions about what to do and requests for reiterating directions that can be observed in many classrooms during independent work sessions. In Case 7.32, Ms. Evans's extra effort to specify her directions beforehand prevented her from wasting allocated time repeating or clarifying directions.

2. To provide real help efficiently to all students when they need it to remain engaged in an independent work session, avoid spending too much time with any one student. For students with adequate reading skills, having steps for task completion spelled out in writing allows you to refer students quickly to what they need to do to help themselves. Ms. Evans used this technique and avoided lengthy exchanges with students. For students who cannot read (e.g., some primary grade students), tasks for independent sessions should be kept extremely simple. If there are, for example, three steps in the completion of a task, the teacher might consider conducting three separate brief independent work sessions, devoting a session to each step.

3. To avoid having early-finishing students idly wait for others to complete the task, sequence independent work sessions so that they are followed by other independent activities with flexible beginning and ending times. The homework assignment Ms. Evans directed her students to begin after they translated the sentences could easily be interrupted when the class is ready to go over the translations and then completed later.

4. Establish some sort of formal routine for requesting help. This minimizes the time students spend waiting and maximizes the time they have for working on the task. Ms. Williams's flag-raising procedure in Case 5.4 is an example of such a formal routine.

Engage in Activity 7.7.

▶ ACTIVITY 7.7

Recall your experiences with teachers conducting independent work sessions. Think of one in whose sessions students tended to be highly engaged. Think of one whose sessions were such that students tended to be disengaged with only little quality participation. In a discussion with a colleague, contrast the two teachers' methods for conducting independent work sessions; point out what they did differently. Compare the differences to the aforementioned four points about independent work sessions.

▶ IDEAS FOR HOMEWORK ASSIGNMENTS

Student Engagement in Homework Assignments

Unlike most other types of learning activities, homework assignments typically require students to allocate their own time for engagement. Some students may have parents nearby encouraging them to be on-task. But parental supervision of students' homework varies extremely according to circumstances in homes, the ages of students, and myriad other factors (Cangelosi, 1992, pp. 20–22). Engagement in a homework assignment usually requires students to (a) understand directions for the assignment, (b) schedule time away from school for the assignment, (c) resist outside-of-school distractions while completing the assigned task, and (d) deliver a report of the completed work in class by a specified deadline.

Many teachers find it so difficult to have students diligently complete homework assignments that they have given up and no longer expect students to do homework. But for most academic subjects, homework is a critical form of learning activity that provides students with needed opportunities for solitary thinking, studying, practicing, and problem solving. The crowded social setting of a classroom is not conducive to the type of concentrated, undisturbed thinking that individuals must engage in to achieve certain cognitive learning objectives. To teach your students to complete homework you assign, you must make sure that engagement in this relatively unsupervised type of learning activity is positively reinforced. In Cases 7.33 and 7.35, Mr. Davis and Ms. Salsevon try both contrived positive reinforcement and contrived punishment to motivate students extrinsically to do homework. Ms. Hanzlik and Mr. Sampson, in Cases 7.34 and 7.36, use intrinsic motivation because the positive reinforcers for doing homework and the punishment for not doing it are naturally occurring:

▶ **CASE 7.33**

Mr. Davis directs his 28 third graders to complete the 25 multiplication computations from Exercise 8.6 of their mathematics workbook for homework. The next day he collects the workbooks and returns them with a smiling-face sticker on the homework of each student who has at least 20 correct answers. Four students who did not even attempt the exercise are verbally reprimanded in front of the class.

▶ **CASE 7.34**

Ms. Hanzlik carefully examines the 25 multiplication computations from Exercise 8.6 of her third graders' mathematics workbooks. For their homework, she selects the 12 computational exercises that she thinks will provide her students with practice in each of the possible problem areas typically encountered by students attempting this particular computational process. The next day she collects the work and does a quick error-pattern analysis (Ashlock, 2001). The papers are returned to the students with a clear indication of which steps in the computational process they did correctly and which they did not. Because she had carefully selected the computations, she is able to provide more helpful feedback with fewer computations than she would have been able to offer on all 25 computations or on randomly assigned ones.

While the rest of the students are going over her error-pattern analysis, correcting their mistakes, and beginning another assignment, Ms. Hanzlik calls the four students—Tim, Gail, Mary Jo, and Phil—who did not complete the assignment aside to speak with them. Ms. Hanzlik: "I'm sorry you didn't give me the opportunity to help you learn how to do this kind of multiplication." Phil: "I would've done it but—" Ms. Hanzlik interrupts, saying, "It doesn't make any difference why you didn't do it. Let's just figure out when you can get this done so I can analyze it and get it back to you before you leave school today. I need to do that for you before you can continue to learn math." Gail: "I forgot—" Ms. Hanzlik: "Please, just let me think of how I can help you. I know! Here's what we'll do. I'll let you do those 12 exercises right after lunch today. That's when the rest of the class will be baking pumpkin bread. You can finish it then, and I'll go over it right after school and get it back to you in time for you to catch your buses."

▶ **CASE 7.35**

As part of a unit on writing library papers, Ms. Salsevon directs her eighth-grade English class to choose a topic, find at least four references from the library on that topic, develop an outline for writing a report on the topic, and write an essay of five to eight pages following the outline. The assignment is due in two weeks. In the meantime, procedures for using the library, using references, outlining, and writing essays will be explained in class. The students are told that 40 percent of their grade for the unit will be based on whether or not this homework assignment is turned in on time. The other part of the grade will result from the exam given at the end of the unit.

▶ **CASE 7.36**

As part of a unit on writing library papers, Mr. Sampson provides his 26 eighth-grade English students with a list of topics and assigns the following homework: "Examine the list of topics. Pick three topics that interest you more than the others. For each of the three, write one paragraph explaining why that topic is more interesting to you than some of the others. Bring your paragraphs to class tomorrow."

The next day Mr. Sampson asks each student in class, "What three topics did you write about?" If the student lists three, then Mr. Sampson asks the student to read her or his favorite paragraph to the class. The nine students who do not have the assignment completed exactly as Mr. Sampson had directed are not asked to read to the class. After the last of 17 students reads, Mr. Sampson collects the papers and makes the following announcement: "Based on what you read to the class and what I read in these papers, I will assign each of you a topic for a project to be completed in the next two weeks."

The next day Mr. Sampson assigns topics by distributing to each student a slip of paper with the name of the topic. Those who had followed Mr. Sampson's directions with the previous homework assignment are given the popular, favored topics for their projects. Those who did not write paragraphs expressing their preferences are assigned the leftover topics. Mr. Sampson announces to the class, "For homework, go to the library and find four references about the topic for your project. Write out the title of each reference, its author, and one sentence on what the reference is about. Bring your list to class tomorrow." Six students raise their hands. Mr. Sampson calls on Allison. Allison: "What's a *reference*?" Mr. Sampson: "I'm glad you asked that! What did you want to say, Jessie?" Jessie: "I don't know what we're supposed to do." Mr. Sampson: "Allison doesn't know what a *reference* is, and Jessie doesn't know what to do for homework because I haven't explained these things to you yet. We're going to spend the rest of today's class explaining just how to do tonight's homework assignment." The rest of the day's English period is devoted to learning activities on how to find and report on references in the library.

The next day the learning activities focus on the lists of library references that the students bring to class. Some time is spent in explaining how to develop outlines for writing library papers. The homework assignment for the next day involves refining the reference lists and developing the first drafts of the outlines. This inextricable association between homework assignments and in-class learning activities continues throughout the unit until students are writing the final draft of the library paper for homework.

Students' grades for the unit are determined strictly by their performances on the in-class examination given at the end of the unit. But items on the exam require students to refer to how they used library references for their project, to refer to their outline, to refer to their final library paper, and to attach a copy of both their outline and the library paper.

Eight Points about Homework Assignments

Your students are more likely to complete homework assignments on time if you keep the following thoughts in mind when planning those assignments:

1. Plan learning activities, especially early in a school term, to teach students how to budget time for homework and procedures for completing homework. Students do not automatically know how to schedule their time for homework, study efficiently, or present homework as a teacher expects it.

2. Simple, uncomplicated homework assignments are more likely to be followed than complex ones. Unlike Ms. Salsevon, Mr. Sampson divided a complex, multistep assignment into numerous simple assignments.

3. Students tend to delay the completion of assignments until just before they are due. Thus, for long-range assignments, set short-range deadline dates for completion of intermediate steps that eventually lead to final completion. Rather than simply requiring the library paper to be completed at the end of the two-week period, Mr. Sampson had students complete specific tasks leading to the final paper throughout that two-week period.

4. All homework assignments should clearly be an integral part of an overall plan of learning activities designed to help students achieve worthwhile goals. Some teachers assign homework only because it's expected. Consequently, the assignment does not tie in very well to in-class learning activities. These teachers' students learn to consider homework to be a useless waste of time. Using homework as punishment or withholding homework assignments as a reward are destructive forms of punishment or positive reinforcement that teach students to resent having to do homework.

5. Student behavior patterns of diligently doing homework assignments are encouraged when their efforts are positively reinforced by feedback provided by their teachers. Mr. Davis's students only found out whether their final answers on their homework were right or wrong. Ms. Hanzlik, on the other hand, provided her students with helpful feedback on just how to execute the computations.

6. Ms. Salsevon attempted to motivate her students to complete a homework assignment by making students' grades contingent on whether or not the assignment was completed on time. Mr. Sampson, on the other hand, treated the assignment as a learning activity, not a test. But he made it clear that the homework assignment helped the students achieve exactly the same learning goals that the graded examination would test. Students can learn the importance of diligently doing homework when there is a clear link between homework assignments and tests. To help students make this association early in the school year, consider giving tests requiring students to complete tasks that are nearly identical to those assigned for homework. Do this early in a school term; and until students develop behavior patterns of doing homework, virtually always test after every homework assignment.

7. If teachers use homework in the class session in which it is due, students who fail to complete the assignment can experience naturally occurring punishment

by being unable to participate fully in class. Similarly, students who have completed the assignment on time can be positively reinforced by the success they experience in class. Mr. Sampson tied each homework assignment in his unit on writing library papers to in-class learning activities. Students who failed to complete homework as specified by his directions felt clearly disadvantaged in the class period when the assignment was due.

8. If the potential for parents to encourage or supervise their children's homework is ever to be realized, teachers, at the very least, must keep parents apprised of homework expectations. Some teachers have parents sign agreements indicating that they will supervise and encourage children to do homework.

Engage in Activity 7.8.

▶ **ACTIVITY 7.8**

Recall your experiences with teachers' homework assignments. Think of assignments in which you willingly engaged and found to be productive learning experiences. Think of some that you either skipped or engaged in only reluctantly. Think of some that were a waste of your time. In a discussion with a colleague, compare the homework assignments and how they differed with respect to the aforementioned eight points about homework.

▶ CLASSROOM DESIGNS THAT ENHANCE STUDENT ENGAGEMENT

To implement some of the ideas presented here for conducting engaging learning activities, you must be able to move easily and quickly about your classroom. Your classroom's acoustical characteristics need to allow students to hear what you intend them to hear without disturbing reverberations and background noise. Students can hardly be engaged in a learning activity in which visual presentations are used if they cannot comfortably see what is displayed. Transition time cannot be minimized when major rearrangements of furniture are required between learning activities. Furthermore, it is difficult for you to take one or several students aside and hold a conference if there is no convenient area for doing so while still supervising the rest of the students.

Questions regarding optimum classroom size and ideal room shape have been studied (Louglin, 1992). Acoustics can be vastly improved by the installation of sound-absorbing material on walls, a carpet, and FM amplification equipment (Berg, 1987, 1990; Worner, 1988). On-task student behaviors tend to improve with such installations (Allen & Patton, 1990). Unfortunately, teachers typically have virtually no control over the size and shape of their classrooms or any equipment permanently installed in them. Teachers are assigned rooms that they did not design to accommodate groups of students whom they did not select. Despite these unfavorable conditions, many teachers maximize their resources and enhance their learning environments by carefully and creatively arranging their classrooms (Cangelosi, 1992, pp. 9–15; Evertson, Emmer, & Worsham, 2006). Case 7.37 is an example.

▶ CASE 7.37

In her first year as an English and Spanish teacher at Vanguard High School, Ms. Del Rio is assigned Room 129 for homeroom and for teaching two remedial reading classes with 23 and 27 students, respectively, one American literature class of 30, and two Spanish 1 classes with 29 and 30 students, respectively. Room 129's initial arrangement and the way Ms. Del Rio uses it for the first month is depicted in Figure 7.9.

Because Ms. Del Rio stresses problem-solving and student-centered learning activities, she finds Room 129's initial arrangement inconvenient. It is difficult for her and the students to move

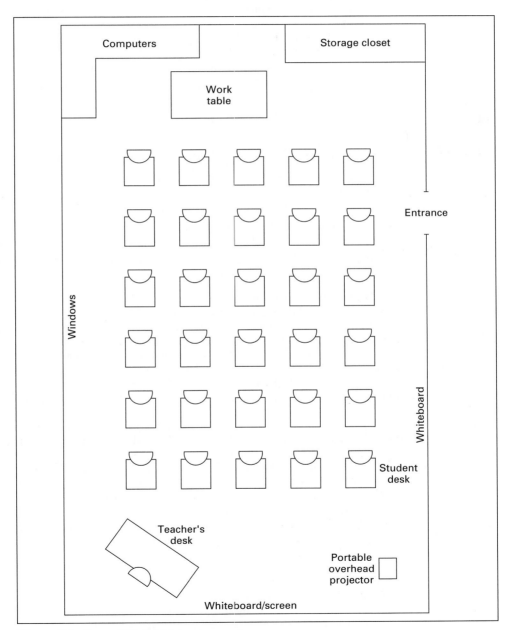

Figure 7.9. Room 129's Initial Arrangement

around. She laments, "I have to negotiate an obstacle course to provide individual help to students located near the center of the room. I jab myself at least twice a day on the corners of these desks!" She is unable to move conveniently and smoothly in the vicinity of students whom she notices drifting off-task. Furthermore, the arrangement does not provide for separation between sound-producing group activity areas (e.g., for multimedia presentations) and quiet areas (e.g., where individual reading or computer-based instruction is taking place).

Dissatisfied with the inflexible arrangement, Ms. Del Rio makes a list of the accommodations she wants her room to provide:

1. Quick and easy access for her between any two points in the room

2. A designated quiet area for students to engage in individualized work

3. A designated large-group activity area for an entire class to congregate for discussions, lectures, tutorial sessions, and media presentations

4. Small-group activity areas for cooperative groups to conduct their business

5. Storage space for equipment and materials to be kept out of sight

6. A secure teacher's desk in a location with a favorable vantage point

7. A silent reading room and minilibrary that can comfortably accommodate several students at a time

8. A time-out room for isolating students

9. A private room in which Ms. Del Rio can hold uninterrupted conferences with individuals (e.g., a student with his or her parents) when a class is not in session

10. A two-way communication device (e.g., a telephone) with which she can quickly summon backup support in crisis situations

Ms. Del Rio doesn't believe she can possibly build all the features on her wish list into her classroom, but she does begin modifying Room 129 to resemble more closely her ideal classroom. In the third month of the school year, she manages to have the school administration exchange the 30 traditional student desks for ten 6.5 feet by 2.67 feet elliptical tables and 30 folding chairs. Her arrangement with three students per table is diagrammed in Figure 7.10. Although she would prefer students to have their own desks rather than share tables, this new arrangement provides more work areas in the back of the room and makes it easier for her to move about the room from one student to another. For small-group discussions, she can quickly have students rearrange tables and chairs to follow the pattern given in Figure 7.11.

Ms. Del Rio needs the storage space provided by the large closet in the back of the room. But she also needs more space in that part of the room for the quiet-area work section. To remedy that situation, she gets the school's maintenance manager to install a closet with a whiteboard and projection screen on the doors in each of the two corners in the front of the room. These two front corners had only been dead space. With this latest modification, depicted in Figure 7.12, Room 129 has more viewable board and screen areas, storage space is maintained, and additional floor areas are available in the back of the room.

Following the news report of a violent tragedy at a school in another state, Vanguard's principal makes a public appeal to fund a safe-school program. The school board provides each teacher with a portable phone to be used for crisis situations.

During the summer break after her first year, Ms. Del Rio calls on the generosity and skills of some of her students and their parents. They partition off an 8 foot by 10 foot area in the back of Room 129 to serve as a combination minilibrary, reading room, time-out room, conference room, and out-of-class-hours escape room for Ms. Del Rio to work undisturbed. Used book shelves, a low-standing table, a sofa, and two chairs—all labeled "surplus" in the school district's warehouse—furnish the new room. While the volunteer carpenters are walling in the room,

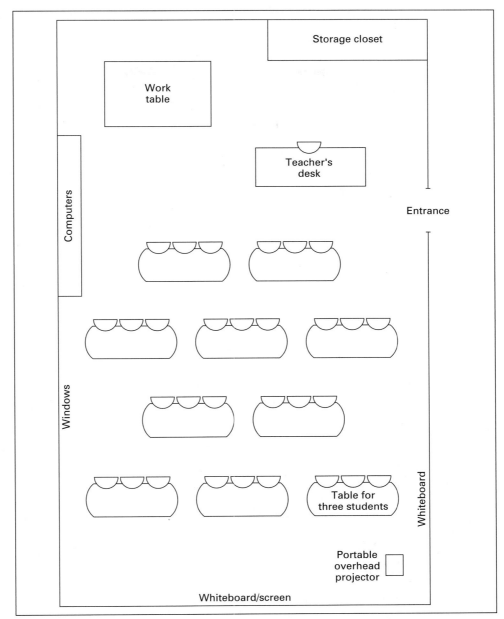

Figure 7.10. Ms. Del Rio's First Rearrangement of Room 129, Set Up for Large-Group Activities

Ms. Del Rio mentions that it would be nice to have individual work stations with the computers in the quiet area in the back of the room. Mr. Singleton, a cabinetmaker by profession, custom-makes the stations to her specifications. Figure 7.13 depicts how Room 129 appears on the first day of Ms. Del Rio's second year at Vanguard. Ms. Del Rio finds it easier to keep students on-task in her second year at Vanguard than she did in her first. An additional year's experience plays a major role

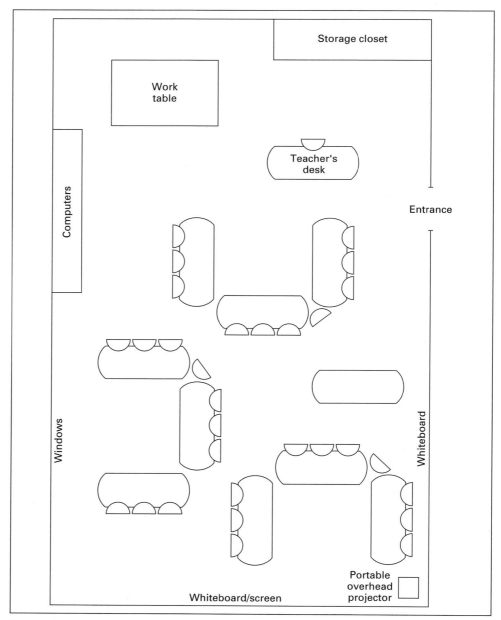

Figure 7.11. Ms. Del Rio's First Rearrangement of Room 129, Set Up for Small-Group Activities

as do the modifications to Room 129. But she sometimes finds the noise from the learning activities in the front of the room disturbing to the individualized activities in the rear. The problem is mitigated after she makes a presentation for Vanguard's Home and School Association and offers a tour of her room. Members are so impressed with her initiative and need for sound separation that they appropriate funds for installing two doors and a sound-insulated glass wall in Room 129. The

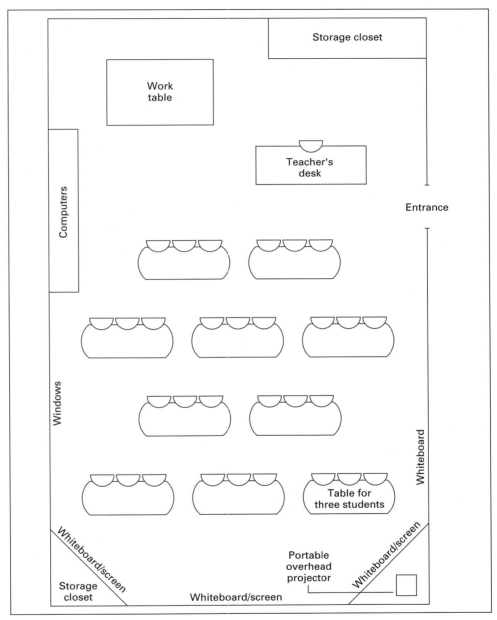

Figure 7.12. Ms. Del Rio Provides for More Space in the Rear of Room 129

project is completed over the December holiday break, and Room 129 appears as in Figure 7.14. Ms. Del Rio would have continued to improve Room 129 had she not accepted a position for the following year at Rose Park High. Room 244, which she will be assigned at Rose Park, is similar to the one depicted in Figure 7.9.

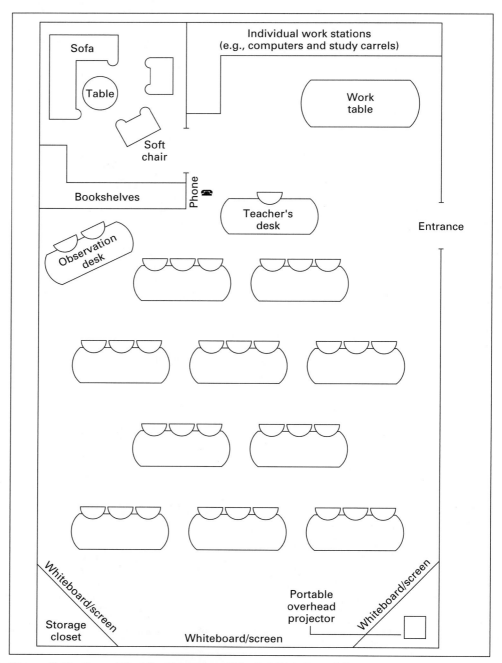

Figure 7.13. Room 129 at the Beginning of Ms. Del Rio's Second Year

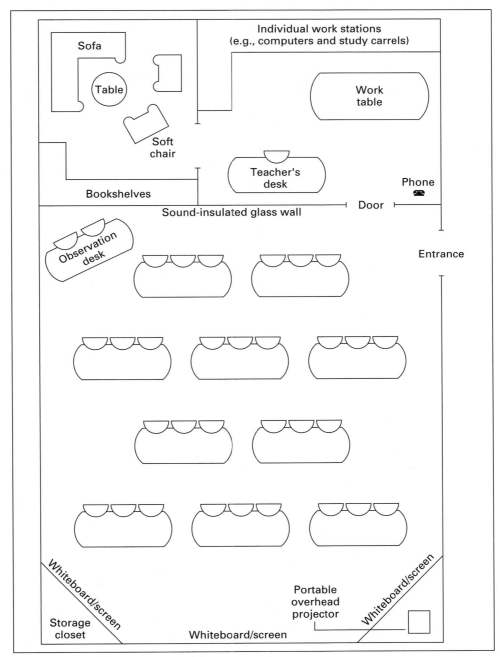

Figure 7.14. Room 129 as Ms. Del Rio Finally Left It

Case 7.38 involves an elementary school classroom.

▶ **CASE 7.38**

Figure 7.15 is a diagram of Room 9 in Public School 157, where Mr. Hawkoos is assigned to teach 27 third graders. Through tactics similar to those used by Ms. Del Rio, Mr. Hawkoos's room is modified as diagramed in Figure 7.16.

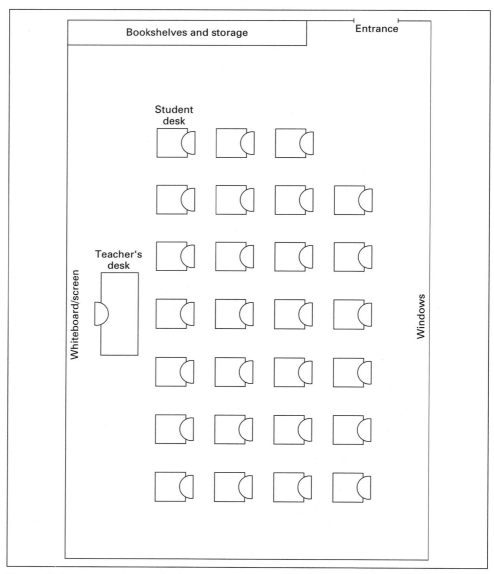

Figure 7.15. Room 9, P.S. 157 When Mr. Hawkoos First Took Charge

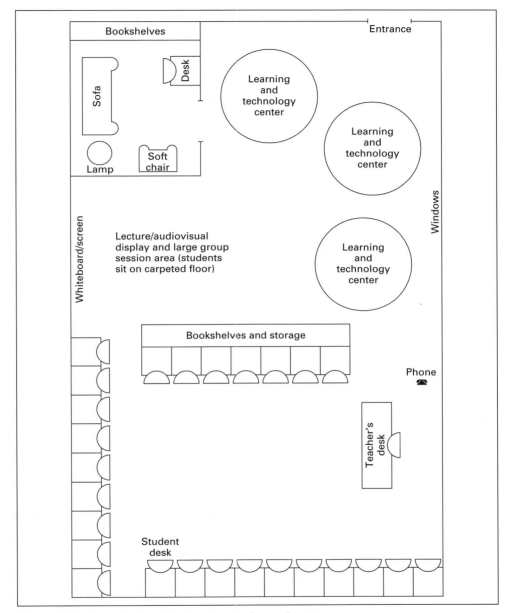

Figure 7.16. Room 9, P.S. 157 After Mr. Hawkoos' Alterations

▶ SYNTHESIS ACTIVITIES FOR CHAPTER 7

I. Develop two overall unit plans for teaching a four-year-old how to count from 1 to 20. Design the first plan so that it does not use problem-based learning activities. Design the second plan so that it does use problem-based learning activities. Discuss with two or three colleagues how the two unit plans differ.

II. Discuss with a colleague the advantages and disadvantages—relative to keeping students engaged—of using a problem-based instructional approach instead of non-problem-based approach.

III. Did you include the following points in the discussion when you responded to Transitional Activity II's prompt?

> In general, students tend to be intrinsically motivated to engage in problem-based learning activities because they discover they can accomplish some of the things that are important to them through engagement in the learning activities. Because problem-based learning activities tend to be more student-centered and indirect than traditional styles of teaching, students may initially consider them unusual and unstructured. Consequently, they may tend to be off-task until they are taught on-task behaviors for this new type of activity. Problem-based learning activities should not be thrust all at once on students who are not used to them.

IV. Develop a lesson plan for teaching an objective within one of your teaching specialties. Plan the lesson so that during learning activities you are in an advantageous position to monitor student engagement. Describe in some detail how you will deliver directions to students for the lesson's learning activities. Compare your plan with those of colleagues with respect to (a) strategies for monitoring student engagement and (b) consistency of the directions with the points enumerated in this chapter's section "Nine Points about Directions."

V. Reread Case 7.4. With a colleague, discuss why you agree or disagree with the following statements:

- The variety of learning activities in Ms. Piscatelli's unit prevents lessons from being monotonous.

- Ms. Piscatelli's problem-based approach to unit design leads to lessons that are more complex than traditional lessons. Thus, to keep students engaged in the various types of learning activities, she needs to be even more explicit with her directions than do teachers whose practices are more traditional.

VI. Design a lecture activity within one of your teaching specialities. In one or two paragraphs, describe your plan for conducting the lecture. Compare your lecture plan with those of colleagues and analyze the plans for consistency with the suggestions implied by the section "Fourteen Points about Lectures."

VII. Design a cooperative group-learning activity within one of your teaching specialties. In one or two paragraphs, describe your plan for conducting the activity. Compare your plan with those of colleagues and analyze the plans for consistency with the suggestions implied by the section "Ten Points about Cooperative Learning Sessions."

VIII. Design a high-level discussion activity within one of your teaching specialties. In one or two paragraphs, describe your plan for conducting the session. Compare your plan with those of colleagues and analyze the plans for consistency with suggestions implied by the section "Seven Points about Discussion Sessions."

IX. Design a reasoning-level questioning activity within one of your teaching specialties. In one or two paragraphs, describe your plan for conducting the session. Compare your plan with those of colleagues and analyze the plans for consistency with the suggestions implied by the section "Six Points about Questioning Sessions."

X. Design an independent work activity within one of your teaching specialties. In one or two paragraphs, describe your plan for conducting the session. Compare your plan with those of colleagues and analyze the plans for consistency with the suggestions implied by the section "Four Points about Independent Work Sessions."

XI. Design a homework activity within one of your teaching specialties. Write out the assignment. Compare your assignment with the assignments of colleagues and analyze them for consistency with the suggestions implied by the section "Eight Points about Homework Assignments."

XII. Examine a classroom used to teach students in one of your teaching specialties. Make a detailed sketch of the room arrangement. Decide how you would rearrange the room to make it more conducive to students' being on-task. Sketch your modified arrangement. Compare your classroom rearrangement with those of colleagues. Which features from Ms. Del Rio's list of 10 in Case 7.37 did you incorporate?

► TRANSITIONAL ACTIVITY FROM CHAPTER 7 TO CHAPTER 8

In preparation for your work with Chapter 8, discuss with two or more colleagues the following questions.

I. What are some strategies for decisively and effectively dealing with student misbehaviors?

II. What responsibilities do teachers have regarding the building of the character of their students?

III. How do effective strategies for dealing with isolated incidents of off-task behavior differ from effective strategies for dealing with off-task behavior patterns?

IV. How can teachers act as classroom disciplinarians without having students feel they're being robbed of their dignities?

V. What are some strategies teachers employ to discourage student misbehavior when misbehaving students are not readily identified?

VI. Is corporal punishment ever an appropriate response to student misbehavior? Why or why not?

VII. How far does the authority of a teacher extend when dealing with student discipline problems?

PART IV

CONFRONTING AND SOLVING DISCIPLINE PROBLEMS

Approaching Off-Task Behaviors Systematically

▶ CHAPTER 8'S GOAL AND OBJECTIVES

The goal of this chapter is for you to develop strategies for responding to off-task student behaviors. Specifically, Chapter 8 is designed to lead you to achieve the following objectives:

1. Apply the teaching cycles model to systematically deal with student off-task behaviors rather than reacting without careful consideration of how to teach students to supplant off-task behaviors with on-task behaviors.

2. Develop your own ideas for implementing each of the following suggestions for responding to student off-task behaviors: (a) Deal with misbehaviors well before they "get to you." (b) Either respond decisively to an off-task behavior or ignore it altogether. (c) Distinguish between teaching students to be on-task and building character. (d) Distinguish between isolated off-task behaviors and off-task behavior patterns. (e) Control the time and place for dealing with off-task behavior. (f) Provide your students with dignified ways to terminate off-task behaviors. (g) Avoid playing detective. (h) Use the help of colleagues, parents, and supervisors. (i) Use alternative lesson plans. (j) Do not use corporal punishment. (k) Know your rights and limitations. (l) Maintain your options. (m) Know your students and yourself.

▶ DEAL WITH OFF-TASK BEHAVIORS VIA THE TEACHING CYCLES MODEL

A Mechanism for Focusing

Compare Cases 8.1 and 8.2.

▶ CASE 8.1

Ms. Blythe is lecturing to her eighth-grade class when Jane, one of her 26 students, begins looking around and tapping her pencil against her desk. Ms. Blythe finds Jane's behavior annoying and judges it to be a potential distraction to others in the class. From her position in the front of the room and without much thought, Ms. Blythe interrupts herself to complain to Jane, "Will you stop that infernal tapping, Jane? Can't you ever do what you're supposed to?"

▶ **CASE 8.2**

Ms. Guevarra is lecturing to her eighth-grade class when Jeanne, one of her 26 students, begins looking around and tapping her pencil against her desk. Ms. Guevarra finds Jeanne's behavior annoying and judges it to be a potential distraction to others in the class. Within the span of three seconds and without interrupting her lecture, Ms. Guevarra thinks to herself: "Jeanne needs to pay attention and quit making that noise. This isn't a chronic behavior for Jeanne; I've never had to deal with it from her before. I will get her to stop and return her attention to the lecture. How should I accomplish this? I'll continue to lecture, but I'll move near her and make eye contact. If that doesn't get her attention or she continues to tap, I'll gently touch the pencil she's tapping. If that fails, I'll think of another tactic."

Continuing her lecture, she walks to a point near Jeanne. Jeanne ceases looking around and appears to attend to the lecture, but she keeps tapping her pencil. Ms. Guevarra gently touches the pencil. Jeanne stops tapping and hardly any of the other class members even notice the silent communication between Ms. Guevarra and Jeanne. Ms. Guevarra continues to monitor how well Jeanne and the other students attend to the lecture.

Unlike Ms. Blythe, Ms. Guevarra systematically dealt with an off-task behavior as she would deal with any other student learning need. She approached Jeanne's off-task behavior using the same steps of the teaching cycles model that she would use to teach a learning unit in science, social studies, physical education, or any other curriculum content area. In a matter of seconds she executed the following steps:

1. *Identified a student need:* She decided that Jeanne should stop tapping and pay attention.

2. *Determined a learning objective:* She decided that she would somehow get Jeanne to stop tapping and become engaged in the lecture session.

3. *Planned a learning activity:* She decided to stand by Jeanne, make eye contact, and gently touch Jeanne's pencil as she continued with her lecture.

4. *Prepared for the learning activity:* She moved into position to carry out her plan. (This whole incident happened so fast that Ms. Guevarra had virtually no need to prepare for the rather simple learning activity in this example. Admittedly, a point is stretched here to remind you of all six steps of the teaching cycles model. In more complicated examples of teachers dealing with off-task behaviors, preparation for the learning activity may be quite elaborate.)

5. *Conducted the learning activity:* She actually stood by Jeanne trying to make eye contact and gently touching her pencil.

6. *Evaluated how well the learning objective was achieved:* She observed Jeanne to see if she would begin to tap and look around again.

Ms. Blythe's response to Jane's off-task behavior appeared to be an unthinking reaction to being annoyed. Instead of focusing on the problem of getting Jane to terminate the disruptive behavior in favor of engaged behavior, Ms. Blythe interrupted her lecture and attacked Jane's personality with an irrelevant rhetorical question. Such tactics may get Jane to stop tapping and look forward, but she would be a very unusual adolescent if she listened to and thought about the substance of Ms. Blythe's lecture immediately after being asked, "Can't you ever do what you're supposed to?" Jane was probably thinking about what she considered to be Ms. Blythe's insulting and embarrassing attack in front of her peers. Furthermore, the engagement of other students was disrupted.

Of course, Ms. Blythe's approach to Jane's off-task behavior was understandable. Teachers are continually faced with the problem of orchestrating a group of young people who can manage to display very annoying behaviors. Students *ought* to behave cooperatively without teachers having to apply creative tactics to lead them to do what they should do on their own. It's no wonder that Ms. Blythe sometimes reacts thoughtlessly to her students' displays of disruptive behaviors. Although her tactics were understandable, they're ineffectual. To overcome the temptation to respond to students' annoying behaviors with ineffective displays of emotion, you would do well to train yourself to be constantly mindful of the teaching cycles model. By having your thoughts organized according to the six steps of the model, you can systematically respond to students' displays of off-task behaviors, even the annoying ones, as Ms. Guevarra did.

More Elaborate Applications

In Cases 8.3 and 8.4, teachers deal with off-task behaviors systematically by applying the teaching cycles model. Unlike the students in Cases 8.1 and 8.2, these students exhibit off-task behaviors that are behavior patterns rather than isolated occurrences. Consequently, the tactics used need to be more elaborate than Ms. Guevarra's.

▶ CASE 8.3

Al, one of Ms. Reid's fourth graders, is engaged in a small-group learning activity with four other students playing geography bingo. The game leader calls out, "The largest continent." Paul exclaims, "Bingo! It's Asia, and I've got it right here for bingo!" Al stands up and yells at Paul, "You stupid asshole! I had that one too! I could've got bingo!" Al shoves Paul down and upsets the other students' game cards. Ms. Reid moves directly to Al and briskly ushers him to a point just outside the classroom door. Looking directly into Al's face, she calmly says, "Wait here while I check to see if Paul is hurt." Without giving Al a chance to speak, she turns and walks back to where the incident occurred as other students gather around Paul. Although he is still lying on the floor, Paul is beginning to communicate his plans for retaliation. Ms. Reid interrupts Paul, saying, "I'm sorry that Al pushed you down, but I'm happy that you are not hurt." Helping Paul to his feet, Ms. Reid continues speaking without giving anyone else a chance to complain about Al or giving Paul a chance to make further threats. Ms. Reid: "Blaine and Carol, I would appreciate your helping each other pick up this mess and getting the bingo game started again. Let's go with just four players this time. Everyone else, please return to your work. Thank you for cooperating." Ms. Reid quickly returns to Al standing in the doorway and says, "Right now, I don't have time to work with you on your misbehavior during geography bingo. I have a class to teach, and it's time for you to work on geography. We'll just have to wait until tomorrow morning to discuss this matter. When your bus arrives tomorrow morning, you come immediately to the classroom and meet me at my desk. Will you remember, or should I phone your house tonight to remind you?" Al: "I'll remember." Ms. Reid: "Fine! Now you still have 13 minutes to work on geography. Go get your geography book and bring it to me at my desk." At her desk, Ms. Reid directs Al to complete a geography exercise at a work table located away from the rest of the class. The exercise is a drill on the same geography skills that the bingo game is designed to develop.

At the end of the school day, when Ms. Reid experiences her first solitary moments after the students have been dismissed, she thinks to herself: "I bought myself some time to figure out what to do about Al's outbursts in class. That was a real chance I took ushering him to the door. With his temper, he might have turned on me. This is the third or fourth time something like this has happened while Al was involved in a group activity. What makes him so aggressive? Well, that's not what I have to worry about right now. My job is to prevent this from happening again. I'll exclude him from any small-group activity for the time being. Today I hope he didn't think the geography book exercise was a punishment. I don't want to teach him to hate geography. Somehow he's got to understand that antisocial behavior isn't tolerated in my classroom! Look at me; I'm getting myself all worked up just sitting here by myself. What do I do? I could explain my dilemma to him and involve him in the design of a solution. That tactic worked really well with Grayson. But Grayson has a different chemistry from Al's. Al isn't ready for that yet. He's too defensive; he'd be telling me how it wasn't his fault. I'd love to know more about his home situation and find out why he's so defensive. But I don't have time to worry about that. I've got a more immediate problem to solve. Okay, here's what I'll do:

1. I don't want to give him a chance to argue and be defensive when we meet tomorrow, so I won't even try to explain the reasons for the way I'm dealing with the problem. I'll simply tell him what we're going to do and not defend the plan.

2. I will assign him to work by himself away from others whenever he would normally be involved in some small-group activity. His independent assignment will cover content similar to the small-group activity in which others will be engaged.

3. I'll watch for indicators that he is modifying his antisocial behavior pattern and becoming more willing to cooperate in group activities.

4. Gradually I'll work him back into group activities as I see encouraging indications that there will be no more trouble. I'll avoid involving him in any sort of competitive activities for a long time.

"Okay, how shall I present this plan to him tomorrow? What will I do if he doesn't show up tomorrow? I'd better prepare for that possibility. . . ."

▶ CASE 8.4

Mr. Mitchelson routinely assigns his eleventh-grade literature class homework that takes students about 45 minutes to complete satisfactorily. Assignments might involve the students in reading a short story, writing an essay, or preparing a reference report. For the first several months of the school session, Mr. Mitchelson finds that only a few students take the time and effort to complete the assignments to his satisfaction. His discussions with students indicate that they view the assignments as busywork that holds little value for them. Most of them fake their way through the assignments, barely doing enough to keep them "out of trouble" with Mr. Mitchelson. In response to this concern Mr. Mitchelson incorporates some of the principles of problem-based learning activities; he makes certain that students recognize the relation between these homework assignments and problems that they feel a need to solve. Gradually, nearly every student is consistently completing the homework in a satisfactory manner.

Wilma, however, is one of the exceptions. Even though Mr. Mitchelson's assignments are now meaningful to the students, Wilma rarely completes homework. The fact that Mr. Mitchelson is now using in-class learning activities that depend on completion of homework assignments compounds Wilma's difficulties because her failure to complete homework makes it nearly impossible for her to participate in class. When queried about homework, Wilma consistently indicates that she tries but just can't get the assignments finished. Mr. Mitchelson believes Wilma has the ability to complete the work satisfactorily. He decides to do something to help her consistently choose to do homework.

As he plans the learning activities for teaching her this on-task behavior pattern, he thinks: "I could subtract points from her grade for not getting assignments in on time, but her literature grade should reflect how well she achieves course goals, not how faithfully she finishes work. I want to base grades on test scores. Of course, if she continues not finishing homework, there's no way she'll achieve the goals; consequently, she'll get poor grades anyway. Maybe I should just let her go, and she'll learn a lesson when she receives a failing grade. That would work nicely as naturally occurring punishment. But what is my purpose here—to teach her some lifelong lesson about being responsible or to help her achieve course goals? I'm not going to take on the problem of trying to change her life, just teach her literature by trying to get her engaged in my learning activities. No, I won't just let it go. The next time she doesn't complete an assignment, I could refer her to Mr. Taylor. But even though he's the counselor, I don't think he'd be much help. Scratch that one. What if I set up a contingency contract with her, working out a system in which privileges depend on completion of homework? I'll save that one for later if something less drastic doesn't work out. What about requiring her to remain after school to complete unfinished work? Then she'd miss her bus, which is fine with me. That would be a nice naturally occurring punishment. But then I'd have to stay with her, and I don't want to do that to myself. Although I'm always here until five o'clock anyway, I need that time for other things, not standing over her pushing her to finish. Scratch another good idea. What I really need to do is find out why she doesn't finish these assignments and then plan something from there.

"She doesn't have a job or anything; she must have the time. Grace says she normally turns in her math homework. Let's see, tomorrow's schedule calls for her to turn in a report expressing why she thinks the people Charley works with in *Flowers for Algernon* are not his friends. And then most of the class has free reading time scheduled at the library. If she doesn't have the report as assigned, I'll require her to finish it in class. There'll be only about five others in the room at that time, and I can observe her working on the assignment."

The next day Wilma has only the introductory paragraph to her report. In that one paragraph, the purpose of the report is accurately stated. As planned, Mr. Mitchelson directs her to complete the report by the end of the 55-minute class period. Wilma sits and stares at her paper for 10 minutes without writing. Mr. Mitchelson goes to her and looks over her shoulder. She asks, "Mr. Mitchelson, is my introduction okay?" "You've stated the purpose with clarity," he replies and moves away. Several minutes later, she comes to Mr. Mitchelson and says, "Were the factory workers Charley's friends or not?" Mr. Mitchelson: "That's a matter of opinion. What do you think?" Wilma: "I don't know." Mr. Mitchelson: "You say you don't know what you think." Wilma: "Well, I don't think the workers were very nice to Charley. Am I wrong?" Mr. Mitchelson: "You can't be wrong. It's a matter of opinion. There is no way to be right or wrong in this case. As you said in your introduction, the purpose of this report is to express your opinion on whether or not the workers were Charley's friends. If you say what you believe, then you are correct whether or not anyone else agrees with you." Wilma: "Oh!" Wilma returns to her seat and writes for five minutes before returning to Mr. Mitchelson with one more line written. "Is this right, Mr. Mitchelson?" she asks. . . .

After the school day, Mr. Mitchelson continues thinking about ways to help Wilma choose to complete assignments: "Wilma really seems reluctant to express her opinions. She finally completed her report in class, but in the meantime she drove me nuts seeking my approval on each line before she'd write the next. She appears afraid to complete one step in an assignment before having the previous step okay'd. Either that or she doesn't trust others and me to accept her opinions. Now that I think about it, just about all the assignments she doesn't do require her to express her opinion. I think Wilma needs to learn that I'm receptive to and value her opinions. It will take some time for her to become convinced of that. In the meantime, as an intermediate step, I should help her get in the habit of completing homework. For now, I'll implement the following plan:

1. I'll privately tell her just what I've decided and that I expect her to complete every assignment.

2. For at least a week, I won't give her assignments requiring her to express her own opinions. For example, with the *Flowers for Algernon* report, instead of directing her to report on why she thinks the people that Charley works with are not his friends, I'll modify it so she's asked to write about somebody else's opinion of whether or not they were Charley's friends. Maybe the assignment for her would be to interview a classmate and report his or her opinion on the question.

3. If Wilma completes these modified assignments every day for a week, I'll gradually begin giving her assignments where she's to express her own opinions. I'll be careful never to judge her opinions; I'll judge only the processes by which she arrives at those opinions. If she doesn't complete all the first week's assignments, then I'll reevaluate the situation, consider other causes, and maybe move to a contingency contract plan to positively reinforce doing homework.

"I need to carefully evaluate how well this works before deciding whether or not to change my strategy."

Engage in Activity 8.1.

▶ *ACTIVITY 8.1*

Discuss with a colleague the advantages and disadvantages of the way Ms. Reid handled Al's disruptive behavior in Case 8.3 and the way Mr. Mitchelson handled Wilma's failure to complete assignments in Case 8.4.

Staying Calm and Organizing Thoughts

In Cases 8.2 to 8.4, Ms. Guevarra, Ms. Reid, and Mr. Mitchelson viewed the problem of eliminating off-task behavior as they would view the problem of helping a student to achieve any other learning objective. By applying teaching techniques to the task of helping students choose on-task behaviors instead of off-task ones, they were able to focus their time, energy, and thoughts on the important issues confronting them. Ms. Reid, for example, did not try to moralize about the evils of fighting. She realized that telling Al about the evils of fighting—something he's likely to have already heard—would serve nothing. Teachers such as Ms. Blythe who do not systematically focus on the behavior to be altered tend to compound difficulties by dwelling on irrelevant issues (e.g., whether or not Jane can ever do what she's supposed to do). Teachers who fail to focus on the goal of getting and keeping students on-task and engaged in learning activities sometimes feel offended when students are disruptive or do not pay attention. These teachers may deal with their own hurt feelings by retaliating against students rather than focusing on getting the students to behave as they should.

The teaching cycles model provides you with a way of organizing your thoughts about teaching students to behave as they should. As you apply this model, you will need to design strategies for dealing with off-task behaviors. The remainder of this chapter provides you with 14 suggestions for devising strategies. Chapter 9 focuses on ways for you to develop strategies that help students supplant off-task behavior patterns with on-task behavior patterns. Chapter 10 is concerned with ideas for dealing with nondisruptive off-task behaviors; Chapter 11's concern is disruptive behaviors.

▶ DEAL WITH MISBEHAVIORS BEFORE THEY "GET TO YOU"

Too often, teachers allow off-task behavior to continue until they become so irritated that they are too stressed to handle the situation constructively. Consider Case 8.5.

▶ CASE 8.5

As part of a process-writing lesson, Mr. Edwards's students are paired off, two to a computer, editing one another's essays. Mr. Edwards notices that Clarence and Paige's discussion centers more on gossiping about Florence, one of their classmates, than on writing. Hoping their ratio of on-task talk to gossip will soon increase, Mr. Edwards does not intervene. Three minutes later, he notices their gossiping has spread to a neighboring pair. Now four students are spending less time on editing and more time whispering about Florence who is situated on the other side of the room. In addition to his concern for keeping students engaged in the activity, he now worries that Florence will overhear the unkind things being said. Not wanting to call her attention to their rudeness, Mr. Edwards's anger rises. Still, he does nothing until more and more off-task conversations erupt around the room. No longer containing himself, Mr. Edwards yells, "Because so many of you don't seem to be worried about getting your papers edited, we'll just have you all print out right now and turn in the essays the way they are!" Most students have no idea what Mr. Edwards is referring to when he declares, "Some people in here have to put down other people to feel better about themselves!"

By the time Mr. Edwards judged he should no longer tolerate the disruptive talking, he was too agitated to think through an effective intervention plan. His agitation clouded his thoughts; consequently, he badly mishandled the episode. Initially he acted passively instead of assertively. Typically, passive behavior explodes into hostile behavior, as in Case 8.5. As Figure 8.1 shows, you should decisively and assertively deal with off-task behaviors well before they approach levels you consider intolerable.

▶ EITHER RESPOND DECISIVELY TO AN OFF-TASK BEHAVIOR OR IGNORE IT ALTOGETHER

Consider Case 8.6.

▶ CASE 8.6

Ms. Hillyard is busy explaining some rules for capitalizing words to her class of 31 fifth graders. "Now, who can tell me which words in this sentence should begin with a capital letter?" she asks as she begins to write on the whiteboard, "my friend eddie said 'looking for ghosts' was a—" Just then, she hears some students talking among themselves. Looking over her shoulder, she sees Don, Abby, and Lyle involved in a conversation. "Hey, you chatterboxes, stop talking and pay attention," she says as she finishes writing the sentence, "—funny movie." The three students continue talking. They hardly heard Ms. Hillyard's message because she failed to get their attention before speaking. Ms. Hillyard continues her explanation for several more minutes before once again trying to quiet Don, Abby, and Lyle: "Okay, I told you to knock it off already. This time I mean no more talking!" She continues her lesson as they continue talking.

It would be inadvisable for Ms. Hillyard to ignore her students' inappropriate talking; however, ignoring the misbehavior in the example would not have been as destructive as

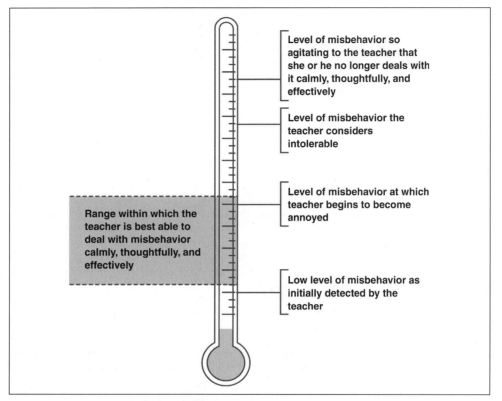

Figure 8.1. Deal with Misbehaviors Before They "Get to You"

her weak, halfhearted response. Not only were her efforts for dealing with the off-task behaviors ineffectual, but her actions displayed to the students in the class that they need not seriously consider her directions. In general, an indecisive, perfunctory attempt at dealing with one incident of off-task behavior compounds a teacher's difficulties in effectively dealing with subsequent occurrences. Here is why:

- When a teacher demonstrates that he or she is aware of off-task behaviors but does not make an effective effort to lead the students to supplant off-task with on-task behaviors, students tend to generalize that the teacher is not serious about expecting them to be on-task. Such an attitude detracts from the businesslike climate that should prevail in a classroom.

- A teacher (e.g., Ms. Hillyard) who tells students how to behave without taking action to lead them to follow what is said conditions students not to bother to listen. Some teachers will repeat demands for students to be on-task (e.g., "Pay attention") over and over without compliance until the teacher finally gets angry and upset. Such a practice conditions students not to listen until the teacher becomes angry and upset.

- Halfhearted efforts that are nonproductive or counterproductive waste a teacher's valuable energy and time.

If you are confronted with an off-task student behavior but are not, at that moment, in a position to apply a strategy that has a reasonable chance of working, then you should delay your response until help can be obtained or you can design and apply a suitable strategy.

In Case 8.7, Mr. Clark's response to students' off-task behavior is more decisive than Ms. Hillyard's was.

▶ **CASE 8.7**

Mr. Clark is busy explaining some rules for capitalizing words to his class of 31 fifth graders. "Now, who can tell me which words in this sentence should begin with a capital letter?" he asks as he begins to write on the whiteboard, "my friend eddie said 'looking for ghosts' was a—" Just then, he hears some students talking among themselves. He stops writing, pivots, and faces the class to see Jim, Oral, and Mavis carrying on a conversation. Walking directly over to them, he takes the book, paper, and pencil off Jim's desk and says, "Jim, please take these over to that empty seat. Mavis, you take your stuff and work from the desk in front of Mike." Confident that his directions will be followed, he quickly returns to the front of the room and continues his explanation.

▶ DISTINGUISH BETWEEN TEACHING STUDENTS TO BE ON-TASK AND BUILDING CHARACTER

A Teacher's Responsibilities and Capabilities

In Case 8.3, Ms. Reid used the teaching cycles model to deal with Al's disruptive behavior; she focused on helping Al to terminate an in-class, antisocial behavior pattern. Ms. Reid recognized that she is responsible for keeping her students engaged in learning activities designed to help them achieve worthwhile learning goals. She believes that developing Al's character and teaching him to be an upstanding, moral human being are outside the realm of her responsibilities and capabilities. Her method for stopping the clash between Al and Paul and quickly getting everyone reengaged in the learning activity was effective partly because she focused on her responsibilities as a teacher.

Sometimes when a teacher reacts in anger to an annoying off-task student behavior, that teacher loses sight of where his or her responsibilities begin and end. Case 8.8 is an example.

▶ **CASE 8.8**

While her first graders are working in intraclass reading groups, Ms. Blanchard sees Todd yank Celia's hair so hard that the child falls over backward and begins crying. Ms. Blanchard yells to Todd, "Come here, boy!" Todd comes over as all the other students stop their work to watch. "How would you like me to pull your hair? You think you're tough! I can be a lot tougher than you! I'll make you sorry for ever being a bully! Suppose I let Celia pull your hair? Would you like that? Well, would you?" Todd: "I didn't pull that—" Ms. Blanchard: "You didn't what? Wait until one of the big second or third graders picks on you! You'll learn not to be so mean!"

Focusing on the Task

Ms. Blanchard's anger clouded her focus. Instead of taking effective action to prevent a recurrence of such intolerable misbehavior, she got off track trying to get Todd to feel sorry for *being* mean. Rather than deal with the incident, she focused on Todd's meanness. In Case 8.9, Mr. Wagoner helps a student substitute engaged behavior for off-task behavior without allowing himself to be sidetracked into thinking he's building character:

▶ **CASE 8.9**

Libba, an eleventh grader, stops at a convenience store on her way to school. She buys and consumes three cans of beer before her 8:45 A.M. homeroom period. Neither her homeroom nor her first-period history teacher notices anything strange in her behavior. But, as second period begins, she appears tipsy to Mr. Wagoner, her science teacher. Mr. Wagoner directs two students to begin setting up an experiment that he plans to demonstrate to the class. Meanwhile, he subtly beckons Libba to the doorway and out in the hall. Detecting the odor of alcohol on her breath, he says, "It's your business if you want to mess up your life. But it's my business to teach you science, and I can't teach it to you when you're in that condition. When we've completed this conversation, you go back to your desk. Just keep quiet and concentrate on facing straight ahead. Did you hear me?" Libba: "Yes, sir." Mr. Wagoner: "Fine. Tomorrow morning come to this room at 8:15. We'll discuss the matter then. Can you remember to be here, or should I remind you with a call tonight?" Libba: "I'll remember; I'll be here."

At 8:15 the next morning, Libba appears in Mr. Wagoner's classroom. He tells her, "If you ever come into my class again while under the influence of alcohol or any other drug, I will immediately send you to Ms. Swindle's office. I will inform Mr. Giradeau that I refuse to teach you in that condition. And I will inform your parents of the situation. Do you understand?" Libba: "Yes, but I'm not the only—" Mr. Wagoner [interrupting]: "I am not talking about others, only you. I don't discuss your problems with other students, and I won't discuss theirs with you. Do you understand?" Libba: "Yes!" Mr. Wagoner: "Yesterday, while you were out of it, we were analyzing the experiment described here in my teacher's manual. I want you to take my manual home tonight and analyze the experiment as it is described on pages 79 through 84. Bring in your results; I'll be happy to give you feedback on them as soon as I find the time. That should catch you up with the rest of the class. You won't be behind anymore. Okay?" Libba: "Okay." Mr. Wagoner: "See you in class. Keep smiling."

Engage in Activity 8.2.

▶ *ACTIVITY 8.2*

Discuss with a colleague the advantages and disadvantages of the way Mr. Wagoner handled Libba's intoxication in Case 8.9. Discuss some of the legal implications of what he did or didn't do. Consider how a teacher's choice of strategies would be influenced by whatever the school-wide discipline policies are in place.

▶ DISTINGUISH BETWEEN ISOLATED OFF-TASK BEHAVIORS AND OFF-TASK BEHAVIOR PATTERNS

Strategies used to terminate isolated off-task behaviors are different from those for off-task behavior patterns. Although off-task behavior patterns are usually more difficult to terminate than isolated incidents, teachers have the luxury of taking time to plan strategies for dealing with patterns; in contrast, isolated off-task behaviors are typically dealt with as they occur. You can effectively use behavior modification principles (e.g., extinction and shaping) explained in Chapter 9 to teach students to eliminate off-task behavior patterns. You need to be mindful of behavior modification principles when dealing with isolated off-task behaviors to guard against off-task behavior patterns developing from the isolated incidents. If an isolated off-task behavior is positively reinforced, then an off-task behavior pattern may emerge.

► CONTROL THE TIME AND PLACE FOR DEALING WITH OFF-TASK BEHAVIORS

Once Ms. Reid stopped Al and Paul from fighting in Case 8.3, she reengaged the class in learning activities and arranged for a more convenient time to take measures for preventing recurrences of Al's disruptive behaviors. She waited to speak with Al (a) after she had time to collect her thoughts and develop a plan of action, (b) at a time and place in which she wouldn't be burdened with having to supervise other students, (c) when and where no other students would be around so Al would feel free to communicate with her without concern for what his peers were thinking, and (d) after they both had time to cool off.

Like Ms. Reid in Case 8.3 and Mr. Wagoner in Case 8.9, you will be more effective in dealing with off-task behaviors if you manage to control the times and places for interacting with students about their misbehaviors. Typically, students are more concerned with the images they portray for their peers than they are with what you or any other teachers are trying to do for them. Consequently, you are more likely to achieve a productive interchange about preventing recurrences of off-task behaviors in a private conference with a student than in a situation when both of you are worried about others in the vicinity. Do not make a major issue out of one student's off-task behavior in front of other students to exhibit the undesirability of the off-task behavior. Such strategies usually lead to feelings of embarrassment and resentment that detract from the cooperative, businesslike climate you want for your classroom.

William Glasser (2001) suggested that one-to-one conferences are useful to help students identify a particular problem behavior, make a value judgment regarding the behavior, and commit to supplant the problem behavior with on-task behavior. Case 8.10 is an example.

► CASE 8.10

For two consecutive days during the times that Mr. Dean has allocated for his high school industrial technology students to work on a project, Elmo either sits and stares into space or sleeps. Responding to this display of off-task behavior, Mr. Dean meets privately with Elmo. Mr. Dean takes a seat directly in front of Elmo so that he can readily achieve eye contact during the following conversation:

Mr. Dean: Thank you for coming. Tell me, Elmo, were you in industrial tech class today?

Elmo: Yeah, you saw me there.

Mr. Dean: How long were you in industrial tech class today?

Elmo: I was there the whole time; I didn't skip out or nothin'! Somebody else might of slipped out, but I didn't.

Mr. Dean: I don't want to talk about anybody else, just what you did in industrial tech class today.

Elmo: Maybe, Sandra was the one who—

Mr. Dean: (interrupting) We're not going to talk about Sandra or anyone other than you and me. What did you do during the 55 minutes you spent in industrial tech today?

Elmo: I don't know.

Mr. Dean: Tell me one thing you remember doing in industrial tech today.

Elmo: I watched you show us how to use that new machine.

Mr. Dean: And what did you do after I finished showing you how to use the drill press?

Elmo: I dunno, I guess I went to sleep.

Mr. Dean: Do you remember what I asked you to do right before you went to sleep?

Elmo: Work on my project, but I was tired.

Mr. Dean: I'm sorry you were tired, but would it be better for you to sleep in class or get your project done?

Elmo: But the project is so boring!

Mr. Dean: I'm sorry you find the project boring. What happens if you don't finish your project by next Monday?

Elmo: I know; you told us. We don't pass the class.

Mr. Dean: Not passing industrial technology, is that good or bad for you?

Elmo: That's bad; that's real bad!

Mr. Dean: Do you want to pass the class?

Elmo: Of course!

Mr. Dean: What will it take for you to pass industrial tech?

Elmo: Do my project.

Mr. Dean: By when?

Elmo: Monday.

Mr. Dean: What will you do so that you'll have it done by Monday?

Elmo: I'll have to work on it this week.

Mr. Dean: When will you have time to work on it?

Elmo: In class, that's the only time you let us work on it.

Mr. Dean: And there are only two more class days for you to get it done. You don't have any time to waste. What are you going to do in class tomorrow when I direct the class to work on projects?

Elmo: I'm going to work on my project.

Mr. Dean: What if you're tired?

Elmo: I'll work on my project anyway.

Mr. Dean: You've made a smart choice. Would you be willing to write a note telling me that you will work on your project for the last 45 minutes of industrial tech class tomorrow? I'll use the note to remind myself to leave you at least 45 minutes of class for your project and I'll make a copy for you to keep to remind you of your commitment.

Engage in Activity 8.3.

Discuss with a colleague the advantages and disadvantages of Mr. Dean waiting until after class to deal with Elmo's failure to work on the assigned project.

Discuss Mr. Dean's communication style. Was it descriptive rather than judgmental and assertive rather than passive or hostile?

▶ PROVIDE STUDENTS WITH DIGNIFIED OPTIONS FOR TERMINATING OFF-TASK BEHAVIORS

Consider Case 8.11.

▶ CASE 8.11

Ms. Fabian is conducting a writing lesson in which her third graders are taking turns writing three-word sentences on the chalkboard. "Okay, Valerie, it's your turn. Please put your sentence on the board," she says. Valerie just looks away and doesn't get out of her chair. Ms. Fabian: "Valerie, please write your sentence on the board." Valerie: "I don't have one." Ms. Fabian: "Here, we'll help you. I'll give you two of the three words, and you use them in a three-word sentence. How about 'John loves'? You find a third word and make a sentence that starts 'John loves.'" Valerie: "No!" Ms. Fabian feels threatened by Valerie's refusal. She fears that if she allows Valerie to win the struggle of wills in front of the class, others will also refuse to follow her directions. Ms. Fabian: "Valerie, you had better be up and writing on the board before I count to five!" Valerie: "I won't." Ms. Fabian: "I'm counting! One, two, three, four. Valerie, you'll be sorry—five! Okay, young lady, you had your chance; now we'll see that you learn to do what you're told!" Valerie: "Okay, okay! I'll write your sentence." Valerie gets up and walks to the front of the room. Ms. Fabian: "It's too late now. I already counted to five. You had your chance." Valerie: "I said, I'll write the sentence." Ms. Fabian: "Not until I receive an apology. You tell me you're sorry for your rudeness, and you apologize to the class for wasting their time." Valerie faces the class and says, with her head down and a sheepish grin on her face, "Sorry!" Ms. Fabian: "And what do you say to me?" "I'm sorry, Ms. Fabian," she mutters, glaring. Ms. Fabian: "That's more like it!"

What could Ms. Fabian ever expect to gain by insisting that Valerie apologize? Did the apology reestablish Ms. Fabian's authority after her counting-to-five strategy failed? The apology might have temporarily helped Ms. Fabian to feel better about herself, but unfortunately such power games only create an atmosphere of unhealthy competitiveness between teacher and students. Such competitiveness precludes the development of dignified, businesslike attitudes that are so vital for a classroom to be characterized by cooperative student engagement.

If you expect dignified behaviors from your students, you need to avoid doing anything that leads them to fear that their dignities are in jeopardy. Thus, your strategies for dealing with their off-task behaviors—even rude and annoying ones—should provide them with face-saving ways to supplant off-task behaviors with on-task ones. This is not always easily done. When students behave rudely, it is tempting for teachers to respond with clever comebacks or put-downs. Not only does this practice destroy a healthy classroom climate, but it can also easily backfire on a teacher, as it does in Case 8.12.

▶ **CASE 8.12**

Mr. Sceroler is urging his eighth-grade class to get homework in on time. He says, "There's nothing I can do if you don't have the work in my hands." Ronald, from the back of the room in a barely audible tone, quips to the student next to him, "He could always go jack off!" Overhearing the comment, Mr. Sceroler yells at Ronald, "What was that you said?" Ronald begins to grin and look around at his classmates. Mr. Sceroler: "You were trying to show off for us, and now you can't say anything! What did you say?" Ronald whispers with his head down, "Nothing." Mr. Sceroler, seeing Ronald back down, begins to feel confident. He continues, "What was that? Speak up. What did you say?" Now facing Mr. Sceroler, Ronald says in a loud voice, "I said I didn't say nothin'!" Mr. Sceroler retorts, "You can't even use decent English. Of course you didn't say anything. You aren't capable of saying anything, are you?" Some class members laugh. Enjoying the audience, Mr. Sceroler smiles. Ronald, very concerned about what his classmates are thinking, suddenly stands up and shouts at Mr. Sceroler, "I said you could always go jack off, but then I forgot, you don't have a dick!"

By trying to outwit Ronald instead of giving him a face-saving way of getting back on-task, Mr. Sceroler turned a self-terminating incident into an unfortunate confrontation with unhappy consequences for all concerned. If Mr. Sceroler heard Ronald's first rude remark, why did he ask him, "What was that you said?" Ronald tried to end the episode by not replying, but Mr. Sceroler persisted and left Ronald with the choice of either lying about what he said or repeating what would surely be interpreted as an obscenity. Had Mr. Sceroler not behaved like an insecure adult intent on proving his superiority over an adolescent, he might have left Ronald a dignified way to return to on-task behavior by either ignoring the original remark or politely directing Ronald to visit with him at a more convenient time.

▶ AVOID PLAYING DETECTIVE

You also encourage competitiveness between you and your students by playing the game of detective, as Mr. Brubacher does in Case 8.13.

▶ **CASE 8.13**

Some students in Mr. Brubacher's biology class begin regularly amusing themselves by covertly screeching "whoop-whoop!" while he speaks to the class. At first, he tries laughing the disruptions off with comments such as "There's a bird in here, and I've got a hunting license!" But after a couple of days, Mr. Brubacher no longer finds any humor in the rudeness. To the delight of his students, he vows to catch the pranksters and put an end to the whoop-whooping. Unsuccessfully, he tries to identify the source of the annoying sounds. More and more students get into the act and are becoming bolder and more creative in devising ways to emit the sound without getting caught.

In Case 8.14, Ms. Fisher also deals with an ongoing disruptive behavior from an unidentified source, but she refuses to play the detective game with her students.

▶ **CASE 8.14**

After a day in which Ms. Fisher's students have amused themselves by covertly screeching "whoop-whoop!" when she speaks to the class, she thinks to herself: "I wish I knew who's responsible for that horrible whoop-whooping. But I'm not going to play their little game with them, so I'm not going to try to find out. I just won't tolerate it anymore. They know that noise annoys me, so I shouldn't act as though it doesn't. Tomorrow, I'll be ready with an alternative lesson plan if they try the whoop-whooping while I'm explaining things to them."

The next day Ms. Fisher is lecturing on the digestive system when "whoop-whoop" is heard and some of the students begin to laugh. Abruptly, Ms. Fisher stops the lecture and silently and calmly displays a transparency on the overhead with the following message: "I cannot explain the digestive system to you while that noise is going on. I won't try to do what you won't allow me to do. But I am responsible for seeing that you learn this material. So please open your book to page 179. Study pages 179 through 191. Most of what we planned to talk about today is covered in those pages. Do not forget that we have a test on the unit objectives scheduled for Monday. Good luck!" Several students glare at two others who appear rather sheepish.

Ms. Fisher believes that most of her students would prefer attending to her explanations rather than depending solely on reading the text. Thus, she believes that if she continues to move abruptly to her alternative lesson plan each time her lectures and explanations are disrupted, enough peer pressure will be exerted to stop the unidentified sources of the dreaded noise.

Engage in Activity 8.4.

▶ *ACTIVITY 8.4*

Discuss with a colleague the advantages and disadvantages of Ms. Fisher's handling of the group's disruptive behavior in Case 8.14.

▶ USE ALTERNATIVE LESSON PLANS

When implementing a planned learning activity, you should, of course, expect students to cooperate with you and become engaged. By being confident that they will be on-task, you communicate your expectations and thus increase the chances that they will be on-task and engaged. Nevertheless, you need to be prepared for the possibility that all students' cooperation is not as forthcoming as you expect. In Case 8.3, Ms. Reid gets Al engaged in an alternate geography learning activity after his behavior excluded him from the geography bingo plan. Ms. Fisher in Case 8.14 dealt with a recurrence of her students' "whoop-whooping" with an alternative learning activity communicating that she considers learning serious business and demands courteous cooperation in her classroom.

A well-designed, appropriate learning activity should not be aborted simply because things don't go as smoothly as planned. Do not give up on your well-thought-out ideas. However, being prepared with alternative plans can sometimes save the day when students' off-task behaviors render your original plan unworkable.

▶ USE THE HELP OF COLLEAGUES

Refer to Mr. Zeltsman's checklist in Case 3.5 for preparing for the opening of a new school year. Item L under "Classroom Organization and Ongoing Routines" reads, "Whom, among building personnel, can I depend on to help handle short-range discipline problems and long-range problems?" In Case 5.4, Ms. Williams has an arrangement with her colleague, Mr. Demery, that allows the two of them to deal more effectively with off-task behaviors than they could working alone. You would do well to seek out a few teachers in your school on whom you can depend to (a) work out cooperative arrangements for handling discipline problems and (b) share ideas and provide counsel on how to teach students who get off-task to be on-task.

Dealing with off-task behaviors is one of a teacher's more difficult jobs. Do not play "macho teacher" and be too embarrassed to seek help. Routinely share ideas with trusted colleagues and seek help when confronted with particularly difficult situations. Ms. Reid in Case 8.3 arranged some think time for herself before confronting Al's antisocial behavior. She may have used some of that time to confer with another teacher or an instructional supervisor who has experience in dealing with similar problems. Of course, it is assumed that you will seek the help of other professionals like yourself without violating the professional trust that exists between you and your students.

▶ USE THE HELP OF PARENTS AND INSTRUCTIONAL SUPERVISORS

The Myth of the "Good Teacher"

In *Assertive Discipline: A Take-Charge Approach for Today's Educator,* Canter and Canter (1976, pp. 6–7) asserted:

> Today's teachers must contend with the "Myth of the Good Teacher." This myth basically goes as follows: "A 'good' teacher should be able to handle all behavior problems on her own, and within the confines of the classroom." This means if you are competent, you should never need to go to your principal or the child's parents for assistance. . . . No one teacher, no matter how good she is, or how much experience or training she has, is capable of working successfully with each and every child without support. There are many students today whose behavior is so disruptive that a teacher must have assistance from both the principal and the parent(s) in order to deal effectively with the child and his behavior.
>
> This "myth" places a burden of guilt upon teachers who encounter problems with their students. According to the myth, if they were "really good" they wouldn't have these problems. These guilt-ridden, inadequate feelings tend to keep teachers from asking for the help they need with certain students.

Canter and Canter (2002) advise you to "ask for assistance from the student's parents," insisting that "you have the right to ask the parents or principal for whatever assistance you deem necessary, in order to maximize your potential influence with a child!" The success of many of the strategies presented in this book for dealing with off-task behaviors depends on teachers' eliciting the cooperation of students' parents (e.g., Case 8.3, in which Ms. Reid communicated her willingness to involve Al's parents by asking, "Will you remember, or should I phone your house tonight to remind you?").

Undeniably, parents have a responsibility for helping teachers teach their children to cooperate in school. Often, however, obstacles to using the help of parents are difficult to overcome. Some parents, for one reason or another, are unavailable or unwilling to help. The Canters' "Myth of the Good Teacher" leads some misdirected teachers to contact parents only as a last resort, when it is too late to deal efficiently with a discipline problem.

Assertiveness

Some teachers, burdened by the myth, approach parents so apologetically that their lack of assertiveness precludes the effective communication necessary for acquiring constructive parental help. Canter and Canter (1976, pp. 156–160) stated (reprinted by permission):

Many teachers feel threatened and overwhelmed by parents, especially if the parents are pushy or manipulative. Thus, many teachers have difficulty in being assertive with parents; they do not clearly and firmly let the parents know what they want or need from them, nor do they stand up for their rights. As a result, all too often we hear teachers being woefully nonassertive. For example, when calling parents:

- *They apologize for bothering parents:* "I'm really sorry to bother you at home with this . . ."
- *They downgrade the problem:* "We had a 'small' problem with your son today." (In reality he had a violent tantrum which disrupted the entire class for 20 minutes.)
- *They belittle themselves:* "I just don't know what to do with your son." (Yes, you do! You need the cooperation of the parents to discipline him at home for his tantrums.)
- *They do not clearly state their needs:* "I know you are busy, working and all, but if you could find the time I'd appreciate it if you talked to your son about his tantrums." (You want her to discipline her son at home—period!)
- *They downgrade the consequences of the child's behavior:* "I don't know what will happen if he doesn't change his behavior in class." (Yes, you do! He will need to be suspended.)

Often teachers confuse being assertive with being hostile. They are afraid that if they are assertive, the parent will be offended and go to the principal. However, hostility means that you express wants and needs in a manner that offends others or violates their self-dignity. The difference between nonassertive, hostile, and assertive communications with parents can best be illustrated by a direct comparison of the different responses:

Situation: You call the parents to discuss the behavior problems of their child. During the conference, the parents become angry and unfairly blame you for their child's problems at school:

- *Nonassertive Response:* You sit there and passively take the criticism without expressing your concerns and feelings.
- *Hostile Response:* You get defensive and tell the parents off, blaming them for their child's problems.
- *Assertive Response:* You listen to the criticism. You express your recognition of their feelings. *Again,* you express that you called them to arrange some constructive cooperation between you, which will help their child's behavior.

Situation: A child comes to school dirty and unkempt. You call the parents to express your concern about the child's cleanliness, and request that he come to school better kempt. The parents balk at your request, as they have in the past:

- *Nonassertive Response:* You listen to the parents and don't press your demands.
- *Hostile Response:* You tell the parents that it is a disgrace the way they send their child to school, and they should be ashamed of themselves.
- *Assertive Response:* You firmly repeat your demand, and let the parents know that in the best interest of their child, you will contact the appropriate agency, if the situation does not improve.

Situation: You call the parents to ask their cooperation in following through at home on the contract you have with their child, as a result of the behavior problems he has in your class. The parents are very reluctant to do so:

- *Nonassertive Response:* You give up and don't press your wants.
- *Hostile Response:* You tell the parents how inadequate they are, and that they had better learn to discipline their child.
- *Assertive Response:* You firmly repeat your demands, and let the parents know the consequences if their child continues to do poorly in school.

As you have seen, in the assertive responses of each situation, the teacher stated her position and stuck to it. It was firm, not passive, not hostile. You, as a teacher, need to let the parents know where you stand and then allow them to *choose* whether to cooperate with your wishes. When you are nonassertive (passive), you allow the parents to "control you." You feel "lousy" and don't receive the support or action you need to help the child. When you are hostile, you "put down" the parents. They will become threatened, and again, you will not get what you want and need from them.

We have found that teachers can learn to be more assertive and, thus, more effective in their relations with parents. The model we utilize is simple, easily learned and implemented:

1. Assert yourself and contact parents as soon as you see that there is, or possibly will be, a situation with the child where you will need the parents' cooperation.
2. Know what you want from your meeting or conversation with the parents. (Goal)
3. Plan how you will achieve the goal. (Objectives)
4. Know why you want parents' cooperation and assistance. (Rationale)
5. Be prepared to explain what you feel will occur if the parents are not cooperative. (Consequences)
6. Have documentation to support your comments.

Of course, eliciting the help of parents to address students' off-task behavior problems is much easier when you have already established an efficient line of communication with those parents before being confronted by the problems. Mr. Perkins in Case 4.55 and Mr. Bertolli with his newsletter—displayed in Figure 4.4—make it easier for themselves to use parental help by keeping parents apprised of classroom goals and expectations. Knowing parents before a discipline problem arises also gives you an advantage in deciding how to handle the problem. Ms. Jackson in Case 10.16 deals with the problem of three students who show up in her class high on marijuana. Before the incident she had communicated with the students' parents; therefore, she is able to develop her strategy for preventing a recurrence of the misbehaviors in light of what she already knows about the help or hindrances she can expect from each set of parents. As you will see when you read Case 10.16, she decides to involve the parents of two of the students but not those of the third.

▶ DO NOT USE CORPORAL PUNISHMENT

Corporal Punishment

From your work with Chapter 2, you made a distinction between naturally occurring punishment and contrived punishment. A punishment for a person's behavior is naturally occurring if an aversive stimulus is experienced by that person as a direct consequence of that behavior. Punishment that is intentionally and artificially imposed following a behavior is contrived punishment. Cases 2.19 and 2.20 illustrate the difference between the two types of punishment.

Corporal punishment is a form of contrived punishment in which physical pain or discomfort is intentionally inflicted on an individual for the purpose of trying to get that person to be sorry he or she displayed a particular behavior. Naturally occurring punishment, even if it is physically painful or uncomfortable, is *not* considered corporal punishment. For example, the pain Henry experiences in Case 8.15 is not corporal punishment because the pain is a direct consequence of the behavior itself.

▶ CASE 8.15

Ignoring Lakeland Elementary School's "no running in the halls" rule, Henry sprints toward the cafeteria, trying to be first in line. He trips and falls, suffering a painful bruise on his elbow.

Cases 8.16 to 8.20 are examples of corporal punishment.

▶ CASE 8.16

For repeated violations of the school dress code, Bonnie is sent to Mr. Bailey, the assistant principal, who administers three swats to Bonnie's buttocks with his infamous "board of education." In accordance with local school district policy, Mr. Bailey's secretary witnesses the punishment as protection against accusations of abuse.

▶ CASE 8.17

John is busily carving a picture in his desktop with the point of a compass when Ms. Salsberry, his fifth-grade teacher, surprises him from behind, twisting his ear and asking, "Do you think this will help you remember not to abuse your desk?" John shrieks in pain.

▶ CASE 8.18

While supervising her prekindergarten class on the playground, Ms. Barfuss notices Raymond running toward a traffic-filled street. Ms. Barfuss chases him down, slaps his thigh twice with her hand, and says, "No, Raymond! Don't go into that street. You could be killed!" Raymond's leg stings for about 25 seconds after the incident.

▶ CASE 8.19

Ms. Loycano's third graders are supposed to be quietly working problems in workbooks when the teacher notices Theresa and Eva involved in a conversation. "Would you two please come up here?" Ms. Loycano asks. Theresa: "What in the shit for?" Ms. Loycano responds, "I don't appreciate hearing that kind of language in the classroom, Theresa. You stay in here when the rest go to lunch, and we'll help you remember how to speak in here." When the other students leave, Ms. Loycano is ready for Theresa with a bar of soap and a wet towel, which she uses to wash out the inside of Theresa's mouth.

▶ CASE 8.20

As she is conducting a group discussion on citizenship for her fourth graders, Ms. Xavier notices Lyman starting to pass a note to Becky. Ms. Xavier: "Let's see the note, Lyman." "I don't got no note!" Lyman says as he quickly sits on the note. Ms. Xavier walks over to Lyman and says, "Stand up." Rather than stand, Lyman squirms in his chair, and the note falls to the floor. Ms. Xavier grabs it and with a smile says, "I think I'll read it to the class!" Lyman stands up and screams, "No!" and kicks Ms. Xavier in the shin. "Ouch!" she screams and kicks him back. "Boy, that'll teach you never to think of touching me again!" she yells.

Do not confuse corporal punishment with other uses of physical force. Cases 8.21 and 8.22 are *not* examples of corporal punishment.

▶ CASE 8.21

Mr. Triche is conducting his eighth-grade mathematics class when a student, not in his class, enters his room and exclaims, "Please, Mr. Triche, hurry! Andy and Todd are beating up Bennie!" Mr. Triche dashes out of his room and follows the alarmed student to the site of the assault. Andy and Todd are kicking Bennie as he lies on the floor. Mr. Triche puts a headlock on both offenders and pulls them off Bennie. Andy and Todd struggle in an attempt to free themselves, but Mr. Triche's grip holds firm. Mr. Triche directs the student who had alarmed him to seek first aid for Bennie from a nearby teacher. Maintaining his headlocks, he forcibly escorts Andy and Todd to the school office where he turns the matter over to the principal.

▶ CASE 8.22

Ms. Marlin is delivering a history lecture to her high school class when she notices John listening to music through the earphones he's wearing. Ms. Marlin: "Would you please put your player away until class is over?" John: "What for?" Ms. Marlin: "Because I don't want you in here unless you are going to pay attention to the lesson." John: "You can't make me leave!" Ms. Marlin walks over to John and says, "John, let's have this discussion out in the hall. We can settle it without the others having to listen to us." John: "I ain't going out there with you." Ms. Marlin puts her hand on John's arm and says, "There's no reason to turn this into a major incident; just come with me and everything will be all right." John stands up and yells, "Don't touch me, you old bitch!" and shoves Ms. Marlin, toppling her over backward. Standing over her, he starts to throw a punch at her, but before he can, she kicks him in the groin. As John drops to the floor in pain, Ms. Marlin scrambles to her feet, quickly moves away from John, stands in the doorway, and gives the following orders to the class: "Everyone but John, get out in the hall immediately! Cynthia, you run to the office, tell them what happened, and get us some help." Before John can rise from the floor, enough students are already moving out of the room and into the hall so that the path between him and Ms. Marlin is blocked.

Mr. Triche used physical force for the sole purpose of terminating the assault on Bennie. Although Andy and Todd probably experienced pain as a consequence of his force, the purpose of the force was not to inflict pain. The purpose was to get them under control to end the assault and get them to the principal. Similarly, Ms. Marlin's violent response to John's attack is not corporal punishment because the purpose of the response was to protect herself and restore order. Had she continued to strike out at John after she had successfully immobilized him, then she would have been administering corporal punishment. In contrast, Mr. Bailey, Ms. Salsberry, Ms. Barfuss, Ms. Loycano, and Ms. Xavier administered corporal punishment because their physical force was applied with the intent of giving students physically painful or uncomfortable experiences that would cause them to regret their misbehaviors.

Arguments for and against Corporal Punishment

Should corporal punishment ever be used in schools? If so, under what circumstances should it be used, and how should it be applied? These questions continue to be debated, as they have been for at least the past 300 years—not so much in academic circles, where the issues have been pretty well put to rest, but in political, judicial, and religious arenas (Roy, 2002). A report from the Center for Effective Discipline (2002) states, "Every industrialized country in the world now prohibits school corporal punishment except the U.S., Canada, and one state in Australia." Corporal punishment in schools is prohibited statewide in 27 of the 50 U.S. states. Corporal punishment as defined herein is absolutely banned in most school districts; in some others it is officially sanctioned and even encouraged (Center for Effective Discipline, 2002; Van Dyke, 1984). U.S. courts have consistently upheld educators' rights to administer corporal punishment as long as it isn't "excessive" or "unreasonable" (Hinchey, 2004; Roy, 2002). Virtually everyone seems to agree—at least publicly—that students should be protected from abusive corporal punishment that results in serious physical trauma or that is applied thoughtlessly. Research findings, however, suggest that all corporal punishment is abusive because of its deleterious effects on both the long-term welfare of students and the educational environment of the school (MacMillan et al. 1999; National Center for the Study of Corporal Punishment and Alternatives, 2002; Rose, 1984; Stokley, 2004; Welsh, 1985). Virtually every prominent professional organization concerned with schools and the welfare of children has issued strong statements opposing the use of corporal punishment in schools (e.g., American Academy of Pediatrics, American Federation of Teachers, American Medical Association, American Psychiatric Association, American Psychological Association, Council for Exceptional Children, National Association for Elementary School Principals, and National Education Association).

Research-based arguments opposing any use of corporal punishment are compelling and long-standing:

- Opposition to corporal punishment is *not* opposition to firm, strict discipline. Sparing the rod does not mean spoiling the child if other, more effective means for handling misbehaviors are employed.

- Research does not support the notion that corporal punishment is an effective tool in teaching students to supplant off-task behaviors with on-task ones (Bongiovanni, 1979; Paolucci & Violato, 2004).

- Corporal punishment is an extremely destructive form of contrived punishment. Even when it serves to discourage one misbehavior, the long-range side effects can be far less desirable than the original misbehavior (Andero & Stewart, 2002; Hyman & Wise, 1979; Stokley, 2004). Welsh (1985, p. 25) reported that no one has ever demonstrated the utility of spanking a child. "When spanking does work, it is not unlike whacking your watch with your hand to make it tick. This crude procedure may work for a while, but the long-term consequences of hitting one's watch is likely to be detrimental to the delicate mechanism. Our research suggests that the watch analogy also holds for whacking children." The association between children's experiences with corporal punishment and their development of aggressive or violent behavior patterns is both well documented and well publicized (Azrin, Hake, & Hutchinson, 1965; Azrin, Hutchinson, & Sallery, 1964; Bandura, 1965; Delgado, 1963; Ulrich & Azrin, 1962; Welsh, 1985).

- Corporal punishment shatters any semblance of a businesslike classroom climate in which mutual respect, cooperation, and seriousness of purpose prevail (Cangelosi, 1990, pp. 60–64; Kohut & Range, 1979; Strike & Soltis, 1986; Sulzer-Azaroff & Mayer, 1977). The sanctity of the learning environment is violated whenever any sort of violent behavior is tolerated. Corporal punishment is not only tolerated violence but *condoned* violence that is modeled by school personnel.

- Research findings indicate that school personnel who rely on corporal punishment tend to be less experienced, more close minded, more neurotic, less thoughtful, and more impulsive than their counterparts who do not use corporal punishment (Bogacki, Armstrong, & Weiss, 2005; Rust & Kinnard, 1983).

But supporters of corporal punishment as a response to off-task school behavior in some circumstances appear to be more influenced by tradition than by research-based principles. They offer the following arguments:

- A proverb says, "Spare the rod and spoil the child."
- The Bible (e.g., Proverbs 13:24, 12:15, 23:13) supports corporal punishment as a means of moral development.
- What else works?
- Some students do not understand anything else.
- Teachers need to be able to protect themselves.
- Corporal punishment builds character and, for boys, masculinity.
- There are harsher, more dangerous forms of punishment such as sustained psychological embarrassment.
- Students want corporal punishment. It provides the firm guidance that students need to feel secure.
- It leads students to respect teachers and other forms of authority.
- Parents want their children to be disciplined at school.
- Unlike many other ways of handling off-task behaviors, corporal punishment can be swiftly administered so that the student can quickly return to the business of being engaged in learning activities.

- Using corporal punishment for one student's off-task behavior may deter others from modeling that behavior.

- Judicial courts in the United States have consistently upheld the right of school officials to use corporal punishment unless it is "excessive" (Kerr & Nelson, 1998, p. 401; Wilson, 2004; Zirkel & Gluckman, 1996).

- The abuses of corporal punishment can be prevented by allowing its application only under clearly specified, strictly controlled circumstances. Different school districts have developed their own guidelines. The following is a sample of rules from the guidelines of a variety of districts:

  ▶ Corporal punishment shall only be used as a last resort after other, more desirable means have failed.

  ▶ Corporal punishment may be administered only to students whose parents have provided the school with written permission.

  ▶ Corporal punishment may be administered only by the school principal or his or her designee.

  ▶ Corporal punishment shall be prescribed only for those who will profit from it.

  ▶ Students are not required to submit to corporal punishment, providing that they are willing to accept the alternative noncorporal punishment prescribed by the school discipline official.

  ▶ To give those involved a cooling-off period, no corporal punishment may be administered within one hour of the violation.

  ▶ Whenever corporal punishment is administered, at least two professional adults must be present.

  ▶ Corporal punishment may be administered only for certain student offenses as specified in the *Disciplinary Code Handbook.*

  ▶ Corporal punishment may be administered to boys only.

  ▶ The severity of corporal punishment is strictly limited.

Corporal Punishment: A Poor Choice

If you happen to work in a school district in which it is legal to use corporal punishment, under what circumstances should you either administer it yourself or refer students to another person who is authorized to administer it? Although the tactic is still used in many schools and may sometimes seem to be a swift, decisive way of dealing with certain off-task behaviors, there are no circumstances when you should depend on corporal punishment. How can one possibly resolve the inconsistency between using corporal punishment and being a professional educator once the following have been considered? (a) the availability of more effective alternatives for dealing with off-task behaviors (see subsequent chapters of this text), (b) the long-range side effects of corporal punishment, and (c) its corrupting influence on the businesslike air of respect and cooperation that contributes so much to keeping students on-task and engaged in learning activities.

▶ KNOW YOUR RIGHTS AND LIMITATIONS

In most school districts you would face legal problems for doing anything that even resembles corporal punishment. In a relatively few districts, you may be required to explain why you failed to use corporal punishment in certain circumstances. When addressing off-task behavior problems, you need to be mindful of the limitations of your rights and responsibilities as a professional teacher. Those rights and responsibilities vary considerably from school district to school district. Unfortunately, there is no foolproof way for you to protect yourself fully from legal suits stemming from circumstances that arise in your school. Mr. Triche was commended by his principal, fellow teachers, and Andy's parents for the way he handled the delicate situation in Case 8.21. Neither Todd nor Andy was injured in the incident, and according to virtually everyone involved, Mr. Triche prevented Bennie from sustaining serious injuries. Yet several months later, Andy's and Todd's parents sued Mr. Triche for brutality in the incident. The suit failed, but only after two years of expensive litigation. How do you protect yourself from this kind of action? Being aware of school district policies and principles of accepted professional practice can help—as can a habit of being reflective before taking a course of action. Mr. Triche did not, in fact, violate any law or school policy by his actions, and he did think about what to do before acting. Repeatedly, he indicates that he does not regret handling the situation as he did. He does, however, resent being suspended from his teaching position while having to fight a legal battle as a consequence of doing the right thing.

Fortunately, legal actions against teachers who fulfill their professional responsibilities and do not exceed the limits of their authority when dealing with discipline problems are unlikely occurrences. Before having to wrestle with a sticky situation, find out just what kind of backing you can expect from your school administrators, supervisors, and professional association. Know, for example, if you have the right to bar a student from your classroom until some contingency you've specified has been met. Come to an agreement on these matters with your principal before the start of a school year.

▶ MAINTAIN YOUR OPTIONS

Two clichés may help make the point of this section: "Don't back yourself into a corner" and "Hold on to your last card." Once you're aware of the extent of your authority, do not exhaust it. If, for example, you tell a student, "Either sit down immediately or you're out of this classroom for good," you have committed yourself to what, in most situations, is the extent of any teacher's authority. If the student doesn't sit down immediately, you have left yourself little recourse. Did you really want things to go that far? Before exhausting your options regarding a situation, seek the help of supervisors.

▶ KNOW YOURSELF AND YOUR STUDENTS

Routinely take time to examine your own motives for the methods you use with students. Why do you handle things the way you do? How far are you willing to go with a plan? How much time and energy are you willing and able to invest to solve a particular problem? What are you willing to risk? To handle off-task behaviors effectively, you must provide yourself with honest answers to these questions. For some off-task behavior problems under certain circumstances, you should tell yourself that your priorities lead you to be unwilling to spend the time and energy necessary to effect solutions. In such instances, implement only the first stage of the teaching cycles model by recognizing that there is a student need with which you are not prepared to deal.

Be receptive to individual differences among your students. Measures that effectively deal with the off-task behavior of one student may be disastrous with another. Be conservative in attempting new ideas with students you don't know well until you have found the ideas to be workable with familiar students. On the other hand, don't give up on an idea because it doesn't work for all students all the time.

The better you understand yourself and your students, the more effectively you will be able to respond to displays of off-task behavior with decisiveness, sensitivity, and flexibility.

▶ SYNTHESIS ACTIVITIES FOR CHAPTER 8

I.   Ms. Odle follows the teaching cycles model to plan and conduct a two-week learning unit on drug, alcohol, and tobacco abuse for her fifth-grade class. She completes stage 1 by determining that her students need to be aware of the physiological and psychological effects of using such substances. In light of that need, she determines the objectives for the unit and thus completes stage 2. For stages 3, 4, and 5 she plans, prepares, and conducts learning activities that include, among other things, small-group discussions, guest lecture presentations, poster projects, and formative tests. Near the end of the two-week period, she administers a comprehensive test, the results of which help her complete step 6, in which she makes a summative evaluation about what students gained from the unit.

Ms. Odle also uses the teaching cycles model to deal with students' off-task behaviors as they occur during time allocated for the unit's learning activities. Cases 8.23 and 8.24 are two such episodes. For each, specify in writing exactly what Mrs. Odle did for each of the six stages in the teaching cycles model to handle the off-task behavior:

▶ CASE 8.23

Ms. Odle is sitting in the back of her classroom as Mr. Boisvert speaks to the 27 fifth graders about his experiences as a counselor at a drug rehabilitation center. She is disturbed by the general lack of attentiveness to Mr. Boisvert's lecture. Some students are huddled together, whispering to one another and giggling; only a few appear to be engaged in the learning activity. As she sits in the rear of the room deciding if she should act and how, Mr. Boisvert directs his remarks more to her than to the students. Their lack of attentiveness coupled with Ms. Odle's display of interest encourage him to address Ms. Odle instead of the students. Ms. Odle thinks to herself: "They should be listening to him. He's taking time from his busy schedule to share some very important ideas; the least we can do is to listen courteously. I'm going to do something to get them reengaged in Mr. Boisvert's lecture. But what? I'd like to avoid dramatizing the fact that the students aren't listening. He might find that embarrassing, and there's no need to let him know that I know that they don't find his talk engaging. I know! But I've got to wait for the opportune moment in his talk. . . ."

"—and it seems that most of the kids I see just don't think that much of themselves," Mr. Boisvert is saying as Ms. Odle stands up from her place in the back of the room and interrupts: "Excuse me, Mr. Boisvert. You've just made such an important point that I want to make sure everyone understands it." She walks to the front of the room, thinking to herself, "Maybe if I stand up front, just a little behind him, he'll quit directing his remarks to me and I'll be in a position to maintain eye contact with the class. They're more likely to at least pretend to be attending if they see me watching them. They know me well enough!" Moving to a point near Mr. Boisvert but looking directly at the class, she asks him, "Would you please explain a little more about what it means for a person not to think much of him or herself?" As Mr. Boisvert continues, Ms. Odle positions herself slightly behind him and to one side where she can monitor the class with her best "be quiet, eyes ahead, sit up straight and listen, or else life in here as you now know it will cease to exist" look on her face. For the remainder of the talk, Ms. Odle observes for indications of how well her tactics are working.

► **CASE 8.24**

For some time, Ms. Odle has believed that Treva should break her habit of making a joke out of what other students say during learning activities. Up till now, Ms. Odle hasn't decided to do anything about this off-task behavior. A few days into the learning unit on substance abuse, Treva goes into her "drunken stupor" act in response to another student's serious comments about the effects of alcohol. After school that day, Ms. Odle thinks to herself, "It wouldn't be so bad if Treva didn't wait for some of the more serious, thought-provoking moments in our discussions to start the class laughing. Then it's hard to get them back into a serious, thoughtful vein. Besides, she's conditioning some students to keep their mouths shut out of fear that their words will be twisted into a joke. I'm going to help Treva reduce the frequency of her clowning. But how should I approach it?"

Ms. Odle designs and implements a plan for (1) identifying the positive reinforcers for her clowning (e.g., the attention she receives from others' laughing at her), (2) taking steps to prevent her clowning from being positively reinforced (e.g., just before one discussion session, Ms. Odle shows the class a video she thinks will bring home the point that taking drugs is never funny), (3) providing positive reinforcers for an appropriate alternative behavior (e.g., drawing attention to Treva when she makes serious, on-task comments in class), and (4) gathering data for deciding how well the plan is working.

II. Compare your response to Synthesis Activity I's prompt with that of a colleague. Also check to see if they contain the general ideas suggested by the following:

In Case 8.23, Ms. Odle followed the teaching cycles model in responding to her students' inattentiveness during Mr. Boisvert's guest lecture presentation. She (a) identified student needs by deciding that the students ought to be politely paying attention to the talk, (b) determined a learning goal by deciding that she would do something to get them to attend silently to the lecture, (c) determined a learning activity by deciding to interrupt Mr. Boisvert discreetly at an opportune moment and applying her "I mean business" body language technique, (d) prepared for the learning activity by moving into position, (e) conducted a learning activity by saying what she did and standing as she did in front of the class, and (f) evaluated how well the goal was achieved by deciding how well her tactics worked.

In Case 8.24, she used the six stages in dealing with Treva's disruptive behavior pattern by (a) determining a student need when she decided that Treva should break her habit of inappropriate joking, (b) determining a learning goal by deciding to do something to help Treva reduce the frequency of clowning in class, (c) designing a learning activity by developing a plan for getting Treva to extinguish her behavior pattern of clowning in class, (d) preparing for at least one component of the learning activity by arranging to show the video, (e) conducting a learning activity by carrying out her plan with such activities as showing the videotape, and (f) evaluating how well Treva is progressing by using the data she gathers.

III. For each of the following statements, write a half-page essay that argues for or against the statement:

    A. Although it is not generally advisable to ignore the off-task behaviors of students, ignoring an incident of off-task behavior is preferable to dealing with it halfheartedly.

    B. Teaching students to be on-task differs from molding students' characters.

    C. If a teacher simply terminates a student's disruptive behavior in class and doesn't take measures to prevent recurrences until after class, other students in the class will think that they, too, can get away with disruptive behaviors.

    D. Students are very concerned about what their peers think of them. Thus, humbling a student in front of the class for disruptive behavior is an effective means of preventing such disruptions in the future.

    E. Sometimes it is better for a teacher to fail to identify the perpetrators of a classroom disruption than to play the detective game with students.

    F. Experienced teachers who apply sound classroom management principles do not need the help of colleagues, supervisors, or parents in dealing with off-task behaviors.

    Exchange your responses with those of colleagues. Discuss differences and similarities.

IV. Design a learning activity for helping students within your teaching specialty achieve a particular learning objective. Now develop an alternative learning activity that you might use in case students do not cooperate with your first plan. Have your plan and alternate plan critiqued by a colleague; return the favor.

V. Visit the following Web site and examine some of the links with articles about alternatives to teachers or parents using corporal punishment: www.temple.edu/education/pse/NCSCPA .html.

▶ TRANSITIONAL ACTIVITY FROM CHAPTER 8 TO CHAPTER 9

In preparation for your work with Chapter 9, discuss with two or more colleagues the following questions:

I. What strategies do teachers employ to lead students to supplant off-task behavior patterns with on-task patterns?

II. How can teachers avoid accidentally encouraging students to develop off-task behavior patterns?

III. How can teachers avoid accidentally discouraging students from developing on-task behavior patterns?

9

Modifying Off-Task Behavior Patterns

► CHAPTER 9'S GOAL AND OBJECTIVES

The goal of this chapter is for you to develop strategies for leading students to supplant off-task behavior patterns with on-task behavior patterns. Specifically, Chapter 9 is designed to lead you to achieve the following objectives.

1. Design learning activities to teach students to supplant off-task behavior patterns with on-task behavior patterns.

2. Understand how the following principles of behavior modification influence the development of behavior patterns: (a) extinction, (b) alternative behavior patterns, (c) shaping, (d) reinforcement schedules, (e) cuing, (f) generalization and discrimination, (g) modeling, and (h) satiation.

► SYSTEMATIC TECHNIQUES FOR CHANGING HABITS

The Formations and Elimination of Behavior Patterns

Theories associated with behavioristic psychology provide explanations for how behavior patterns are formed; they also provide a basis for strategies used to teach students to terminate off-task behavior patterns in favor of on-task ones. Positive reinforcement, punishment, and negative reinforcement in conjunction with the behavior modification principles of extinction, alternative behavior patterns, reinforcement schedules, shaping, cuing, generalization, discrimination, modeling, and satiation are particularly powerful forces for you to understand and use in dealing with your students' off-task behavior patterns.

Behavior modification principles are continually influencing both the formation and elimination of your students' behavior patterns. Taking advantage of these principles to help students break off-task habits and acquire on-task ones is, of course, preferable to having them operate out of your control. You achieve success with the behavior modification principles explained in this chapter by (a) consciously considering their influence when planning learning activities and interacting with students and (b) applying them systematically to off-task behavior problems.

3 days prior to program	2 days prior to program	1 day prior to program	1st day of program	2nd day of program	3rd day of program
ЖГ ЖГ ЖГ	ЖГ ЖГ ЖГ	ЖГ ЖГ ЖГ	ЖГ ЖГ ЖГ ЖГ ЖГ	ЖГ ЖГ ЖГ ЖГ ЖГ ЖГ ЖГ ЖГ	ЖГ ЖГ ЖГ ЖГ ЖГ ЖГ ЖГ ЖГ ЖГ

Figure 9.1. Mr. Washington's Perception of Jana's Yelling

The Need for Systematic Observation

As demonstrated in Case 9.1, being systematic is particularly valuable in evaluating how well a behavior modification plan is working.

▶ **CASE 9.1**

Jana, one of Mr. Washington's first graders, habitually yells out to him while he is busy working with other students. Mr. Washington decides to apply both the principles of extinction and alternative behavior patterns in devising a scheme to deal with her disruptive behavior pattern. After some thoughtful consideration, he decides that Jana's yelling is positively reinforced by the attention it gains her. Thus, he plans to ignore her whenever she yells for him and to give her special attention when she acts in a more appropriate fashion. He tries his plan, but he doesn't systematically gather data on how the plan is working. Instead, he depends only on his informal perceptions, which leave him with the impression that the frequency of Jana's yelling is increasing, not decreasing. Figure 9.1 depicts what appears to be happening according to Mr. Washington's unsystematically formed impression. Consequently, he aborts his plan after only three days.

Had Mr. Washington been more systematic and maintained records, he might not have given up so quickly. If, for example, he had kept a tally sheet to mark down every time Jana yelled, a somewhat different picture might have emerged. Figure 9.2 depicts what his results might actually have been.

Is such a discrepancy between perceived frequency of yelling and actual frequency likely? Research results suggest that such differences are quite likely (Cangelosi, 1982, pp. 116–118). Compare the tallies perceived by Mr. Washington (i.e., Figure 9.1) with the actual tallies reflected by Figure 9.2. Speculate about what may have caused the discrepancies.

The actual baseline data differ very little from what Mr. Washington thought. According to both Mr. Washington's perception and the systematically collected tallies, Jana's screams increase in frequency right after the plan is implemented. Does this surprise you? Jana's screaming had gained her attention in the past. When Mr. Washington began ignoring her, she could be expected at least initially to attempt with greater vigor and frequency what had previously worked.

3 days prior to program	2 days prior to program	1 day prior to program	1st day of program	2nd day of program	3rd day of program
卌 卌 卌 l	卌 卌 llll	卌 卌 卌 lll	卌 卌 卌 卌 卌 l	卌 卌 卌 卌 l	卌 l

4th day of program	5th day of program
llll	lll

Figure 9.2. Jana's Actual Frequency of Yelling

It is after the plan had been in operation for a couple of days that Mr. Washington's perceptions appear distorted. How might that phenomenon be explained? Perhaps Mr. Washington's expectations changed when he began implementing his plan. Jana's yelling is an annoying habit that he wants her to terminate. He's developed a plan that ought to work; he expects it to work. Because Mr. Washington expects the plan to work, Jana's every yell appears to echo louder and to be more annoying than her yells before he was working to stop the behavior.

▶ APPLYING THE PRINCIPLE OF EXTINCTION

The Principle

Whenever the positive reinforcers for a person's voluntary behavior pattern are removed or cease to exist, the person will begin to discontinue that behavior pattern. This phenomenon is the *principle of extinction*. Students begin to break habits when they discover those habits are no longer rewarding. One voluntarily establishes a particular behavior pattern only in the presence of positive reinforcers. The removal of those reinforcers will, in time, extinguish that behavior pattern. Both desirable (e.g., on-task) and undesirable (e.g., off-task) behavior patterns are extinguished by either conscious design or unplanned changes in situations.

Unintentional Extinction

Case 9.2 is an example of an unplanned extinction of a desirable behavior pattern.

► **CASE 9.2**

Ruth, a sixth grader, begins stopping by her school's library to browse and pick up books. During some of her initial visits, Ruth helps Ms. Tolbert, the librarian, shelve books and do other chores. Ms. Tolbert enthusiastically expresses her appreciation and carries on lively conversations with Ruth as they work together. Ruth enjoys Ms. Tolbert's companionship and feels that her efforts are appreciated. Ruth begins coming every day after school to help. After about a month, Ms. Tolbert becomes accustomed to Ruth's help and is less attentive to her. She is not as inclined to carry on lively conversations with Ruth and expresses her appreciation for Ruth's help less often than she did before. Soon Ruth's after-school library visits become less frequent until she no longer shows up at all.

Initially, Ruth's help in the library was positively reinforced by Ms. Tolbert's expressions of appreciation and companionship. Ruth was motivated to continue to help in the library after school as long as that behavior pattern was positively reinforced. The principle of extinction was unwittingly applied by Ms. Tolbert when she ceased providing the positive reinforcement for Ruth's habit.

Intentional Extinction

You can sometimes take conscious advantage of the principle of extinction to teach students to eliminate certain off-task behavior patterns by (a) specifying the exact behavior pattern to be extinguished; (b) identifying the positive reinforcers for the behavior; (c) developing a plan for eliminating the positive reinforcement; (d) in light of baseline data, establishing a realistic time schedule for reducing the frequency of the behavior; (e) implementing the plan; and (f) evaluating how well the pattern is being broken. In Case 9.3, a teacher plans to use the principle of extinction to help students break an off-task behavior habit.

► **CASE 9.3**

Ms. Goldberg, a mathematics teacher, has been using a procedure in which each student's grade is determined by the number of points accumulated during a semester. A student has two means for gaining points. (a) Half the total possible points are based on test scores. (b) The rest of the points are awarded for homework that, when turned in on time, is scored according to the number of correct responses.

Ms. Goldberg begins to notice that increasingly more students receive high marks on homework but low marks on test papers. Under her system, these students are still able to pass the course. She analyzes the situation, collects some baseline information, and realizes that these students are simply copying their homework from others. Understanding that her grading system positively reinforces this habit of copying instead of actually doing homework, she decides to alter her grading procedure so that those positive reinforcers are eliminated. Under the new system, homework will still be assigned but no longer factored into the semester grade. Instead, she will use the homework strictly as a learning activity that provides students with practice and feedback relative to the skills that they will be asked to display on the tests. The tests will be the sole source of data for determining semester grades.

After explaining her new grading procedure to the class, she implements it and assesses whether or not homework copying diminishes and test scores improve.

Engage in Activity 9.1.

▶ *ACTIVITY 9.1*

With a colleague, discuss the advantages and disadvantages of Ms. Goldberg's handling of the copying-homework problem in Case 9.3. Also address the following questions:

1. By eliminating the positive reinforcement for copying homework, is she not also eliminating the positive reinforcement for doing homework at all?

2. According to her plan, how—if at all—will students be positively reinforced for doing homework?

3. Should she be concerned about another undesirable behavior pattern replacing students' copying-homework behavior pattern?

Extinction is not the only method for helping students to eliminate off-task behavior patterns. Other methods (e.g., punishment) are more appropriate when the positive reinforcers for an off-task behavior pattern cannot be identified or efficiently controlled.

▶ ALTERNATIVE BEHAVIOR PATTERNS

Students, like all living persons, are always behaving in some manner. Sleeping, running, remembering, watching television, doing homework, waiting in line, thinking about schoolwork, thinking about an embarrassing moment, worrying about appearance, listening, talking, being angry, and daydreaming are only a minute portion of the cognitive, affective, and psychomotor behaviors that contribute to a person's behavior complex at any given moment. Because students are always displaying some type of behavior, whenever one behavior pattern is extinguished, an alternate or replacement behavior pattern emerges. Consequently, when you are trying to help a student terminate one undesirable behavior pattern, you should guard against that student's replacing the current pattern with another undesirable pattern, possibly even worse. Ms. Goldberg, in Case 9.3, needs to guard against students' replacing "copying homework" behavior with "cheating on tests" behavior.

When you apply the principle of extinction, you should specify a suitable alternative behavior pattern that you plan to have positively reinforced. Ideally, the alternative on-task behavior pattern is incompatible with the off-task one that is to be extinguished. For example, it would be wise for Ms. Goldberg to provide feedback on her students' homework to enhance their chances of improving test scores. Students who did not make the effort to do their homework, either correctly or incorrectly, would discover that they were at a grave disadvantage on tests. Thus, the teacher would have positively reinforced the alternative on-task behavior pattern of completing homework assignments.

In Case 9.4, a teacher deals with an off-task behavior pattern by positively reinforcing an alternative on-task behavior pattern, one that is incompatible with the off-task pattern.

▶ CASE 9.4

Jerry habitually litters the area where his teacher, Mr. Archer, conducts industrial technology class. Mr. Archer places Jerry in charge of the daily cleanup crew responsible for seeing that the work area is clean before any class session can be dismissed. The work crew is directed to begin its duties five minutes before the scheduled end of a period. As soon as the area is clean, the class is free to leave. The promise of leaving early and the responsibility of being in charge of the crew positively reinforce Jerry's alternative pattern of cleaning up. Cleaning up is incompatible with the original off-task pattern of littering.

▶ APPLYING THE PRINCIPLE OF SHAPING

Consider Case 9.5.

▶ CASE 9.5

Abby hardly ever speaks up in Mr. Arata's class. Mr. Arata sets a goal for Abby to answer questions voluntarily, make comments, and raise questions during group learning activity sessions. During a lecture–discussion session on protecting endangered wild animals, Mr. Arata notices that Abby brings up her hand to stroke her hair. Mr. Arata quickly says to her, "Yes, Abby, what did you want to say?" Abby: "Nothing." Mr. Arata: "I thought I saw you raise your hand. You looked like you disagreed with the way the location of the dam was decided." Abby: "No, I agree with the process." Realizing that most of the others also agree, Mr. Arata tells the class, "Those of you who agree with Abby raise your hands." Most of the students lift their hands. Mr. Arata: "Danny, why do you agree with Abby?" Danny: "Well, I think she's right because. . . ." A faint grin drifts across Abby's face.

During the ensuing weeks, Mr. Arata controls class discussions so that any move Abby makes indicating that she is beginning to open up in class is followed by positive reinforcers. Mr. Arata has discovered that although Abby does not enjoy being the center of attention, she does enjoy having others believe what she believes. He uses this knowledge to design the positive reinforcers for any contribution she makes to class discussions.

Mr. Arata attempted to apply the principle of shaping to help Abby develop an engaged behavior pattern of contributing her comments during discussion sessions. The emergence of a student's behavior pattern is due to *shaping* when the following occurs: (a) Some seemingly random action by the student (e.g., Abby's stroking her hair) that has some characteristic similarity to the behavior to be learned (e.g., Abby's raising her hand to speak up in class) is positively reinforced. (b) Subsequent actions by the student that are more like the behavior to be learned than previous actions are positively reinforced. (c) Subsequent actions by the student that are less like the behavior to be learned than previous actions are not positively reinforced.

In Case 9.6, a kindergarten teacher applies the principle of shaping to help students develop a habit of using courteous, thoughtful language.

▶ CASE 9.6

When Ms. Harris's students speak to her, she makes a concerted effort to provide them with intense eye contact and displays of interest as long as they are speaking positively about others and using expressions such as "thank you," "please," "excuse me," and "if you don't mind." When they speak unkindly of others, use demanding tones, or fail to use the aforementioned kinds of expressions, then she uses fewer active listening techniques and appears less interested in what they are telling her. At the beginning of a conversation, she searches for any, even accidental, display of thoughtfulness in the student's conversation. She makes sure that the student recognizes her appreciation of that display.

Case 9.7 is the classic example of shaping.

▶ **CASE 9.7**

Students in a college psychology class decide to use shaping to play a practical joke on their professor. They appear very attentive to the professor's lecture whenever he makes any movement toward the doorway of the lecture hall. Any movement away from the door or any failure to move at all is met with inattentiveness. After a week, the professor is lecturing from the doorway.

Engage in Activity 9.2.

▶ *ACTIVITY 9.2*

In a discussion with a colleague, compare the three behavior modification principles of extinction, alternative behavior pattern, and shaping with respect to the following questions.

1. Which of the three principles targets the development of new behavior patterns? Which targets the elimination of existing behavior patterns?

2. What role does positive reinforcement play in the principle of extinction?

3. What role does positive reinforcement play in the principle of alternative behavior pattern?

4. What role does positive reinforcement play in the principle of shaping?

5. How do these three principles complement one another with respect to teaching students to supplant off-task behavior patterns with on-task behavior patterns?

▶ MAINTAINING DESIRABLE BEHAVIOR CHANGES

Reinforcement Schedules

How long a behavior pattern—either on-task or off-task—persists is largely dependent on the scheduling of positive reinforcers. Two types of reinforcement schedules are of particular concern in dealing with off-task behaviors in the classroom: *fixed* and *intermittent*.

Fixed Schedules

Fixed schedules of positive reinforcement can be either fixed intervals or fixed ratios. *Fixed interval schedules* provide for a positive reinforcer to occur routinely after a set amount of time elapses in which a prescribed behavior has been displayed. *Fixed ratio schedules* provide for a positive reinforcer to occur routinely after a prescribed behavior has been displayed to a specified degree or with a specified frequency. Students on fixed positive reinforcement schedules should always be able to predict how and when they will be rewarded for displaying the prescribed behavior. In Case 9.8, a teacher uses a fixed interval schedule of positive reinforcement; in Case 9.9 the schedule is fixed ratio.

▶ **CASE 9.8**

Ms. Mecke makes arrangements with a local theater chain to provide enough movie passes for her to carry out a strategy she has devised to help her manage her class. Each day, she checks to see whether or not students have completed all required work and cleaned up their work areas. Those students who have maintained a perfect record for a school week are given a movie pass. Each student begins on Monday morning with a fresh record and the opportunity of receiving a pass on Friday.

▶ **CASE 9.9**

Nearly every time Mr. Schwartz asks a question in class, David blurts out an answer. Mr. Schwartz speaks to David about the problem, but David has difficulty controlling his tendency to share his thoughts on whatever topic is raised. Finally, Mr. Schwartz and David work out the following agreement: For every sequence of questions that Mr. Schwartz raises for the class, Mr. Schwartz will call on David to answer every fifth question, providing that David has sat quietly through the previous four questions and listened to others give their responses.

Ms. Mecke's students knew exactly what they would have to do for five consecutive days to earn a movie pass on Friday. David understood that he had to display quiet listening behavior through four straight questions and answers before he could be rewarded with a chance to speak out in class. The agreement that Mr. Schwartz and David worked out is a rather simple form of a *contingency contract*. Contingency contracts are commonly associated with fixed schedules of positive reinforcers. You enter into a contingency contract with a student by agreeing to provide rewards or privileges in return for the student's displaying a prescribed behavior. *Contingency proclamations* are similar except that the teacher imposes the prescription on the student rather than working out the arrangement cooperatively. Look ahead to Figure 10.1 for an example of a formal contingency contract.

Intermittent Schedules

Fixed schedules of positive reinforcers are particularly powerful in motivating students to initiate a behavior pattern. But *intermittent schedules* are far more powerful in getting students to retain a behavior pattern once the pattern has been started (Lewis & Doorlag, 1991, pp. 124–127; Martin & Pear, 1996, pp. 77–89; Ormrod, 2006, pp. 301–310). The student whose behavior pattern is being positively reinforced cannot accurately predict when rewards will occur because an intermittent schedule of reinforcement is irregular. Most unplanned reinforcement schedules are intermittent. An unplanned intermittent reinforcement schedule leads to an undesirable behavior pattern in Case 9.10.

▶ **CASE 9.10**

Fourteen-year-old Michelle consumes a significant quantity of wine for the first time. Although the taste does not appeal to her, she begins to feel lightheaded and temporarily relieved from the pressures and anxieties of being an adolescent. Her drinking is positively reinforced by this feeling of relief. A week later, she is feeling unhappy and drinks again. This time, however, she feels no high, so she drinks more until she feels better. On other occasions, she feels no relief, only terribly sick. She continues to drink in the hope that it will make her feel better; sometimes it does, and sometimes it doesn't. She can't predict how much she must drink to feel better or even if any one drinking bout will provide her with relief at all.

The intermittent positive reinforcement schedule for Michelle's drinking will likely lead to a permanent habit unless some incompatible, alternative behavior pattern is positively reinforced. The classic example of an intermittent schedule is that of the unpredictable rewards associated with gambling behavior. Gambling, of course, can become compulsive.

Planned Schedules of Reinforcement

A *planned schedule* of positive reinforcers, which is commonly used in conjunction with shaping, provides (a) a generous fixed schedule during the stage in which the behavior pattern is to be initiated, (b) a meager fixed schedule after the pattern has been exhibited for a time, and (c) an intermittent schedule to maintain the pattern until the student becomes intrinsically motivated to continue the pattern without outside intervention. Case 9.11 is an example.

▶ **CASE 9.11**

Milan tends to display disruptive behaviors during in-class reading assignments, and Mr. Devlin experiences difficulty in getting Milan to complete them. After giving the matter considerable thought, Mr. Devlin decides to use shaping to teach Milan to choose to read books. One day Mr. Devlin sees Milan pick up a magazine, thumb through it, and put it down. Mr. Devlin: "If you read any one article in that magazine, you can tell me about it during the Cubs game tomorrow night. I have an extra ticket." Milan: "You mean you'd take me to see the Cubs?" Mr. Devlin: "If you read the article." Milan: "It's a deal!" After the game, Mr. Devlin hands Milan a short story on baseball and says, "When you get through reading this, maybe we can talk about it at another game."

In time Milan reads more, but Mr. Devlin schedules payoffs farther apart and makes them contingent on more ambitious readings. Eventually, Milan learns to enjoy reading without the anticipation of an extrinsic reward. The extrinsic motivation that stemmed from a desire to attend baseball games is eventually replaced by the intrinsic motivation derived from Milan's enjoyment of reading.

Engage in Activity 9.3.

▶ *ACTIVITY 9.3*

With one or two colleagues, collaboratively respond to the following prompts.

1. In Case 9.8, Ms. Mecke used a fixed schedule of positive reinforcement to extrinsically motivate students to be on-task. Imagine some possible scenarios in which the positive reinforcement is destructive. Also imagine some possible scenarios in which over time her fixed schedule of positive reinforcement works so well that students become intrinsically motivated to be on-task so that the promise of theater passes is no longer needed.

2. What are the advantages and disadvantages of Mr. Schwartz's tactics in Case 9.9 for dealing with David's blurting-out-answers behavior pattern?

3. What are the advantages and disadvantages of the way Mr. Devlin varied the schedule of positive reinforcement to shape Milan's behavior in Case 9.11?

▶ CUING

A *cue* is a signal that stimulates a person (e.g., a student) to exhibit a previously learned voluntary behavior pattern. Consider Cases 9.12 to 9.14.

▶ CASE 9.12

Ms. Setzer's second graders are working in pairs. The noise level in the classroom begins to rise to an unacceptable level. Saying nothing, Ms. Setzer calmly walks over to the light switch and blinks the lights once. The noise level drops to an acceptable level.

▶ CASE 9.13

Mr. Weaver is vocally giving directions to his chemistry students who are working at laboratory tables. As they follow his directions, they become somewhat noisy in their efforts to help one another. Mr. Weaver continues to speak but gradually lowers his voice so that it is no longer audible to those in the noisy room. The students begin signaling one another to quiet down until the noise level drops below Mr. Weaver's volume.

▶ CASE 9.14

Five minutes ago, Ms. Peterson assigned Tyrone and his sixth-grade classmates some exercise problems to work on in class. After working out one problem, Tyrone doodles and gazes around the room. Ms. Peterson walks over to Tyrone and silently looks at his paper. Tyrone's attention returns to the exercise problems.

It appeared that Ms. Setzer had conditioned her students to lower their voices in response to the blinking-light cue. Similarly, students responded to Mr. Weaver's lowering his voice as a cue to quiet down. Ms. Peterson's proximity to Tyrone cued him back on-task.

Teaching students to respond to cues, especially nonverbal ones, is invaluable to an efficient, smoothly operating classroom. Recall how Ms. Morrison used posters in her classroom as cues to facilitate smooth transitions between learning activities in Case 3.21. As will be suggested by a number of examples in Chapters 10 and 11 (e.g., Mr. Legget's method of dealing with Rosalie's habitual mind wandering in Case 10.5), efficient cues can sometimes be worked out with students to signal that they are exhibiting an off-task behavior and should immediately replace that behavior with a previously agreed-upon alternative behavior. Krumboltz and Krumboltz (1972, p. 67) stated, "Cuing seems to work better under some circumstances than under others. When cues are verbal, they are sometimes confused with nagging but there is an important distinction. Nagging is persistent unpleasant urging or scolding by finding fault. Cuing is a simple nonhostile direction when the child needs a reminder or when he needs help in learning."

▶ GENERALIZATION AND DISCRIMINATION

The Idea

The communication style that Ms. Sowel uses with her seventh graders in Cases 9.15 and 9.16 should not be emulated in any respect. But her conversations with two students reflect the idea of the principles of generalization and discrimination.

▷ **CASE 9.15**

Betty is busily trying to write an essay in Ms. Sowel's class. She frowns, crumples her paper, and tosses it on the floor. Ms. Sowel turns to Betty and says, "Young lady, pick up that paper right now! Do you throw trash on your living room floor at home?" Betty: "No, ma'am. I'm sorry." Ms. Sowel: "Well, if you don't throw trash on the floor of your living room, then you shouldn't throw it on the floor of your classroom either!"

▷ **CASE 9.16**

As Ms. Sowel's seventh-grade English students file into her room, Roy shoves Hildreth from behind. Hildreth spins around face to face with Roy and says, "Look motherfucker, don't start any of your shit with me!" Ms. Sowel dashes to Hildreth, turns him by his shoulders to face her, and loudly exclaims. "Maybe that filthy language is tolerated around your home, but it will not be tolerated in my classroom!"

The Principle of Generalization

In her crude manner, Ms. Sowel attempted in Case 9.15 to help Betty exhibit a behavior pattern in the classroom (i.e., disposing of trash in a proper container) that Betty practiced at home. Ms. Sowel wanted Betty to *generalize* a behavior pattern from one situation to another. Students generalize by responding to a new set of stimuli in a manner similar to the way in which they have been conditioned to respond to a different—but similar—set of stimuli. Students tend to generalize between two situations and thus respond similarly in both situations because they focus on commonalities instead of differences. You teach students to generalize between two situations by providing them with cues that remind them of what is common to both situations.

The Principle of Discrimination

By throwing paper on her classroom floor when she wouldn't have done so at home, Betty displayed that she was *discriminating*, rather than generalizing, between the stimuli presented by the classroom and those presented by her home. Ms. Sowel attempted to get her to generalize her disposal-of-trash behavior at home to the classroom. In Case 9.16, Ms. Sowel made a poorly conceived attempt to get Hildreth to discriminate between his home—where, according to Ms. Sowel's rude remark, a type of language is acceptable—and her classroom—where that type of language is unacceptable. Students discriminate by responding to a new set of stimuli in a manner dissimilar to the way in which they have been conditioned to respond to a different—but similar—set of stimuli. Students tend to discriminate between two situations and thus respond differently in one situation from the way they do in the other because they focus on differences rather than commonalities. You teach students to discriminate between two situations by providing them with cues that remind them of what is different about the two situations.

Distinguishing between Generalizing and Discriminating

In Cases 9.17 to 9.20, Vern, Stephen, Amanda, and Alyson appear to be generalizing.

▶ **CASE 9.17**

Whenever Vern watches television at his house, he relaxes—never trying to follow what is being said very closely. Vern's teacher shows his class a videotaped lecture on the Declaration of Independence. Although Vern's teacher indicated that they would be tested on the content of the video, Vern is very relaxed as he watches the video monitor—not following what is said very closely.

▶ **CASE 9.18**

Eight-year-old Stephen tells his mother, "Sidney took my ball away from me at school today!" "What did you do about it?" his mother asks. "I slugged him and took it back," he replies. "Good!" his mother says. "You have to take care of yourself." A few days later, Stephen's four-year-old brother grabs a book that Stephen is reading. Stephen hits his brother and grabs back the book.

▶ **CASE 9.19**

In addition to diligently completing history assignments, Amanda reads some unassigned history books. Afterward, she obtains a grade of *A* in history. Amanda begins diligently working on her science course and seeks additional work in science.

▶ **CASE 9.20**

Alyson notes that her mother is more responsive to her requests when she says "please." She asks her teacher, "May I please play with a puzzle?"

In Cases 9.21 to 9.24, Shauna, Mickey, Nancy, and Chris appear to be discriminating.

▶ **CASE 9.21**

Whenever Shauna watches television at her house, she relaxes, never trying to follow what is being said very closely. Shauna's teacher shows her class a videotaped lecture on the Declaration of Independence. Although the medium is similar to the television in her home, Shauna realizes that she will be tested on the content of the video. She takes notes and listens closely as she watches the video monitor.

▶ **CASE 9.22**

Mickey speaks openly about his sexual fantasies to his buddies, but he never mentions them to his father.

▶ **CASE 9.23**

Nancy always does homework for Mr. Clancy's class, but she rarely does it for Ms. Taylor's class.

▶ **CASE 9.24**

Twelve-year-old Chris tries to win and uses his hardest slam when playing table tennis against Amy, his older sister. But when he plays table tennis against his five-year-old brother, he just pats the ball back to him and never slams.

▶ APPLYING THE PRINCIPLE OF MODELING

Individuals are *modeling* behavior when they initiate a behavior pattern they have observed others display. Marilyn, Sandy, Scott, Phil, Ms. Shelly's students, and Ms. Loyacono's students are learning behavior patterns through modeling in Cases 9.25 to 9.30.

▶ CASE 9.25

Marilyn is a student in Mr. Bomgars's class. He asks the class, "If y equals 6 divided by the quantity $x - 3$, where x is a real number between 0 and 3, what happens to y as x approaches its minimum? George?" George: "Well, I think—" Interrupting George, Mr. Bomgars says, "*You* think! That must be a new experience for you! I've never known you to think before!" A few class members roar with laughter. The next day a friend tells Marilyn, "I'm late for a meeting; I'd better hurry." Marilyn, in a loud voice, says, "*You* hurry! How can you hurry while carrying around that stomach?"

▶ CASE 9.26

As part of a problem-solving learning activity for her ninth-grade class, Ms. Rogers assigns Sandy to a cooperative group with Ed and Diane. Initially, Sandy has little motivation for working on the task and solving the problem. But as she associates with Ed and Diane, who enthusiastically and diligently work on the project, Sandy gains an interest in working on the task herself.

▶ CASE 9.27

Several days after Scott's mother spanks him, he hits his younger sister.

▶ CASE 9.28

Phil and Dudley are confronted by a drug pusher on their school's grounds, who offers to sell them some dope. Phil declines the offer: "No, I don't use the stuff." Dudley pulls out some money and says, "Okay, I'll try it." As soon as Dudley completes the transaction, Phil pulls out his own money and tells the pusher, "Yeah, I'll have some, too."

▶ CASE 9.29

Three times a week, Ms. Shelly makes an hour available to her fifth graders to read silently any selection from a large collection of trade books available in her classroom. During the free-silent-reading periods, Ms. Shelly catches up on paperwork. Only about half of Ms. Shelly's students enthusiastically read during these periods.

▶ CASE 9.30

Three times a week, Ms. Loyacono makes an hour available to her fifth graders to read silently any selection from a large collection of trade books available in her classroom. During the free-silent-reading periods, Ms. Loyacono always silently reads books of her own choosing. Virtually all her students enthusiastically read during these periods.

Modeling is a form of generalization in which a person reasons, "If it's okay for them, it's okay for me." Because children and adolescents tend to follow the examples set by others, modeling is a particularly powerful means for teaching behavior patterns to students. But you should guard against using the destructive and ineffective tactic of comparing one student's behavior to that of another. If, for example, Tom is told, "Why don't you behave more like Bill? Bill never gives me trouble!" Tom is likely to resent Bill and begin protecting his own ego by acting as un-Bill-like as he can. You effectively use modeling by quietly serving as an example of the behavior pattern you want students to follow or by grouping students who need to learn to follow the behavior pattern with those who already display it. In Case 9.30, Ms. Loyacono applied the former tactic; in Case 9.26, Ms. Rogers applied the latter.

Engage in Activity 9.4.

► **ACTIVITY 9.4**

In a discussion with a colleague, compare the four behavior modification principles of cuing, generalization, discrimination, and modeling with respect to the following questions.

1. Which of the four principles targets the development of new behavior patterns? Which targets the elimination of existing behavior patterns? Note that some of the principles may be applied to teach both new behavior patterns as well the elimination of existing behavior patterns.

2. What role does cuing play in the principle of generalization?

3. What role does cuing play in the principle of discrimination?

4. What role does generalization play in the principle of modeling?

5. What role does discrimination play in the principle of modeling?

► APPLYING THE PRINCIPLE OF SATIATION

In Case 9.31, Ms. Elkins attempts to apply the principle of satiation.

► CASE 9.31

Andy is distributing magazines to his eleventh-grade classmates in Ms. Elkins's literature class. Andy places a magazine in front of James, who hands it back to Andy and says, "Hey, I don't take anything from you!" "You gotta take it now 'cause you already put your nigger hands on it!" replies Andy. James leaps to his feet, and the two square off at each other. Two other students and Ms. Elkins step in and take charge. Without further incident, Ms. Elkins sends them both to the dean's office.

Andy and James have been antagonizing one another since school began two months ago. Ms. Elkins does not want to have them suspended, as they usually conscientiously engage in learning activities and are both progressing well toward learning goals. Except for behaviors related to their volatile relationship, neither tends to be disruptive. This latest incident, however, is just one more in a continuing series of confrontations between the two. Ms. Elkins refuses to conduct her class with the fear that Andy and James will break out in a fight. She decides to try one more tactic before recommending suspensions.

Her plan calls for Andy and James to work closely on assigned tasks in which the success of one depends on the success of the other. Initially, she assigns them to work on a joint project for which they will receive the same grade. Ms. Elkins believes that, while working together, they will become so saturated with antagonizing each other that they might eventually choose to cooperate instead. She knows she is gambling, but she considers the current situation intolerable and suspension undesirable.

Ms. Elkins attempted to apply the *principle of satiation*. According to that principle, if an established learned behavior is allowed to continue unchecked, the person exhibiting the behavior may soon become tired of the pattern and elect to terminate it. If, as in the case of Andy and James, immediate, naturally occurring punishment is a consequence of the behavior pattern, the satiation principle may be applicable. Of course, if the naturally occurring punishment is severe, one may not be able to afford to apply the satiation principle. You wouldn't, for example, apply the satiation principle in dealing with a child who habitually runs into a busy street. You should consider satiation as a method for terminating off-task behavior patterns only when (a) the naturally occurring punishment is a consequence of the behavior pattern, (b) the naturally occurring punishment is not dangerous, and (c) you are willing to tolerate the off-task behavior pattern long enough for the satiation principle to take effect.

▶ SYNTHESIS ACTIVITIES FOR CHAPTER 9

I. Following is a list of 11 concepts or principles from behavioristic psychology that can be used in the design of learning activities to help students supplant off-task behavior patterns with on-task ones. Classify each according to one of the following: (a) focuses on terminating an existing behavior pattern, (b) focuses on developing a new behavior pattern, or (c) can focus on either terminating an existing pattern or developing a new one.

    A. Positive reinforcement

    B. Punishment

    C. Negative reinforcement

    D. Extinction

    E. Alternative behavior

    F. Shaping

    G. Cuing

    H. Generalization

    I. Discrimination

    J. Modeling

    K. Satiation

II. Check your responses to Synthesis Activity I's prompt against the following: B, D, and K focus on terminating existing behaviors; A, C, E, F, and J focus on developing new behaviors; G, H, and I could be either. Cuing could be either because cues can be used to remind students to initiate a behavior or remind them to stop a behavior they are exhibiting. Generalization could be either because students can generalize that what is appropriate under one circumstance is also appropriate under another or they can generalize that what is inappropriate in one situation is also inappropriate in another. Discrimination could be either because students can recognize that because a behavior is appropriate in one situation does not mean it's appropriate in another, or they can recognize that inappropriate behavior for one set of circumstances may be appropriate for another.

III. Describe an example of each of the following:

    A. A student's generalizing between two situations leads to an on-task behavior.

    B. A student's generalizing between two situations leads to an off-task behavior.

C. A student's discriminating between two situations leads to an on-task behavior.

D. A student's discriminating between two situations leads to an off-task behavior.

E. A teacher (a) identifies an off-task behavior pattern exhibited by a student, (b) identifies an alternative on-task behavior pattern for that student to develop, and (c) devises a plan for applying the principle of extinction to help the student eliminate the off-task pattern and for positively reinforcing the alternative pattern.

F. A teacher uses a destructive positive reinforcer to encourage an on-task behavior pattern.

G. A teacher uses the principle of shaping to help a student develop an on-task behavior pattern.

H. A teacher unwittingly uses the principle of shaping to lead a student to develop an off-task behavior pattern.

Compare and discuss your examples with those of colleagues.

IV. Milton is a seventh grader who habitually fails to bring the required uniform to physical education class:

A. Describe a scenario in which Milton's teacher uses contrived punishment to deal with this off-task behavior pattern.

B. Describe a scenario in which Milton's teacher uses a naturally occurring punishment.

C. Describe a scenario in which Milton's teacher uses negative reinforcement.

Compare and discuss your scenarios with those of colleagues.

► TRANSITIONAL ACTIVITY FROM CHAPTER 9 TO CHAPTER 10

In preparation for your work with Chapter 10, discuss with two or more colleagues the following questions:

I. Why is it critical for teachers to discourage students from being off-task even when the off-task behaviors are nondisruptive?

II. What strategies do teachers employ to deal with the following types of off-task behaviors?

- Mind wandering and daydreaming
- Refusing to participate in class activities
- Failing to complete homework assignments
- Being under the influence of debilitating drugs
- Being absent or tardy
- Cheating on tests

Dealing with Nondisruptive Off-Task Behaviors

▶ **CHAPTER 10'S GOAL AND OBJECTIVES**

The goal of this chapter is for you to develop strategies for constructively dealing with students' nondisruptive off-task behaviors. Specifically, Chapter 10 is designed to lead you to achieve the following objectives.

1. Design learning activities to teach students to supplant the following types of off-task behavior patterns with on-task behavior patterns: (a) mind wandering, (b) daydreaming, (c) refusing to participate in class activities, (d) failing to complete homework assignments, (e) failing to bring needed materials to class, (f) being under the influence of debilitating drugs during class, (g) being absent or tardy, and (h) cheating on tests.
2. Effectively handle isolated incidents of the types of nondisruptive off-task behaviors that are listed under Objective 1.

▶ **NONDISRUPTIVE OFF-TASK BEHAVIORS**

Nondisruptive off-task behaviors can easily be overlooked by teachers. Such behaviors (e.g., daydreaming) do not interfere with the learning activities of a class as a whole; a student interferes only with his or her own learning by exhibiting nondisruptive off-task behaviors. A student usually suffers only minor consequences from one isolated incident of nondisruptive off-task behavior. But there are three reasons why you should deal with rather than disregard nondisruptive off-task behaviors—even isolated ones.

- Whenever students are off-task, they are failing to benefit from your planned learning activities and consequently are diminishing their chances of achieving learning goals. Because you are responsible for helping students achieve learning goals, it follows that you are responsible for helping students be on-task.
- Off-task behavior patterns begin with isolated off-task behaviors that are positively reinforced.
- Students exhibiting nondisruptive off-task behaviors tend to fall behind in a lesson. Once students miss one part of a learning activity, they are unlikely to

understand subsequent parts, even if they become reengaged. Students who are unable to follow a learning activity may become bored, frustrated, and disruptive.

The efficacy of the solutions you prescribe for any off-task behavior problem is dependent on your understanding of the students, the peculiarities of the situation, and yourself. Please keep in mind that the examples of teachers dealing with off-task behaviors given in this chapter and Chapter 11 are only examples. The teachers' tactics in these examples worked or didn't work because of individual characteristics of the involved persons and circumstances. You and other teachers can learn from them, but you must develop your own individual style for handling the unique cases you confront.

▶ MIND WANDERING AND DAYDREAMING

Detection and Response

Mind wandering and daydreaming may be the most common forms of student off-task behaviors. *Mind wandering* is an uncontrolled coursing of ideas and mental images (Dewey, 1933, pp. 3–12). *Daydreaming* is similar to mind wandering except that the daydreamer cognitively controls the thoughts and images (Klinger, 1978). Traditionally, children have been reprimanded, embarrassed, and punished for allowing their thoughts to deviate from school tasks. Nevertheless, daydreaming seems to serve a critical purpose in cognitive development (Gold & Cundiff, 1980). There appears to be a direct relation between the frequency of daydreams and an individual's level of creative achievement (Lyerly, 1982). Mind wandering and especially daydreaming per se shouldn't be discouraged, but students need to learn to control mind wandering and time their daydreams so that engagement in learning activities isn't disrupted.

Because teachers cannot directly observe mind wandering and daydreaming as they can other off-task behaviors (e.g., inappropriate talking), it is difficult to detect this form of student disengagement. Shrewd and concerned teachers learn to read body language, recognize vacant stares, and use questioning techniques to detect students who are quietly drifting out of touch with learning activities. Contrast Cases 10.1 to 10.3.

▶ CASE 10.1

Mr. Minchot is explaining to his ninth-grade science class how Darwin and Wallace each arrived at his theory of natural selection. Most of the class listens intently. Sitting erect, Amelia stares directly at Mr. Minchot and imagines herself along a riverbank galloping on a horse. Mr. Minchot, pleased with his class's silence, continues to speak, unaware of Amelia's disengagement.

▶ CASE 10.2

Ms. Searcy is explaining to her ninth-grade science class how Darwin and Wallace each arrived at his theory of natural selection. Most of the class listens intently. Sitting erect, Amy stares directly at Ms. Searcy and imagines herself along a riverbank galloping on a horse. Ms. Searcy, who watches her students' faces as she lectures, notices the blank look in Amy's eyes. Suspicious that Amy is not engaged in the lesson, she pauses and asks, "What do you think about that, Amy?" Amy: "About what?" Ms. Searcy: "About what I said." Amy: "I don't know what you said." Ms. Searcy: "You don't know what I said because you were daydreaming. Amy, the daydreamer, off in a world of her own! Okay, daydreamer, let's listen from now on." Amy: "Yes, ma'am, I will."

"Off in a world of her own—Amy, the daydreamer!" Amy thinks to herself as she stares directly at Ms. Searcy and nods her head as if agreeing with what Ms. Searcy is saying. Amy keeps pondering those words; she likes the sound of "a daydreamer, off in her own world."

▶ **CASE 10.3**

Ms. Smith is explaining to her ninth-grade science class how Darwin and Wallace each arrived at his theory of natural selection. Most of the class listens intently. Sitting erect, Anita stares directly at Ms. Smith and imagines herself along a riverbank galloping on a horse. Ms. Smith, who watches her students' faces as she lectures, notices the blank look in Anita's eyes. Suspicious that Anita is not engaged in the lesson, she pauses and asks the class, "Why do you suppose Darwin waited so long before publishing his theory? Anita?" Anita: "What's the question?" Ms. Smith: "Please repeat the question for those of us who missed it, Michael." Michael: "You asked why Darwin took so long before publishing his stuff." Ms. Smith: "Thanks, Mike. What's your opinion, Debbie?" Debbie expresses her opinion and the lecture–discussion continues. Ms. Smith subtly observes Anita to see if the strategy worked.

If Amelia continues to enjoy her daydreaming during Mr. Minchot's lecture, she may soon develop a pattern of daydreaming in his classes. The beginning of a lecture may serve as a cue for Amelia to daydream. Ms. Searcy dealt with Amy's daydreaming, but she disrupted her own learning activity to belabor Amy's behavior and destructively characterize Amy as a daydreamer. Ms. Smith hopes that her one question for Anita cued her back on-task without disrupting the rest of the class or positively reinforcing the daydreaming.

Strategies

Teachers employ strategies to check mind wandering in Cases 10.4 and 10.5.

▶ **CASE 10.4**

Mr. Cavallaro's second graders are working on independent computational exercises. He circulates among them, checking on their engagement. Richard stares into space; Mr. Cavallaro doesn't believe Richard is thinking about one of the exercise problems. He moves into Richard's line of vision and makes eye contact. Richard seems to return to work. But Mr. Cavallaro begins noticing that more and more students appear to have wandering minds. Convinced that their attention spans are inadequate for the exercise to continue efficiently, he calls for their attention, directs them to stop their computing, and takes them outside where he conducts a five-minute session of calisthenics—not as a punishment, but to give them a change of pace from mental activity. After the exercises, they return to the classroom and complete the computations.

▶ **CASE 10.5**

Mr. Legget detects that a number of his seventh-grade English students frequently allow their minds to wander from the planned topic during learning activities. By watching students' faces and raising questions, he determines that this form of disengagement is particularly prevalent during large-group sessions in which he lectures and conducts discussions. He decides to attempt a strategy with Rosalie, who appears to daydream habitually, and evaluate how well it works with her. If successful, he will try the strategy with others and eventually develop a plan for the entire class. In a one-to-one conference, Mr. Legget and Rosalie verbalize the problem and agree to the following plan.

Mr. Legget is to provide Rosalie with a tiny, flat, rubber image of a frog that can easily be attached to and removed from her desktop. Mr. Legget will keep a statue of a frog facing the class on his desk. During large-group learning activities, Rosalie is to attach the rubber frog to her desktop. Every time she sees the frog on her desk looking at her, she is to glance at the frog on Mr. Legget's desk and be reminded that it is not time to daydream.

The success of the plan depends on the frog's cuing Rosalie to discriminate between when daydreaming is appropriate and when it is not. She does not attach the frog to her desk at times when daydreaming is appropriate. After a two-week trial, Rosalie and Mr. Legget both agree that the frequency with which she daydreams during large-group learning activities is significantly lower than it was before they started the program. The time frame for the plan is extended.

Pleased with Rosalie's success, Mr. Legget initiates a similar strategy with Mike. But Mike tends to stare upward and not see anything when he daydreams, and the plan fails. Mr. Legget decides to use a sound-cue approach with Mike, and they agree that Mr. Legget will watch for signs that Mike's attention is drifting. When he believes Mike's thoughts have wandered, he will wait for an appropriate point in the lecture or discussion and rap a pencil, which he always carries, against the backside of the ring he wears. When he hears the unique sound, Mike is to remind himself to focus his thoughts on the lesson.

The plan works fairly well with Mike, and Mr. Legget experiments with other cues for other students. Some work well; others do not. After a month, Mr. Legget is having trouble keeping up with what cues whom. Finally, he calls a class meeting to relate a plan for the entire class to combat daydreaming and mind wandering during lectures and discussions. The plan calls for him to trigger the beeper on the chronograph he wears on his wrist any time he detects at least three students who are drifting off.

While deciding on his approach, Mr. Legget had considered, among many other things, placing a small gong on his desk and striking it whenever he deems that a "stay with us" cue is needed. The gong, he thought, would have a dramatic effect. But he can't carry the gong with him, so he rejected it to retain the mobility afforded by the beeper on his chronograph. After implementing his plan for two weeks, he evaluates its success. He decides that, although it doesn't seem to help some students, it is worthwhile continuing because it is working for others.

Engage in Activity 10.1.

► *ACTIVITY 10.1*

With a colleague, collaboratively respond to the following prompts.

1. Discuss the advantages and disadvantages of Mr. Cavallaro's tactics for dealing with students' mind wandering in Case 10.4.

2. Speculate on specific empirical observations Mr. Cavallaro and Mr. Leggett might have made to enable them to detect students' mind wandering and daydreaming in Cases 10.4 and 10.5.

3. Discuss the advantages and disadvantages of the tactics Mr. Leggett used to deal with Rosalie's daydreaming in Case 10.5.

4. Discuss the advantages and disadvantages of the tactics Mr. Leggett used to combat mind wandering and daydreaming for the whole class in Case 10.5.

▶ REFUSING TO PARTICIPATE IN CLASS ACTIVITIES

In Cases 10.6 to 10.9, teachers effectively deal with students' disengagement during in-class learning activities; in these examples, reasons other than mind wandering or daydreaming interfere with the students' in-class participation.

▶ CASE 10.6

Ms. Webb has just directed her first-grade students to carry out assignments in five-member cooperative groups. Five classmates—Sophonia, Scott, April, Heather, and Louis—are assigned to work together and plan a mural for the classroom. Scott, April, Heather, and Louis move to their work area and begin discussing the project. Sophonia remains at her desk on the other side of the room. Ms. Webb observes the situation for a minute, collects her thoughts, and discreetly goes to Sophonia and says to her in a soft voice, "You are not working with your group. May I help you?" Sophonia: "No, I'm okay." Ms. Webb: "Why did you decide to stay here instead of working with your group?" Sophonia: "Because of Scott; he makes me mad." Ms. Webb: "Why did you get mad?" Sophonia: "He calls me 'dummy'!" Ms. Webb: "I understand why you would get mad. I don't like it when someone calls me 'dummy.'" Reading Sophonia's expression, Ms. Webb believes Sophonia received the supportive communication and has dealt with her feelings. Thus, Ms. Webb confidently says, "Now hurry and get with your group. We need your ideas so that we'll have the best mural possible!" As Sophonia moves toward her task group, Ms. Webb decides to be especially attentive to Sophonia and Scott's group, thinking that her presence will reduce the chances that Scott will call Sophonia "dummy." As Ms. Webb continues to supervise the activities in the room, she thinks to herself, "What, if anything, should I do if I hear Scott call Sophonia 'dummy'?"

▶ CASE 10.7

Mr. Sabid directs his French class to translate 12 sentences before the end of the class period; he plans to collect their work and give them feedback the next day. As other students begin the work, Derald puts his head down on his desk and falls asleep. Mr. Sabid thinks, "I could just let him go and require him to complete those translations before he leaves school today. But I'd rather stop his sleeping in class before it becomes a distraction to others. I wonder what's going on with him today. It's not like him to do this. Well, for whatever reason, I'm not going to allow him to develop a habit of sleeping in my class. I know! I'll write a note to him. A note won't disturb the others, nor will it call attention to him." Mr. Sabid writes:

> Derald:
>
> If I do not receive your complete translations before I leave today at 4:30, I will not be able to give you feedback on them in tomorrow's class. If you don't finish them by the end of the period, turn them in to me at 4:20 P.M. today in room 143. I will be working in there then.—Mr. Sabid

Quietly, Mr. Sabid walks over to Derald, inconspicuously and gently shakes him until he opens his eyes, and hands him the note. Mr. Sabid immediately walks away, not giving Derald an opportunity to make a comment. If Derald does not either complete the work by the end of the class or meet Mr. Sabid with the work at 4:20, Mr. Sabid plans to contact Derald's parents.

▶ CASE 10.8

Mr. Burns-Whittle notices that one of his fifth graders, Jamie, is just sitting at his desk instead of working on the assigned in-class word recognition exercise. Mr. Burns-Whittle discreetly goes over to Jamie, makes eye contact, and signals him to begin working. Jamie just looks away without taking the cue. Mr. Burns-Whittle then whispers directly to Jamie, "I need you to begin the exercise now." Assuming Jamie will begin, Mr. Burns-Whittle confidently walks away. Twenty seconds later, he sees that Jamie has still not begun. He beckons Jamie to meet him just outside the room in the hall. There he softly asks Jamie, "Why have you not begun your work?" Jamie: "Because I don't want to." Mr. Burns-Whittle: "I understand that you don't want to do this exercise, but I suggest that you get it over with now so you won't need to worry about it later today." Jamie: "I'm not going to do it." Mr. Burns-Whittle: "Jamie, do you know what the word 'option' means?" Jamie: "No." Mr. Burns-Whittle: "An option is a choice. It's an opportunity to choose. Right now, you have an option. You have a choice to make. What did I just say?" Jamie: "I have a choice." Mr. Burns-Whittle: "You have the option of going to Ms. Cook's office and waiting there for me until two o'clock when I have the time to work with you. Or you have the option of quietly returning to your desk and completing the assignment. Which option do you choose?" Jamie: "I don't want to go to Ms. Cook's office." Mr. Burns-Whittle: "So give me your choice. I have to get back to our class." Jamie: "Okay, I won't go to Ms. Cook." Mr. Burns-Whittle: "Then you've made your choice."

Jamie returns to his place and reluctantly begins working. Mr. Burns-Whittle thinks, "If he doesn't continue working, I'll send him to the office and direct the staff to have him wait for me until I get there at two. That'll give me time to decide what to do."

▶ CASE 10.9

Mr. Cobb is a junior high school social studies teacher who does not design learning activities around problems that students have a felt need to solve. Throughout his years as a teacher, Mr. Cobb has had difficulty with students habitually failing to participate in class activities, failing to complete homework assignments, failing to bring materials to class, and skipping his classes. Consequently, he finds it necessary to initiate the following plan for each of his social studies classes that meet five days a week for 55 minutes per meeting.

The last 30 minutes of each Wednesday's meeting and the entire 55 minutes of each Friday's meeting are designated as "option times" in which students may spend their time in one of the following ways:

Option 1: A supervised study session in which students are required to work individually and silently on school-related tasks of their choice

Option 2: A free activity in which students do as they please (e.g., watch a videotape, listen to CDs, socialize, play games, go to the library, or attend supervised study hall) within a predetermined set of specific guidelines

Option 3: Work under Mr. Cobb's direction completing certain tasks (e.g., filing, collating papers, cleaning the classroom, duplicating materials, or performing classroom maintenance) within a predetermined set of specific guidelines

The specific guidelines that pertain to the plan are printed in a book of classroom regulations given to every student. Mr. Cobb gives each student the opportunity of signing a contingency contract similar to the one that appears in Figure 10.1. Students who do not sign such a contract automatically exercise option 1 during each option time. Those who sign will exercise either option 2 or 3 during option times, depending on how well they have fulfilled the contingencies of their contract during any given week.

Although some of Mr. Cobb's colleagues criticize his plan because it cuts into regularly scheduled class time, Mr. Cobb continues to use it. He believes that the plan's overall impact leads to a richer participation in learning activities because students are more diligent with in-class activities, homework, and attendance. His data indicate that each student lost far more than 85

CONTINGENCY CONTRACT

Contract Period:

Beginning   Ending

We the undersigned,   (here
referred to as "Teacher") and   (hereafter referred to as "Student") do hereby enter into a contract
with the following provisions:

The teacher will maintain a record of option credits* for the
student in a ledger book (hereafter referred to as "the ledger")
during the contract period according to the following schedule:

ATTENDANCE (10 credits per day maximum):
10 credits for each regularly scheduled social studies class at
which the student attends for a complete 55 minutes. 5 credits for each such class that the student attends for less than
the 55 minutes.

HOMEWORK (10 credits per day maximum):
Homework assignments completed and returned by the deadline established by the teacher will be rated for completeness
and effort on a scale of 1 to 10 by the teacher. Homework
received after the deadline will be rated for completeness and
effort on a scale of 1 to 5.

IN-CLASS ASSIGNMENTS (10 credits per day maximum):
In-class assignments completed and returned by the deadline established by the teacher will be rated for completeness
and effort on a scale of 1 to 10 by the teacher. In-class assignments received after the deadline will be rated for completeness and effort on a scale of 1 to 5.

HAVING MATERIALS IN CLASS (5 credits per day
maximum):
5 credits are earned each day that the student has all of his/
her materials (e.g., books, pens, and paper) for full class
participation.

The student may choose to exercise option 2** during option
times on a Wednesday by forfeiting 50 of his/her option credits.
Otherwise the student is required to exercise option 3** on the
Wednesday. The student may exercise option 2 during option time
on a Friday by forfeiting 100 of his/her option credits. Otherwise

Figure 10.1. Mr. Cobb's Contingency Contract

the student is required to exercise option 3 on Friday. The student must have a ledger balance of at least 50 option credits before a Wednesday class period begins and 100 option credits before a Friday class begins to be in a position to choose option 2 on that day.

The student's option credit balance shall not in any way influence decisions which the teacher makes (e.g., course grades) other than whether or not the student may choose option 2 on Wednesdays and Fridays.

Nothing in this contract shall supersede classroom, school, or school system policies and regulations.

This contract may be voided before its ending date by mutual agreement of both the student and the teacher.

---

*Option Credits are defined on page 6 of "Classroom Regulations."
**Options 2 and 3 are defined on page 8 of "Classroom Regulations."

Teacher   /   date

Student   /   date

Witness   /

Witness   /

Figure 10.1. (*continued*)

minutes of class time per week before implementation of the plan because of time Mr. Cobb spent dealing with student disengagement.

Engage in Activity 10.2.

▶ *ACTIVITY 10.2*

With a colleague, collaboratively respond to the following prompts.

1. Discuss the advantages and disadvantages of the following in Case 10.6: (a) Ms. Webb's use of supportive communications as she conferred with Sophonia, (b) Ms. Webb not immediately interacting with Scott regarding what Sophonia said, and (c) Ms. Webb closely monitoring Sophonia and Scott's group. Discuss tactics Ms. Webb might consider if she hears Scott speak rudely during the group activity.

2. Discuss the advantages and disadvantages of the following in Case 10.7: (a) Mr. Sabid waking Derald instead of leaving him alone and allowing naturally occurring punishment to do its work, (b) Mr. Sabid using a note instead of oral speech to communicate with Derald, and (c) Mr. Webb gently shaking Derald to wake him instead of using a method that didn't require physical contact.

3. Discuss the advantages and disadvantages of the tactics Mr. Burns-Whittle used to deal with Jamie's failure to follow directions in Case 10.8.

4. Discuss the advantages and disadvantages of Mr. Cobb's tactics for motivating students to participate in class activities in Case 10.9.

▶ FAILING TO COMPLETE HOMEWORK ASSIGNMENTS

Meaningful Homework

Consider Case 10.10.

▶ **CASE 10.10**

While conducting a learning activity within a unit on modern poetry for one of her high school English classes, Ms. Ramsen provides definitions and explanations of the following concepts: rhythm, meter, iamb foot, trochee foot, anapest foot, and dactyl foot. Ronny, Stacy, and most of the other students listen to Ms. Ramsen and record the definitions in their notes. Ms. Ramsen then assigns homework in which they are to read and analyze several poems, classifying them according to rhythm and meter. The assignment specifies exactly what is expected. At the end of the period, Ronny complains to Stacy, "How can Ramsen expect me to do this when I don't even know what she's talking about? Iambs! Trochees! She must be crazy! Those definitions don't make any sense to me. She didn't teach them to us!" Stacy: "No one understood her today; I don't know how to do the homework." That night as Ronny struggles through Ms. Ramsen's assignment, the concepts introduced in class that day begin to come clear to him. After he analyzes several poems, the differences between an iamb foot and a trochee foot are apparent.

For many learning objectives, in-class learning activities only provide direction, stimulate thinking, and explain assignments; actual student objective achievement occurs after class when students individually think, practice, and work out problems on their own. In many circumstances, the most efficient time for students to conceptualize, memorize, or polish skills is when they are working on out-of-class assignments. Unfortunately, some teachers don't adhere to the suggestions implied by Chapter 7's section "Eight Points about Homework Assignments." They tend to assign homework mindlessly. Mr. Davis's students in Case 10.11 are given busywork that is hardly relevant to student attainment of any goal that addresses their needs.

▶ **CASE 10.11**

Mr. Davis says to his history class: "For tonight's homework, complete exercise 5.3 beginning on page 83 of your workbook. I will check it first thing tomorrow. Anyone who doesn't have every blank filled will get 10 points deducted from his or her grade total. Is that clear?"

Exercise 5.3 consists of 27 fill-in-the-blank statements such as, "The first state to enter the union after the original _____ colonies was _____ in _____." The workbook is published as a supplement to the history text used in Mr. Davis's class. To complete the assignment, a student spends about an hour searching the textbook for what goes in the blanks. Chapter 5 of the history text contains each of the 27 completed statements nearly verbatim. Few students see value in doing this assignment other than to keep them in Mr. Davis's good graces and prevent them from losing points off their grades.

The concern of this section of the chapter is to show how teachers (e.g., Ms. Ramsen in Case 10.10) can deal with situations in which students choose not to attempt *meaningful* homework assignments. It is debatable whether it is even desirable for students to complete assignments such as Mr. Davis's for which there is no worthwhile rationale. There are no naturally occurring consequences for failing to complete meaningless assignments. With his point-deduction scheme, Mr. Davis imposed a contrived punishment for students' failure to fill in all the blanks.

Strategies

Recall how Ms. Hanzlik dealt with students' failure to complete homework in Case 7.34. In Case 10.12, Mr. Benge uses another strategy.

► CASE 10.12

The goal of Mr. Benge's first unit in the English course he is just starting with an eighth-grade class involves improving students' essay-writing abilities. His first homework assignment requires students to choose a topic for a two-page essay dealing with something from their neighborhood and then construct an outline listing the subtopics for the introduction, the main body, and the ending. A number of students ask Mr. Benge questions about how to do the assignment "right." Instead of answering their questions, he tries to assure them that they only need to do it the best way they know how so he can learn how to help them do it right. He tells them that he will collect the work the next day and make suggestions on it that will help them fix it up so that eventually they will be ready to start writing the complete two-page essay. Although he will collect and comment on the work, it will not be graded. "How many points is this worth?" asks one student. "Zero," replies Mr. Benge.

Christine, who like most members of the class does not yet know Mr. Benge well enough to trust what he says, thinks to herself, "I've never made an outline before. I don't know how to do this and because he's not grading us on it, I won't do it." The next day Christine and several others do not have topics and outlines ready. Others present their attempts to Mr. Benge, but, as he expected, few are anything near a finished product. Mr. Benge analyzes each outline he receives and returns it to its owner with helpful suggestions and encouraging comments. Students refine their outlines in class using Mr. Benge's suggestions and then individually show their revised outlines to him. He either makes further suggestions for refinement or okays the work and directs them to begin writing their essays.

Christine feels left out of the activities because she did not give Mr. Benge the opportunity to help her. She asks Mr. Benge if she can turn in the work the next day. He replies, "If you bring a draft of your outline tomorrow, I'll try to get to it and make suggestions. But I may not have time. Do not write your essay until after I've approved your outline." At no time does Mr. Benge ask Christine or others why they did not do the initial assignment, nor is he receptive to hearing their excuses. He concerns himself only with the business of getting the work done—not with why it was not done in the past.

The following day, Mr. Benge busies himself helping those who are on schedule with their assignments. He does not find time to annotate the late ones. He takes those home and returns with them the next day. Until all those students who have kept up with the work have satisfactory essays in hand, the procedures continue with students' presenting homework to Mr. Benge who then makes suggestions and gives the next assignment. Mr. Benge administers a unit test that includes a prompt to write an essay. Christine feels her chances of doing well on the test are diminished because she was one day behind schedule throughout the unit and never had the opportunity to have her final homework checked by Mr. Benge before taking the test. She vows to keep up with Mr. Benge's assignments more diligently in the future.

Engage in Activity 10.3.

With a colleague, collaboratively respond to the following prompts.

1. Discuss the differences between meaningful homework assignments (e.g., Mr. Benge's in Case 10.12) and homework assignments that are not meaningful (e.g., Mr. Davis's in Case 10.10). Unless the assignment is meaningful, why will there be no naturally occurring consequences for not doing it?

2. Discuss the advantages and disadvantages of the following in Case 10.12: (a) Mr. Benge directing students to develop an outline before most were confident that they understood how to do the work, (b) Mr. Benge acting unconcerned about why students didn't do the homework assignment, and (c) Mr. Benge devoting more time to working with students who did the homework than with students who didn't.

▶ FAILING TO BRING NEEDED MATERIALS TO CLASS

Teachers deal with students' failure to bring necessary materials to school in Cases 10.13 to 10.15.

▶ CASE 10.13

Ms. Watham directs her class to begin an in-class written assignment. Instead of beginning, Andrea tells her, "I don't have anything to write with. I forgot my pencil." Ms. Watham: "Here, you may borrow one of mine this time. Please don't make a habit of this." Andrea: "I won't. Thank you." Ms. Watham thinks to herself, "I'd better develop some strategies if this 'forgetting' becomes habitual."

▶ CASE 10.14

Because failing to bring supplies and borrowing among students has become a problem for Ms. Murphy's fourth-grade class, the class has established the following rules:

Borrowing supplies among students is not allowed during class. A student who does not have needed school supplies may choose either to (a) purchase the needed items from the class storeroom, paying the marked price immediately or (b) take the needed items from the storeroom and provide twice as many items to the storeroom supply the morning of the next school day. For example, if three sheets of paper are taken, six are provided the next day. Students who fail to replace twice what they took will be required to work off the price of the items during the free period the day after the items are taken. The work tasks will be determined by Ms. Murphy and will involve jobs such as cleaning up the classroom or straightening up the storeroom.

▶ CASE 10.15

Mr. Emery requires the boys in his junior high physical education classes to dress in clean uniform shorts, T-shirts, socks, sneakers, and athletic supporters. Before class, while other students are changing into their uniforms, Mark engages Mr. Emery in the following conversation:

Mark: Coach, I brought my P.E. clothes home to wash, and I forgot to bring them back today.

Mr. Emery: Well, you need to work out today but not in those street clothes. What are you missing?

Mark: My shirt, shorts, socks, and jock.

Mr. Emery: You've got your sneakers?

Mark: Yes.

Mr. Emery: Wait here. I can lend you some extra stuff, but you'll have to bring them back tomorrow clean.

Mark: Okay, Coach.

Mr. Emery goes to his supply of P.E. clothes and purposely selects tight shorts and an oversized shirt. Returning, he gives them to Mark. As he dresses, Mark looks at the ill-fitting outfit and thinks, "I hope I never forget my uniform again!"

Engage in Activity 10.4.

► **ACTIVITY 10.4**

With a colleague, collaboratively respond to the following prompts.

1. Discuss the advantages and disadvantages of the way Ms. Watham responded to Andrea's failure to bring a pencil to class in Case 10.13.

2. Discuss the advantages and disadvantages of Ms. Murphy's rules in Case 10.14. Are you concerned that the rules disadvantage students according to how much money they have available to them?

3. Discuss the advantages and disadvantages of the way Mr. Emery dealt with Mark's failure to bring P.E. clothes to class in Case 10.15.

► BEING UNDER THE INFLUENCE OF DEBILITATING DRUGS

Teachers' Attitudes

Every school day in numerous urban, suburban, and rural school districts, tens of thousands of elementary, middle, junior high, and high school students attend classes under the debilitating influence of drugs (e.g., alcohol, marijuana, cocaine, crack, legal prescription drugs, barbiturates, amphetamines, and heroin) (Brendtro & Long, 1995; Cangelosi, 2006). According to the Center for Disease Control and Prevention, 25% of high school students report that they abused drugs at least 20 times; 79% report having experimented with alcohol at least once (National Center for Addiction and Substance Abuse at Columbia University, 2002). Strangers to a community who want to buy illegal drugs typically first try areas near high schools, junior high schools, and middle schools. Teachers respond to student drug use in a variety of ways.

- Many teachers never become aware of their students' drug use, although it occurs at their schools and affects the success of their learning activities. Such teachers remain naïve because they do not see individual personalities in their classes. They visualize their classes as a mass of faceless students and think, for example, of their "third-period European literature class" rather than "Clarence, Jean, Barbara, Mano, Sam, Oramya," and so on. Typically, such teachers spend much of their time talking to their groups while staring at the back walls of their classroom. They do not look into individual students' eyes and do not distinguish between glassy-eyed stupors and bright-eyed alertness. Subtle and even dramatic personality changes go undetected. Students who are depressive in the morning and manic in the afternoon appear the same all day to these teachers.

- Some teachers, who believe they have never before been around drug users, are so frightened by the prospect of drugs in their classrooms that they do not allow themselves to accept the possibility. "Deny what you don't like and you won't have to deal with it" is the deceptive message in which they find comfort. These teachers avoid drug awareness seminars and believe that motion-picture dramatizations of heroin addicts in the acute stages of withdrawal indicate how all drug users act. They are not familiar with the wealth of resources available on dealing with drugs in schools (e.g., see www.casacolumbia.org)

- Some teachers welcome the mellow, nondisruptive behaviors displayed by many students under the influence of certain drugs (e.g., marijuana and barbiturates). "I wish he didn't use drugs at all, but I'd rather have him doped up than misbehaving," one teacher admitted. She continued, "He can sleep it off in my class. That way, he's not disturbing those who want to learn. I can't control their habits, so why try?" Similarly, there are teachers who encourage parents to obtain medication for their "hyperactive" children.

- Some teachers react to student drug use by initiating a personal crusade against this "evil." Moralizing on reasons for why drugs should be avoided is usually ineffectual. Teachers who preach to students about the evils of drug use are often dealing with their own feelings of inadequacy. They may not be doing anything to stem drug use effectively, but they can tell themselves, "I'm trying to do something about the problem."

- Some teachers do not moralize about drug use, but they do attempt to help students become more knowledgeable regarding the effects of drugs. These teachers alter curricula so that specific units about drugs are taught and problems involving drugs are used to motivate students intrinsically to engage in learning activities in science, mathematics, social studies, physical education, language arts, music, and other academic areas. Chapter 6's section, "Problem-Based Learning," suggested ideas for using this approach. These teachers believe that knowledge will help students make enlightened decisions regarding drug use.

- There are teachers who realize that they cannot be all things to their students and concentrate on helping students attain only those goals for which they are responsible. But they also realize that students cannot be completely engaged in learning activities and thus efficiently achieve those goals while under the influence of crack, marijuana, uppers, downers, acid, cocaine, and other common mind-altering substances (Grossman, 1995, pp. 502–504; Ormrod, 2006, p. 372; Santrock, 1984, pp. 606–635). Such teachers believe that, although they may not be able to control drug use outside their own classrooms, they are responsible for and can teach students to choose not to be under the influence of such substances when under their supervision.

Strategies

The teachers in Cases 10.16 to 10.18 use the last of the aforementioned six approaches to student drug use.

▶ **CASE 10.16**

Royal, Paul, and Jake return from their lunch break to their seventh-grade classroom grinning and glancing at one another. Ms. Jackson, their teacher, observes them carefully and finds their behavior, although not disruptive, strange for them. Ms. Jackson ignores the three boys for the first 10 minutes while she conducts a large-group activity. As the class divides into smaller work groups and begins a second learning activity, Ms. Jackson individually engages each of the three in a conversation. She notices that Paul and Jake are less coherent than usual and that all three respond more slowly to questions. Their eyes seem more dilated than one would expect in the daytime, and she detects a sweet, musky odor when she stands near Royal. She believes the three boys smoked marijuana during the lunch break. She thinks to herself, "I'm pretty sure this is the first time they've shown up in class stoned. I need to make sure it's the last. I have to prevent others from modeling what they've done. They first need to understand that this won't be tolerated in our classroom. I should get them out of here while I think of what to do, but they should also be kept apart. I don't want them enjoying each other's company right now."

Ms. Jackson goes over to Royal, directs him to follow her out of the room. Just out of earshot of the other students, she calmly says, "You're in no condition right now to learn. There is no sense in your remaining here for this lesson." Royal: "But I didn't do anything!" Ms. Jackson: "You're just not thinking as well as you usually do, and I think it's because you've been smoking marijuana or something else that messes up your mind. You wait for me in the time-out room until I have time to come and get you." Royal enters the time-out room adjoining the classroom. Ms. Jackson thinks, "Now for the other two. I don't want them together. They should be alone to think. Where can I put Paul? Let's see. The library? No, Ms. Green wouldn't understand. She'd likely do something stupid. I know; I'll send a note to Ms. Lobianco in the office and ask if she can find a couple of inconspicuous places for Paul and Jake to wait separately. She'll understand." Ms. Jackson writes the following note and seals it in an envelope addressed to Ms. Lobianco, the principal's receptionist–secretary:

Ms. Lobianco:

I need to send Jake and Paul out of my room until 2:20 when I can retrieve them. Can you immediately locate two inconspicuous, quiet places (one for each as I don't want them together or anyone talking to them now)? My time-out room is occupied, and I don't want either in the library.

Please return this note by way of Tyrone indicating whether or not you can work this out. If you can, I'll send Paul first and then Jake five minutes later. If either doesn't make it, send an aide to my room to let me know.

Thanks for your help.

Wilma Jackson

Ms. Jackson directs Tyrone to take the note. In two minutes, he returns with a reply from Ms. Lobianco: "It's all worked out; glad to help." Ms. Jackson directs Paul and then Jake to the office in a manner similar to the way she handled Royal. She thinks, "Now what do I do? I'd like to turn the whole matter over to their parents. Jake's parents would handle it effectively. But Royal's parents would probably just beat him. I don't want that. I'm not sure about Paul's parents. I wouldn't be surprised if they share their dope with him. They seem so emotionally immature. I'll call Jake's and Paul's parents tonight. But Royal's parents will just mishandle it and not help him at all. I'm going to refer him to the guidance office; Mr. Hodge will handle it right."

After school, Ms. Jackson enters the time-out room and engages Royal in the following conversation:

Ms. Jackson: I never want you to come into our class after smoking marijuana.

Royal: I didn't smoke anything!

Ms. Jackson: I'm surprised, because you show signs of having smoked something.

Royal: Well, I didn't!

Ms. Jackson: Whatever you've already done or have not done is in the past. I just want to make sure that you won't ever take anything like marijuana before coming to class in the future. Do you understand?

Royal: Yes, but I didn't!

Ms. Jackson: What is it that I'm trying to tell you?

Royal: Not ever to show up in our class stoned.

Ms. Jackson: Very well; you understand. Now to help you from ever letting this happen, I am going to ask Mr. Hodge to assist you. If he agrees, he'll be calling you into his office to speak with you either tomorrow or the next day. Do you have anything you'd like to say?

Royal: What about Paul and Jake; don't they have to do anything?

Ms. Jackson: We're not concerned with Paul and Jake right now; only with you. Do you have anything else to say?

Royal: No, nothing.

Ms. Jackson: Now hurry along so you won't miss your bus. Have a pleasant night; I'll see you tomorrow.

Ms. Jackson brings Paul to the time-out room and engages him in the following conversation:

Ms. Jackson: Paul, I never want you to come to class after smoking marijuana.

Paul: Who said I smoked it? Was it Royal? He smoked a lot more than me! Why are you puttin' it on me?

Ms. Jackson: Be cool, Paul. I don't want to talk about Royal. It's you I'm asking never to use any kind of dope before or during school. I can't teach you when your mind's messed up. Tonight I'm going to call your parents to get their help in preventing this from happening again. I don't expect it to happen again, but if it does, I'm not going to call your parents again. I'm going to send you to Principal Bannon. Do you know what that means?

Paul shrugs his shoulders.

Ms. Jackson: What do you suppose Ms. Bannon will do if I send you to her office?

Paul shrugs again.

Ms. Jackson: I don't know what that means.

Paul: I don't know what she'll do.

Ms. Jackson: Let's brainstorm the possibilities. You go first.

Paul: (grinning shyly) She could just let it go.

Ms. Jackson: (not grinning at all) That's one possibility. Here's another. She could expel you. Now it's your turn.

Paul: She could call the police.

Ms. Jackson: That's a very real possibility. Or she could call the juvenile authorities. I think we understand one another. That's good. Now I know you've got somewhere to go, so be on your way. But first, how about a nice firm handshake? Take care; I'll see you tomorrow.

Jake takes his turn speaking with Ms. Jackson in the time-out room:

Ms. Jackson: Jake, I think you smoked marijuana or something that messes up your mind at lunch break today.

Jake: Yes.

Ms. Jackson: Thank you for being up front with me. I never expect you to come into our class in that condition again.

Jake: Okay.

Ms. Jackson: Now I have a favor to ask of you. I want you to relate the whole incident to either your mother or your father after you get home. Have one of them call me to discuss it at this number and time.

She writes down her phone number and a time interval and hands it to Jake.

Ms. Jackson: That's between 7 and 10 o'clock tonight. If I haven't heard from one of them by 10, I'll call your house. Okay?

Jake: All right.

Ms. Jackson: You take care; I'll see you tomorrow.

▶ **CASE 10.17**

Jim comes into Mr. Terrell's fourth-period business law class glassy-eyed and moving in a peculiar mechanical fashion. As Mr. Terrell watches him sit down at his desk, Jim's head bobs around his shoulders like a doll with a spring neck. Jim seems to be making an effort to appear straight, but Mr. Terrell is not deceived. Mr. Terrell decides not to deal with the situation at present. After class, he writes out an anecdotal account describing Jim's behavior in class that day. He sends copies to the principal and a trusted school counselor with notes requesting advice about how he should handle the matter.

▶ **CASE 10.18**

Through 10 years of schooling, Ray was never instructed by a teacher who used learning activities designed around problems that he felt a need to solve. Not being intrinsically motivated to participate, Ray learned in ninth grade that by coming to class high on drugs, time seemed to pass more quickly and the boredom was not as insufferable. The drugs also seemed to relieve the anxiety he felt over his concern for peer approval.

In the beginning of Ray's eleventh school year, Ms. Koo-Kim, Ray's literature teacher, becomes aware that he is habitually stoned in her class. She thinks to herself: "I will not tolerate Ray or any other student who wastes time in my class being strung out. I'll definitely do something to teach him to show up straight or not at all. But how? What strategy should I try? Maybe I should give him one warning and then let the office handle him if he shows up like this again. But unless they catch him with the stuff on him, what can they do? There's no school rule against being high, just one for possession and trafficking. First, I'll see if I can entice him into wanting to participate in class. Maybe intrinsic motivation isn't just a textbook dream. I need to find out more about Ray."

After some observations, Ms. Koo-Kim thinks that Ray might have some interest in being an entertainer. She decides to assign him the role of Macbeth in an upcoming class play during a unit on Shakespeare. She hopes he will discover that he cannot learn to perform to the satisfaction of his classmates when he is high. She figures that the responsibility of having them depend on him will either make or break him in the literature class.

Ms. Koo-Kim implements her plan, and Ray begins to realize that he is unable to remember the lines he studies the night before when he is under the influence of drugs in class. Classmates' performances are affected by how well Ray does. Several times Ray and other students suggest that he be replaced for the production. Ms. Koo-Kim persists in her expression of confidence in

Ray's will to succeed. Ray resolves to control his drug use at least so that it does not interfere with his ability to be engaged during the unit on Shakespeare. Ms. Koo-Kim hopes that this is the beginning of the end of Ray's attending her class under the influence of drugs.

Engage in Activity 10.5.

▶ *ACTIVITY 10.5*

With a colleague, collaboratively respond to the following prompts.

1. Discuss the advantages and disadvantages of the following in Case 10.16: (a) Ms. Jackson telling Royal she thinks he smoked marijuana even though she did not actually observe him do it, (b) Ms. Jackson separating Royal, Paul, and Jake so she can speak with each privately without them conferring with one another, (c) Ms. Jackson calling Jake's and Paul's parents while referring Royal to Mr. Hodge, and (d) the way Ms. Jackson interacted with each of the three students.

2. Discuss how Ms. Jackson's tactics in Case 10.16 should depend on the school's discipline policies.

3. Discuss the advantages and disadvantages of the tactics Mr. Terrell used in Case 10.17.

4. Discuss the advantages and disadvantages of Ms. Koo-Kim's tactics in Case 10.18.

▶ BEING ABSENT OR TARDY

Schoolwide Policies for Extrinsically Motivating Student Attendance

The attendance policy related in Case 10.19 typifies those of many secondary and middle schools.

▶ **CASE 10.19**

Gloster High's handbook includes the following attendance policy:

- A student who is absent for an entire school day or from an entire class during a school day may not be admitted back into any of the classes that he or she missed before bringing a note, signed by a parent, explaining the reason for the absence. The note will be evaluated by the school attendance official to classify the absence as either "excused" or "unexcused." The official will provide the student with an admit slip, which teachers are required to initial before allowing the student to return to individual classes.

- A student who arrives at school after the beginning of homeroom period or is late for any class must explain the reason for the tardiness to the attendance officer who will provide the student with an admit slip and categorize the tardiness as either "excused" or "unexcused." Teachers shall not allow tardy students into their classes without admit slips.

- A student who accumulates three unexcused absences for a class during one grade-reporting period or a student who accumulates a combined total of five unexcused absences and incidents of tardiness for a class period during one grade-reporting period shall receive a failing grade for that class for that grade-reporting period.

- A student may make up work missed during an excused absence or excused tardiness. Students may not make up work missed during any unexcused absence or unexcused tardiness.

- A student will be suspended from attending school for a week each time he or she accumulates a total of five unexcused absences.

Teachers' Policies for Extrinsically Motivating Student Attendance

Sometimes individual teachers—especially secondary school teachers—have policies for their classes similar to the ones in Case 10.20.

▶ **CASE 10.20**

Ms. Keane includes the following in her course syllabus.

Each student's course grade will be based on attendance, completion of assignments, scores on weekly tests, score on the final examination, and conduct in class. During the 45-day grading period, students have the opportunity to earn up to 500 points distributed as follows:

1. Attendance (90 points): For each complete class attended, the student will receive 2 points. A student who is tardy receives 1 point for that day. No points are received on days a student is absent.

2. Completion of assignments (90 points): For each day a student satisfactorily turns in assigned homework on time and completes all in-class work, that student is credited with 2 points. Only 1 point is given on days in which assignments are either turned in late or unsatisfactorily done. No points are given on days that assignments are not turned in at all.

3. Scores on weekly tests (160 points): Eight 20-point weekly tests will be given.

4. Final exam score (100 points): The final exam will be an opportunity for each student to earn up to 100 points.

5. In-class conduct (60 points): Each student will begin the grade-reporting period with 60 points. A student who is disruptive in a class or violates a classroom regulation will have points subtracted from that total in proportion to the seriousness of each offense.

A student's report grade will be determined by the number of points obtained during the grading period as follows: A for 468 to 500 points, B for 428 to 467 points, C for 388 to 427 points, D for 348 to 387 points, and F for 0 to 347 points.

Irrationality of Some Popular Attendance Policies

Schools and teachers with policies similar to those in Cases 10.19 and 10.20 attempt to extrinsically motivate students to attend classes using a system of rewards and punishments that largely depend on students' desires to obtain high grades on reports. The rationale for such systems is untenable for at least four reasons:

- The purpose of grades is to communicate teachers' summative evaluations of students' achievement of learning goals. If in-class learning activities are relevant to student attainment of goals and grades are assigned based on students' achievement of those goals, then there is no need to tie grades artificially to class attendance. Students who are absent from classes in which *worthwhile* learning activities take place are far less likely to receive high grades than students who engage in those worthwhile learning activities. It is only when what goes on in class does not help students achieve goals that making grades directly contingent on attendance even remotely makes sense. In such unfortunate cases, the rationale is "We want students to attend classes. Because what goes on in classes doesn't really help them achieve and thus does not naturally help their grades, we'll fabricate a relation between attendance and grades."

- Many students, especially those with a history of obtaining low grades, are simply not motivated by the desire for high grades or the fear of low grades.

- Not allowing a student to make up work missed for unexcused absences or tardiness is an admission that schoolwork is unimportant. If work missed by an absent student is critical to that student's goal attainment, then not allowing her or him to do that work is leaving the student with a learning gap. How is a teacher supposed to deal with that student for the remainder of the school year when the student lacks some knowledge, skill, ability, or attitude that is a prerequisite for subsequent learning?

- Responding to habitual absenteeism with suspensions seems counterproductive. Is the principle of satiation being applied?

Strategies

Rather than depend on schemes for artificially tying grades to attendance, you, as a teacher, can make sure that students discover the natural connection among attendance, achievement, and grades. Teachers deal with students' absenteeism in Cases 10.21 to 10.23.

▶ CASE 10.21

As part of a language arts exercise, Mr. Kacala's third-grade students compose letters to the mayor of their city suggesting ideas for reducing crime. The letters are written in class on a day when April is not in attendance. The next day, when April returns, Mr. Kacala has the letters for the mayor displayed on the wall. He tells the students, "Select a letter to talk about to the class. In your talk, explain what you agree with in the letter and what you disagree with. You may talk about a letter only if its author agrees to talk about the letter *you* wrote."

As the students go about reading the letters hanging on the walls and deciding who will critique whose letter, April says, "I want to talk about Steve's letter!" Steve: "Okay, then I get to do yours." April: "I don't have one because I wasn't here yesterday." Steve: "Let's ask Mr. Kacala what to do." Hearing about their problem, Mr. Kacala replies, "I'm sorry, but if April does not have a letter, then she won't be able to talk about another person's today." April: "But it wasn't my fault; I was sick yesterday!" Mr. Kacala: "I'm really sorry that you were sick yesterday. It's terrible that you didn't get to write a letter." April: "But I want to—" Mr. Kacala: "I know you do. I'll tell you what. Just listen to the others talk about the letters today, and after you get home, you write your letter. Bring it tomorrow. Gretchen isn't here today. If she agrees, you can talk about each other's letters tomorrow or on whatever day she's back in school." April: "But I want to do Steve's today!" Mr. Kacala has already moved toward another group of students and is conversing with them.

▶ CASE 10.22

Due to a dental appointment, Singh misses Mr. Shapiro's health science class one Tuesday. The next day Singh listens to Mr. Shapiro's lecture. He is befuddled and unable to follow the trend of thought. Several times within his lecture, Mr. Shapiro prefaces statements with "As we discussed yesterday." Not having discussed anything with the class yesterday, Singh feels frustrated about not being able to follow the lecture.

Afterward, Singh approaches Mr. Shapiro with "Man! I'm absent one day, and now I'm two days behind! I couldn't follow a thing you said today just because I had an excused absence. You know I had to go to the dentist yesterday." Mr. Shapiro: "Yes, I was just thinking it was unfortunate that you didn't schedule that appointment at another time. Anyway, after class find someone who is willing to let you copy yesterday's notes. After you've gone over the notes, check with me at 7:45 in here tomorrow morning. I'll answer any questions I can before homeroom period begins. I'll also lend you some reading matter that'll help you catch up." Singh: "Thank you."

▶ **CASE 10.23**

Willie engages Ms. Grimes, his college botany teacher, in the following conversation:

Willie: Ms. Grimes, will we have a test on Tuesday of next week?

Ms. G.: I'm not sure yet. It depends on how much progress we make before then. If the test isn't Tuesday, it'll be on Thursday of that week.

Willie: I have to be out of town that Tuesday, and I don't want to miss a test. If we have one, will I be allowed to make it up? I really hate to miss, but I can't help it because—

Ms. G.: [interrupting] Why you'll be absent is irrelevant. Let's concern ourselves with what we should do about it.

Willie: Okay.

Ms. G.: Actually, I'd much rather you miss a test than a regular class meeting. I can administer an equivalent form of the test to you at another time.

Willie: And you won't take off points because it's a makeup?

Ms. G.: Why would I do that?

Willie: That's what other teach—Hey, that's great!

Ms. G.: But if we have a regular class on Tuesday, that does present us with a problem. Whom do you know in class that you trust to help us and you can easily get in touch with?

Willie: Lamona or Edgar. Either one will help.

Ms. G.: Ask one of them to bring a recorder to class that Tuesday. I'll record the session for you, and they can get the disk to you. As soon as you return to town, listen to the recording, get their notes, find out the assignment, and discuss the session with Lamona or Edgar. After you've done that, e-mail me to make an appointment to address any further questions you might have.

Willie: Thank you. I'll do it. Really, I wouldn't miss your class if it wasn't for—

Ms. G.: [interrupting] Good-bye, Willie.

Engage in Activity 10.6.

▶ *ACTIVITY 10.6*

With a colleague, collaboratively respond to the following prompts:

1. Discuss the advantages and disadvantages of Mr. Kacala's tactics for teaching April the importance of attending class in Case 10.21.

2. Discuss the advantages and disadvantages of Mr. Shapiro's tactics for teaching Singh the importance of attending class in Case 10.22.

3. Discuss the advantages and disadvantages of the way Ms. Grimes interacted with Willie in Case 10.23. What messages did she communicate to Willie about the importance of being in class? How, if at all, did her conversation with Willie help set a businesslike tone for her classroom?

▶ CHEATING ON TESTS

Ten Incidents

Some students are quite resourceful in devising ways to cheat; consider Cases 10.24 to 10.33.

▶ CASE 10.24

Angee gets up from her chair, walks over to the classroom pencil sharpener, and returns to her desk to complete the multiple-choice science test she and the rest of her sixth-grade classmates are taking. During her walk, Angee looked at several other students' papers to find out how they responded to prompts.

▶ CASE 10.25

Calculus teacher Mr. Kruhl scores test papers by writing down the number of points off next to each prompt a student doesn't correctly answer. Mr. Kruhl does not mark anything next to correctly answered prompts; he simply subtracts the number of points for incorrect responses from the maximum possible score of 100. Jack, one of Mr. Kruhl's students, realizes this after his first calculus test is returned. When Jack is about to begin taking the second calculus test, he thinks, "I'll never have time to complete this 12-page monster in the 90 minutes Kruhl's allowing us. I'll just rip out pages 6 and 9 and discard them. He'll probably just pass over them and not realize they're missing. If he does catch it, I'll say they were never there." Several days later, Mr. Kruhl returns Jack's paper with a score derived by subtracting the number of points off for incorrect prompts from 100. Jack's score is the same as it would have been if Jack had correctly responded to all of the prompts on pages 6 and 9.

▶ CASE 10.26

June did not study for the history exam that Ms. Tolbert is giving today. Instead, June memorized the answers to an old unit test that Ms. Tolbert had administered to one of June's friends in a previous class. June is overjoyed when Ms. Tolbert hands her a test identical to the one her friend shared.

▶ CASE 10.27

Ms. Lem-Davis directs her family and consumer science class to write an essay on the role of the family. She specifies that the paper should be about five double-spaced, typed pages in length with between five and 10 different reference sources to be cited in the text and listed in the bibliography. For each student, the paper will "count" 150 possible points toward the 500 points for the term grade. It is due in one week.

Tamika goes to her home computer, accesses www.speedypaper.com, on the Internet and specifies Ms. Lem-Davis's parameters for the paper. An hour later, the Web-based paper writing service e-mails Tamika a completed six-page essay with seven citations listed in the bibliography. Tamika waits several days before turning in the paper with her own name to Ms. Lem-Davis.

Another student, Benjamin, addresses Ms. Lem-Davis' assignment by cutting and pasting pieces of others' works he finds on Web sites and turning the writing in as if it were his own.

▶ CASE 10.28

Twelfth graders Kraemer, Tom, and Arthur engage Ms. Hubert in a lively conversation before school as their co-conspirator, Mary Ellen, steals four copies of the final physics exam scheduled for that afternoon from Ms. Hubert's desk. During morning study hall, the four students jointly figure out the answers, and each fills out a copy of the test. To avoid suspicion, they make sure that there are some discrepancies among their papers. When Ms. Hubert administers the test, the four carefully substitute their completed copies for the ones distributed by Ms. Hubert.

▶ **CASE 10.29**

Sonia, an eighth-grade student, runs a popular service for her schoolmates at Abraham Lincoln Middle School. Sonia searches trash containers for test materials that have been discarded in the faculty workroom or school office. From her growing test file, she provides test information to her many "friends." Sonia feels very popular with her peers.

▶ **CASE 10.30**

"May I please be excused to go to the restroom?" Mickey asks Mr. Green during a fourth-grade spelling test. Mr. Green: "Yes, but hurry so you will have plenty of time to finish your test." Mickey: "I will. Thank you very much." In the restroom, Mickey extracts his spelling list, which earlier in the day he had hidden under a toilet. He quickly checks the spelling of the four words from the test that he does not know.

▶ **CASE 10.31**

Freda takes a lengthy psychology test and leaves several short-answer, written-response items blank. Her teacher, Mr. Zabriski, scores the test and returns them to the class the following day. The items Freda left blank are marked with zeroes, but she quickly fills in the answers and approaches Mr. Zabriski: "Mr. Zabriski, don't I get any credit for these? I thought they were at least partly correct!"

▶ **CASE 10.32**

As Mr. Duetchman supervises a large group of high school students taking a two-day-long achievement test battery, he finds it curious that Donna frequently brings her elbows together and stares down the neckline of her dress. Not knowing what to do, he dismisses her behavior as a reflection of adolescent self-consciousness. Actually, Donna has a cheat sheet attached to the inside of her bra.

▶ **CASE 10.33**

Ms. Bolden instructs her first graders to keep their test papers covered and not let classmates see their answers while taking a mathematics test. Ashley and Monica are sitting at the same table taking the test when Monica turns to Ashley. Pointing to one of her test prompts, Monica says, "I forgot what this one is." Ashley: "Ms. Bolden said you weren't supposed to show me your paper! Cover it up." Monica: "Sorry! But I need some help on this one." Ashley: "Okay, don't show me your paper. Just read it to me." Monica: "What's this called?" Monica draws a rectangle in the air with her finger. Ashley: "Let me see what I just put for that. But don't look on my paper while I look. It's not allowed." Ashley turns back to Monica, still carefully covering her paper, and says, "It's a rectangle."

Prevalence and Causes of Cheating

By violating rules under which a test is administered so they can correctly respond to prompts that they could not answer otherwise, students contaminate the validity of that test. In other words, in addition to being an unethical, distasteful practice, cheating leads to inaccurate and misleading test results.

How prevalent is cheating in elementary, middle, and secondary school classrooms? Estimates of the ratio of test-taking behaviors involving cheating and test-taking behaviors free of cheating vary considerably from study to study, but the vast majority of studies examining the prevalence of cheating—most using self-report techniques but some using direct observations—indicate that cheating is commonplace. According to McCabe (2001), cheating is widespread among high school students with 74% reporting that they have cheated on tests and 72% on written assignments. More than 30% of the 4,500 students questioned by McCabe indicated that they cheat repetitively; 52% indicated they copied from Web sites without citing their sources.

Evans and Craig (1990) indicated that 50.1% of middle school teachers, 61.4% of middle school students, 70% of high school teachers, and 71.3% of high school students perceive cheating to be a serious problem in their schools. Cheating is observed at all grades K through 12, but its practice appears to increase with grade level (Cangelosi, 1993). Within the past five years, *cybercheating* (i.e., using the Internet to download documents and claim them as one's own as Tamika did in Case 10.27 or using the words and ideas of others without referencing them as Benjamin did in Case 10.27) has become popular. Students are able to download or have complete essays and library papers written to specifications by using Web sites (e.g., www.speedypapers.com, www.cheathouse.com, www.schoolsucks.com, and www.termpapers-on-file.com).

Students would hardly be inclined to cheat on tests if they believed in the benefits of their teachers' *accurately* assessing what has been learned. Why, then, do many students cheat? Studies examining school conditions associated with student cheating and reasons for cheating professed by students have addressed this question (Cangelosi, 2006; Evans & Craig, 1990; McCabe, 2001). Whether or not students attempt to cheat appears to be more a function of teacher-controlled factors and students' perceptions of classroom situations than a function of personality and demographic characteristics of the students themselves (Bushway & Nash, 1977; Cangelosi, 1993). In general, students are more inclined to cheat when they have the following perceptions:

- They need to compete for high grades to gain or retain self-esteem, approval, or other rewards extrinsic to learning itself (e.g., a scholarship or an academic letter).
- There is little or no value in the content on which they are being tested.
- The opportunity to cheat exists with a low probability of being detected.
- The teacher lacks withitness.
- The classroom does not have a businesslike climate.
- The school's administrators value test performance more than learning. (For example, regular learning activities may be disrupted for several weeks to prepare for an upcoming standardized test battery to "make our school look good" or "outscore a rival school." Students are directed to make extraordinary

preparations for these testing events, including changes in eating and sleeping patterns, and visitors are barred from the school during the week of the test battery. The approach is similar to the way in which coaches prepare teams for championship games. Keep in mind that some forms of cheating are acceptable parts of many sports (e.g., basketball players are taught to fall to the floor to deceive referees into thinking they've been fouled).)

Strategies

As the previous section mentioned, students would have no inclination to cheat on a test if they believed that accurate information about their achievement is more beneficial than misinformation. Once again, three vital principles become apparent:

- The self-worth that students perceive and the respect, love, and esteem that others—including teachers—feel for them should never depend on their achievements.
- Formative evaluations of students' achievements should be emphasized far more than summative evaluations.
- Grades should be used only to communicate summative evaluations; they should not be used as a reward for achievements.

Given the unfortunate fact that there is almost universal violation of these principles, you are virtually assured of encountering students inclined to cheat on tests. But even with these students, cheating is unlikely when you adhere to the following suggestions:

- You set a businesslike tone and display an attitude that communicates that students are expected not to cheat.
- Test administrations are closely supervised. Please note, however, that, as Case 10.33 illustrates, the concept of cheating is not well developed in children under the age of nine. Primary-school children do not differentiate between obtaining a correct response with unauthorized aid and obtaining it without unauthorized aid (Pulaski, 1980; Rogoff, 1990, pp. 42–61). Teachers should observe whether or not young children respond on their own or with unauthorized aid. Steps should be taken so that such aid is not available. But warning young students not to cheat or punishing them for behaviors that adults consider to be cheating is, for them, a frustrating experience that only teaches them they are not trusted. Even with older students, warnings "not to cheat" are futile and should be avoided. Nevertheless, students should not be given reasonable opportunities to cheat.
- The same form of a test is not used repeatedly.
- You account for each copy of a test that is duplicated—copies can be numbered—and keep materials such as duplicating masters or electronic versions of originals secure.
- You score students responses' to test prompts using detailed rubrics (e.g., see Cangelosi, 2000, pp. 35–37, 186–189) so that points are added for correct responses rather than subtracting points for incorrect ones. Not only do rubrics—along with annotations—provide helpful feedback to students,

but they also help you remember why you scored responses as you did. Students are less likely to manipulate responses after the tests are returned if you have already commented on their answers and used detailed rubrics.

- Students are directed to check whether or not their test copies contain all pages and are properly collated before beginning the test.

- Students are not tested on the recall of material that seems unnecessary to memorize. When students perceive that obtaining a grade on a test is the sole purpose for memorizing, using crib notes seems like a sensible thing to do.

- If you direct students to produce papers such as Ms. Lem-Davis did in Case 10.27, guard against cybercheating by employing some of the electronic resources for teachers to check on whether unauthorized sources were used (e.g., see www.plagerism.org, www.turnitin.com, or www.academicintegrity.org). Such software helps you to demonstrate withitness.

Because a student cheats on a test is not a reason for recording a low score. Cheating does not reflect learning-goal attainment—except in the rare case in which the learning goal is for the student to be honest. Thus, if a teacher knows that a student has cheated on a test, then the test results are not valid and no score should be recorded. A student's understanding of biology, for example, should not be judged by whether or not that student cooperated with the test-taking procedures. Judgments of how well learning goals are achieved should be withheld until after the student no longer displays the dishonest behavior and a valid measurement of achievement can be obtained (Cangelosi, 1982, pp. 237–238). The teachers in Cases 10.34 to 10.36 deal with some sticky situations.

► **CASE 10.34**

While scoring a unit test he had administered to his tenth-grade first-aid class, Mr. Broussard notices some inconsistencies in Joe's test responses. Joe's responses to a couple of the more difficult prompts on the test are correct, while he missed a number of others that measured simple rudimentary knowledge. Mr. Broussard asks himself, "How could he get these correct without knowing this?" Later, while scoring Remy's paper, Mr. Broussard notices that Remy answers the same difficult items using words very similar to those in Joe's responses. Mr. Broussard compares their two sets of responses and notices some peculiar similarities. On the multiple-choice portions of the test, Joe's choices nearly always agree with Remy's. He finds it curious that the two would consistently choose the same distractors or foils for multiple-choice prompts that they both missed.

Suspicious that Joe copied from Remy's paper, Mr. Broussard begins planning how to deal with the situation. He thinks, "I should confront them both with this. Scare the heck out of them! But if I'm wrong, I'll only teach them they're not trusted. That could be damaging. They might cheat from now on because they figure there is no trust to lose. But I really can't put any stock in Joe's test results, and I need to know what he got out of this unit. I need an accurate score on him. Also, I don't want Joe to get away with this. I don't think he's cheated before. I should block any positive reinforcement so this doesn't become a pattern. I'll just disregard his test paper and schedule a retest for him with an equivalent form."

The next day Mr. Broussard distributes the scored and annotated test papers. Joe says from his desk: "Mr. Broussard, you didn't give my test back." Mr. Broussard: "No, I didn't. Please come up here." Joe arrives, and Mr. Broussard says softly, "You didn't get your paper back. What do you think happened?" Joe: "I don't know. I took the test." Mr. Broussard: "Yes, I know. I remember going over it." Mr. Broussard pulls out his grade book and says, "Here, Joe, let's see if I recorded a score for you. No, there's no score here. Look." Joe sees the empty square. Mr. Broussard: "We'll just schedule a retest. How about tomorrow? I'll give you a test tomorrow." Joe: "That's not fair for me to have to take another test." Mr. Broussard: "Things don't always seem fair. Now, let's see when we can schedule it. . . ."

▶ CASE 10.35

Mr. Stoddard validates each sociology test that he administers to his classes before allowing the test results to influence evaluations he makes regarding students' achievement levels. From analysis of one set of test results and his observations of some curious student behaviors during the administration of that test, Mr. Stoddard suspects that student cheating contaminated the accuracy of the test results. At the next class meeting, Mr. Stoddard announces, "The results I received from the test are invalid. There are some major discrepancies among the scores. Statistical analyses indicate the test was too unreliable to indicate your levels of achievement accurately. Therefore, I discarded the results and we will take a refined version of the test under more controlled conditions on Wednesday."

▶ CASE 10.36

Ms. Maggio administers a problem-solving test to her fifth graders in which they are directed to work out in their heads a sequence of tasks that are presented on pages 39 and 40 of one of their textbooks. She instructs them to look at only those two pages in their books while working out the solutions and expressing answers on a sheet of paper. Ms. Maggio notices that one student, Nettie, is keeping an eye on her during the test. Nettie seems to manipulate her book suddenly whenever Ms. Maggio comes near or looks at her. Ms. Maggio suspects that Nettie has surreptitiously turned to the back of the book in which answers to the problems are given.

After the test, Ms. Maggio examines Nettie's answer sheet. Most of the responses are correct. She then engages Nettie in a private conference and presents one of the problems that Nettie answered on the test and asks her to solve it. Nettie is unable to come up with a solution this time. Nettie fails twice more to reproduce answers that she had written on the test earlier in the day. Ms. Maggio: "Nettie, I do not understand why you cannot figure out these answers now if you solved the problems during the test." Nettie: "I don't know." Ms. Maggio: "I will not check off that you can do these types of problems until you demonstrate to me that you can."

Engage in Activity 10.7.

▶ *ACTIVITY 10.7*

With a colleague, collaboratively respond to the following prompts.

1. Discuss the advantages and disadvantages of the way Mr. Broussard dealt with the suspected cheating incident in Case 10.34.

2. Discuss the advantages and disadvantages of the way Mr. Stoddard dealt with the invalid test results in Case 10.35.

3. Discuss the advantages and disadvantages of the way Ms. Maggio interacted with Nettie in Case 10.36. How, if at all, did her conversation with Nettie help set a businesslike tone for the classroom?

▶ SYNTHESIS ACTIVITIES FOR CHAPTER 10

I. Which of the six attitudes about students' abuse of drugs listed in the section "Teachers' Attitudes" do you most closely associate with your own philosophy? Explain in a paragraph why you prefer this approach. Argue your point of view with a colleague whose opinion differs from yours.

II.   Observe the students in a classroom. Search for indicators of student daydreaming and mind wandering. Describe what you observed in those students' behaviors that led you to believe that they had quietly become disengaged from the learning activity. Compare your descriptions with those of a colleague.

III.   When you and some colleagues engaged in Chapter 5's Synthesis Activity XI, you designed a school discipline policy. Review that policy with your colleagues; expand and modify it in light of your work with Chapters 9 and 10.

▶ TRANSITIONAL ACTIVITY FROM CHAPTER 10 TO CHAPTER 11

In preparation for your work with Chapter 11, discuss with two or more colleagues the following questions.

I.   Why is it necessary for teachers to control disruptive student behaviors to fulfill their responsibilities to all their students?

II.   What strategies do teachers employ to deal with the following types of disruptive behaviors?

- Disruptive talking
- Interrupting a speaker
- Clowning
- Being discourteous
- Failing to clean up after a learning activity
- Vandalizing property
- Threatening a student or teacher
- Fighting
- Assaulting a student or teacher

11

Dealing with Disruptive Behaviors

► CHAPTER 11'S GOAL AND OBJECTIVES

The goal of this chapter is for you to develop strategies for constructively dealing with students' disruptive off-task behaviors. Specifically, Chapter 11 is designed to lead you to achieve the following objectives.

1. Design learning activities to teach students to supplant the following types of off-task behavior patterns with on-task, prosocial behavior patterns: (a) disruptive talking, (b) interrupting, (c) clowning, (d) being discourteous, (e) failing to clean up, (f) bullying, (g) fighting, (h) attacks on teachers, and (i) vandalizing.
2. Effectively handle isolated incidents of the types of disruptive behaviors that are listed under Objective 1.

Disruptive Behaviors

When students reject opportunities to learn by displaying nondisruptive off-task behaviors, they suffer the consequences of their own choices. But students who behave disruptively also tread on the rights of other students to learn. You, as their teacher, can hardly ignore disruptive student behaviors.

This chapter includes cases in which teachers deal one way or another with disruptive student behaviors. From these examples, you are urged to extract strategies that will work for you and your students. Reflect on the pros and cons of how these teachers handle disruptions, but please don't simply copy their methods.

► DEALING WITH NONVIOLENT DISRUPTIONS

Disruptive Talking

Consider Cases 11.1 to 11.4.

► CASE 11.1

Ms. Bravo usually plans each school day so that her fourth-grade students alternate learning activities in which they need to be rather quiet with learning activities in which talking with one another is not disruptive. Her students typically look forward to the learning activities that have hardly any restrictions on talking. One day during a quiet session in which the class is supposed to be engaged in an independent learning activity, sporadic conversations erupt among the students. Ms. Bravo finds the noise disturbing to those working on the assigned task. Realizing that students are anticipating playing "Who Am I?" in 30 minutes, she blinks the classroom lights to get their attention and announces, "There is much, too much talk for us to think on our own. I am starting my stopwatch now." She pushes a button on the chronograph on her wrist and continues: "I will keep my stopwatch running as long as there is noise in here. When the noise stops, my watch will stop. When the noise starts again, my watch will also. We will begin playing 'Who Am I?' only after 30 minutes of silence for working out these problems." In five minutes the class is quiet and working, and Ms. Bravo stops her timer. Eight minutes later, talking disrupts the work, and Ms. Bravo accumulates another six minutes on the stopwatch waiting for silence. The required total of 30 minutes of silence is finally obtained after one more three-minute interruption. She directs the class to begin playing "Who Am I?" 14 minutes after the game was scheduled to start. But the starting time for the silent learning activity scheduled right after "Who Am I?" is not delayed. A number of students complain that the game was too short and they did not have enough time to finish.

▶ CASE 11.2

There are 30 minutes remaining in Ms. Allen's fourth-period Russian II class when she directs the students to begin work on a translation exercise from their textbooks. A number of students carry on conversations that disturb others. Ms. Allen motions for silence, but talking continues to spring up around the classroom. Ms. Allen calls a halt to the translations, saying, "Class, please let me have your attention.—I think each of us needs silence to translate these sentences properly. I'm sorry, but I see this isn't working. Let's hold off on these translations until you can get away by yourselves—either at home or during your free period. Just have them ready for class tomorrow. Right now, put your books away and we'll work together on our conversational Russian. Here's what we'll do. . . ."

▶ CASE 11.3

Mr. Haimowitz is explaining Ohm's law to his physics class when he becomes annoyed by a conversation between two students, Walt and Henry. Without missing a word in his explanation, he moves between the students and continues speaking to the class. The two boys stop talking and appear to pay attention as long as Mr. Haimowitz is between them. Five minutes later, with Mr. Haimowitz lecturing from another area of the room, Walt and Henry are conversing again. This time Mr. Haimowitz, continuing with his lecture, goes over to them, picks up Henry's papers from the top of his desk, and motions Henry to follow him to another part of the room where there is a vacant desk. Mr. Haimowitz places Henry's papers on the desktop, and Henry takes a seat. At no time during the incident does Mr. Haimowitz speak directly to either Henry or Walt, nor does he miss a word in his explanation of Ohm's law.

▶ CASE 11.4

Leora and Nan, two sixth graders, consider themselves best friends. At school they are almost constant companions. Ms. Helmick, their teacher, believes their relationship is healthy and doesn't want to discourage it. But they have developed a pattern of talking, note passing, giggling, and looking at one another during quiet learning activities. Ms. Helmick has dealt with cases of their disruptive talking individually, as she would for isolated off-task behaviors. She now decides that their pattern of disruptive talking must somehow be modified. Careful thought leads her to formulate the following alternative three plans:

1. Ms. Helmick will confront the two with the problem they have been creating. She will explain that each time she recognizes that they are talking at an inappropriate time, she will signal them to leave the area where the learning activity is going on and to continue their conversation in the time-out room. They are to remain there until the learning activity that they disturbed is over.

2. Ms. Helmick will frequently schedule "free talk" sessions after quiet learning activities. Participation in the free talk sessions, in which students can socialize within certain guidelines, will be contingent on all students' having quietly engaged in the previous quiet learning activity. Time wasted during the quiet activity due to disruptive talking is made up from time scheduled for the free talk session.

3. Each time Leora and Nan's talking disrupts a learning activity, Ms. Helmick will use the stopwatch she wears on her wrist to keep account of the amount of time wasted. Leora and Nan will then be required to make up the lost time after school that day. Leora's and Nan's parents will be made aware of this plan so they can cooperate in having the two students get home on days they miss their buses.

Ms. Helmick is not yet sure which of the three plans she will try first. She has confidence in the first plan because she doesn't believe that Leora and Nan want to be excluded from class activities. In fact, incidents during class activities often stimulate their in-class talking. Furthermore, the principle of satiation may take effect; the girls could become "talked out." In the time-out room they would be deprived of much of the stimulation (e.g., seeing other students) for their conversations. Ms. Helmick thinks the second plan would bring peer pressure on Leora and Nan to control their disruptive talking. The third plan uses the power of negative reinforcement because the girls would control when Ms. Helmick stops her timer.

Engage in Activity 11.1.

▶ *ACTIVITY 11.1*

With a colleague, collaboratively respond to the following prompts:

1. Discuss the advantages and disadvantages of the following in Case 11.1: (a) Ms. Bravo alternating allocated times in which students need to be quiet with allocated times in which talking is part of the activity and the fact that students are aware that this is how their school days are planned and (b) Ms. Bravo's tactic of using her timer.

2. Discuss the advantages and disadvantages of the tactics Ms. Allen used to deal with disruptive talking in Case 11.2.

3. Discuss the advantages and disadvantages of the tactics Mr. Haimowitz used to deal with disruptive talking in Case 11.3. Also discuss some possible strategies Mr. Haimowitz might have used if Henry had refused to comply with the directive to follow him to the other desk. Keep in mind that you and your colleague do not know Walt and Henry as individuals nor do you know about the relationship Mr. Haimowitz has developed with them. Imagine some different students that you do know as individuals; discuss how the tactics would work with them.

4. Discuss the relative advantages and disadvantages of each of Ms. Helmick's three plans that she considers in Case 11.4. Imagine some different students that you know as individuals; discuss how each plan might work with each of them.

Interrupting

What motivates Sandy's behavior in Case 11.5?

▶ **CASE 11.5**

During a questioning session, Mr. Caldwell asks Lorene, "What number multiplied by 7 is 42?" Lorene: "Uhh, let's see. I think—" Sandy interrupts, "Six because 42 divided by 7 is 6!" Lorene appears relieved to be off the hook. Sandy smiles. Mr. Caldwell is frustrated because his planned questioning strategy in which Lorene was to reason deductively has been disrupted. Sandy's interruption deprived Lorene of a learning experience. Mr. Caldwell, appearing quite disgusted, turns to Sandy: "Why did you interrupt?" Sandy: "I was just helping her out."

But Sandy did not help Lorene at all. Unfortunately, students are often conditioned from their experiences with IRE cycles to believe that all that teachers want from them are the "right" answers. They don't think that processes and thinking skills concern teachers. Furthermore, these students have learned to believe that they are constantly being tested. Thus, by popping up with the right answer, Sandy felt she could seize an opportunity to show off her knowledge and either gain Lorene's favor for helping her or outdo Lorene in a competition of "Who knows the answer?" Mr. Caldwell faced a dilemma. On one hand, he did not want to discourage Sandy's enthusiasm for the lesson. On the other hand, he needed to discourage such disruptions. Of course, teachers who apply research-based principles for conducting questioning and discussion sessions (e.g., those elaborated on in Chapter 2's section, "True Dialogues Instead of IRE Cycles," and Chapter 7's section, "Ideas for Questioning Sessions") are less likely than Mr. Caldwell to be faced with this dilemma.

Teachers effectively deal with students' interruptions in Cases 11.6 to 11.8.

▶ **CASE 11.6**

Ms. Brittain has established the following procedure for her fourth graders to follow during large-group discussions:

During a discussion session only the one person who has the floor may speak. A student may obtain the floor by raising his or her hand and being recognized by the student who at the time has the floor. A student who has the floor must relinquish it within one minute after another raises a hand. Ms. Brittain will intervene at any time in the process to ensure each student a fair opportunity to speak and to keep the discussion focused on the agreed-upon topic.

While discussing the differences between living in a large city and a small town, Crystal has the floor. She is explaining why she thinks it is easier to travel in a small town. Without raising his hand, Oral interrupts: "Yeah, but in a big city you can take a subway and—" Crystal (interrupting): "I have the floor! I didn't call on you!" Oral: "But—" Ms. Brittain (interrupting): "Oral, the procedure is to raise your hand and wait to be recognized before speaking. Now, I want to hear what Crystal was saying about traveling in a small town." The discussion continues as Ms. Brittain carefully monitors the session.

▶ **CASE 11.7**

Mr. Rutknecht is explaining how to bisect an angle with a straightedge and compass when Debbie, one of his 34 students, interrupts: "What size radius do you need for the first arc?" Mr. Rutknecht appreciates that Debbie has asked a question relevant to the topic. He wants to encourage her interest and that type of question, but he doesn't want to positively reinforce interruptions. He responds to Debbie's out-of-turn question with a frown and continues his explanation, watching for Debbie and other students to raise their hands. Momentarily, Lynn raises her hand, and Mr. Rutknecht immediately recognizes her. Lynn asks a question and raises a point on which Mr. Rutknecht elaborates. Five students, including Debbie, raise their hands, and two speak out without being recognized. Mr. Rutknecht cuts off the interrupting students and calls on those with hands raised. At one point, he thanks a student for her patience in waiting to be recognized.

▶ **CASE 11.8**

"People moved west because—" Maureen is saying to Mr. Peck's class, when another student, Hugh, interrupts: "They never would have moved if. . . ." Mr. Peck has had to deal with Hugh's interruptions in the past; he resolves to do something about the pattern. That night Mr. Peck thinks: "I will use the principle of extinction to help Hugh break this habit of interrupting speakers during class. I first need to identify the payoff he realizes from interrupting. What's the positive reinforcement? I think he likes being noticed—wanting the rest of the class and me to know what he knows. He thinks others are upstaging him by talking. It is a competitive thing. If it's attention he wants, I'll make sure he gets it when he's patiently waiting for his turn to talk. I'll keep him from getting attention when he interrupts. Each time he interrupts, I'll cut him off immediately by repeating the last words of whomever he interrupted. I won't even look at him. I'll just jump in and say, 'You were saying,' and repeat the words of the other student. If he interrupts Sue, for example, I'll interrupt him and say to Sue, 'Excuse me, Sue, you were saying you thought that,' and I'll let Sue go on. When Hugh remains quiet, I'll ask him for a comment or an opinion. That should positively reinforce a desirable alternative behavior. Now I'd better make a tally sheet to help me measure how much progress Hugh makes while he's on this plan."

Engage in Activity 11.2.

▶ *ACTIVITY 11.2*

With a colleague, collaboratively respond to the following prompts:

1. Discuss the advantages and disadvantages of the following in Case 11.6: (a) The specific procedure Ms. Brittain had in place prior to Oral's interruption and (b) the way Ms. Brittain interacted with Oral and Crystal.

2. Discuss the advantages and disadvantages of the tactics Mr. Rutknecht used to deal with students' interruptions in Case 11.7.

3. Discuss the relative advantages and disadvantages of Mr. Peck's plan for modifying Hugh's habit of interrupting in Case 11.8.

Clowning

Consider how the teachers in Cases 11.9 to 11.11 deal with student clowning.

▶ **CASE 11.9**

Mr. Holt's sixth-grade class is engaged in a large-group learning activity on nutrition when Vickie responds to one of Mr. Holt's questions: "I'm not just going to eat anything. I'm careful about what I stick in my body." Woodrow stands up and yells out, "Here's something you can stick in your body!" Woodrow momentarily grabs his crotch. Laughter erupts around the room. Because

Mr. Holt has previously thought about handling this type of situation and follows the teaching cycles model, he is able to process the following thoughts in his mind without a moment's delay: "Woodrow has never pulled this stunt before. He's only looking for attention. It's too bad they laughed at him. That's positive reinforcement, and this could be the beginning of a pattern. I need to prevent this from happening again. But how? I have numerous options. I need to maintain a stern, but unflustered expression—show disapproval, but not shock. I can't pretend it didn't happen because they laughed at him. Criticizing what he did right here would just draw more attention to him. That's what he wants. Of course, he's left himself very vulnerable for a comeback. It would be easy for me to turn this around and embarrass him with his own words. That might serve as a punishment—a destructive one. It's never helpful to have a child lose face in front of peers. That could easily turn into a competitive thing between us; I can't afford that. I'm only glad no one in the class had a comeback for him. I must make sure I don't label him in any way. If I called him 'dirty' or 'rude,' he might learn to live up to that expectation. I could pretend that I did not understand the sexual connotation of his comment and respond as if he were really talking about nutrition. But that would be obvious dishonesty. No, I've got to handle this one head-on."

Because Mr. Holt's mind is busy with the aforementioned thoughts in the moments immediately following the outburst of laughter, he is able to maintain a serious expression throughout. The class quickly realizes that Mr. Holt does not find Woodrow's clowning humorous. He turns to Woodrow and says, "I know you are trying to make us laugh. But I do not like to hear that kind of joke. You and I will talk about this right after the class leaves for lunch today." Turning to Vickie, Mr. Holt says, "Excuse the interruption, Vickie. You were telling us that you choose your food carefully. Please continue."

▶ CASE 11.10

It is the first week of the school year in Ms. Giminski's kindergarten class. Students have just begun working individually on a language-arts task. Brian jumps up and begins dancing in front of the others saying, "Watch me! Watch me!" Two students stop their work and giggle, but most just ignore him. Ms. Giminski thinks, "I hope this isn't a pattern for Brian. This may be what he does for attention at home." She picks up Brian's paper, takes him by the hand, and walks him to an area of the room that is out of the view of the other students. She softly tells Brian, "Please sit here and finish your paper. Bring it to me only after all these spaces are colored in. What are you going to do?" Brian: "Color all this and bring it to you." Ms. Giminski: "That is what you are to do."

Over the next several days, Ms. Giminski watches for signs of Brian's wanting to show off. She makes an effort to see that he gets attention at times when he is not trying to show off.

▶ CASE 11.11

Holly's frequent quips, gestures, and facial contortions evoke laughter among her peers in Mr. Smith's tenth-grade English class. Mr. Smith considers occasional clowning humorous and a healthy diversion from work. But Holly's clowning has become so frequent that it is impeding class progress. Mr. Smith is beginning to fear what Holly will come up with and consequently phrases his words with care to avoid having her turn a serious comment into a joke. He decides to help her control her in-class clowning and thinks to himself, "I'm not going to continue to stand for Holly's habitual clowning. She's modifying my behavior so that I'm not as relaxed in class as I used to be. I'm afraid to smile for fear she'll think it's her cue to be on stage. If I ask her why she is clowning or turn her jokes back on her, it would embarrass her and she might quit. Or would she? She'd more likely try to regain face with the class by trying even harder to be funny. No, I never want her to be embarrassed. That would make matters worse. She does it to gain favor and relieve her boredom. I know! I'll call her in for a private conference and be perfectly frank with her. I'll explain that her clowning is making it difficult for me to do my job. I'll request her cooperation. If she agrees to try, I'll agree to help her succeed. We'll set up a secret code between us so that I can signal her when she is being disruptive and should stop whatever she's doing at the moment. The rest of the class doesn't need to know. She can also have a signal worked out for me when she feels the urge to clown; I'll help her pick an appropriate time and set her stage. We'll establish a real cooperative relationship. But I'd better come up with some alternative plans in case she doesn't go for this one. I hope she goes for the original idea, or else I may have to sacrifice her welfare for the good of the class."

Engage in Activity 11.3.

▶ *ACTIVITY 11.3*

With a colleague, collaboratively respond to the following prompts:

1. Discuss the advantages and disadvantages of the following in Case 11.9: (a) Mr. Holt responding to Woodrow's inappropriate clowning via the teaching cycles model rather than reacting emotionally to such rude and potentially sexually harassing behavior, (b) Mr. Holt waiting until after class to work on a plan to prevent Woodrow from repeating such inappropriate behavior, (c) Mr. Holt not responding in a way that assumes Vickie had been victimized by Woodrow's rudeness (e.g., by not requiring Woodrow to apologize), and (d) the way Mr. Holt interacted with Woodrow and Vickie. Also discuss how Mr. Holt's handling of the incident needs to be influenced by school-wide discipline policies (e.g., whether or not the school has a policy with respect to sexually suggestive conduct).

2. Discuss the advantages and disadvantages of the tactics Ms. Giminski used to deal with Brian's clowning in Case 11.10. What behavioral modification principles did she appear to have in mind?

3. Discuss the advantages and disadvantages of the tactics Mr. Smith used to deal with Holly's clowning in Case 11.11. What behavioral modification principles did he appear to have in mind?

Being Discourteous

Learning activities are generally more effective when they are conducted in a businesslike atmosphere of cooperation and mutual respect among participants. Thus, it is usually disruptive for students to treat others in the classroom in a disrespectful or thoughtless manner. Although conventional customs of decorum and courtesy vary among the subcultures represented in many school populations, a teacher is responsible for establishing an environment in which students are unlikely to feel insulted, uncomfortable, or inconvenienced as a consequence of the rudeness of others. In Cases 11.12 to 11.15, teachers deal with discourteous student behaviors.

▶ CASE 11.12

Mr. Lowder assigns Mitch and Ward to be on the same basketball team during one physical education session. Mitch complains aloud in front of the class, "I don't want Ward on my team; he's gay! I'd rather not play." Mr. Lowder immediately thinks, "Mitch is so competitive. I should just tell him, 'Fine! Then you don't play.' He could just sit on the sidelines. Maybe I could play in his place and show Ward that I'd like to be on his team. But I don't want to give the class the impression that their participation isn't critical. I'd like to do something to protect Ward's feelings. I know he has already allowed them to be damaged, and I may make things worse by making a big deal out of this incident. I'll let it slide for now; if it recurs, I'll intervene. Maybe I should catch Mitch by himself and let him know that I don't approve of such behavior. I will. In fact, I'll hold a conference with him to lead him to examine the consequences of such discourtesy."

▶ **CASE 11.13**

Several of Ms. Belcher's second graders begin jockeying and shoving to obtain a place near the front of the line that they are forming in preparation for going to the auditorium for a puppet show. "Hey, I'm first; get away!" Jack yells, as Ellis pushes his way to the front. Ms. Belcher observes students moving up to the front of the line by being aggressive. In a calm voice, she announces, "Keep your places in line. We're going to stretch our legs a bit and take a walk around the room before leaving." Noticing that Cheri is last in the line, Ms. Belcher continues: "Cheri, you lead the line around the back wall, over along the side wall, past the front, and then out the door. I'll get in behind Ellis and shut the door as I leave." Surprised by the strange route they take exiting the room, the students turn silently and follow Cheri to the auditorium. Cheri beams as Ellis and Jack roll their eyes in disgust.

▶ **CASE 11.14**

Susan, a seventh grader, is working on a problem-solving assignment when she exclaims in a curt voice to Ms. Comeaux, her teacher, "I can't do this asshole crap! It's so stupid!" Ms. Comeaux: "I can tell you're frustrated. The problems are difficult. When you are ready for me to help you with them, tell me in a courteous way, using only words that are acceptable to me."

▶ **CASE 11.15**

Mr. Turner's social studies students are engaged in cooperative group discussions when he overhears Kendall tell Russ, "You wouldn't think that if you weren't such an ugly slob!" Mr. Turner: "Kendall, I get so angry when you speak rudely that I cannot understand what you're trying to say." Mr. Turner hopes that he has reminded the group that impolite, thoughtless talk is unacceptable during learning activities. He wants to avoid an inane, nonproductive exchange about why Kendall spoke rudely. He does not think that it would be wise to appear as if he were trying to protect Russ, so he doesn't say anything like "Russ is not an ugly slob! I like him very much." He believes that would display a lack of confidence in Russ's being able to deal with his own feelings. The focus is on terminating the rude behavior and getting on with the business at hand.

Engage in Activity 11.4.

▶ *ACTIVITY 11.4*

With a colleague, collaboratively respond to the following prompts.

1. Discuss the advantages and disadvantages of the tactics Mr. Lowder used to deal with Mitch's rudeness in Case 11.12. Imagine a student you know as an individual. If he or she had done what Mitch did in Case 11.12, what would you plan to

say in the private conference? Imagine another student you know as an individual. If he or she had been the intended target of a rude remark, how would you plan to interact with that student over the incident?

2. Discuss the advantages and disadvantages of the tactics Ms. Belcher used to deal with her second

graders' discourtesy in Case 11.13. What behavioral modification principles did she appear to have in mind?

3. Discuss the advantages and disadvantages of the tactics Ms. Comeaux used to deal with Susan's

discourtesy in Case 11.14. What respo... described in Chapter 4 did she employ?

4. Discuss the advantages and disadvantages of the tactics Mr. Turner used to deal with Kendall's rudeness in Case 11.15.

Failing to Clean Up

A classroom in disarray, a littered playing field, inaccessible equipment, unattractive surroundings, damaged supplies, and an unprepared activity area interfere with the effectiveness of learning activities. Thus, by failing to clean up after themselves, students can be disruptive. Teachers in Cases 11.16 to 11.18 deal with this problem.

▶ CASE 11.16

Ms. Johnson frequently schedules her third graders' school days so that learning activities that require students to pick up materials afterward are followed by activities that students genuinely enjoy. Initiation of an anticipated enjoyable activity is always contingent on the classroom's being in acceptable order as specified by Ms. Johnson.

▶ CASE 11.17

Ms. Lambert usually gives her tenth-grade biology students some time to begin their homework assignment in class. But she never informs them of the assignment until after the lab area meets her standards for cleanliness and order.

▶ CASE 11.18

Each student in Mr. Diffy's art class has a container for supplies. Mr. Diffy directs his students to clean their materials and put them away for the next day. Juan and Candy leave out some of their brushes, paints, cloth, and paper. Mr. Diffy notices this before they depart but says nothing. He cleans up after them, placing their equipment in the general art supply closet. The next day Juan complains, "Where's my thin brush? And I'm out of paper; I had plenty yesterday!" Candy: "I can't find my green paint." Mr. Diffy: "Oh, that must have been your stuff I cleaned up yesterday. I'm sorry, but I mixed them up with the general supplies. You need to purchase more."

Engage in Activity 11.5.

▶ *ACTIVITY 11.5*

With a colleague, collaboratively respond to the following prompts.

1. Discuss how the advantage Ms. Johnson gains in Case 11.16 by having enjoyable activities scheduled after activities in which students need to pick up after themselves is similar to the

advantage gained by Ms. Bravo in Case 11.1, who schedules activities in which students may talk following silent-work activities.

2. Discuss the advantages and disadvantages of the tactics Ms. Lambert used in Case 11.17 to encourage her students to pick up after themselves.

3. Discuss the advantages and disadvantages of the tactics Mr. Diffy used to deal with Juan and Candy's failure to clean up their art supplies in Case 11.18. Relate Case 11.18 to Case 2.19—the case in which Ms. Brock illustrated the differences in the effects of naturally occurring and contrived punishment.

► DEALING WITH VIOLENT DISRUPTIONS

Safe-School Programs in Place

From your work with Chapter 5's section, "Developing Safe-School Programs," you understand that violence-prevention strategies must be implemented throughout your school to enable you to teach in a safe and nurturing environment that is conducive to the business of learning. How well you can deal with violent student behaviors (e.g., bullying, fighting, attacks on teachers, and vandalizing) depends on your being able to rely on your school's security system and the schoolwide implementation of policies for effectively responding to antisocial conduct. The cases described in this section are taken from schools with reasonably dependable safe-school programs in place.

Bullying

Generally speaking, if a student threatens or strikes a teacher or other adult school personnel, that student is in serious trouble with school authorities and possibly with law-enforcement authorities. Expulsion or suspension from the school is a likely consequence. Although society tends to view the unarmed assault of one student on another as less serious than assault on an adult, students have as much a right as teachers to feel safe and secure from violence at school. Students who fear for their safety can hardly be expected to enthusiastically engage in learning activities. Thus, students' bullying others—even outside the classroom—is disruptive to your planned learning activities. *Bullying* is antisocial behavior intended to intimidate and threaten the well-being of another. The following report from Walker, Colvin, and Ramsey (1995, p. 189) is consistent with more recent findings (Cook, 2005; Whitted & Dupper, 2005):

> Shelly (1985) found that approximately 80% of high school students and 90% of elementary and middle school students in the United States reported that they had been bullied at some point in school. The advent of gangs both on and off school grounds provides an ominous new dimension to the historic problems of bullies and bullying. A significant number of students who bring weapons to school do so because they feel they need them for protection. Many schools have become trading centers for the exchange and sale of weapons; most of the student body is usually aware of these activities. Students frequently believe that school officials and other adults cannot adequately protect them from bullying and the specter of gang victimization; in many cases they are right. Thus, the behavioral interactions that occur between antisocial and non-antisocial students under adult supervision (for example, in the classroom) are mediated and strongly affected by what has occurred or may occur between them in unsupervised situations where adults are not present. It is important for school staff and parents to be aware of such constraints in the ongoing peer relations of children and youth.

Fear of being bullied is a major cause of student absenteeism (Smith, 2004). I 11.19, a teacher develops a plan for dealing with a situation involving bullying.

▶ **CASE 11.19**

Ms. Duke finds it odd that Frank, Maunsell, Mickey, and a few other of her fifth-grade boys choose to spend their time before school and during recess in the classroom with her. "Why don't you men go out and get some fresh air while you still have the chance?" she asks. They shrug sheepishly and remain with her. She finds Mickey's absentee pattern curious. He seems perfectly healthy on Monday, Wednesday, and Friday, while being excused for "illness" on Tuesday and Thursday. Other puzzling occurrences involving the boys (e.g., their homework papers are wet and crumpled all on the same day with no apparent explanation) cause Ms. Duke to wonder what is going on. These boys choose to spend their time at school in her company, yet Ms. Duke has the distinct impression that they are uncomfortable around her and would prefer being elsewhere. The students offer no explanation.

Ms. Duke begins making observations. Instead of staying in her room just before school begins in the mornings, she walks the grounds where most of her students are at that time. She notices that Bobby, Ronald, Stan, and Winslow nearly always hang around together and that her "shadows," Frank, Maunsell, and Mickey, appear particularly uneasy as Bobby and his companions greet her with "Good morning, Ms. Duke!" Soon Ms. Duke surmises that Bobby, Ronald, Stan, and Winslow are terrorizing fellow students to the point that Frank's, Mickey's, and Maunsell's opportunities to learn are being hindered.

She thinks to herself: "I can't stand bullying! What do those creeps think they get out of terrorizing others? They must really be miserable with themselves to act so miserably toward their classmates! I can't conduct effective learning activities in an environment filled with fear. What should I do? If I confront that bunch with what I suspect, they'll think Maunsell and the rest of the victims tattled on them, and they'll just make life more miserable for them. We need intense adult supervision on the school grounds, the bus stop, the buses, the halls! Good grief! Do we need a police state? I'll try one tactic, and if it doesn't work, I'll find a way to sit on those bullies so they become the ones imprisoned by having to hang around me all day. But first I'll try this. I'll pair Maunsell and Bobby in a joint project where they have to meet me before school. That'll begin breaking up the bully group before school, and maybe the two will start cooperating. If that seems to show some progress, I'll work some of the other bullies into cooperating roles with the victims. Oh! Listen to me! I'm labeling them. I'd better watch my language and not even think about characterizations such as 'bullies' and 'victims.' I don't know if this plan will work at all. Why should I force them together? Maybe I should call a class meeting instead and discuss the problem openly with the group and have them initiate a proposal. They'd probably come up with a vigilante plan with Bobby and his bunch as the main 'hit squad.' That's an idea! Put them in charge of keeping the school grounds peaceful. Forget it. I'll stick with the plan of splitting the gang and motivating some cooperation between the antagonists. I need to work out the details...."

Ms. Duke's plan has a chance of working because she focused on her task of making the learning environment conducive to on-task behavior. She was not overly concerned with punishing those who perpetrated the terror or teaching them a lifelong moral lesson. She concentrated on stopping the disruptive behaviors and preventing recurrences. She controlled her anger. She abhorred Bobby's, Ronald's, Stan's, and Winslow's antisocial behaviors and determined not to tolerate such activities. But she also recognized that they need a more constructive way of dealing with their own insecurities—a way that doesn't step on the rights of others. This realization made it possible for her to think calmly through a plan for dealing with the situation.

Engage in Activity 11.6.

With a colleague, collaboratively respond to the following prompts.

1. Discuss the advantages and disadvantages of the tactics Ms. Duke used in Case 11.19 to break the cycle of bullying among her students.

2. Revisit Case 5.4. Discuss the advantages and disadvantages of Ms. Williams's tactics for teaching her students to adhere to the conduct standard "Respect your own rights."

3. Visit the following Web site of the Teaching Tolerance Project of the Southern Poverty Law Center: www.tolerance.org. Go to the link for teachers; insert the word "bullying" in the search engine. Sample some of the articles and teachers' suggestions for preventing and dealing with bullying.

Fighting

Fights between students tend to follow three stages, each lasting about a minute (Lee Canter & Associates, 1994c):

1. *Posturing and provocation*: Before any physical violence occurs, the students often taunt and threaten one another and demonstrate to one another and observers that they are preparing for action. Such "getting ready for battle" activity is more common in male combatants than in females.

2. *Intense physical aggression*: If no teacher or other responsible person intervenes successfully during stage 1, the verbal aggression and posturing escalate into intense physical fighting.

3. *Lull*: As the students become tired, the fight becomes less intense, and the students may pause momentarily. The student who is faring worse may attempt to look for a way to terminate the fight altogether. In the absence of a successful intervention during the lull, the fight is likely to escalate once again.

In Case 11.20, a teacher intervenes during the first stage, preventing escalation into intense physical fighting; then she refers the two students to the school's peer-mediation program to reduce the chance of subsequent altercations.

▶ CASE 11.20

As Ms. Daines is moving from the main building of Seaside Middle School to one of the portable classroom buildings for her fourth-hour history class, she notices students congregating around two eighth-grade boys confronting one another. Quickly moving into the group of onlookers, she observes one of the boys remove some of his jewelry and the keys from his pocket. The other takes off his jacket and says, "Come on, I'm ready for you!" Ms. Daines thinks, "I don't know either one of these kids; I'd better proceed with caution. I don't want them to turn on me." In a low voice she asks one of the onlookers, "What are their first names?" The student answers, "Ernie is on the left; Steve is the other one."

Moving about three meters from the two, she commands in a calm but firm and loud voice, "Steve, Ernie, stop now. Let's talk about this." Steve glances at Ms. Daines while Ernie continues glaring ahead, leaving Ms. Daines with the impression that Steve may be the one who is more likely to seek a way out of the confrontation and thus more likely to comply with her commands. "Steve, come with me now. Ernie, be cool; stay right there." Directing her attention to the onlookers, she says, "Get on with your business; get to your next class or wherever you should be. There's nothing for you to see here."

As Steve walks to Ms. Daines, the crowd begins to disperse, but Ernie stalks after Steve. Ms. Daines: "Ernie, stop right there. We can settle this without fighting. Fighting will get you into trouble." "He's already in trouble with me!" Ernie shouts as he stops. "Steve, where are you scheduled to be during fourth hour?" she asks. Steve: "In art class." Ms. Daines: "Go there right now while Ernie stays here with me." Ernie: "Why does he get to—" As Steve begins to leave, Ms. Daines interrupts Ernie's complaint, engaging him in the following conversation:

Ms. Daines: Ernie, who is your homeroom teacher?

Ernie: Why should I tell you?

Ms. Daines: Because I'm going to ask Mr. Blankenship to meet with you and Steve to work this out in peer mediation. If you tell me your homeroom teacher's name, it'll be easier for me to arrange it rather than have security track you down to handle this problem.

Ernie: Ms. Berdeaux.

Ms. Daines: Thank you. Now, where are you supposed to be?

Ernie: Art class, just like him!

Ms. Daines: Walk with me to my class to give you and Steve a little time to cool down. I'll write a note for you so you won't get into trouble for being late for art class.

Between fourth and fifth period Ms. Daines informs Mr. Blankenship of the incident and suggests that he arrange for the two to engage in peer-mediation sessions to work out their conflict without resorting to violence.

Ms. Daines's successful intervention during stage 1 was aided by her use of short, clear commands to the students. By addressing them by name and detecting which one looked at her first, she made the calculated gamble that Steve was the more likely to comply with her directions. She provided an initial alternative to catch their attention by saying, "Let's talk about this." Then she followed through by arranging for peer mediation.

Not knowing the students, Ms. Daines was careful not to put herself between the potential combatants, who might have turned on her. But because she succeeded in preventing escalation into intense fighting, the situation was less dangerous for her than for the teacher in Case 11.21.

► CASE 11.21

"Hey, there's a fight in the hall!" a student shouts to Mr. Wessels as he sits at his desk during his lunch hour at Ben Franklin High School. Mr. Wessels jumps up and runs down the hall to find about 15 students surrounding Quinn and Carlos, who are rolling on the floor, punching and kicking one another. Assessing the intense fighting as dangerous, he decides against trying to separate the boys physically. Mr. Wessels looks at the crowd of students, noticing several students who are taunting the combatants to continue and some who are only passively watching. Turning to a student he knows, he says, "Benito, quickly go to Ms. Gywn's office and ask whoever is there to send help immediately." Thinking that the crowd is fueling the aggression, he decides to clear the onlookers from the scene. "Everybody, get out of this area. Leave this area right now before security arrives. Now—right now!" he demands. Most begin to back away, but a few stay. Moving between the remaining crowd and the combatants but still staying out of reach of

Figure 11.1. Mr. Wessels Intervenes during Stage 2 of a Fight

Quinn and Carlos, he commands in a calm but loud voice, "Stop fighting. Stop fighting now!" The fight continues intensely, but he anticipates a lull. He begins clearing the area of objects that the combatants might use as weapons or fall on—a chair, trash cans, and pencils on the floor. As he does this, he moves around the perimeter of the fight, leading the few remaining students to back away from the combatants (see Figure 11.1).

"Stop fighting," he commands again, but with no detectable impact on the two. He grabs a trash can and bangs it on the floor several times to make a distracting noise. Still holding the trash can, he shouts, "Stop fighting now!" Carlos looks at him. Mr. Wessels: "Carlos, be cool and back off. Do the smart thing. Quinn, stop now before it's too late. There's still time to do the smart thing!" Both boys are suffering from lacerations and contusions; Carlos looks worse than Quinn. Finally, a lull begins. Mr. Wessels continues to clear the area of the last two or three onlookers. Two staff members from the office arrive, and Mr. Wessels feels it is safe enough for him to make his demands in closer proximity to the two boys. Without an audience of peers and only in the presence of the three adults, the boys finally back off and are escorted to the principal's office.

Mr. Wessels's initial assessment of the situation led him to realize that he was in no position to separate the combatants safely during the intense fighting stage.

Thus, he tried only verbal commands and dealt with those factors he could safely and successfully control—sending for help, removing the audience, removing dangerous objects, monitoring the fight to identify openings for intervention, preparing to intervene during the lull, and waiting for backup.

In Case 11.22, a teacher deals with fighting in her classroom.

▶ **CASE 11.22**

Ms. Solberg's fourth graders are working individually at their places on an assignment as she helps Zachary at his desk. Suddenly, from behind her, she hears Beth scream, "Stop it!" She turns to see Roxanna on the floor crying, "Ow! Oh, ow!" Roxanna has fresh scratch marks extending from one cheek down the side of her neck. Beth is standing over her. "She clawed me!" screams Roxanna, continuing to cry. Ms. Solberg is uncertain about what happened, but rather than investigate the cause, she decides to deal with Roxanna's immediate need. She bends over Roxanna, cradles her head with an arm, and says, "You are hurt. I'm sorry." Ms. Solberg softly strokes Roxanna's hair and says, "I can see why you're crying." Roxanna: "She clawed me! I hate—" Ms. Solberg (interrupting): "Don't talk now; we have to clean those scratches." Beth: "Well, she poked me first—" Ms. Solberg (interrupting and not looking at Beth): "Enough talk. I don't want to hear anything until we've taken care of Roxanna's scratches. Zachary, please go get two tissues from my desk. Wet one at the sink and leave one dry and bring them both to me. Nadine, bring me the first-aid kit, please. The rest of you get back to work."

As Ms. Solberg helps Roxanna to her feet and walks her to the back of the room, she thinks to herself, "I've bought some time to figure out how to handle this and prevent recurrences. This will also give those two time to cool off. I can deal with them more effectively when they're less angry." She thanks Nadine and Zachary for their help and administers to Roxanna's scratches. Ms. Solberg thinks: "I'll talk to both of them together and get them to examine their own actions. But when? This has to be handled before they leave school today. It's going to be inconvenient, but I must meet them after school. It'll be hard on me today but a lot easier in the long run if I deal with this today. If this behavior becomes a pattern with Beth, I'll be dealing with misery for the rest of the year. The inconvenience today will be a good investment for the future."

Nine minutes after everyone is back on-task, Ms. Solberg beckons Beth and Roxanna to her desk. Ms. Solberg: "Roxanna, what are you planning to do after the final bell today?" Roxanna: "I have a Girl Scout meeting. Mrs. Sheirer is picking us up." Ms. Solberg: "Where is the meeting and how long will it last?" Roxanna: "At Ellie's house." Ms. Solberg: "When will it be over?" Roxanna: "I don't know." Ms. Solberg: "Is Ellie's house far from here?" Roxanna: "It's just over the other side of the hill." Ms. Solberg: "Could you show me how to get there?" Roxanna: "Yes." Ms. Solberg: "Thank you. Beth, what do you do after school today?" Beth: "I catch bus 57." Ms. Solberg: "Do you go straight home from the bus?" Beth: "Yes." Ms. Solberg: "Who will be there when you arrive?" Beth: "My dad." Ms. Solberg: "Is your dad there now?" Beth: "Probably; he works the night shift. He's probably sleeping." Ms. Solberg: "Thank you." Beth: "Ms. Solberg, Roxanna poked—" Ms. Solberg (interrupting): "Not now, Beth. We'll talk about it after school." Roxanna: "But I've got a Girl Sc—" Ms. Solberg (interrupting): "You will miss your bus today, Beth. So I will call your dad and make arrangements for you to get home. Roxanna, I'll meet Ms. Sheirer and explain to her that you'll be late for Girl Scouts. Both of you are to stay right here after the last bell so we can talk about how to prevent today's incident from ever happening again. I'll make arrangements for you to get to where you need to be after our talk. Now go back to your places and get on with your work."

After the last bell, Roxanna and Beth wait in the classroom as Ms. Solberg informs Ms. Sheirer that Roxanna will be late for the meeting and that she'll drive her to Ellie's house herself. Ms. Solberg then phones Beth's father and arranges for him to pick up Beth in 30 minutes. Arriving back in the classroom, she sits with Beth and Roxanna with no one else present:

Ms. Solberg: Beth, your father will pick you up in front of school in 30 minutes. We have until then to talk about what happened today.

Roxanna: I didn't do nothin' to her!

Beth: [interrupting] I guess jabbin' me through my ribs is nothin'!

Roxanna: I was just playing. You didn't have to try and kill me with your claws!

Beth: [holding up her hands in a clawlike manner] You ain't seen nothin' yet!

Roxanna: [flinching] Look, Ms. Solberg, she's gonna do it again!

Ms. Solberg: No, she isn't. Would you like to know what I think, Beth?

Beth: [returning to nonthreatening posture] What?

Ms. Solberg: Please answer me with a more pleasant tone.

Beth: Yes, ma'am.

Ms. Solberg: Roxanna, are you ready to hear what I think?

Roxanna: Yes, ma'am.

Ms. Solberg: I think Roxanna poked Beth as she passed her desk. And Roxanna did it to be friendly, sort of like saying, "Hello, Beth. Look at me. I'm here." Is that right, Roxanna?

Roxanna: Yes.

Beth: But—

Ms. Solberg: [interrupting] Shh! But Roxanna poked Beth too hard, and it disturbed her while she was working. Is that right, Beth?

Beth: Yes, ma'am.

Ms. Solberg: And Beth got so annoyed that, without thinking, she struck out at Roxanna and hurt her. If Beth had thought first, she would not have scratched Roxanna. Now I don't care who was right and who was wrong. I only care that none of my students hurts another again. If Beth hadn't lost control of her temper and had just ignored Roxanna's poke, everything would be OK now. And if Roxanna hadn't bothered Beth while she was working, this wouldn't have happened. Am I correct?

Beth and Roxanna both nod in agreement.

Ms. Solberg: Beth, will this ever happen again?

Beth: Not if she doesn't—

Ms. Solberg: [interrupting] Beth, either one of you is capable of keeping this from happening again. No matter what anyone else does, are you going to let this happen again?

Beth: No, I won't.

Roxanna: Me neither.

Ms. Solberg: Wonderful! We'll wait here until it's time for Beth's dad to be out front; then I'll take Roxanna to her Girl Scout meeting.

In Case 11.23, a teacher intervenes in a fight involving a deadly weapon. Her strategy of placing herself between the students is inadvisable for the vast majority of situations. In Case 11.23, however, the teacher's knowledge of the student with the weapon gave her confidence that she was not endangering herself. She would not have used this strategy with students with whom she had not previously established a healthy relationship.

▶ **CASE 11.23**

Ms. Saunders, a librarian at Bishop Vincent High School, is supervising activities in the library when Stanley, an eleventh-grade student, bursts into the room and confronts Ronny, another student who is seated at a table. Stanley: "You little piece of shit! You owe me!" Ronny pulls a small knife from his pants, gets up, and faces Stanley. Displaying the knife, he says, "Get away from me, or I'll cut your goddamn throat out!" Stanley: "You wouldn't—" Ms. Saunders has made her way to the two and yells, "Enough!" Convinced the two see her, she steps between them with her back to Stanley and faces Ronny. She attempts to present a stern but nonthreatening posture to Ronny. She does not want to further escalate their states of anxiety. "Stanley," she firmly says, "I want you to turn around and walk out the door right now. You can wait for us in the hall." Some of the other students in the library are gathering around as others back away from the scene. Stanley: "I don't have to—" Ms. Saunders [still with her back to Stanley]: "Be cool, Stanley. You're right. You don't have to, but be cool and do it anyway." Ronny: "Yeah, why don't—" Ms. Saunders [interrupting]: "Ronny, shut up! And the rest of you in here get back to what you were doing. This whole incident is over. Hurry up! You've got work to do." Surprised, Stanley leaves; other students hesitatingly move back to their places. Ronny and Ms. Saunders are left alone standing face-to-face with the knife between them. Calmly and softly, Ms. Saunders tells Ronny, "It's okay now. There's no longer a need for that knife, so put it back in your pocket. After I report this incident to Mr. Civello, he'll be calling you to his office. If I were you, I'd get rid of that knife before he calls you. You can dispose of it yourself after you're through working here. Or if you like, I'll take care of it for you now."

Ronny lowers the knife and puts it back into his pocket. Ms. Saunders walks back to her desk where she calls Mr. Civello's office to report the situation. Ronny returns to where he was seated before but then immediately gets up, goes over to Ms. Saunders, and asks, "If you take this for me, will it go easier on me?" Ms. Saunders: "It might." Ronny: "Here." He hands her the knife. With Ronny still standing there, Ms. Saunders completes her report over the phone. The dean of students, Mr. Civello, handles the matter, taking disciplinary action with both students.

Ms. Saunders's strategy worked, but only because she was confident that Ronny would not hurt her. In general, you need to be more concerned about your own safety when a student brandishes a weapon. Teachers need to be trained in strategies for confronting situations, students, and intruders who threaten them and their students with weapons—especially guns. On the videotape program *Intervening Safely During Fights*, Ron Garrison (Lee Canter & Associates, 1994c) provides the following suggestions in such frightening situations:

- *Remain calm.* Take a deep breath and remember that you need to proceed calmly and rationally—for your safety and the safety of others.

- *Use slow deliberate movements.* Quick, unexpected movements may startle the assailant and cause him or her to react violently.

- *Use the "three-step turn-and-withdraw" technique.* Slowly and carefully, take three steps back while turning your body sideways. With hands opened, slowly lower your arms to let the assailant know that you are not armed. This puts distance between you and the assailant, gives the assailant a smaller target, and uses the bones in your arm and in your leg to protect your vital organs.

- *Inform the assailant that you are clearing the area.* Tell the assailant that you are clearing the area of students. Then ask students to slowly step back and leave the area.

- *Offer options.* Offer options to the assailant—especially the option of escape. Say, for example, "Please leave. We don't need trouble. Please go now." This is critical because the assailant may be looking for a way out of the confrontation.

- *Comply with demands.* Comply with any demands the assailant requests provided you believe they will not bring harm to anyone.

- *Summon help.* It is critical to obtain backup support in a crisis situation. Plan ahead of time what actions will be taken to ensure that available personnel would arrive at the scene in a manner that would facilitate a safe resolution to the problem.

Engage in Activity 11.7.

▶ *ACTIVITY 11.7*

With a colleague, collaboratively respond to the following prompts:

1. Discuss the advantages and disadvantages of the tactics Ms. Daines used in Case 11.20 to deal with the confrontation between Steve and Ernie. Did she interact with them in a manner consistent with suggestions from Chapter 4? How, if at all, was she inconsistent with the spirit in which peer mediation is to be conducted by suggesting that Steve and Ernie consider peer mediation. Keep in mind the following: (a) they had already threatened one another, but had not yet engaged in physical fighting, (b) peer mediation is for dealing with conflicts *before* any schoolwide policies are violated, and (c) participation in peer mediation is supposed to be voluntary.

2. Discuss the advantages and disadvantages of the following in Case 11.21: (a) Mr. Wessels not jumping in and physically separating Quinn and Carlos, (b) Mr. Wessels sending for help before dealing with onlookers' taunting or Quinn and Carlos' fighting, (c) how Mr. Wessels went about dispersing the onlookers, (d) Mr. Wessels repeating the command to "stop fighting," (e) Mr. Wessels banging the trash can on the floor to distract the combatants, and (f) Mr. Wessels speaking to Carlos, who was the first to look at him. What is the significance of Carlos looking at Mr. Wessels before Quinn? Why might that suggest that Carlos may be more likely to comply with Mr. Wessels' directives than Quinn?

3. Discuss the advantages and disadvantages of the following in Case 11.22: (a) Ms. Solberg dealing with Roxanna's injuries before addressing the students' behaviors, (b) the way Ms. Solberg interacted with Beth, Roxanna, and the rest of the class, (c) the way Ms. Solberg arranged for the two girls to meet with her after school, (d) Ms. Solberg taking Roxanna to the Girl Scout meeting—keeping in mind the dangers of a teacher being alone in a car with a student, and (e) the overall tactics Ms. Solberg used—keeping in mind that you don't know the students as individuals.

4. Discuss the advantages and disadvantages of the following in Case 11.23: (a) Ms. Saunders stepping between Ronny and Stanley contrary to the sound advice presented herein, (b) Ms. Saunders speaking to Stanley with her back turned to him, (c) the way Ms. Saunders interacted with Ronny and Stanley, (d) Ms. Saunders' offer to take care of the knife for Ronny, and (e) the overall tactics Ms. Saunders used to get the two students—whom she knew as individuals—to terminate the confrontation.

Attacks on Teachers

Causes

Students make the mistake of physically attacking teachers for a variety of complex reasons. Some of the more common factors are the following.

- The student feels backed into a corner, and striking out at the teacher is the only way to save face with peers. Case 11.24 is an example.

▶ **CASE 11.24**

Ms. Mildred is lecturing to one of her eighth-grade classes when she becomes annoyed by Jim and Jan's off-task conversation. Ms. Mildred stops her lecture and scolds, "Can't you two be quiet? You're forever chattering. Jim, if you'd listen in class instead of mooning over Jan all the time, you wouldn't be flunking!" Jim is overwhelmed with embarrassment. He is very fond of Jan and feels that Ms. Mildred has challenged his status with Jan and his peers. He tries to save face by verbally striking out: "I never mooned anybody!" Ms. Mildred gets embarrassed herself and yells, "What? That's not what I meant! You come right here, young man, and apologize to me!" Jim slowly shuffles up to Ms. Mildred with a grin on his face, shifting his eyes to see who is watching him. Ms. Mildred: "Wipe that stupid grin off your face! There's nothing funny about your impudence!" Jim looks down, trying not to laugh, but he is overcome by his concern for what his classmates are thinking and covers his fear and anger with laughter. "You wipe that smile off and apologize," says Ms. Mildred standing face-to-face with Jim. Jim wipes his mouth with his hand and says, "There, I wiped it off." But he bursts out laughing as he hears others in the room giggling. Furious, Ms. Mildred thinks that Jim is making her look bad in front of the class. She tries to gain the upper hand with a show of authority: "You know I can make you sorry you ever set foot in this school! You either say 'I'm sorry' to me right now, or you'll find out just how tough I can be!" Jim believes that this confrontation has gone too far for him to back down without losing the respect of his classmates. Panicked and knowing no desirable way out of the situation, he suddenly changes demeanor. Gritting his teeth, he says in a low voice, "Go play with yourself, you old bitch!" Jim shoves Ms. Mildred, using both hands on her shoulders. She tumbles over backward as he runs out of the room.

Within a week, Jim is expelled from the school and enrolled in an alternative school for students who have committed first-class offenses according to school board policy.

- • The teacher is an accessible target for the student at a moment when the student is reacting angrily. Cases 11.25 to 11.27 are examples.

▶ **CASE 11.25**

Mr. Diel is returning to his classroom where several tenth graders are waiting for the beginning of the next period. Suddenly he observes Kraemer leap at Danny and yell, "What did you call me? Don't ever say that to me again! Understand?" Danny is about to respond when Mr. Diel arrives. From behind he touches Kraemer on the right shoulder and says, "Easy, Kraemer." Kraemer wheels around and swings his right arm so that his elbow catches Mr. Diel in the mouth. A tooth is broken and blood spurts from Mr. Diel's lip.

▶ **CASE 11.26**

Finis is a 15-year-old student participating in an intramural basketball game refereed by Mr. Leblanc, a physical education teacher. The game is closely contested when Mr. Leblanc calls a personal foul on Finis. "You, number 32," Mr. Leblanc yells, coming face-to-face with Finis in the tradition of basketball officials. Finis believes that he is not guilty of the foul; he thinks he was fouled instead. "Get your hand up, 32!" Mr. Leblanc yells in Finis's face. Finis: "I didn't do—" Mr. Leblanc (interrupting): "Technical foul!" Finis, frustrated and helpless, lashes out at the nearest accessible target, striking Mr. Leblanc on the nose with his fist.

▶ **CASE 11.27**

Ms. Blouin teaches a class of 11 students who are classified as EBD. Two of her students, Suzanne and Paul, habitually express their feelings by physically striking out at Ms. Blouin. Ms. Blouin has been kicked, bitten, pushed, scratched, and slapped by these two students. To help her deal with the situation, avoid being victimized by them, and prepare for similar situations in the future, Ms. Blouin completes a course in self-defense techniques especially designed for teachers. Ms. Blouin is now better able to protect herself from such abuse without a high risk of injury to Suzanne, Paul, or any other student who might attack her or attack another student. The self-defense techniques she uses are designed to immobilize students without harming them.

- The student attempts to exert control over authorities, win favor with peers, seek revenge on an authority, or relieve boredom by carrying out a prank that endangers the well-being of teachers. Case 11.28 is an example.

► **CASE 11.28**

Ms. Heidingsfelder, a teacher at Blackhawk Trail High School, is driving home after work when she is startled by the sound of an explosion from under her car. A tire blows out, she loses control of the vehicle, crosses a lane with oncoming traffic, and comes to a stop on the side of the road. Fortunately, she is uninjured, and the car suffers only a damaged tire.

Ms. Heidingsfelder does not suspect that the accident is anything more than that until the following school day. Several students in her third-period class question her: "Ms. H, are you okay?" "Did you drive your wheels to school today?" "Did anything happen to you after school yesterday?" Thinking quickly, she concludes that she has been a victim of a booby trap. Believing she can hardly find the responsible criminals among the students, she decides not to give them the satisfaction of knowing that the prank worked. She replies, "I'm fine; it's awfully nice of you to ask. Why do you ask if anything out of the ordinary happened after school yesterday?"

- The student feels obliged to defend herself or himself against a perceived danger posed by the teacher. Case 11.29 is an example.

► **CASE 11.29**

Mr. Moe, an assistant principal at Greenfield Creek Junior High, is six feet, five inches tall and weighs nearly 300 pounds. He believes his reputation as a strict disciplinarian who'll "knock off your head rather than look at you" helps him with his primary responsibility of maintaining order in the school. One day Mr. Moe surprises Rudolph, an eighth grader, smoking crack in a restroom. Panicked at the sight of the enormous man with the infamous reputation, Rudolph spots a large wrench inadvertently left on the floor by a custodian. He grabs it and throws it at Mr. Moe's head.

Strategies

You can reduce your chances of being a victim of student violence by adhering to the following principles:

- You are not intimidated by the threat of violence.
- You do not pose a threat to students. This includes not perpetrating violence on them (e.g., using corporal punishment, roughly touching them, or violating their space) or competing with them for esteem from others—especially their peers. You never try to show up a student.

- You use physical force with students *only* in drastic situations in which it is the only reasonable means for restraining them from harming themselves or another. Physical force is never used to punish or hurt, only to restrain in certain unusual situations.

- You are sensitive to potentially volatile situations and do not make yourself available as a target when students might unthinkingly react aggressively.

- You avoid making ultimatums in which the consequence of students' noncompliance is the most severe sanction you can levy. If you commit yourself to administering the severest penalty available to you, then students have nothing left to lose by displaying even less-desirable behaviors than those that initially led to the unpleasant situation.

- You never tolerate violent behavior in your presence. You have every right to use the full power of the legal system to prevent violence or the threat of violence from preventing you from effectively meeting your professional responsibilities.

- You build positive relationships with students, respecting them and earning their respect for you.

- You and your colleagues consistently implement a sound safe-school program.

Vandalizing

Vandalism, like discourtesy and an unkempt classroom, can be extremely disruptive to a learning environment. School-level vandalism (e.g., painting graffiti on walls, breaking windows, or arson) should be handled by school administrators and law-enforcement authorities. It is wise for you, as a teacher, to avoid playing the role of detective with your own students. Antagonism between teacher and students is a likely consequence when the teacher tries to detect the identities of culprits among students. Repeated vandalism may be encouraged by students who desire to continue the "cops and robbers" game that a teacher has been duped into playing. In addition to reporting vandalism to authorities and cooperating with their investigations, you may try to prevent acts of vandalism from being positively reinforced. Consider Case 11.30.

▶ **CASE 11.30**

Ms. Romano enters her equipment room to prepare for the day's physical education classes when she discovers the soccer balls she plans to use are deflated and flattened. The nets of the six portable soccer goals are cut and unusable. In horror she thinks, "Who would have done this? This screws up my whole day! The girls will be on the field in six minutes, and we are scheduled to play soccer first period. If I ever catch the little—!" Ms. Romano composes herself and begins thinking: "Barbara, Evelyn, Tamaria, and some of the others have been complaining about having to play soccer during first period. They said it was too hot and their hair was a mess the rest of the day. I wonder if it's one of them. Well, I don't know that. I could hardly find out if I tried. But I do know that a lot of the girls would love to use this as an excuse to avoid going out and working up a sweat."

Ms. Romano walks over to the locker room where her students are changing. She announces, "Let's go, ladies! We meet on the soccer field at exactly 9:20." "Do we have to? It's too hot today!" complains one student. Ms. Romano makes no response and heads for the field. Outside, she tells the class, "We will not be able to play soccer today because the equipment has been damaged." Barbara: "Then why are we on the soccer field?" Ms. Romano: "Because it is critical that we do an anaerobic activity today, and the soccer field is as good a place as any to get your hearts and lungs working. Just because we can't play soccer doesn't mean we can't get the same benefits that a vigorous soccer game affords us." Some students begin to moan and complain to one another. Ms. Romano puts them through an especially fatiguing routine of calisthenics. After the session, the students are dragging and perspiring. They enter the showers with tousled hair. Ms. Romano reports the vandalism to her immediate supervisor who makes arrangements to repair the damage and prepares a report for the principal.

▶ SYNTHESIS ACTIVITIES FOR CHAPTER 11

I. Observe the students in a colleague's classroom. Identify three incidents of disruptive student behaviors. For each, write two paragraphs describing the disruptive behavior and what the teacher did to deal with it. Limit your report to descriptions of what happened; do not include your value judgments regarding the teacher's method of handling the disruption. Discuss the episodes with the teacher, eliciting her or his rationale for the methods of responding to the disruptions.

II. When you and some colleagues engaged in Chapter 10's Synthesis Activity III, you expanded and modified the school discipline policy you originated when engaging in Chapter 5's Synthesis Activity XI. Review that revised policy with your colleagues; expand and modify it further in light of your work with Chapter 11.

▶ TRANSITIONAL ACTIVITY FROM CHAPTER 11 TO CHAPTER 12

In preparation for your work with Chapter 12, discuss with two or more colleagues the following questions.

I. Why do proven methods for managing student behavior sometimes fail?

II. What advantages do experienced teachers have over beginning teachers relative to gaining and maintaining students' cooperation?

III. How can instructional supervision, self-assessments, and action research be used to refine individual teachers' classroom management strategies?

PART V

MAKING CLASSROOM MANAGEMENT STRATEGIES WORK FOR YOU

Incorporating Classroom Management Strategies into Your Teaching Style

▶ **CHAPTER 12'S GOAL**

The goal of this chapter is to heighten your awareness of the following.

1. The art of teaching is far too complex for even proven strategies to succeed fully in the hands of novices who have yet to accumulate adequate experiences for refining their teaching talents.

2. You need to cultivate your teaching strategies, techniques, and style continually so that your ability to apply classroom management strategies for gaining and maintaining students' cooperation improves as your experiences grow.

▶ **BUILDING ON EXPERIENCES**

Some methods for gaining students' cooperation may not work as effectively as you'd like until you've had some experience trying them out and tailoring them to your own situations. Consider the following examples.

- From your work with Chapter 4, you understand the importance of establishing productive communication patterns with your students by using descriptive instead of judgmental language. But most people are not in the habit of considering their words carefully enough to use descriptive language consistently. Consequently, you may find that it takes a concerted effort to practice descriptive language with your students before descriptive phrases flow from your tongue and you begin to reap the benefits of this technique.

- While working with Chapter 7, you were encouraged to use problem-based learning activities to motivate student engagement intrinsically (e.g., in Case 7.4). But teachers need to spend time observing students and becoming thoroughly familiar with the subject matter before they will be readily able to identify interesting problems on which to focus. Familiarity with both students and subject matter increases with teaching experience. If you are not used to conducting problem-based learning activities but are convinced of the advantages of doing so, begin on a small scale with teaching units that lend themselves to that approach. In time you will build both your repertoire of teaching units that use the problem-based approach and your ability to design such units.

- Throughout this text, especially in Chapter 8, you have been encouraged to respond to your students' off-task behaviors using the teaching cycles model, just as you do for academic teaching units. In Case 8.3, Ms. Reid effectively handled a rather nasty situation because she organized her thoughts around the teaching cycles model. You may have to face a number of discipline problems before you have used the teaching cycles model often enough to make it consistently and efficiently work to your advantage.

- As indicated in Chapter 9, the principle of extinction can be a powerful weapon in your arsenal against off-task behavior patterns. Nevertheless, unless you can identify positive reinforcers that lead students habitually off-task, you can hardly take advantage of extinction. As an observant, reflective teacher, you will—with experience—develop your abilities to identify what positively reinforces your students' habits.

▶ INSTRUCTIONAL SUPERVISION

Preservice teacher preparation programs provide beginning teachers with necessary, but insufficient, competencies to be successful in-service teachers. The success of instructional practice depends on teachers' further developing those competencies from in-service experiences. To be consistently effective, especially in the first few years of their careers, in-service teachers need support, guidance, and feedback as they practice their complex art (Corcoran, 1995; Smith, 2001).

Instructional supervision means collaborating with teachers to help them enhance their effectiveness with students (Cangelosi, 1991, pp. 6, 122–158). Two promising and frequently practiced instructional supervisory models are peer coaching and mentoring (Oliva & Pawlas, 2001, pp. 410–456). *Peer coaching* involves two or more teachers sharing ideas and providing formative feedback on one another's teaching. *Mentor teachers* work with beginning teachers to help them through their first few years.

Case 12.1 (adapted from Cangelosi, 1991, pp. 148–157) illustrates the type of collegial communication that grows out of peer coaching and mentoring relationships:

▶ CASE 12.1

Two primary-grade teachers, Kristine Scott and Ebony Del Rio, engage in the following conversation:

Kristine: Do you have any ideas on dealing with a student who habitually interrupts classmates when they have the floor?

Ebony: The prescription has to fit the student and the situation. Why do you ask? Does one of your students have that problem?

Kristine: I don't know. Tim Ziegler seems to be developing a pattern of interrupting classmates. I'm not sure if he needs me to teach him to break the habit or if it's something I should deal with like an isolated disruption, instance by instance.

Ebony: Apparently it's bothering you enough that the problem merits some attention.

Kristine: In the last three days, I'd bet he's interrupted someone speaking in class at least four times.

Ebony:　What were the circumstances—group discussions, recitations, what?

Kristine:　At least twice that I can remember, it was during a class meeting when we have very strict procedures governing who may speak. That's when I first began thinking he might be developing a habit. In the past, I hadn't really paid attention to it.

Ebony:　Sounds like you need to collect some baseline data. That'll give us a better idea if it's habitual or not. Why don't you keep a chart indicating. . . .

The conversation continues. The two decide to meet to analyze the baseline data that Kristine collects. If they decide that Kristine should treat Tim's interruptions as a habit, Kristine will propose an intervention plan that Ebony will critique.

After three days spent collecting baseline data, Kristine is convinced that Tim has a persistent pattern that she needs to teach him to modify. Thus, she already has an objective formulated the next time she meets with Ebony:

Kristine:　Tim's definitely developed a habit. What do you think of this objective?

Ebony:　(reading) "Tim will reduce the frequency of interrupting classmates who are speaking from his baseline ratio of 35 percent of the time to a ratio of less than 10 percent within two weeks." Wow! Pretty ambitious.

Kristine:　It's either that or I have to keep reacting to each incident one at a time, which means he's just going to get deeper and deeper into trouble.

Ebony:　We don't want that. But I have one question. This objective suggests you're going to focus on his breaking the habit. What have you got in mind for intervention?

Kristine:　I haven't worked it out yet, but I guess I should apply the principle of extinction.

Ebony:　But then you'd have to identify the positive reinforcers. For this type of behavior, that's going to be difficult to do and then control.

Kristine:　I agree. Do you have a suggestion?

Ebony:　If you change your objective so that it focuses on teaching him an on-task behavior pattern that's incompatible with his pattern of interruptions—

Kristine:　Oh! Like quietly listening when others are speaking and raising his hand to speak.

Ebony:　Exactly. Then a principle like shaping would apply and that would be more efficient for this situation.

Kristine:　So I'll restate the objective. Give me a minute.—How does this sound? "Tim will exhibit a pattern of quiet listening behaviors by waiting his turn to speak and raising his hand to be recognized at least 90% of the time that classmates are speaking. Two weeks after intervention begins, this pattern will have emerged." What do you think?

Ebony:　I think your chances of succeeding with that objective are favorable.

Kristine:　Now I've got to design the intervention. I'll work on it tonight. May I show it to you tomorrow?

Ebony:　You bet; I'm anxious to see what you come up with.

The following day, their conversation focuses on the next stage of the teaching cycles model:

Ebony:　So what have you planned for your intervention?

Kristine:　My plans aren't finalized, but I'll continue to maintain a record of his behavior during relevant situations—just for baseline. I'll try to anticipate the times when other students have the floor and be near Tim so I can use non-attention-getting body language to intercept his interruptions quickly. Now if that will control his interruptions, then there's a chance shaping can work.

Ebony:　How do you propose to use shaping?

Kristine:　I'll really have to monitor him closely. Then when he's displaying some patience and makes any kind of movement that even vaguely resembles raising his hand, I'll call on him to make a comment. I'd have to get on a gradually decreasing schedule of reinforcement for waiting to speak in turn.

Ebony: Do you think he finds attention rewarding?

Kristine: Not in general; I think he's just got a lot to say.

Ebony: So you'll give him opportunities to speak as rewards for waiting.

Kristine: Right, but first I've got to get him to begin raising his hand. That's the real key.

Ebony: I think it'll work if you consistently stick to your reinforcement schedule.

Kristine: But I really have to know when to jump in and when to back off. It's not going to be easy. Will you spot-check me occasionally with a few observations?

Ebony: Yes, and you can also share what happens each day with me. We can discuss how closely you're sticking to the plan.

Three times during the first week of Kristine's attempt to teach Tim to raise his hand habitually and patiently wait his turn to speak, she and Ebony discuss how the plan is progressing. Here is a portion of the next conference:

Kristine: This morning, just before I pulled the four reading groups together to share stories with one another, I moved right by Tim and then stayed with him for the whole discussion. Anytime he even looked like he was going to interrupt, I'd be right between him and the rest of the class.

Ebony: Did he ever interrupt?

Kristine: Not once this morning. But here's the best part! Because I was blocking his view, he began to wiggle in his chair to look around me. That's when I pretended to think he was raising his hand and I called on him, thanking him for raising his hand.

Ebony: What did he say?

Kristine: What didn't he say? He talked on and on about the story his group read! I let him talk longer than I usually do to reinforce his waiting to be called on.

Ebony: But did others get bored?

Kristine: Some appeared restless.

Ebony: So that's going to be a complicating factor.

Kristine: That's not the only one. . . .

Ebony observes Kristine's class twice during the following week. As they continue to discuss strategies for Tim and assess his progress, they learn from one another, stimulating each other's abilities to formulate strategies for a wide variety of complex situations.

▶ ASSESSING YOUR OWN TEACHING

Some teachers expertly and systematically evaluate their own instruction; others use more haphazard approaches. But none can avoid making judgments about their own performances. Teachers' self-assessments—accurate or not—influence their strategies, preparation, and activities. With video cameras generally available for classroom and household use, you can easily view your own instructional performances in the privacy of your home. But to realize the potential of this resource, you should acquaint yourself with some of the systematic self-assessment tools (Cangelosi, 1991, pp. 127–130). Struyk (1990), for example, developed and validated a video-based instrument and procedure by which teachers evaluate the efficiency of their own classroom management strategies for transition time.

▶ ACTION RESEARCH

In their quest to improve their own performances and be better prepared to exchange ideas with colleagues, many teachers conduct action research projects. They experiment with different strategies and techniques and compare outcomes. Case 12.2 (adapted from Cangelosi, 1992, pp. 30–31) is an example.

▶ CASE 12.2

Although convinced of the benefits of cooperative learning activities and knowledgeable on how to use them, Ms. Olson worries that her students will display far more disruptive off-task behaviors during such activities than they normally do during the large-group and independent work sessions she's used to conducting. She's simply not ready to commit a major share of her instructional time to cooperative learning activities if the consequences are an increase in off-task behaviors—no matter what the academic benefits might be.

To help her resolve the question, she experiments with the lessons in a writing unit by conducting six comparable learning activities over a two-week period so that two of the activities are large group, two are independent work sessions, and two involve cooperative small groups. To compare the three types of activities relative to levels of student cooperation and on-task behaviors, she videotapes the sessions using a tripod stationed in the rear of the room. To reduce the effects of being videotaped on student behavior during the experimental sessions, she videotaped class sessions during the previous week so the students would be used to having the camera in the classroom.

After the six experimental sessions are complete, she views the videotapes, carefully counting incidences of student off-task behaviors and noting evidence of student cooperation. Her comparisons reveal no major differences in students' cooperation and on-task behaviors according to the type of activity. She also gains insights about what she might do to improve her classroom management techniques. She concludes that as long as cooperative learning activities are carefully planned and orchestrated, students are just as likely to be on-task as they are during other types of learning activities. Thus, she plans to include more cooperative group activities in subsequent units.

▶ YOUR UNIQUENESS

Because of differences among you and other teachers and your circumstances and theirs, what is advisable for other teachers may be inadvisable for you. Nevertheless, your knowledge of what other teachers do to teach their students to be on-task is a major source of ideas for originating your own systematic approaches. For example:

- Ms. Phegley's activities in Case 3.8 exemplify research-based strategies for the first week of a school term to establish a learning environment that encourages students to cooperate. There are probably legitimate reasons why you should not try to copy exactly what Ms. Phegley did when you begin your next new term as a teacher. Unlike Ms. Phegley, you may not feel comfortable putting your hands on your head as a cue for your students to listen to your directions. Maybe your students are too old for that sort of thing. But surely you can learn from Ms. Phegley's tactics by thinking of ways that you can nonverbally but comfortably establish cues for your students to follow during the first week of a school term.

- Mr. Brown used a democratic process to determine a classroom procedure in Case 5.6. Perhaps a democratic process is too inefficient for you to use in establishing your own classroom procedures or standards of conduct. Even if you choose not to follow Mr. Brown's example, your knowledge of what he did can give you ideas about things such as how to distinguish clearly for your students those times when the class is to focus on management matters from those times when the concern is on achieving some academic learning objective.

- In Case 10.5, Mr. Legget took some rather extraordinary steps to deal with the problem of students' mind wandering and daydreaming. Most teachers would not choose to try his elaborate scheme. But his method illustrates some important strategies that can be incorporated into more conventional approaches.

It is inadvisable for you to try to revolutionize your teaching style all at once; new ideas and methods should be tried cautiously and conservatively. But they *should* be tried if they have a documented record of success. Those suggested by this book do have such a success record for gaining students' cooperation. For some that you try, you can expect immediate success; others must be practiced before the benefits are enjoyed. Please reread the first section of Chapter 1, "Teaching Experiences: Satisfying or Frustrating." May your teaching career be dominated by satisfying experiences.

References

Abernathy, S., Manera, E., & Wright, R. (1985). What stresses student teachers most? *Clearing House, 58*, 361–362.

Alberti, R., & Emmons, M. (1995). *Your perfect right* (7th ed.). San Luis Obsipo, CA: Impact.

Allen, L. A., & Patton, D. M. (1990, November). *Effects of sound field amplification on students' on-task behavior*. Paper presented at the Listening in the Classroom Teleconference, Logan, UT.

American Psychiatric Association. (2000). *Diagnostic and statistical manual of mental disorders, text revision: DSM-IV-TR* (4th ed.). Washington, DC: Author.

American Speech-Language-Hearing Association. (1993). Definitions of communications disorders and variations. *Asha, 35*(10), 40–41.

Andero, A. A., & Stewart, A. (2002). Issues of corporal punishment: Reexamined. *Journal of Instructional Psychology, 29*(2), 90–96.

Ashlock, R. B. (2001). *Error patterns in computation: Error patterns to improve instruction* (8th ed.). Upper Saddle River, NJ: Prentice Hall.

Avery, N. (2005). Our multicultural classroom. *Teaching preK-8, 36*(2), 52–53.

Azrin, N. H., Hake, D. G., & Hutchinson, R. R. (1965). Elicitation of aggression by a physical blow. *Journal of Experimental Analysis of Behavior, 8*, 55–57.

Azrin, N. H., Hutchinson, R. R., & Sallery, R. D. (1964). Pain-aggression toward inanimate objects. *Journal of Experimental Analysis of Behavior, 7*, 223–228.

Baenen, J. (2000). *Transescent seminar* [Videotape]. Platteville, WI: Center of Education for the Young Adolescent.

Ballard, M. B., Argus, T., & Remley, T. P. (1999). Bullying and school violence: A proposed prevention program. *NASSP Bulletin, 83*, 38–47.

Bandura, A. (1965). Behavior modification through modeling procedures. In L. Krasner & L. P. Ullman (Eds.), *Research in behavior modification* (pp. 310–340). New York: Holt, Rinehart & Winston.

Banks, J. A., & Banks, C. A. M. (Eds.). (2001). *Multicultural education: Issues and Perspectives* (4th ed.). New York: Wiley.

Berg, F. S. (1987). *Facilitating classroom listening*. Boston: College-Hill Press.

Berg, F. S. (1990). Sound field FM: A new technology for the classroom. *Clinical Connection, 4*, 14–17.

Black, S. (2006). Respecting differences. *American School Board Journal, 193*(1), 34–36.

Bodine, R. J., & Crawford, D. K. (1998). *The handbook of conflict resolution education: A guide to building quality programs for schools*. San Francisco: Jossey-Bass.

Bogacki, D. F., Armstrong, J. J., & Weiss, K. J. (2005). Reducing school violence: The corporal punishment scale and its relationship to authoritarianism and pupil-control ideology. *The Journal of Psychiatry and Law, 33*, 367–386.

Bongiovanni, A. F. (1979). An analysis of research on punishment and its relation to the use of corporal punishment in the schools. In I. A. Hyman & J. Wise (Eds.), *Corporal punishment in American education* (pp. 351–372). Philadelphia: Temple University.

Borkowski, J. G. (1992). Metacognitive theory: A framework for teaching literacy, writing, and math skills. *Journal of Learning Disabilities, 25*, 253–257.

Boston high schoolers have wide exposure to school violence, polls find. (2006, January 4). *Education Week, 25*, 4.

Bowers, C. A., & Flinders, D. J. (1990). *Responsive teaching: An ecological approach to classroom patterns of language and thought*. New York: Teachers College Press.

Bradley, A. (2006, January 25). Florida middle schooler dies after standoff with police. *Education Week, 25*, 6.

Brandenburg, N. A., Friedman, R. M., & Silver, S. E. (1990). The epidemiology of childhood psychiatric disorders: Prevalence findings from recent studies. *Journal of the American Academy of Child and Adolescent Psychiatry, 29*, 76–83.

Brendtro, L., & Long, N. (1995). Breaking the cycle of conflict. *Educational Leadership, 52*, 52–56.

Brock, S. E., Sandoval, J., & Lewis, S. (2001). *Preparing for crises in the schools: A manual for building school crisis response teams* (2nd ed.). New York: Wiley.

Brown, J. H., and Brown, D. (2006). Resilient leadership and why "at risk" is at risk. *Education Digest, 71*(5), 24–28.

Bucher, K. T., & Manning, M. L. (2005). Creating safe schools. *Clearing House, 79*(1), 55–60.

Bushway, A., & Nash, W. (1977). School cheating behavior. *Review of Educational Research, 47,* 623–632.

Caldwell, J. (2005, December 20). Kerry's courage. *Advocate,* Issue 953, 38–44.

Cameron, J., & Pierce, W. D. (1994). Reinforcement, reward, and intrinsic motivation: A meta-analysis. *Review of Educational Research, 64,* 363–423.

Cangelosi, B. R. (2000). Who you dissn', dude? At-risk students learn assertive communication skills. *English Journal, 89,* 111–118.

Cangelosi, B. R., & Petersen, M. L. (1998, November). *Empowering students' interpersonal skills through assertive communications.* A colloquium presentation at the annual conference of the National Council of Teachers of English, Nashville, TN.

Cangelosi, J. S. (1980). *Project G.R.E.A.T. needs assessment report.* Tallahassee: Florida Department of Education.

Cangelosi, J. S. (1982). *Measurement and evaluation: An inductive approach for teachers.* Dubuque, IA: Wm. C. Brown.

Cangelosi, J. S. (1990). *Cooperation in the classroom: Students and teachers together* (2nd ed.). Washington, DC: National Education Association.

Cangelosi, J. S. (1991). *Evaluating classroom instruction.* New York: Longman.

Cangelosi, J. S. (1992). *Systematic teaching strategies.* New York: Longman.

Cangelosi J. S. (1993, April). *Cheating on tests: Issues in elementary and secondary school classrooms.* A paper presented at a joint session of the American Educational Research Association and the National Council for Measurement in Education, Atlanta, GA.

Cangelosi, J. S. (2000). *Assessment strategies for monitoring student learning.* New York: Addison-Wesley/Longman.

Cangelosi, J. S. (2003). *Teaching mathematics in secondary and middle school: An interactive approach* (3rd ed.). Upper Saddle River, NJ: Merrill/Prentice Hall.

Cangelosi, J. S. (2006). *Classroom management practices and schoolwide discipline policies.* An unpublished study. Logan: Utah State University.

Canter, L., & Canter, M. (1976). *Assertive discipline: A take-charge approach for today's educator.* Seal Beach, CA: Canter and Associates.

Canter, L., & Canter, M. (2002). *Assertive discipline: Positive behavior management for today's schools* (3rd ed.). Santa Monica, CA: Lee Canter & Associates.

Carnes, J. (Ed.). (1999). *Responding to hate at school: A guide to teachers, counselors, and administrators.* Montgomery, AL: Southern Poverty Law Center.

Cazden, C. B. (1988). *Classroom discourse: The language of teaching and learning.* Portsmouth: NH: Heinemann.

Center for Effective Discipline. (2002). *Facts about corporal punishment.* [Website: www.stophitting.com] Columbus, OH: Author.

Chandler, L. (2005). False data. *IRE Journal, 28* (6), 23–25.

Charles, C. M. (2005). *Building classroom discipline* (8th ed.). Boston: Pearson/Allyn and Bacon.

Charney, R. (1993). Teaching children nonviolence. *Journal of Emotional and Behavior Problems, 2*(1) 46–48.

Clancy, J. (2005). Headteacher? Not me—yet. *Times Educational Supplement,* Issue 4653, 4.

Cohen, E. G., & Lotan, R. A. (1995). Producing equal-status interaction in the heterogeneous classroom. *American Educational Research Journal, 32,* 99–120.

Cook, G. (2005). A new study shows the prevalence of bullying and harassment at school. *American School Board Journal, 192*(12), 4–6.

Corcoran, T. B. (1995). *Transforming professional development for teachers: A guide for state policymakers.* Washington: National Governors Association.

Delgado, J. M. R. (1963). Cerebral heterostimulation in a monkey colony. *Science, 141,* 161–163

Deutsch, M. (1973). *The resolution of conflict.* New Haven, CT: Yale University Press.

DeVoe, J. F., Peter, K., Kaufman, P., Rudy, S. A., Miller, A. K., Planty, M., Snyder, T. D., & Rand, M. R. (2003). *Indicators of school crime and safety*: 2003 (NCES 2004–004/NCJ 201257). Washington, DC: U.S. Department of Education and Justice.

Dewey, J. (1933). How we think (rev. ed.). Boston: D. C. Heath.

Dill, V. S., & Haberman, M. (1995). Building a gentler school. *Educational Leadership, 52,* 69–71.

Dishion, T. J., Nelson, S. E., and Yasui, M. (2005). Predicting early adolescent gang involvement from middle school adaptation. *Journal of Clinical Child and Adolescent Psychology, 34*(1), 62–73.

Dreikurs, R. (1968). *Psychology in the classroom* (2nd ed.). New York: Harper & Row.

Dreikurs, R., Grunwald, B., & Pepper, F. (1982). *Maintaining sanity in the classroom* (2nd ed.). New York: Harper & Row.

Dunlap, K. (1919). Are there instincts? *Journal of Abnormal Psychology, 14,* 307–311.

Dunn, M. J. (2001). Break the bullying cycle. *American School and University, 73,* 38–39.

Dunne, M., Humphreys, S., & Leach, F. (2006). Gender violence in school in the developing world. *Gender and Education, 18*(1), 75–98.

Evans, E. D., & Craig, D. (1990). Teacher and student perceptions of academic cheating in middle and senior high schools. *Journal of Educational Research, 84*, 44–52.

Evertson, C. M. (1989). Classroom organization and management. In M. C. Reynolds (Ed.), *Knowledge base for the beginning teacher* (pp. 59–70). Oxford, England: Pergamon.

Evertson, C. M., Emmer, E. T., & Worsham, M. E. (2006). *Classroom management for elementary teachers* (7th ed.). Boston: Pearson/Allyn and Bacon.

Federal Register. (1977, December 29). *Procedures for evaluating specific learning disabilities*. Washington, DC: Department of Health, Education, and Welfare.

Fisher, C. W., Berliner, D. C., Filby, N. N., Marliave, R., Cahen, L. S., & Dishaw, M. M. (1980). Teaching behaviors, academic learning time, and student achievement: An overview. In C. Denham & A. Lieberman (Eds.), *Time to learn* (pp. 7–32). Washington, DC: National Institute of Education.

Flannery, M. E. (2005). The D word. *NEA Today, 24* (Issue 1), 22–29.

Fleischman, H. L., & Hopstock, P. J. (1993). *Descriptive study of services to limited English proficient students*. Arlington, VA: Development Associates.

Franklin, J. (2001). The diverse challenges of multiculturalism. *Education Update, 43*, 1, 3, & 8.

Garbarino, J. (1992). *Children in danger: Coping with the consequences of community violence*. San Francisco: Jossey-Bass.

Ginott, H. G. (1965). *Parent and child*. New York: Avon Books.

Ginott, H. G. (1972). *Teacher and child*. New York: Avon Books.

Glasser, W. (1985). *Control theory in the classroom*. New York: Perennial Press.

Glasser, W. (2001). *Every student can succeed*. Chatworth, CA: William Glasser Incorporated.

Gold, S. R., & Cundiff, G. (1980). Increasing the frequency of daydreaming. *Journal of Clinical Psychology, 36*, 116–121.

Gordon, T. (1974). *T.E.T.: Teacher effectiveness training*. New York: Peter H. Wyden.

Gordon, T. (1989). *Discipline that works: Promoting self-discipline in children*. New York: Random House.

Gottfried, A. E., Fleming, J. S., & Gottfried, A. W. (2001). Continuity of academic instrinsic motivation from childhood through last adolescence: A longitudinal study. *Journal of Educational Psychology, 93*, 3–13.

Grossman, H. (1995). *Classroom behavior management in a diverse society* (2nd ed.). Mountain View, CA: Mayfield.

Guanci, J. A. (2002). Peer mediation: A winning solution. *The Education Digest, 67*, 26–33.

Guerrero, A. (2005). Youth violence prevention in a problem-based clerkship curriculum. *American Journal of Preventive Medicine, 29*, 206–210.

Haefner, J., Cangelosi, J., Lindahl, A., Koebbe, J., Mueller, D., & Powell, J. (2001). *BioMathLab: Modeling Biological Processes in the Laboratory*. Report to the Department of Education Office of Postsecondary Education (FIPSE) Comprehensive Program, Washington.

Hallahan, D. P., Gajar, A. H., Cohen, S. B., & Tarver, S. G. (1978). Selective attention and locus of control in learning disabled and normal children. *Journal of Learning Disabilities, 4*, 47–52.

Hallahan, D. P., & Kauffman, J. M. (1997). *Exceptional learners: Introduction to special education* (7th ed.). Boston: Allyn & Bacon.

Hennemann, T. (2005, September 27). Protectors of youth. *Advocate*, Issue 947, 44–47.

Heward, W. L. (2006). *Exceptional children: An introduction to special education* (8th ed.). Upper Saddle River, NJ: Pearson/Merrill/Prentice Hall.

Hinchey, P. H. (2004). Corporal punishment: Legalities, realities, and implications. *The Clearing House, 77*(3), 96–100

Hoover, J., & Juul, C. (1993). Bullying in Europe and the U.S. *Journal of Emotional and Behavioral Problems, 2*(1), 25–29.

Hyman, I. A., & Wise, J. H. (Eds.). (1979). *Corporal punishment in American education*. Philadelphia: Temple University Press.

Jansen, A., Smeets, T., Martijn, C., & Nederkoorn, C. (2006). I see what you see: The lack of self-serving body-image bias in eating disorders. *British Journal of Clinical Psychology, 45*, 123–135.

Jesunathadas, J. (1990). *Mathematics teachers' instructional activities as a function of academic preparation*. Doctoral dissertation, Utah State University, Logan, UT.

Johnson, D. W., & Johnson, R. T. (1989). *Cooperation and competition: Theory and research*. Edina, MN: Interaction.

Johnson, D. W., & Johnson, R. T. (1991). *Teaching students to be peacemakers*. Edina, MN: Interaction.

Johnson, D. W., & Johnson, R. T. (1992). *Creative controversy: Intellectual challenges in the classroom*. Edina, MN: Interaction.

Johnson, D. W., & Johnson, R. T. (1994). *Teaching students to be peacemakers: Results of five years of research*. Minneapolis: University of Minnesota Cooperative Learning Center.

Johnson, D. W., & Johnson, R. T. (1995). Why violence prevention programs don't work—and what does. *Educational Leadership, 52*, 63–67.

Johnson, J. R. (1997). *Geometry portfolio projects*. Presentation at the Western Regional Conference of the National Council of Teachers of Mathematics, Salt Lake City, UT.

Jones, F. (1979). The gentle art of classroom discipline. *National Elementary Principal, 58*, 26–32.

Jones, F. (2001). *Fred Jones' tools for teachers*. Santa Cruz, CA: Frederic H. Jones & Associates.

Jones, F. (2002). *The video toolbox*. Santa Cruz, CA: Frederic H. Jones & Associates.

Jones, F. (2003). Tools for teaching. http://www.fredjones.com.

Jones, V., & Jones, L. (2004). *Comprehensive classroom management: Creating communities of support and solving problems* (7th ed.). Boston: Pearson/Allyn and Bacon.

Kapos, K. (1995). Schools studying 220-day year. *Salt Lake Tribune, 250*(36), B1–B3.

Kapos, K. (1998). Adding hours to school day is not enough. *Salt Lake Tribune, 256*(69), D1+.

Kauffman, J. M. (1997). *Characteristics of emotional and behavioral disorders of children and youths* (6th ed.). New York: Merrill/Macmillan.

Keith, S., & Martin, M. E. (2005). Cyber-bullying: Creating a culture of respect in a cyber world. *Reclaiming Children and Youth, 13*(4), 224–228.

Kerr, M. M., & Nelson, C. M. (1998). *Strategies for managing behavior problems in the classroom* (3rd ed.). Upper Saddle River, NJ: Prentice Hall.

Khisty, L. L. (1997). Making mathematics accessible to Latino students: Rethinking instructional practice. In J. Tretacosta & M. J. Kenney (Eds.), *Multicultural and gender equity in the mathematics classroom: The gift of diversity* (1997 Yearbook) (pp. 92–101). Reston, VA: National Council of Teachers of Mathematics.

Klinger, E. (1978). Modes of normal conscious flow. In K. S. Pope & J. L. Singer (Eds.), *The stream of consciousness*. New York: Plenum Press.

Knipper, K. J., & Dugan, T. J. (2006). Writing to learn across the curriculum: Tools for comprehension in content area classes. *Reading Teacher, 59*(5), 462–470.

Kobrin, K. (1992). *In there with kids: Teaching in today's classrooms*. Boston: Houghton Mifflin.

Kohut, S., & Range, D. G. (1979). *Classroom discipline: Case studies and viewpoints*. Washington, DC: National Education Association.

Kondrasuk, J. N., Greene, T., Waggoner, J., Edwards, K., & Nyak-Rhodes, A. (2005). Violence affecting school employees. *Education, 125*, 638–647.

Kounin, J. (1977). *Discipline and group management in classrooms* (rev. ed.). New York: Holt, Rinehart & Winston.

Kounin, J. S., & Doyle, P. H. (1975). Degree of continuity of a lesson's signal system and the task involvement of children. *Journal of Educational Psychology, 67*, 159–164.

Kounin, J. S., & Gump, P. V. (1974). Signal systems of lesson settings and the task-related behavior of preschool children. *Journal of Educational Psychology, 66*, 554–562.

Kounin, J. S., & Sherman, L. (1979). School environments as behavior settings. *Theory into Practice, 18*, 145–151.

Krisberg, B., & Austin, J. (1993). *Reinventing juvenile justice*. Newbury Park, CA: Sage.

Krumboltz, J. D., & Krumboltz, H. B. (1972). *Changing children's behavior* (pp. 180–201). Englewood Cliffs, NJ: Prentice Hall.

Kumarakulasingam, T., & Harrington, R. G. (2006). Relationship between classroom management, teacher stress, burnout, and levels of hope. In R. G. Harrington & L. Holub (Ed.), *Taking sides: Clashing views on controversial issues in classroom management* (pp. 25–32). Dubuque, IA: McGraw-Hill/Dushkin.

Latham, G. I. (1984). *Time-on-task and other variables affecting the quality of education of handicapped students*. Logan: Utah State University.

Lavoie, R. D. (1989). *Understanding learning disabilities: How difficult can this be? The F.A.T. city workshop* [Videotape]. Greenwich, CT: Eagle Hill Outreach. A Peter Rose Production distributed by PBS Video.

Lee Canter & Associates. (1994a). *Dealing with the potentially violent student* [Videotape]. Santa Monica, CA: Author.

Lee Canter & Associates. (1994b). *Developing a school safety plan* [Videotape]. Santa Monica, CA: Author.

Lee Canter & Associates. (1994c). *Intervening safely during fights* [Videotape]. Santa Monica, CA: Author.

Lee Canter & Associates. (1994d). *Preventing conflict and violence in the classroom* [Videotape]. Santa Monica, CA: Author.

Lee Canter & Associates. (1994e). *Preventing gang activity in school* [Videotape]. Santa Monica, CA: Author.

Lee Canter & Associates. (1994f). *Using peer mediation to resolve conflicts* [Videotape]. Santa Monica, CA: Author.

Levin, J., & Shanken-Kaye, J. M. (1996). *The self-control classroom*. Dubuque, IA: Kendall/Hunt.

Lewis, R. B., & Doorlag, D. H. (1991). *Teaching special students in the mainstream* (3rd ed.). New York: Macmillan.

Lindquist, B., & Molnar, A. (1995). Children learn what they live. *Educational Leadership, 52*, 50–51.

Long, N. J. (1990, Spring). Managing highly resistant students. *Perspective*, 6–9.

Louglin, C. E. (1992). Classroom physical environment. In M. C. Alkin (Ed.), *Encyclopedia of educational research* (6th ed., pp. 161–164). New York: Macmillan.

Lyerly, K. Z. (1982). *Daydreaming and its implications to reading instruction among gifted children*. Master's thesis, University of North Florida, Jacksonville, FL.

MacMillan, H. L., Boyle, M. H., Wong, M. Y., Duku, E. K., Fleming, J. E., & Walsh, C. A. (1999). Slapping and spanking in childhood and its association with lifetime prevalence of psychiatric disorders in a general population sample. *Canadian Medical Association Journal, 161*(7), 805–809.

Marco, T. (2006, January 17). Fighting for fairness. *Advocate*, Issue 954, 30–31.

Martin, G., & Pear, J. (1996). *Behavior modification: What it is and how to do it* (5th ed.). Englewood Cliffs, NJ: Prentice Hall.

Maslow, A. H. (1987). *Motivation and personality* (3rd ed.). New York: Harper & Row.

McCabe, D. L. (2001). Student cheating in American high schools (Web site: www.academicintegrity.org). Durham, NC: The Center for Academic Integrity.

McCormick, C. B., & Pressley, M. (1997). *Educational psychology: Learning, instruction, and assessment*. New York: Longman.

Mendler, A., & Curwin, R. (2001). *Discipline with dignity* (rev. ed.). Upper Saddle River, NJ: Merrill/Prentice Hall.

National Center for Addiction and Substance Abuse at Columbia University. (2002). Substance use and sexual health among teens and young adults in the U.S. (Web site: www.casacolumbia.org). New York: Author.

National Center for the Study of Corporal Punishment and Alternatives. (2002). *Discipline research* (Web site, www.temple.edu/education/pse/NCSCPA.html). Philadelphia: Author.

National Commission on Excellence in Education. (1983). *A nation at risk: The imperative of educational reform*. Washington, DC: U.S. Government Printing Office.

National Joint Committee on Learning Disabilities. (1989, September). *Letter from NJCLD to member organizations. Topic: Modifications to the NJCLD definition of learning disabilities*. Washington, DC: Author.

Norris, M. (2005). San Diego County students win school lawsuit. *Lesbian News, 30*(12), 15.

Obenchain, K. M., & Taylor, S. S. (2005). Behavior management: Making it work in middle and secondary schools. *Clearing House, 79*, 7–11.

Oliva, P. F., & Pawlas, G. E. (2001). *Supervision for today's schools* (6th ed.). New York: Wiley.

Opotwo, S. (2000). Aggression and violence. In M. Deutsch & P. T. Coleman (Eds.), *The handbook of conflict resolution: Theory and practice* (pp. 403–427). San Francisco: Jossey-Bass.

Ormrod, J. E. (2006). *Educational psychology: Developing learners* (5th ed.). Upper Saddle River, NJ: Pearson/Merrill/Prentice Hall.

Paolucci, E. O., & Violato, C. (2004). A meta-analysis of the published research on the affective, cognitive, and behavioral effects of corporal punishment. *The Journal of Psychology, 138*(3), 197–221.

Parsons, R. D., Hinson, S. L., & Sardo-Brown, D. (2001). *Educational psychology: A practitioner-researcher model of teaching*. Belmont, CA: Wadsworth.

Paul, R., & Elder, L. (2005). Critical thinking . . . and the art of substantive writing, part 1. *Journal of Developmental Education, 29*(1), 40–41.

Peebles-Wilkins, W. (2006). Affirm diversity: "Mix it up." *Children and Schools, 28*(1), 3.

Pulaski, M. A. S. (1980). *Understanding Piaget: An introduction to children's cognitive development* (2nd ed.). New York: Harper & Row.

Pysch, R. (1991). Discipline improves as students take responsibility. *NASSP Bulletin, 75*, 117–118.

Quina, J. (1989). *Effective secondary teaching: Going beyond the bell curve*. New York: Harper & Row.

Redl, F., & Wattenberg, W. (1959). *Mental hygiene in teaching* (rev. ed.) New York: Hardcourt, Brace, and World.

Reeves, J. R. (2006). Secondary teacher attitudes toward including English-language learners in mainstream classrooms. *The Journal of Educational Research, 99*, 131–142.

Reid, K. S. (2005). ACLU says KY district not providing anti-bias training. *Education Week, 24*(43), 5.

Robert, H. R., Evans, W. J., Honemann, D. H., & Balch, T. J. (2004). *Robert's rules of order: Newly revised in brief*. Cambridge, MA: Perseus Books Group.

Roberts, J., & Olinger, D. (2005). Numbers game. *IRE Journal, 28* (6), 26–27.

Rogoff, B. (1990). *Apprenticeship in thinking*. New York: Oxford University Press.

Rose, T. L. (1984). Current uses of corporal punishment in American public schools. *Journal of Educational Psychology, 76*, 427–441.

Roy, L. (2002). Corporal punishment in American public schools and the rights of the child. *Journal of Law and Education, 30*, 554–563.

Rust, J. O., & Kinnard, K. Q. (1983). Personality characteristics of the users of corporal punishment in the schools. *Journal of School Psychology, 21*, 91–105.

Salmivalli, C. (2001). Peer-led intervention campaign against school bullying: Who considered it useful, who benefitted? *Educational Research, 43*, 263–278.

Salmivalli, C., Kaukiainen, A., & Voeten, M. (2005). Anti-bullying intervention: Implementation and outcome. *British Journal of Educational Psychology, 75*, 465–487.

Sandy, S. V., & Cochran, K. M. (2000). Aggression and violence. In M. Deutsch & P. T. Coleman (Eds.), *The handbook of conflict resolution: Theory and practice* (pp. 316–342). San Francisco: Jossey-Bass.

Santini, J. (1998). Longer school days on the way? *Herald Journal, 89*(140), 1 ff.

Santrock, J. W. (1984). *Adolescence: An introduction* (2nd ed.). Dubuque, IA: Wm. C. Brown.

Santrock, J. W. (2001). *Educational psychology*. Boston: McGraw-Hill.

School bullying. (2006, November 22). *Advocate*, Issue 951, 16.

Schrumpf, E., Crawford, D., & Usadel, H. (1991). *Peer mediation: Conflict resolution in schools*. Champaign, IL: Research Press.

Schunk, D. H. (1989). Self-efficacy and cognitive achievement: Implications for students with learning problems. *Journal of Learning Disabilities, 22*, 14–22.

Seligman, M. E. (1992). *Helplessness: On depression, development, and death*. San Francisco: W. H. Freeman.

Setati, M. (2005). Teaching mathematics in a primary multilingual classroom. *Journal for Research in Mathematics Education, 36*, 447–466.

Shaprio, J. P., Burgoon, J. D., & Welker, C. J. (2002). Evaluation of the Peacemakers program: School-based violence: Prevention for students in grades four through eight. *Psychology in the Schools, 39*, 87–100.

Shaw, T. (2006). Simple questions, difficult answers. *Multimedia & Internet @ Schools. 13*(1), 38–40.

Shelly, L. (1985). American crime: An international anomaly? *Comparative Social Research, 8*, 81–95.

Shorr, P. W. (2006). The new digital wave. *Instructor, 115*(5), 24–27.

Short, E. J., & Weissberg-Benchell, J. (1989). The triple alliance of learning: Cognition, metacognition, and motivation. In C. B. McCormick, G. E. Miller, & M. Pressley (Eds.), *Cognitive strategy research: From basic research to educational applications* (pp. 33–63). New York: Springer-Verlag.

Silva, H. (1985). The children of Mariel from shock to integration: Cuban refugee children in south Florida schools. ERIC ED 261 136.

Silver, A. A., & Hagin, R. A. (2002). *Disorders of learning in childhood* (2nd ed.). New York: Wiley.

Singer, E. (2005). The strategies adopted by Dutch children with dyslexia to maintain their self-esteem when teased at school. *Journal of Learning Disabilities, 38*(5), 411–423.

Skemp-Arit, K. M. (2006). Body image dissatisfaction and eating disturbances among children and adolescents. *JOPERD: The Journal of Physical Education, Recreation & Dance, 77*(1), 45–51.

Skiba, R., & Peterson, R. (1999). The dark side of zero tolerance: Can punishment lead to safe schools? *Phi Delta Kappan, 80*, 372–376, 381–382.

Skinner, B. F. (1953). *Science and human behavior*. New York: Macmillan.

Skinner, B. F. (1954). The science of learning and the art of teaching. *Harvard Educational Review, 24*, 86–97.

Smith, M. S. (2001). *Practiced-based professional development for teachers of mathematics*. Reston, VA: NCTM.

Smith, P. K. (2004). *Bullying in schools: How successful can intervention be?* New York: Cambridge University Press.

Stainburn, S. (2005). Straight talk. *Teacher Magazine, 17*(3), 36–39.

Steffenhagen, J. (2005). Child safety and administrative oversight. *Education Canada, 45*(4), 64.

Stevahn, L., Munger, L., & Kealey, K. (2005). Conflict resolution in a French immersion elementary school. *Journal of Educational Research, 99*(1), 3–18.

Stokley, A. (2004). The negative impact of corporal punishment. *Points of View: Corporal Punishment, 1*, 1–4.

Strike, K., & Soltis, J. (1986). Who broke the fish tank? And other ethical dilemmas. *Instructor, 95*, 36–39.

Struyk, L. R. (1990). *A self-evaluation model for examining transition time in the classroom*. Doctoral dissertation, Utah State University, Logan, UT.

Sulzer-Azaroff, B., & Mayer, G. R. (1977). *Applying behavior analysis procedures with children and youth*. New York: Holt, Rinehart and Winston.

Teaching tolerance. (2005). *NEA Today, 26*(7), 34–36.

Tierno, M. J. (1994). Responding to the socially motivated behaviors of early adolescents:

Recommendations for classroom management. In K. M. Cauley, F. Linden, & J. H. McMillan (Eds.), *Educational psychology 94/95* (pp. 200–204). Guilford, CT: Duskin.

Tobin, K., Tippins, D. J., & Gallard, A. J. (1994). Research on instructional strategies for teaching science. In D. L. Gabel (Ed.), *Handbook of research on science teaching and learning* (pp. 45–93). New York: Macmillan.

Tonn, J. (2005, November 30). Federal agencies cite drop in school crime since 1992. *Education Week, 25,* 4.

Torok, W. C., & Trump, K. S. (1994). Gang intervention: Police and school collaboration. *FBI Law Enforcement Bulletin, 63,* 13–17.

Turnbull, H. R., & Turnbull, A. P. (1998). *Free appropriate public education* (5th ed.). Denver: Love Publishing.

Ulrich, R. E., & Azrin, N. H. (1962). Reflexive fighting in response to aversive stimulation. *Journal of Experimental Analysis of Behavior, 5,* 511–520.

Underwood, J. (2004). Legal protections gay students must receive. *Education Digest, 70*(4), 16–26.

U.S. Department of Education. (2003). *Twenty-fifth annual report to Congress on implementation of the Individuals with Disabilities Education Act.* Washington, DC: Author.

Urdan, T., Ryan, A. M., Anderman, E. M., & Gheen, M. H. (2002). Goals, goal structures, and avoidance behaviors. In C. Midgley (Ed.). *Goals, goal structures, and patterns of adaptive learning* (pp. 55–83). Mahwah, NJ: Erlbaum.

VanDeWeghe, R. (2005). Research matters. *English Journal, 95*(2), 97–100.

Van Dyke, H. T. (1984). Corporal punishment in our schools. *Clearing House, 57,* 296–300.

Van Horn, K. L. (1982, April). *The Utah pupil/teacher self-concept program: Teacher strategies that invite improvement of pupil and teacher self-concept.* A

paper presented at the annual meeting of the American Educational Research Association, New York, NY.

Velez, H. (2006, January 31). Dancing against harassment. *Advocate,* Issue 955, 21.

Walker, H. M., Colvin, G., & Ramsey, E. (1995). *Antisocial behavior in school strategies and best practices.* Pacific Grove, CA: Brooks/Cole.

Watson, J. B. (1914). *Behavior: An introduction to comparative psychology.* New York: Holt, Rinehart & Winston.

Watson, R. (1995). A guide to violence prevention. *Educational Leadership, 52,* 57–59.

Weber, W. A. (1990). Classroom management. In J. M. Cooper (Ed.), *Classroom teaching skills* (4th ed., pp. 229–306). Lexington, MA: D. C. Heath.

Webster's third new international dictionary. (1986). Chicago: Merriam-Webster.

Weinstein, C. S., & Mignano, A. (1993). *Organizing the elementary school classroom: Lessons from research and practice.* New York: McGraw-Hill.

Welsh, R. S. (1985). Spanking: A grand old American tradition? *Children Today, 14,* 25–29.

Whitted, K. S., and Dupper, D. R. (2005). Best practices for preventing or reducing bullying in schools. *Children and Schools, 27*(3), 167–175.

Willert, H. J. (2002). Do sweat the small stuff: Stemming school violence. *American Secondary Education, 30,* 2–13.

Wilson, B. (2004). The benefits of corporal punishment. *Points of View: Corporal Punishment, 1,* 1–3.

Woolfolk, A. E. (1993). *Educational psychology* (5th ed.). Boston: Allyn & Bacon.

Worner, W. (1988). An inexpensive group FM amplification system for the classroom. *Volta Review, 90,* 29–39.

Zirkel, P. A., & Gluckman, I. B. (1996). Is corporal punishment child abuse? *Principal, 76,* 60–61.

Index

Abernathy, S., 10, 391

Absences, student, 350–353

Accommodating individual students' needs, 180–230

Action research, 389

Active listening. *See* Communications, supportive replies. *See also* Listening

Administrative duties, teachers', 79–80, 83

Aggression. *See* Antisocial behavior *See also* Communications, hostile. *See also* Violence

Alberti, R., 115, 391

Alkin, M. C., 395

Allen, L. A., 276, 391

Allocated time. *See* Time, allocated

Alternative behavior patterns, principle of, 322–323

American Academy of Pediatrics, 311

American Federation of Teachers, 311

American Medical Association, 311

American Psychiatric Association, 213, 311, 391

American Psychological Association, 311

American Speech-Language-Hearing Association, 193, 391

Anderman, E. M., 37, 397

Andero, A. A., 44, 312, 391

Antisocial behavior, 11–12, 37, 48–49. *See also* Bullying. *See also* Fighting. *See also* Violence and violence prevention

Argus, T., 155, 391

Armstrong, J. J., 312, 391

Ashlock, R. B., 273, 391

Assertiveness. *See* Communications, assertive

Assessing teaching, 388–389

Atmosphere and climate, classroom. *See* Classroom, atmosphere and climate

Attacks on teachers, 378–381

Attendance at school, students', 20–27, 350–353

Attention deficit disorder. *See* Learning disabilities, students with

Austin, J., 155, 394

Aversive stimuli. *See* Punishment

Avery, N., 225, 391

Azrin, N. H., 312, 391, 397

Baenen, J., 35, 391

Balch, T. J., 151, 395

Ballard, M. B., 155, 391

Bandura, A., 312, 391

Banks, C., 225, 391

Banks, J., 225, 391

Beginning a new year or school term, 20–27, 59–74

Behavioral disorders, students with, 212–215. *See also* Antisocial behavior

Behavioristic psychology, 37–45

Behavior modification, 37, 318–333. *See also* Patterns, behavior

Bender, L., 153

Berg, F., 276, 391

Berliner, D. C., 393

Bilingual education, 220. *See also* English as a second or other language (ESOL)

Black, S., 225, 391

Bodine, R. J., 162, 391

Body language. *See* Communications, body language

Bogacki, D. F., 312, 391

Bongiovanni, A. F., 311, 391

Boredom, student. *See* Engagement. *See also* Motivation, student

Borkowski, J. G., 208, 391

Bowers, C. A., 28, 31, 391

Boyle, M. H., 395

Bradley, A., 48, 391

Brandenburg, N. A., 213, 391

Brendtro, L., 153, 154, 167, 345, 391

Brock, S. E., 154, 173, 174, 391

Brown, D., 153, 391

Brown, J. H., 153, 391

Bucher, K. T., 173, 391

Bullying, 154, 155, 173, 189, 370–372. *See also* Antisocial behavior. *See also* Violence and violence prevention

Burgoon, J. D., 156, 396

Bushway, A., 356, 391

Businesslike atmosphere, 57–59, 111

Cahen, L. S., 393

Caldwell, J., 189, 392

Cameron, J., 48, 392

Cangelosi, B. R., 121, 122, 129, 185, 392

Cangelosi, J. S., 3, 5, 12, 20, 28, 32, 34, 44, 48, 79, 86, 106, 117, 125, 135, 147, 152, 162, 175, 176, 187, 236, 244, 267, 273, 276, 312, 319, 345, 356, 357, 358, 386, 388, 389, 392, 393

Canter, L., 34, 115, 175, 306, 307, 392

Canter, M., 34, 115, 175, 306, 307, 392

Carnes, J., 225, 392

Cauley, K. M., 396

Cazden, C. G., 31, 392

Center for Disease Control and Prevention, 345

Center for Effective Discipline, 311, 392

Chandler, L, 48, 392

Characterizing students. *See* Communications, judgmental

Charles, C. M., 12, 19, 392

Charney, R., 156, 392

Cheating on tests, 354–359

Clancy, J., 3, 392

Classroom arrangement and design, 276–285

Classroom atmosphere and climate, 57–231

Cleaning up after learning activities, 42–43, 369–370

Clowning, student, 365–367

Cochran, K. M., 156, 396

Cohen, E. G., 89, 392

Cohen, S. B., 208, 393

Coleman, P. T., 395, 396

Collaboration among teachers, 149, 305–306, 386–389

Colvin, G., 163, 370, 397

Communication impairments, students with, 189–194

Communications, 34, 90, 94–135
    assertive, 115–129, 166, 306–308
    body language, 102–106
    descriptive, 90, 94–99, 187–189
    hostile, 115–121, 308
    judgmental, 94–98
    parents, with, 63–67, 96, 130–135, 306–308
    passive, 115–121, 307–308
    privileged, 134–135
    supportive, 108–110, 167

Community, learning, 87–88, 168–178. *See also* Classroom atmosphere and climate

Conflict management and resolution, 154–162

Contingency contracts and proclamations, 325, 340–341

Cook, G., 370, 392

Cooper, J. M., 397

Cooperative learning. *See* Learning activities, cooperative learning sessions

Cooperative relationships, establishing, 94–135,

Corcoran, T. B., 386, 392

Corporal punishment.
    See Punishment, corporal

Council for Exceptional Children, 311

Court, student, 162

Craig, D., 356, 392

Crawford, D. K., 157, 162, 391, 396

Cues, 83–84, 327

Cundiff, G., 335, 393

Curwin, R., 34, 395

Cyberbullying, 173

Cybercheating, 356–358

Daydreaming, 79, 335–337

Delgado, J. M., 312, 392

Denham, C., 393

Descriptive language.
    See Communications, descriptive

Deutsch, M., 156, 392, 395, 396

Developmental psychology studies, implications for classroom management, 34–37

DeVoe, J. F., 48, 392

Dewey, J., 335, 392

Dill, V. S., 168, 169, 175, 392

Direct instructional strategies, 20–27

Directions, giving. *See* Learning activities, directions for

Disabilities, students with.
    See Exceptionalities, student

Discipline policies. *See* Standards for conduct. *See also* Schoolwide discipline policies

Discrimination, principle of, 327–329

Discussion sessions. *See* Learning activities, discussion sessions

Dishaw, M. M., 393

Dishion, T. J., 163, 166, 392

Disruptive behaviors, 9–16 79, 111, 182–185, 291–315, 361–382. *See also* Bullying. *See also* Clowning, student. *See also* Interruptions, student. *See also* Language, offensive. *See also* Rudeness. *See also* Talking, disruptive student. *See also* Temper tantrums. *See also* Violence

Diversity among students.
    See Students, individual differences among. *See also* Multicultural education

Doorlag, D. H., 213, 325

Doyle, P. H., 71, 394

Dreikurs, R., 34, 43, 392

Drug and substance abuse, students', 37, 165, 185–186, 345–350

Dugan, T. J., 13, 394

Duku, E. K., 395

Dunlap, K., 37, 392

Dunn, M. J., 155, 392

Dunne, M., 49, 392

Dupper, D. R., 153, 370

Eating disorders, 187–188

Edwards, K., 49, 394

Elder, L., 13, 395

Emmer, E. T., 276, 393

Emmons, M., 115, 391

Emotional or behavioral disorders (EBD), students with, 212–220

Engagement, student, 9–16, 235–287

English as a second or other language (ESOL), 36–37, 215, 220–224

Evaluation of student achievement, communicating, 121–132, 357–359. *See also* Monitoring students' learning and behavior
    formative, 121–131, 357
    summative, 122, 125, 129, 357

Evans, E. D., 356, 392

Evans, W. J., 151, 395

Evertson, C. M., 12, 276, 393

Exceptionalities, students', 37, 189–224

Extinction, principle of, 320–322

Extrinsic rewards. *See* Motivation, extrinsic

Fear of trying, students', 87–88

Feelings, accepting. *See* Communications, supportive

Fighting, 372–378. *See also* Violence

Filby, N. N., 393

Fisher, C. W., 12, 86, 258, 393

Fixed schedules of reinforcement.
    See Positive reinforcers, schedules for

Flannery, M. E., 3, 393

Fleischman, H. L., 220, 393

Fleming, J. E., 395

Fleming, J. S., 48
Flinders, D. J., 28, 31, 391
Formative evaluation.
See Evaluation of student
achievement, communicating,
formative
Franklin, J., 225, 393
Friedman, R. M., 213, 391

Gabel, D. L., 397
Gajar, A. H., 208, 393
Gallard, A. J., 267, 397
Gang activity at school, reducing,
163–167
Garbarino, J., 154, 393
Garrison, R., 174
Generalization, the principle of,
327–329
Gheen, M. H., 37, 397
Ginott, H. G., 19, 34, 89, 94, 95, 115,
136, 393
Glasser, W., 34, 36, 115, 301, 393
Gluckman, I. B., 313, 397
Goals, learning. See Teaching cycles
model
Gold, S. R., 335, 393
Gordon, T., 34, 108, 115, 393
Gottfried, A. E., 48, 393
Gottfried, A. W., 48, 393
Grading, 130, 357–359. See also
Evaluation of student
achievement, communicating
Graffiti, 164. See also Vandalism
Greene, T., 49, 394
Grossman, H., 220, 346, 393
Grouping, intraclass, 86, 258–262
Grunwald, B., 43, 392
Guanci, J. A., 162, 393
Guerrero, A., 154, 393
Gump, P. V., 71, 394

Haberman, M., 168, 169, 175, 392
Habits. See Patterns, behavior
Haefner, J., 28, 98, 393
Hagin, R. A., 202, 207, 396
Hake, D. G., 312, 391
Hallahan, D. P., 193, 207, 208,
213, 393
Harrington, R. G., 12, 394
Hearing impairments, students with,
189–194, 200–205

Hennemann, T., 189, 393
Heward, W., L., 34, 191, 192, 207,
213, 393
Hinchey, P. H., 311, 393
Hinson, S. L., 35, 89, 395
Holub, L., 394
Homework assignments.
See Learning activities,
homework assignments
Honemann, D. H., 151, 395
Hoover, J., 155, 393
Hopstock, P. J., 220, 393
Hostility. See Antisocial behavior.
See also Violence. See also
Communications, hostile
Humphreys, S., 49, 392
Hutchinson, R. R., 312, 391
Hyman, I. A., 44, 312, 391, 393
Hyperactivity. See Learning
disabilities, students with

Impoliteness. See Rudeness
Incentives. See Positive reinforcers.
See also Motivation
Inclusion of special populations.
See Exceptionalities, student
Inclusion of students who are
marginalized by "mainstream"
society, 185–189
Independent work sessions.
See Learning activities,
independent work sessions
Individual differences among
students, 181–230
Individualized Education Program
(IEP), 190–224
Individuals with Disabilities
Education Act (IDEA),
191–193
Inquiry instructional strategies,
20–27, 265–269. See also
IRE cycles
Intermittent schedules of
reinforcement. See Positive
reinforcers, schedules for
Interrupting speakers, students',
364–365
Intraclass grouping. See Grouping,
intraclass
Intrinsic rewards. See Motivation,
student, intrinsic

Intruders on the school campus,
176–178
IRE cycles (Initiate-respond-
evaluate), 28–34, 98,
188, 264
Isolated behaviors, 38–39, 300–301

Jansen, A., 187, 393
Jesunathadas, J., 236, 393
Johnson, D. W., 154, 156, 162, 393
Johnson, J. R., 230, 394
Johnson, R. T., 154, 156, 162, 393
Jones, F., 16, 86, 102, 103, 394
Jones, L., 12, 394
Jones, V., 12, 394
Judgmental language.
See Communications,
judgmental
Juul, C., 155, 393

Kapos, K., 12, 394
Karen, R., 153
Kauffman, J. M., 193, 207, 208, 213,
393, 394
Kaufman, P., 392
Kaukiainen, A., 153, 396
Kealey, K., 153, 156, 396
Keith, S., 173, 394
Kenney, M. J., 394
Kerr, M. M., 213, 313, 394
Khisty, L. L., 221, 394
Kinnard, K. Q., 312, 396
Klinger, E., 335, 394
Knipper, K. J., 13, 394
Kobrin, K., 34, 394
Koebbe, J., 393
Kohut, S., 312, 394
Kondrasuk, J. N., 49, 394
Kounin, J., 34, 71, 74, 103, 185, 394
Krasner, L., 391
Krisberg, B., 155, 394
Krumboltz, H. B., 327, 394
Krumboltz, J. D., 327, 394
Kumarakulasingam, T., 12, 394

Labeling students. See Communi-
cations, judgmental
Language, offensive, 170–171
Language usage. See Communi-
cations
Latham, G. I., 12, 394

Lavoie, R. D., 210, 231, 394
Leach, F., 49, 392
Learning activities, 20–27, 235–287
  alternative, 293–294, 305
  cooperative learning sessions,
    5–7, 258–264
  directions for, 80–84, 240–244.
    See also Procedures,
    routine classroom
  discussion sessions, 262–264
  homework assignments, 20–27,
    272–276, 294–296,
    342–344
  independent work sessions,
    86–87, 103–104,
    270–272
  lecture sessions, 252–258
  questioning sessions, 265–269
Learning disabilities, students with,
  206–212
Learning theory, implications for
  classroom management
  strategies, 20–27
Lecture sessions. *See* Learning
  activities, lecture sessions
Lee Canter & Associates, 162, 164,
  166, 167, 174, 175, 372, 377,
  394
Lessons. *See* Learning activities
Levin, J., 213, 394
Levy, D., 153
Lewis, R. B., 213, 325, 394
Lewis, S., 154, 173, 391
Lieberman, A., 393
Limited English proficiency (LEP),
  221–224
Lindahl, A., 393
Linden, F., 396
Lindquist, B., 155, 394
Listening in the classroom, 98–109,
  276. *See also* Communi-
  cations, supportive
Long, N., 153, 154, 167, 345, 391,
  395
Lotan, R. A., 89, 392
Louglin, C. E., 276, 395
Lyerly, K. Z., 335, 395

MacMillan, H. L., 311, 395
Mainstreaming, *See* Exceptionalities,
  student

Manera, E., 10, 391
Manning, M. L., 173, 391
Marco, T., 189, 395
Marliave, R., 393
Martign, C., 187, 393
Martin, G., 325, 395
Martin, M. E., 173, 394
Marty, M., 154
Maslow, A., 89, 395
Mayer, G. R., 312, 396
McCabe, D. L., 356, 395
McCormick, C. B., 31, 395, 396
McCray, S., 167
McMillan, J. H., 396
Mendler, A., 34, 395
Mentor teacher. *See* Supervision,
  instructional
Midgley, C., 397
Mignano, A., 12, 397
Miller, A. K., 392
Miller, G. E., 396
Mind-wandering, 335–337
Misbehavior. *See* Off-task behaviors
Modeling, 111, 169, 186, 330–331
Molnar, A., 155, 394
Monitoring students' learning and
  behavior, 71–72, 244–252,
  319–320. *See also* Teaching
  cycles model. *See also*
  Withitness
Motivation, student, 46–48,
  235–287. *See also* Positive
  reinforcement
  extrinsic, 46–48
  intrinsic, 46–48, 235–240
Mueller, R., 393
Multicultural education, 34–37,
  224–230
Munger, L., 153, 156, 396
Myth of the "good teacher," 302,
  306–308

Nash, W., 356, 391
National Association for Elementary
  School Principals, 311
National Center for Addiction and
  Substance Abuse at Columbia
  University, 345, 395
National Center for the Study of
  Corporal Punishment and
  Alternatives, 311, 395

National Commission on Excellence
  in Education, 12, 395
National Council on Crimes and
  Delinquency, 155
National Education Association, 311
National Joint Commission on
  Learning Disabilities, 207,
  395
Nederkoorn, C., 187, 393
Negative reinforcement, 5–8, 45,
Nelson, C. M., 213, 313, 394
Nelson, S. E., 163, 166, 392
Norris, M., 189, 395
Nyak-Rhodes, A., 49, 394

Obenchain, K. M., 10, 395
Obscenity. *See* Language, offensive
Off-task behaviors, 6–16, 291–382
Olinger, D., 48, 395
Olivia, P. F., 386, 395
On-task behaviors, 9–16, 19. *See
  also* Engagement, student
Opotow, S., 155, 395
Ormrod, J. E., 19, 34, 35, 36, 38, 46,
  48, 89, 96, 186, 258, 325, 346,
  395

Paolucci, E. O., 311, 395
Parents, students'. *See* Communi-
  cations, with parents
Parson, R. D., 35, 89, 395
Passive. *See* Communications,
  passive
Patterns, behavior, 38–39, 300–301,
  318–333
Patton, D. M., 276, 391
Paul, R., 13, 395
Pawlas, G. E., 386, 395
Pear, J., 325, 395
Peebles-Wilkins, W., 225, 395
Peer acceptance. *See* Social
  acceptance
Peer mediation, 156–162
Pepper, F., 43, 392
Permissiveness. *See* Communi-
  cations, passive
Peter, K., 392
Petersen, M. L., 203, 392
Peterson, R., 155, 396
Physical impairments, students with,
  193–205

Pierce, W. D., 48, 392
Planty, M., 392
Pope, K. S., 394
Positive reinforcers, 39–42, 88–89
    destructive, 40–41, 88–89,
        186–188
    schedules for, 324–326
Powell, J., 393
Praise. *See* Communications,
    judgmental
Pre-service teacher education,
    181–185
Pressley, M., 231, 395, 396
Privileged information.
    See Communications,
    privileged
Problem-based learning, 48,
    235–240
Procedures, routine classroom,
    142–144. *See also* Learning
    activities, directions
Prosocial behavior, 11–12
Public Law 94–142. See *Individuals
    with Disabilities Education
    Act (IDEA)*
Pulaski, M. A. S., 357, 395
Punishment, 42–44
    contrived, 42–43, 309
    corporal, 44, 309–314
    destructive, 44, 186, 309–313
    naturally occurring, 42–43, 309
    unwittingly administered, 44
Pysch, R., 36, 395

Questioning sessions. *See* Learning
    activities, questioning sessions
Quina, J., 256, 257, 395

Ramsey, E., 163, 370, 397
Rand, M. R., 392
Range, D. G., 312, 394
Redl, F., 34, 395
Reeves, J. R., 220, 395
Refusing to participate, students',
    301–303, 338–339, 341
Reid, K. S., 189, 395
Remley, T. P., 155, 391
Research bases for classroom
    management strategies,
    18–53
Responsibility for one's own
    conduct, 112–115

Rewards. *See* Positive reinforcers
Reynolds, M. C., 393
Robert, H. R., 151, 395
Roberts, J., 48, 395
Rogoff, B., 357, 395
Rose, T. L., 311, 395
Roy, L., 311, 395
Rudeness, students', 367–368
Rudy, S. A., 392
Rules for conduct. *See* Standards for
    conduct
Rust, J. O., 312, 396
Ryan, A. M., 37, 397

Safe school policies and plans,
    153–178
Safety audits, 173
Sallery, R. D., 312, 391
Salmivalli, C., 153, 155, 396
Sandavol, J., 154, 173, 391
Sandy, S. V., 156, 396
Santini, J., 26, 396
Santrock, J. W., 35, 46, 346, 396
Sardo-Brown, D., 35, 89, 395
Satiation, principle of, 331–332
Schedules of reinforcement.
    See Positive reinforcers,
    schedules for
Schoolwide discipline policies,
    151–178. *See also* Safe school
    policies and plans
Schrumpf, E., 157, 396
Schunk, D. H., 208, 396
Self-confidence, 35
Self-concept and self-esteem,
    See Social acceptance
Seligman, M. E., 208, 396
Setati, M., 225, 396
Sexual orientation, students',
    185–189
Shanken-Kaye, J. M., 213, 394
Shaping, principle of, 323–324
Shaprio, J. P., 156, 396
Shaw, T., 86, 396
Shelly, L., 370, 396
Sherman, L., 71, 394
Shorr, P. W., 85, 396
Short, E. J., 208, 396
Silva, H., 220, 396
Silver, A. A., 202, 207, 396
Silver, S. E., 213, 391

Singer, E., 189, 396
Singer, J. L., 394
Skemp-Arit, K. M., 187, 396
Skiba, R., 155, 396
Skinner, B. F., 37, 396
Smeets, T., 187, 393
Smith, M. S., 386, 396
Smith, P. K., 371, 396
Snyder, T. D., 392
Social acceptance, 88–90, 95–98,
    185–189, 206
Social interaction and
    communications studies,
    implications for classroom
    management strategies,
    27–34
Socratic method. *See* Learning
    activities, questioning sessions
Soltis, J., 307, 312, 396
Special needs, students with.
    See Exceptionalities, student.
Stainburn, S., 189, 396
Standards for conduct, 140–153,
    182–185, 188–189
Steffenhagen, J., 153, 156, 396
Stevahn, 153, 396
Stewart, A., 44, 312, 391
Stokley, A, 311, 312, 396
Strike, K., 312, 396
Struyk, L. R., 12, 86, 396
Student court, 162
Substance abuse. *See* Drug and
    substance abuse
Sulzer-Azaroff, B., 312, 396
Summative evaluation.
    See Evaluation of student
    achievement, communicating,
    summative
Supervision, instructional, 386–389
Supplies, students' failure to bring,
    344–345
Supportive replies. *See* Communi-
    cations, supportive
Syllabus, course, 73–77, 351

Talking, disruptive student, 156,
    361–365
Tardiness, student, 20–27, 350–353
Tarver, S. G., 208, 393
Taylor, S. S., 10, 395
Teaching cycles model, 4–9, 72–73,
    121, 148, 291–296

Teaching students to communicate
assertively, 103–111, 138
Technology for classroom
management and school
safety, 67, 70, 85–86,
175–178
Tierno, M. J., 36, 396
Time
allocated, 9–16, 78–81
engaged. *See* Engagement,
student
saving, 74, 78–81
transition, 9–16, 74, 78–79, 388
Tippins, D. J., 267, 397
Tobin, K., 267, 397
Tonn, J., 48, 397
Torok, W. C., 166, 397
Transitions. *See* Time, transition
Trentacosta, J., 394
True dialogues, 28–34
Trump, K. S., 166, 397
Turnbull, A. P., 191, 192, 213, 397
Turnbull, H. R., 191, 192, 213, 397

Ullman, L. P., 391
Ulrich, R. E., 312, 397
Underwood, J., 189, 397
United States Department of
Education, 213, 397

Urdan, T., 37, 397
Usadel, H., 157, 396

Vandalism, 163–166,
381–382
VanDeWeghe, R., 13, 397
Van Dyke, H. T., 311, 397
Van Horn, K. L., 95, 397
Velez, H., 189, 397
Violato, C., 311, 395
Violence and violence prevention,
48–49, 87–88, 153–178,
182–185, 370–382. *See also*
Antisocial behavior. *See also*
Bullying. *See also*
Punishment, corporal
Visual impairments, students with,
193–194
Voeten, M., 153, 396
Voice tone, 105–106

Waggoner, J., 49, 394
Wait time. *See* Learning activities,
questioning sessions
Walker, H. M., 163, 370, 397
Walsh, C. A., 395
Watson, J. B., 37, 397
Watson, R., 153, 172, 173, 397
Wattenberg, W., 34, 395

Weapons at school, 48. *See also*
Fighting. *See also* Attacks on
teachers
Weber, W. A., 43, 397
Weinstein, C. S., 12, 397
Weiss, K. J., 312, 391
Weissberg-Benchell, J.,
208, 396
Welker, C. J., 156, 396
Welsh, R. S., 311, 312, 397
Whitted, K. S., 153, 370, 397
Wilbert, H. J., 155, 397
Wilson, B., 313, 397
Wise, J. H., 44, 312, 391, 393
Withitness, 34, 71–72, 103,
244–252, 358. *See also*
Monitoring students' learning
and behavior
Wong, M. Y., 395
Woolfolk, A. E., 12, 397
Worner, W., 276, 397
Worsham, M. E., 276, 393
Wright, R., 10, 391

Yasui, M., 163, 166, 392

Zero-reject implications,
192–193
Zirkel, P. A., 313, 397